CASES AND MATERIALS ON THE LAW GOVERNING LAWYERS

Fourth Edition

CASES AND MATERIALS ON THE LAW GOVERNING LAWYERS

Fourth Edition

James E. Moliterno
Vincent Bradford Professor of Law
Washington & Lee University School of Law

Library of Congress Cataloging-in-Publication Data

Moliterno, James E., 1953-
    Cases and materials on the law governing lawyers / James E. Moliterno. — 4th ed.
    p. cm.
    ISBN 978-1-4224-9866-8 (hard cover)
    1. Practice of law — United States — Cases. 2. Lawyers — United States — Cases. 3. Attorney and client — United States — Cases. 4. Legal ethics — United States — Cases. I. Title.
    KF300.M65 2012
    340.023 dc23   2011047641

NOTE TO USERS

To ensure that you are using the latest materials available in this area, please be sure to periodically check the LexisNexis Law School web site for downloadable updates and supplements at www.lexisnexis.com/lawschool.

Editorial Offices
121 Chanlon Rd., New Providence, NJ 07974 (908) 464-6800
201 Mission St., San Francisco, CA 94105-1831 (415) 908-3200
www.lexisnexis.com

MATTHEW◆BENDER

(2012–Pub.3511)

Dedication

To Timothy, Emily, and Greg —J.E.M.

Preface to Fourth Edition

This casebook is now in its 12th year and the time was right for a general refreshment. In this fourth edition, an effort was made to tighten every case edit and every law journal excerpt. Dated materials have been replaced with more contemporary ones. The result is a leaner, more efficient casebook that is easier to read and use.

Materials have been added to reflect issues that have emerged in the last five years. In general the move toward a global legal profession has been reflected in expanded International Notes.

Preface to the Third Edition

The lawyer's world is shrinking. More commercial transactions than ever have international implications. More clients move more comfortably in global environments. U.S. lawyers being educated today need to be aware of differences in the law governing lawyers in non-U.S. jurisdictions. Those differences will evolve over the new lawyer's career, but today's lawyers need an awareness that such differences exist and some sense of when and how to apply another jurisdiction's lawyer law.

Aside from the deletion of a few cases and the insertion of a couple of new ones, the main feature of this third edition is the addition of "International Notes." Each of these will provide a brief contrast between U.S. lawyer law and that of another jurisdiction, most often the EU or Japan or China, but others as well. This exposure is not sufficient to say that students using this book will learn the lawyer law of these other jurisdictions. To do that, a supplemental book would be needed. But these International Notes do provide a sense of the international treatment of several core lawyer law issues. With this sense, new lawyers will be better prepared to function in the shrinking, global environment.

Preface to the Second Edition

The primary motivation for producing a second edition has been the important work of the ABA's Ethics 2000 Commission. The Commission has worked long and hard to accomplish its mission of revising the Model Rules of Professional Conduct. The work was largely completed in February 2002, when the ABA House of Delegates approved the Commission's Report, thereby amending the Model Rules in a number of significant respects. Of course, these amendments have affected the law governing lawyers and will undoubtedly have greater effect in the future. The amendments will almost immediately affect the law governing lawyers in some federal courts and agencies because by local rule many federal courts look to the ABA Model Rules as either their governing rules of ethics or as important guidance. Until states adopt the amendments, of course, their greatest impact will be inchoate. And it remains to be seen whether the states will adopt these amendments quickly (as they adopted the Model Code in the 1970s), slowly-but-surely (as they adopted the Model Rules in the 1980s and 90s), or not at all (as some states have declined to adopt past amendments and some of the original provisions of the Model Rules). However they are accepted by the states, the Ethics 2000 Commission revision of the Model Rules is important material to consider in the study of the law governing lawyers both because of the enormous energy and thought that the Commission has given to the project and because the new Model Rules will become the centerpiece text for the Multistate Professional Responsibility Bar Exam.

Interspersed through this second edition are various entries titled, "Notes on the February 2002 Amendment to Model Rule X." Through this device, the materials present all of the significant changes wrought by the work of the Ethics 2000 Commission. As the next few years pass, these entries may become more significant as states adopt or reject the new ABA approach to the particular issues. Two critical topics facing the profession were left incompletely addressed by Ethics 2000: multidisciplinary practice and multijurisdictional practice. The latter is being thoroughly treated by the ABA Commission on Multijurisdictional Practice, having delivered its final report to the ABA for action at the 2002 annual meeting. Materials have been added to this edition that will allow classroom discussion of the main features of the multijurisdictional practice debate. Multidisciplinary practice presents perhaps the thorniest, weightiest, and most revealing issue currently facing the legal profession. Can the legal profession survive if it does not embrace multidisciplinary practice? Can it survive if it *does* embrace multidisciplinary practice? On no other question facing the profession are more divergent views held more strongly. Materials have been added to this edition to allow a classroom discussion of multidisciplinary practice issues. The international aspects of both issues loom large.

Not insignificantly, discussion problems have been added as well, allowing treatment of the material through class discussions of these hypotheticals. Finally, the inevitable changes, re-editing of cases, and adding of notes and questions have occurred. I am grateful to those who have used the book and been kind enough to offer suggestions. I hope you will recognize your suggestions in the changes that have been made.

Preface to the First Edition

The Professional Responsibility course (by whatever name it is called at your school) is about the law and ethics that govern relationships lawyers have with clients, other lawyers, the profession, the justice system, and the public. It is the only substantive law course in the typical law school curriculum that is about what lawyers do. In Torts, Contracts, and so on, you study law that affects clients' relationships with others and that lawyers interact with as an expert a step removed from the actual effect of the law. In Professional Responsibility, by contrast, the law you study is directly about your future role as a lawyer. In other words, Professional Responsibility is the course in which the lawyer is the "client," the one on whom the law studied actually operates. Arguably, Professional Responsibility is the most important course in the law school curriculum. At least it is the course whose subject matter will affect you most frequently and most directly.

The law governing lawyers is a complicated mix of many different areas of substantive law from many different sources. Most obvious are the organized bar's self-regulations, enforced through the courts (as ethics codes adopted in the states), but other law fields have important applications to the various relationships of which lawyers are a part. Agency, contract, tort, procedure and evidence law, among others, have specific applications to lawyers. All of these are interwoven in this casebook.

In particular, the organized bar, through the American Bar Association, has promulgated model ethics codes. The ABA models have dominated the law of lawyering because these models, with some modification, have been adopted by the states as law. These models have also dominated law school courses in Professional Responsibility. They have dominated law school teaching of the subject because they are easily accessible and because they serve as simple proxies for what the law of lawyering is in the states.

Between the two models, the Model Code and the Model Rules, the Rules now dominate. The Code was originally adopted by the ABA in 1969 and was amended from time to time thereafter. When the Rules were adopted by the ABA in 1983, the ABA ceased its effort to amend and update the Model Code. The Code is now almost entirely out-of-date in some respects. States whose law reflects the Model Code as their basis have gone from a high point of nearly fifty to under three and falling. More than forty-five states now have adopted ethics codes based on the Model Rules. This casebook takes the approach with regard to the models that has come to be most prevalent in law school courses: The Model Rules are the basic document of study; the Model Code is used as contrast in particular areas.

All of this talk of ethics codes must not be read to mean that law other than the ethics codes is unimportant. On the contrary, the other significant trend in Professional Responsibility courses is toward the recognition that lawyers' conduct is governed largely by law outside the ethics codes and by control systems other than the bar disciplinary system. Malpractice liability, litigation sanctions, regulatory agency control, the evidentiary privilege, civil and criminal liability, among others, all serve to control lawyer conduct, most often with greater effect than the bar disciplinary process. That law, and those other systems, are a significant part of this casebook.

TABLE OF CONTENTS

TABLE OF CONTENTS

TABLE OF CONTENTS

TABLE OF CONTENTS

TABLE OF CONTENTS

TABLE OF CONTENTS

TABLE OF CONTENTS

TABLE OF CONTENTS

TABLE OF CONTENTS

TABLE OF CONTENTS

TABLE OF CONTENTS

Chapter I

INTRODUCTION TO THE ROLE OF LAWYER

The lawyer's role in its various forms is at the center of the law governing lawyers. The law governing lawyers is about the relationships of lawyers to their clients, their peers, the justice system, the profession, and the public. Relationships involve role-sensitive activities. Study of the law governing lawyers must begin with an introduction to the role of lawyer.

A. MORAL PHILOSOPHY, RIGHT AND WRONG, AND THE LAW GOVERNING LAWYERS

Moral philosophy is the pursuit of an understanding of moral and ethical choice. Moral philosophy informs the study of the law governing lawyers, but moral philosophy does not replace legal analysis as the tool for determining the application of the law governing lawyers. Occasionally someone will say that all you must do to be an ethical lawyer is to practice what your parents taught you or to remember what you learned in kindergarten about golden rules, playing nicely, respect for others, and sharing belongings. No one should forget any of those good lessons, and cheating or stealing will produce predictably bad results when engaged in by lawyers. But there is a great deal more to the law governing lawyers than the difference between right and wrong. Many of the rules that govern lawyers are counterintuitive. Many are based on special role-based morality that attends the lawyer's role. Some are grounded in the organized bar's self-interest. Above all else, the law governing lawyers is law. It must be studied and mastered like any other law field.

The law governing lawyers is a complicated mix of many different areas of substantive law from many different sources. Most obvious are the organized bar's self regulations (the ethics rules as adopted in the states and enforced through the courts), but other fields of law have important applications to the various relationships of which lawyers are a part. Agency, contract, tort, procedure and evidence law, among others, have specific applications to lawyers.

Important to an understanding of lawyer ethics is the concept of role morality. Certain roles, thought necessary to the continued existence of an ordered society, implicate moral choices for those in the particular role. Those choices, if they are consistent with the effective execution of the role, are by definition moral.

The lawyer occupies a critical role in the system of justice. To the extent that the justice system is thought to be moral and the lawyer's role within it essential, the lawyer who effectively carries out the lawyer's role is moral. This role morality supplants the generally applicable moral standards where the two conflict. For example, a lawyer owes a duty of confidentiality to a client and adherence to it, as modified by its exceptions is necessary to the adversary system of dispute resolution. When a lawyer interviews a client, say a criminal defendant, and learns that the client has committed the crime with which he is charged and that he has no valid defenses, the lawyer's maintenance of the confidence and continued zealous representation of the client is moral. It comports with and fulfills the lawyer's role in the dispute resolution system.

Lawyers' moral decision-making involves a balancing process. Lawyers owe many duties, not all of which point in a single direction at any given moment. Lawyers owe duties to clients, the justice system, third parties generally, opposing parties, the society, and the profession. There is a hierarchy among these duties, but all difficult legal ethics questions involve an attempted balancing among these duties. The law governing lawyers, at least the profession's self-regulation/rules, are essentially an attempted balance among the competing duties in given contexts. For example, a lawyer owes a duty of loyalty to a client and a duty of candor to the court. If a lawyer's client commits perjury, the lawyer's decision-making will involve a balancing, according to the rules of the law of lawyering, between these two competing duties. The Model Rules' effort to produce an answer for the lawyer to this balance-question, MR 3.3, creates a set of contingent answers that depend on the time at which the lawyer learns that the client's testimony was false. The timing of the lawyer's knowledge brings into the balancing mix factors such as the level of lawyer complicity in the perjury and the interests of finality of court proceedings. General notions of the right or wrong of revealing a client's perjury are a factor but not the exclusive factor in this balancing process.

When there is talk of "higher" standards for lawyers, it usually masks the speaker's preference for one competing duty over another. The legal rules that govern lawyers are nearly all an attempted balance among competing duties: an effort to find a wise line that divides in particular contexts between devotion to one duty over another. Different standards in such a context are not really higher or lower, they merely strike the balance between the competing duties in a different place.

B. THE ROLE OF LAWYER

During the 1990's criminal trial of O.J. Simpson, a great many media experts on the professional responsibility of lawyers were created and profusely displayed in the mass media. Such experts are now a staple of news coverage. One of the experts described the conduct of one of the trial lawyers as follows: "Today in court, [that lawyer] was demonic, nearly unethical." The expert may think that a lawyer must be somehow worse than demonic to violate the professional responsibility rules. More likely, though, this odd comment is a reminder that being morally good or morally bad is not the primary inquiry when applying the law governing lawyers. The professional responsibility codes are an attempted expression of the limits of conduct by people acting in the role of lawyer.

1. Conceptions of the Lawyer's Role

The most common, standard concept of the lawyer's role sees the practice of law as a public profession in which the lawyer operates with reference to basic role premises. An early, classic expression of the lawyer's devotion to the interests of the client, and the role implications of such a commitment, is that of Lord Brougham:

> An advocate, in the discharge of his duty, knows but one person in all the world, and that person is his client. To save that client by all means and expedients, and at all hazards and costs to other persons, and amongst them, to himself, is his first and only duty; and in performing this duty he must not regard the alarm, the torments, the destruction which he may bring upon others.[1]

Although Brougham's description of the advocacy duty is often regarded as overstated, it is not substantially so. A much more mainstream, middle-of-the-road member of the profession, Justice Lewis Powell, said this in a Supreme Court opinion that struck down state bar rules that required lawyers to be citizens of the United States.

> Lawyers frequently represent foreign countries and the nationals of such countries in litigation in the courts of the United States, as well as in other matters in this country. In such representation, the duty of the lawyer, subject to his role as an "officer of the court," is to further the interests of his clients by all lawful means, even when those interests are in conflict with the interests of the United States or of a State. But this representation involves no conflict of interest in the invidious sense. Rather, it casts the lawyer in his honored and traditional role as an authorized but independent agent acting to vindicate the legal rights of a client, whoever it may be.

In re Griffiths, 413 U.S. 717, 724 n.14 (1973). Lawyers are meant to be client-favoring, even when some injustice may occur. Some of the law governing lawyers describes these client-favoring duties such as loyalty, maintenance of confidentiality, fiduciary duties, and conflict avoidance. Some of the law governing lawyers sets boundaries beyond which client-favoring conduct may not go.

William H. Simon, *The Ideology of Advocacy: Procedural Justice and Professional Ethics*
1978 Wis. L. Rev. 29, 36–38[2]

The first principle of conduct is the <u>principle of neutrality</u>. This principle prescribes that the lawyer remain detached from his client's ends. The lawyer is expected to represent people who seek his help <u>regardless of his opinion of the justice of their ends</u>. In some cases, he may have a duty to do so; in others, he may have the personal privilege to refuse. But whenever he takes a case, he is not

[handwritten margin note: must be neutral]

---

[1] 2 Trial of Queen Caroline 8 (J. Nightingale ed., 1820-21).

[2] Copyright © 1978 by Wisconsin Law Review. Reprinted with permission.

considered responsible for his client's purposes. Even if the lawyer happens to share these purposes, he must maintain his distance. In a judicial proceeding, for instance, he may not express his personal belief in the justice of his client's cause.

The second principle of conduct is partisanship. This principle prescribes that the lawyer work aggressively to advance his client's ends. The lawyer will employ means on behalf of his client which he would not consider proper in a non-professional context even to advance his own ends. These means may involve deception, obfuscation, or delay. Unlike the principle of neutrality, the principle of partisanship is qualified. A line separates the methods which a lawyer should be willing to use on half of a client from those he should not use. Before the lawyer crosses the line, he calls himself a representative; after he crosses it, he calls himself an officer of the Court. Most debates within the Ideology of Advocacy concern the location of this line. . . . The principles of neutrality and partisanship describe the basic conduct and attitudes of professional advocacy. The two principles are often combined in the terms "adversary advocacy" or "partisan advocacy". . . . However, it should be noted that the two principles are distinct in important respects. Many occupational roles, for instance the bureaucrat and the doctor, are expected to serve the general public without regard to the ends of those who seek their help. Yet, they are not expected to engage in the partisan pursuit of individual ends. On the other hand, political representatives are expected to be partisan, but they are not expected to serve all comers without regard to their ends. Only the lawyer seems to insist on making a virtue of both neutrality and partisanship.

Two further principles, though less obvious, are also assumed. . . . The first is the principle of procedural justice. In its most general usage, procedural justice holds that the legitimacy of a situation may reside in the way it was produced rather than its intrinsic properties. Another aspect of the principle is that, given adequate procedures, one can act justly by conforming to them regardless of the consequences to which one's conduct contributes. In this essay, the term "procedural justice" is used more specifically to refer to the notion that there is an inherent value or legitimacy to the judicial proceeding (and to a more qualified extent, the entire legal system) which makes it possible for a lawyer to justify specific actions without reference to the consequences they are likely to promote. . . .

The second foundation principle of the Ideology of Advocacy is professionalism. In its most general usage, the term professionalism refers to the notion that social responsibility for the development and application of certain apolitical and specialized disciplines should be delegated to the practitioners of these disciplines. In this paper, the term is used more specifically to describe the notion that the law is an apolitical and specialized discipline and that its proper development and application require that legal ethics be elaborated collectively by lawyers in accordance with criteria derived from their discipline. . . . [Commentators assume that questions about the limits of advocacy] are to be resolved in terms of legal doctrine and that they should be resolved by lawyers collectively in their occupational capacities and not by lawyers individually in terms of personal or social norms or by broad-based political institutions.

A competing conception of the lawyer's role, described as the "morally activist lawyer" by its advocate David Luban, suggests a lawyer who recognizes the limits on the moral value of the justice system within which the lawyer's role-morality justifications exist. The morally activist lawyer shares responsibility with the client for the goals and the means of the representation. The morally activist lawyer will attempt to persuade the client to do what is morally right, not merely what is legally required or permitted, and will refrain from representation activities that the lawyer finds morally objectionable.

DAVID J. LUBAN, LAWYERS AND JUSTICE
xix–xxiii (1988)[3]

An intellectually powerful picture dominates academic as well as professional discussions of legal ethics. In broad terms, this dominant picture consists of three elements: the theory of role morality (the ethical system that F.H. Bradley styled "my station and its duties"); the adversary system excuse; and the standard conception of the lawyer's role.

The theory of role morality takes off from a distinction between universal moral duties that bind us all because we are all moral agents and special duties that go with various social roles or "stations" in life. The moment we draw this distinction, we observe that conflicts sometimes arise between "common morality" and "role morality" — for example, when a lawyer's role morality demands that she bend her talents and ingenuity toward getting a guilty, violent criminal back out on the street. When such conflicts arise, the theory asserts that role morality must take precedence. On this conception, morality consists in performing the duties of my station. This notion, at the level of general ethical theory, explains how people in certain social roles may be morally required to do things that seem immoral.

The adversary system excuse accounts for the reasons lawyers in particular are governed by a role morality that differs from common morality. The adversary system of justice, which lies at the core of Anglo-American legal procedure, lays the responsibility on each party to advocate its own case and to assault the case of the other party. Since this battle of arguments is conducted by lawyers, they have a heightened duty of partisanship toward their own clients and a diminished duty to respect the interests of their adversaries or of third parties. The adversary system thus excuses lawyers from common moral obligations to nonclients.

The adversary system excuse carries as a corollary the standard conception of the lawyer's role, consisting of (1) a role obligation (the "principle of partisanship") that identifies professionalism with extreme partisan zeal on behalf of the client and (2) the "principle of nonaccountability," which insists that the lawyer bears no moral responsibility for the client's goals or the means used to attain them.

These three elements form a highly coherent picture that resonates with so much of our familiar experience and contains so many points of plain truth that it

---

[3] Copyright © 1988 by Princeton University Press. Reprinted by permission of Princeton University Press.

Clients first

is hard to argue with. All of us, after all, are familiar with special social roles carrying unique duties that may offend common morality. We know that soldiers may be called on to kill, that journalists must snoop and publish and then let the chips fall where they may. All of us, secondly, are familiar with the adversary system; and finally, we want and expect our own lawyer to give our interests absolute priority and to refrain from sitting in judgment over us. According to a recent survey, 38 percent of those polled said that the single most positive aspect of lawyers is that their "first priority is to their clients."

All three elements of the dominant picture have been around for a long time, and it is my view that they have always informed the ethical ideals of legal practice in the adversary system. But the harsh consequences of this argument were not explicitly drawn until Monroe Freedman wrote his 1966 article, *Professional Responsibility of the Criminal Defense Lawyer: The Three Hardest Questions*, and his book LAWYERS' ETHICS IN AN ADVERSARY SYSTEM. Freedman spelled out the dominant picture with great clarity and used it to argue that criminal defense lawyers have a moral obligation to go along with the testimony of perjurious clients and to discredit — brutally, if necessary — opposing witnesses known to be telling the truth.

Freedman's conclusions embarrassed leaders of the bar and scholars who had tended to cloak the subject of legal ethics in euphemisms and happy-talk, as though role morality, the adversary system excuse, and the standard conception of the lawyer's role harmonize effortlessly with everyday moral views. The embarrassment caused by Freedman's candor was all to the good. But Freedman's argument was not just embarrassing; his deductions of unappetizing conclusions were also intellectually devastating. And although many authorities on legal ethics disagreed with Freedman's most controversial conclusions, they did not come to terms with the tangle of complicated theoretical claims on which the dominant picture rests. On the contrary, even Freedman's critics tended to agree with the three elements of the dominant picture. For that reason, they failed to convince.

And yet the dominant picture yields a terribly disquieting conclusion — in Macaulay's words, that a lawyer "with a wig on his head, and a band round his neck [will] do for a guinea what, without those appendages, he would think it wicked and infamous to do for an empire."

Never mind Macaulay's guinea. Resentment of lawyers' fees is of course part of public disquiet with the profession. But the fundamental complaint is that a role morality such as the standard conception amounts simply to an institutionalized immunity from the requirements of conscience. This is the impasse. What I have called the dominant picture of lawyers' ethics is clearly a serious and plausible one, but its conclusions fill us with unease.

* * *

[I suggest an alternative to the dominant picture, which] I call "moral activism." The morally activist lawyer shares and aims to share with her client responsibility for the ends she is promoting in her representation; she also cares more about the means used than the bare fact that they are legal. As a result, the morally activist lawyer will challenge her client if the representation seems to her morally unworthy; she may cajole or negotiate with the client to change the ends or means; she may find herself compelled to initiate action that the client will view as betrayal; and she will not fear to quit. She will have none of the principle of nonaccountability, and she sees severe limitations on what partisanship permits.

*   *   *

An outrageous-looking professional act, such as assisting a man convicted of incest to regain custody of his children (the example is a real one), can be justified only by the lawyer's obligation to represent a client's interests zealously. That obligation is an essential facet of the role of partisan advocate, and the partisan advocate is a creature of the adversary system. Ultimately, then, . . . the adversary system excuse is only as good as the adversary system itself.

INTERNATIONAL NOTES

1.   The "umbrella" bar association of the European Union, the CCBE, Preamble addresses the role of the lawyer in the following way:

> In a society founded on respect for the rule of law, the lawyer fulfills a special role. His duties do not begin and end with the faithful performance of what he is instructed to do so far as the law permits. A lawyer must serve the interests of justice as well as those rights and liberties he is trusted to assert and defend and it is his duty not only to plead his client's cause but to be his advisor.

Preamble to CODE OF CONDUCT FOR LAWYERS IN THE EUROPEAN UNION (2002)

> A lawyer's function therefore lays on him a variety of legal and moral obligations toward: the client; the courts and other authorities before whom the layer pleads the client's cause or acts on his behalf; the legal profession in general and each fellow member of it in particular; the public for whom the existence of a free and independent profession itself is an essential means of safeguarding human rights in face of the power of the state and the other interests in society.

Id.

2.   In November 2004, Japanese attorneys established new ethical standards, which also apply to registered foreign business attorneys. The new ethical rules characterize an attorney's role and duties as follows: (1) An attorney shall be aware that his or her mission is to protect fundamental human rights, to realize social justice, and to strive to attain this mission. (2) An attorney shall respect freedom and independence in his or her duties. (3) An attorney shall be aware of the importance of attorney autonomy and strive to maintain and develop this self-governing system. (4) An attorney shall protect the independence of the judiciary and strive to contribute to the sound development of the justice system. (5) An attorney shall respect truth, be faithful, and perform his or her duties fairly and in good faith. (6) An attorney shall value honor, maintain credibility, unsullied integrity, and strive to ennoble himself or herself at all times. (7) An attorney shall develop his or her culture and strive to study in order to be deeply versed in statutes

and legal business. (8) An attorney shall strive to participate and practice public interest activities that are appropriate to this mission. Kyoko Ishida, *Ethical Standards of Japanese Lawyers: Translation of the Ethics Codes for Six Categories of Legal Service Providers*, 14 PAC. RIM L. & POL'Y J. 383 (2005).

2. Differences Between Lawyers' Litigation and Planning Roles

PROBLEM 1-1

It's April, and Maria Lucano has two new clients. Both of their matters involve the application of the same Internal Revenue Service regulation. William Severino has asked Lucano to fashion a transaction that will comply with the IRS regulation and provide certain tax advantages. Paul Deliquattro has been charged by the IRS with fraud in the creation of a transaction through which he claimed those same tax advantages pursuant to the same regulation. How will Lucano's work and approach differ in representing Severino and Deliquattro?

In a litigation context, most of the lawyer's work will be backward looking. The litigation will seek to assess legal responsibility for the client's and the opposing party's past conduct. The lawyer's work will involve the operation of the justice system on the client's behalf. In the planning context, most of the lawyer's work will be forward looking. The planning lawyer will seek to predict the consequences of proposed future conduct. In both legal and moral terms, a lawyer bears more responsibility for the client's acts in the planning context than in the litigation context. The lawyer's planning work, advice, and assistance in execution will help shape future client conduct. As such, a lawyer bears greater legal and moral responsibility for a client's acts in the planning as opposed to the litigation context.

WESTLAKE v. ABRAHAMS
565 F. Supp. 1330 (N.D. Ga. 1983)

This action was brought by a purchaser of two commodity futures options from Lloyd, Carr & Co. (hereinafter Lloyd, Carr) under the [securities and commodity trading laws] [B]efore the Court is a motion of Bushnell, Gage & Reizen; Mr. Bushnell; Mr. Gage; Mr. Reizen; Ms. Shecter; and Mr. Henry (the aforesaid defendants will be collectively referred to herein as either "the defendants" or the firm of "Bushnell, Gage & Reizen") for summary judgment.

FACTUAL AND PROCEDURAL BACKGROUND

The complaint, filed March 30, 1978, alleges that the plaintiff purchased from defendant Lloyd, Carr, a commodity futures option broker, certain interests denominated "commodity futures options."

* * *

The plaintiff seeks to recover actual and punitive damages for himself and for a class of similarly situated purchasers for losses resulting from their purchases, with interest thereon, together with the costs of this suit and reasonable attorney's fees. The defendants, whose motions for summary judgment are now before the Court for consideration, were members of the law firm of Busnell, Gage & Reizen and were named as defendants because the plaintiff alleges that they acted as general counsel for Lloyd, Carr and were, by virtue of and through their activities as general counsel, "controlling persons" of Lloyd, Carr within the meaning of section 15 of the Securities Act and section 20 of the Exchange Act, and in addition were "aiders and abettors" in the illegal acts, practices, and course of business allegedly pursued by Lloyd, Carr.

*   *   *

[B]oth the plaintiff and defendant Gage conducted substantial discovery, including the depositions or sworn statements of defendant Gage, plaintiff Westlake, and Frank Post, former staff counsel to Lloyd, Carr. In addition, documents in defendant Gage's law offices in Southfield, Michigan, were examined. . . . By order dated November 26, 1980, published at 504 F. Supp. 337 (N.D. Ga. 1980), the Court denied Gage's motion for summary judgment. Therein, the Court determined that a genuine issue existed as to whether defendant Gage was a "controlling person" of Lloyd, Carr under the federal securities laws. In addition, the Court determined that there was a genuine issue remaining as to whether the plaintiff's investment constituted a security under the federal securities laws.

*   *   *

. . . On February 24, 1981, the plaintiff filed his amended complaint naming as additional defendants: the law firm of Bushnell, Gage & Reizen; Mr. Bushnell, Jr.; Mr. Reizen; Ms. Shecter; and Mr. Henry. The aforementioned additional defendants were all members of the law firm Bushnell, Gage & Reizen and occupy the same position in relation to the plaintiff in this suit as does defendant Gage.

*   *   *

[P]ursuant to substantial discovery which includes among other things the deposition of Lloyd, Carr's former "staff counsel" Frank Post and the affidavits of defendants Mr. Bushnell, Mr. Gage, Mr. Reizen, Ms. Schecter, and Mr. Henry, the defendants, filed the pending motions for summary judgment.

*   *   *

Defendants' Motion for Summary Judgment

The standard for summary judgment . . . require[s] an inquiry into the merits of the parties' claims. Under Rule 56, the party seeking summary judgment bears the exacting burden of demonstrating that there is no actual dispute as to any material fact. Summary judgment should be granted when the moving party is entitled to judgment as a matter of law, when it is clear what the truth is, and when no genuine issue remains for trial. In assessing whether the party moving for summary judgment has borne his burden of demonstrating want of actual dispute as to a material fact, the Court should view all evidence introduced and all factual inferences from that evidence in the light most favorable to the party opposing the motion, and all reasonable doubts about the facts should be resolved in favor of the nonmoving litigant. However, denials or allegations by the nonmoving party in the form of legal conclusions unsupported by specific facts have no probative value and are thus insufficient to create issues of material fact that would preclude summary judgment.

*   *   *

Securities Act

*   *   *

[T]he plaintiff asserts that by their activities as general counsel for Lloyd, Carr, the defendants are liable as "controlling persons" of Lloyd, Carr under section 15 of the Securities Act.

*   *   *

Controlling Person Liability

The Court now considers the defendants' motion for summary judgment with regard to controlling person liability under section 15 of the Securities Act, 15 U.S.C. § 77o, which provides:

> Every person who, by or through stock ownership, agency, or otherwise, or who pursuant to or in connection with an agreement or understanding with one or more other persons by or through stock ownership, agency, or otherwise controls any person liable under section 11 or 12, shall also be jointly and severally with and to the same extent as such controlled person to any person to whom such controlled person is liable, unless the controlling person had no knowledge of or reasonable grounds to believe in the existence of the facts by reason of which the liability of the controlled person is alleged to exist.

The Securities and Exchange Commission has articulated a standard for determining who is a controlling person in 17 C.F.R. § 230.405(f) (1979) . . . . :

> The term "control" (including the terms "controlling," "controlled by" and "under common control with") means the possession, direct or indirect, of the power to direct or cause the direction of the management and policies of a person, whether through the ownership of voting securities, by contract or otherwise.

Case law has further defined "control" as the ability to exert influence, directly or indirectly, over the decision-making process of another person. Even if control is demonstrated, a controlling person may defend the assertion of liability by proof that he acted without "knowledge of or reasonable grounds to believe in the existence of the facts by reason of which the liability of the controlled person is alleged to exist." Section 15 of the Securities Act, 15 U.S.C. § 77o. The burden of establishing control in the first instance is on the plaintiff, while the burden of establishing the "lack of knowledge" defense is on the defendants. Therefore, the analysis of the controlling person liability proceeds in two stages. The plaintiff must first establish that the defendant is a statutory controlling person. If the plaintiff is able to make such a showing, then in order to avoid liability, the defendant must demonstrate that he meets the requirements of the "lack of knowledge" defense.

In its order of November 26, 1980, this Court addressed, among other things, defendant Gage's prior motion for summary judgment with regard to the statutory controlling person issue. At that time, the plaintiff argued that because defendant Gage as general counsel for Lloyd, Carr was frequently in contact with Lloyd, Carr management, was aware of Lloyd, Carr's disputes with administrative agencies, and had knowledge of Lloyd, Carr's unconventional sales methods as well as knowledge of certain allegations of fraud made against Lloyd, Carr, defendant Gage was a controlling person of Lloyd, Carr under the "otherwise" provision in section 15 of the Securities Act. The Court relied mainly on the uncontroverted sworn statement of Frank Post, former Lloyd, Carr staff counsel, in which he stated that Bushnell, Gage & Reizen served Lloyd, Carr in a general advisory capacity; that James Carr as president and Jim Brien as vice president, or both, would consult the law firm regarding any major decisions; that he Frank Post, as staff counsel, looked to the law firm for approval of any course of action that he took; that he was instructed to consult with Ms. Schecter, Mr. Henry, or Mr. Gage before disposing of any reparations claims by unpaid customers; and that he looked to the law firm and not Lloyd, Carr principals for approval of his activities as Lloyd, Carr staff counsel. To support his motion, defendant Gage relied on his own affidavit in which he swore that he acted as litigation counsel and that he was not in a position to control Lloyd, Carr. Based on the uncontroverted Post February 8, 1980, statement and the Gage affidavit, the Court concluded that a genuine issue of material fact remained as to whether defendant Gage actually controlled Lloyd, Carr through control of the Lloyd, Carr staff counsel and through the dependence of James Carr and Jim Brien on defendant Gage's advice. The Court, furthermore, held that whether defendant Gage had a "good faith" or "lack of knowledge" defense under the controlling persons statutes was inappropriate for summary judgment resolution because it directly involved defendant Gage's credibility.

*   *   *

Subsequent to the denial by the Court of defendant Gage's motion for summary judgment in November 1980, the defendants conducted extensive discovery which includes the deposition, affidavit, or sworn statement of Frank Post, James Carr, Jim Brien, Mr. Cosulich, Mr. Labus, Mr. Bushnell, Mr. Reisen, Mr. Henry, and Ms. Schecter. Based upon the record now before the Court, the defendants move for summary judgment in their favor on the ground that no genuine issue of material fact exists as to whether the defendants were controlling persons under section 15 of the Securities Act.

First, the defendants point to the testimony of Frank Post at his deposition when he was specifically questioned about his testimony found on page 14 of his statement upon which the Court relied in denying defendant Gage's prior motion for summary judgment on the "controlling person" issue. Mr. Post admitted that he was not a member of the Lloyd, Carr "board," that he did not regularly attend the board meetings, and that he was not generally privy to conversations which may have taken place between Bushnell, Gage & Reizen and either Mr. Carr or Mr. Brien. Mr. Post admitted that he had no personal knowledge upon which to base this part of his prior testimony. Furthermore, Mr. Post testified that the only "major decisions" known to him on which Bushnell, Gage & Reizen was consulted dealt with matters of litigation. Mr. Post was unable to cite to even one specific occasion when Bushnell, Gage & Reizen gave advice to Lloyd, Carr on anything other than a litigated matter.

The defendants point out that Rule 56(e) of the Federal Rules of Civil Procedure provides that opposing affidavits must be made on personal knowledge and shall set forth such facts as would be admissible in evidence. Because Mr. Post has admitted that he has no personal knowledge of any business decisions on which Lloyd, Carr consulted Bushnell, Gage & Reizen, his testimony at page 14 of the sworn statement cannot be considered in opposition to the defendants' motion.

Second, the defendants argue that the uncontradicted testimony on personal knowledge of these defendants and of the principals or board members of Lloyd, Carr, i.e., Mr. Carr, Mr. Brien, Mr. Cosulich, and Mr. Labus, unequivocally establishes that Bushnell, Gage & Reizen was not a controlling person of Lloyd, Carr. While the defendants swore that neither they nor the firm gave any general business, tax, commodities, or securities advice to Lloyd, Carr and that their substantive representations related entirely to matters involving litigation, they admit that the firm assisted Lloyd, Carr in a few "ministerial" matters, such as filing the necessary forms to qualify to do business in various states. It is not disputed that the Lloyd, Carr board members, in particular James Carr, had actual control over the management of Lloyd, Carr. The members of that board uniformly swore that Bushnell, Gage & Reizen had no involvement whatsoever in the alleged fraudulent practices of Lloyd, Carr. In addition, Mr. Brien, who was responsible for the day-to-day liaison with Lloyd, Carr's attorneys, states that Bushnell, Gage & Reizen's relationship with Lloyd, Carr was that of outside counsel handling matters of pending or threatened litigation. Further, Mr. Brien stated that Bushnell, Gage, & Reizen did not give, nor was it asked to give, advice on securities laws, commodities laws, or any general business law related to the sale practices and activities of Lloyd, Carr. In view of the above direct evidence, the defendants assert that being described as "general counsel" alone is insufficient to raise a genuine of fact precluding summary judgment.

Simply stated, the thrust of the plaintiff's opposition to the defendants' motion for summary judgment on the controlling person issue is that Bushnell, Gage & Reizen, through its litigation activities, had absolute control over the very essence of Lloyd, Carr because Bushnell, Gage & Reizen used threats and litigation tricks to deter the authorities' efforts to shut down Lloyd, Carr. Furthermore, the plaintiff asserts that although Lloyd, Carr had been officially advised that continued operation without registration and compliance with antifraud provisions was illegal, the established policy of Lloyd, Carr under the unrestricted direction of Bushnell, Gage & Reizen was to use "litigation" as a sword to intimidate the CFTC and to allow Lloyd, Carr to continue unfettered in its illegal activities.

To support his contention, the plaintiff relies mainly on evidence [that the litigation work was part of an overall strategy to keep Lloyd,Carr in business.]

In their March 4, 1983, letter brief, the defendants respond that the facts concerning Bushnell, Gage & Reizen's litigation activities referred to by the plaintiff do not justify a trial to determine whether lawyers, acting as litigation counsel, can by that activity incur controlling person liability under the Securities Act. The defendants maintain that the evidence establishes that Bushnell, Gage & Reizen did nothing more than zealously represent in litigation its client, Lloyd, Carr, as demanded by Canon 7 of the Model Code of Professional Responsibilities (1979) (hereinafter CPR). Furthermore, the defendants maintain that as litigation counsel they "obviously" had knowledge of the underlying issues and claims against Lloyd, Carr. In addition, the defendants maintain that as litigation counsel, they represented Lloyd, Carr in matters which, if decided adversely to their client, would unsurprisingly affect its business. The defendants argue that there is no evidence to show that Bushnell, Gage & Reizen controlled the day-to-day operations of Lloyd, Carr.

The defendants, furthermore, assert that Bushnell, Gage & Reizen had no power to "control" Lloyd, Carr but only had the lawyer's ability to make recommendations to James Carr which would be accepted or rejected. Consequently, the defendants maintain that James Carr operated Lloyd, Carr as he pleased, notwithstanding the legal advice from Bushnell, Gage & Reizen. The defendants specifically point out one instance when a temporary restraining order (TRO) was issued against Lloyd, Carr and Bushnell, Gage & Reizen vigorously advised James Carr to comply with the TRO by closing the Michigan operations. James Carr, however, responded to that advice by saying: "Hell no, I am not going to close my office!" The defendants also refer the Court to the direct evidence previously submitted and relied upon in their briefs which uniformly supports the defendants' position that they acted as litigation counsel and their litigation advice was accepted or rejected upon the decision of James Carr.

Because research has revealed no legal precedent with regard to whether and under what circumstances litigation counsel should be held liable as controlling persons under section 15 of the Securities Act, the Court herein has set forth the legal positions of the respective parties in substantial detail. While the plaintiff brings to the attention of the Court several cases discussing the duties of attorneys in the area of securities law, those cases are inapposite to the case at bar involving attorneys in their role as litigators or advocates because the cited cases involve attorneys acting only in their role as advisors in the area of securities. Cases involving attorneys who zealously represent the interests of their clients are distinguishable from cases involving attorneys who advise their clients how the securities laws apply to particular situations or where the attorneys prepare or assist in preparing offering circulars or opinion letters containing incorrect information, as in those cases cited by the plaintiff. In asserting a position on behalf of his client, an advocate for the most part deals with past conduct and must take the facts as he finds them. By contrast, an attorney serving as an advisor primarily assists his client in determining courses of future conduct and relationships. While serving as an advocate, an attorney should resolve in favor of his client doubts as to the bounds of the law. In serving as an advisor, an attorney should give his professional opinion as to what the ultimate decisions of the courts would likely be as to the applicable law.

While this Court has previously noted that an attorney could be found to be liable as a controlling person when, for example, the attorney is in some sense a culpable participant in the acts perpetrated by the controlled person, . . . the Court during oral argument on February 22, 1983, stated its opinion that an attorney cannot be held to be a controlling person under the federal securities laws for vigorously performing legitimate litigation activities for his client. Unless the plaintiff shows that an attorney participated in fraud or a similarly culpable act or unless the plaintiff shows that the attorney pursued legal representation in blatant violation of the CPR, Canon 7, he cannot be held to be a controlling person merely because he renders legal advice in pursuing litigation on behalf of his client. Simply because a client is legally attacked and is perhaps unlikely to prevail in court does not mean that the client is not entitled to legal representation. On the contrary, such an individual is not only entitled to but in need of zealous legal representation within the bounds of the law. This Court declines to discourage such representation.

Considering the facts and factual inferences in a reasonable light most favorable to the plaintiff, the Court concludes that no genuine issues of material fact remain as to whether the defendants were "controlling persons" of Lloyd, Carr under the Securities Act. The plaintiff's arguments seem implicitly to assume that a law firm called "general counsel" is automatically a controlling person, but the Court does not believe such assumption is warranted. The Court focuses upon what the defendants actually did, rather than upon their title. . . . In order to reach the conclusions argued by the plaintiff, a fact finder would have to contort the record facts and resort to pure speculation. After profound consideration of the motions, the briefs, and the record, the Court determines that the plaintiff has failed to raise facts or inferences sufficient to preclude the defendants' motions for summary judgment on the "controlling person" issue under the Securities Act.

Chapter II

REGULATION OF THE LEGAL PROFESSION AND CONTROLS ON LAWYER CONDUCT

The first part of this chapter relates to the organizational structure of the profession while the second part introduces various mechanisms that are used to govern lawyer conduct.

A. INSTITUTIONAL FRAMEWORK

1. Organization of the Legal Profession

The legal profession has organized itself in a variety of ways. Membership in some organizations is voluntary while membership in others is required of those who wish to practice law in a particular jurisdiction.

a. The American Bar Association

The American Bar Association (ABA) is a national, voluntary association of lawyers. The ABA was created largely to serve social functions in 1888. By the early 20th century, it had turned attention to efforts to speak for the legal profession with a single voice. At that time, however, it could boast of only modest membership of less than 10% of licensed lawyers. Because membership in the organization was by "invitation-only" at that time, that 10% was a select group of elite lawyers whose clients were among the leaders in American business and industry. Some of the ABA's early work is tainted by the self- and client-interested (or at the very least myopic) motivations and views of the organization's membership. Early stances and actions against ethnic immigrant lawyers and African-American lawyers, increases in educational requirements for admission to practice, and restrictions on advertising, all bear the mark of the ABA's early flaws of elitism.

Today, ABA membership is open to anyone licensed to practice law in any state. Currently, approximately 50% of licensed lawyers belong to the ABA. The ABA does not license individuals to practice law. As a voluntary association, the ABA has no direct regulatory authority over any lawyer. Nonetheless, its views on issues affecting the law of lawyering and its model ethics codes have tremendous influence. In addition to its work on directly lawyer-related issues, the ABA takes positions on a wide variety of social issues, generates model statutes, and lobbies for their adoption by legislatures.

b. Alternative National Bar Associations

National organizations of lawyers have been established, in some instances to express alternative views from those held by the ABA. The National Lawyers Guild was established in 1936 as a more liberal, more progressive organization of lawyers. It continues to be active in a variety of public interest areas. The National Bar Association was established in 1909 as an organization for Black lawyers who until the 1940s were largely denied membership in the ABA. Along with the National Conference of Black Attorneys, which was formed in 1969, the NBA plays an active role in legal and political issues. The National Association of Women Lawyers, with its roots in the Women Lawyers' Club of New York City of 1909 and the Women Lawyers' Association of 1911, exists to promote legal and political positions of its members. A wide variety of other voluntary associations of lawyers exist, organized, for example, by race or ethnicity (e.g., The Asian Bar Association), sexual preference (e.g., The National Lesbian and Gay Bar Association), religion (e.g., The Christian Legal Society), employer (e.g., The Federal Bar Association), practice subject matter (e.g., The Customs Bar), and practice activity (e.g., Association of Trial Lawyers of America and The American College of Trial Lawyers).

[handwritten margin note: Other organizations]

c. State Bar Associations

The ABA does not license lawyers to practice law. States, through their courts and sometimes legislatures, license lawyers to practice law within the relevant jurisdiction. State bar associations, with delegated authority to recommend licensure and discipline of lawyers, assist courts in their supervision of lawyers and operate as professional organizations for the particular state's lawyers.

Lawyers from individual states began to organize statewide bar associations in the 1870s. At first, all of these were voluntary organizations. In many states they remain so. In some states, membership in the state bar association is mandatory, effectively a part of the licensing process. This mandatory membership establishes what is called an "integrated bar" of which all the lawyers licensed to practice in the state are members. State courts and legislatures have the power to create integrated/mandatory bars in the states.

[handwritten margin note: some state bars are mandatory]

The Bar of California is considered an "integrated bar," an association of attorneys in which membership and dues are required as a condition of practicing law, created under state law to regulate the State's legal profession. In fulfilling its broad statutory mission to "promote the improvement of the administration of justice," the Bar used its membership dues for self-regulatory functions, such as formulating rules of professional conduct and disciplining members for misconduct. Until 1990, it also used dues to lobby the legislature and other governmental agencies, file amicus curiae briefs in pending cases, hold an annual delegates conference for the debate of current issues and the approval of resolutions, and engage in educational programs. Some California lawyers complained that in some respects, their dues were being used to advance political and ideological causes to which they do not subscribe, in violation of their First and Fourteenth Amendment rights to freedom of speech and association. The lower courts ruled for the Bar, saying that as a government agency, it can expend its budget to advance what it regards as being in the public interest. The Supreme Court reversed, ruling that the

State Bar's use of members' compulsory dues to finance political and ideological activities with which petitioners disagree violates their First Amendment right of free speech when such expenditures are not necessarily or reasonably incurred for the purpose of regulating the legal profession or improving the quality of legal services. Furthermore, the Court determined that the State Bar is not a typical "government agency." The Bar's principal funding comes from dues levied on its members rather than from appropriations made by the legislature; its membership is composed solely of lawyers admitted to practice in the State; and its services by way of governance of the profession are essentially advisory in nature, since the ultimate responsibility of such governance is reserved by state law to the State Supreme Court. By contrast, there is a substantial analogy between the relationship of the Bar and its members and that of unions and their members. Just as it is appropriate that employees who receive the benefit of union negotiation with their employer pay their fair share of the cost of that process by paying agency-shop dues, it is entirely appropriate that lawyers who derive benefit from the status of being admitted to practice before the courts should be called upon to pay a fair share of the cost of the professional involvement in this effort. The state bar was created, not to participate in the general government of the state, but to provide specialized professional advice to those with the ultimate responsibility of governing the legal profession. These differences between the state bar and traditional government agencies subjects the state bar to the same constitutional rule with respect to the use of compulsory dues as are labor unions. *Keller v. State Bar of California*, 496 U.S. 1 (1990).

NOTES, QUESTIONS, AND EXAMPLES

1. In 1997, following budget disputes between the State Bar of California and the governor, the State Bar of California "closed." Disciplinary processes halted; no one answered the ethics hot line; complaints regarding lawyer misconduct were placed in a warehouse. A leaner budget and the bar dues to support the disciplinary process, but little else, were finally approved by the State Supreme Court in late 1998. A state of affairs somewhat closer to normalcy has returned since then.

2. As a voluntary association of lawyers, the ABA can do with its members dues what the Supreme Court rules the state bars cannot do. The ABA is an extremely active force in a wide range of social issues that are not directly lawyer-related.

3. Consider the Court's analogy of bar associations to labor unions. For the purposes of the *Keller* Court, lawyers are no different from bakers or plumbers or truck drivers. On what other sorts of lawyer issues can you imagine such an analogy being relevant?

INTERNATIONAL NOTES

1. Admission to practice law in most Member States of the European Union typically consists of three aspects: education, examination, and practical training. Educational programs vary in duration among member states, but all are considered part of an undergraduate education. *See* Wayne J. Carroll, *Liberalization of National Legal Admissions Requirements in the European Union: Lessons and*

Implications, 22 PENN ST. INT'L L. REV. 563, 566 (2004). Uniformity among the educational programs is being advanced through a series of higher education standards agreements. These agreements seek to make movement among European universities more fluid and also to make degree requirements from various universities more uniform. The so-called "Bologna Declaration" articulates these principles and has been a driving force in European higher education reform. Aspiring EU lawyers generally must take a state-administered examination before being allowed to engage in the practice of law. *Id.* However, Spain remains one exception to this rule. In Spain, an undergraduate degree and payment of a license are sufficient to obtain a law license. A law requiring a bar exam was adopted by the Spanish parliament, but as of 2011, the law has yet to be implemented.

2.   Traditionally, to practice law in Japan as an attorney, judge, or public prosecutor, a person was required to pass Japan's national bar examination, complete an 18-month apprenticeship at the Legal Training Institute of the Supreme Court, and then pass a completion test. Alternatively, a person may practice law if they passed the bar examination and then worked for five years or more in positions of specialized legal work in the courts, Ministry of Justice, House of Representatives, House of Councilors, or other government institution. Reforms to the profession training system have been underway since 2001, and beginning in 2006, aspiring attorneys must complete a law school curriculum or alternatively pass a preliminary test to sit for the bar examination. *See* Japan Federation of Bar Associations, *Japanese   Attorney   Systems,   available   at*   http://www.nichibrenren.or.jp/en/about/system.html.

2.   Sources of the Law Governing Lawyers

The law that governs lawyers comes from a variety of sources and exists in a variety of forms, including ethics codes, inherent court power, statutes and court rules, and constitutional provisions. Much of the law that governs lawyers is the law of other substantive areas such as contracts, torts, and agency.

a.   Ethics Codes

Every state has an adopted code of ethics for lawyers that operates as a set of mandatory legal rules governing lawyer conduct.

Beginning in 1908, the ABA adopted a series of three model ethics codes that have served as models for state adoption. Because the ABA is a voluntary, non-license granting organization, none of these three has ever been directly controlling on a lawyer's conduct. The models have, however, been the chief source from which states have created their own codes. Additionally, federal courts have frequently looked both to the ABA models as well as the code for the state in which the particular federal court sits for governing ethics rules.

The 1908 Canons of Ethics were adopted by the ABA but were not initially expected to be adopted by states or routinely enforced as rules by courts and bar authorities. The Canons are largely aspirational in tone; only the rules on advertising and solicitation are written in mandatory terms. The Canons consist of 32 statements (canons) describing appropriate and inappropriate lawyer conduct.

The Canons were adopted by the ABA at a time when its membership represented less than 10% of the practicing lawyers in the United States. That 10%, furthermore, was the elite element of the bar. Except for the addition of prohibitions on advertising, the Canons were based on, indeed drawn almost verbatim from, the 1887 Alabama Code of Ethics, which had itself been copied largely from GEORGE SHARSWOOD, AN ESSAY ON PROFESSIONAL ETHICS (1854). Arguably, the Canons were 50 years out-of-date on the date of their adoption.

The Model Code of Professional Responsibility (1969) was the ABA's first genuine effort to influence the setting of mandatory, national standards for lawyer conduct. Following its Preamble and Preliminary Statement, which includes important definitional material, the Model Code consists of three types of provisions: Canons, Disciplinary Rules, and Ethical Considerations. The nine Canons are broad statements of basic norms. Within each Canon are Disciplinary Rules, which are the mandatory prescriptions "that state a minimum level of conduct below which no lawyer can fall without being subject to disciplinary action." Model Code, Preliminary Statement. A group of Ethical Considerations (ECs) are associated with each of the nine Canons, giving flesh to the Disciplinary Rules. The ECs were meant to be aspirational rather than mandatory, but courts have at times used them as if they were mandatory.

The Model Code was immensely successful in terms of adoption by the states. By 1974, 49 states had adopted an ethics code based on the ABA Model Code. In terms of longevity, they were less successful, being seriously called into question a mere few years after their adoption. The early 1970s Watergate scandal, and the many lawyers who were involved in it, created the impetus for a more law-like set of ethics rules.

The 1983 Model Rules of Professional Conduct were drafted and then adopted during this time of serious questioning of the quality of the ABA Model Code. The Model Rules largely abandoned the aspirational tone of the Canons and the Ethical Consideration portion of the Model Code in favor of a "rule and comment," Restatement-like organizational scheme. The result has been a more rule-of-law treatment of the law of lawyering than was possible under the former, more aspirational, spirit-of-the-profession tone codes. Nearly all states have replaced their Model Code-based ethics codes with Model Rules-based ethics codes.

In 1997, the ABA created the Ethics 2000 Commission to evaluate and revise the Model Rules. Although some believed that this revision would develop into the adoption of an entirely new code potentially with a different format from the Model Rules, the Commission confined itself to revision rather than replacement of the Model Rules. Most of the Commission's extensive proposals were adopted by the ABA in February 2002, resulting in the most wide-reaching and extensive amendments to the Model Rules since their 1983 adoption.

States adopt lawyer ethics codes either by legislation or by rule-making action by the state's court of last resort.

b.   Case Authority and Inherent Court Power

In several ways, courts make the law governing lawyers. Courts interpret the existing ethics codes and as such make the law of lawyering in their interpretive activities in the same way as courts interpreting statutes make law. Because courts have inherent power to regulate lawyers, who are officers of the court, a common law of lawyer regulation also exists.

CHAMBERS v. NASCO, INC.
501 U.S. 32 (1991)

WHITE, J.

This case requires us to explore the scope of the inherent power of a federal court to sanction a litigant for bad-faith conduct. Specifically, we are asked to determine whether the District Court, sitting in diversity, properly invoked its inherent power in assessing as a sanction for a party's bad-faith conduct attorney's fees and related expenses paid by the party's opponent to its attorneys. We hold that the District Court acted within its discretion, and we therefore affirm the judgment of the Court of Appeals.

I

This case began as a simple action for specific performance of a contract, but it did not remain so. Petitioner G. Russell Chambers was the sole shareholder and director of Calcasieu Television and Radio, Inc. (CTR), which operated television station KPLC-TV in Lake Charles, Louisiana. On August 9, 1983, Chambers, acting both in his individual capacity and on behalf of CTR, entered into a purchase agreement to sell the station's facilities and broadcast license to respondent NASCO, Inc., for a purchase price of $18 million. The agreement was not recorded in the parishes in which the two properties housing the station's facilities were located. Consummation of the agreement was subject to the approval of the Federal Communications Commission (FCC); both parties were obligated to file the necessary documents with the FCC no later than September 23, 1983. By late August, however, Chambers had changed his mind and tried to talk NASCO out of consummating the sale. NASCO refused. On September 23, Chambers, through counsel, informed NASCO that he would not file the necessary papers with the FCC.

NASCO decided to take legal action. On Friday, October 14, 1983, NASCO's counsel informed counsel for Chambers and CTR that NASCO would file suit the following Monday in the United States District Court for the Western District of Louisiana, seeking specific performance of the agreement, as well as a temporary restraining order (TRO) to prevent the alienation or encumbrance of the properties at issue. NASCO provided this notice in accordance with Federal Rule of Civil Procedure 65 and Rule 11 of the District Court's Local Rules, both of which are designed to give a defendant in a TRO application notice of the hearing and an opportunity to be heard.

The reaction of Chambers and his attorney, A.J. Gray III, was later described by the District Court as having "emasculated and frustrated the purposes of these rules and the powers of [the District] Court by utilizing this notice to prevent NASCO's access to the remedy of specific performance." On Sunday, October 16, 1983, the pair acted to place the properties at issue beyond the reach of the District Court by means of the Louisiana Public Records Doctrine. Because the purchase agreement had never been recorded, they determined that if the properties were sold to a third party, and if the deeds were recorded before the issuance of a TRO, the District Court would lack jurisdiction over the properties.

To this end, Chambers and Gray created a trust, with Chambers' sister as trustee and Chambers' three adult children as beneficiaries. The pair then directed the president of CTR, who later became Chambers' wife, to execute warranty deeds conveying the two tracts at issue to the trust for a recited consideration of $1.4 million. Early Monday morning, the deeds were recorded. The trustee, as purchaser, had not signed the deeds; none of the consideration had been paid; and CTR remained in possession of the properties. Later that morning, NASCO's counsel appeared in the District Court to file the complaint and seek the TRO. With NASCO's counsel present, the District Judge telephoned Gray. Despite the judge's queries concerning the possibility that CTR was negotiating to sell the properties to a third person, Gray made no mention of the recordation of the deeds earlier that morning. That afternoon, Chambers met with his sister and had her sign the trust documents and a $1.4 million note to CTR. The next morning, Gray informed the District Court by letter of the recordation of the deeds the day before and admitted that he had intentionally withheld the information from the court.

Within the next few days, Chambers' attorneys prepared a leaseback agreement from the trustee to CTR, so that CTR could remain in possession of the properties and continue to operate the station. The following week, the District Court granted a preliminary injunction against Chambers and CTR and entered a second TRO to prevent the trustee from alienating or encumbering the properties. At that hearing, the District Judge warned that Gray's and Chambers' conduct had been unethical.

Despite this early warning, Chambers, often acting through his attorneys, continued to abuse the judicial process. In November 1983, in defiance of the preliminary injunction, he refused to allow NASCO to inspect CTR's corporate records. The ensuing civil contempt proceedings resulted in the assessment of a $25,000 fine against Chambers personally. Two subsequent appeals from the contempt order were dismissed for lack of a final judgment.

Undeterred, Chambers proceeded with "a series of meritless motions and pleadings and delaying actions." These actions triggered further warnings from the court. At one point, acting sua sponte, the District Judge called a status conference to find out why bankers were being deposed. When informed by Chambers' counsel that the purpose was to learn whether NASCO could afford to pay for the station, the court canceled the depositions consistent with its authority under Federal Rule of Civil Procedure 26(g).

At the status conference nine days before the April 1985 trial date,[1] the District Judge again warned counsel that further misconduct would not be tolerated.[2] Finally, on the eve of trial, Chambers and CTR stipulated that the purchase agreement was enforceable and that Chambers had breached the agreement on September 23, 1983, by failing to file the necessary papers with the FCC. At trial, the only defense presented by Chambers was the Public Records Doctrine.

In the interlude between the trial and the entry of judgment during which the District Court prepared its opinion, Chambers sought to render the purchase agreement meaningless by seeking permission from the FCC to build a new transmission tower for the station and to relocate the transmission facilities to that site, which was not covered by the agreement. Only after NASCO sought contempt sanctions did Chambers withdraw the application.

The District Court entered judgment on the merits in NASCO's favor, finding that the transfer of the properties to the trust was a simulated sale and that the deeds purporting to convey the property were "null, void, and of no effect." Chambers' motions, filed in the District Court, the Court of Appeals, and this Court, to stay the judgment pending appeal were denied. Undeterred, Chambers convinced CTR officials to file formal oppositions to NASCO's pending application for FCC approval of the transfer of the station's license, in contravention of both the District Court's injunctive orders and its judgment on the merits. NASCO then sought contempt sanctions for a third time, and the oppositions were withdrawn.

When Chambers refused to prepare to close the sale, NASCO again sought the court's help. A hearing was set for July 16, 1986, to determine whether certain equipment was to be included in the sale. At the beginning of the hearing, the court informed Chambers' new attorney, Edwin A. McCabe, that further sanctionable conduct would not be tolerated. When the hearing was recessed for several days, Chambers, without notice to the court or NASCO, removed from service at the station all of the equipment at issue, forcing the District Court to order that the equipment be returned to service.

Immediately following oral argument on Chambers' appeal from the District Court's judgment on the merits, the Court of Appeals, ruling from the bench, found the appeal frivolous. The court imposed appellate sanctions in the form of attorney's fees and double costs, pursuant to Federal Rule of Appellate Procedure 38, and remanded the case to the District Court with orders to fix the amount of appellate sanctions and to determine whether further sanctions should be imposed for the manner in which the litigation had been conducted.

On remand, NASCO moved for sanctions, invoking the District Court's inherent power, Fed. Rule Civ. Proc. 11, and 28 U.S.C. § 1927. After full briefing and a hearing, the District Court determined that sanctions were appropriate "for the manner in which this proceeding was conducted in the district court from October

---

[1] [2] The trial date itself reflected delaying tactics. Trial had been set for February 1985, but in January, Gray, on behalf of Chambers, filed a motion to recuse the judge. The motion was denied, as was the subsequent writ of mandamus filed in the Court of Appeals.

[2] [3] To make his point clear, the District Judge gave counsel copies of Judge Schwarzer's then recent article, *Sanctions Under the New Federal Rule 11 — A Closer Look*, 104 F.R.D. 181 (1985).

14, 1983, the time that plaintiff gave notice of its intention to file suit to this date." At the end of an extensive opinion recounting what it deemed to have been sanctionable conduct during this period, the court imposed sanctions against Chambers in the form of attorney's fees and expenses totaling $996,644.65, which represented the entire amount of NASCO's litigation costs paid to its attorneys.[3] In so doing, the court rejected Chambers' argument that he had merely followed the advice of counsel, labeling him "the strategist," behind a scheme devised "first, to deprive this Court of jurisdiction and, second, to devise a plan of obstruction, delay, harassment, and expense sufficient to reduce NASCO to a condition of exhausted compliance."

In imposing the sanctions, the District Court first considered Federal Rule of Civil Procedure 11. It noted that the alleged sanctionable conduct was that Chambers and the other defendants had "(1) attempted to deprive this Court of jurisdiction by acts of fraud, nearly all of which were performed outside the confines of this Court, (2) filed false and frivolous pleadings, and (3) attempted, by other tactics of delay, oppression, harassment and massive expense to reduce plaintiff to exhausted compliance." The court recognized that the conduct in the first and third categories could not be reached by Rule 11, which governs only papers filed with a court. As for the second category, the court explained that the falsity of the pleadings at issue did not become apparent until after the trial on the merits, so that it would have been impossible to assess sanctions at the time the papers were filed. Consequently, the District Court deemed Rule 11 "insufficient" for its purposes. The court likewise declined to impose sanctions under § 1927,[4] both because the statute applies only to attorneys, and therefore would not reach Chambers, and because the statute was not broad enough to reach "acts which degrade the judicial system," including "attempts to deprive the Court of jurisdiction, fraud, misleading and lying to the Court." The court therefore relied on its inherent power in imposing sanctions, stressing that "[t]he wielding of that inherent power is particularly appropriate when the offending parties have practiced a fraud upon the court."

The Court of Appeals affirmed. [W]e granted certiorari.

---

[3] [5] In calculating the award, the District Court deducted the amounts previously awarded as compensatory damages for contempt, as well as the amount awarded as appellate sanctions. . . . The court also sanctioned other individuals, who are not parties to the action in this Court. Chambers' sister, the trustee, was sanctioned by a reprimand; attorney Gray was disbarred and prohibited from seeking readmission for three years; attorney Richard A. Curry, who represented the trustee, was suspended from practice before the court for six months; and attorney McCabe was suspended for five years. Although these sanctions did not affect the bank accounts of these individuals, they were nevertheless substantial sanctions and were as proportionate to the conduct at issue as was the monetary sanction imposed on Chambers. Indeed, in the case of the disbarment of attorney Gray, the court recognized that the penalty was among the harshest possible sanctions and one which derived from its authority to supervise those admitted to practice before it.

[4] [6] That statute provides: "Any attorney . . . who so multiplies the proceedings in any case unreasonably and vexatiously may be required by the court to satisfy personally the excess costs, expenses, and attorneys' fees reasonably incurred because of such conduct." 28 U.S.C. § 1927.

II

Chambers maintains that 28 U.S.C. § 1927 and the various sanctioning provisions in the Federal Rules of Civil Procedure reflect a legislative intent to displace the inherent power. At least, he argues that they obviate or foreclose resort to the inherent power in this case. We agree with the Court of Appeals that neither proposition is persuasive.

A

It has long been understood that "[c]ertain implied powers must necessarily result to our Courts of justice from the nature of their institution," powers "which cannot be dispensed with in a Court, because they are necessary to the exercise of all others." *United States v. Hudson*, 7 Cranch 32, 34 (1812). For this reason, "Courts of justice are universally acknowledged to be vested, by their very creation, with power to impose silence, respect, and decorum, in their presence, and submission to their lawful mandates." *Anderson v. Dunn*, 6 Wheat. 204, 227 (1821). These powers are "governed not by rule or statute but by the control necessarily vested in courts to manage their own affairs so as to achieve the orderly and expeditious disposition of cases." *Link v. Wabash R. Co.*, 370 U.S. 626, 630-31 (1962).

Prior cases have outlined the scope of the inherent power of the federal courts. For example, the Court has held that a federal court has the power to control admission to its bar and to discipline attorneys who appear before it. *See Ex parte Burr*, 9 Wheat. 529, 531 (1824). While this power "ought to be exercised with great caution," it is nevertheless "incidental to all Courts."

In addition, it is firmly established that "[t]he power to punish for contempts is inherent in all courts." This power reaches both conduct before the court and that beyond the court's confines, for "[t]he underlying concern that gave rise to the contempt power was not . . . merely the disruption of court proceedings. Rather, it was disobedience to the orders of the Judiciary, regardless of whether such disobedience interfered with the conduct of trial." *Young v. United States ex rel. Vuitton et Fils S.A.*, 481 U.S. 787, 798 (1987).

*   *   *

B

We discern no basis for holding that the sanctioning scheme of the statute and the rules displaces the inherent power to impose sanctions for the bad-faith conduct described above. These other mechanisms, taken alone or together, are not substitutes for the inherent power, for that power is both broader and narrower than other means of imposing sanctions. [W]hereas each of the other mechanisms reaches only certain individuals or conduct, the inherent power extends to a full range of litigation abuses. At the very least, the inherent power must continue to exist to fill in the interstices. . . .

Like the Court of Appeals, we find no abuse of discretion in resorting to the inherent power in the circumstances of this case.

* * *

IV

We review a court's imposition of sanctions under its inherent power for abuse of discretion. Based on the circumstances of this case, we find that the District Court acted within its discretion in assessing as a sanction for Chambers' bad-faith conduct the entire amount of NASCO's attorney's fees.

NOTES, QUESTIONS, AND EXAMPLES

1. Attorney Gray was disbarred from practicing before the federal courts in which this case was heard. The federal court lacks the power to affect his license to practice before state courts in jurisdictions in which he is admitted to practice. Nonetheless, a common disciplinary scenario involves one court disciplining a lawyer based on the record of misconduct before another disciplining court.

2. Attorney Gray and his client engaged in numerous fraudulent acts to stymie the administration of justice. When does aggressive, zealous advocacy become sanctionable abuse? State and local bar associations have been adopting lawyer creeds in recent years. The creeds exist independently from the mandatory codes of ethics and are meant to encourage by aspiration good conduct among lawyers, that is, civility. For an interesting case that blurs the line between civility and mandatory ethics rule enforcement, see *Dondi Properties Corp. v. Commerce Savings & Loan Ass'n*, 121 F.R.D. 284 (N.D. Tex 1988).

c. Ethics Opinions

Both the ABA and state bar associations issue non-binding ethics opinions that are frequently relied upon by courts in law of lawyering cases. These opinions are often generated by the submission of a hypothetical question (usually based on a situation currently being confronted by the questioner) to a state bar committee whose responsibility it is to answer such questions and publish the opinions. Such opinions are not binding on the parties and are advisory only. Nonetheless, it is not uncommon to find courts relying on them as secondary, persuasive authority.

d. Constitutional Constraints

Like any other area of state or federal regulation, the law governing lawyers is subject to constitutional limitations. In effect, the Constitution operates as an overriding element of the law of lawyering. Constitutional limitations are most prominent in areas such as lawyers' commercial speech (advertising and solicitation of clients) (*see* Chapter IX), which is afforded considerable First Amendment protection, lawyers' general speech rights (e.g., *Gentile v. State Bar of Nevada*, excerpted in Chapter VII), and states' efforts to impose residency requirements for entry to practice, in cases such as *Supreme Court of New Hampshire v. Piper*, 470 U.S. 274 (1985), summarized later in this chapter.

e.   "Other Law"

The law of a wide variety of other substantive areas, whether statute-, rule-, or case-based, forms an essential part of the law of lawyering. In some instances, other substantive legal rules are incorporated into the ethics codes while in other instances, these substantive rules exist in a way that governs lawyers qua lawyers in much the same way they govern others.

Contract law, as modified by fiduciary constraints, governs, for example, the lawyer-client contractual relationship. Tort law governs, for example, lawyer liability to clients for malpractice, lawyer liability to third parties for intentional wrongful acts and in some cases incompetence. Tort law also plays a major role in the law of contingent fee arrangements. Fiduciary law governs the special relationship and duties of lawyers to clients and certain other beneficiaries of lawyer and client acts. Agency law governs and informs much of the relationship between lawyer and client, with the lawyer acting as the client's agent. Criminal law governs lawyer criminal liability not only for the lawyer's individual acts but also possible liability as an accomplice or conspirator with a client who is engaged in criminal conduct. Criminal and civil procedural law govern lawyer conduct, particularly in litigation contexts, and include, for example, rules that implicate the imposition of court sanctions for a variety of lawyer conduct. Antitrust law governs, for example, bar association efforts to restrain trade (e.g., *Goldfarb v. Virginia State Bar*, 421 U.S. 773 (1975) (holding that bar enforced minimum fee schedules violate antitrust principles)). Administrative law in a wide range of topic areas governs lawyers in special ways. The areas include, for example, tax, banking, securities, environmental, and occupational safety regulations. Employment law, including employment discrimination laws, applies to law firm and entity employment of lawyers. (*See* Chapter VIII.)

INTERNATIONAL NOTE

Consider the most basic complication of cross-border practice. Imagine a Polish lawyer and a Pennsylvania lawyer who represent two commercial entities wishing to collaborate on establishing a manufacturing facility in Croatia. The two lawyers meet while each happens to be in Madrid. As they share vino tinto at a Madrid terrace restaurant, they begin discussing the legal issues that must be resolved if their clients' venture is to succeed. Each lawyer, no doubt, would like to know how candid and forthright the other lawyer must be in these discussions. But before they can even begin to know, they must know what set of ethics rules each lawyer must follow, and what culture of lawyering each lawyer belongs to. Do they follow Polish lawyer ethics law? Spanish? EU? Pennsylvanian? Croatian? Lawyer ethics codes have choice of law provisions, instructing bar authorities on what ethics law to apply to a "home" lawyer practicing across borders. The EU rule, the Polish rule, and the ABA Model Rule, for example, are as follows. Which is most helpful? Why?

EU Choice of Law

When practising cross-border, a lawyer from another Member State may be bound to comply with the professional rules of the Host Member State. Lawyers have a duty to inform themselves as to the rules which will affect them in the performance of any particular activity. Member organizations of the CCBE are obliged to deposit their codes of conduct at the Secretariat of the CCBE so that any lawyer can get hold of the copy of the current code from the Secretariat. CODE OF CONDUCT FOR EUROPEAN LAWYERS § 2.4 (2006).

Polish Choice of Law

It is the obligation of each advocate practising his profession abroad to observe the norms of this code, in addition to the norms of the ethical code applying in the host country.

POLISH SUPREME BAR COUNCIL'S COMPENDIUM OF RULES ON ADVOCATES' ETHICS AND THE DIGNITY OF THE PROFESSION ch. 1, §§ 1, 4.

U.S. Choice of Law

Model Rule 8.5 Disciplinary Authority; Choice of Law[5]

(a) Disciplinary Authority. A lawyer admitted to practice in this jurisdiction is subject to the disciplinary authority of this jurisdiction, regardless of where the lawyer's conduct occurs. A lawyer not admitted in this jurisdiction is also subject to the disciplinary authority of this jurisdiction if the lawyer provides or offers to provide any legal services in this jurisdiction. A lawyer may be subject to the disciplinary authority of both this jurisdiction and another jurisdiction for the same conduct.

(b) Choice of Law. In any exercise of the disciplinary authority of this jurisdiction, the rules of professional conduct to be applied shall be as follows:

(1) for conduct in connection with a matter pending before a tribunal, the rules of the jurisdiction in which the tribunal sits, unless the rules of the tribunal provide otherwise; and

(2) for any other conduct, the rules of the jurisdiction in which the lawyer's conduct occurred, or, if the predominant effect of the conduct is in a different jurisdiction, the rules of that jurisdiction shall be applied to the conduct. A lawyer shall not be subject to discipline if the lawyer's conduct conforms to the rules of a jurisdiction in which the lawyer reasonably believes the predominant effect of the lawyer's conduct will occur.

---

[5] ABA Model Rules of Professional Conduct, 2011 Edition. Copyright © 2011 by the American Bar Association. Reprinted with permission. Copies of ABA Model Rules of Professional Conduct, 2008 Edition, are available from Service Center, American Bar Association, 321 North Clark Street, Chicago, IL 60654, 1-800-285-2221.

3. Admission to Practice

A license to practice law is a prerequisite to a person's lawful engagement in the activities of lawyering. Education, knowledge, and character requirements are the chief hurdles in the path of the applicant for admission to the practice of law.

a. Territorial Restrictions

SUPREME COURT OF NEW HAMPSHIRE v. PIPER
470 U.S. 274 (1985)

Appellee, a resident of Vermont, was allowed to take, and passed, the New Hampshire bar examination. But pursuant to Rule 42 of the New Hampshire Supreme Court, which limits bar admission to state residents, she was not permitted to be sworn in. After the New Hampshire Supreme Court denied appellee's request that an exception to the Rule be made in her case, she filed an action in federal district court. The district court granted appellee's motion for a summary judgment. The court of appeals affirmed.

The Supreme Court affirmed, finding that Rule 42 violated the Privileges and Immunities Clause of Art. IV, 2. [L]ike the Commerce Clause, the Privileges and Immunities Clause was intended to create a national economic union. "[O]ne of the privileges which the Clause guarantees to citizens of State A is that of doing business in State B on terms of substantial equality with the citizens of that State." *Toomer v. Witsell*, 334 U.S. 385, 396 (1948). Moreover, although a lawyer is "an officer of the court," he does not hold a position that can be entrusted only to a "full-fledged member of the political community" and thus is not an "officer" of the State in any political sense. *In re Griffiths*, 413 U.S. 717 (1973). Therefore, a nonresident's interest in practicing law is a "privilege" protected by the Clause. A State may discriminate against nonresidents only where its reasons are "substantial" and the difference in treatment bears a close or substantial relationship to those reasons. None of the reasons offered by appellant for its refusal to admit nonresidents to the bar — nonresidents would be less likely to keep abreast of local rules and procedures, to behave ethically, to be available for court proceedings, and to do pro bono and other volunteer work in the State — meets the test of "substantiality," and the means chosen do not bear the necessary relationship to the State's objectives.

NOTES, QUESTIONS, AND EXAMPLES

1. The Court later held that rules for admission on motion (that is, being admitted to practice in state B by virtue of a lawyer's admission and longevity of practice in state A) must treat residents and non-residents alike. *Supreme Court of Virginia v. Friedman*, 487 U.S. 59 (1988).

2. Do *Piper* and *Friedman* mean that states have lost the ability to exclude lawyers already licensed in other states?

3. The unsuccessful arguments made by the State of New Hampshire in favor of territorial restrictions on licensure are similar to current arguments opposed to

multijurisdictional practice proposals. *See* Section 4 of this chapter. After reading the materials on multijurisdictional practice, consider whether the *Piper* arguments should be more or less effective in the MJP context than they were in the residency context.

4. In a move that could foreshadow broader arrangements in the future, three states (Washington, Oregon, and Idaho) have created a form of regional admission to practice. The states have agreed to permit any lawyer in good standing in any one of the three states to be licensed to practice in the other two states without taking the bar exam in those other two states. Unlike the usual reciprocity arrangements existing in most states that allow admission on motion, this agreement does not require that the lawyer has been in practice for a fixed number of years (usually five or seven).

5. The European Union has established fairly simple, unrestrictive rules for cross-border practice within the EU. The CCBE, the umbrella bar association for the EU states, provides the ethics rules to be followed when a European lawyer practices across European borders.

b. Education, Knowledge, and Good Character

PROBLEM 2-1

Sandy Morris was a "troublemaker" at his school. He has graduated from State U. Law School despite engaging in repeatedly obnoxious acts. He had, among many other things, played a wide variety of "practical jokes" on classmates and faculty members and sold t-shirts emblazoned with a nude caricature of his law school's dean. How should State Bar treat Morris's application to sit for the bar exam?

PROBLEM 2-2

Jon Wetzel took and passed the bar exam. The application form asked whether the applicant had ever belonged to a group that advocated the violent overthrow of the government, similar to that in *Wadmond, infra*, but gave the applicant three response choices: Yes, No, and Decline to Answer. Wetzel chose "Decline to Answer," and the bar authorities have refused to process his application further without receiving a Yes or No answer to the question. What result? Is the applicant entitled to use whatever choices are on the questionnaire or is he evading the lawful inquiries of the bar authorities, à la Mr. DeBartolo in the case that follows?

———

All states impose educational requirements on applicants for admission to practice law. All but a few states require graduation from an ABA accredited law school for admission to practice. A few states, most notably California, permit applications from graduates of state-accredited law schools that are not ABA accredited. A few states allow as a substitution for law school graduation, "reading the law" in the offices of a licensed lawyer on a prescribed and approved schedule.

An examination (the bar exam) is administered in each state to test applicants' knowledge of legal rules and principles. States determine whether or not an applicant has satisfied the knowledge requirement based on the exam results. A few states, dwindling in number, provide for a waiver of the bar examination requirement for graduates of selected, in-state law schools. New Hampshire Rule 42 permits an alternative form of the bar exam: law students in New Hampshire who take certain courses can have their success in those courses stand as their bar exam.

To be a successful applicant for admission to practice law, one must be found to be of good character. States require the completion of questionnaires from applicants, and in some states, recommendations from law school personnel, currently licensed lawyers, or others. The issue in the bar's character examination is the same as is often present in lawyer disciplinary actions: Does this individual have the good character necessary to the practice of law? A wide range of past conduct, including criminal convictions, arrests, civil litigation, and job performance, may be considered by the admission authorities. Some crimes, because they involve fraud or dishonesty, are sufficient grounds, standing alone, for denial of an application for admission to the bar, such as fraud, perjury, embezzlement, bribery, theft, and robbery. An applicant need not have committed a crime for bar authorities to find a lack of good character. The questions asked and the information gathered, however, must bear a relationship to the purpose of the inquiry: the applicant's fitness for the practice of law. Political activity has been a particularly active area of inquiry by bar admission authorities. Because the lawyer must take an oath to uphold the federal and state constitutions, political activity is a legitimate area of inquiry but one that is constrained by First Amendment speech and association rights.

IN RE LAMMERS
62 Ohio St. 3d 322, 581 N.E.2d 1359 (1991)

Applicant, Maximillian Paul Lammers, Jr., attended the University of Bridgeport School of Law from 1981 through 1984. As of May 1984, Lammers needed to complete a two-hour legal writing seminar in order to have the eighty-six credit hours required to graduate. Knowing that he would not have his legal writing assignment completed on time, Lammers received an extension of time in which to submit it.

Despite his credit-hour deficiency, Lammers was permitted to participate in the school's commencement exercises. He also applied to take the July 1984 Ohio Bar Examination. As part of his application, he submitted the required Certificate of Law School that must be completed by the dean of the applicant's law school. On that form, the dean was to certify whether the applicant "has been" or "will be" awarded a Juris Doctor degree prior to the bar examination. On Lammers' certificate, a line was drawn through both choices and an asterisk placed above the "has been" selection. No explanation or comment accompanied the asterisk.

In July 1984, Lammers took the Ohio Bar Examination. Lammers passed the test and was admitted to the practice of law in November 1984. Lammers secured employment and has continued to practice law since. To date, however, Lammers has not completed his legal writing seminar and, consequently, has never received his law degree.

In early 1989, University of Bridgeport School of Law Associate Dean Robert C. Farrell contacted Lammers and stated that the school had learned of Lammers' admission, without a law degree, to the Ohio bar. In response, Lammers requested, and was denied, another extension of time in which to complete his legal writing assignment. On May 11, 1989, Farrell relayed his information to this court. The matter was referred to the Board of Commissioners on Character and Fitness of the Supreme Court on August 29, 1990.

A special investigator appointed by the board confirmed that Lammers had never received his law degree. The investigator could not determine who altered Lammers' Certificate of Law School. Dean Howard Glickstein acknowledged his signature on the document but denied making any alteration. Lammers and registrar Mary Ellen Durso also denied making the alteration.

On June 5, 1991, the matter was heard by a board-appointed panel. Lammers testified that he was aware when he took the bar examination that a law degree was a precondition to eligibility for the examination. He was also aware that he lacked a law degree. He explained that he intended to eventually complete the seminar paper and did not believe, at the time, that the unfinished assignment would preclude him from taking the bar examination. As time passed, the paper "became this thing in the back of my mind," but was never completed.

Lammers accepted full responsibility for his conduct and recognized the gravity of his actions. He expressed eagerness to do whatever was necessary to correct the situation. In addition, Lammers submitted letters from Richard C. Sahli, Dale T. Vitale and Grant W. Wilkinson, all of whom supervised Lammers at his most recent employment with the Ohio Environmental Protection Agency. All the supervisors commented on Lammers' forthrightness in bringing the current matter to their attention. The supervisors also highly praised Lammers' enthusiasm, professionalism, legal knowledge and work ethic and stated that Lammers was a valuable employee.

The panel concluded that Lammers' lack of a law degree disqualified him from admission to the practice of law under Gov. Bar R. I(1)(C). The panel recommended that Lammers' license be revoked and that upon obtaining his law degree, he be readmitted to the practice of law without undergoing further examination. The board adopted the panel's findings of fact and recommendation. Lammers filed objections to the board's report, urging this court to stay the proposed revocation until Lammers had a chance to obtain his degree.

Effective October 8, 1991, this court, at 62 Ohio St.3d 1427, 578 N.E.2d 820, issued an order immediately revoking Lammers' license and conditioning reinstatement on receipt of his law degree and successful recompletion of the Ohio Bar Examination.

Charles W. Kettlewell, Columbus, for applicant.

Timothy J. Ucker, Special Investigator, Columbus, for the Bd.

PER CURIAM.

Per Curiam. Under Gov. Bar R. I(1), an applicant for admission to the practice of law in Ohio must:

" * * * (C) [H]ave earned a degree from a law school which is approved by the American Bar Association * * *." It is undisputed that applicant Lammers has not satisfied this requirement. The only question that remains is the appropriate action to be taken.

In reaching our decision, we recognize the high professional regard in which the applicant is held by his most recent employer. Against this, however, we must balance seven years of deliberate disregard for rules of this court, Lammers' continued misrepresentation of his status as a law school graduate, and his conspicuous lack of initiative to remedy this situation prior to it being brought to our attention.

Lammers knew in 1984 that a law degree was necessary to take Ohio's bar examination. He took the test anyway. Lammers also knew that a law degree was a prerequisite to admission to the practice of law in this state. He took his professional oath nonetheless. This clear disregard of the rules of this court is not minimized by the applicant's claim that he intended to eventually complete his seminar paper and receive his degree.

Additionally, as Lammers continued to function as a licensed attorney, he inherently misrepresented himself as a law school graduate. The record also contains evidence of at least one instance of Lammers' deliberate misrepresentation of his graduate status. Lammers admittedly misrepresented himself as an 1984 law school graduate in his employment application with the Lake County Public Defender's Office.

Finally, we find Lammers' delay in taking remedial action to be significant. In the approximately five years preceding initiation of this matter, Lammers made no effort to secure his degree. This is despite a conversation he had with a former classmate, Mitch Lieberman, who warned him that the law school had not forgotten about Lammers' uncompleted seminar class. Lammers testified that in 1987 or 1988, Lieberman passed along word from a University of Bridgeport law professor that the issue of Lammers' unfinished seminar paper had been raised in a recent faculty meeting. Lammers, however, did nothing and continued to ignore the situation until the law school contacted him shortly before these proceedings were commenced. Lammers' prolonged inactivity convinces us that Lammers had abandoned any intention of completing the writing seminar and would have continued to practice without a degree indefinitely.

Lammers urges us to stay revocation of his law license, citing our recent decisions in *In re July 1986 Ohio Bar Examination Applicant No. 719* (1991), 60 Ohio St.3d 605, 573 N.E.2d 593, and *1986 Ohio Bar Examination Applicant No. 1327* (1991), 60 Ohio St.3d 606, 573 N.E.2d 38. In those cases, the applicants were notified that they had passed the July 1986 bar examination. In each instance, the passing score was based, in part, on a multi-state bar examination ("MBE") score that warranted a random check of only two of twelve essay booklets. Both applicants were admitted to the practice of law in November 1986.

Subsequent review revealed that the applicants' MBE scores were lower than originally thought and, as such, all the essay booklets should have been graded. We concluded that the applicants were improperly afforded a presumption of passing. However, since the essay booklets had been destroyed, the applicants' true performances could not be determined.

We suspended applicants from the practice of law until they were able to demonstrate compliance with the bar admission requirements by successfully retaking the Ohio Bar Examination. Suspension, however, was stayed pending application for and successful completion of the next scheduled bar examination.

Those two cases differ substantially from that currently at bar. In the earlier decisions, the circumstances giving rise to the test-score controversy were beyond the applicants' control. In this case, Lammers was solely responsible for the incidents precipitating revocation.

In consideration of the above, we confirm our order issued effective October 8, 1991.

Order confirmed.

Moyer, C.J., and Sweeney, Holmes, Douglas, Wright, Herbert R. Brown and Resnick, JJ., concur.

CLARK v. VIRGINIA BOARD OF BAR EXAMINERS
880 F. Supp. 430 (E.D. Va. 1995)

Memorandum Opinion

The issue before the Court is whether a question appearing on the Virginia Board of Bar Examiners' "Applicant's Character and Fitness Questionnaire" addressing an applicant's history of mental or emotional disorders violates the Americans with Disabilities Act, 42 U.S.C. §§ 12101 et seq. (1994). . . .

For the reasons set forth below, the Court finds that Question 20(b) is framed too broadly and violates the Plaintiff's rights under the Americans with Disabilities Act. Accordingly, judgment is entered in favor of the Plaintiff and the Virginia Board of Bar Examiners is enjoined from requiring that future applicants answer Question 20(b).

I. Findings of Fact

Plaintiff Julie Ann Clark brings this action against the Virginia Board of Bar Examiners (the "Board") to have Question 20(b) stricken from the Board's "Applicant's Character and Fitness Questionnaire" (the "Questionnaire") because it violates the Americans with Disabilities Act (the "ADA"). The Board maintains that Question 20(b) is posed appropriately and is necessary to identify applicants with mental disabilities that would seriously impair their ability to practice law and protect their clients' interests. The Court, after reviewing the evidence, authorities and arguments of counsel, makes the following findings of fact.

A. The Parties to the Case

Plaintiff Julie Ann Clark, a resident of Virginia, graduated from George Mason University Law School in June of 1993. She is currently employed as a children's program specialist at the Bazelon Center for Mental Health Law. . . . Ms. Clark suffers from a condition previously diagnosed as "major depression, recurrent." Because the details of Ms. Clark's condition were disclosed in an affidavit filed under seal, they are not reviewed here. In an unsealed affidavit, Ms. Clark avers that, as a result of her condition, she "effectively lost much of [her] ability to concentrate, act decisively, sleep properly, orient [her]self, and maintain ordinary social relationships." This condition, which occurred a few years ago, affected her for thirteen months.

The Virginia Board of Bar Examiners, an entity created under the authority of Virginia Code § 54.1-1319 (1994), is responsible for the examination of applicants for licenses to practice law in Virginia. [T]he Board must determine, prior to licensing, that each applicant is a "person of honest demeanor and good moral character, is over the age of eighteen and possesses the requisite fitness to perform the obligations and responsibilities of a practicing attorney at law." The Board makes this determination "from satisfactory evidence produced by the applicant in such form as the board may require." As a precondition to licensure, the Board requires that applicants answer all of the questions contained in its Questionnaire, including Question 20(b).

[T]he Board promulgated rules governing the admission of bar applicants. Section III of these Rules, titled Character Requirements, explains that the burden is on the applicant to produce evidence satisfactory to the Board that he or she possesses the requisite fitness to perform the obligations of a practicing attorney. The stated purpose of the character and fitness review is to ensure the protection of the public and safeguard the system of justice. The revelation or discovery of characteristics suggesting a lack of fitness to practice law, including evidence of mental or emotional instability, may be treated as cause for further inquiry by the Board. The application does not, however, inquire into physical disabilities which may impair one's ability to practice law.

B. Application for Admission to the Virginia State Bar

On or about December 13, 1993, Plaintiff completed the Questionnaire and filed it with the Board. Plaintiff declined to answer Questions 20(b) and 21 of the Questionnaire on the grounds that they violated Title II of the ADA Questions 20(b) and 21, and the preamble introducing these questions, read as follows:

> The Board is required to assess effectively the fitness of each applicant to perform the obligations and responsibilities of a practicing attorney at law. In this regard, a lawyer's chemical dependency or untreated or uncontrolled mental or emotional disorders may result in injury to the public. Questions 20 and 21 request information essential to the Board's assessment. The members of the Board recognize that stress of law school, as well as other life factors, frequently result in applicants seeking psychiatric or psychological counseling. The Board encourages you to

obtain counseling or treatment if you believe that you may benefit from it. Because generally only severe forms of mental or emotional problems will trigger an investigation or impact on bar admission decisions, your decision to seek counseling should not be colored by your bar application. . . .

* * *

20. (b) Have you within the past five (5) years, been treated or counseled for a mental, emotional or nervous disorders?

* * *

21. If your answer to question 20 (a), (b) or (c) is yes, complete the following that apply:

(a) Dates of treatment or counseling;

(b) Name, address and telephone number of attending physician or counselor or other health care provider;

(c) Name, address and telephone number of hospital or institution;

(d) Describe completely the diagnosis and treatment and the prognosis and provide any other relevant facts. You may attach letters from your treating health professionals if you believe this would be helpful.

On February 8, 1994, the Board advised Ms. Clark that her refusal to provide relevant information would prevent her from taking the bar examination. Pursuant to agreement of counsel, the Board subsequently agreed to allow Ms. Clark to sit for the February bar examination without answering Questions 20(b) and 21 of the Questionnaire. However, the Board indicated that it would not grant her a license until she completed the Questionnaire.

Ms. Clark took the Virginia bar examination on February 22 and 23, 1994 and passed it. She completed all of the application procedures with the exception of answering Questions 20(b) and 21. The Board concedes that, but for her refusal to answer Questions 20(b), it has no reason to believe that Ms. Clark lacks the requisite character and fitness to practice law in Virginia. As the only thing preventing Ms. Clark's licensure is her refusal to answer Question 20(b), the issue of whether Question 20(b) violates the ADA is properly framed for the Court.

C. Application Procedures of the Virginia Board of Bar Examiners

The Board reviews approximately 2,000 applications per year. Because it lacks the resources to review all of these applications in-depth, the Board relies on the self-reporting of verifiable facts to obtain relevant information about each applicant. The Board sends the applications to the NCBE [National Conference of Bar Examiners], which prepares a character and fitness report on each applicant. The NCBE verifies all of the answers to the Questionnaire, including Question 20(b). To verify an affirmative answer to Question 20(b), the NCBE inquires from the health care professional disclosed in Question 21 whether the information disclosed is true.

After preparation of the character and fitness report, the NCBE returns the applications and verifying information to the Board for reevaluation. Upon receipt from the NCBE, employees of the Board review and mark the applications for items that may be pertinent to applicants' character and fitness, such as convictions, unpaid debts, job terminations, drug or alcohol use, mental health counseling, and institutionalization.

The Secretary-Treasurer of the Board, Mr. W. Scott Street, III, reviews the marked applications and decides which should be brought to the attention of the full Board for further examination. Although neither Mr. Street nor any member of the Board has any training in psychiatric or psychological problems, the Board assesses the disclosed mental health information to determine whether further investigation is warranted. The Board has broad authority to conduct additional hearings to determine an applicant's fitness, and to subpoena witnesses and documents at such hearings. In the twenty-three years Mr. Street has served as the Secretary-Treasurer, he has never brought to the attention of the Board an application disclosing the mere receipt of treatment or counseling for stress, depression, or marital or adjustment problems. Further, no applicant has been denied the right to sit for the bar examination based on their answer to Question 20(b).

In the last five years, forty-seven applicants have answered "yes" to Questions 20(b). Of these forty-seven applicants, only two cases warranted further inquiry by the Board. In those two cases, the Board asked each applicant to provide letters from current health care providers stating that they were fit to practice law.[6] Both applicants provided the requested letters, but, because one applicant failed the bar examination, only one applicant was licensed by the Board.

Unlike the practice in some other states, the Board does not grant conditional licenses to practice law. Although licensed attorneys are subject to certain ethical constraints, the Board cannot impose requirements, such as continued counseling or treatment, as a condition to licensing. As the Board lacks any ability to ensure the mental fitness of applicants post-licensure, it must identify and screen out the unfit applicants prior to licensing. The Board avers that Question 20(b) is essential to the identification of such unfit applicants.

D. Battle of the Experts

Plaintiff maintains that Question 20(b) must be rejected because it is overbroad and is ineffectual in identifying those applicants unfit to practice law. Plaintiff offered the testimony of Dr. Howard V. Zonana, Director of the Law and Psychiatric Division and Professor of Clinical Psychology at the Yale University School of Medicine, to support its contention that there is no correlation between past mental health counseling and fitness to practice law. Dr. Zonana testified that Question

---

[6] One applicant had a bipolar disorder, had attempted suicide, and was voluntarily hospitalized on numerous occasions. The applicant's refusal to take prescribed medications resulted in further institutionalization. Upon receipt of a letter from the health care provider stating that the applicant had gained insight into the nature of the disease, was in compliance with a plan of treatment, and was fit to engage in the practice of law, the applicant was licensed. The second applicant was diagnosed with a manic depressive disorder and refused to acknowledge the existence of the problem. Untreated, the applicant engaged in irrational behavior such as spending money wildly. Although the applicant provided the requested letter attesting to his mental fitness, the applicant failed the bar exam.

20(b) elicits information that, unlike evidence of past behavior, is unrelated to applicants' present ability to practice law and has little or no predictive value. According to Dr. Zonana, there is little evidence to support the ability of bar examiners, or even mental health professionals, to predict inappropriate or irresponsible future behavior based on a person's history of mental health treatment. Dr. Zonana believes that evidence of past behavior, as elicited by the Board's other "characterological" questions, provides the best indicator of an applicant's present ability to function and work.[7]

The credibility of Dr. Zonana's position is supported by its consistency with the position of the American Psychiatric Association (the "APA"). According to the APA, psychiatric history should not be the subject of applicant inquiry because it is not an accurate predictor of fitness. . . .

The [APA] Guidelines' focus on current ability to function, versus prior history of treatment or counseling, echoes the testimony offered by Dr. Zonana. Plaintiff contends that Question 20(b) is framed to identify mental or emotional illnesses that do not currently affect the applicant.

In support of maintaining Question 20(b), the Board offered the testimony of Dr. Charles B. Mutter, a psychiatrist, assistant professor of Psychiatry and Family Medicine at the University of Miami School of Medicine, and member of the Florida Board of Bar Examiners from 1989 to 1993. Dr. Mutter, drafter of a question similar to Question 20(b) included in Florida's bar application, testified that Question 20(b) is appropriate as posed. He stated that attorneys, as protectors of clients' rights and assets, hold a special position of trust with the public which must be safeguarded with mental health pre-screening. Further, Dr. Mutter insisted that broad mental health questions are essential for collecting complete information regarding applicants' fitness to practice law. Narrower mental health questions, in Dr. Mutter's view, are inadequate because they allow applicants to filter their responses and provide self-promoting answers.

Dr. Mutter's immoderate position, however, is unsupported by objective evidence and is discordant with a contemporary understanding of mental health questions under the ADA. For one, Dr. Mutter was unable point to any evidence proving a correlation between mental health questions and an inability to practice law. Despite this absence of correlative evidence, Dr. Mutter expressed the view that broad psychological pre-screening should be used in other professions, such as medicine, banking, law enforcement, and firefighting. Significantly, Dr. Mutter's somewhat extreme advocacy of mental health inquiry is controverted by the official position of the APA, a fact of which Dr. Mutter, an APA member, was unaware. Further, Dr. Mutter's position has been rejected by the Florida Board of Bar Examiners which, pursuant to a settlement agreement in *Ellen S. v. Florida Board of Bar Examiners, et al.*, 859 F. Supp. 1489 (S.D. Fla. 1994), struck the mental health question drafted by Dr. Mutter. Accordingly, the Court finds that, although

---

[7] Unlike mental health questions, "characterological" or "behavioral" questions are those questions which are designed to elicit information about applicants' character from evidence of past behavior (e.g., work experience, military service, academic achievements, etc.). Most of the questions on the Questionnaire are behavioral or characterological in nature. The Court uses the terms "characterological" and "behavioral" interchangeably.

both doctors have impressive curricula vitarum, Dr. Zonana's position is more credible and persuasive than that of Dr. Mutter.

E. Need for Inquiry into Mental Health

The Court accepts that an attorney's uncontrolled and untreated mental or emotional illness may result in injury to clients and the public. . . . Dr. Zonana acknowledged that there are many mental illnesses which may adversely affect, or even preclude, a person's ability to practice law. He also indicated that, while responses to behavioral questions are better indicators of mental health, inquiry into an applicant's mental health is necessary for a complete evaluation of their fitness to practice law. Thus, it is clear from the facts before the Court that, at some stage in the application proceeding, some form of mental health inquiry is appropriate.

F. Efficiency of Question 20(b)

Assuming that a mental health question is allowed under the ADA, the Court must determine whether Question 20(b) is a permissible mental health inquiry. . . .

According to testimony presented by both Plaintiff and Defendant, approximately twenty percent of the population suffers from some form of mental or emotional disorder at any given time. However, despite reviewing some 2000 applications per year, the Board has received only forty-seven affirmative answers to its mental health questions in the past five years. This affirmative response rate, or "hit" rate, of less than one percent is far below the expected rate of twenty percent. The Board has presented no evidence to suggest, nor is there any reason to believe, that bar applicants are not reflective of the general population. Thus, the great discrepancy between the Board's hit rate and the reported percentage of persons suffering from mental impairment indicates that Question 20(b) is ineffective in identifying applicants suffering from mental illness.

Notwithstanding its receipt of forty-seven affirmative responses, the Board has never denied a license on the basis of prior mental health counseling. Although the Virginia State Bar has suspended attorneys for mental disability, the Board is unable to point to a single instance where an affirmative answer to Question 20(b) has prevented licensure. Thus, based on the Board's own experience, Question 20(b) has failed to serve its purpose of preventing the licensure of applicants lacking the fitness to practice law.

G. Deterrent Effect

In addition to being ineffectual, Plaintiff argues that Question 20(b) has a deterrent effect which inhibits applicants from getting necessary mental health counseling or treatment. Plaintiff presented the deposition testimony of Dean Paul M. Marcus, Acting Dean and Professor of Law at the Marshall-Wythe School of Law at the College of William and Mary, and Philip P. Frickey, Professor of Law at the University of Minnesota Law School, on the deterrent effect of broad mental health questions, like Question 20(b). Drawing on his experience counseling law students as both a teacher and administrator, Dean Marcus concluded that questions such as Question 20(b) deter law students from seeking counseling or treatment from which they might otherwise benefit. Similarly, Professor Frickey stated that broad mental health questions like Question 20(b) have a strong negative effect upon many law students, often discouraging them from seeking beneficial mental health counseling.

*   *   *

H. Data from other Jurisdictions and Authorities

The imposition of mental health questions like Question 20(b) is not unique to Virginia. All fifty states and the District of Columbia have moral character qualifications which applicants are required to demonstrate as a condition of admission to the bar. Not all of these jurisdictions inquire into applicants' mental health, however, and many states inquire only into hospitalization or institutionalization for mental illness. The various approaches of the bar examiners in the other forty-nine states can be broken down as follows:

Two (2) states, Arizona and Massachusetts ask no mental health questions.

Five (5) states have recently stricken their mental health questions. These include: Hawaii, Illinois, New Mexico, Pennsylvania and Utah.

Ten (10) states and the District of Columbia ask only about hospitalization or institutionalization for mental impairment or illness. The states include: California, Georgia, Iowa, Kansas, Louisiana, Montana, New Hampshire, New Jersey, South Dakota, and Vermont.

Thirty-two (32) states ask broad questions concerning treatment or counseling for mental and emotional disorder or illness. These thirty-two states are further divided into two groups:

One (1) state, Arkansas limits inquiry to continuous treatment for mental or emotional disorder.

Thirteen (13) states limit their question to specific diagnoses or ask applicants if they have any mental disorder which they believe will affect their ability to practice law. This group includes: Alabama, Alaska, Connecticut, Delaware, Florida, Idaho, Maine, Maryland, Minnesota, New York, Rhode Island, Texas, and Washington.

Eighteen (18) states which ask broad mental health questions like Question 20(b). These include: Colorado, Indiana, Kentucky, Michigan, Mississippi, Missouri, Nebraska, Nevada, North Carolina, North Dakota, Ohio, Oklahoma, Oregon, South Carolina, Tennessee, West Virginia, Wisconsin and Wyoming.

In the wake of the passage of the ADA, which became effective for public entities in January 1992, the inclusion of mental health questions on bar applications has gained new significance. At least eight states, including Connecticut, Florida, Maine, Minnesota, New York, Pennsylvania, Rhode Island and Texas, have recently altered their mental health questions in light of potential or actual litigation under the ADA.

The changes in these states are reflected in similar adjustments in the policies of the American Bar Association ("ABA") and the NCBE, two leading national legal organizations.

II. CONCLUSIONS OF LAW

The Court finds, based on the affidavit Plaintiff filed under seal, that Ms. Clark is a person with a disability or, alternatively, a person with a past record of impairment within the meaning of the ADA. Further, Ms. Clark has shown that she can meet the essential eligibility requirements of practicing law and is "a qualified person with a disability" under the ADA. While Defendant argues that Ms. Clark is not an "otherwise qualified individual" because she failed to answer Question 20(b), this argument begs the question of whether Question 20(b) must be answered at all.

The Board has presented no evidence to suggest that all or most of the applicants answering Question 20(b) affirmatively threaten the health or safety of the public. Nor is there any evidence that the Board engaged in any individualized assessment in formulating Question 20(b). Absent a showing that Ms. Clark would pose a direct threat to the health or safety of others, the Court finds that Ms. Clark meets all of the "essential eligibility requirements" for admission to the bar of the Commonwealth of Virginia.

* * *

III. CONCLUSION

. . . The imposition of Question 20(b) by the Board violates the ADA. While the licensure of attorneys implicates issues of public safety, the Board has failed to show that Question 20(b), as posed, is necessary to the Board's performance of its licensing function. Accordingly, judgment is entered for the Plaintiff and the Virginia Board of Bar Examiners is enjoined from requiring that future applicants answer Question 20(b) of the Questionnaire.

LAW STUDENTS CIVIL RIGHTS RESEARCH COUNCIL, INC. v. WADMOND
401 U.S. 154 (1971)

MR. JUSTICE STEWART delivered the opinion of the Court.

An applicant for admission to the Bar of New York must be a citizen of the United States [This requirement was later struck down as violative of the Equal Protection Clause by the Court in *In re Griffiths*, 413 U.S. 717 (1973)], have lived in the State for at least six months, and pass a written examination conducted by the State Board of Law Examiners. In addition, New York requires that the Appellate Division of the State Supreme Court in the judicial department where an applicant resides must "be satisfied that such person possesses the character and general fitness requisite for an attorney and counsellor-at-law." This case involves a broad attack, primarily on First Amendment vagueness and overbreadth grounds, upon this system for screening applicants for admission to the New York Bar.

I

The three-judge District Court, although divided on other questions, was unanimous in finding no constitutional infirmity in New York's statutory requirement that applicants for admission to its Bar must possess "the character and general fitness requisite for an attorney and counsellor-at-law." We have no difficulty in affirming this holding. *See Konigsberg v. State Bar*, 366 U.S. 36, 40-41; *Schware v. Board of Bar Examiners*, 353 U.S. 232, 247 (Frankfurter, J., concurring).

II

[B]efore he may be finally admitted to practice, an applicant must swear (or affirm) that he will support the Constitutions of the United States and of the State of New York. Reflecting these requirements, Rule 9406 of the New York Civil Practice Law and Rules directs the Committees on Character and Fitness not to certify an applicant for admission "unless he shall furnish satisfactory proof to the effect" that he "believes in the form of the government of the United States and is loyal to such government."

The appellants constitutional attack is mounted against the requirement of belief "in the form of" and loyalty to the Government of the United States, and upon those parts of the questionnaires directed thereto.

We do not understand the appellants to question the constitutionality of the actual oath an applicant must take before admission to practice. In any event, there can be no doubt of its validity. It merely requires an applicant to swear or affirm that he will "support the constitution of the United States" as well as that of the State of New York.

If all we had before us were the language of Rule 9406, which seems to require an applicant to furnish proof of his belief in the form of the Government of the United States and of his loyalty to the Government, this would be a different case. For the language of the Rule lends itself to a construction that could raise substantial constitutional questions, both as to the burden of proof permissible in such a context under the Due Process Clause of the Fourteenth Amendment, and as to the permissible scope of inquiry into an applicant's political beliefs under the First and Fourteenth Amendments. But this case comes before us in a significant and unusual posture: the appellees are the very state authorities entrusted with the definitive interpretation of the language of the Rule. We therefore accept their interpretation, however we might construe that language were it left for us to do so.

The appellees have made it abundantly clear that their construction of the Rule is both extremely narrow and fully cognizant of protected constitutional freedoms. There are three key elements to this construction. First, the Rule places upon applicants no burden of proof. Second, "the form of the government of the United States" and the "government" refer solely to the Constitution, which is all that the oath mentions. Third, "belief" and "loyalty" mean no more than willingness to take the constitutional oath and ability to do so in good faith.

Accepting this construction, we find no constitutional invalidity in Rule 9406. There is "no showing of an intent to penalize political beliefs." *Konigsberg v. State Bar*, 366 U.S. at 54. At the most, the Rule as authoritatively interpreted by the appellees performs only the function of ascertaining that an applicant is not one who "swears to an oath pro forma while declaring or manifesting his disagreement with or indifference to the oath." *Bond v. Floyd*, 385 U.S. 116, 132.

III

As this case comes to us from the three-judge panel, the questionnaire applicants are asked to complete contains only two numbered questions reflecting the disputed provision of Rule 9406.[8] They are as follows:

26. (a) Have you ever organized or helped to organize or become a member of any organization or group of persons which, during the period of your membership or association, you knew was advocating or teaching that the government of the United States or any state or any political subdivision thereof should be overthrown or overturned by force, violence or any unlawful means?

If your answer is in the affirmative, state the facts below.

(b) If your answer to (a) is in the affirmative, did you, during the period of such membership or association, have the specific intent to further the aims of such organization or group of persons to overthrow or overturn the government of the United States or any state or any political subdivision thereof by force, violence or any unlawful means?

27. (a) Is there any reason why you cannot take and subscribe to an oath or affirmation that you will support the constitutions of the United States and of the State of New York? If there is, please explain.

(b) Can you conscientiously, and do you, affirm that you are, without any mental reservation, loyal to and ready to support the Constitution of the

---

[8] [18] The District Court ordered the elimination or revision of the following questions contained in the questionnaires at the time this litigation was commenced:

26. Have you ever organized or helped to organize or become a member of or participated in any way whatsoever in the activities of any organization or group of persons which teaches (or taught) or advocates (or advocated) that the Government of the United States or any State or any political subdivision thereof should be overthrown or overturned by force, violence or any unlawful means? If your answer is in the affirmative, state the facts below.

27 (a). Do you believe in the principles underlying the form of government of the United States of America?

31. Is there any incident in your life not called for by the foregoing questions which has any favorable or detrimental bearing on your character or fitness? If the answer is "Yes" state the facts. [In the Second Department the words "favorable or" did not appear.]

None of the above questions is in issue here.

United States?

Question 26 is precisely tailored to conform to the relevant decisions of this Court. Our cases establish that inquiry into associations of the kind referred to is permissible under the limitations carefully observed here. We have held that knowing membership in an organization advocating the overthrow of the Government by force or violence, on the part of one sharing the specific intent to further the organization's illegal goals, may be made criminally punishable. It is also well settled that Bar examiners may ask about Communist affiliations as a preliminary to further inquiry into the nature of the association and may exclude an applicant for refusal to answer. *Konigsberg v. State Bar*, 366 U.S. at 46-47. Surely a State is constitutionally entitled to make such an inquiry of an applicant for admission to a profession dedicated to the peaceful and reasoned settlement of disputes between men, and between a man and his government. The very Constitution that the appellants invoke stands as a living embodiment of that ideal.

As to Question 27, there can hardly be doubt of its constitutional validity in light of our earlier discussion of Rule 9406 and the appellees' construction of that Rule. The question is simply supportive of the appellees' task of ascertaining the good faith with which an applicant can take the constitutional oath. Indeed, the "without any mental reservation" language of part (b) is the same phrase that appears in the oath required of all federal uniformed and civil service personnel. New York's question, however, is less demanding than the federal oath. Taking the oath is a requisite for federal employment, but there is no indication that a New York Bar applicant would not be given the opportunity to explain any "mental reservation" and still gain admission to the Bar.

The judgment is Affirmed.

*   *   *

[JUSTICE BLACK' s dissenting opinion has been omitted.]

JUSTICE MARSHALL, whom JUSTICE BRENNAN joins, dissenting.

This litigation began with a comprehensive constitutional attack by appellants on longstanding state rules and practices for screening applicants for admission to the New York Bar. During the course of the litigation some of these practices were changed by appellees; others were found wanting by the three-judge court below, and changed as a result of that court's opinion and its final order. Now we face the residuum of the appellants' original challenge, and the Court today ratifies everything left standing by the court below. I dissent from that holding because I believe that appellants' basic First Amendment complaint, transcending the particulars of the attack, retains its validity. The underlying complaint, strenuously and consistently urged, is that New York's screening system focuses impermissibly on the political activities and viewpoints of Bar applicants, that the scheme thereby operates to inhibit the exercise of protected expressive and associational freedoms by law students and others, and that this chilling effect is not justified as the necessary impact of a system designed to winnow out those applicants demonstrably unfit to practice law.

As an abstract matter I do not take issue with the proposition that some inquiry into the qualifications of Bar applicants may be made, beyond such obvious threshold qualifications as residence or success in a regularly administered written examination. Accordingly, I would not upset the general rules which charter an inquiry as to the "fitness" of applicants, absent a showing not made here, that in practice the general rules work an impermissible result. But this is hardly the end of the case. For New York is not content with a politically neutral investigation into the fitness of Bar applicants to practice law. Screening officials are specifically directed by state law to assess an applicant's political beliefs and loyalties, and to scrutinize his associational and other political activities for signs that the applicant holds certain viewpoints. Such an inquiry, in my view, flatly offends the First Amendment, and state laws or administrative rules that license such an inquiry must be struck down.

* * *

I have no doubt whatever that Rule 9406, if read to mean what it says, must fall as violative of settled constitutional principles, or that any inquisition designed to implement a rule so written must equally be barred. Rule 9406 directs screening officials to probe the contents of an individual's political philosophy in order to ascertain whether he entertains certain beliefs as a matter of personal faith. The Rule, which charters an inquisition, fastens, not upon overt conduct, nor even on activities that incidentally involve the public exposure or advocacy of ideas, but on personal belief itself. Yet it is a settled principle of our constitutional order that, whatever may be the limits of the freedom to act on one's convictions, the freedom to believe what one will "is absolute." *Cantwell v. Connecticut*, 310 U.S. 296, 303 (1940). As we said not long ago in *Stanley v. Georgia*, 394 U.S. 557, 565 (1969), "Our whole constitutional heritage rebels at the thought of giving government the power to control men's minds." The premise that personal beliefs are inviolate is fundamental to the constitutional scheme as a whole, and the premise is not questioned even in cases where this Court has divided sharply over the extent of the First Amendment's protections. In the present case we have a rule of New York law which, as written, sanctions systematic inquiry into the beliefs of Bar applicants, and excludes from the practice of law persons having beliefs that are not officially approved. This inquiry and this criterion for exclusion are impermissible. However wayward or unorthodox a man's political beliefs may be, he may not be kept out or drummed out of the Bar or any other profession on that account.

There are several flaws in the Court's analysis. We are told that while the Rule may be too sweeping, the administrative construction is narrow enough, so the construction saves the Rule. But this argument cannot merit embrace unless, in the first instance, we are able to ascertain the meaning and the sweep of the administrative interpretation itself. The majority opinion points to no New York case law that shows what the proffered interpretation means. Nor, I think, can the Court comfortably point to appellees' past practice as a guide to the proper interpretation of Rule 9406. For the opinions below and the papers in this case reveal that these appellees, prior to the launching of this litigation, thought it their duty to make virtually unlimited inquiry into an applicant's associational, political, and journalistic activities.[9] Thus past administrative practice, which may sometimes be helpful in clarifying the sweep of a doubtful law, in this case is no help at all in settling constitutional doubts concerning the reach of Rule 9406. Appellees' announcement that they will be more restrained, and will focus their inquiries on "sincerity," is of course entitled to the full respect of a reviewing court. Nonetheless, I do not believe that Rule 9406 is saved by the announcement. At any rate, we certainly are not confronted by "long usage" giving "well-defined contours," to appellees' proposed construction of the challenged Rule.

The revised questionnaires for the two departments, the ones passed upon by the court below, had eliminated the most obvious constitutional defects of the original questionnaires. Still, certain remaining questions were found wanting in the District Court's opinion — for example, the precursor to present Question 26. In fact, the only question in the present questionnaire that appears to reflect an "extremely narrow" focus on insincerity of a prospective oath taker — Question 27(a) — was drafted by the District Court as part of its final order. Appellees' own proposed rewording was rejected.

For the reasons stated I would strike down the portions of Rule 9406 discussed herein, as written and construed, and also Questions 26 and 27(b). To that extent I would reverse the District Court.

NOTES, QUESTIONS, AND EXAMPLES

1. The footnotes in the full *Clark* opinion include the text of mental health questions asked in all 50 states.

2. The district judge in *Clark* expressed much concern about the deterrent effect of detailed mental health questions on students seeking counseling. He also made much of the fact that the bar's inquiry had produced very few investigations and even fewer decisions disqualifying applicants. Yet the Supreme Court in *Wadmond* credits the bar authorities for their restraint in not disqualifying any applicant based on answers to the loyalty questions. How can these views be reconciled?

3. The communist threat has subsided. Cases like *Wadmond* now involve white supremacists such as Matthew Hale of Illinois, who was denied admission to the bar based on his extremist views. *See, e.g., Court Rejects Hale's Appeal for Law License*, STATE JOURNAL REGISTER (Springfield, Illinois), June 27, 2000, at 9; Tony Mauro, *Court Will Not Hear Appeal of Would-Be Lawyer Matthew Hale*, LEGAL

---

[9] [7] Judge Motley's separate opinion below states portions of appellees' original, unrevised questionnaires that give some idea of appellees' original conception of their mission under Rule 9406. These questionnaires, utilized in the First or the Second Judicial Department, or both, asked inter alia for a list of all "unfavorable incidents in your life," a list containing "each and every club, association, society or organization of which you are or have been a member," a list of "any articles for publication" written by an applicant. An applicant was asked whether he had ever "contributed in any way or signed a petition for" any subversive organization, or had "participated in any way whatsoever" in such organization's activities. Each applicant was required to "state . . . in not less than 100 words" what he thought were the "principles underlying the form of government of the United States."

INTELLIGENCER, June 27, 2000, at 4. How should the *Wadmond* analysis apply in such cases?

c. Misconduct in the Application Process

PROBLEM 2-3

David Brickmeyer graduated from law school seven years ago, but has not applied to take the bar exam until now. He accumulated significant debt while in law school, some of it student loans and some credit card debt. During the seven years since graduation, he has worked various jobs but is delinquent on his student loans and in default on most of his credit card debt. Some of the debt has gone to collection agencies and two collection claims have been filed against him in court. On his bar application, he answered "No" when asked if he is a party to any pending court action. How should the bar authorities respond to his application? Would the result be different if he revealed the pending court matters?

An applicant to the bar may not make any material false statement and must not "fail to disclose a fact necessary to correct any misapprehension known by the [applicant] to have arisen in the matter . . . ." MR 8.1(b). Misconduct and lack of candor in the application process are common reasons given by bar authorities for disqualifying applicants.

IN RE DE BARTOLO
488 N.E.2d 947 (Ill. 1986)

JUSTICE MILLER delivered the opinion of the court.

Following an investigation and hearing, the Committee on Character and Fitness for the First Judicial District refused to certify to the State Board of Law Examiners that the petitioner, Frederick Francis DeBartolo, possessed the good moral character and general fitness necessary for the practice of law. He has filed in this court a petition for relief from the committee's refusal to certify his character and fitness, and we now deny the petition.

The petitioner graduated from the John Marshall Law School in June 1981, and he passed the bar examination given in July of that year. More than a year later, in August 1982, the committee informed the petitioner that it had decided to refuse to certify that he possessed the requisite character and fitness for the practice of law. The petitioner requested a hearing on that decision, and he was supplied with a list of the specific matters that concerned the committee. After hearing testimony, the committee voted to refuse to certify the petitioner's character and fitness; a written report of the committee's findings and conclusions was filed later. This petition followed.

As described in the committee's report, the sworn "Questionnaire and Statement of Applicant" submitted by the petitioner in applying for admission to the Illinois bar contained inaccurate information regarding his high school education and omitted a number of his residences. Moreover, the committee was disturbed that the petitioner had incurred some 200 to 400 parking tickets, as he had indicated on his application. Finally, the committee found that the petitioner twice had falsely represented himself to others as a police officer. Concluding that those matters raised questions regarding the petitioner's stability, integrity, and character, the committee refused to certify him for admission to the bar.

The committee based its determination on the petitioner's responses on his application and on the evidence that was introduced at the hearing. The matters in question may be considered briefly. The petitioner indicated on his application that he had incurred between 200 and 400 parking tickets while in law school and that they either had been paid or contested successfully in court. At the hearing the petitioner discounted their significance: he believed that many of the tickets were unfairly given, as when he put money in the meter but received a ticket anyway, and he asserted too that the tickets provided an important source of revenue for the city and that the meters were patrolled zealously in the area where he normally parked.

On his application the petitioner gave inaccurate information concerning his high school education. On the application he said that he had attended St. Ignatius High School from 1970 to 1974; at the hearing he acknowledged, however, that he actually had attended a different high school, Proviso West, for a different period of time, 1971 to 1975. He offered no explanation for those discrepancies and attributed them to his haste and neglect in filling out the application.

The petitioner's application was deficient in another respect. On it he indicated that he had resided in Westchester, Illinois, at his parents' home for the preceding 10 years. He testified at the hearing, however, that he had lived at five different addresses in Chicago during the several years preceding his application, which apparently confirmed the committee's investigation of the matter. He occupied those places for only short periods, ranging from one day to eight months, and generally was not required to pay rent. The petitioner believed that the application called only for a list of domiciles, which in his case remained his parents' address at all times. We would note, however, that the petitioner used several of the other addresses in registering to vote and in applying for various official documents such as a driver's license, a firearm owner's identification card, a city of Chicago vehicle license, and a car registration. He also used an address other than the one in Westchester in applying for a job with the Chicago police department.

Finally, the committee found that the petitioner had on at least two occasions misrepresented himself to others as a police officer. Chicago police officer Russell J. Luchtenburg, a college classmate of the petitioner, testified that one day at school sometime in 1977 he refused petitioner's request to borrow his badge and gun. According to Luchtenburg, the petitioner told him that he had left his own badge and gun at home and wanted to borrow Luchtenburg's so that he could arrest some persons whom he had seen smoking marijuana. At the hearing the petitioner denied the occurrence. Joseph Burke, who had investigated the petitioner's application for employment with the Chicago police department, testified that the petitioner admitted to him that he had falsely represented himself as a police officer once while in a tavern with friends. Although the petitioner contests the point, this evidence supports the committee's determination that the petitioner had in fact made the misrepresentations.

A number of persons, including relatives, lawyers, and friends, testified in the petitioner's behalf at the hearing; they attested to his integrity, stability, and overall fitness to practice law. The petitioner was employed as a commodities trader, and a co-worker described their responsibility in that capacity. At the time of the hearing the petitioner had no record of moving traffic violations or criminal convictions, nor had he been involved in any civil actions that would bring his general fitness into question.

An applicant for admission to the bar must show that he possesses the good moral character and general fitness necessary for the practice of law, and the petitioner has failed to demonstrate that here. Remarkably, on his application he provided incorrect information regarding his high school attendance, and he failed to list his numerous residences. An applicant for admission to the bar of this State must submit to the Committee on Character and Fitness "an affidavit in such form as the Board of Law Examiners shall prescribe concerning his history." The decisions of this court have emphasized the importance of candor and completeness in filling out the application; the failure to respond fully and accurately to the various questions betrays a lack of concern for the truth and, moreover, frustrates the committee in its examination of the applicant. In other respects, too, the petitioner's conduct has been questionable. He has misrepresented himself as a police officer and has shown disregard for the law by amassing some 200 to 400 parking tickets over a short period of time.

Based on the record before us, then, we agree with the committee that the petitioner did not at that time demonstrate the good moral character and general fitness that are necessary to qualify him for admission to the bar of this State. The committee's decision to refuse to certify that the petitioner possessed those qualities is not, as he contends, harsh and unwarranted.

Although the committee's decision was appropriate, we do not believe that the petitioner's conduct here must necessarily bar him for life from the practice of law. Just as an attorney who has been disbarred, disbarred upon consent, or suspended until further order of the court may, after passage of the applicable period of time, seek reinstatement, by analogy the petitioner here should be allowed to reapply for admission, and he may do so at this time. Upon the petitioner's reapplication, the committee may consider all matters that are relevant to his moral character and general fitness to practice law, including his conduct since the hearing held here and his candor in filling out his new application and in responding to whatever inquiry the committee makes.

For the reasons indicated, the petition for admission to the bar of this State is denied.

NOTES, QUESTIONS, AND EXAMPLES

1. Licensed lawyers are duty bound not to assist in the admission of an unqualified applicant, MR 8.1, but must account for client confidentiality constraints when a bar applicant consults the lawyer qua lawyer. MR 8.1(b).

2.   Two years before beginning law school, Applicant was convicted of possession of marijuana, a criminal offense in his state. The bar application asks Applicant to state and describe any criminal convictions. Applicant concludes that the marijuana conviction is unimportant and writes, "None" in the blank provided to answer the questionnaire. Applicant submits the questionnaire. If Applicant is successful in obtaining admission to the bar, will Applicant be subject to discipline?

3.   Each federal court maintains a bar, a list of licensed lawyers, separate from the states in which they sit. Typically, a lawyer who is licensed to practice and in good standing in a state need only be introduced by a current member of the federal bar in order to be licensed in that federal court. Some federal courts administer their own bar examination for admission to practice in the particular federal district.

d. Pro Hac Vice Admission

When a lawyer who is licensed to practice in one state has an occasional, nonrecurring need to represent a client before the courts of another state, the lawyer requests admission before that state's courts "pro hac vice," "for this turn only." The application is made by the lawyer filing a motion with the particular court before which the lawyer wants permission to appear. For such a motion to be granted, states typically require that the lawyer's home state have a policy of reciprocating when its lawyers have a similar need to practice in the applying lawyer's home state's courts. Many states require that the applying lawyer associate for purposes of that case with a lawyer who is licensed in the state. This requirement is based on the expectation that the locally licensed lawyer will inform the visiting lawyer of local norms of behavior including ethics requirements, and on the state's need to maintain some control over counsel in the instant case. A judge has broad discretion in ruling on an application to practice pro hac vice and may consider a broad range of factors in ruling on the application.

LEIS v. FLYNT
439 U.S. 438 (1979)

Per Curiam.

Petitioners, the judges of the Court of Common Pleas of Hamilton County, Ohio, and the Hamilton County prosecutor, seek relief from a decision of the United States Court of Appeals for the Sixth Circuit. The Court of Appeals upheld a Federal District Court injunction that forbids further prosecution of respondents Larry Flynt and Hustler Magazine, Inc., until respondents Herald Fahringer and Paul Cambria are tendered a hearing on their applications to appear pro hac vice in the Court of Common Pleas on behalf of Flynt and Hustler Magazine. Petitioners contend that the asserted right of an out-of-state lawyer to appear pro hac vice in an Ohio court does not fall among those interests protected by the Due Process Clause of the Fourteenth Amendment.

Because we agree with this contention, we grant the petition for certiorari and reverse the judgment of the Sixth Circuit.

Flynt and Hustler Magazine were indicted on February 8, 1977, for multiple violations of Ohio Rev. Code Ann. § 2907.31 (1975), which prohibits the dissemination of harmful material to minors. At the arraignment on February 25, local counsel for Flynt and Hustler presented an entry of counsel form that listed Fahringer and Cambria as counsel for both defendants. Neither lawyer was admitted to practice law in Ohio. The form was the one used by members of the Ohio Bar, and it neither constituted an application for admission pro hac vice nor alerted the court that Fahringer and Cambria were not admitted to practice in Ohio. The judge presiding at the arraignment routinely endorsed the form but took no other action with respect to the two out-of-state lawyers.

The case was transferred as a matter of course to Judge Morrissey, who had before him another active indictment against Flynt and Hustler Magazine. Fahringer and Cambria made no application for admission pro hac vice to him or any other judge. At a pretrial conference on March 9, Judge Morrissey advised local counsel that neither out-of-state lawyer would be allowed to represent Flynt or Hustler Magazine. Fahringer and Cambria appeared in person before Judge Morrissey for the first time at a motions hearing on April 8, where they expressed their interest in representing the defendants. Judge Morrissey summarily dismissed the request. Respondents then commenced a mandamus action in the Ohio Supreme Court seeking to overturn the denial of admission. They also filed an affidavit of bias and prejudice seeking to remove Judge Morrissey from the case. The Ohio court dismissed the mandamus action but did remove Judge Morrissey, stating that while it found no evidence of bias or prejudice, trial before a different judge would avoid even the appearance of impropriety. The new trial judge ruled that the Ohio Supreme Court's dismissal of the mandamus action bound him to deny Fahringer and Cambria permission to represent Flynt and Hustler Magazine, but he did allow both of them to work with instate counsel in preparing the case.

Respondents next filed this suit in the United States District Court for the Southern District of Ohio to enjoin further prosecution of the criminal case until the state trial court held a hearing on the contested pro hac vice application. The court ruled that the lawyers' interest in representing Flynt and Hustler Magazine was a constitutionally protected property right which petitioners had infringed without according the lawyers procedural due process. Further prosecution of Flynt and Hustler Magazine therefore was enjoined until petitioners tendered Fahringer and Cambria the requested hearing. The Sixth Circuit affirmed, holding that the lawyers could not be denied the privilege of appearing pro hac vice "without a meaningful hearing, the application of a reasonably clear legal standard and the statement of a rational basis for exclusion."

As this Court has observed on numerous occasions, the Constitution does not create property interests. Rather it extends various procedural safeguards to certain interests "that stem from an independent source such as state law." The Court of Appeals evidently believed that an out-of-state lawyer's interest in appearing pro hac vice in an Ohio court stems from some such independent source. It cited no state-law authority for this proposition, however, and indeed noted that "Ohio has no specific standards regarding pro hac vice admissions . . . ." Rather the court referred to the prevalence of pro hac vice practice in American courts and instances in our history where counsel appearing pro hac vice have rendered distinguished service. We do not question that the practice of courts in most States is to allow an out-of-state lawyer the privilege of appearing upon motion, especially when he is associated with a member of the local bar. In view of the high mobility of the bar, and also the trend toward specialization, perhaps this is a practice to be encouraged. But it is not a right granted either by statute or the Constitution. Since the founding of the Republic, the licensing and regulation of lawyers has been left exclusively to the States and the District of Columbia within their respective jurisdictions. The States prescribe the qualifications for admission to practice and the standards of professional conduct. They also are responsible for the discipline of lawyers.

A claim of entitlement under state law, to be enforceable, must be derived from statute or legal rule or through a mutually explicit understanding. The record here is devoid of any indication that an out-of-state lawyer may claim such an entitlement in Ohio, where the rules of the Ohio Supreme Court expressly consign the authority to approve a pro hac vice appearance to the discretion of the trial court. . . . There simply was no deprivation here of some right previously held under state law.

The petition for writ of certiorari is granted, the judgment of the Sixth Circuit is reversed, and the case is remanded for further proceedings consistent with this opinion.

JUSTICE STEVENS, with whom JUSTICE BRENNAN and JUSTICE MARSHALL join, dissenting.

A lawyer's interest in pursuing his calling is protected by the Due Process Clause of the Fourteenth Amendment. The question presented by this case is whether a lawyer abandons that protection when he crosses the border of the State which issued his license to practice.

The Court holds that a lawyer has no constitutionally protected interest in his out-of-state practice. In its view, the interest of the lawyer is so trivial that a judge has no obligation to give any consideration whatsoever to the merits of a pro hac vice request, or to give the lawyer any opportunity to advance reasons in support of his application. The Court's square holding is that the Due Process Clause of the Fourteenth Amendment simply does not apply to this kind of ruling by a state trial judge.[10]

The premises for this holding can be briefly stated. A nonresident lawyer has no right, as a matter of either state or federal law, to appear in an Ohio court. Absent

---

[10] [2] Although the Court does not address it, this case also presents the question whether a defendant's interest in representation by nonresident counsel is entitled to any constitutional protection. The clients, as well as the lawyers, are parties to this litigation. Moreover, the Ohio trial judge made it perfectly clear that his ruling was directed at the defendants, and not merely their counsel. After striking the appearances of Fahringer and Cambria, the trial judge stated:

I will tell you this then, Mr. Flynt. [The] case is set for the 2d of May, 1977. . . . The only thing is that you will be restricted to having an attorney that's admitted to practice in the State of Ohio.

any such enforceable entitlement, based on an explicit rule or mutual understanding, the lawyer's interest in making a pro hac vice appearance is a mere "privilege" that Ohio may grant or withhold in the unrestrained discretion of individual judges. The conclusion that a lawyer has no constitutional protection against a capricious exclusion seems so obvious to the majority that argument of the question is unnecessary. Summary reversal is the order of the day.

* * *

I

The notion that a state trial judge has arbitrary and unlimited power to refuse a nonresident lawyer permission to appear in his courtroom is nothing but a remnant of a bygone era. [T]he nature of law practice has undergone a metamorphosis during the past century. Work that was once the exclusive province of the lawyer is now performed by title companies, real estate brokers, corporate trust departments, and accountants. Rules of ethics that once insulated the local lawyer from competition are now forbidden by the Sherman Act and by the First Amendment to the Constitution of the United States. Interstate law practice and multistate law firms are now commonplace. Federal questions regularly arise in state criminal trials and permeate the typical lawyer's practice. Because the assertion of federal claims or defenses is often unpopular, "advice and assistance by an out-of-state lawyer may be the only means available for vindication." The "increased specialization and high mobility" of today's Bar is a consequence of the dramatic change in the demand for legal services that has occurred during the past century.

History attests to the importance of pro hac vice appearances. As Judge Merritt, writing for the Court of Appeals, explained:

> Nonresident lawyers have appeared in many of our most celebrated cases. For example, Andrew Hamilton, a leader of the Philadelphia bar, defended John Peter Zenger in New York in 1735 in colonial America's most famous freedom-of-speech case. Clarence Darrow appeared in many states to plead the cause of an unpopular client, including the famous Scopes trial in Tennessee where he opposed another well-known, out-of-state lawyer, William Jennings Bryan. Great lawyers from Alexander Hamilton and Daniel Webster to Charles Evans Hughes and John W. Davis were specially admitted for the trial of important cases in other states. A small group of lawyers appearing pro hac vice inspired and initiated the civil rights movement in its early stages. In a series of cases brought in courts throughout the South, out-of-state lawyers Thurgood Marshall, Constance Motley and Spottswood Robinson, before their appointments to the federal bench, developed the legal principles which gave rise to the civil rights movement.

> There are a number of reasons for this tradition. "The demands of business and the mobility of our society" are the reasons given by the American Bar Association in Canon 3 of the Code of Professional Responsibility. That Canon discourages 'territorial limitations' on the practice of

law, including trial practice. There are other reasons in addition to business reasons. A client may want a particular lawyer for a particular kind of case, and a lawyer may want to take the case because of the skill required. Often, as in the case of Andrew Hamilton, Darrow, Bryan and Thurgood Marshall, a lawyer participates in a case out of a sense of justice. He may feel a sense of duty to defend an unpopular defendant and in this way to give expression to his own moral sense. These are important values, both for lawyers and clients, and should not be denied arbitrarily.

The modern examples identified by Judge Merritt, though more illustrious than the typical pro hac vice appearance, are not rare exceptions to a general custom of excluding nonresident lawyers from local practice. On the contrary, appearances by out-of-state counsel have been routine throughout the country for at least a quarter of a century. The custom is so well recognized that, as Judge Friendly observed in 1966, there "is not the slightest reason to suppose" that a qualified lawyer's pro hac vice request will be denied.

This case involves a pro hac vice application by qualified legal specialists; no legitimate reason for denying their request is suggested by the record. They had been retained to defend an unpopular litigant in a trial that might be affected by local prejudices and attitudes. It is the classic situation in which the interests of justice would be served by allowing the defendant to be represented by counsel of his choice.

The interest these lawyers seek to vindicate is not merely the pecuniary goal that motivates every individual's attempt to pursue his calling. It is the profession's interest in discharging its responsibility for the fair administration of justice in our adversary system. The nature of that interest is surely worthy of the protection afforded by the Due Process Clause of the Fourteenth Amendment.

*   *   *

Accordingly, I respectfully dissent from the Court's summary disposition of a question of great importance to the administration of justice.

4. Unauthorized Practice

By the nature of the licensing requirements, lawyers licensed to practice in a given state have a state-created monopoly on the practice of law in that state. When a person engages in the unauthorized practice of law, civil and sometimes criminal penalties attach.

In order to determine what activities constitute the unauthorized practice of law, you need to determine what activities amount to the practice of law. Court appearance constitutes the core of the practice of law for purposes of unauthorized practice analysis. Nothing is more centrally, and visibly, lawyer's work than appearing on behalf of a client in court. Although giving legal advice is clearly lawyer's work, courts are understandably more reluctant to attempt to monitor and police the unauthorized practice of giving legal advice. If the advice-giving is accompanied by either a fee or document drafting or both, the activity is seen as more clearly impinging the lawyer monopoly.

Unauthorized practice may occur when a licensed lawyer practices outside the jurisdiction in which the license was granted or when those not licensed in any state engage in the practice of law. Lawyers licensed in one jurisdiction commit unauthorized practice violations when they practice in another jurisdiction without obtaining permission from the second jurisdiction's courts. Civil and criminal penalties are not the only consequences of extraterritorial practice.

RANTA v. McCARNEY
391 N.W.2d 161 (N.D. 1986)

VANDEWALLE, J.

Robert P. McCarney appealed from a judgment of the Burleigh County Court in favor of Esko E. Ranta for recovery of fees for legal services. We reverse and remand.

Ranta is an attorney licensed to practice in Minnesota. Since 1966 he has traveled to North Dakota to provide various legal advice to McCarney, primarily in the area of taxation. He never has been licensed to practice law in the State of North Dakota. Details of the fees to be charged were traditionally left open, with Ranta billing McCarney the amount Ranta believed was fair and reasonable for the services rendered. Ranta states that they never had any problems so far as fees were concerned, and that McCarney "referred to me at least twenty clients in this area . . . ." At one point, Ranta opened what he called a "branch office" in Bismarck, apparently to serve those additional clients.[11]

Although in-State practice before a Federal court pursuant to that court's rules commonly has been construed as an authorized practice of law, this Court has no knowledge of any special exception given to persons practicing in the area of tax law. The unlicensed practice of law in this State by nonresident attorneys is allowed only when court permission, pursuant to the applicable Federal or State court rules, is granted for the limited purposes of appearing in relation to a particular matter before the court. Any other unauthorized practice of law is prohibited by § 27-11-01, N.D.C.C.

McCarney hired Ranta in 1977 in connection with the sale of McCarney's Ford, Inc. On November 7, 1977, the final documents selling the business were negotiated and signed in an all-day closing in Bismarck. On or about June 1, 1978, McCarney paid Ranta $5,000. At the end of that month Ranta sent McCarney his bill of $22,500, showing the $5,000 paid as a credit and a $17,500 balance due. The bill contained no statement of hours or costs incurred. At trial office records that showed approximately sixty-one hours of work on behalf of McCarney were

---

[11] [1] Ranta freely admitted at trial to rendering services to "at least twenty clients in this area" and opening a branch office in Bismarck. Ranta gave the following justification for providing McCarney with legal advice in this State:

> I know it's a criminal act as far as the courts are concerned, but to take matters like tax planning or representing clients before the Internal Revenue Service, I have had clients in at least half of the fifty states that I have represented on tax matters, and the question has never been raised. This was basically a tax matter that I was counselling Mr. McCarney on.

submitted. According to Ranta, the only other time records were kept in his mind.

At the end of the trial McCarney moved to amend his answer to include the *McCarney sues saying Ranta never licensed*
defense that Ranta never was licensed to practice law in the State of North Dakota
and therefore could not recover compensation. The trial court granted the motion,
but in a later memorandum opinion stated that McCarney "has received the total
benefits of the contract and should not now be allowed to claim that Mr. Ranta is
not entitled to his fee. There is nothing in the law of the State of North Dakota
which prohibits Mr. Ranta from collecting his fee, and in addition, the doctrine of
equitable estoppel should preclude Mr. McCarney from advancing such an
argument."

Section 27-11-01, N.D.C.C., prohibits the practice of law in this State without
proper authorization:

> Except as otherwise provided by state law or supreme court rule, a
> person may not practice law, act as an attorney or counselor at law in this
> state, or commence, conduct, or defend in any court of record of this state,
> any action or proceeding in which he is not a party concerned, nor may a
> person be qualified to serve on a court of record unless he has:
>
> 1. Secured from the supreme court a certificate of admission to the
> bar of this state; and
>
> 2. Secured an annual license therefor from the state bar board.
>
> Any person who violates this section is guilty of a class A misdemeanor.

This Court defined "the practice of law" by quoting *In re Opinion of the Justices,*
194 N.E. 313, 317 (Mass. 1935):

> . . . Practice of law, under modern conditions consists in no small part of
> work performed outside of any court and having no immediate relation to
> proceedings in court. It embraces conveyancing, the giving of legal advice
> on a large variety of subjects, and the preparation and execution of legal
> instruments covering an extensive field of business and trust relations and
> other affairs. Although these transactions may have no direct connection
> with court proceedings, they are always subject to become involved in
> litigation. They require in many aspects a high degree of legal skill, a wide
> experience with men and affairs, and great capacity for adaptation to
> difficult and complex situations. These "customary functions of an attorney
> or counsellor at law" . . . bear an intimate relation to the administration of
> justice by the courts. No valid distinction, . . . can be drawn between that
> part which involves appearance in court and that part which involves advice
> and drafting of instruments in his office. The work of the office lawyer is the
> ground work for future possible contests in courts. It has profound effect on
> the whole scheme of the administration of justice. It is performed with that
> possibility in mind, and otherwise would hardly be needed. . . . It is of
> importance to the welfare of the public that these manifold customary
> functions be performed by persons possessed of adequate learning and
> skill, of sound moral character, and acting at all times under the heavy trust
> obligation to clients which rests upon all attorneys.

The underlying reasons which prevent corporations, associations and individuals other than members of the bar from appearing before the courts apply with equal force to the performance of these customary functions of attorneys and counsellors at law outside of courts. . . .

The court went on to state that "if compensation is exacted either directly or indirectly, 'all advice to clients, and all action taken for them in matters connected with the law,' constitute practicing law." Ranta's conduct constituted the practice of law in this State.

Although our statutory law does not specifically prohibit compensation of out-of-State attorneys who practice law in the State in violation of § 27-11-01, the statute is clearly intended to provide protection to our citizens from unlicensed and unauthorized practice of law. As we stated recently in *Niska*, "North Dakota has a compelling interest in regulating the practice of law within its boundaries." Section 27-11-01 "is aimed at preventing the harm caused by unqualified persons performing legal services for others." Although Ranta may be competent (a factor which is irrelevant), he is not authorized to practice law in this State. The purpose of the statute is to determine before an individual practices in this State whether that person is competent and qualified to do so.

* * *

Ranta's qualifications came from his having been a lawyer for forty years specializing in the area of tax law.

We believe a fair reading of Section 27-11-01 indicates a preference by both the Legislature and our Court of furthering the strong policy considerations underlying the prohibition against the unauthorized practice of law that occurs in this State by barring compensation for any such activities. The statute is intended to protect the public from unlicensed attorneys and is to be liberally construed "with a view to effecting its objects and to promoting justice." Section 1-02-01, N.D.C.C. An out-of-State lawyer who is not authorized to practice law in this State (such as Ranta) sits in the same position as a suspended attorney previously admitted to practice law in this State; such a person cannot lawfully practice law in this State, nor can that person charge a fee for such services. We therefore hold that an out-of-State attorney who is not licensed to practice law in this State cannot recover compensation for services rendered in the State of North Dakota. This position is in accord with the majority view on the issue. *See generally* cases cited in 11 A.L.R.3d 907 (1967 & Supp. 1985); 7 Am. Jur. 2d Attorneys at Law § 242 (1980); 7A C.J.S. Attorney & Client § 285 (1980 & Supp. 1985). We further hold that a violation of § 27-11-01 precludes the application of equitable principles, such as equitable estoppel, because such a violation constitutes unclean hands.

* * *

The judgment is reversed and remanded.

ERICKSTAD, C.J., GIERKE, J., LEVINE, J. dissent. MESCHKE, J. respectfully dissenting.

I agree that the purpose of 27-11-01 is to protect the public from unqualified legal advisors. But I disagree that Mr. Ranta is the unqualified legal advisor intended to be protected against.

Mr. Ranta . . . is trained in the law. Against Mr. Ranta's efforts to practice law in this State, the public needs no protection. Mr. Ranta . . . is not a suspended attorney. To the contrary, he is an attorney in good standing in Minnesota with 40 years of experience in tax law. Small wonder that Mr. McCarney sought out Ranta and maintained a working relationship with him over many years. The only protection effected by the holding in this case is the protection of the economic interests of the attorneys of this State and the estate of Mr. McCarney. While there may be some justification for the former, the question is whether that justification outweighs the forfeiture to Ranta and windfall to McCarney occasioned by our holding. I do not believe it does and, therefore, I dissent.

The majority reasons that our statute's purpose is to determine before an individual practices in this State whether he is competent and qualified to do so. While I agree with this principle, I disagree that this purpose has not been fulfilled. The fact that Mr. Ranta holds a Minnesota license is precisely the determination that our statute seeks to accomplish. That such determination has been made by the Minnesota authorities, not ours, does not frustrate the statute's purpose. That trust [in Minnesota bar authorities] recognizes that modern demands of business and the mobility of our society — indeed the public interest, require a sensitivity to the ramifications of regulating the practice of law.

Our State, of course, has legitimate interests in maintaining control over who may provide legal services within its borders. We are properly concerned over ensuring that legal representation be provided by persons of sound training, ethics and familiarity with not only the general principles of law, but the particular features of North Dakota law. Here, that was accomplished. Therefore, the interests weighing in favor of enforcement of McCarney's promise to pay Ranta for legal services, i.e. the avoidance of unjust enrichment and forfeiture, are more substantial than the regulatory purpose of the statute.

Accordingly, I respectfully dissent.

NOTES, QUESTIONS, AND EXAMPLES

1.   Professionals and others whose businesses border the law may not engage in the legal work that border their other professional duties. Real estate agents, bankers, and insurance professionals are the usual examples.

2.   "Do-It-Yourself" lawyering kits and services have been increasing in the marketplace. Especially when these are marketed by non-lawyers, bar authorities have sought to shut such operations down. *See, e.g., Florida Bar v. Brumbaugh*, 355 So. 2d 1186 (Fla. 1978). What issues are presented for lawyers and bar associations in such instances? Is it clear that the whole story is being told when the *Brumbaugh* court says:

The reason for prohibiting the practice of law by those who have not been examined and found qualified to practice is frequently misunderstood. It is not done to aid or protect the members of the legal profession either in creating or maintaining a monopoly or closed shop. It is done to protect the public from being advised and represented in legal matters by unqualified persons over whom the judicial department can exercise little, if any, control in the matter of infractions of the code of conduct which, in the public interest, lawyers are bound to observe.

3.   Disbarred Lawyer advised pro se bankruptcy clients regarding bankruptcy forms and filings. Should this activity be regarded as the unauthorized practice of law? *See Iowa v. Sturgeon*, 635 N.W.2d 679 (Iowa 2001).

4.   Unauthorized practice of law, as well as definitions of multidisciplinary practice, depends on an understanding of what it means to practice law. Many states have such definitions embedded in their unauthorized practice statutes and rules. The ABA set a task force to work on drafting a model definition of the practice of law. After producing an expansive definition in its draft, the task force received criticism from the Antitrust Division of the Department of Justice and the Federal Trade Commission. The criticism suggested that the draft definition would exclude many nonlawyers from engaging in currently lawful activities, quelling competition and raising prices for legal and related services. On March 28, 2003, the task force abandoned its effort to create a national standard, encouraging the states to continue efforts to create their own definitions. At one extreme, the Utah legislature adopted a statute (which may never become effective if efforts to identify ways of expanding access to legal services are successful) that confines the practice of law to court activities. Utah Code § 78-9-102. By contrast, the Arizona Supreme Court adopted a rule that more broadly defines lawyer's work (including, for example, "preparing or expressing legal opinions" and "negotiating legal rights"), but also authorizes the certification of nonlawyers to prepare basic legal forms for certain routine transactions. Ariz. R. Sup. Ct. 31.

5.   Multijurisdictional Practice

A wide range of simple realities of life and law practice have created a powerful impetus for the states to allow lawyers licensed in other states or countries to engage in regular but temporary practice in states where they are not licensed as the needs of their clients dictate. More than admission to practice pro hac vice, the movement to create multijurisdictional practice rules addresses activities in and out of court. Consider the following case and report of the ABA's Commission on Multijurisdictional Practice.

RITTENHOUSE v. DELTA HOME IMPROVEMENT, INC.
(IN RE DESILETS)
291 F.3d 925 (6th Cir. 2002)

[handwritten: Bankruptcy]

Boggs, Circuit Judge. Allan J. Rittenhouse appeals the judgment of the district court that he is not an attorney as defined by the Bankruptcy Code, 11 U.S.C. § 101(4). Because the district court erred in its interpretation of the relevant section of the Bankruptcy Code, we reverse.

[handwritten: R/ Rittenhouse fed ok TX]

I

Allan J. Rittenhouse was counsel of record for debtor Ernest J. Desilets. During Desilets's bankruptcy proceeding, Delta Home Improvement, Inc. (Delta) moved the court to suspend Rittenhouse from practicing before the bankruptcy courts, to require him to disgorge fees, and to sanction him for the unauthorized practice of law. Because Rittenhouse had not been authorized by the State Bar of Michigan to practice law in the State of Michigan, the bankruptcy court held that Rittenhouse was not an "attorney" within the meaning of the Bankruptcy Code, 11 U.S.C. § 101(4). The bankruptcy court held that Rittenhouse was a "bankruptcy preparer" under 11 U.S.C. § 110(a), and because he had failed to comply with several requirements imposed by the Code on bankruptcy preparers, ordered him to pay a $3500 fine and disgorge fees of $872.

[handwritten: Lower ct said not lawyer]

[handwritten: FACTS]

A brief factual synopsis is useful. Rittenhouse graduated from the South Texas College of Law, and was admitted to practice law in Texas in 1992. In December 1992, he moved to Wisconsin. His applications for admission to the Wisconsin and Michigan bars were denied. In February 1994, Rittenhouse applied for admission to the bar of the United States District Court for the Western District of Michigan, and was admitted. Rittenhouse has an office in his home in Wisconsin. He also has an office in Iron Mountain, Michigan. His practice was limited to bankruptcy matters in federal court.

[handwritten: Texas lawyer]

[handwritten: Wisc. & Mich Denied but got into fed.]

[handwritten: Bankruptcy law in Mich.]

In July 1995, the State Bar of Michigan informed Rittenhouse by letter that his conduct constituted the unauthorized practice of law. Rittenhouse responded to the letter and argued that a practice limited to federal bankruptcy did not constitute the unauthorized practice of law. The Michigan Bar took no further action until December 9, 1999, when it instituted a suit in state court to enjoin Rittenhouse from unauthorized practice. This state court action was terminated on August 18, 2000, by the issuance of a stipulated injunction prohibiting Rittenhouse from engaging in conduct deemed to be the unauthorized practice of law.

The bankruptcy court fined Rittenhouse and required him to return fees for engaging in the unauthorized practice of law, while referring the matter of his suspension for *en banc* consideration by the bankruptcy court. *En banc* review resulted in an order indefinitely suspending Rittenhouse from appearing before the bankruptcy court.

Rittenhouse appealed to the district court, which affirmed the bankruptcy court determination. Rittenhouse now timely appeals the district court's decision.

II

Rittenhouse does not dispute any of the facts established by the bankruptcy or district courts. We determine the remaining statutory questions *de novo*.

All parties agree that Rittenhouse was eligible for admission to the bar of the Western District of Michigan, and was properly admitted pursuant to Local Rule (W.D. Mich.) 83.1, which reads in pertinent part:

> *Eligibility* — A person who is duly admitted to practice in a court of record of a state, and who is in active status and in good standing, may apply for admission to the bar of this Court . . . .

We look to 11 U.S.C. § 101(4) for the definition of "attorney" for purposes of the bankruptcy code:

> "attorney" means attorney, professional law association, corporation, or partnership, authorized under applicable law to practice law; . . . .

The central issue of the case is, therefore, whether the "applicable law" authorizing an attorney to practice before the bankruptcy court consists solely of the federal rules for admission to the federal bar, or also includes the state rules for admission to the state bar, even when not referenced in the federal rules.

This question has not been resolved by our Circuit. We turn therefore to persuasive authority. In *In re Poole*, 222 F.3d 618 (9th Cir. 2000), the Ninth Circuit determined that federal standards control admission to the federal bar. *Poole* concerned an attorney admitted to the Illinois State Bar, and admitted to practice in the Arizona federal courts. The trustee in a bankruptcy proceeding moved to require the attorney to disgorge his fees because he was not an "attorney" under 11 U.S.C. § 101(4). The Ninth Circuit rejected this argument. In so doing, the court noted:

> Admission to practice law before a state's courts and admission to practice before the federal courts in that state are separate, independent privileges. The two judicial systems of courts, the state judicatures and the federal judiciary, have autonomous control over the conduct of their officers, among whom, in the present context, lawyers are included . . . . In short, a federal court has the power to control admission to its bar and to discipline attorneys who appear before it.

The plaintiff in *Poole* argued, as does Delta here, that a lawyer not admitted in the forum state is not an "attorney" as defined in 11 U.S.C. § 101(4). The *Poole* plaintiff argued that the "applicable law" was Arizona law, and that under Arizona law, the defendant attorney could not practice law, including practice before a federal court.

The *Poole* court found that the states did not have the power to determine who could be admitted to the federal bar. The court stated:

> As we have discussed, and as nearly a century of Supreme Court precedent makes clear, practice before federal courts is not governed by state court rules. Further, and more importantly, suspension from federal practice is not dictated by state rules.

See also Chambers v. NASCO Inc., 501 U.S. 32 (1991) ("a federal court has the power to control admission to its bar"); *Theard v. United States*, 354 U.S. 278 (1957) (disbarment by federal courts does not necessarily flow from disbarment by state courts); *In re Ruffalo*, 390 U.S. 544 (1968) (accord). Since the state and federal systems are separate and independent, the court held that the "applicable law" to which 11 U.S.C. § 101(4) refers was federal rather than Arizona law.

Further, in *Sperry v. Florida ex rel. the Florida Bar*, 373 U.S. 379, 385 (1963), the United States Supreme Court held that the State of Florida could not apply its licensing provisions to the defendant attorney to prevent him from preparing patent applications, because he was registered to practice before the United States Patent Office. The district court in the instant case cited *Sperry* as holding that when federal and state law do not directly conflict, state law need not give way. This misstates the holding of *Sperry*. There, the Court held that when a state licensing law excludes a lawyer from practice that federal rules expressly allow, the two rules *do* conflict, and the state law must give way.

Sperry provides strong guidance for the current case. The *Sperry* Court noted:

> A State may not enforce licensing requirements which, though valid in the absence of federal regulation, give the State's licensing board [in *Sperry*, the Florida Bar Association] a virtual power of review over the federal determination that a person or agency is qualified and entitled to perform certain functions, or which impose upon the performance of activity sanctioned by federal license additional conditions not contemplated by Congress.

The only plausible distinction between *Sperry* and *Poole* is that the enabling Congressional statute in *Sperry* expressly allowed for the prosecution of patents by nonlawyers.[12] This is a distinction without a difference, given that Rittenhouse is a duly licensed lawyer who meets the requirements for admission to the Bar of the Western District of Michigan.

There is countervailing persuasive authority. The bankruptcy court and district court relied primarily on a Connecticut bankruptcy court decision, *In re Peterson*, 163 B.R. 665 (Bankr. D. Conn. 1994). In *Peterson,* the court determined that an attorney was engaged in the unauthorized practice of law because he maintained an extensive federal bankruptcy practice in Connecticut, while being licensed in New York. The *Peterson* court held that when the attorney maintained an office and conducted significant business in Connecticut, he violated Connecticut state rules prohibiting the unauthorized practice of law.

In response to the argument that the attorney was allowed to practice law before the federal courts because he was admitted to the federal bar, the *Peterson* court

---

[12] [1] The court in *In re Peterson*, 163 B.R. 665 (Bankr. D. Conn. 1994), attempted to distinguish *Sperry* by arguing that patent practice cases were different than bankruptcy practice cases, because the federal government enacted a specific statute that gave the power to practice law to patent attorneys. In both cases, Congress has confided the ability to control a federal bar to a federal entity. Although it seems clear, we need not go so far as to hold that the statutes granting federal courts the ability to regulate their bars would allow federal courts to admit practitioners unlicensed by any state. A state (Texas) has licensed Rittenhouse to practice law.

held that there was a difference between the right to practice law, and the right to practice before a court. *Peterson*, 163 B.R. at 673. The court cited *Leis v. Flynt*, 439 U.S. 438 (1979), as holding that the licensing and regulation of lawyers is generally left to the states. The *Peterson* court reasoned that since state law was the source of the ability to practice law, federal law did not, alone, grant that ability. Thus, the court held, state law governed who was allowed to practice law in federal courts.

The persuasive weight of *Peterson* is dependant on the soundness of its reading of *Leis*. In *Leis*, the Supreme Court held that state rules governed practice in *state* courts. *Leis* does not hold that state rules govern practice in *federal* courts. Although federal courts often reference state rules in their requirements (as did the rule at issue here — an applicant must be properly licensed by a state to be admitted), they need not do so.

Contrary to *Peterson's* reading of *Leis*, federal courts have the right to control the membership of the federal bar. "Congress has provided in 28 U.S.C. § 2071 that the district courts may prescribe rules for the conduct of their business. It is clear from 28 U.S.C. § 1654 that the authority provided in § 2071 includes the authority of a district court to regulate the membership of its bar." *Frazier v. Heebe*, 482 U.S. 641 (1987) (Rehnquist, dissenting). The power to admit and regulate attorneys is not, as the *Peterson* court asserts, the sole bailiwick of the states. Since both the federal courts and state bars have the ability to regulate attorneys, the question becomes which has the greater power to regulate admission to the federal bar. The bankruptcy judge, below, answered this question succinctly: "if this court is unable to reconcile Michigan's laws governing the practice of law with the federal court rules relating to the subject, the State's rules must yield." *In re Desilets*, 247 B.R. 660, 668 (Bankr. W.D. Mich. 2000).

The bankruptcy court in the instant case determined that the applicable state and federal rules are compatible. The bankruptcy court argued that the sole power granted by the federal rules was the ability to practice in federal court; the grant, the court argued, was not of a general power to practice law. *Desilets*, 247 B.R. at 669-70. Since the bankruptcy court interpreted the local federal rules only to authorize practice in the court, and not the practice of law, the court found no conflict between state and federal rules.

We disagree, on two grounds. First, this argument is incorrect on the face of the federal rule. Local Rule (W.D. Mich.) 83.1(a)(iii) defines the phrase "practice in this Court" to mean:

> in connection with an action or proceeding pending in this Court, to appear in, commence, conduct, prosecute the action or proceeding; appear in open court; sign a paper; participate in a pretrial conference; represent a client at a deposition; counsel a client in the action or proceeding for compensation; or otherwise practice in this Court or before an officer of this Court.

This statement authorizes activities beyond those involved in appearance before the bankruptcy court. In particular, the rule authorizes the attorney to "counsel a client in the action or proceeding for compensation." This is what Rittenhouse did, and what the courts below determined he was not allowed to do, based on their reading of state law. When state licensing laws purport to prohibit lawyers from doing that which federal law expressly entitles them to do, the state law must give way. *Sperry*, 373 U.S. at 385.

[handwritten margin note: Fed trumps state.]

Second, Rittenhouse does have a valid state source of the authority to practice law: he is properly licensed by Texas. There is no slip 'twixt the cup and the lip; Rittenhouse is admitted to the practice of law in Texas, and the local rule requires only that an attorney be duly admitted to practice in a court of record of a state in order to practice before the Western District of Michigan.

[handwritten margin note: Texas said good.]

The bankruptcy court, district court, and the Michigan Bar seem in fact to be exercised on practical, not legal, grounds. They have noticed that Rittenhouse has an office and practices federal bankruptcy law in a state in which he is not licensed to practice law generally; presumably he competes for federal bankruptcy business with properly licensed Michigan lawyers. However, this was also the motivating force behind the controversy in *Sperry*, where the Florida Bar sought to prevent attorneys not licensed by Florida from practicing patent law in Florida.

The bankruptcy court's analysis also suffers from a practical failing; it did not realistically distinguish between Rittenhouse and those attorneys who have their offices across the border, but do all of their work before the Michigan federal courts.[13] The bankruptcy court's analysis would equally extend to lawyers working for large New York firms, who happened to do most of their legal work in Michigan for Michigan (or multistate, or multinational) clients. We do not believe that the Western District of Michigan Local Rules and 11 U.S.C. § 101(4) can be read to prohibit Rittenhouse's practice, while permitting these other quotidian forms of practice.

[handwritten margin note: NY lawyers do it.]

Because Rittenhouse was properly admitted to the federal bar under the applicable rule, and because federal standards govern practice before the federal bar, we reject the bankruptcy court's determination as adopted by the district court.

III

For the foregoing reasons, the district court's judgment is

Reversed.

MERRITT, CIRCUIT JUDGE, dissenting.

I did not know until I read Judge Boggs' opinion that for lawyers it is now a regular, everyday practice — part of the profession's "quotidian forms of practice" (to use the court's words) — for lawyers to practice daily in the federal courts of

---

[13] [2] In fact, Rittenhouse does have an office in his home in Wisconsin, and has undertaken to rent office space in Texas in response to the court's rulings below. The argument that would be advanced to distinguish Rittenhouse from out-of-state attorneys who regularly take cases in Michigan is presumably that the reason out-of-state attorneys may represent clients before the Western District of Michigan is that the state rules allow them to, on a *pro hac vice* basis. This is a circular argument: that Michigan chooses not to exclude all out-of-state attorneys from federal court is better evidence for the proposition that it lacks the power to do so, rather than the proposition that it may do so but has simply exercised extraordinary restraint up until now.

State A, say Michigan or Tennessee, while living and being licensed to practice only in State B, say New York or Florida. I recognize that law practice is changing. But I had thought that a lawyer still needs to pass the bar exam and be admitted to practice in the state where the lawyer routinely engages in state and federal litigation. I did not know that the routine, "quotidian" practice of law in the federal courts of a state where a lawyer is not licensed to practice is a right that may not be regulated or affected by the local rules of the federal court in which the lawyer appears.

In addition, if we follow Judge Boggs' reasoning for the court, licensing in federal court becomes an exclusively federal matter without giving credence or comity to the licensing requirements of the state courts. Federalism may be waning, but I am not ready to set up a national system for licensing, removing and regulating federal practice. I am not ready to say, along with my colleagues, that " 'applicable law' authorizing an attorney to practice . . . consists solely of the federal rules for admission to the federal bar" without regard to "state rules for admission to the state bar." I would continue the longstanding practice of the federal courts in rendering comity to the state courts in regulating the practice of law. *See, e.g., Leis v. Flynt*, 439 U.S. 438, 442 (1979) (noting that it is well established that the States, not federal courts, "prescribe the qualifications for admission to practice and the standards of professional conduct" as well as be "responsible for the discipline of lawyers"). We do not need an elaborate national agency to regulate licensing, removing and disciplining federal lawyers, and the federal courts themselves are not equipped to handle this task alone without the help of the state courts and their rules of practice. Further, if Rittenhouse can practice regularly before the Michigan bankruptcy court with a Texas law license, he has successfully circumvented the Michigan state bar exam and requirements for admission. Opening the door to such a practice places an undue burden on federal courts to regulate and discipline attorneys who are no longer under the oversight of their local state bar and additionally encourages prospective attorneys to forum shop among state bars for the easiest requirements.

REPORT OF THE ABA COMMISSION ON MULTIJURISDICTIONAL PRACTICE[14]
American Bar Association
August 2002

INTRODUCTION AND OVERVIEW

* * *

In the early twentieth century, states adopted "unauthorized practice of law" (UPL) provisions that apply equally to lawyers licensed in other states and to nonlawyers. These laws prohibit lawyers from engaging in the practice of law except in states in which they are licensed or otherwise authorized to practice law. UPL

---

restrictions have long been qualified by *pro hac vice* provisions, which allow courts or administrative agencies to authorize an out-of-state lawyer to represent a client in a particular case before the tribunal. In recent years, some jurisdictions have adopted provisions authorizing out-of-state lawyers to perform other legal work in the jurisdiction.

Jurisdictional restrictions on law practice were not historically a matter of concern, because most clients' legal matters were confined to a single state and a lawyer's familiarity with that state's law was a qualification of particular importance. However, the wisdom of the application of UPL laws to licensed lawyers has been questioned repeatedly since the 1960s in light of the changing nature of clients' legal needs and the changing nature of law practice. Both the law and the transactions in which lawyers assist clients have increased in complexity, requiring a growing number of lawyers to concentrate in particular areas of practice rather than being generalists in state law. Often, the most significant qualification to render assistance in a legal matter is not knowledge of any given state's law, but knowledge of federal or international law or familiarity with a particular type of business or personal transaction or legal proceeding. Additionally, modern transportation and communications technology have enabled clients to travel easily and transact business throughout the country, and even internationally. Because of this globalization of business and finance, clients sometimes now need lawyers to assist them in transactions in multiple jurisdictions (state and national) or to advise them about multiple jurisdictions' laws.

[handwritten margin note: Complex]

[handwritten margin note: easy travel small world]

Although client needs and legal practices have evolved, lawyer regulation has not yet responded effectively to that evolution. As the work of lawyers has become more varied, specialized and national in scope, it has become increasingly uncertain when a lawyer's work (other than as a trial lawyer in court) implicates the UPL law of a jurisdiction in which the lawyer is not licensed. Lawyers recognize that the geographic scope of a lawyer's practice must be adequate to enable the lawyer to serve the legal needs of clients in a national and global economy. They have expressed concern that if UPL restrictions are applied literally to United States lawyers who perform any legal work outside the jurisdictions in which they are admitted to practice, the laws will impede lawyers' ability to meet their clients' multi-state and interstate legal needs efficiently and effectively.

This concern was sharpened by the California Supreme Court decision, *Birbrower, Montalbano, Condon & Frank, P.C. v. Superior Court of Santa Clara County*, 949 P.2d 1 (Cal. 1998), which held that lawyers not licensed to practice law in California violated California's misdemeanor UPL provision when they assisted a California corporate client in connection with an impending California arbitration under California law, and were therefore barred from recovering fees under a written fee agreement for services the lawyers rendered while they were physically or "virtually" in California. Although the state law was subsequently and temporarily amended to allow out-of-state lawyers to obtain permission to participate in certain California arbitrations, concerns have persisted.

[handwritten margin note: CA OOS can't help clients in CA stuff]

In response to professional concerns about the regulation of multijurisdictional law practice, ABA President Martha Barnett appointed the Commission in July 2000 . . . .

SUMMARY OF RECOMMENDATIONS

"Multijurisdictional practice" ("MJP") describes the legal work of a lawyer in a jurisdiction in which the lawyer is not admitted to practice law. As this report discusses, a wide variety of practices falling within this rubric have been called to the attention of the MJP Commission. The guiding principle that informs the Commission's recommendations is simple to state: we searched for the proper balance between the interests of a state in protecting its residents and justice system, on the one hand; and the interests of clients in a national and international economy in the ability to employ or retain counsel of choice efficiently and economically. . . .

The Commission's recommendations are, in summary, that:

The ABA affirms its support for the principle of state judicial regulation of the practice of law.

The ABA re-title Rule 5.5 of the Model Rules of Professional Conduct as "Unauthorized Practice of Law; Multijurisdictional Practice of Law".

The ABA amend Rule 5.5(a) of the ABA *Model Rules of Professional Conduct* to provide that a lawyer may not practice law in a jurisdiction, or assist another in doing so, in violation of the regulations of the legal profession in that jurisdiction.

The ABA adopt proposed Rule 5.5(b) to prohibit a lawyer from establishing an office or other systematic and continuous presence in a jurisdiction, unless permitted to do so by law, or another provision of Rule 5.5; or holding out to the public or otherwise representing that the lawyer is admitted to practice law in a jurisdiction in which the lawyer is not admitted.

The ABA adopt proposed Rule 5.5(c) to identify circumstances in which a lawyer who is admitted in a United States jurisdiction, and not disbarred or suspended from practice in any jurisdiction, may practice law on a temporary basis in another jurisdiction. These would include:

- Work on a temporary basis in association with a lawyer admitted to practice law in the jurisdiction, who actively participates in the representation;

- Services ancillary to pending or prospective litigation or administrative agency proceedings in a state where the lawyer is admitted or expects to be admitted *pro hac vice* or is otherwise authorized to appear;

- Representation of clients in, or ancillary to, an alternative dispute resolution ("ADR") setting, such as arbitration or mediation; and

- Non-litigation work that arises out of or is reasonably related to the lawyer's practice in a jurisdiction in which the lawyer is admitted to practice.

The ABA adopt proposed Rule 5.5(d) to identify multijurisdictional practice standards relating to (i) legal services by a lawyer who is an employee of a client and (ii) legal services that the lawyer is authorized by federal or other law to render in a jurisdiction in which the lawyer is not licensed to practice law.

* * * .

The Basis for Change

Background: state licensing and jurisdictional restrictions

State admissions and regulation. Lawyers in the United States are not licensed to practice law on a national basis, but are licensed by a state judiciary to practice law within the particular state. In general, state admissions processes are intended to protect the public by ensuring that those who are licensed to practice law in the state have the requisite knowledge of that state's laws and the general fitness and character to practice law.

So know State's part. law.

The state-based licensing process originated more than two centuries ago when the need for legal services was locally based and often involved the need for representation in court. Over time, the nature of law practice has expanded. Increasingly, lawyers counsel and assist clients outside the courthouse.

* * *

As a practical matter, a lawyer who seeks to engage in a national law practice cannot presently gain admission to the bar of every state. States generally require out-of-state lawyers to pass the state's bar examination to be licensed. Bar examinations generally differ from state to state, although the degree of difference has narrowed over the years, as states have come to rely increasingly on a standardized examination. Being a member in good standing of another state's bar generally does not qualify a lawyer for "reciprocal" admission, although many states do allow lawyers to be admitted on motion upon a showing of good standing and a demonstrated record of active law practice elsewhere for a specific period.

* * *

States sanction members of their own bar for misconduct occurring outside the jurisdiction, and some states also bring disciplinary proceedings predicated on misconduct committed in the state by a lawyer who is licensed elsewhere. . . .

Geographical boundaries. In general, a lawyer may not represent clients before a state tribunal or otherwise practice law within a particular state unless the lawyer is licensed by the state or is otherwise authorized to do so.

gen.

* * *

Today, no state categorically excludes out-of-state lawyers and there is general agreement that, as a practical matter, lawyers cannot serve clients effectively unless accommodations are made for multijurisdictional law practice, at least on a temporary or occasional basis. For example, every jurisdiction permits *pro hac vice* admission of out-of-state lawyers appearing before a tribunal, although the processes and standards for *pro hac vice* admission differ.

States allow it.

For transactional and counseling practices, and other work outside court or agency proceedings, there is no counterpart to *pro hac vice* admission, but, as discussed below, multijurisdictional law practice is common for certain types of practitioners. The laws of two states, Michigan and Virginia, specifically authorize occasional or incidental practice by out-of-state lawyers. Michigan's UPL statute provides that it does not apply to an out-of-state lawyer who is "temporarily in [Michigan] and engaged in a particular matter." The Virginia rules permit an out-of-state lawyer occasionally to provide legal advice or services in Virginia "incidental to representation of a client whom the attorney represents elsewhere." As noted earlier, California now specifically authorizes out-of-state lawyers to represent clients in arbitrations. Some state courts have identified similar exceptions in judicial decisions.

Some states also accommodate certain out-of-state lawyers who seek to establish a law office in the state or to practice law in the state on a regular basis. For example, states have adopted provisions permitting in-house corporate lawyers, or lawyers employed generally by organizational clients, to provide legal services on behalf of the organization from an office located in a state where the lawyer is not licensed. Typically, the lawyer is required to register and to submit to the state's regulatory authority.

With respect to foreign lawyers, approximately half of the states, beginning with New York in 1974, have adopted "foreign legal consultant" provisions, which allow members of the legal professions of foreign jurisdictions to be licensed without examination to engage in the practice of law in the state on a restricted basis. In 1993, the ABA adopted a resolution recommending that all states adopt such a provision and approved a *Model Rule for the Licensing of Legal Consultants. The increasing prevalence of multijurisdictional practice.*

Testimony before the Commission was unanimous in recognizing that lawyers commonly engage in cross-border legal practice. Further, there was general consensus that such practice is on the increase and that this trend is not only inevitable, but necessary. The explosion of technology and the increasing complexity of legal practice have resulted in the need for lawyers to cross state borders to afford clients competent representation.

In ADR proceedings as well, it is common for lawyers to render services outside the particular states in which they are licensed. Sometimes, the parties choose to conduct the ADR proceeding in a state that has no relation to the parties or the dispute, because they prefer a neutral site. Because particular knowledge of state law and procedure is not necessary, the parties often select lawyers based on other considerations, such as the lawyers' prior knowledge of the relevant facts or a preexisting client-lawyer relationship.

Lawyers who provide legal advice or assistance in transactions also commonly provide services in states in which they are not licensed. Like litigators, transactional lawyers who are representing clients in the state in which they are licensed travel outside the state in order to conduct negotiations, gather information, provide advice, or perform other tasks relating to the representation. Lawyers also travel outside their home states in order to provide assistance to clients who are in special need of their expertise. For example, lawyers who concentrate their practice in federal law — such as securities, antitrust, labor, or intellectual property law — are often retained by clients outside their home states because of the clients' regard for their particular expertise. The same is true of foreign lawyers whose expertise in foreign law is sought, as well as of other lawyers, such as bond lawyers or mergers-and-acquisition lawyers, who practice in specialized areas.

For some lawyers, multijurisdictional practice grows out of an ongoing relation- *travel*
ship with a client. Sometimes, the work is for a client who resides in the lawyer's *w/ client*
home state but who has business dealings outside the state. Other times, the work
is for a client who has moved out of state. A lawyer who drafts a will for a client in
one state may be asked by that client to draft a codicil to the will after the client has
moved to another state. For in-house lawyers in particular, ongoing work for a
corporate employer commonly involves travel to the different states where the
corporation has offices or business interests.

The impact of jurisdictional restrictions on legal practice

Lawyers have general understandings about how jurisdictional restrictions apply
to their work in states where they are not licensed. These understandings are
shaped less by the wording of the UPL provisions or by decisional law, which is
sparse, than by conventional wisdom or by what the U.S. Supreme Court has called
"the lore of the profession." On one hand, lawyers understand that they may not
open a permanent office in a state where they are not licensed and also that they
may not appear in the court of a state where they are not licensed without judicial
authorization. On the other hand, lawyers recognize that they may give advice in
their own states concerning the law of other jurisdictions, that they may represent
out-of-state clients in connection with transactions and litigation that take place
where the lawyer is licensed, and that they may travel to other jurisdictions in
connection with legal work on behalf of clients who reside in and have matters in the
state where the lawyer is licensed.

Lawyers' general understandings are, to some extent, reinforced by the sporadic
enforcement of state UPL laws. Regulatory actions are rarely brought against
lawyers who assist clients on a temporary basis in connection with multi-state or
interstate matters. This might fairly suggest that there is a profession-wide
understanding that the UPL laws, however broadly they may be written and
however they may be interpreted in theory, will be interpreted by courts and
enforcement agencies to accommodate reasonable and conventional professional
practices. Further, one might assume that, because of the sporadic nature of
proceedings to enforce jurisdictional restrictions, lawyers may comfortably rely on
their professional understandings and that, therefore, there is no need to reform
existing laws, however inconsistent or nonspecific they may be. These assumptions
would be mistaken, however.

[E]ven if lawyers felt free to ignore UPL laws in areas where there is a
professional consensus that the laws are outmoded and there appears to be a tacit
understanding that they will not be enforced, it is undesirable to retain the laws as
written, rather than amending them to accord with contemporary understandings
and practices that serve clients well. Keeping antiquated laws on the books breeds
public disrespect for the law, and this is especially so where the laws relate to the
conduct of lawyers, for whom there is a professional imperative to uphold the law.

[The Commission's 10 recommendations are not reproduced here. —Ed.]

6.   Self-Governance and the Duty to Report Misconduct

PROBLEM 2-4

Bar Applicant goes to a quiet restaurant to consult with Lawyer. They reasonably believe they are having a private conversation in low tones at a corner table. Bar Applicant tells Lawyer about a serious criminal matter in Bar Applicant's past that she believes has not come to the attention of the bar admission authorities. Bar Applicant asks Lawyer, as her lawyer, whether she is obliged to report the criminal matter on her bar application. Lawyer says, "No, don't do it. What they don't know won't hurt them." Despite their efforts to be confidential, Other Lawyer, who recognizes both Bar Applicant and Lawyer, overhears the conversation. What, if any, reporting obligations do Lawyer and Other Lawyer have?

PROBLEM 2-5

Robert Lewis has been victimized by the fraudulent transfer of property by Jessica Wallace. Wallace is a lawyer who has significant real estate holdings. Wallace has apparently been engaged in a series of frauds extending over a period of years, pledging and selling the same parcels of unimproved real property to multiple buyers and lenders. Lewis was such a buyer. Lewis meets with Taylor Gregory regarding his possible claims against Wallace. After some investigation, Gregory concludes that Lewis has an easily provable fraud claim against Wallace. Gregory is also concerned about the pattern of frauds being perpetrated by Wallace, some of which have undoubtedly victimized individuals who are not yet aware of their plight. Gregory discusses settlement possibilities with Wallace and they tentatively agree (subject to Lewis' approval) that Wallace will pay Lewis a settlement in monthly installments over the next four years. Gregory discusses the proposal with Lewis and informs Lewis that Gregory may have a duty to report Wallace to the Bar authorities. Lewis is flabbergasted. "If Wallace is suspended or disbarred, how will she pay me the settlement? I'll accept the settlement, but don't report him." Lewis has a point. What should Gregory do?

Among the chief features of the legal profession's claim to be self-governing is the requirement of reporting a fellow lawyer's or judge's serious misconduct to the appropriate professional authority. MR 8.3.

Before a duty to report misconduct can arise, the lawyer must have "knowledge that another lawyer has committed" the misconduct. MR 8.3(a). Personal knowledge of the misconduct obviously satisfies the "knowledge" requirement. While it would be counterproductive to require a lawyer to report every courthouse rumor about another lawyer's misconduct (i.e., the lawyer in such an instance does not "know" of the misconduct), the knowledge requirement is satisfied when a lawyer has been informed of the misconduct from a credible person and there is some independent corroboration. Put another way, "knowledge" as used in this rule means actual knowledge, but actual knowledge may be inferred from the circumstances. Model Rules, Terminology.

The rule does not require a lawyer to report all misconduct of which the lawyer has knowledge. It requires a lawyer to report misconduct "that raises a substantial question as to that lawyer's honesty, trustworthiness or fitness as a lawyer in other respects." MR 8.3(a). "Substantial" means a "material matter of clear and weighty importance." Model Rules, Terminology.

The rule does not require a report of misconduct when the lawyer has learned of the misconduct through confidential communications that would be protected by the ethical duty of confidentiality under Model Rule 1.6. MR 8.3(c). Clearly, this provision eliminates the reporting requirement when a lawyer is consulted as a lawyer by the lawyer who has engaged in the misconduct. But it must also be remembered that the exceptions to the duty of confidentiality continue to apply with equal force in this setting as in any other. Less clear is whether the confidentiality aspect of Model Rule 8.3 eliminates the reporting requirement when a lawyer learns from a client about another lawyer's misconduct.

IN RE HIMMEL
533 N.E.2d 790 (Ill. 1988)

JUSTICE STAMOS delivered the opinion of the court.

This is a disciplinary proceeding against respondent, James H. Himmel. On January 22, 1986, the Administrator of the Attorney Registration and Disciplinary Commission (the Commission) filed a complaint with the Hearing Board, alleging that respondent violated Rule 1-103(a) of the Code of Professional Responsibility (the Code) by failing to disclose to the Commission information concerning attorney misconduct. On October 15, 1986, the Hearing Board found that respondent had violated the rule and recommended that respondent be reprimanded. The Administrator filed exceptions with the Review Board. The Review Board issued its report on July 9, 1987, finding that respondent had not violated a disciplinary rule and recommending dismissal of the complaint. We granted the Administrator's petition for leave to file exceptions to the Review Board's report and recommendation.

We will briefly review the facts, which essentially involve three individuals: respondent, James H. Himmel, licensed to practice law in Illinois on November 6, 1975; his client, Tammy Forsberg; and her former attorney, John R. Casey.

The complaint alleges that respondent had knowledge of John Casey's conversion of Forsberg's funds and respondent failed to inform the Commission of this misconduct. The facts are as follows.

In October 1978, Tammy Forsberg was injured in a motorcycle accident. In June 1980, she retained John R. Casey to represent her in any personal injury or property damage claim resulting from the accident. Sometime in 1981, Casey negotiated a settlement of $35,000 on Forsberg's behalf. Pursuant to an agreement between Forsberg and Casey, one-third of any monies received would be paid to Casey as his attorney fee.

In March 1981, Casey received the $35,000 settlement check, endorsed it, and deposited the check into his client trust fund account. Subsequently, Casey converted the funds.

Between 1981 and 1983, Forsberg unsuccessfully attempted to collect her $23,233.34 share of the settlement proceeds. In March 1983, Forsberg retained respondent to collect her money and agreed to pay him one-third of any funds recovered above $23,233.34.

Respondent investigated the matter and discovered that Casey had misappropriated the settlement funds. In April 1983, respondent drafted an agreement in which Casey would pay Forsberg $75,000 in settlement of any claim she might have against him for the misappropriated funds. By the terms of the agreement, Forsberg agreed not to initiate any criminal, civil, or attorney disciplinary action against Casey. This agreement was executed on April 11, 1983. Respondent stood to gain $17,000 or more if Casey honored the agreement. In February 1985, respondent filed suit against Casey for breaching the agreement, and a $100,000 judgment was entered against Casey. If Casey had satisfied the judgment, respondent's share would have been approximately $25,588.

The complaint stated that at no time did respondent inform the Commission of Casey's misconduct. According to the Administrator, respondent's first contact with the Commission was in response to the Commission's inquiry regarding the lawsuit against Casey.

In April 1985, the Administrator filed a petition to have Casey suspended from practicing law because of his conversion of client funds and his conduct involving moral turpitude in matters unrelated to Forsberg's claim. Casey was subsequently disbarred on consent on November 5, 1985.

A hearing on the complaint against the present respondent was held before the Hearing Board of the Commission on June 3, 1986. In its report, the Hearing Board noted that the evidence was not in dispute. The evidence supported the allegations in the complaint and provided additional facts as follows.

Before retaining respondent, Forsberg collected $5,000 from Casey. After being retained, respondent made inquiries regarding Casey's conversion, contacting the insurance company that issued the settlement check, its attorney, Forsberg, her mother, her fiancé and Casey. Forsberg told respondent that she simply wanted her money back and specifically instructed respondent to take no other action. Because of respondent's efforts, Forsberg collected another $10,400 from Casey. Respondent received no fee in this case.

The Hearing Board found that respondent received unprivileged information that Casey converted Forsberg's funds, and that respondent failed to relate the information to the Commission in violation of Rule 1-103(a) of the Code. The Hearing Board noted, however, that respondent had been practicing law for 11 years, had no prior record of any complaints, obtained as good a result as could be expected in the case, and requested no fee for recovering the $23,233.34. Accordingly, the Hearing Board recommended a private reprimand.

Upon the Administrator's exceptions to the Hearing Board's recommendation, the Review Board reviewed the matter. The Administrator now raises three issues for review: (1) . . . ; (2) whether the Review Board erred in concluding that respondent had not violated Rule 1-103(a); and (3) whether the proven misconduct warrants at least a censure.

As to respondent's argument that he did not report Casey's misconduct because his client directed him not to do so, we again note respondent's failure to suggest any legal support for such a defense. A lawyer, as an officer of the court, is duty-bound to uphold the rules in the Code. The title of Canon 1 reflects this obligation: "A lawyer should assist in maintaining the integrity and competence of the legal profession." A lawyer may not choose to circumvent the rules by simply asserting that his client asked him to do so.

As to the second issue, the Administrator argues that the Review Board erred in concluding that respondent did not violate Rule 1-103(a). The Administrator urges acceptance of the Hearing Board's finding that respondent had unprivileged knowledge of Casey's conversion of client funds, and that respondent failed to disclose that information to the Commission. The Administrator states that respondent's knowledge of Casey's conversion of client funds was knowledge of illegal conduct involving moral turpitude. Further, the Administrator argues that the information respondent received was not privileged under the definition of privileged information. Therefore, the Administrator concludes, respondent violated his ethical duty to report misconduct under Rule 1-103(a). According to the Administrator, failure to disclose the information deprived the Commission of evidence of serious misconduct, evidence that would have assisted in the Commission's investigation of Casey.

Respondent contends that the information was privileged information received from his client, Forsberg, and therefore he was under no obligation to disclose the matter to the Commission. Respondent argues that his failure to report Casey's misconduct was motivated by his respect for his client's wishes, not by his desire for financial gain. To support this assertion, respondent notes that his fee agreement with Forsberg was contingent upon her first receiving all the money Casey originally owed her. Further, respondent states that he has received no fee for his representation of Forsberg.

Our analysis of this issue begins with a reading of the applicable disciplinary rules. Rule 1-103(a) of the Code states:

> (a) A lawyer possessing unprivileged knowledge of a violation of [a disciplinary rule] shall report such knowledge to a tribunal or other authority empowered to investigate or act upon such violation.

107 Ill. 2d R. 1-103(a).

* * *

The question whether the information that respondent possessed was protected [*issue*] by the attorney-client privilege, and thus exempt from the reporting rule, requires application of this court's definition of the privilege. We have stated that " '(1) [w]here legal advice of any kind is sought (2) from a professional legal adviser in his [*Privilege*] capacity as such, (3) the communications relating to that purpose, (4) made in confidence (5) by the client, (6) are at his instance permanently protected (7) from disclosure by himself or by the legal adviser, (8) except the protection be waived.' " [Q]uoting 8 J. Wigmore, Evidence § 2292 (McNaughton rev. ed. 1961). We agree with the Administrator's argument that the communication regarding Casey's conduct does not meet this definition. The record does not suggest that this information was communicated by Forsberg to the respondent in confidence. We have held that information voluntarily disclosed by a client to an attorney, in the presence of third parties who are not agents of the client or attorney, is not privileged information. In this case, Forsberg discussed the matter with respondent at various times while her mother and her fiancé were present. Consequently, unless the mother and fiancé were agents of respondent's client, the information communicated was not privileged. Moreover, we have also stated that matters intended by a client for disclosure by the client's attorney to third parties, who are not agents of either the client or the attorney, are not privileged. The record shows that respondent, with Forsberg's consent, discussed Casey's conversion of her funds with the insurance company involved, the insurance company's lawyer, and with Casey himself. Thus, . . . the information was not privileged.

[handwritten margin note: b/c others were present]

Though respondent repeatedly asserts that his failure to report was motivated not by financial gain but by the request of his client, we do not deem such an argument relevant in this case. This court has stated that discipline may be appropriate even if no dishonest motive for the misconduct exists. In addition, we have held that client approval of an attorney's action does not immunize an attorney from disciplinary action. . . .

Respondent does not argue that Casey's conversion of Forsberg's funds was not illegal conduct involving moral turpitude under Rule 1-102(a)(3) or conduct involving dishonesty, fraud, deceit, or misrepresentation under Rule 1-102(a)(4). It is clear that conversion of client funds is, indeed, conduct involving moral turpitude. We conclude, then, that respondent possessed unprivileged knowledge of Casey's conversion of client funds, which is illegal conduct involving moral turpitude, and that respondent failed in his duty to report such misconduct to the Commission. Because no defense exists, we agree with the Hearing Board's finding that respondent has violated Rule 1-103(a) and must be disciplined.

[handwritten margin note: Holding]

In evaluating the proper quantum of discipline to impose, we note that it is this court's responsibility to determine appropriate sanctions in attorney disciplinary cases. We have stated that while recommendations of the Boards are to be considered, this court ultimately bears responsibility for deciding an appropriate sanction. We reiterate our statement that " '[w]hen determining the nature and extent of discipline to be imposed, the respondent's actions must be viewed in relationship "to the underlying purposes of our disciplinary process, which purposes are to maintain the integrity of the legal profession, to protect the administration of justice from reproach, and to safeguard the public.' "

This failure to report resulted in interference with the Commission's investigation of Casey, and thus with the administration of justice. Perhaps some members of the public would have been spared from Casey's misconduct had respondent reported the information as soon as he knew of Casey's conversions of client funds. We are particularly disturbed by the fact that respondent chose to draft a settlement agreement with Casey rather than report his misconduct.

*   *   *

Accordingly, it is ordered that respondent be suspended from the practice of law for one year.

NOTES, QUESTIONS, AND EXAMPLES

1.   The *Himmel* case is based on the view that the reporting requirement trumps a client's desire that the misconduct of the client's former lawyer not be reported. This view is not unanimously held; authority from other states has opined the contrary. *See, e.g.*, Md. Ethics Op. 89-46 (1989). Which interest ought to prevail?

2.   Illinois Rule 1-103, modeled after the ABA Model Code provision, is different from the analogous Model Rule provision. Unlike DR 1-103, which on its face mandates the reporting of rule violations no matter what their magnitude, Model Rule 8.3(a) requires the reporting of violations "that raise a substantial question as to [the violating lawyer's] honesty, trustworthiness, or fitness as a lawyer." Would that difference have affected the *Himmel* decision in any way?

3.   The *Himmel* court uses the evidentiary privilege as the measure of the rule's limitation on reporting "unprivileged" information about misconduct. (Notice the citation to *Wigmore*.) Should the evidentiary privilege or the broader ethical duty of confidentiality be the right measuring stick for this purpose? (Take a look at Model Rule 8.3 to see which it uses.)

4.   Consider the different control systems for policing lawyer conduct. Forsberg filed a complaint with the bar regarding Casey's conduct. She also retained Himmel to file a civil claim to recover damages from Casey. Which of the two has the greater affect on Casey? On Forsberg?

5.   Lawyer hears from credible sources about serious misconduct by Fellow Lawyer. Lawyer believes the information and reports Fellow Lawyer to bar authorities. The charges against Fellow Lawyer prove false. Fellow Lawyer sues Lawyer for defamation. What result? *See Weber v. Cueto*, 568 N.E.2d 513 (Ill. App. Ct. 1991).

B.   CONTROL DEVICES INTRODUCED

This part of Chapter II introduces the various control devices that operate to limit lawyer conduct. Read the materials in this section to acquire a sense of the parameters and procedures of each of the control systems. Many of the cases excerpted in this casebook are other than bar disciplinary cases; they will provide a further exposure to the nuances of the various control systems. Consider in this section's introduction to the control systems the advantages, strengths, and weaknesses of the various control systems for controlling lawyer conduct. What sanctions are available? What motivation exists for an aggrieved party to pursue a particular action against a lawyer? Which processes will be most efficient in the control of which aspects of lawyer conduct?

Just as there is a tendency to think only of the lawyer ethics codes when thinking about the sources of the law that governs lawyers, there is a tendency to think only of the bar disciplinary process when thinking about the control systems and mechanisms that affect lawyer conduct. In both instances, such a view is too narrow. In addition to ethics codes and the bar disciplinary process, malpractice, criminal codes, civil liability other than malpractice, judges' in-court power, litigation sanctions, and other litigation devices all limit and control lawyer conduct.

In fact, because of the small likelihood of bar disciplinary proceedings and sanctions, these other limitations are far more effective controls than are the lawyer ethics codes themselves for controlling at least some forms of lawyer conduct. However, because a violation of the lawyer ethics code often supports, directly or indirectly, the application of one of the other control devices, the analysis of the ethics codes remain a high priority. Each of the sets of controls has its own set of substantive standards for determining whether lawyer conduct has triggered the imposition of the particular control device. And each of the sets of controls has its own set of sanctions or remedies that are connected to the particular control device (e.g., suspension, disbarment, reprimand for bar discipline; money sanctions for Rule 11 violations; damages for malpractice; disqualification for conflict disqualification motions; fines and jail time for contempt of court; etc.). Each system, of course, is animated by its own set of policies that are key to understanding the analysis of cases decided within each system.

1. Bar Discipline

Discipline imposed at the hands of the organized bar is the most often referred to and studied, but much less often actually imposed, control on lawyer conduct. Discipline by the bar and then the court system operates by authority of the licensing of lawyers. The entity that grants the lawyer a license to practice law, the highest court in a particular state, usually through the action of the organized bar of the state, has authority to discipline lawyers who violate the ethics code of the jurisdiction. Discipline must be contrasted with malpractice liability. Discipline is imposed for the protection of the public generally and for the benefit of the profession, while malpractice is a tort or contract-based civil action that is meant to compensate victims of a lawyer's negligence or contract breach. The differing policies underlying the malpractice liability system and the bar discipline system dictate differing treatment of single acts of negligence.

FLORIDA BAR v. NEALE
384 So. 2d 1264 (Fla. 1980)

Per Curiam.

William J. Neale, a member of The Florida Bar, petitions this Court for review of a referee's recommendation in a bar grievance procedure. We have jurisdiction.

In 1978 the Eighteenth Judicial Circuit Grievance Committee "C" found probable cause in four complaints made against Neale. The referee found for Mr. Neale on three of those but recommended that he be found guilty of violating

Disciplinary Rule 6-101(A)(2) and 6-101(A)(3)[15] on the remaining complaint. He further recommended an eighty-nine-day suspension followed by a two-year conditional probation. At its September 1979 meeting, the bar's board of governors voted to accept the referee's recommendation of dismissing the three cases. The board voted to reject the referee's recommendations concerning the fourth case, however, believing a one-year suspension with required proof of rehabilitation to be more appropriate. Following the board's action, Neale filed his petition for review.

This complaint against Neale arose from his representation of a Mrs. Mitchell for a claim of injuries she suffered as a result of being bitten by a dog in 1970. After attempts to negotiate a settlement failed, Neale filed suit on Mitchell's behalf in 1973. A few days before trial, Neale learned that the dog had a history of biting and that punitive damages might be available. His motion to amend the original complaint in order to allege punitive damages was denied, and Neale, believing that a four-year statute of limitations controlled, took a voluntary nonsuit with his client's concurrence. At that time, however, the statute of limitations on strict liability arising from dog bites was three years, and the defendants successfully raised this defense in the subsequent suit. On appeal, the district court affirmed the trial court's judgment against Mrs. Mitchell.

The referee found that Neale's late discovery of the dog's propensity to bite reflected inadequate preparation under the circumstances because Neale did not properly interrogate his client or make an independent investigation that would have resulted in his learning of the dog's history of biting.

Neale learned a fact that he deemed important late in the game. He then overlooked or misconstrued the statute of limitations on his statutory remedy. This neglect, however, is not of sufficient magnitude to warrant conviction of an ethical violation under Canon 6.

The power to disbar or suspend a member of the legal profession is not an arbitrary one to be exercised lightly, or with either passion or prejudice. Such power should be exercised only in a clear case for weighty reasons and on clear proof.

There is a fine line between simple negligence by an attorney and violation of Canon 6 that should lead to discipline. The rights of clients should be zealously guarded by the bar, but care should be taken to avoid the use of disciplinary action under Canon 6 as a substitute for what is essentially a malpractice action.[16]

We therefore reject the recommendations of both the referee and the bar and dismiss the charges against the respondent.

It is so ordered.

----

[15] [1] A lawyer shall not: . . .

　(2) Handle a legal matter without preparation adequate in the circumstances.

　(3) Neglect a legal matter entrusted to him.

[16] [3] *House of Maddox*, 46 Ill. App. 3d 68, 4 Ill. Dec. 644, 360 N.E.2d 580 (App. Ct. 1977), holds that an attorney's allowing the statute of limitations to run in a dog bite case is malpractice.

Discipline may be based on an incredibly wide range of conduct both within and without the lawyer's role. It may be imposed for violations of the ethics code rules, for acts involving moral turpitude, for criminal conduct, for dishonesty, fraud and deceit, and for acts that are prejudicial to the administration of justice. A lawyer is subject to discipline when she violates a mandatory rule of the relevant state's adopted ethics code. All other grounds for discipline are implicitly included in this category, since the adopted ethics code typically includes provisions that in one way or another require a lawyer to refrain from conduct that is criminal, is fraudulent, involves moral turpitude, or prejudices the administration of justice. Model Rule 8.4 is the trigger for any finding of misconduct under the Model Rules. Read its provisions and note especially that even attempts to violate the ethics code can produce bar discipline.

IN RE WARHAFTIG
524 A.2d 398 (N.J. 1987)

Per Curiam.

In this disciplinary proceeding, arising out of a presentment filed by the District XII Ethics Committee, respondent is charged with invading trust account funds by withdrawing anticipated legal fees in advance of real-estate closings. The Disciplinary Review Board (DRB or Board) concluded that respondent had engaged in unethical conduct, but that knowing misappropriation had not been established by clear and convincing evidence. The Board therefore recommended that respondent be publicly reprimanded. Because we conclude that respondent's conduct clearly constituted knowing misappropriation, we decline to adopt the DRB's recommendation, and instead order that respondent be disbarred.

I

The charges filed against respondent were the result of a random compliance audit conducted by the Office of Attorney Ethics. The audit took place in November and December, 1983, and covered the two-year period ending on October 31st of the same year. The audit findings were summarized in the Board's Decision and Recommendation:

> The audit disclosed that respondent continually issued checks to his own order for fees in pending real estate matters. He would replace the "advance" when the funds were received for the real estate closing.

In one case, a real estate closing occurred on September 19, 1983. Funds totaling $70,722.33 were deposited into respondent's trust account on September 20, 1983. In another case, a real estate closing took place on October 28, 1983. The funds totaling $150,686.27 were deposited into his trust account on October 31, 1983. However, respondent had issued a check to his order for $910 on June 16, 1983 which represented his fee of $455 for each of these two closings. The audit report revealed other instances where respondent similarly took advance fees.

* * *

Respondent maintained his own lists of fees taken in advance. This list contained the names of clients and the amounts he anticipated earning from these clients in pending real estate closings. As a closing occurred and the fee was earned, respondent would delete the client's name and fee. When an anticipated closing fell through, respondent would replace the fee he had earlier advanced to himself.

* * *

When respondent received notice of the audit, he contacted his accountant who advised him that if his trust account was short he should immediately replace the funds. Respondent borrowed $11,125 from accounts in the names of his two teenage sons and deposited the money into his trust account to cover the withdrawn fees. Respondent made this deposit about five days before the originally scheduled audit date of October 4, 1983.

The auditor was not able to determine which clients' monies respondent had taken because of the size of respondent's real estate practice. Money continually flowed in and out of the trust account. Respondent, at the ethics hearing, maintained that he never failed to make the proper disbursements at the closings and that no one ever lost money as a result of his practice. He discontinued this practice in September 1983 when he received notice of the audit.

At the Ethics Committee hearing, respondent explained that his withdrawal of advance fees from the trust account was necessitated by the "gigantic cash flow burden" he experienced beginning in the early 1980s. Such pressures were the result of a precipitous decline in his real-estate practice. At the same time, an additional strain on respondent's finances was created by his wife's having to undergo treatment for cancer, and by his son's need for extensive psychiatric counseling. According to respondent, only a small portion of these expenses was covered by insurance.

Respondent was also questioned at the hearing as to whether he knew, at the time the advance-fee scheme was implemented, that his conduct constituted an ethical violation. Respondent stated:

> I was aware that what I was doing was wrong, and I was also aware that no one was being hurt by what I was doing. And what I was doing, especially by keeping lists like this, was making sure that nobody would get hurt by what I was doing.

* * *

> My perspective on the taking of the money was it was wrong, it was a violation of the rules. But I was so certain that no one could possibly be hurt by it that I didn't feel that I was stealing, certainly not stealing.

In a presentment filed on June 28, 1985, the Ethics Committee concluded that respondent had failed to comply with the record-keeping provisions of Rule 1:21-6; that several checks he had drawn on business accounts were dishonored for insufficient funds; that he had made false entries in his trust account records, contrary to DR 9-102; and that he had misappropriated clients' funds, also a violation of DR 9-102. Specifically, the presentment stated that "[r]espondent's conduct was clearly unethical in that he did deliberately and repeatedly take funds from his trust account equal to anticipated fees." The panel therefore recommended that respondent be publicly disciplined, but directed the attention of the DRB to several mitigating factors it found to be present in the case.

The DRB adopted these conclusions in its decision.

The Board concluded that the record did not support a finding that knowing misappropriation had occurred in this case. The Board, in recommending a public reprimand, also noted the existence of several mitigating factors: respondent's discontinuance of the practice at issue; his cooperation with the Office of Attorney Ethics; the acknowledgment of his wrongdoing; and the fact that no clients were actually injured by respondent's conduct.

A single member of the Board dissented from its recommendation, noting that [r]espondent withdrew funds from his trust account to pay himself for services rendered and to be rendered to a particular client without necessarily having funds belonging to that particular client in his trust account. In short, he was using funds belonging to client A to pay fees owed and to be owing by client B. Under *In re Wilson*, 81 N.J. 451 (1979), this "borrowing" of client funds constitutes a misappropriation and warrants disbarment.

II

In recommending public discipline, the DRB recognized that *In re Wilson*, which requires the disbarment of an attorney who knowingly misappropriates his clients' funds, controls the outcome of this case. However, the Board emphasized a perceived distinction between respondent's conduct, which it characterized as the "premature withdrawal of . . . monies to which he had a colorable interest[,]" and the knowing misappropriation described in *Wilson*. Apparently, the Board was persuaded by respondent's contention that while he was aware that he was violating a Disciplinary Rule, he "didn't feel that [he] was stealing . . . ."

The distinction drawn by the DRB cannot be sustained under the *Wilson* rule. [K]nowing misappropriation under *Wilson* "consists simply of a lawyer taking a client's money entrusted to him, knowing that it is the client's money and knowing that the client has not authorized the taking." We have consistently maintained that a lawyer's subjective intent, whether it be to "borrow" or to steal, is irrelevant to the determination of the appropriate discipline in a misappropriation case. In *Wilson*, we articulated the reason for this strict approach:

> Lawyers who "borrow" may, it is true, be less culpable than those who had no intent to repay, but the difference is negligible in this connection. Banks do not rehire tellers who "borrow" depositors' funds. Our professional standards, if anything, should be higher. Lawyers are more than fiduciaries: they are representatives of a profession and officers of this Court.

In view of our conclusion that respondent knowingly misappropriated client funds, we order that he be disbarred. Respondent shall reimburse the Ethics Financial Committee for appropriate administrative costs.

ORDER

It is ORDERED that ARNOLD M. WARHAFTIG of UNION, who was admitted to the bar of this State in 1968, be disbarred and that his name be stricken from the roll of attorneys of this State, effective immediately; and it is further

ORDERED that ARNOLD M. WARHAFTIG be and hereby is permanently restrained and enjoined from practicing law; and it is further

ORDERED that respondent comply with Administrative Guideline No. 23 of the Office of Attorney Ethics dealing with disbarred attorneys; and it is further

ORDERED that respondent reimburse the Ethics Financial Committee for appropriate administrative costs.

NOTES, QUESTIONS, AND EXAMPLES

1. If any of Warhaftig's clients had filed a conversion claim against him, what would have been their damages?

2. Notice the formalist analysis of the court. (The rule prohibits X; lawyer did X; discipline results.) Such analysis is typical of bar disciplinary decisions, while a more policy-oriented, legal realist analysis is more typical of modern legal analysis. William Simon has noticed and analyzed this anomaly. *See* WILLIAM H. SIMON, THE PRACTICE OF JUSTICE (1998). Could it be that when lawyers are the "clients," lawyer-controlled legal analysis becomes much more certain, less indeterminate? Could it be that the odd mixture of policies underlying the lawyer ethics rules, including the strong dose of profession self-interest, makes a policy-driven analysis of lawyer ethics codes less compelling? Might this phenomenon simply be a cost of self-regulation?

a. Acts Indicating Moral Turpitude

Formerly, the standard for whether an act reflected adversely on a lawyer's fitness (and therefore subjected the lawyer to discipline) was whether the act involved moral turpitude. DR 1-102(A)(3). This standard, thought too broad and amorphous, is no longer the explicit standard under the Model Rules. *See* MR 8.4. Nonetheless, moral turpitude language finds its way into the court decisions applying Model Rule 8.4. The explicit standard, under Model Rule 8.4, is more functional. The act is disciplinable misconduct if it "reflects adversely on the lawyer's honesty, trustworthiness, or fitness as a lawyer in other respects."

b. Criminal Conduct

A lawyer is subject to discipline when he engages in criminal conduct that reflects adversely on the lawyer's fitness as a lawyer. Minor criminal conduct, such as small-amount possession of controlled substances or criminal trespass during a civil rights demonstration, that says little about the lawyer's honesty, trustworthiness, or fitness as a lawyer in other respects, will not subject the lawyer to discipline. Under the Model Code rubric, such conduct amounts to a criminal act not involving moral turpitude. Criminal conduct outside the role of lawyer that reflects adversely on the lawyer's fitness will subject the lawyer to discipline. ABA Formal Op. 336 (1974). Fraud in a lawyer's private business transactions, setting a fire on the lawyer's office or residence as insurance fraud, or engaging in drug trafficking are all examples of criminal conduct outside the role of lawyer that would subject the lawyer to discipline.

c. Dishonesty, Fraud, and Deceit

Acts, whether in or out of the lawyer's role, that involve dishonesty, fraud and deceit, even if not rising to the level of criminal conduct, subject the lawyer to discipline. MR 8.4(c). This rule overlaps coverage with a variety of other ethics code rules that prohibit deceitful conduct of one kind or another. *See, e.g.*, MR 3.3, 3.4, and 4.1.

d. Conduct Prejudicial to the Administration of Justice

This prohibition is a broad, catch-all category including various forms of misconduct, much of which is also prohibited by more specific rules. MR 8.4(d). This rule is most often invoked to discipline litigation conduct that is regarded as tactically out-of-bounds. Disregarding court orders, rude conduct in open court, being intoxicated in court, paying witnesses to engage in inappropriate conduct, and the like are the most frequent examples. The "administration of justice" rules are vague and have been used to support discipline for widely variant forms of bad behavior. These rules have been challenged as being unconstitutionally void for vagueness and violative of First Amendment expression rights, but have been upheld. *See Howell v. State Bar of Texas*, 843 F.2d 205 (5th Cir.), *cert. denied*, 488 U.S. 982 (1988).

IN RE SNYDER
472 U.S. 634 (1985)

Burger, C.J., delivered the opinion of the Court, in which all other Members joined except Blackmun, J., who took no part in the decision of the case.

We granted certiorari to review the judgment of the Court of Appeals suspending petitioner from practice in all courts of the Eighth Circuit for six months.

I

In March 1983, petitioner Robert Snyder was appointed by the Federal District Court for the District of North Dakota to represent a defendant under the Criminal Justice Act. After petitioner completed the assignment, he submitted a claim for $1,898.55 for services and expenses. The claim was reduced by the District Court to $1,796.05.

Under the Criminal Justice Act, the Chief Judge of the Court of Appeals was required to review and approve expenditures for compensation in excess of $1,000. Chief Judge Lay found the claim insufficiently documented, and he returned it with a request for additional information. Because of technical problems with his computer software, petitioner could not readily provide the information in the form requested by the Chief Judge. He did, however, file a supplemental application.

The secretary of the Chief Judge of the Circuit again returned the application, stating that the proffered documentation was unacceptable. Petitioner then discussed the matter with Helen Monteith, the District Court Judge's secretary, who suggested he write a letter expressing his view. Petitioner then wrote the letter that led to this case. The letter, addressed to Ms. Monteith, read in part:

> In the first place, I am appalled by the amount of money which the federal court pays for indigent criminal defense work. The reason that so few attorneys in Bismarck accept this work is for that exact reason. We have, up to this point, still accepted the indigent appointments, because of a duty to our profession, and the fact that nobody else will do it.
>
> Now, however, not only are we paid an amount of money which does not even cover our overhead, but we have to go through extreme gymnastics even to receive the puny amounts which the federal courts authorize for this work. We have sent you everything we have concerning our representation, and I am not sending you anything else. You can take it or leave it.
>
> Further, I am extremely disgusted by the treatment of us by the Eighth Circuit in this case, and you are instructed to remove my name from the list of attorneys who will accept criminal indigent defense work. I have simply had it.
>
> Thank you for your time and attention.

The District Court Judge viewed this letter as one seeking changes in the process for providing fees, and discussed these concerns with petitioner. The District Court Judge then forwarded the letter to the Chief Judge of the Circuit. The Chief Judge in turn wrote to the District Judge, stating that he considered petitioner's letter "totally disrespectful to the federal courts and to the judicial system. It demonstrates a total lack of respect for the legal process and the courts."

The Chief Judge expressed concern both about petitioner's failure to "follow the guidelines and [refusal] to cooperate with the court," and questioned whether, "in view of the letter" petitioner was "worthy of practicing law in the federal courts on any matter." He stated his intention to issue an order to show cause why petitioner should not be suspended from practicing in any federal court in the Circuit for a period of one year. Subsequently, the Chief Judge wrote to the District Court again, stating that if petitioner apologized the matter would be dropped. At this time, the Chief Judge approved a reduced fee for petitioner's work of $1,000 plus expenses of $23.25.

After talking with petitioner, the District Court Judge responded to the Chief Judge as follows:

> He [petitioner] sees his letter as an expression of an honest opinion, and an exercise of his right of freedom of speech. I, of course, see it as a youthful and exuberant expression of annoyance which has now risen to the level of a cause. . . .

He has decided not to apologize, although he assured me he did not intend the letter as you interpreted it.

The Chief Judge then issued an order for petitioner to show cause why he should not be suspended for his "refusal to carry out his obligations as a practicing lawyer and officer of [the] court" because of his refusal to accept assignments under the Criminal Justice Act. Nowhere in the order was there any reference to any disrespect in petitioner's letter of October 6, 1983.

Petitioner requested a hearing on the show cause order. In his response to the order, petitioner focused exclusively on whether he was required to represent indigents under the Criminal Justice Act. He contended that the Act did not compel lawyers to represent indigents, and he noted that many of the lawyers in his District had declined to serve.[17] He also informed the court that prior to his withdrawal from the Criminal Justice Act panel, he and his two partners had taken 15 percent of all the Criminal Justice Act cases in their district.

At the hearing, the Court of Appeals focused on whether petitioner's letter of October 6, 1983, was disrespectful, an issue not mentioned in the show cause order. At one point, Judge Arnold asked: "I am asking you, sir, if you are prepared to apologize to the court for the tone of your letter?" Petitioner answered: "That is not the basis that I am being brought forth before the court today." When the issue again arose, petitioner protested: "But, it seems to me we're getting far afield here. The question is, can I be suspended from this court for my request to be removed from the panel of attorneys."

Petitioner was again offered an opportunity to apologize for his letter, but he declined. At the conclusion of the hearing, the Chief Judge stated:

> I want to make it clear to Mr. Snyder what it is the court is allowing you ten days lapse here, a period for you to consider. One is, that, assuming there is a general requirement for all competent lawyers to do pro bono work that you stand willing and ready to perform such work and will comply with the guidelines of the statute. And secondly, to reconsider your position as Judge Arnold has requested, concerning the tone of your letter of October 6.

Following the hearing, petitioner wrote a letter to the court, agreeing to "enthusiastically obey [the] mandates" of any new plan for the implementation of the Criminal Justice Act in North Dakota, and to "make every good faith effort possible" to comply with the court's guidelines regarding compensation under the Act. Petitioner's letter, however, made no mention of the October 6, 1983, letter.

The Chief Judge then wrote to Snyder, stating among other things:

> The court expressed its opinion at the time of the oral hearing that interrelated with our concern and the issuance of the order to show cause was the disrespect that you displayed to the court by way of your letter

---

[17] [2] A resolution presented by the Burleigh County Bar Association to the Court of Appeals on petitioner's behalf stated that of the 276 practitioners eligible to serve on the Criminal Justice Act panel in the Southwestern Division of the District of North Dakota, only 87 were on the panel.

addressed to Helen Montieth [*sic*], Judge Van Sickle's secretary, of October 6, 1983. The court expressly asked if you would be willing to apologize for the tone of the letter and the disrespect displayed. You serve as an officer of the court and, as such, the Canons of Ethics require every lawyer to maintain a respect for the court as an institution.

Before circulating your letter of February 23, I would appreciate your response to Judge Arnold's specific request, and the court's request, for you to apologize for the letter that you wrote.

Please let me hear from you by return mail. I am confident that if such a letter is forthcoming that the court will dissolve the order.

Petitioner responded to the Chief Judge:

I cannot, and will never, in justice to my conscience, apologize for what I consider to be telling the truth, albeit in harsh terms. . . .

It is unfortunate that the respective positions in the proceeding have so hardened. However, I consider this to be a matter of principle, and if one stands on a principle, one must be willing to accept the consequences.

After receipt of this letter, petitioner was suspended from the practice of law in the federal courts in the Eighth Circuit for six months. The opinion stated that petitioner "contumaciously refused to retract his previous remarks or apologize to the court." It continued:

[Petitioner's] refusal to show continuing respect for the court and his refusal to demonstrate a sincere retraction of his admittedly "harsh" statements are sufficient to demonstrate to this court that he is not presently fit to practice law in the federal courts. All courts depend on the highest level of integrity and respect not only from the judiciary but from the lawyers who serve in the court as well. Without public display of respect for the judicial branch of government as an institution by lawyers, the law cannot survive. . . . Without hesitation we find Snyder's disrespectful statements as to this court's administration of CJA contumacious conduct. We deem this unfortunate.

We find that Robert Snyder shall be suspended from the practice of law in the federal courts of the Eighth Circuit for a period of six months; thereafter, Snyder should make application to both this court and the federal district court of North Dakota to be readmitted.

* * *

The en banc court opinion stayed the order of suspension for 10 days, but provided that the stay would be lifted if petitioner failed to apologize. He did not apologize, and the order of suspension took effect.

We granted certiorari. We reverse.

II

A

Petitioner challenges his suspension from practice on the grounds (a) that his October 6, 1983, letter to the District Judge's secretary was protected by the First Amendment, (b) that he was denied due process with respect to the notice of the charge on which he was suspended, and (c) that his challenged letter was not disrespectful or contemptuous. We avoid constitutional issues when resolution of such issues is not necessary for disposition of a case. Accordingly, we consider first whether petitioner's conduct and expressions warranted his suspension from practice; if they did not, there is no occasion to reach petitioner's constitutional claims.

Courts have long recognized an inherent authority to suspend or disbar lawyers. This inherent power derives from the lawyer's role as an officer of the court which granted admission. The standard for disciplining attorneys practicing before the courts of appeals is set forth in Federal Rule of Appellate Procedure 46:

> *(b) Suspension or Disbarment. When it is shown to the court that any member of its bar has been suspended or disbarred from practice in any other court of record, or has been guilty of conduct unbecoming a member of the bar of the court, he will be subject to suspension or disbarment by the court.* The member shall be afforded an opportunity to show good cause, within such time as the court shall prescribe, why he should not be suspended or disbarred. Upon his response to the rule to show cause, and after hearing, if requested, or upon expiration of the time prescribed for a response if no response is made, the court shall enter an appropriate order. (Emphasis added.)

The phrase "conduct unbecoming a member of the bar" must be read in light of the "complex code of behavior" to which attorneys are subject. Essentially, this reflects the burdens inherent in the attorney's dual obligations to clients and to the system of justice. Justice Cardozo once observed:

> "Membership in the bar is a privilege burdened with conditions." [An attorney is] received into that ancient fellowship for something more than private gain. He [becomes] an officer of the court, and, like the court itself, an instrument or agency to advance the ends of justice.

As an officer of the court, a member of the bar enjoys singular powers that others do not possess; by virtue of admission, members of the bar share a kind of monopoly granted only to lawyers. Admission creates a license not only to advise and counsel clients but also to appear in court and try cases; as an officer of the court, a lawyer can cause persons to drop their private affairs and be called as witnesses in court, and for depositions and other pretrial processes that, while subject to the ultimate control of the court, may be conducted outside courtrooms. The license granted by the court requires members of the bar to conduct themselves in a manner compatible with the role of courts in the administration of justice.

Read in light of the traditional duties imposed on an attorney, it is clear that "conduct unbecoming a member of the bar" is conduct contrary to professional standards that shows an unfitness to discharge continuing obligations to clients or the courts, or conduct inimical to the administration of justice. More specific guidance is provided by case law, applicable court rules, and "the lore of the profession," as embodied in codes of professional conduct.[18]

B

Apparently relying on an attorney's obligation to avoid conduct that is "prejudicial to the administration of justice,"[19] the Court of Appeals held that the letter of October 6, 1983, and an unspecified "refusal to show continuing respect for the court" demonstrated that petitioner was "not presently fit to practice law in the federal courts." Its holding was predicated on a specific finding that petitioner's "disrespectful statements [in his letter of October 6, 1983] as to this court's administration of the CJA [constituted] contumacious conduct."

We must examine the record in light of Rule 46 to determine whether the Court of Appeals' action is supported by the evidence. In the letter, petitioner declined to submit further documentation in support of his fee request, refused to accept further assignments under the Criminal Justice Act, and criticized the administration of the Act. Petitioner's refusal to submit further documentation in support of his fee request could afford a basis for declining to award a fee; however, the submission of adequate documentation was only a prerequisite to the collection of his fee, not an affirmative obligation required by his duties to a client or the court. Nor, as the Court of Appeals ultimately concluded, was petitioner legally obligated under the terms of the local plan to accept Criminal Justice Act cases.

We do not consider a lawyer's criticism of the administration of the Act or criticism of inequities in assignments under the Act as cause for discipline or suspension. The letter was addressed to a court employee charged with administrative responsibilities, and concerned a practical matter in the administration of the Act. The Court of Appeals acknowledged that petitioner brought to light concerns about the administration of the plan that had "merit," and the court instituted a study of the administration of the Criminal Justice Act as a result of petitioner's complaint. Officers of the court may appropriately express criticism on such matters.

The record indicates the Court of Appeals was concerned about the tone of the letter; petitioner concedes that the tone of his letter was "harsh," and, indeed it can be read as ill-mannered. All persons involved in the judicial process — judges,

---

[18] [6] The Court of Appeals stated that the standard of professional conduct expected of an attorney is defined by the ethical code adopted by the licensing authority of an attorney's home state, and cited the North Dakota Code of Professional Responsibility as the controlling expression of the conduct expected of petitioner. The state code of professional responsibility does not by its own terms apply to sanctions in the federal courts. Federal courts admit and suspend attorneys as an exercise of their inherent power; the standards imposed are a matter of federal law.

[19] [7] This duty is almost universally recognized in American jurisdictions. *See, e.g.*, Disciplinary Rule 1-102(A)(5), North Dakota Code of Professional Responsibility; Rule 8.4(d), American Bar Association, Model Rules of Professional Conduct (1983); Disciplinary Rule 1-102(A)(5), American Bar Association, Model Code of Professional Responsibility (1980).

litigants, witnesses, and court officers — owe a duty of courtesy to all other participants. The necessity for civility in the inherently contentious setting of the adversary process suggests that members of the bar cast criticisms of the system in a professional and civil tone. However, even assuming that the letter exhibited an unlawyerlike rudeness, a single incident of rudeness or lack of professional courtesy — in this context — does not support a finding of contemptuous or contumacious conduct, or a finding that a lawyer is "not presently fit to practice law in the federal courts." Nor does it rise to the level of "conduct unbecoming a member of the bar" warranting suspension from practice.

Accordingly, the judgment of the Court of Appeals is

Reversed.

e. Forms of Discipline and Procedural Issues

Discipline generally comes in the form of disbarment, suspension, or reprimand, either public or private. Courts also may require disciplined lawyers to engage in professional responsibility educational programs. Disbarment is an indefinite dismissal from the rolls of lawyers licensed to practice in the particular jurisdiction. In most jurisdictions, a disbarred lawyer may petition for readmission after a designated time period has elapsed. Nonetheless, disbarment is the most serious form of discipline and most often effectively ends a lawyer's legal career. Suspension is a fixed period revocation of the license to practice law. Reprimand is a statement of reproach issued by the bar to the disciplined lawyer. Reprimands may either be private or public. When a reprimand is public, the reprimand will be published in a newspaper.

Typical procedures for bar discipline involve a complaint, an informal finding of probable cause, an investigation by a bar committee, a hearing before a bar hearing committee, appeals through appeals panels through to the state's court of last resort, which has the final disciplining authority. The bar bears the burden of proof and the accused has no jury trial right. The person filing the complaint with the bar is not a party to the proceedings. Instead, the bar association pursues the matter as it chooses, largely as a prosecutor pursues criminal charges without regard to the wishes of a crime victim.

IN RE RUFFALO
390 U.S. 544 (1968)

Justice Douglas delivered the opinion of the Court.

Petitioner was ordered indefinitely suspended from the practice of law by the Supreme Court of Ohio on two findings of alleged misconduct. *Mahoning County Bar Assn. v. Ruffalo*, 176 Ohio St. 263, 199 N.E.2d 396. That order became final and is not here on review. The Federal District Court, after ordering petitioner to show cause why he should not be disbarred, found that there was no misconduct. *In re Ruffalo*, 249 F. Supp. 432 (D.C.N.D. Ohio). The Court of Appeals likewise ordered petitioner to show cause why he should not be stricken from the roll of that court on the basis of Ohio's disbarment order. The majority held that while one of the two charges might not justify discipline, the other one did; and it disbarred petitioner from practice in that Court. 370 F.2d 447 (6th Cir.). The dissenting judge thought that neither charge justified suspension from practice. The case is here on a writ of certiorari.

Petitioner was an active trial lawyer who handled many Federal Employers' Liability Act cases. The Association of American Railroads investigated his handling of claims and referred charges of impropriety to the President of the Mahoning County Bar Association who was also local counsel for the Baltimore & Ohio Railroad Co. The Mahoning County Bar Association then filed the charges against petitioner.[20]

In the state court proceedings, upon which the decision of the Court of Appeals relied, the Ohio Board of Commissioners on Grievances and Discipline originally charged petitioner with 12 counts of misconduct. Charges Nos. 4 and 5 accused petitioner of soliciting FELA plaintiffs as clients through an agent, Michael Orlando. At the hearings which followed, both Orlando and petitioner testified that Orlando did not solicit clients for petitioner but merely investigated FELA cases for him. It was brought out that some of Orlando's investigations involved cases where his employer, the Baltimore & Ohio Railroad, was defendant. Immediately after hearing this testimony, the Board, on the third day of hearings, added a charge No. 13 against petitioner based on his hiring Orlando to investigate Orlando's own employer. Counsel for petitioner objected, stating:

> Oh, I object to that very highly. There is nothing morally wrong and there is nothing legally wrong with it. . . . When does the end of these amendments come? I mean the last minute you are here, [counsel for the county Bar Association] may bring in another amendment. I think this gentleman [petitioner] has a right to know beforehand what the charges are against him and be heard on those charges.

Motion to strike charge No. 13 was denied, but the Board gave petitioner a continuance in order to have time to respond to the new charge.

The State Board found petitioner guilty of seven counts of misconduct, including No. 13. On review, the Supreme Court of Ohio found the evidence sufficient to sustain only two charges, one of them being No. 13, but concluded that the two violations required disbarment. The only charge on which the Court of Appeals acted was No. 13, which reads as follows:

---

[20] [Mr. Ruffalo was a quite successful plaintiffs' personal injury lawyer who, as the Court notes, handled many cases against various railroads. He, like many such lawyers before him, was reported to the bar by the lawyers representing the corporate clients who were regularly defendants in his clients' cases. The charges brought against the plaintiffs' lawyer in most such cases were for solicitation of clients and for providing financial assistance to clients during pending litigation. *See* Section C[2] [e] in Chapter V, "Conflicts of Interest," and Section A in Chapter IX, "Advertising and Solicitation." In one such case, the railroads hired an investigator to impersonate a railroad worker, fake injuries, retain the target personal injury lawyer, defraud doctors and the court, and thereby entrap the target personal injury lawyer into participating in a fraud on the court. *Chicago Bar Ass'n. v. McCallum*, 173 N.E.2d 827 (Ill. 1930). —Ed.]

That Respondent did conspire with one, Michael Orlando, and paid said Michael Orlando moneys for preparing lawsuits against the B. & O. Railroad, the employer of said Michael Orlando, during all the periods of time extending from 1957 to July of 1961, well knowing that said practice was deceptive in its nature and was morally and legally wrong as respects the employee, Michael Orlando, toward his employer, the B. & O. Railroad Company.

Though admission to practice before a federal court is derivative from membership in a state bar, disbarment by the State does not result in automatic disbarment by the federal court. Though that state action is entitled to respect, it is not conclusively binding on the federal courts.

Petitioner, active in the trial of FELA cases, hired a railroad man to help investigate the cases. He was Orlando, a night-shift car inspector for the Baltimore & Ohio Railroad Co. There was no evidence that Orlando ever investigated a case in the yard where he worked as inspector. There was no evidence that he ever investigated on company time. Orlando had no access to confidential information; and there was no claim he ever revealed secret matters or breached any trust. It is clear from the record that petitioner chose a railroad man to help him investigate those claims because Orlando knew railroading.

As noted, the charge (No. 13) for which petitioner stands disbarred was not in the original charges made against him. It was only after both he and Orlando had testified that this additional charge was added. Thereafter, no additional evidence against petitioner relating to charge No. 13 was taken. Rather, counsel for the county bar association said:

We will stipulate that as far as we are concerned, the only facts that we will introduce in support of Specification No. 13 are the statements that Mr. Ruffalo has made here in open court and the testimony of Mike Orlando from the witness stand. Those are the only facts we have to support this Specification No. 13.

There was no de novo hearing before the Court of Appeals. Rather, it rested on the Ohio court's record and findings:

We have before us, and have reviewed, the entire record developed by the Ohio proceedings, but think it proper to dispose of the matter primarily upon the charges on which the Ohio Court disciplined Mr. Ruffalo. The facts as to these are not in dispute. We consider whether we find insupportable the Ohio Court's determination that such facts disclosed unprofessional conduct warranting the discipline imposed and whether they warrant similar discipline by us.

* * *

We turn then to the question whether in Ohio's procedure there was any lack of due process.

Disbarment, designed to protect the public, is a punishment or penalty imposed on the lawyer. He is accordingly entitled to procedural due process, which includes fair notice of the charge. [W]hen proceedings for disbarment are "not taken for matters occurring in open court, in the presence of the judges, notice should be given to the attorney of the charges made and opportunity afforded him for explanation and defence." Therefore, one of the conditions this Court considers in determining whether disbarment by a State should be followed by disbarment here is whether "the state procedure from want of notice or opportunity to be heard was wanting in due process."

In the present case petitioner had no notice that his employment of Orlando would be considered a disbarment offense until after both he and Orlando had testified at length on all the material facts pertaining to this phase of the case. As Judge Edwards, dissenting below, said, "Such procedural violation of due process would never pass muster in any normal civil or criminal litigation."

These are adversary proceedings of a quasi-criminal nature. The charge must be known before the proceedings commence. They become a trap when, after they are underway, the charges are amended on the basis of testimony of the accused. He can then be given no opportunity to expunge the earlier statements and start afresh.

How the charge would have been met had it been originally included in those leveled against petitioner by the Ohio Board of Commissioners on Grievances and Discipline no one knows.

This absence of fair notice as to the reach of the grievance procedure and the precise nature of the charges deprived petitioner of procedural due process.

2. Malpractice

Malpractice is a civil claim for relief intended to remedy a wrong done by a professional (in this case a lawyer) to an individual client or group of clients. Contract theory malpractice actions have the common contract elements of agreement, breach, and damage. Damage measurement under contract theories is more limited than that of tort theories. Under tort theories, the most used of the malpractice theories, the elements are the familiar negligence elements of duty, breach, causation, and damages. The lawyer's duty to the client is measured by the skill and knowledge of ordinary lawyers in the community. A lawyer owes this duty to a client irrespective of whether any fee is being paid for the lawyer's service. Thus, appointed counsel and pro bono counsel, for example, owe the same duty as a lawyer who is charging a fee for service. Lawyers are expected to have general knowledge of the law and its fundamental principles. A lawyer is expected to be sufficiently familiar with research techniques and to use them to discover the law that applies to a client's matter. Nonetheless, a lawyer does not owe a duty to know every possible nuance in the law. Specialists in a particular field (tax, for example) are held to a higher standard than that of the ordinary lawyer in the community. The standard will be set by the knowledge and skill of those specializing in the particular field.

TOGSTAD v. VESELY, OTTO, MILLER & KEEFE
291 N.W.2d 686 (Minn. 1980)

J/P/App/Aff.

PER CURIAM.

Jury award to P

This is an appeal by the defendants from a judgment of the Hennepin County District Court involving an action for legal malpractice. The jury found that the defendant attorney Jerre Miller was negligent and that, as a direct result of such negligence, plaintiff John Togstad sustained damages in the amount of $610,500 and his wife, plaintiff Joan Togstad, in the amount of $39,000. Defendants (Miller and his law firm) appeal to this court from the denial of their motion for judgment notwithstanding the verdict or, alternatively, for a new trial. We affirm.

FACTS

In August 1971, John Togstad began to experience severe headaches and on August 16, 1971, was admitted to Methodist Hospital where tests disclosed that the headaches were caused by a large aneurism on the left internal carotid artery.

[The court describes the nature of Plaintiff's underlying medical malpractice claim. —Ed.]

About 14 months after her husband's hospitalization began, plaintiff Joan Togstad met with attorney Jerre Miller regarding her husband's condition. Neither she nor her husband was personally acquainted with Miller or his law firm prior to that time. John Togstad's former work supervisor, Ted Bucholz, made the appointment and accompanied Mrs. Togstad to Miller's office. Bucholz was present when Mrs. Togstad and Miller discussed the case.

P told lawyer her case - he said their isn't a case

no money

Mrs. Togstad testified that she told Miller "everything that happened at the hospital," including the nurses' statements and conduct which had raised a question in her mind. She stated that she "believed" she had told Miller "about the procedure and what was undertaken, what was done, and what happened." She brought no records with her. Miller took notes and asked questions during the meeting, which lasted 45 minutes to an hour. At its conclusion, according to Mrs. Togstad, Miller said that "he did not think we had a legal case, however, he was going to discuss this with his partner." She understood that if Miller changed his mind after talking to his partner, he would call her. Mrs. Togstad "gave it" a few days and, since she did not hear from Miller, decided "that they had come to the conclusion that there wasn't a case." No fee arrangements were discussed, no medical authorizations were requested, nor was Mrs. Togstad billed for the interview.

no exp. in medical

it isn't seek another att. b/c she relict on D's Adv.

Mrs. Togstad denied that Miller had told her his firm did not have expertise in the medical malpractice field, urged her to see another attorney, or related to her that the statute of limitations for medical malpractice actions was two years. She did not consult another attorney until one year after she talked to Miller. Mrs. Togstad indicated that she did not confer with another attorney earlier because of her reliance on Miller's "legal advice" that they "did not have a case."

On cross-examination, Mrs. Togstad was asked whether she went to Miller's office "to see if he would take the case of [her] husband . . . ." She replied, "Well, I guess it was to go for legal advice, what to do, where shall we go from here? That is what we went for." Again in response to defense counsel's questions, Mrs. Togstad testified as follows:

> And it was clear to you, was it not, that what was taking place was a preliminary discussion between a prospective client and lawyer as to whether or not they wanted to enter into an attorney-client relationship?

> I am not sure how to answer that. It was for legal advice as to what to do.

> And Mr. Miller was discussing with you your problem and indicating whether he, as a lawyer, wished to take the case, isn't that true?

> Yes.

[handwritten margin note: Whether Miller wanted to take the case.]

On re-direct examination, Mrs. Togstad acknowledged that when she left Miller's office she understood that she had been given a "qualified, quality legal opinion that [she and her husband] did not have a malpractice case."

Miller's testimony was different in some respects from that of Mrs. Togstad. Like Mrs. Togstad, Miller testified that Mr. Bucholz arranged and was present at the meeting, which lasted about 45 minutes. According to Miller, Mrs. Togstad described the hospital incident, including the conduct of the nurses. He asked her questions, to which she responded. Miller testified that "the only thing I told her [Mrs. Togstad] after we had pretty much finished the conversation was that there was nothing related in her factual circumstances that told me that she had a case that our firm would be interested in undertaking."

[handwritten margin note: Miller's side. firm not interested.]

Miller also claimed he related to Mrs. Togstad "that because of the grievous nature of the injuries sustained by her husband, that this was only my opinion and she was encouraged to ask another attorney if she wished for another opinion" and "she ought to do so promptly." He testified that he informed Mrs. Togstad that his firm "was not engaged as experts" in the area of medical malpractice, and that they associated with the Charles Hvass firm in cases of that nature. Miller stated that at the end of the conference he told Mrs. Togstad that he would consult with Charles Hvass and if Hvass's opinion differed from his, Miller would so inform her. Miller recollected that he called Hvass a "couple days" later and discussed the case with him. It was Miller's impression that Hvass thought there was no liability for malpractice in the case. Consequently, Miller did not communicate with Mrs. Togstad further.

[handwritten margin note: says he told her to go to another att'l.]

On cross-examination, Miller testified as follows:

> Now, so there is no misunderstanding, and I am reading from your deposition, you understood that she was consulting with you as a lawyer, isn't that correct?

> That's correct.

> That she was seeking legal advice from a professional attorney licensed to practice in this state and in this community?

> I think you and I did have another interpretation or use of the term "Advice." She was there to see whether or not she had a case and whether the firm would accept it.

We have two aspects; number one, your legal opinion concerning liability of a case for malpractice; number two, whether there was or wasn't liability, whether you would accept it, your firm, two separate elements, right?

I would say so.

Were you asked on page 6 in the deposition, folio 14, "And you understood that she was seeking legal advice at the time that she was in your office, that is correct also, isn't it?" And did you give this answer, "I don't want to engage in semantics with you, but my impression was that she and Mr. Bucholz were asking my opinion after having related the incident that I referred to." The next question, "Your legal opinion?" Your answer, "Yes." Were those questions asked and were they given?

expert witness

Kenneth Green, a Minneapolis attorney, was called as an expert by plaintiffs. He stated that in rendering legal advice regarding a claim of medical malpractice, the "minimum" an attorney should do would be to request medical authorizations from the client, review the hospital records, and consult with an expert in the field. John McNulty, a Minneapolis attorney, and Charles Hvass testified as experts on behalf of the defendants. McNulty stated that when an attorney is consulted as to whether he will take a case, the lawyer's only responsibility in refusing it is to so inform the party. He testified, however, that when a lawyer is asked his legal opinion on the merits of a medical malpractice claim, community standards require that the attorney check hospital records and consult with an expert before rendering his opinion.

Hvass stated that he had no recollection of Miller's calling him in October 1972 relative to the Togstad matter.

should tell abt the SoL

Hvass stated, however, that he would never render a "categorical" opinion. In addition, Hvass acknowledged that if he were consulted for a "legal opinion" regarding medical malpractice and 14 months had expired since the incident in question, "ordinary care and diligence" would require him to inform the party of the two-year statute of limitations applicable to that type of action.

jury found Att-client relationship

but for Miller's bad advice - they would have won med-mal suit

This case was submitted to the jury by way of a special verdict form. The jury found that Dr. Blake and the hospital were negligent and that Dr. Blake's negligence (but not the hospital's) was a direct cause of the injuries sustained by John Togstad; that there was an attorney-client contractual relationship between Mrs. Togstad and Miller; that Miller was negligent in rendering advice regarding the possible claims of Mr. and Mrs. Togstad; that, but for Miller's negligence, plaintiffs would have been successful in the prosecution of a legal action against Dr. Blake; and that neither Mr. nor Mrs. Togstad was negligent in pursuing their claims against Dr. Blake. The jury awarded damages to Mr. Togstad of $610,500 and to Mrs. Togstad of $39,000.

* * *

In a legal malpractice action of the type involved here, four elements must be shown: (1) that an attorney-client relationship existed; (2) that defendant acted negligently or in breach of contract; (3) that such acts were the proximate cause of the plaintiffs' damages; (4) that but for defendant's conduct the plaintiffs would have been successful in the prosecution of their medical malpractice claim.

We believe it is unnecessary to decide whether a tort or contract theory is preferable for resolving the attorney-client relationship question raised by this appeal. The tort and contract analyses are very similar in a case such as the instant one,[21] and we conclude that under either theory the evidence shows that a lawyer-client relationship is present here. The thrust of Mrs. Togstad's testimony is that she went to Miller for legal advice, was told there wasn't a case, and relied upon this advice in failing to pursue the claim for medical malpractice. In addition, according to Mrs. Togstad, Miller did not qualify his legal opinion by urging her to seek advice from another attorney, nor did Miller inform her that he lacked expertise in the medical malpractice area. Assuming this testimony is true, as this court must do we believe a jury could properly find that Mrs. Togstad sought and received legal advice from Miller under circumstances which made it reasonably foreseeable to Miller that Mrs. Togstad would be injured if the advice were negligently given. Thus, under either a tort or contract analysis, there is sufficient evidence in the record to support the existence of an attorney-client relationship.

Defendants argue that even if an attorney-client relationship was established the evidence fails to show that Miller acted negligently in assessing the merits of the Togstads' case. They appear to contend that, at most, Miller was guilty of an error in judgment which does not give rise to legal malpractice. However, this case does not involve a mere error of judgment. The gist of plaintiffs' claim is that Miller failed to perform the minimal research that an ordinarily prudent attorney would do before rendering legal advice in a case of this nature. The record contains sufficient evidence to support plaintiffs' position.

The defect in defendants' reasoning is that there is adequate evidence supporting the claim that Miller was also negligent in failing to advise Mrs. Togstad of the two-year medical malpractice limitations period and thus the trial court acted properly in refusing to instruct the jury in the manner urged by defendants. One of defendants' expert witnesses, Charles Hvass, testified:

> Now, Mr. Hvass, where you are consulted for a legal opinion and advice concerning malpractice and 14 months have elapsed [since the incident in question], wouldn't — and you hold yourself out as competent to give a legal opinion and advice to these people concerning their rights, wouldn't ordinary care and diligence require that you inform them that there is a two-year statute of limitations within which they have to act or lose their rights?

---

[21] [4] Under a negligence approach it must essentially be shown that defendant rendered legal advice (not necessarily at someone's request) under circumstances which made it reasonably foreseeable to the attorney that if such advice was rendered negligently, the individual receiving the advice might be injured thereby. *See, e.g., Palsgraf v. Long Island R. Co.*, 248 N.Y. 339, 162 N.E. 99, 59 A.L.R. 1253 (1928). Or, stated another way, under a tort theory, "an attorney-client relationship is created whenever an individual seeks and receives legal advice from an attorney in circumstances in which a reasonable person would rely on such advice." 63 MINN. L. REV. 751, 759 (1979). A contract analysis requires the rendering of legal advice pursuant to another's request and the reliance factor, in this case, where the advice was not paid for, need be shown in the form of promissory estoppel. *See* 7 C.J.S., *Attorney and Client*, § 65; RESTATEMENT (SECOND) OF CONTRACTS, at § 90.

[handwritten margin note: expert said he should have told her abt SOL]

Yes. I believe I would have advised someone of the two-year period of limitation, yes.

Consequently, based on the testimony of Mrs. Togstad, i.e., that she requested and received legal advice from Miller concerning the malpractice claim, and the above testimony of Hvass, we must reject the defendants' contention, as it was reasonable for a jury to determine that Miller acted negligently in failing to inform Mrs. Togstad of the applicable limitations period.

* * *

There is also sufficient evidence in the record establishing that, but for Miller's negligence, plaintiffs would have been successful in prosecuting their medical malpractice claim. Dr. Woods, in no uncertain terms, concluded that Mr. Togstad's injuries were caused by the medical malpractice of Dr. Blake. Defendants' expert testimony to the contrary was obviously not believed by the jury. Thus, the jury reasonably found that had plaintiff's medical malpractice action been properly brought, plaintiffs would have recovered.

Based on the foregoing, we hold that the jury's findings are adequately supported by the record. Accordingly we uphold the trial court's denial of defendants' motion for judgment notwithstanding the jury verdict.

* * *

Affirmed.

NOTES, QUESTIONS, AND EXAMPLES

1. Lawyers are not guarantors of particular results any more than doctors guarantee recovery from illness. Often, a variety of reasonable strategies will be available from which to choose. When a lawyer chooses a reasonable course of action, and that course later produces bad results, the lawyer has not breached the duty of care owed to the client. Actions by a lawyer that are below the applicable standard of care breach the duty to the client.

2. For a malpractice claim to exist, the lawyer's breach of duty must cause the client's damages. Often, this means that the client will have to prove that she would have prevailed in the matter had the lawyer not breached the duty of care. This requirement is called the "case within a case." The malpractice plaintiff must prove the value of the underlying case in order to prevail in the malpractice case.

3. To establish the standard of care and its breach, expert opinion is usually required in a lawyer malpractice action.

3. Liability for Complicity in Client Conduct

Lawyers are prohibited under the Model Rules from "counselling a client to engage or assisting a client in conduct that the lawyer knows is criminal or fraudulent." MR 1.2(d). While this provision sets up the disciplinary exposure of a lawyer who violates the rule, under a variety of theories a lawyer may also be criminally and civilly liable for the wrongs of the clients that the lawyer assists. The *Westlake v. Abrahams* case (excerpted in Chapter I) is just such a case.

4. Contempt of Court

Judges' contempt power is a considerable control on lawyer conduct in the litigation setting. The contempt power is meant to give judges reasonable control over the courtroom and to enforce standards of courtroom behavior among litigants.

TAYLOR v. HAYES
418 U.S. 488 (1974)

JUSTICE WHITE delivered the opinion of the Court.

The question in this case concerns the validity of a criminal contempt judgment entered against petitioner by reason of certain events occurring in the course of a criminal trial in the courts of the Commonwealth of Kentucky. Petitioner was retained counsel for Narvel Tinsley, a Negro, who along with his brother Michael was charged with the murders of two police officers. According to the Kentucky Court of Appeals, the "murders created some considerable sensation in Louisville . . . and . . . newspaper coverage was overly abundant." Trial before respondent trial judge began on October 18, 1971, and was completed on October 29.

On nine different occasions during this turbulent trial, respondent, out of the hearing of the jury and most often in chambers, informed petitioner that he was in contempt of court. The first charge was immediately reduced to a warning and no sentence was imposed at the time of charge in that or any other instance. Petitioner was permitted to respond to most, but not all, of the charges.

At the conclusion of the trial on October 29 and after a guilty verdict had been returned, respondent, in the presence of the jury, made a statement concerning petitioner's trial conduct. Refusing petitioner's request to respond and declaring that "I have you" on nine counts, respondent proceeded to impose a jail term on each count totaling almost four and one-half years: 30 days on the first count, 60 days on the second, 90 days on the third, six months on counts four, five, six, and seven, and one year each on counts eight and nine, "all to run consecutive."[22] A few

---

[22] [2] The following is the complete transcript of the proceedings on October 29, 1971, with respect to the contempt charges against petitioner:

> The Court: Mr. Taylor, the Court has something to take up with you sir, at this time.
>
> Mr. Taylor: Well, I'll be right here, Judge.
>
> The Court: I've for two weeks sit here and listen to you. Now, you're going to listen to me.
> Stand right here, sir.
>
> For two weeks I've seen you put on the worst display I've ever seen an attorney in my two years of this court and 15 years of practicing law. You've quoted that you couldn't do it any other way. You know our court system is completely based upon, particularly criminal law, the Doctrine of Reasonable Doubt. That's exactly what it means, reason. It doesn't mean that it's based upon deceit; it doesn't mean that it's based upon trickery; it doesn't mean it's based upon planned confusion.

days later, petitioner was also barred from practicing law by respondent in his division of the Criminal Branch of the Jefferson Circuit Court.

While petitioner's appeal was pending, on March 2, 1972, respondent entered a corrected judgment containing a "certificate" which described the nine charges of contempt[23] but eliminated the first charge as having been reduced to a warning and

---

Sometimes I wonder really what your motive is, if you're really interested in the justice of your client, or if you have some ulterior motive, if you're interested in Dan Taylor or Narvel Tinsley.

It's a shame that this court has to do something that the Bar Association of this State should have done a long time ago.

As far as a lawyer is concerned, you're not. I want the jury to hear this; I want the law students of this community to hear this, that you're not the rule, you're the exception to the rule. —

Mr. Taylor: (Interrupting) Thank you.

The Court: I want them to understand that your actions should not be their actions because this is not the way that a court is conducted. This is not the way an officer of a court should conduct itself.

Mr. Taylor: I would respond to you, sir —

The Court: (Interrupting) You're not responding to me on anything.

Mr. Taylor: (Interrupting) Oh yes, I will.

The Court: Yes, you're not, either. Mr. Taylor: Yes, I will.

The Court: The sentence is on Count One —

Mr. Taylor: (Interrupting) Unless you intend to gag me —

The Court: (Interposing) I'll do that —

Mr. Taylor: (Interposing) My lawyers will respond to you —

The Court: (Interposing) I'll do that, sir.

Mr. Taylor: My lawyers will respond to you, sir.

The Court: You be quiet, or you'll — there will be some more contempts —

Mr. Taylor: (Interrupting) No, you heard what I said.

The Court: I have you nine counts. First Count, 30 days in jail; Second Count, 60 days in jail; Third Count, 90 days in jail; Fourth Count, six months in jail; Fifth Count, six months in jail; Sixth Count, six months in jail; Seventh Count, six months in jail; Eighth Count, one year in jail; Ninth Count, one year in jail, all to run consecutive.

Take him away.

Mr. Taylor: We will answer you in court.

The Court: I'd be glad to see you.

[23] [3] The nine charges of contempt were described in the certificate as follows:

Contempt 1. Mr. Taylor, in questioning a prospective juror, on the second day of Voir Dire, repeatedly ignored the Court's order not to continue a certain line of questioning and to ask his questions of the jury as a whole. He evidenced utter disrespect for prospective jurors (T.E. 335-347).

Contempt 2. The court sustained the Commonwealth objection on the use of a prior statement to cross examine Officer Hogan and not to go into the escape of Narvel Tinsley. Mr. Taylor repeatedly and completely ignored the court's ruling (T.E. 1071-1080).

Contempt 3. During the playing of a tape recording of the voice of witness David White, Mr. Taylor wrote on a blackboard. After the playing of the tape it was ordered that the blackboard be removed from the court and Mr. Taylor was advised by the court that he could use it in his final summation to the jury. Mr. Taylor was disrespectful to the court by his tone of voice and manner when he replied, 'I'll certainly keep that in mind, your Honor' (T.E. 1355).

Contempt 4. During cross-examination of Narvel Tinsley, by Mr. Schroering, Mr. Taylor interrupted and moved for a recess, was overruled by the court, and then became most disrespectful to the court and

reduced the sentence on each of the last two counts to six months in jail. The corrected judgment was silent as to whether the sentences were to run concurrently or consecutively.

The Kentucky Court of Appeals affirmed, holding that petitioner was guilty of each and every contempt charged. In its view, petitioner's actions "were deliberate, delaying, or planned disruptive tactics which did in fact create such an atmosphere in the court that he, if permitted to continue, would have appeared to be the star performer in the center ring of a three-ring circus." Petitioner had committed "innumerable acts . . . which clearly reflected his contempt for the court as well as the judicial system of this Commonwealth . . . ." and had been "overbearing, contemptuous, and obnoxiously persistent in his questions and objections . . . ." The Court of Appeals also concluded that petitioner had not launched any "personal attack" on the trial judge and that the judge had neither conducted himself as an " 'activist seeking combat' " nor had become so personally embroiled that he was disqualified to sit in judgment on the charges of contempt, although his remarks prior to entering judgment of contempt at the conclusion of the trial were "inappropriate."

The Court of Appeals further ruled that because the amended judgment did not "direct that the sentences, as amended, be served consecutively . . . they must be served concurrently." Thus, "[the] penalty actually imposed on Daniel Taylor [was] six months in jail," and his conviction and sentence without a jury trial were deemed constitutionally permissible. The Kentucky Court of Appeals ruled, however, that it had exclusive authority to discipline or disbar attorneys and that,

---

refused to take his seat at counsel's table as ordered.

Contempt 5. Complete and utter disrespect by Mr. Taylor in the questioning of Mr. Irvin Foley, and [*sic*] attorney and Legal Advisor to the Louisville Police Department when he continually disobeyed the court's ruling regarding a press conference which the court had ruled on unadmissible [*sic*]. Mr. Taylor accused the court of disallowing admittance of black persons in the courtroom during the examination of this witness and made a statement in the presence of the jury inferring that only white police officers could enter the courtroom. It has always been the rule of this court that there will be no interruption during the examination of a witness or during closing arguments by people coming and going into and from the courtroom, which rule was known to Mr. Taylor (T.E. 1950-1955).

Contempt 6. The witness Jesse Taylor, a Louisville Police Officer, read a statement by witness, David White. A Ruling was made by the court that the statement spoke for itself, had been introduced in evidence and could not be commented on by Officer Taylor, who merely took the statement. Mr. Taylor continued to disregard the court's order and ruling by continually reading parts of the statement out of context (T.E. 2008-2016).

Contempt 7. Mr. Taylor in examining Mr. Norbert Brown, again referred to a press conference that the court had previously ordered him not to go into. He also waved his arms at the witness in a derogatory manner indicating the witness was not truthful and showing utter contempt of the court's ruling (T.E. 2030-2032).

Contempt 8. The court directed Mr. Taylor to call his next witness. He called Lt. Garrett, Louisville Police Department. After the witness was sworn and took the stand, a deputy Sheriff advised the court that Mr. Taylor's aide was not searched, as everyone else had been upon entering the courtroom. Mr. Taylor ordered the deputy to search his aide. The court ordered Mr. Taylor to begin his examination, which he refused to do until he was cited for contempt in the court's chamber (T.E. 2068-2069).

Contempt 9. Mr. Taylor repeatedly asked the same question of witness Floyd Miller that the court had held improper. He was also disrespectful in his tone of voice when referring to a certain police officer as 'this nice police officer' (T.E. 2169-2172).

in any event, the rule in Kentucky since 1917 had been that suspension from practice was not a permissible punishment for criminal contempt. The order prohibiting petitioner from practicing in the Jefferson Circuit Court, Criminal Branch, Second Division, was therefore reversed. We granted certiorari limited to specified issues.

I

Petitioner contends that any charge of contempt of court, without exception, must be tried to a jury. Quite to the contrary, however, our cases hold that petty contempt like other petty criminal offenses may be tried without a jury and that contempt of court is a petty offense when the penalty actually imposed does not exceed six months or a longer penalty has not been expressly authorized by statute. Hence, although petitioner was ultimately found guilty and sentenced separately on eight counts of contempt, the sentences were to run concurrently and were, as the Kentucky Court of Appeals held, equivalent to a single sentence of six months. The original sentences imposed on the separate counts were to run consecutively and totaled almost four and one-half years, with two individual counts each carrying a year's sentence. But the trial court itself entered an amended judgment which was understood by the Kentucky Court of Appeals to impose no more than a six-month sentence. The eight contempts, whether considered singly or collectively, thus constituted petty offenses, and trial by jury was not required.

II

We are more persuaded by petitioner's contention that he was entitled to more of a hearing and notice than he received prior to final conviction and sentence. In each instance during the trial when respondent considered petitioner to be in contempt, petitioner was informed of that fact and, in most instances, had opportunity to respond to the charge at that time. It is quite true, as the Kentucky Court of Appeals held, that "[the] contempt citations and the sentences coming at the end of the trial were not and could not have been a surprise to Taylor, because upon each occasion and immediately following the charged act of contempt the court informed Taylor that he was at that time in contempt of court." But no sentence was imposed during the trial, and it does not appear to us that any final adjudication of contempt was entered until after the verdict was returned. It was then that the court proceeded to describe and characterize petitioner's various acts during trial as contemptuous, to find him guilty of nine acts of contempt, and to sentence him immediately for each of those acts.

It is also plain from the record that when petitioner sought to respond to what the Kentucky Court of Appeals referred to as the trial court's "declaration of a charge against Taylor based upon the judge's observations" during trial, respondent informed him that "[you're] not responding to me on anything" and even indicated that petitioner might be gagged if he insisted on defending himself. The trial court then proceeded without further formality to impose consecutive sentences totaling almost four and one-half years in the county jail and to bar petitioner forever from practicing before the court in which the case at issue had been tried.

This procedure does not square with the Due Process Clause of the Fourteenth Amendment. We are not concerned here with the trial judge's power, for the purpose of maintaining order in the courtroom, to punish summarily and without notice or hearing contemptuous conduct committed in his presence and observed by him. *Ex parte Terry*, 128 U.S. 289 (1888). The usual justification of necessity is not nearly so cogent when final adjudication and sentence are postponed until after trial. Our decisions establish that summary punishment need not always be imposed during trial if it is to be permitted at all. In proper circumstances, particularly where the offender is a lawyer representing a client on trial, it may be postponed until the conclusion of the proceedings. [We have] noted that "[summary] punishment always, and rightly, is regarded with disfavor . . . ? 343 U.S. at 8. "[We] have stated time and again that reasonable notice of a charge and an opportunity to be heard in defense before punishment is imposed are 'basic in our system of jurisprudence.' " Even where summary punishment for contempt is imposed during trial, "the contemnor has normally been given an opportunity to speak in his own behalf in the nature of a right of allocution."

On the other hand, where conviction and punishment are delayed, "it is much more difficult to argue that action without notice or hearing of any kind is necessary to preserve order and enable [the court] to proceed with its business." . . . This is not to say, however, that a full-scale trial is appropriate. Usually, the events have occurred before the judge's own eyes, and a reporter's transcript is available. But the contemnor might at least urge, for example, that the behavior at issue was not contempt but the acceptable conduct of an attorney representing his client; or, he might present matters in mitigation or otherwise attempt to make amends with the court.[24]

These procedures are essential in view of the heightened potential for abuse posed by the contempt power. . . . Due process cannot be measured in minutes and hours or dollars and cents. For the accused contemnor facing a jail sentence, his "liberty is valuable and must be seen as within the protection of the Fourteenth Amendment. Its termination calls for some orderly process, however informal."

Because these minimum requirements of due process of law were not extended to petitioner in this case, the contempt judgment must be set aside.

---

[24] [8] The American Bar Association Advisory Committee on the Judge's Function has recommended, *inter alia*:

> Notice of charges and opportunity to be heard.

> Before imposing any punishment for criminal contempt, the judge should give the offender notice of the charges and at least a summary opportunity to adduce evidence or argument relevant to guilt or punishment.

> Commentary

> Although there is authority that in-court contempts can be punished without notice of charges or an opportunity to be heard, *Ex parte Terry*, 128 U.S. 289 (1888), such a procedure has little to commend it, is inconsistent with the basic notions of fairness, and is likely to bring disrespect upon the court. Accordingly, notice and at least a brief opportunity to be heard should be afforded as a matter of course. Nothing in this standard, however, implies that a plenary trial of contempt charges is required.

American Bar Association Project on Standards for Criminal Justice, The Function of the Trial Judge § 7.4, p. 95 (Approved Draft 1972).

* * *

Nothing we have said here should be construed to condone the type of conduct described in the opinion of the Kentucky Court of Appeals and found by that court to have been engaged in by petitioner. Behavior of this nature has no place in the courtroom which, in a free society, is a forum for the courteous and reasoned pursuit of truth and justice.

The judgment of the Kentucky Court of Appeals is reversed and the case is remanded to that court for further proceedings not inconsistent with this opinion.

So ordered.

5. Disqualification Motions and Other Litigation-Driven Controls

Powerful constraints on lawyer conduct exist in the form of various litigation motions, including Federal Rule of Civil Procedure ("FRCP") 11 and its state counterparts and disqualification of counsel motions. Such motions have become much more used (some say overused) during the last 30 years. These motions, when granted, have an immediate and significant impact on the lawyer against whom they were filed.

a. Disqualification for Conflict of Interest

When a lawyer perceives that an opposing lawyer may have a conflict of interest in litigation, the lawyer may request that the court disqualify opposing counsel from further participation in the case. When such a motion is granted, counsel is no longer permitted to be employed by her client in that matter. Losing a client, at least for the particular case, and the associated fee is a weighty consequence. The standards for when a disqualification motion should be granted are substantially the same as the underlying conflict of interest standards including the shield or "Chinese Wall" defense. Because litigation consequences are at stake instead of lawyer disciplinary consequences, courts take into account interests in addition to the typical conflicts of interest concerns. The following interests, along with all of the usual conflicts of interest policies, will be considered and weighed by a court considering a disqualification motion. Granting a motion to disqualify almost always means delay in the court proceedings while new counsel becomes sufficiently familiar with the matter to proceed. Courts consider the delay and court inefficiency in determining whether to grant disqualification motions. The moving party seeks a litigation advantage by filing the motion to disqualify. A court will consider the conduct of the moving party, especially as it relates to the timing of the motion. In particular, a court will consider whether the moving party has made the motion promptly after learning of the grounds for the motion or has instead waited until close to trial when the conflicted lawyer's party would be most disadvantaged by loss of counsel. In extreme cases, the moving party may be found to have intentionally created the conflict for the opposing party's lawyers. When that occurs, courts will be reluctant to grant the motion to disqualify. Clients, who have presumably retained their counsel of choice, are disadvantaged, usually without fault, when a disqualification motion is granted. Courts will take this into account when considering the motion. Several cases excerpted in Chapter V, "Conflicts of Interest," are disqualification motion decisions.

b.   FRCP 11 and Its State Law Counterparts

Money sanctions are available against an offending lawyer under various frivolous claim prohibition rules, especially Federal Rule of Civil Procedure 11. Most states have an analogous statute or rule of procedure that governs proceedings in state court. These motions for sanctions have become very popular litigation tools, leading, many say, to added hostility between lawyers contesting such motions. The money sanctions make Rule 11 a significant lawyer control device.

Ethics code rules exist, specifically Model Rule 3.1, that are analogous to FRCP 11. In general, when a lawyer has committed an egregious violation of FRCP 11, that lawyer is also subject to discipline, although few instances of bar discipline for frivolous claim filing have occurred. (*See Lawyer Disciplinary Board v. Neely and Hunter*, excerpted in Chapter VII.) To avoid frivolous claim liability, a claim must have a basis in fact and must have a basis in law. A claim that lacks arguable merit under existing law and lacks a good faith argument for an extension or modification of existing law is frivolous and exposes the filer of the claim to sanctions. A lawyer is obligated by FRCP 11 to make a reasonable fact investigation prior to filing a claim and determine that there are reasonable factual grounds to support the allegations in the complaint.

Under the 1993 amendments to FRCP 11, a safe harbor provision exists. Before one may file a FRCP 11 motion, notice must be given to the alleged offending lawyer. Twenty-one days must pass after notice before the motion may be filed. During that 21-day period the offending lawyer may take actions to eliminate the violation. Such actions typically involve withdrawing or amending the complained-of paper or allegation. The provision of FRCP 11 that creates this warning period has been called the "safe harbor" provision. Also, under the 1993 amendments to FRCP 11, sanctions may be imposed by the court on both the lawyer who signed the frivolous court paper and the lawyer's firm.

A few other sanctions provisions that are similar to FRCP 11 exist to govern lawyer frivolous argument conduct, especially on appeal. *See, e.g.,* 28 U.S.C. § 1927.

Rule 11. Signing of Pleadings, Motions, and Other Papers; Representations to Court; Sanctions

(a) **Signature.** Every pleading, written motion, and other paper shall be signed by at least one attorney of record in the attorney's individual name, or, if the party is not represented by an attorney, shall be signed by the party. Each paper shall state the signer's address and telephone number, if any. Except when otherwise specifically provided by rule or statute, pleadings need not be verified or accompanied by affidavit. An unsigned paper shall be stricken unless omission of the signature is corrected promptly after being called to the attention of the attorney or party.

(b) Representations to Court. By presenting to the court (whether by signing, filing, submitting, or later advocating) a pleading, written motion, or other paper, an attorney or unrepresented party is certifying that to the best of the person's knowledge, information, and belief, formed after an inquiry reasonable under the circumstances—

(1) it is not being presented for any improper purpose, such as to harass or to cause unnecessary delay or needless increase in the cost of litigation;

(2) the claims, defenses, and other legal contentions therein are warranted by existing law or by a nonfrivolous argument for the extension, modification, or reversal of existing law or the establishment of new law;

(3) the allegations and other factual contentions have evidentiary support or, if specifically so identified, are likely to have evidentiary support after a reasonable opportunity for further investigation or discovery; and

(4) the denials of factual contentions are warranted on the evidence or, if specifically so identified, are reasonably based on a lack of information or belief.

(c) Sanctions. If, after notice and a reasonable opportunity to respond, the court determines that subdivision (b) has been violated, the court may, subject to the conditions stated below, impose an appropriate sanction upon the attorneys, law firms, or parties that have violated subdivision (b) or are responsible for the violation.

(1) How Initiated.

(A) By Motion. A motion for sanctions under this rule shall be made separately from other motions or requests and shall describe the specific conduct alleged to violate subdivision (b). It shall be served as provided in Rule 5, but shall not be filed with or presented to the court unless, within 21 days after service of the motion (or such other period as the court may prescribe), the challenged paper, claim, defense, contention, allegation, or denial is not withdrawn or appropriately corrected. If warranted, the court may award to the party prevailing on the motion the reasonable expenses and attorney's fees incurred in presenting or opposing the motion. Absent exceptional circumstances, a law firm shall be held jointly responsible for violations committed by its partners, associates, and employees.

(B) On Court's Initiative. On its own initiative, the court may enter an order describing the specific conduct that appears to violate subdivision (b) and directing an attorney, law firm, or party to show cause why it has not violated subdivision (b) with respect thereto.

(2) Nature of Sanction; Limitations. A sanction imposed for violation of this rule shall be limited to what is sufficient to deter repetition of such conduct or comparable conduct by others similarly situated. Subject to the limitations in subparagraphs (A) and (B), the sanction may consist of, or include, directives of a nonmonetary nature, an order to pay a penalty into court, or, if imposed on motion and warranted for effective deterrence, an order directing payment to the movant of some or all of the reasonable attorneys' fees and other expenses incurred as a direct result of the violation.

    (A)   Monetary sanctions may not be awarded against a represented party for a violation of subdivision (b)(2).

    (B)   Monetary sanctions may not be awarded on the court's initiative, unless the court issues its order to show cause before a voluntary dismissal or settlement of the claims made by or against the party which is, or whose attorneys are, to be sanctioned.

  (3) **Order.** When imposing sanctions, the court shall describe the conduct determined to constitute a violation of this rule and explain the basis for the sanction imposed.

(d) Inapplicability to Discovery. Subdivisions (a) through (c) of this rule do not apply to disclosures and discovery requests, responses, objections, and motions that are subject to the provisions of Rules 26 through 37.

28 U.S.C. § 1927. Counsel's Liability for Excessive Costs

Any attorney or other person admitted to conduct cases in any court of the United States or any Territory thereof who so multiplies the proceedings in any case unreasonably and vexatiously may be required by the court to satisfy personally the excess costs, expenses, and attorneys' fees reasonably incurred because of such conduct.

Chapter III

FORMAL ASPECTS OF THE LAWYER-CLIENT RELATIONSHIP

This chapter is about a variety of formal aspects of the lawyer-client relationship, such as when the lawyer-client relationship begins and how it ends, how the lawyer functions as a fiduciary, and how the lawyer and client arrange fees. When the lawyer-client relationship begins and how it ends have implications for lawyer duties such as confidentiality (*see* Chapter IV), the potential for liability for malpractice (*see* Chapter II), and the measure of loyalty owed. The onset of those duties will in turn dictate the conflicts of interest analysis that must be done in multiple client situations (*see* Chapter V). The lawyer is a fiduciary and special property handling duties come with that role. Contract law dictates some aspects of the lawyer-client fee relationship, but the existence of the lawyer's fiduciary role modifies contract law to create a special body of law that governs lawyer-client fee agreements. Because they are so much a part of the lawyer-client relationship, basic duties of competence, diligence, and communication and shared decision-making are treated in this chapter.

[handwritten margin note: extra fiduciary duties]

A. UNDERTAKING REPRESENTATION

Before a lawyer has formally undertaken representation, a limited set of lawyer-to-client duties exist including the confidentiality duty that is owed to prospective clients (*see* Chapter IV). Undertaking representation signifies the beginning of the formal lawyer-client relationship. When a lawyer-client relationship begins, the full range of duties from lawyer to client exists.

1. Duty to Undertake Representation

In general, lawyers have no duty to undertake a particular representation. A lawyer is not like a public utility that must accept every customer who is willing to pay the necessary fee. In general, then, a lawyer chooses which clients the lawyer will agree to represent. Unlike an individual lawyer, the population of lawyers as a group has something in common with public utilities. Lawyers have a state-granted monopoly over the provision of legal services. Lawyers in many states take an oath when they are admitted to practice that provides, in part, that the lawyer will never reject for personal reasons the causes of the defenseless and oppressed. One may infer from this oath and the existence of the monopoly on the provision of legal services, a limited duty of every lawyer to accept a fair share of representation of the defenseless and oppressed. This same oath is often cited as support for the pro bono service requirements. MR 6.1 (*see* Chapter VII). Here consider the lawyer's duty to accept court appointments to represent clients except when good cause exists to decline. MR 6.2.

BROWN v. BOARD OF COUNTY COMMISSIONERS OF WASHOE COUNTY
451 P.2d 708 (Nev. 1969)

The issue, presented to us by an original proceeding for a writ of mandate, is whether NRS 7.260 limiting compensation to $300 for a court appointed attorney in a non-capital criminal case, is unconstitutional if applied to the circumstances before the court. It is not contended that the statute is unconstitutional per se.

The petitioner, attorney Stanley Brown, seeks to compel the County Commissioners to provide funds from which the county auditor may draw his warrant in the sum of $11,624.23 payable to petitioner, and from which the County Treasurer may pay the same. Brown was appointed to represent an indigent defendant in a non-capital criminal case prosecuted by the State of Nevada. He practices alone. By reason of the complexity and length of the trial, he was forced to associate counsel in other matters; was unable to see other clients for over two months; lost several regular clients, and was compelled to return retainers in excess of $1,000. He filed several petitions for compensation with various departments of the district court, and orders were entered thereon awarding compensation in the total amount of $11,624.23. These court orders were tendered to the County Auditor and referred by him to the County Commissioners who denied the claims as being in excess of the statutory limit of $300. This proceeding ensued.

1. In the absence of a statute providing for compensation a lawyer, upon court order, is obliged to represent an indigent without recompense. Essential service without regard to financial reward is one of the great traditions of the legal profession. "I will never reject, from any consideration personal to myself, the cause of the defenseless or oppressed," reads the oath of an attorney.

Of course, a lawyer does not owe free representation to any and every indigent who chooses to demand it of him. His duty is owed to the court and it is the court's call that he is obliged to answer. It follows that the duty thus imposed is an incident of the license to practice law, and the power to deal with it reposes in the judicial branch of government which is charged with the responsibility for the terms and conditions of the right to practice. Whether that power carries with it an authority to direct compensation for professional services beyond limits legislatively imposed is the question before us.[1]

2. In 1879 this court ruled that the legislative limit for compensation could not be enlarged by court order. At that time the statute provided that court appointed counsel was entitled to receive such fee as the court may fix "not to exceed fifty

---

[1] [9] Statutes enacted to cover this situation fall generally into two groups, those allowing a "reasonable sum" as compensation to be determined by the court, and those fixing a maximum limit within which the court may exercise its discretion. And even those states which allow a reasonable compensation to be fixed by the court recognize that what may be reasonable for the representation of an indigent defendant may be far from what is considered reasonable as between counsel and a solvent client in a private transaction.

dollars." The court there noted that in the absence of statute the attorney would be obliged to honor the court appointment and to defend without compensation.

During the past decade new constitutional concepts of criminal justice and the complexity of our social problems have dramatically increased the burden upon the legal profession. The announced goal is equal justice for the rich and poor alike. The presence and assistance of counsel now is required at all critical stages of a criminal proceeding, and sometimes to press collateral post-conviction applications. The enlargement of federally protected rights demands a greater degree of specialized knowledge and proficiency on the part of assigned counsel. The cost of criminal justice is increasing. As a consequence, many jurisdictions have adopted a public defender system for the indigent accused, thereby placing the cost upon the taxpayer. The federal government has enacted the Criminal Justice Act which provides greater relief for assigned counsel than exists under state statutes similar to ours. It is apparent that the members of the bar should not be required to absorb the full costs of the defense of the indigent. A permanent solution of this problem properly rests with the legislative branch of our government since it is charged with the responsibility of appropriating public funds for public purposes, and we invite legislative action.

3. In extraordinary circumstances the Illinois Supreme Court ruled that court appointed attorneys representing indigents were entitled to receive compensation in excess of the statutory limit. The court found that its inherent power to appoint counsel "necessarily includes the power to enter an appropriate order ensuring that counsel do not suffer an intolerable sacrifice and burden and that the indigent defendants' right to counsel is protected."

The circumstances before the Illinois court were indeed extraordinary. The court appointed counsel were engaged in defending four indigent inmates who were indicted for the alleged murders of three prison guards during the course of a riot at the prison. The trial occurred in a county some distance from the homes and offices of counsel, and they were forced to maintain two residences, spend large out-of-pocket sums for investigation costs and expert witness fees, and were totally unable to carry on their private practice of law. The first nine weeks of the trial were consumed in selecting a jury. When the petition for fees and motion to withdraw as counsel was presented to the trial court, the state had examined 16 witnesses and intended to call 60 to 100 more during its case in chief. One of the attorneys was on the brink of insolvency, and the others were unable to continue payment of current trial costs. In short, court appointed counsel were faced with financial ruin if compelled to continue the trial without relief. Further, had counsel been permitted to withdraw the trial would have had to start anew. In these extreme circumstances the court came to the relief of counsel and distinguished its prior decision of *People v. Zuniga*, 202 N.E.2d 31 (Ill. 1964), which disallowed an award of fees in excess of the statutory maximum, pointing out that in the latter case there had been no showing of undue hardship, or that the indigent's right to counsel had in any way been impaired.

In the case at hand the petitioner's situation does not meet the "extraordinary circumstances" test of the *Randolph* case. His showing below implies no more than a reduction in income, but by no means can be classified as indicating financial ruin.

For this reason we decline to apply the rationale of the *Randolph* decision to the circumstances of this case.

The obligation of counsel to assume the burden of defending indigents necessarily involves personal sacrifice. It is to be presumed that courts charged with the appointment of counsel will never so burden one, or a few, members of the bar to the exclusion of others. We commend the petitioner for his services in this case. His willingness to assist the court is in the highest tradition of our profession, and brings honor to him, and to the bar as well. Our commendation may be an inadequate exchange for his personal sacrifice. Nonetheless, it is sincerely offered, and we repeat our invitation for legislative correction. This burden should be passed to the taxpayers, and the members of the bar, as taxpayers, will, of course, share in it.

Petition denied.

BATJER, J., concurring:

I concur with the other members of the court in this opinion. The legislature of this state has long ago determined that lawyers appointed to represent indigents should be compensated for their services. The inequity that presently exists in the statutory compensation should be alleviated by the legislature.

I agree with the holding in the case of *People v. Randolph*, 219 N.E.2d 337 (Ill. 1966), but I would go further and hold that courts have the inherent power to enter an appropriate order ensuring that counsel do not suffer an intolerable sacrifice and burden. No particular segment of our population should be required to bear an unreasonable financial burden that belongs to society as a whole.

In the event the legislature fails to provide a system of reasonable compensation for lawyers appointed to defend indigents, this court should invoke its inherent power.

MALLARD v. UNITED STATES DISTRICT COURT FOR THE SOUTHERN DISTRICT OF IOWA
490 U.S. 296 (1989)

JUSTICE BRENNAN delivered the opinion of the Court.

We are called upon to decide whether 28 U.S.C. § 1915(d) authorizes a federal court to require an unwilling attorney to represent an indigent litigant in a civil case. We hold that it does not.

I

Section 1915(d) provides: "The court may request an attorney to represent any [person claiming in forma pauperis status] unable to employ counsel and may dismiss the case if the allegation of poverty is untrue, or if satisfied that the action is frivolous or malicious." In *Nelson v. Redfield Lithograph Printing*, 728 F.2d 1003,

1005 (1984), the Court of Appeals for the Eighth Circuit ordered "the chief judge of each district to seek the cooperation of the bar associations and the federal practice committees of the judge's district to obtain a sufficient list of attorneys practicing throughout the district so as to supply the court with competent attorneys who will serve in pro bono situations," such as in forma pauperis proceedings conducted under 28 U.S.C. § 1915. The District Court for the Southern District of Iowa heeded the Court of Appeals' command. Under the system in force since February 1986, once the District Court has determined that an indigent party qualifies for representation under § 1915(d), the Clerk of the Court forwards a copy of the court file to the Volunteer Lawyers Project (VLP), a joint venture of the Legal Services Corporation of Iowa and the Iowa State Bar Association. The VLP keeps a copy of a roster prepared by the District Court of all attorneys admitted to practice before the court and in good standing. After deleting the names of lawyers who have volunteered for VLP referrals of pro bono state-court cases, the VLP selects lawyers from the list non-alphabetically for § 1915(d) assignments.[2] Lawyers who are chosen under the plan may apply to the District Court for reimbursement of out-of-pocket costs. They may also keep any fee award provided by statute, but are not guaranteed even minimal compensation for their own services. The VLP assists lawyers assigned to litigate in areas of the law with which they are unfamiliar by providing written materials, holding periodic seminars, and facilitating consultations with experienced attorneys.

Petitioner Mallard was admitted to practice before the District Court in January 1987, and entered his first appearance the following month. In June 1987 he was asked by the VLP to represent two current inmates and one former inmate who sued prison officials under 42 U.S.C. § 1983, alleging that prison guards and administrators had filed false disciplinary reports against them, mistreated them physically, and endangered their lives by exposing them as informants. After reviewing the case file, Mallard filed a motion to withdraw with the District Court. In his motion, petitioner stated that he had no familiarity with the legal issues presented in the case, that he lacked experience in deposing and cross-examining witnesses, and that he would willingly volunteer his services in an area in which he possessed some expertise, such as bankruptcy and securities law. The VLP opposed petitioner's motion, claiming that he was competent, that he had an ethical duty to do whatever was necessary to try the case, and that permitting an exception to the rule of assignment would create a dangerous precedent. A Magistrate denied petitioner's motion.

Mallard then appealed to the District Court. Although he reiterated his unfamiliarity with § 1983 actions, he contended that he should be permitted to withdraw not because of his inexperience in interpreting the statute and its case law, but because he was not a litigator by training or temperament. Forcing him to represent indigent inmates in a complex action requiring depositions and discovery, cross-examination of witnesses, and other trial skills, Mallard asserted,

---

    [2] [1] In February 1986, the Iowa State Bar Association sent a letter to all lawyers licensed to practice before the United States District Courts for the Northern and Southern Districts of Iowa describing the referral system. According to the letter, 130 appointments were made between June 1984 and June 1985. The combined lists for both Districts embraced roughly 3,500 lawyers. Each lawyer was eligible to be chosen every third year, making her odds of being selected roughly 1 in 9 in those years.

would compel him to violate his ethical obligation to take on only those cases he could handle competently and would exceed the court's authority under § 1915(d).

Unmoved, the District Court upheld the Magistrate's decision. Based on the quality of petitioner's brief in support of his motion to withdraw, the court pronounced him competent, notwithstanding his very slight acquaintance with trial litigation. The court also held that § 1915(d) empowers federal courts to make compulsory appointments in civil actions. In November 1987, Mallard sought a writ of mandamus from the Court of Appeals for the Eighth Circuit to compel the District Court to allow his withdrawal. The Court of Appeals denied the petition without opinion. We granted certiorari to resolve a conflict among the Courts of Appeals over whether § 1915(d) authorizes compulsory assignments of attorneys in civil cases. We now reverse.

II

Interpretation of a statute must begin with the statute's language. Section 1915(d)'s operative term is "request": "The court may request an attorney to represent" an indigent litigant. The import of the term seems plain. [The Court proceeds to analyze the plain meaning of the statute's key word, "request," distinguishing it from the language used in most similar state statutes, either "assign" or "appoint." —Ed.]

IV

We emphasize that our decision today is limited to interpreting § 1915(d). We do not mean to question, let alone denigrate, lawyers' ethical obligation to assist those who are too poor to afford counsel, or to suggest that requests made pursuant to § 1915(d) may be lightly declined because they give rise to no ethical claim. On the contrary, in a time when the need for legal services among the poor is growing and public funding for such services has not kept pace, lawyers' ethical obligation to volunteer their time and skills pro bono publico is manifest. Nor do we express an opinion on the question whether the federal courts possess inherent authority to require lawyers to serve. Although respondents and their amici urge us to affirm the Court of Appeals' judgment on the ground that the federal courts do have such authority, the District Court did not invoke its inherent power in its opinion below, and the Court of Appeals did not offer this ground for denying Mallard's application for a writ of mandamus. We therefore leave that issue for another day. We hold only that § 1915(d) does not authorize the federal courts to make coercive appointments of counsel. Accordingly, the judgment of the Court of Appeals is reversed, and the case is remanded for further proceedings consistent with this opinion.

So ordered.

JUSTICE STEVENS, with whom JUSTICE MARSHALL, JUSTICE BLACKMUN, and JUSTICE O'CONNOR join, dissenting.

The relationship between a court and the members of its bar is not defined by statute alone. The duties of the practitioner are an amalgam of tradition, respect for the profession, the inherent power of the judiciary, and the commands that are set forth in canons of ethics, rules of court, and legislative enactments. This case involves much more than the parsing of the plain meaning of the word "request" as used in 28 U.S.C. § 1915(d). This case also does not concern the sufficiency of the lawyer's reasons for declining an appointment[3] or the sanctions that may be imposed on an attorney who refuses to serve without compensation. There are, of course, many situations in which a lawyer may properly decline such representation. He or she may have a conflict of interest, may be engaged in another trial, may already have accepted more than a fair share of the uncompensated burdens that fall upon the profession, or may not have the qualifications for a particular assignment. As this case comes to us, however, the question is whether a lawyer may seek relief by way of mandamus from the court's request simply because he would rather do something else with his time. For me, the answer is quite plain.

The lawyer's duty to provide professional assistance to the poor is part of the ancient traditions of the bar long recognized by this Court and the courts of the several States. As Justice Field, then sitting on the California Supreme Court, declared more than a century ago:

> [I]t is part of the general duty of counsel to render their professional services to persons accused of crime, who are destitute of means, upon the appointment of the Court, when not inconsistent with their obligations to others; and for compensation, they must trust to the possible future ability of the parties. Counsel are not considered at liberty to reject, under circumstances of this character, the cause of the defenseless, because no provision for their compensation is made by law.

Rowe v. Yuba County, 17 Cal. 61, 63 (1860).

Or, as Justice Sutherland declared for the Court more recently: "Attorneys are officers of the court, and are bound to render service when required by such an appointment." *Powell v. Alabama*, 287 U.S. 45, 73 (1932).

* * *

Section 1915(d) embodies this authority to order counsel to represent indigent litigants even if it does not exhaust it. The statute was passed to give federal courts the same authority to allow in forma pauperis actions that the courts in the most progressive States exercised. In 1892, state courts had statutory authority to order lawyers to render assistance to indigent civil litigants in a dozen States, and common law power to appoint counsel in at least another 10 States. Congress intended to "open the United States courts" to impoverished litigants and "to keep

---

[3] [1] The petitioner tried to persuade the Magistrate that he had valid reasons for not wanting to represent convicted felons in litigation against their prison guards, but those reasons were found insufficient by the District Court, and this Court does not question the accuracy of that finding.

pace" with the laws of these "[m] any humane and enlightened States." H.R. Rep. No. 1079, 52d Cong., 1st Sess. 1-2 (1892). Congress also intended to ensure that the rights of litigants suing diverse parties in the most liberal of these States would not be defeated by the defendant's removal of the suit to federal court. To be faithful to the congressional design of ensuring the poor litigant equal justice whether the suit is prosecuted in federal or state court, the statute should be construed to require counsel to serve, absent good reason, when requested to do so by the court.

The program adopted by the District Court for the Southern District of Iowa to provide representation for indigent litigants was in operation when petitioner became a member of that court's bar. In my opinion his admission to practice implicitly included an obligation to participate in that program.[4] When a court has established a fair and detailed procedure for the assignment of counsel to indigent litigants, a formal request to a lawyer by the court pursuant to that procedure is tantamount to a command.

In context, I would therefore construe the word "request" in § 1915(d) as meaning "respectfully command." If that is not what Congress intended, the statute is virtually meaningless. There is no substance to the Court's speculation that Congress enacted this provision because of a concern that a court's requests to represent a poor litigant might otherwise be "disregarded in the mistaken belief that they are improper." There is no anecdotal or historical evidence to support this highly improbable speculation. In my opinion Congress gave its endorsement to these judicial "requests," assuming that it would be "unthinkable" for a lawyer to decline without an adequate reason.

Justice Blackmar of the Missouri Supreme Court expressed precisely my sentiments in dissent from a decision denying the courts of that State the power to compel attorneys to represent indigents in civil cases:

> I have often served in court appointments, and I am sure that my brethren have also. When a judge said, "help me out," I really felt that I had no choice. Perhaps I had in mind the old army maxim that the commanding officer's desire is the subaltern's command. Perhaps I thought that the court could use its coercive power. I found, however, that judges were sensitive when good reasons for declining appointments were advanced, and were willing to explore alternatives. By issuing our absolute writ, we strip the respondent [the trial judge] of her bargaining power.

State ex rel. Scott v. Roper, 688 S.W.2d 757, 773 (1985).

I respectfully dissent.

---

4 [7] "[R]epresentation of indigents under court order, without a fee, is a condition under which lawyers are licensed to practice as officers of the court, and . . . the obligation of the legal profession to serve without compensation has been modified only by statute. An applicant for admission to practice law may justly be deemed to be aware of the traditions of the profession which he is joining, and to know that one of these traditions is that a lawyer is an officer of the court obligated to represent indigents for little or no compensation upon court order." *United States v. Dillon,* 346 F. 2d 633, 635 (9th Cir. 1965), *cert. denied,* 382 U.S. 978 (1966).

NOTES, QUESTIONS, AND EXAMPLES

Although usually regarded as an exclusively legislative function, a New York State trial judge ordered an increase in the hourly rate for New York lawyers appointed to represent indigents in criminal and family court matters. In so ruling, the judge said, "This court finds serious and imminent danger of ineffective assistance of counsel to indigent litigants in New York City family and criminal courts resulting from inadequate compensation rates paid to assigned counsel." *New York County Lawyers' Association v. New York*, 192 Misc. 2d 424, 745 N.Y.S.2d 376 (Sup. Ct. 2002). The judge-ordered rates increased to $90 per hour from $40 and $25 for in and out of court time respectively.

Virginia has the lowest statutorily imposed compensation caps for court-appointed lawyers in the nation, thus strongly discouraging counsel from spending more than a few hours on circuit court cases and even less on district court cases. The actual figures are shocking — a court-appointed attorney cannot receive more than a total of $112 for a misdemeanor or juvenile delinquency charge punishable by confinement, $1,096 for a felony charge punishable by more than 20 years of confinement, and $395 for all other non-capital felony charges. Public defenders, who handled approximately 37% of the criminal indigent defendant caseload in 2002, carry caseloads that far exceed national standards. Public defender offices operate without fundamental tools of legal practice, such as internet access, paralegals or updated computers, and few litigation resources are provided to the offices. Both private, court-appointed lawyers and public defenders struggle with "hide the ball" discovery rules and practices. Experts, which can be necessary to wage an adequate defense in cases involving medical, forensic, and scientific evidence, are rarely available in Virginia's indigent defendant cases. Assigned counsel rarely employ the use of investigators, for whom payment must be authorized by the court. They perform their own investigation or none at all. http://www.americanbar.org/content/dam/aba/migrated/legalservices/downloads/sclaid/indigentdefense/va_report2004.authcheckdam.pdf at 1–2.

INTERNATIONAL NOTES

1. The European standards for beginning client-attorney relationships, like most other areas of legal ethics, are more diverse than the unitary standards of a country such as the United States, even though as a matter of state law, each U.S. state has its own standards for beginning the lawyer-client relationship. The CCBE Code does not make mention to the specifics of such a relationship. It simply requires that lawyers obey the standards of the court before which they appear. However, individual countries have taken different approaches on the matter. For example, Italy and the Czech Republic have a system of court appointments by which a lawyer is forbidden from refusing to provide assistance when the court orders them to do so. For the most part, lawyer-client relationships are governed by the countries' applicable contract law, as the majority of these relationships are contractual in nature.

2. In England, the "cab-rank" rule generally obligates a barrister to accept any case offered, regardless of the barrister's personal views of the case or the client.

The Code of Conduct provides:

> A barrister who supplies advocacy services must not withhold services: (a) on the ground that the nature of the case is objectionable to him or to any section of the public; (b) on the ground that the conduct opinions or beliefs of the prospective client are unacceptable to him or to any section of the public; (c) on any ground relating to the source of any financial support which may properly be given to the prospective client for the proceedings in question.

Bar Council of England and Wales, Code of Conduct, Rule 601. The cab-rank rule has several exceptions, some of which mirror reasons permitting a U.S. lawyer to decline a court appointment under MR 6.2. For example, a barrister does not have to accept a case for an insufficient fee, nor a case that she is not competent to handle, nor a case that conflicts with the barrister's existing schedule. *See* BAR COUNCIL OF ENGLAND AND WALES, CODE OF CONDUCT, Rule 604; GEORGE HARRIS & JAMES MOLITERNO, GLOBAL ISSUES IN LEGAL ETHICS 29, 46 (2007).

2. Duty to Reject Representation

Unlike the general rule that a lawyer has no duty to accept every client's matter, lawyers are prohibited from accepting (that is, lawyers must reject) representation in several different situations. MR 1.16(a). When accepting representation will violate an ethics rule, the lawyer has a duty to reject the representation.

3. Lawyer-Client Contracts and the Beginning of the Lawyer-Client Relationship

The lawyer-client relationship is governed in the first instance by the particular contract entered into by the lawyer and client and by general contract principles. Irrespective of contract obligations, that lawyer-client contract is modified by the various duties that lawyers owe clients. These duties, such as the duty to safeguard client property, and the duties of confidentiality and loyalty, are imposed by the ethics rules or by general fiduciary duty law and general agency law without regard to what the particular lawyer-client contract might say.

The lawyer-client relationship formally begins when a client reasonably believes that the lawyer has undertaken to provide the client with legal service. The relationship does not depend for its onset on the existence of a written contract nor a fee payment. (Remember *Togstad*, Chapter II.)

B. FEES

Although the disciplinary system regulation of lawyer's fees is relatively light and rarely enforced, it does exist. Fees are regulated for their amount and their nature. More significant than bar discipline regulation of fees are direct court supervision of fees and, in insurance defense practice, the influence of the insurer.

1. The Reasonableness Standard

A lawyer's fee must be reasonable. MR 1.5. Under the Model Code, the fee regulation required that a lawyer's fee not be "clearly excessive." DR 2-106(A). Under the 1908 ABA Canons, which preceded the Model Code, a fee was only subject to discipline if it was "so exorbitant and wholly disproportionate to the services performed as to shock the conscience of those to whose attention it was called." *Goldstone v. State Bar*, 6 P.2d 513, 516 (Cal. 1931).

The reasonableness standard applies to all forms of lawyer fee, including contingent fees.

Fees Rule 1.5 ABA Model Rules of Professional Conduct[5]

(a) A lawyer shall not make an agreement for, charge, or collect an unreasonable fee or an unreasonable amount for expenses. The factors to be considered in determining the reasonableness of a fee include the following:

(1) the time and labor required, the novelty and difficulty of the questions involved, and the skill requisite to perform the legal service properly;

(2) the likelihood, if apparent to the client, that the acceptance of the particular employment will preclude other employment by the lawyer;

(3) the fee customarily charged in the locality for similar legal services;

(4) the amount involved and the results obtained;

(5) the time limitations imposed by the client or by the circumstances;

(6) the nature and length of the professional relationship with the client;

(7) the experience, reputation, and ability of the lawyer or lawyers performing the services; and

(8) whether the fee is fixed or contingent.

(b) The scope of the representation and the basis or rate of the fee and expenses for which the client will be responsible shall be communicated to the client, preferably in writing, before or within a reasonable time after commencing the representation, except when the lawyer will charge a regularly represented client on the same basis or rate. Any changes in the basis or rate of the fee or expenses shall also be communicated to the client.

(c) A fee may be contingent on the outcome of the matter for which the service is rendered, except in a matter in which a contingent fee is prohibited by paragraph (d) or other law. A contingent fee agreement shall be in a writing signed by the client and shall state the method by which the fee is to be determined, including the percentage or percentages that shall accrue to the lawyer in the event of settlement, trial or appeal; litigation and other expenses to be deducted from the

---

[5] ABA Model Rules of Professional Conduct, 2011 Edition. Copyright © 2011 by the American Bar Association. Reprinted with permission. Copies of ABA Model Rules of Professional Conduct, 2008 Edition are available from Service Center, American Bar Association, 321 North Clark Street, Chicago, IL 60654, 1-800-285-2221.

recovery; and whether such expenses are to be deducted before or after the contingent fee is calculated. The agreement must clearly notify the client of any expenses for which the client will be liable whether or not the client is the prevailing party. Upon conclusion of a contingent fee matter, the lawyer shall provide the client with a written statement stating the outcome of the matter and, if there is a recovery, showing the remittance to the client and the method of its determination.

(d) A lawyer shall not enter into an arrangement for, charge, or collect:

(1)   any fee in a domestic relations matter, the payment or amount of which is contingent upon the securing of a divorce or upon the amount of alimony or support, or property settlement in lieu thereof; or

(2)   a contingent fee for representing a defendant in a criminal case.

(e) A division of a fee between lawyers who are not in the same firm may be made only if:

(1)   the division is in proportion to the services performed by each lawyer or each lawyer assumes joint responsibility for the representation;

(2)   the client agrees to the arrangement, including the share each lawyer will receive, and the agreement is confirmed in writing; and

(3)   the total fee is reasonable.

IN RE KUTNER
399 N.E.2d 963 (Ill. 1979)

On July 7, 1976, the Administrator of the Attorney Registration and Disciplinary Commission filed a complaint charging the respondent, Luis Kutner, with unprofessional conduct. The complaint alleged that respondent was guilty of . . . charging an excessive fee in violation of Disciplinary Rule 2-106 of the Illinois Code of Professional Responsibility (1970) (DR 2-106).

Following prolonged hearings, the Hearing Board on June 27, 1978, filed its report and recommendation, concluding that respondent violated DR 2-106 by charging an excessive fee. . . . The Hearing Board unanimously recommended that the Review Board impose a private reprimand. On December 20, 1978, the Review Board issued its report and recommendation, in which it was determined that the appropriate measure of discipline for violation of DR 2-106 should be censure of respondent by this court. This disciplinary action comes before us on respondent's exceptions to the report and recommendation of the Review Board.

On August 14, 1973, the complainant, Warren P. Fisher, was arrested in Glencoe and charged with battery by his sister-in-law, Ruth Fisher. . . . Sometime later, the police arrived and arrested him for battery.

Upon his mother's recommendation, Fisher called respondent and they arranged a meeting to discuss the case. On August 28, 1973, respondent met with him and told him that he would represent him in the defense of the criminal battery charge for $5,000. An additional fee for representation of Fisher in a possible civil suit was also mentioned. . . . Fisher paid the respondent $250 as an initial consultation fee, but indicated that he could not afford to pay the balance of the $5,000 fee. Respondent testified that he then considered the Fisher file closed. However, a few days later, after managing to borrow the additional money, Fisher contacted respondent and advised him that he would send a check for the balance due, $4,750.

Subsequently, Fisher and respondent met to discuss the details of the case. At this second meeting, respondent asked Fisher to provide him with a written summary detailing the facts of the encounter with his sister-in-law. Respondent also discussed further the possibility of a civil suit against the Glencoe police. On September 4, 1973, one day prior to Fisher's court date, respondent called Fisher and advised him that he would not be able to meet Fisher in court and that he was sending attorney Gorman in his place. Fisher was instructed by respondent not to tell Gorman how much respondent was paid to take the case. On the 5th, Fisher met Gorman in the courtroom. When the attorney approached the bench to request a continuance, the complainant, Ruth Fisher, stepped up and asked the judge to drop the charges. The case was then dismissed.

Afterwards, Fisher consulted two attorneys, each of whom advised him that the fee which he had paid respondent was excessive. On October 25, 1973, Fisher wrote a letter to respondent requesting the refund of $4,000, the amount by which Fisher considered he was overcharged. Respondent, however, refused to return any portion of the fee paid by Fisher, who then contacted the Chicago Bar Association. The matter was referred to the Committee on Professional Fees, which initiated steps toward settlement. While Fisher agreed to submit the dispute to binding arbitration, respondent refused. Respondent did, following remand by the Review Board, offer to settle the matter by refunding $1,000.

In his appearances before the Hearing Board, respondent testified at length as to his accomplishments in the legal profession, particularly in international matters and civil rights. He has been practicing law for nearly 49 years, and much of his practice throughout those years has been devoted to pro bono publico work. The Hearing Board found that respondent has received many citations praising his work in those fields and that he is the author of a number of law review and other articles. However, notwithstanding respondent's achievements in the field of civil rights and international law, there is no evidence that respondent had any extensive experience with, or particular expertise in, the defense of routine criminal cases such as the one involving Fisher, particularly in recent years.

Respondent's argument, as we interpret it, is that attorney-client fixed-fee agreements, when freely entered into, are not subject to scrutiny by a disciplinary committee and may not form the basis for disciplinary action against an attorney. Rather, respondent contends that any dispute over a fixed fee must be resolved based on traditional contract principles in a court of law.

The administrator presented the expert testimony of Sherman Magidson, an attorney licensed in 1959 and an experienced practitioner in the field of criminal law. He testified, in response to a hypothetical question which set forth all of the relevant facts, that the fee customarily charged for representation of a client in Fisher's position, assuming it would be necessary to go to trial to defend the battery charge, would be between $750 and $1,250. He testified further that in the event of dismissal of the criminal charge prior to trial, as in the Fisher case, the customary practice is to return a portion of the fixed fee to the client. Magidson further testified that Fisher's case did not appear to be a novel one, that there were no complex legal issues involved, that it did not present unusual time or labor requirements, and that the acceptance of this case would not preclude other employment by the attorney.

The Hearing Board concluded that respondent spent between 5 and 6 hours on Fisher's case, while respondent estimated his total time commitment at approximately 10 hours. Respondent stressed, however, that he did not want this disciplinary action resolved by computing a reasonable fee on an hourly basis. Rather, respondent seeks to rely on, as he refers to it, the "law of fixed fees." However, even a cursory reading of DR 2-106 leads one to the inescapable conclusion that the time required to perform a legal task is a factor to consider in attempting to determine whether a fee is excessive. Even conceding that respondent spent 10 hours on the case, respondent was paid at a rate of $500 per hour.

Considering the time and labor expended, the fee customarily charged, and all of the other elements of DR 2-106, we find a $5,000 fee for representation of Fisher in a routine battery case which never went to trial not only excessive, but unconscionable. We cannot accept respondent's description of the Fisher case as an extraordinary one for which "an involved, unique preparation would be necessary." Rather, we concur in the Hearing Board's characterization of it as a "simple battery case." Furthermore, respondent's arguments that DR 2-106 is unconstitutionally vague or that the disciplinary proceedings herein were tainted by prosecutorial misconduct do not merit discussion.

Accordingly, we agree with the conclusion of the Hearing Board and the Review Board that respondent's conduct in this matter violated DR 2-106 and warrants discipline. Taking into consideration the fact that respondent has practiced law for nearly 50 years during which he has engaged in many pro bono publico activities, together with the absence of any other disciplinary complaints, we believe that censure by this court is the appropriate sanction to impose.

Respondent censured.

JUSTICE CLARK, dissenting:

I must dissent because I think the majority is venturing into troubled waters when it begins to assess the value of a lawyer's services for the purpose of imposing disciplinary sanctions. It is quite within the sphere of proper judicial activity to set legal fees as part of punitive damages, or to approve a fee as reasonable in dissolution-of-marriage or probate cases. It is quite another matter, however, when we hold that an attorney has charged an excessive fee and publicly censure him for so doing.

The majority fails to realize that its opinion says that a lawyer can voluntarily enter into an agreement with a client, based on the mutual agreement of the parties as to the worth of the attorney's services, only to be second-guessed later on.

*   *   *

I would suggest that it is not our function to delve into what is a reasonable fee in a given case precisely because no case is "standard." The negotiation of a fee should be left to the parties. A person may be willing to pay more for the services of a particular attorney at a particular time, when, however, under different circumstances, the attorney's services would not be as valuable. In this connection the question may be asked whether the fee in this case would be excessive if the attorney involved were a nationally famous criminal lawyer? Or, would the fee be considered excessive if a corporate client retained an attorney because of his reputation as an aggressive advocate, and the case was settled shortly thereafter? I doubt it.

Accordingly, because of the reservations I have expressed about the dangers of assessing the value of legal services in order to impose disciplinary sanctions, I must dissent from the majority opinion.

PFEIFER v. SENTRY INSITRANCE
745 F. Supp. 1434 (E.D. Wis. 1990)

THOMAS J. CURRAN, UNITED STATES DISTRICT JUDGE.

Deborah Pfeifer commenced the above-captioned case against the City of Brookfield (Wisconsin), former Brookfield police officer Stephen McNeill, and their insurers seeking compensatory and punitive damages for depriving her of rights guaranteed by the Fourth and Fourteenth Amendments to the United States Constitution.

In her complaint, as amended, Pfeifer claims that she was driving through Brookfield on August 10, 1986, when then-officer Stephen McNeill approached her in his police car, stopped her car, then forced her to perform a sex act. She demanded $450,000.00 in compensatory damages and $350,000.00 in punitive damages from McNeill. Pfeifer's second cause of action was brought against the City of Brookfield.

*   *   *

All the named defendants answered and denied liability. The insurers asserted crossclaims for contribution or indemnification. Then, prior to the scheduled trial, the defendants settled with the plaintiff for $20,000.00.

Now, the only claim remaining in this case is defendant Western World Insurance Company's crossclaim against defendant Sentry Insurance. Western World has moved for summary judgment, asking the court to declare that Sentry had a duty to defend and indemnify the City of Brookfield in this action. In addition, Western World has asked the court to declare that the bill for attorney fees submitted to it by the law firm of von Briesen & Purtell, S.C., is unreasonable and the company has asked the court to determine reasonable fees. The parties agreed to argue these issues in briefs.

* * *

[The court denied the first prong of Western World's motion for summary judgment and entered a declaratory judgment of noncoverage in favor of Sentry. —Ed.]

* * *

III. ATTORNEY FEES

As the second prong of its summary judgment motion, Western World asks this court to declare that the bill for $60,012.72 in attorney fees it received from the law firm of von Briesen & Purtell, S.C., which represented the City of Brookfield in this matter, is unreasonable. Western World also wants the court to determine reasonable fees.

A. Facts

Documents in the record show that, before this federal lawsuit was commenced, the City of Brookfield retained the law firm of von Briesen & Purtell, S.C. The firm represented the City in the administrative disciplinary proceedings against officer Stephen McNeill which were instituted following the incident involving Deborah Pfeifer. These proceedings concluded with McNeill resigning on September 8, 1987.

On May 26, 1988, the City notified the law firm that Deborah Pfeifer had filed a notice of claim against the City. Even though no lawsuit had been filed, von Briesen & Purtell sent two letters to Western World, Brookfield's law enforcement liability insurer, asking that it be allowed to handle the defense of the City. The firm told Western World facts of the case from handling the administrative proceedings and that its experience in civil rights law would enable it to provide economical representation.

On August 9, 1988, Deborah Pfeifer filed a summons and complaint in federal court. She also filed notices of depositions and discovery demands which were returnable within forty days. On August 12, 1988, by telephone, Western World authorized von Briesen & Purtell to respond to the complaint. The firm then filed an answer on behalf of the City of Brookfield, and, at the request of the City's police chief, began to prepare the City's witnesses for the depositions.

On October 13, 1988, Western World wrote a letter to the City reserving its rights under the policy and authorizing von Briesen & Purtell to continue to act as defense counsel for the City. In another letter sent directly to von Briesen & Purtell on October 18, 1988, Western World requested that the firm defend the City of Brookfield. In the same letter Western World included a list of the following eight guidelines for defense counsel:

GUIDELINE 1:

Preliminary workup should be restricted to a review of the Summons and Complaint, Appearance, investigative material, Answer, Demands for Answers to Interrogatories, requests for admission, requests for production of documents and filing of Cross-Complaints, if applicable. No further workup is to be done without express authorization from the Company.

GUIDELINE 2:

Attorneys should not engage in investigation or lengthy and repeated interviews with witnesses or insureds if those procedures can be properly performed by independent adjusters or investigators. If extenuating circumstances cause a deviation from this instruction, authorization must be obtained from the Company.

GUIDELINE 3:

Legal research requirements should be promptly reported to the Company. You are requested to provide a summary of the reasons necessitating research requiring more than two hours, and not undertake same without authorization from the Company.

GUIDELINE 4:

Six-month interim billing is encouraged; however, other arrangements will be entertained. In no case will billing be considered on less than a quarterly basis. Time sheets and details of the services performed are required.

GUIDELINE 5:

If depositions are authorized, we request a "brief" narrative report covering the highlights of the testimony as they refer to the liability and damages. If the testimony simply confirms our prior knowledge of the claim, it is not necessary to highlight that testimony. In no case do we require copies of depositions unless specifically requested.

GUIDELINE 6:

The Company must be promptly advised of court appearances, settlement conferences, pre-trial depositions, and trial. It is required that counsel report twice daily when on trial. If reporting should have to take place after Company local hours, arrangements may be made to report to the handling examiner at home.

GUIDELINE 7:

The Company requests that attorney reports be concise and brief.

GUIDELINE 8:

Reports are to be forwarded directly to the examiner in charge of the file, addressing your correspondence to their individual attention. Single copies of your reports are all that is needed.

In conclusion, Western World stated that:

This letter sets forth guidelines only. It is not expected that it will be possible to follow these guidelines to the letter in every lawsuit that we refer to you. If, as you proceed with the defense, the exercise of your professional responsibility to your client, our insured, you believe a deviation from these guidelines is necessary, please advise us immediately and we will provide you with the necessary authorization.

On behalf of von Briesen & Purtell, Attorney James Reiher wrote to Western World to object to some of the guidelines. In his November 9, 1988 letter, Reiher took issue with the two-hour limit on legal research and with the semi-annual billing policy. Reiher asked that his firm be allowed to send monthly statements. He explained that: "In this way, if a client has a question about the services or the fees, the issue can be raised, discussed, and resolved contemporaneously with the events as they occur and any disputes can be finalized while the case is immediate and in progress." Reiher also asked that the firm's bills be paid quarterly. In the same letter Reiher informed Western World that three von Briesen & Purtell attorneys would be working on the case.

In a reply dated December 6, 1988, Western World stated that it preferred that the case be handled by one attorney and insisted that only one attorney be in attendance at discovery and court proceedings. Western World agreed to the monthly billing and quarterly payments, but asked the law firm to adhere to Guidelines 2, 3, 5, 6, 7 and 8. Despite these negotiations, no bills were ever sent to Western World until November of 1989.

Meanwhile, the City of Brookfield moved to dismiss the complaint on the ground that the plaintiff had only identified herself as "D.P." in the caption of the complaint. The motion was accompanied by a six-page brief. After the plaintiff responded, the motion was denied.

The second, and final, motion filed by the City of Brookfield was a motion to compel the plaintiff to answer questions regarding her sexual history. This motion was also denied.

By June of 1989, the parties had negotiated a $20,000.00 settlement with the plaintiff. The City of Brookfield contributed $4,000.00. The following November, von Briesen & Purtell sent Western World the disputed bill for $55,925.20 in legal fees and $4,087.52 in costs. Western World also received bills from its own counsel (Riordan, Crivello, Carlson, Mentkowski and Steeves, S.C.) and from counsel for defendant McNeill (Schellinger & Doyle, S.C.). Together, these two bills totaled less than $20,000.

B. Legal Standards

Courts have the inherent power to determine the reasonableness of attorney fees and to refuse to enforce any contract that calls for clearly excessive or unreasonable fees. In determining the reasonable value of attorney's fees for services rendered, the proper factors to be considered are: (1) the character and importance of the litigation; (2) the amount of money or value of the interest affected; (3) the professional skill and experience called for and the standing of the attorney in the profession; and (4) the amount and character of the services rendered, the labor, time and trouble involved. When the amount of a fee is challenged, the burden of proof is upon the attorney to prove the reasonableness of the fee. A party who opposes requested fees has a responsibility to state objections with particularity and clarity.

Burden on Attorney to prove Reasonable

C. Discussion

Western World does not take issue with the City's showing in support of the first three factors to be considered in setting a reasonable fee. Therefore, in the absence of any challenge, the court will merely summarize the City's showing as a basis for resolving the parties' dispute over the number of hours billed by von Briesen & Purtell.

1. Character and Importance of Case

In emphasizing the character and importance of this litigation, the City of Brookfield says that "it was the claim against the police department's custom, policies, and practice which was the most complex, required the most timeconsuming work, and faced the most significant consequences from an adverse verdict and judgment." The City makes much of the Brookfield police chief's concern about the "attack" on his department embodied in the lawsuit. The police chief alleges that he asked von Briesen & Purtell to represent the City in this matter, to prepare himself and his officers for their depositions, and to conduct an aggressive and exhaustive defense. The City does not say what authority, if any, the police chief had to direct the tactics and time expenditure of legal counsel engaged to represent the City.

2. Value Affected

The amount of money or value affected by von Briesen & Purtell's handling of this lawsuit was considerable, if measured by the pleadings. The plaintiff demanded $450,000.00 from the City in her Amended Complaint. This claim, plus her claim against Stephen McNeill for another $450,000.00 in compensatory damages and for $350,000.00 in punitive damages, was settled for a total of $20,000.00. One may presume that this result was favorable to the defendants.

3. Attorney Skill and Experience

To establish the skill, experience, and professional standing of the von Briesen & Purtell firm, the City has submitted the affidavits of Gregg Gunta, James Reiher and John Lindquist, three of the six attorneys who worked on the case. These three have outlined their background, experience in civil rights litigation, and work done in connection with this case. The law firm emphasizes that: "The City requested that von Briesen & Purtell defend this civil rights action specifically because of its professional skill and experience in the area and its past relationship with its police department."

4. Amount and Character of Services

The factor over which the parties cannot agree is the amount and character of the services rendered, including the labor, time and trouble involved. To support the number of hours billed (approximately 589 hours) the City has submitted the law firm's itemized bill. Western World has no quarrel with the $95.00 per hour rate charged by von Briesen & Purtell, but the insurance company calls the number of hours billed "excessive." Western World has prepared the following summary of charges billed and charged allowed, which shows ten categories of amounts in dispute:

SUMMARY OF CHARGES BILLED/ALLOWED

		Amount Billed	Amount Allowed
Legal Research:	72.05 Hours at $95.00 per Hour	$6,844.75	$1,900.00
Conferences Among Lawyers at von Briesen & Purtell:	41.10 Hours at $95.00 per Hour	$3,904.50	$475.00
Pleadings: Drafting Answer	6.45 Hours at $95.00 per Hour	$612.75	$237.50 Hour
Unsuccessful Motion to Dismiss:	35.30 Hours at $95.00 per Hour	$3,353.50	$570.00
Conferences With the Insured:	18.30 Hours at $95.00 per Hour	$1,738.50	$-0-
Review of Police Department Documents:	57.10 Hours at $95.00 per Hour	$5,424.50	$950.00
Deposition Summaries:	46.90 Hours at $95.00 per Hour	$4,455.50	$-0-
Preparation for Depositions:	45.90 Hours at $95.00 per Hour	$4,360.50	$950.00
Redundant Time:	127.70 Hours at $95.00 per Hour	$12,131.50	$-0-
Unauthorized Lexis & Westlaw Charges:		$2,117.44	$-0-
Unauthorized Report of Devise and Tweedale, Inc.:		$300.00	$-0-
Total Billing	$60,012.72		
Total of Billings in Issue	-45,243.44		
Allowed Amounts in Issue	+5,082.50		
Total Billings Allowed	$19,851.78		

Von Briesen & Purtell, S.C., has refused to accept Western World's offer of $19,851.78 or to suggest a compromise figure.

It appears that this unfortunate dispute has devolved upon the court because von Briesen & Purtell never sent Western World the monthly statements the law firm had insisted upon and Western World never insisted upon receiving the semi-annual statements required by their Guideline No. 4. Instead, approximately four months after a settlement was reached, von Briesen & Purtell sent Western World its first and only bill. This bill's descriptions of time expended show that von Briesen & Purtell wholly ignored many of the Western World guidelines. At the same time, there is nothing in the record after the letter of December 6, 1987, to show that Western World questioned von Briesen & Purtell's ongoing representation, even though it should have been aware of the activities through its own counsel who was also participating in the litigation.

In support of the magnitude of the bill, the City explains that the number of hours worked by von Briesen & Purtell attorneys far exceeded those worked by the other two law firms because von Briesen & Purtell did the majority of work on the five depositions which were taken and on the two motions which were filed. In addition, the City maintains that the claim against Brookfield was the more complex of the plaintiff's two causes of action. But even if these assertions are true, the City has not met the burden of justifying the number of hours billed by its counsel.

Tracking the summary compiled by Western World, the first area of contention is the $6,844.75 billed for 72.05 hours of legal research. Western World has offered to pay $1,900.00 for twenty hours of research. Obviously, von Briesen & Purtell violated Western World's Guideline No. 3 by not obtaining prior permission before undertaking over two hours of research. The City explains that "much of [the research] was associated with the briefing of two motions . . . ." The remainder of the research time was allegedly spent looking up law in preparation for a contemplated, but never filed, motion for summary judgment.

Research actually used in the form of case citations can only be a rough guide to the productivity of time spent, but in this case the City cited a total of only twenty cases in its motion to dismiss, its motion to compel and its reply brief combined. This works out to a charge of approximately $342.44 per citation. Neither of the two motions touched on the merits of the case. And while the court recognizes that some research into the merits is necessary to answer the complaint and to prepare a general defense strategy, the City has not met its burden of justifying 72.05 hours, especially in the absence of a showing that von Briesen & Purtell sought prior permission from Western World to undertake extensive research and in view of its repeated boasts that its counsel were highly experienced in civil rights litigation. The court will allow thirty hours of research at $95.00 per hour for a total of $2,850.00.

Second, Western World objects to the $3,904.50 charge for 41.1 hours of intraoffice conferences among the City's lawyers. Western World has offered to pay $475.00 for five hours of conferences. It points out that early in the case it asked that this litigation be handled by only one lawyer. Because von Briesen & Purtell violated Western World's directive and has otherwise failed to justify this high number of intra-office conference hours, the court will allow only eighteen hours at a rate of $95.00 per hour or $1,710.00 to be billed for conferences. This represents conference time of approximately one half hour per week from the filing of the complaint to the settlement.

Third, Western World challenges the time spent responding to the complaint. Von Briesen & Purtell charged $612.75 for 6.45 hours spent drafting the City's thirty-three paragraph answer. Western World wants to reduce the fee to $237.50 for 2.5 hours of work on this task because it believes that experienced counsel should not require more time to draft an answer. The court's concern is not so much the amount of time, but the quality of the answer. *See, e.g.*, Answer at para. 27 (raising the affirmative defense of good faith immunity on behalf of the City — a legally unsupportable defense under federal civil rights law). Nevertheless, Western World's stringent Guidelines put no restrictions on drafting pleadings authorized by the company, so the court will only reduce the time billed to 6.15 hours by subtracting .3 hours for the time billed for filing the answer at the courthouse. This is a function that need not be performed by a lawyer. Consequently, the court will approve a fee of $580.25 for drafting the answer.

Western World also objects to von Briesen & Purtell's spending 35.30 hours drafting the City's unsuccessful motion to dismiss. Instead of the $3,353.50 charged, Western World has offered to pay $570.00 for six hours of work. On this point, the court agrees with Western World. The City moved to dismiss the complaint on the sole ground that the plaintiff had failed to identify herself by name. Instead, she used the initials "D.P." Exposing the plaintiff's name could have been accomplished by a simple motion to amend the caption. For these reasons, lavishing almost six hours per page on this motion was clearly unreasonable. Therefore, the court will approve only six hours of time for a charge of $570.00.

Fourth, Western World wants to eliminate 18.3 hours of charges for conferences between von Briesen & Purtell attorneys and City of Brookfield personnel. These are hours which are unrelated to the preparation of discovery responses. In its brief in support of the fee, the City has made no attempt to justify these conferences, so the court will disallow the entire $1,738.50 billed for the 18.3 hours attributed to conferences.

The fifth category of contention is von Briesen & Purtell's review of police department documents. Before being retained by Western World to represent the City of Brookfield, von Briesen & Purtell represented that its attorneys were already well versed in the facts of this case. Western World now professes to be outraged that the attorneys spent an additional 57.10 hours reviewing City of Brookfield documents relevant to this litigation. The fee requested for this task is $5,424.50, but Western World only wants to pay for ten hours of document review at a fee of $950.00.

[T]he court will reduce the amount charged for von Briesen & Purtell's review of City of Brookfield Police Department documents to $3,524.50.

Sixth, Western World asks the court to reject all 46.90 of the hours billed by von Briesen & Purtell for summarizing the transcripts of the five depositions which were taken during the course of this litigation. Western World contends that these summaries would have been unnecessary had one lawyer been handling the case. Moreover, trial was not scheduled until March 19, 1990, so preparation of the summaries for use as a trial tool was premature and, therefore, unnecessary.

> The City, on the other hand, says that the depositions were summarized: as they were taken in order to better prepare for the next depositions to come, as well as to prepare for possible future motions to be filed in the action, including summary judgment. Deposition summaries are not only utilized at trial. These deposition summaries were utilized during the course of this litigation to protect the insured in the discovery stage and to be used in support of any potential defenses as they arose.

Von Briesen & Purtell violated Western World's stringent guidelines by not obtaining prior authorization for depositions and by failing to advise the Company of the pretrial depositions as required by guidelines 5 and 6.

On the other hand, once taken, the firm was required under guideline 5 to prepare "a brief narrative report." The 46.9 hours charged for preparing summaries of five depositions seems to be excessive. More hours were charged for preparing the summaries than was spent taking the depositions according to time sheets. The court feels that three hours summarizing each deposition would be sufficient for a total of 15 hours. The charge for this service is thus reduced to $1,425.00.

The insurance company's seventh objection is to the 45.9 hours of time spent preparing for the five depositions. Western World has offered to pay $950.00 for ten hours of preparation. However, again, von Briesen & Purtell violated the Western World guidelines. The billable hours for the five depositions was approximately 37 hours. An average of four hours preparation for each deposition would normally be considered high, but because of the limited evidence in this regard the court will allow 20 hours and reduce the amount charged to $1,900.00.

As its eighth category of contested time entries, Western World has labeled 127.70 hours as "redundant time." In rejecting the full $12,131.50 charged, the insurer explained to von Briesen & Purtell that:

> This redundant time is the result of having so many different lawyers work on the case. . . . For example, on September 29, 1988 and September 30, 1988, two different attorneys listened to the same audio tape. There was a review of the personnel file four times in four days between September 8, 1988 and September 12, 1988. On June 19, 1989 and June 20, 1989, you had three separate attorneys working on settlement. We noted that you have had three different lawyers meeting with the Brookfield Chief of Police; two separate attorneys meeting with police officers; two attorneys reviewing interrogatory answers; and two attorneys reviewing the plaintiff's prior police records. These are examples of unnecessary work.

However, Western World did not issue its directive that one attorney handle the case until December 6, 1988, so the court will not adjust the fee to deduct "redundant" charges prior to December 6, 1988. Before receiving the Western World directive, von Briesen & Purtell notified Western World that three of its lawyers would be working on the case, and although Western World did not absolutely forbid this arrangement, tacitly allowing more than one lawyer to participate in the litigation is not tantamount to inviting duplication of efforts. For this reason, the court finds that 78.95 hours of the time spent by von Briesen &

Purtell lawyers after December 6, 1988, which Western World has labeled as "redundant," represent unreasonable charges and will be deducted from the law firm's bill.

[T]he City of Brookfield has also wholly failed to put forth any evidence or argument to justify the ninth and tenth items to which Western World objects — the "Unauthorized Lexis and Westlaw Charges" and "Unauthorized Report of Devise and Tweedale, Inc." Consequently, the $2,117.44 cost of the computer-assisted research and the $300.00 cost of the report will be declared unreasonable.

In summary, the court has determined that the reasonable fees for the following categories of work are:

Legal Research 30 hours at $95.00 per hour	$2,850.00
Conferences Among Lawyers at von Briesen & Purtell 18 hours at $95.00 per hour	1,710.00
Pleadings	
Drafting Answer 6.45 hours at $95.00 per hour	580.25
Unsuccessful Motion to Dismiss 6 hours at $95.00 per hour	570.00
Conferences With the Insureds	- 0 -
Review of Police Department Documents 37.10 hours at $95.00 per hour	3,524.50
Deposition Summaries 15.00 hours at $95.00 per hour	1,425.00
Preparation for Depositions 20.00 hours at $95.00 per hour	1,900.00
Redundant Time 48.75 hours at $95.00 per hour	4,631.25
Unauthorized Lexis & Westlaw Charges	- 0 -
Unauthorized Report of Devise and Tweedale, Inc.	- 0 -

Consequently, a reasonable fee to be paid by Western World Insurance Company to von Briesen & Purtell, S.C. for its representation of the City of Brookfield in this litigation is calculated as follows:

Total Billing	$60,012.72
Total of Billings in Issue	− 45,243.44
Allowed Amounts in Issue	+ 17,191.00
Total Reasonable Billings	31,960.28

ORDER

For the reasons explained above, the court ORDERS that defendant Western World Insurance Company's Motion for Summary Judgment (filed April 12, 1990) IS DENIED IN PART AND GRANTED IN PART. The court orders that judgment shall be entered declaring that:

The bill for attorney fees submitted by the law firm of von Briesen & Purtell for its defense of the City of Brookfield in Civil Action No. 88-C-833 brought in the

United States District Court for the Eastern District of Wisconsin is unreasonable in part. A reasonable fee for services rendered is $31,960.28.

IT IS FURTHER DECLARED AND ADJUDGED

that the bill for attorney fees submitted by the law firm of von Briesen & Purtell for its defense of the City of Brookfield in Civil Action No. 88-C-833 brought in the United States District Court for the Eastern District of Wisconsin is unreasonable in part. A reasonable fee for services rendered is $31,960.28.

WONG v. MICHAEL KENNEDY, P.C.
853 F. Supp. 73 (E.D.N.Y. 1994)

MEMORANDUM AND ORDER

GLASSER, UNITED STATES DISTRICT JUDGE:

Plaintiff Kin Cheung Wong ("plaintiff" or "Mr. Wong") moves the court Pursuant to Fed. R. Civ. P. 56, seeking an order (1) granting him partial summary judgment in the amount of $75,000, and (2) directing defendants Michael Kennedy, P.C. and Michael Kennedy ("defendants") to provide a complete accounting of certain funds he deposited in escrow with them. For the reasons described below, the motion for partial summary judgment is granted to the extent that the court declares unenforceable the retainer agreement executed by the parties, and defendants are ordered to provide a more detailed accounting for a portion of the funds deposited in escrow.

FACTS

Plaintiff commenced this action by filing a Complaint on December 7, 1993; jurisdiction is based on diversity of citizenship pursuant to 28 U.S.C. § 1332. The underlying facts are as follows. In July 1990, plaintiff retained defendants to represent him in connection with a criminal proceeding captioned United States v. Wong, 89-CR-679. Plaintiff and defendants entered into a written retainer agreement (the "Retainer Agreement"), which provided that plaintiff would pay defendants a legal fee in the amount of $225,000 "as and for all legal services rendered and to be rendered in connection with" the litigation, "up to and including ten (10) weeks of trial." More specifically, the Retainer Agreement required that $75,000 of the fee be paid "immediately upon signing of this agreement," and that $150,000 be paid two weeks prior to the date of trial. In the event that the trial lasted more than ten weeks, the Retainer Agreement provided that Mr. Wong would pay "a weekly trial fee" of $12,500 per week up to and including fifteen weeks of trial, and a weekly trial fee of $10,000 should the trial last more than fifteen weeks. In addition, the Retainer Agreement, which bore the caption and docket number of the criminal proceeding, contained the following provision:

> It is further agreed and understood that KIN CHEUNG WONG is retaining the legal services of the law office of MICHAEL KENNEDY, P.C.

for legal representation in the United States District Court for the Eastern District of New York under the above captioned present or superseding indictment.

Finally, the Retainer Agreement stated as follows:

> In the event that the legal services of the law office of MICHAEL KENNEDY, P.C. are terminated by KIN CHEUNG WONG prior to trial, any fee actually paid on or prior to the date of such termination shall be deemed earned and no part thereof shall be refundable. If however, such legal services are terminated because of an unforeseen event, then KIN CHEUNG WONG agrees to be billed at the rate of TWO HUNDRED FIFTY DOLLARS (U.S.) ($250.00) per hour for services actually rendered.

Defendants, who are appearing pro se in this matter, allege that the Retainer Agreement was entered into after extensive negotiations among defendants and three attorneys named Ronald Garnett, Lawrence Schoenbach and Dixon Tang (an attorney in Hong Kong), beginning in late May 1990. Mr. Kennedy describes the negotiations more specifically as follows:

> I spent many hours during this time giving the Hong Kong lawyer information about myself and negotiating a retainer agreement. I was told that the case would definitely be tried and that no deal was possible. I was also told that the trial could last up to ten weeks. Mr. Wong wanted my assurance that I would personally try the case and not some associate. He also wanted my assurance that I had time to devote to pre-trial work: many meetings with clients at prison would be necessary, obtaining discovery, preparing motions, particularly, suppression, reviewing discovery with client, and possibly going to Hong Kong for investigation.

Accordingly, defendants allege that the $75,000 to be paid upon the execution of the Retainer Agreement was understood by all parties — including Mr. Wong — to be a "general retainer" that was deemed "earned when paid."[6] Moreover, defendants allege, the $250 per hour figure provided in the Retainer Agreement was understood by all parties to be applicable only if Mr. Kennedy became unavailable due to an unforeseen event; the figure "was by no means intended as rate for the performance of legal services. On the contrary, the $250.00 rate was a reduction of [Mr. Kennedy's] prevailing hourly rate intended to compensate the client for [his] unavailability."

The Retainer Agreement ultimately was executed in July. It is undisputed that defendants received $75,000 upon the execution of the Retainer Agreement. Defendants allege that they thereafter appeared on behalf of plaintiff at his

---

[6] [1] Mr. Kennedy explains the fee structure as follows:

> I would never have agreed to represent Mr. Wong through a possible 10 week trial with extensive pre-trial work without a guaranteed general retainer, such as was executed here. Mine has always been a small 2-3 person firm. We must select our cases and make our commitments carefully. I committed several months of my time to Mr. Wong's defense. I passed up many other lucrative potential cases in order to be able to fulfill my commitment to Mr. Wong. I held up my end of the bargain.

arraignment on July 31, 1990, at which time a motion schedule was set for the month of September. Defendants allege that they did extensive work during the month of August reviewing discovery and extradition materials, meeting with Mr. Wong and generally preparing for trial; plaintiff alleges that Mr. Kennedy met with Mr. Wong on only two occasions, and disputes that defendants expended time reviewing discovery materials because "this Court's records . . . show that Mr. Kennedy never filed any application for discovery."

In late September 1990, approximately two months after being retained, defendants were discharged by plaintiff. Curiously, plaintiff does not explain his reasons for discharging defendants; he simply alleges that he retained Thomas Nooter, Esq. to represent him in the criminal proceeding. Mr. Kennedy alleges that upon being notified by Mr. Nooter that he had been discharged as counsel for Mr. Wong, he visited with Mr. Wong at Otisville. He alleges that Mr. Wong was "very apologetic," but told him that "Mr. Nooter and others had promised him . . . that they would be able to make a deal that would guarantee Mr. Wong little or no time in jail"; as Mr. Kennedy describes the conversation, "Mr. Wong said because they promised a good result and [Mr. Kennedy] could not promise, he had to go with them[.]"[7] Defendants further allege that Mr. Wong told Mr. Kennedy that he was "grateful for all [he] had done, that he expected no money back from [his] retainer and would not ask for any money back."

In May 1991, Mr. Nooter wrote to defendants to request an accounting; Mr. Nooter represented that "although [Mr. Wong] feels he paid a huge sum for what turned out to be a very brief period of representation, [he is] not making any request for a return of fees at this time."

On September 23, 1993, plaintiff's counsel in the present matter requested from defendants an itemized bill for services actually rendered on behalf of plaintiff based on the "agreed hourly rate" of $250, and a refund of any unearned portion of the legal fee received by defendants. In response, defendants wrote "your letter of September 23 contains so many factual and legal inaccuracies that I am obliged to reject your representation that you have been 'retained' by Mr. Wong. I require written authorization from Mr. Wong before I will consider talking to you about this matter." Defendants allege that they never received such authorization.

In addition, plaintiff alleges that defendants have failed to comply with discovery requests for documents concerning services rendered and time spent by defendants on behalf of plaintiff. Defendants submit that because so much time has passed, they are unable to reconstruct with precision the amount of time expended on Mr. Wong's behalf: Mr. Kennedy did not keep detailed time sheets while he actually was doing the work, but, according to Mr. Kennedy, "had Mr. Wong told [him] at the time of discharge that he wanted a refund, or an accounting, [he] would have been able to better recall from memory all [his] hours and the tasks performed."

By this action, plaintiff seeks "return of all sums paid to defendants less any

---

[7] [3] Mr. Kennedy avers that he told plaintiff that the promise made to him by Mr. Nooter was false and unethical, and that he forebore bringing ethics charges against Mr. Nooter and the other attorneys only because Mr. Wong pleaded with him not to do so. He maintains that "at Mr. Wong's insistence, [he] consented to the substitution of Counsel and [he] eventually turned [his] files over to Mr. Nooter."

amounts actually earned by defendantson the grounds that the Retainer Agreement is void and unenforceable as against public policy, and the Retainer Agreement and defendants' failure to refund the fees violate various Rules of the Code of Professional Responsibility and constitute a breach of defendants' fiduciary duty. Plaintiff now seeks partial summary judgment awarding him $75,000.

DISCUSSION

It is axiomatic that "courts have 'traditional authority . . . to supervise the charging of fees for legal services under the courts' inherent and statutory power to regulate the practice of law.' " In this case, plaintiff argues that he is entitled to summary judgment because retainer agreements like the one utilized by defendants here are prohibited under New York law. Defendants, in turn, claim that there is a genuine dispute as to whether the $75,000 received from plaintiff was a "permissible general retainer or a prohibited special nonrefundable retainer." Defendants nonetheless ask the court to award summary judgment in their favor.

I.

Plaintiff relies primarily on the recent decision of the New York Court of Appeals in *Matter of Cooperman*, 1994 WL 84413 (N.Y.) (Mar. 17, 1994), as support for his argument. That case involved a disciplinary proceeding brought against an attorney who repeatedly used special nonrefundable retainer fee agreements with his clients. The Court of Appeals affirmed the order of the Appellate Division suspending the attorney from practice for two years, finding that "special nonrefundable retainer fee agreements clash with public policy and transgress provisions of the Code of Professional Responsibility (*see* DR 2-110[A] [3]; DR 2-110[B] [4]; DR 2-106[A]), essentially because these fee agreements compromise the client's absolute right to terminate the unique fiduciary attorney-client relationship." The court remarked that this absolute right arises from the distinct nature of the attorney-client relationship, which implicates " 'the greatest trust between [people].' " *Id.* (quoting F. Bacon, *Of Counsel, in* THE ESSAYS OF FRANCIS BACON 181 (1846)). . . . Moreover, the court held, the fact that a particular nonrefundable fee may be reasonable "cannot rescue an agreement that impedes the client's absolute right to walk away from the attorney."

In addition, the court noted that its holding was not intended to invalidate the "other types of appropriate and ethical fee agreements"; "minimum fee arrangements and general retainers that provide for fees, not laden with the nonrefundability impediment irrespective of any services, will continue to be valid and not subject in and of themselves to professional discipline."

The dispute in this case turns on whether the $75,000 paid to defendants upon the execution of the Retainer Agreement was a special nonrefundable retainer fee agreement like that invalidated by the Court of Appeals in *Cooperman*, or a general retainer agreement, of the kind expressly left intact by that decision. A description of the different types of retainer agreements follows.

A special retainer is an agreement between attorney and client pursuant to which the client contracts to pay a specified fee in exchange for specified services; the fee may be calculated on an hourly, percentage or other basis, and may be payable in advance or as billed. A nonrefundable retainer is a specific type of special retainer which allows an attorney to keep an advance payment regardless of whether the specified services are rendered. It is this type of agreement that the Court of Appeals found invalid in *Cooperman*.

By contrast, a general retainer is an agreement pursuant to which the client agrees to pay the attorney a fixed sum "in exchange for the attorney's promise to be available to perform, at an agreed price, any legal services . . . that arise during a specified period. Because the general retainer fee is given in exchange for availability, it is a charge separate from fees incurred for services actually rendered. In other words, such fees are 'earned when paid' because the payment is made for availability." *Id.* at 6. *See also* RESTATEMENT OF THE LAW GOVERNING LAWYERS § 46 cmt. e, at 213 (Tent. Draft No. 4, 1991) ("A retainer . . . is a fee paid to ensure that a lawyer will be available for the client if required."); BLACK'S LAW DICTIONARY 1183 (5th ed. 1979) ("['Retainer'] can mean a fee not only for the rendition of professional services when requested, but also for the attorney taking the case, making himself available to handle it, and refusing employment by plaintiff's adversary . . . .").

II.

[N]otwithstanding the averments contained in the Kennedy Affidavit, it is plain from the face of the Retainer Agreement that it is a special nonrefundable retainer agreement. The Retainer Agreement provided that plaintiff was to pay defendants $225,000 for specified services, including all legal services rendered in connection with the captioned litigation, up to and including ten weeks of trial. This fee expressly did not include payment for services rendered beyond ten weeks of trial, or services rendered in connection with an appeal, retrial, or other proceeding. And this fee was made nonrefundable under any circumstances by the provision of the Retainer Agreement stating that "any fee actually paid on or prior to the date of . . . termination shall be deemed earned and no part thereof shall be refundable." Merely reciting the language "shall be deemed earned" does not convert the Retainer Agreement into a general retainer, as defendants would have it; to the contrary, there is nothing in the Retainer Agreement to indicate that the payment was made in exchange for Mr. Kennedy's availability. Moreover, defendants' attempt to characterize the $75,000 as a general retainer and the $150,000 portion of the fee as a special retainer is undermined by the plain meaning of the document; the only apparent distinction between the two sums was that the $75,000 was to be paid upon execution of the contract, while the $150,000 was to be paid two weeks prior to the date of trial. Presumably, had Mr. Wong terminated defendants' services one week before trial and after paying the $150,000, that sum also would have been deemed earned and nonrefundable.

Even though the court concludes that the Retainer Agreement is void as a matter of law, it is not prepared to order defendants to return the $75,000 paid to them by plaintiff. Rather, under the law as set forth in *Cooperman*, counsel is not precluded from recovering payment in quantum meruit for the reasonable value of services actually rendered. In determining the value of counsel's services in quantum meruit, the following factors will be relevant: (1) the difficulty of the questions involved; (2)

the skill required to handle the problem; (3) the time and labor expended; (4) counsel's experience, ability and reputation; (5) the customary fee charged for similar services; and (6) the amount involved.

Accordingly, counsel are hereby directed to contact the court to schedule a hearing to determine the fees, if any, to which defendants are entitled.

* * *

Conclusion

In sum, the court grants plaintiff's motion for summary judgment to the extent that it declares the Retainer Agreement unenforceable. However, the court declines to enter judgment in favor of plaintiff in the amount of $75,000, but rather orders a hearing to determine the reasonable value of any services defendants actually rendered on behalf of plaintiff.

NOTES, QUESTIONS, AND EXAMPLES

1.   In a number of states, New York among them, effective March 2002, all lawyer fee agreements over a specified minimum amount must be in writing. Among its recommendations, the Ethics 2000 Commission proposed that the ABA amend Model Rule 1.5 to require all fee agreements in excess of $500 be in writing. This recommendation was defeated by a narrow margin (129- 108) in the ABA House of Delegates.

2.   New York, like several other states, now requires fee disputes to be submitted to arbitration. 22 NYCRR part 137 (eff. Jan. 1, 2002).

3.   In most instances, regardless of who wins litigation, each side pays his own lawyer. There are fee-shifting statutes, mainly regarding certain civil rights matters, that authorize the court to order a defendant to pay the lawyer fee for a "prevailing" plaintiff. The client, and not the lawyer, owns this fee award until it is paid to the lawyer. The result is that when a fee award is made, the government may attach a portion of it to pay a pre-existing debt owed to the government, such as a tax debt. *Astrue v. Ratliff*, 130 S. Ct. 2521 (2010).

INTERNATIONAL NOTE

In the U.S., except for a few fee-shifting, civil rights statutes, each side pays its own lawyer, regardless of who wins the litigation. The "loser pays rule" is referred to as the "English Rule," but application of the rule in the United Kingdom it is not automatic but a matter within the court's discretion. David A. Root, *Attorney Fee-Shifting in America: Comparing, Contrasting, and Combining the "American Rule" and the "English Rule,"* 15 Ind. Int'l & Comp. L. Rev. 583, 600 (2005). In three categories of cases fees are not ordinarily awarded to the winning party: (1) small claims disputes when the claim does not exceed a certain sum; (2) tribunals in which each party must pay its own costs; and (3) suits where the losing party is funded by legal aid. *Id.* at 591.

2. Contingent Fees

With a few exceptions and restrictions, a lawyer is permitted to charge a fee that is contingent on the outcome of the matter. For example, a lawyer may charge a fee that is equal to 40% of the recovery on the client's claim that results from a trial verdict. The amount of the fee is contingent on the amount of the recovery. Contingent fee arrangements have traditionally been thought of as a way for a client with a meritorious claim but little money with which to pay an hourly or up-front fee to get the claim handled by a lawyer.

The organized bar has a history of suspicion and disapproval of contingent fees. Contingent fees are thought to stir up litigation that would otherwise not be pursued. Of course, if that litigation is meritorious, the fact that contingent fee arrangements make it possible for it to be pursued ought to be regarded as a positive rather than negative effect. When in the late 19th and early 20th century the bar expressed its deep suspicion of contingent fees, it must be remembered that the organized bar was made up nearly exclusively of corporate practitioners whose clients were being named defendants in lawsuits brought by injured workers and consumers. The injured plaintiffs were represented on a contingent fee basis by solo practitioners. Without the contingent fee, these plaintiffs would not have had counsel.

Generally, cases that produce a res, a pool of recovery money from which the contingent fee may be paid, are appropriate for contingent fees. There are two exceptions. A lawyer is prohibited from charging a contingent fee in a domestic relations case when the fee is to be contingent on obtaining a divorce or on the amount of property, child support, or alimony recovered. MR 1.5(d)(1). The intrusion of a lawyer whose fee depends on such matters into sensitive domestic relations matters is thought to be too risky to the sensitive and important relationships between spouses and between parent and child. Also, a lawyer is prohibited from charging a contingent fee to a defendant in a criminal matter in part because no res is produced from which the fee may come and in part because of the special public interest involved in criminal matters. MR 1.5(d)(2).

Because of the heightened dangers of client misunderstanding and of lawyer overreaching, additional restrictions apply to contingent fee arrangements. MR 1.5(c).

Although ordinarily a fee agreement need not be in writing, a contingent fee agreement must be in writing. The written agreement must explain the way in which the fee will be calculated and, in particular, the way in which deductions for expenses will be calculated. MR 1.5(c). The lawyer must provide an ending statement in writing to the client explaining the outcome of the matter and providing the calculation of the fee and expenses. MR 1.5(c).

Reginald Heber Smith, *Justice and the Poor*
Carnegie Foundation for the Advancement of Teaching
Bull. No. Thirteen 85–86 (1919)

The defect in the traditional method of administering justice, of making as an absolute condition precedent to all litigation the retaining of attorneys at prices which parties could not afford to pay, reached its most acute form in this field [of injuries to workers]. Several factors combined to create a thoroughly bad situation. It was about 1880 that the great industrial expansion began, when all the accent of business was on production, on "speeding-up" output, and not on safety. Employment in many industries became more hazardous than military service even in time of war. Thousands of injured workmen, to secure the redress vouchsafed by law, faced long and difficult litigation calling for the expenditure of much money for expenses and lawyer's fees. This same commercial expansion left its mark on the practice of law. Many of the largest and best offices gave up general practice and engaged exclusively in business and corporation law. The charity work which had always been a part of the older type of office was discarded under the pressure of the new era. . . .

As justice was organized and as law practice was conducted, there was no one to help an injured workman. There was a void in the system. To fill the gap came the contingent fee. The system of charging fees depending on the success of the litigation was the necessary result of the conditions which were allowed to exist. Without doubt it was better than nothing. The man whose leg or arm had been cut off would prefer to accept half of the amount awarded him by a jury than to receive nothing through inability to get his day in court. Many honorable lawyers took cases on the contingent basis, conducted their cases honestly, and charged as small a percentage of the recovery as they could.

Nevertheless, the system as a whole has been, and is, the greatest blot on the history of the American Bar. There is little doubt that if a modern contingent fee agreement had been offered to any judge a hundred years ago, it would unhesitatingly have been declared illegal and void. The bar did not sanction it without a struggle, and the courts resorted to fictions before they upheld it. Stripped of verbiage, and in actual practice, the system is one whereby the lawyer gambles on the outcome of litigation. If he loses his investment in one case, he must recoup out of his winnings in the next. It is obviously inconsistent with any theory that the lawyer is a minister of justice; he is an interested Party to the litigation because he is betting on its outcome. However much it might be glossed over, when the acid test was applied this truth was judicially admitted. Contingent fees have been justified on the ground that only by them could the poor obtain justice, but when a poor injured workman applied for permission to sue in forma pauperis, the court refused the petition, saying, "the suit is carried on partially for the benefit of the counsel."

The contingent fee system brought about a thousand abuses of its own. It attracted undesirable persons to become members of the profession. Because the stakes were high and the players essentially gamblers it induced the unholy triumvirate of lawyer-runner-doctor conspiring together to win fraudulent cases. It has degraded expert testimony and served as a cloak for robbery through extortionate fees. Unquestionably it has done more than anything else to bring the bar into deserved disrepute.

Contingent Fees
31 LAW NOTES 144 (1927)

In New York and perhaps some other states, agitation against the practice of taking personal injury cases on contingent fees has recently been revived. It is a practice capable of abuses, and one from which some abuses have grown. But the problem of avoiding those abuses, without opening the door to worse ones is not a simple one. It is a matter of the first importance that a man injured by actionable negligence should, however poor, have the assistance of able and experienced counsel to prosecute his claim. It is of equal importance that he should have that assistance as speedily as possible after he is injured, or the skillful claim agents maintained by large corporations and indemnity insurance companies will get a release from him for an inadequate sum. With this class of defendants there is little of conscience or humanity in the making of settlements, little thought of the future of a crippled man. A thousand cases dealing with the exploits of claim agents and company doctors prove this. On the other hand it is important that individuals and corporations to whom the causing of an accidental injury is a rare and lamentable thing, and who maintain no claim departments to meet guile with guile, should be protected from blackmailing claims urged by shyster lawyers with unscrupulous clients, and if they inflict an actionable injury should have a chance to make an honest settlement without having the amount increased by a fee for needless legal charges. The various phases of the evil have grown so large that it is worth some public expense to cure it. Would it not be feasible to create a body like the Workmen's Compensation Commission, and require all settlements for personal injury to be made, informally and without counsel, before this body? Its functions should of course, be advisory only, but to give some force to its recommendations, the fact that the plaintiff or defendant, as the case may be, has refused to accept a settlement recommended by the Commission, together with the nature of the recommended settlement, should be provable at the trial. In case a suit proves unavoidable the contingent fee contract of the plaintiff's attorney should be required to be filed with and approved by the Commission before suit. Such a system would, it is thought, prevent many settlements unfair to the injured person, produce many just settlements, and discourage many unfair claims. Moreover, in case of a settlement before the Commission it would be possible to give to the settlement the force of a judgment and make it payable in installments, thus avoiding the ruin which an automobile accident or similar disaster may bring to a man of small means. It is generally recognized that Workmen's Compensation Laws have cured practically all the evils which inhered in personal injury litigation between employer and employee, and it would seem that cases arising between third persons could be handled under a similar system at least to the extent of affording a forum in which voluntary adjustment might be attempted.

3.   Fee Splitting

Lawyers in the same firm routinely share fees with one another. That process is a central part of what it means to be a partner in a firm. However, when lawyers who are not members of a firm share fees, or when lawyers seek to share fees with non-lawyers, special problems arise. Fee splitting among lawyers not in the same firm has been a controversial topic in professional responsibility law. In particular, the "forwarding fee" has been thought to be offensive to lawyer ethics. A forwarding fee is a fee charged by a lawyer who does no more than send a prospective client on to another lawyer who actually provides the legal service. The forwarding fee practice raises the specter of lawyers marketing to attract large numbers of clients that they have no intention of serving, but for whom they merely act as a broker. By contrast, the lawyer who interviews a prospective client, realizes that the lawyer lacks the proper expertise for the client's problem, and sends the client to a lawyer who has that expertise has done the client and the profession a service of some consequence.

Some lawyers do act as knowledgeable brokers, advertising to generate significant numbers of clients (typically with personal injury or products liability claims for which a contingent fee would be appropriate), then referring those clients to firms that handle the matters. The referring lawyer receives a percentage of any fee that is generated. Often, the lawyers to whom the clients are referred prefer to refrain from advertising. *See* Michael Freedman, *New Techniques in Ambulance Chasing*, FORBES (Nov. 12, 2001).

MORAN v. HARRIS
131 Cal. App. 3d 913 (1982)

In *Altschul v. Sayble* (1978) 83 Cal. App. 3d 153, fee splitting contracts between lawyers were held to be unearned forwarding fee arrangements and unenforceable as being contrary to public policy. This appeal presents the same question under somewhat different circumstances. At the time *Altschul* was decided, Rules of Professional Conduct, rule 2-108 prohibited fee splitting between attorneys except to the extent that each attorney performed services and/or assumed responsibility for the case. Effective January 1, 1979, the California Supreme Court approved an amendment to the rule which effectively sanctioned forwarding fee arrangements under certain circumstances.[8] We believe this amendment indicates not only that

---

[8] [2] Rule 2-108(A) currently reads:

A member of the State Bar shall not divide a fee for legal services with another person licensed to practice law who is not a partner or associate in the member's law firm or law office, unless:

(1) The client consents in writing to employment of the other person licensed to practice law after a full disclosure has been made in writing that a division of fees will be made and the terms of such division; and

(2) The total fee charged by all persons licensed to practice law is not increased solely by reason of the provision for division of fees and does not exceed reasonable compensation for all services they render to the client.

The 1979 amendment deleted from the rule the provision, first enacted in November of 1972, that the division of fees must be "made in proportion to the services performed or responsibility assumed by each [lawyer]."

referral fee agreements are no longer contrary to public policy, but also that they were not contrary to public policy before the original enactment of rule 2-108 (former rule 22) in November 1972. Since the referral contract at issue in this case was entered into in January 1972, we conclude public policy does not now prohibit its enforcement.

I

In December 1971, Muriel Joseph contacted her lawyer John Moran and discussed what she believed to be the negligence of Tri-City Hospital in caring for her infant granddaughter, Tashia. Moran recommended Tashia's parents should consult a lawyer with expertise in medical malpractice matters. Later, Muriel called Moran and asked him to arrange such an appointment for her son, Kenneth, and his wife, Patricia. Moran selected Gordon Von Kalinowski, an acknowledged legal specialist in the medical malpractice field. Muriel, Kenneth, Patricia and Moran met with Von Kalinowski in January 1972. As a result of that meeting, Kenneth and Patricia retained Von Kalinowski to represent them. They orally agreed Von Kalinowski's contingent fee would be an unspecified percentage of the recovery, the exact percentage to be set and approved by the court in a minor's compromise. After meeting with the clients, Von Kalinowski orally agreed to split his fee equally with Moran.[9] Moran's role was to maintain communication with the Josephs and to perform those services in the case which Von Kalinowski might request. Von Kalinowski was to control the litigation.

Von Kalinowski filed the malpractice complaint on behalf of his clients against Tri-City and others in June 1972. Between February and June of that year, Moran spoke frequently with Muriel, alleviating her concern about the apparent lack of progress in the case. Sometime in the spring of 1973, because of Von Kalinowski's ill health, his work on the Joseph case bogged down.

In September, Wesley Harris learned Von Kalinowski was having some problems keeping current with his work and indicated his willingness to assume responsibility in any case which Von Kalinowski was willing to turn over to him. As a result of this solicitation, Von Kalinowski delivered 20 files to Harris, including the Joseph malpractice case. Harris agreed to be bound by Von Kalinowski's agreement with Moran.

Harris called Moran, told him he was in possession of the Joseph file, and was willing to assume responsibility in the case. Moran and Harris went to the Josephs' residence and obtained Kenneth's and Patricia's consent and signatures to the written substitution of attorneys in favor of Harris. The substitution was signed on January 14 and filed February 5, 1974. By dint of Harris' efforts through January 1975, he effected settlements with the various defendants resulting in attorney's fees of $226,996.37.

Moran's action for damages, the underlying suit here, was filed after Harris

---

[9] [3] At the time of the agreement between Moran and Von Kalinowski, former rule 22 (the predecessor of rule 2-108) prohibiting referral fee arrangements had not yet been adopted. Thus, the contract when entered into was legal.

refused to honor their referral fee agreement. Bound by *Altschul v. Sayble*, the trial court held the contract unenforceable, but nevertheless awarded Moran $25,000 as the reasonable value of his services actually rendered in the case. Pending this appeal by both parties, rule 2-108 was amended to remove the prohibition against referral fee contracts.

II

As a general proposition "courts will not compel parties to perform contracts which have for their object the performance of acts against sound public policy either by decreeing specific performance or awarding damages for breach. This rule is not generally applied to secure justice between [the] parties [to that] contract, but from regard for a higher interest — that of the public, whose welfare demands that certain transactions be discouraged."

* * *

IV

In *Altschul v. Sayble*, the court concerned itself with the enforceability of a referral fee contract entered into before the effective date of former rule 22, which made the parties to such contracts subject to professional discipline. Acknowledging the legality of an agreement is normally determined as of the time of its making, the court relied on the Ethical Considerations noted in the American Bar Association Code of Professional Responsibility in concluding the contract was contrary to public policy when it was entered into.

Viewed with the benefit of hindsight, *Altschul's* reasoning appears precipitous and a bit myopic. The 1979 amendment to rule 2-108, eliminating the prohibition of referral fee contracts, had the effect of placing the State Bar in much the same disciplinary position it was in from 1928 (when the Supreme Court first adopted the Rules of Professional Conduct) until 1972 (when former rule 22 became effective). What *Altschul* described as the clear expression of public policy, nonexistent in the professional rules for about 44 years, disappeared after making a relatively brief appearance for about 7 years. We seriously doubt whether, in the absence of the later passage of rule 22, *Altschul* would have held forwarding fee contracts entered into before November 1972 unenforceable as contrary to public policy.

The practice of forwarding fees among lawyers, part of our legal culture, remains with us even though the detrimental effect upon the client appears obvious. "In an era where recovery in tort is founded primarily upon socialization of the loss occasioned by injury to person and property, the society which bears that loss must be protected against arrangements which prevent the recovery from reaching the party injured, reduced only by necessary legal fees and other expenses of litigation. The pure referral fee, which compensates one lawyer with a percentage of a contingent fee for doing nothing more than obtaining the signature of a client upon a retainer agreement while the lawyer to whom the case is referred performs the work, is far from necessary to the injured person's recovery. To the extent that the referral fee is paid for that purpose, loss has not been socialized. Rather, the obtaining of business by a lawyer who, by his own motion, has conceded his inability to handle it has been subsidized." The honoring of a referral fee is even more puzzling where the referring attorney is merely heeding the Rules of Professional Conduct in rejecting a case which he does not have the requisite skill or experience to handle competently.

Regardless of the logic of this argument, there is another point of view. If the ultimate goal is to assure the best possible representation for a client, a forwarding fee is an economic incentive to less capable lawyers to seek out experienced specialists to handle a case. Thus, with marketplace forces at work, the specialist develops a continuing source of business, the client is benefited and the conscientious, but less experienced lawyer is subsidized to competently handle the cases he retains and to assure his continued search for referral of complex cases to the best lawyers in particular fields.

Whether one argument is better than the other is unimportant. What is important is to recognize there are differing points of view on this subject and those points of view may well have influenced the Legislature, the Supreme Court and the State Bar to refrain from prohibiting referral fee contracts prior to 1972. Presumably, these institutions, each structurally geared to respond to its constituents or the public, acted in response to articulated perceptions.

We should not presume that similar perceptions did not motivate these same institutions to refrain from prohibiting referral fee contracts before 1972.

V

Our expressed views should not be interpreted as an encouragement of referral fee agreements. Nevertheless, there is considerable distance between prohibition and encouragement. That distance may be the "breathing space" necessary to accommodate both the public nature of the legal profession and commercial milieu within which it must survive. Here, Moran did not violate any State Bar rule at the inception of the agreement; no rule would now be violated by its enforcement. Recognizing that lawyers continue to routinely participate in fee splitting arrangements with the apparent approval of those institutions charged with regulating the profession, we conclude the justice system is better served by having Harris bound by his word than by depriving Moran of the benefit of his contract. Judgment reversed with instructions to enter judgment for plaintiff against defendants Wesley H. Harris and Wesley H. Harris, a professional corporation, in the sum of $88,952.59.

*   *   *

Rather than prohibit all fee splitting among lawyers from different firms, the Model Rule drafters crafted a rule to regulate the practice. The fee splitting practice is permitted when the following conditions are met (MR 1.5(e)): (i) The fee splitting lawyers must either share the fee in proportion to the services rendered by each lawyer or agree with the client that the lawyers assume joint responsibility for the representation (MR 1.5(e)(1)); (ii) The client must agree to the fee splitting arrangement by all lawyers involved, and the agreement must be confirmed in writing (MR 1.5(e)(2)); (iii) The total fee charged by all lawyers involved must continue to comply with the general standard of reasonableness of the fee (MR 1.5(e)(3)).

Fee splitting with non-lawyers, essentially partnering with non-lawyers, is prohibited under most circumstances by Model Rule 5.4 and raises the issues implicated by multidisciplinary practice. *See* Section E in Chapter VIII "Duties to the Legal System and Society."

4. Minimum Fee Schedules

GOLDFARB v. VIRGINIA STATE BAR
421 U.S. 773 (1975)

Petitioners, husband and wife, contracted to buy a home in Fairfax County, Va., and the lender who financed the purchase required them to obtain title insurance, which necessitated a title examination that could be performed legally only by a member of respondent Virginia State Bar. Petitioners unsuccessfully tried to find a lawyer who would examine the title for less than the fee prescribed in a minimum-fee schedule published by respondent Fairfax County Bar Association and enforced by respondent Virginia State Bar. Petitioners then brought this class action against respondents, seeking injunctive relief and damages, and alleging that the minimum-fee schedule and its enforcement mechanism, as applied to fees for legal services relating to residential real estate transactions, constitute price fixing in violation of § 1 of the Sherman Act. Although holding that the State Bar was exempt from the Sherman Act, the District Court granted judgment against the County Bar Association and enjoined the publication of the fee schedule. The Court of Appeals reversed, holding not only that the State Bar's actions were immune from liability as "state action," *Parker v. Brown*, 317 U.S. 341, but also that the County Bar Association was immune because the practice of law, as a "learned profession," is not "trade or commerce" under the Sherman Act; and that, in any event, respondents' activities did not have sufficient effect on interstate commerce to support Sherman Act jurisdiction.

The Supreme Court held that the minimum-fee schedule, as published by the County Bar Association and enforced by the State Bar, violates § 1 of the Sherman Act. For the Court, the schedule and its enforcement mechanism constitute price fixing since the record shows that the schedule, rather than being purely advisory, operated as a fixed, rigid price floor. The fee schedule was enforced through the prospect of professional discipline by the State Bar, by reason of attorneys' desire to comply with announced professional norms, and by the assurance that other lawyers would not compete by underbidding. Furthermore, since a significant amount of funds furnished for financing the purchase of homes in Fairfax County comes from outside the State, and since a title examination is an integral part of such interstate transactions, interstate commerce is sufficiently affected for Sherman Act purposes notwithstanding that there is no showing that prospective purchasers were discouraged from buying homes in Fairfax County by the challenged activities, and no showing that the fee schedule resulted in raising fees. Finally, Respondents' activities are not exempt from the Sherman Act as "state action." Neither the Virginia Supreme Court nor any Virginia statute required such activities, and, although the State Bar has the power to issue ethical opinions, it does not appear that the Supreme Court approves them. It is not enough that the anticompetitive conduct is "prompted" by state action; to be exempt, such conduct must be compelled by direction of the State acting as a sovereign. Here the State Bar, by providing that deviation from the minimum fees may lead to disciplinary action, has voluntarily joined in what is essentially a private anticompetitive activity and hence cannot claim it is beyond the Sherman Act's reach.

INTERNATIONAL NOTES

1. Fee schedules are common, however, in Europe and elsewhere, where they are considered a protection against exploitation of unsophisticated clients. The CCBE Code acknowledges and appears to condone fee schedules, providing that fees can "be charged in proportion to the value of the matter handled by the lawyer if this is in accordance with an officially approved fee schedule." CCBE Rule 3.3.3. One German commentator notes that fee schedules are a form of "social engineering" designed to overcompensate attorneys who take higher risk cases, thereby subsidizing legal services for poorer clients. Virginia G. Maur, *Attorney Fee Arrangements: The U.S. and Western European Perspectives*, 19 N.W. J. INT'L L. & BUS. 272, 294–95 (1999).

2. In Italy, a tariff (fee schedule) established by the national bar association (the Consiglio Nazionale Forenze) sets minimum and maximum fees for specific legal tasks. Parties can agree to fees higher than the tariff but are prohibited from agreeing to fees lower than the minimum established by the tariff. KLUWER LAW INT'L & INT'L BAR ASS'N, LAW WITHOUT FRONTIERS: A COMPARATIVE SURVEY OF THE RULES OF PROFESSIONAL ETHICS APPLICABLE TO THE CROSS-BORDER PRACTICE OF LAW 188 (Edwin Godfrey ed., 1995).

In China, litigation fees are set by the Ministry of Justice and approved by the State Council, though local variation is permitted. Fees for non-litigation services, however, may be negotiated between lawyer and client. Regulations provide that such fees should be a flat sum for non-property maters and a percentage of the amount at stake in property-related matters, but may not be based on time spent. *See* LAWYERS COMMITTEE FOR HUMAN RIGHTS, LAWYERS IN CHINA: OBSTACLES TO INDEPENDENCE AND THE DEFENSE OF RIGHTS 20, n.75 (1998).

5. Fee Forfeiture

CAPLIN & DRYSDALE, CHARTERED v. UNITED STATES
491 U.S. 617 (1989)

JUSTICE WHITE delivered the opinion of the Court.

We are called on to determine whether the federal drug forfeiture statute includes an exemption for assets that a defendant wishes to use to pay an attorney who conducted his defense in the criminal case where forfeiture was sought.

Because we determine that no such exemption exists, we must decide whether that statute, so interpreted, is consistent with the Fifth and Sixth Amendments. We hold that it is.

I

In January 1985, Christopher Reckmeyer was charged in a multicount indictment with running a massive drug importation and distribution scheme. The scheme was alleged to be a continuing criminal enterprise (CCE), in violation of 84 Stat. 1265, as amended, 21 U.S.C. § 848 (1982 ed., Supp. V). Relying on a portion of the CCE statute that authorizes forfeiture to the Government of "property constituting, or derived from . . . proceeds . . . obtained" from drug-law violations, § 853(a),[10] the indictment sought forfeiture of specified assets in Reckmeyer's possession. At this time, the District Court, acting pursuant to § 853(e)(1)(A),[11] entered a restraining order forbidding Reckmeyer to transfer any of the listed assets that were potentially forfeitable.

There is no question here that the offenses Reckmeyer was accused of in the indictment fell within the class of crimes triggering this forfeiture provision. Sometime earlier, Reckmeyer had retained petitioner, a law firm, to represent him in the ongoing grand jury investigation which resulted in the January 1985 indictments. Notwithstanding the restraining order, Reckmeyer paid the firm $25,000 for preindictment legal services a few days after the indictment was handed down; this sum was placed by petitioner in an escrow account. Petitioner continued to represent Reckmeyer following the indictment.

On March 7, 1985, Reckmeyer moved to modify the District Court's earlier restraining order to permit him to use some of the restrained assets to pay petitioner's fees; Reckmeyer also sought to exempt from any postconviction forfeiture order the assets that he intended to use to pay petitioner. However, one week later, before the District Court could conduct a hearing on this motion,

---

[10] [1] The forfeiture statute provides, in relevant part, that any person convicted of a particular class of criminal offenses

> shall forfeit to the United States, irrespective of any provision of State law -
>
> (1) any property constituting, or derived from, any proceeds the person obtained, directly or indirectly, as the result of such violation;
>
> . . . .
>
> The court, in imposing sentence on such person, shall order, in addition to any other sentence imposed . . . , that the person forfeit to the United States all property described in this subsection.

21 U.S.C. § 853(a) (1982 ed., Supp. V).

[11] [2] The pretrial restraining order provision states that

> [u]pon application of the United States, the court may enter a restraining order or injunction . . . or take any other action to preserve the availability of property described in subsection (a) of [§ 853] for forfeiture under this section -
>
> (A) upon the filing of an indictment or information charging a violation . . . for which criminal forfeiture may be ordered under [§ 853] and alleging that the property with respect to which the order is sought would, in the event of conviction, be subject to forfeiture under this section.

§ 853(e)(1).

Reckmeyer entered a plea agreement with the Government. Under the agreement, Reckmeyer pleaded guilty to the drug-related CCE charge, and agreed to forfeit all of the specified assets listed in the indictment. The day Reckmeyer's plea was entered, the District Court denied his earlier motion to modify the restraining order, concluding that the plea and forfeiture agreement rendered irrelevant any further consideration of the propriety of the court's pretrial restraints. Subsequently, an order forfeiting virtually all of the assets in Reckmeyer's possession was entered by the District Court in conjunction with his sentencing.

After this order was entered, petitioner filed a petition under § 853(n), which permits third parties with an interest in forfeited property to ask the sentencing court for an adjudication of their rights to that property; specifically, § 853(n)(6)(B) gives a third party who entered into a bona fide transaction with a defendant a right to make claims against forfeited property, if that third party was "at the time of [the transaction] reasonably without cause to believe that the [defendant's assets were] subject to forfeiture." Petitioner claimed an interest in $170,000 of Reckmeyer's assets, for services it had provided Reckmeyer in conducting his defense; petitioner also sought the $25,000 being held in the escrow account, as payment for preindictment legal services. Petitioner argued alternatively that assets used to pay an attorney were exempt from forfeiture under § 853, and if not, the failure of the statute to provide such an exemption rendered it unconstitutional. The District Court granted petitioner's claim for a share of the forfeited assets.

A panel of the Fourth Circuit affirmed, finding that — while § 853 contained no statutory provision authorizing the payment of attorney's fees out of forfeited assets — the statute's failure to do so impermissibly infringed a defendant's Sixth Amendment right to the counsel of his choice. The Court of Appeals agreed to hear the case en banc and reversed sub nom. *In re Forfeiture Hearing as to Caplin & Drysdale, Chartered*, 837 F.2d 637 (1988). All the judges of the Fourth Circuit agreed that the language of the CCE statute acknowledged no exception to its forfeiture requirement that would recognize petitioner's claim to the forfeited assets. A majority found this statutory scheme constitutional; four dissenting judges, however, agreed with the panel's view that the statute so construed violated the Sixth Amendment. Petitioner sought review of the statutory and constitutional issues raised by the Court of Appeals' holding. We granted certiorari, and now affirm.

II

Petitioner's first submission is that the statutory provision that authorizes pretrial restraining orders on potentially forfeitable assets in a defendant's possession, 21 U.S.C. § 853(e) (1982 ed., Supp. V), grants district courts equitable discretion to determine when such orders should be imposed. This discretion should be exercised under "traditional equitable standards," petitioner urges, including a "weigh[ing] of the equities and competing hardships on the parties"; under this approach, a court "must invariably strike the balance so as to allow a defendant [to pay] . . . for bona fide attorneys fees," petitioner argues. Petitioner further submits that once a district court so exercises its discretion, and fails to freeze assets that a defendant then uses to pay an attorney, the statute's provision for recapture of forfeitable assets transferred to third parties, § 853(c), may not operate on such sums.

Petitioner's argument, as it acknowledges, is based on the view of the statute expounded by Judge Winter of the Second Circuit in his concurring opinion in that Court of Appeals' en banc decision, *United States v. Monsanto*, 852 F.2d 1400, 1405-1411 (1988). We reject this interpretation of the statute today in our decision in *United States v. Monsanto*, which reverses the Second Circuit's holding in that case. As we explain in our *Monsanto* decision, whatever discretion § 853(e) provides district court judges to refuse to enter pretrial restraining orders, it does not extend as far as petitioner urges — nor does the exercise of that discretion "immunize" nonrestrained assets from subsequent forfeiture under § 853(c), if they are transferred to an attorney to pay legal fees. Thus, for the reasons provided in our opinion in *Monsanto*, we reject petitioner's statutory claim.

III

We therefore address petitioner's constitutional challenges to the forfeiture law. Petitioner contends that the statute infringes on criminal defendants' Sixth Amendment right to counsel of choice, and upsets the "balance of power" between the Government and the accused in a manner contrary to the Due Process Clause of the Fifth Amendment. We consider these contentions in turn.

*   *   *

A

Petitioner's first claim is that the forfeiture law makes impossible, or at least impermissibly burdens, a defendant's right "to select and be represented by one's preferred attorney." *Wheat v. United States*, 486 U.S. 153, 159 (1988). Petitioner does not, nor could it defensibly do so, assert that impecunious defendants have a Sixth Amendment right to choose their counsel. The Amendment guarantees defendants in criminal cases the right to adequate representation, but those who do not have the means to hire their own lawyers have no cognizable complaint so long as they are adequately represented by attorneys appointed by the courts. "[A] defendant may not insist on representation by an attorney he cannot afford." *Wheat, supra*, at 159. Petitioner does not dispute these propositions. Nor does the Government deny that the Sixth Amendment guarantees a defendant the right to be represented by an otherwise qualified attorney whom that defendant can afford to hire, or who is willing to represent the defendant even though he is without funds. Applying these principles to the statute in question here, we observe that nothing in § 853 prevents a defendant from hiring the attorney of his choice, or disqualifies any attorney from serving as a defendant's counsel. Thus, unlike *Wheat*, this case does not involve a situation where the Government has asked a court to prevent a defendant's chosen counsel from representing the accused. Instead, petitioner urges that a violation of the Sixth Amendment arises here because of the forfeiture, at the instance of the Government, of assets that defendants intend to use to pay their attorneys.

Even in this sense, of course, the burden the forfeiture law imposes on a criminal defendant is limited. The forfeiture statute does not prevent a defendant who has nonforfeitable assets from retaining any attorney of his choosing. Nor is it necessarily the case that a defendant who possesses nothing but assets the Government seeks to have forfeited will be prevented from retaining counsel of choice. Defendants like Reckmeyer may be able to find lawyers willing to represent them, hoping that their fees will be paid in the event of acquittal, or via some other means that a defendant might come by in the future. The burden placed on defendants by the forfeiture law is therefore a limited one.

Nonetheless, there will be cases where a defendant will be unable to retain the attorney of his choice, when that defendant would have been able to hire that lawyer if he had access to forfeitable assets, and if there was no risk that fees paid by the defendant to his counsel would later be recouped under § 853(c).[12] It is in these cases, petitioner argues, that the Sixth Amendment puts limits on the forfeiture statute.

*   *   *

Petitioner's "balancing analysis" . . . rests substantially on the view that the Government has only a modest interest in forfeitable assets that may be used to retain an attorney. Petitioner takes the position that, in large part, once assets have been paid over from client to attorney, the principal ends of forfeiture have been achieved: dispossessing a drug dealer or racketeer of the proceeds of his wrong-doing. We think that this view misses the mark for three reasons.

First, the Government has a pecuniary interest in forfeiture that goes beyond merely separating a criminal from his ill-gotten gains; that legitimate interest extends to recovering all forfeitable assets, for such assets are deposited in a Fund that supports law-enforcement efforts in a variety of important and useful ways. *See* 28 U.S.C. § 524(c), which establishes the Department of Justice Assets Forfeiture Fund. The sums of money that can be raised for law enforcement activities this way are substantial,[13] and the Government's interest in using the profits of crime to fund these activities should not be discounted.

Second, the statute permits "rightful owners" of forfeited assets to make claims for forfeited assets before they are retained by the Government. The Government's interest in winning undiminished forfeiture thus includes the objective of returning property, in full, to those wrongfully deprived or defrauded of it. Where the Government pursues this restitutionary end, the Government's interest in forfeiture is virtually indistinguishable from its interest in returning to a bank the proceeds of a bank robbery; and a forfeiture-defendant's claim of right to use such assets to

---

[12] [4] That section of the statute, which includes the so-called "relation back" provision, states: "All right, title, and interest in property described in [§ 853] vests in the United States upon the commission of the act giving rise to forfeiture under this section. Any such property that is subsequently transferred to a person other than the defendant may be the subject of a special verdict of forfeiture and thereafter shall be forfeited to the United States, unless the transferee establishes" his entitlement to such property pursuant to § 853(n), discussed *supra.* 21 U.S.C. § 853(c) (1982 ed., Supp. V).

[13] [6] For example, just one of the assets which Reckmeyer agreed to forfeit, a parcel of land known as "Shelburne Glebe," was recently sold by federal authorities for $5.3 million. Washington Post, May 10, 1989, at D1, cols. 1-4. The proceeds of the sale will fund federal, state, and local law-enforcement activities.

hire an attorney, instead of having them returned to their rightful owners, is no more persuasive than a bank robber's similar claim.

Finally, as we have recognized previously, a major purpose motivating congressional adoption and continued refinement of the racketeer influenced and corrupt organizations (RICO) and CCE forfeiture provisions has been the desire to lessen the economic power of organized crime and drug enterprises. This includes the use of such economic power to retain private counsel. The notion that the Government has a legitimate interest in depriving criminals of economic power, even insofar as that power is used to retain counsel of choice, may be somewhat unsettling. But when a defendant claims that he has suffered some substantial impairment of his Sixth Amendment rights by virtue of the seizure or forfeiture of assets in his possession, such a complaint is no more than the reflection of "the harsh reality that the quality of a criminal defendant's representation frequently may turn on his ability to retain the best counsel money can buy." *Morris v. Slappy*, 461 U.S. 1, 23 (1983) (Brennan, J., concurring in result). Again, the Court of Appeals put it aptly: "The modern day Jean Valjean must be satisfied with appointed counsel. Yet the drug merchant claims that his possession of huge sums of money . . . entitles him to something more. We reject this contention, and any notion of a constitutional right to use the proceeds of crime to finance an expensive defense."[14]

If appointed counsel is ineffective in a particular case, a defendant has resort to the remedies discussed in *Strickland v. Washington*, 466 U.S. 668 (1984).

It is our view that there is a strong governmental interest in obtaining full recovery of all forfeitable assets, an interest that overrides any Sixth Amendment interest in permitting criminals to use assets adjudged forfeitable to pay for their defense.

We therefore reject petitioner's claim of a Sixth Amendment right of criminal defendants to use assets that are the Government's — assets adjudged forfeitable, as Reckmeyer's were — to pay attorney's fees, merely because those assets are in their possession.[15] See also *Monsanto*, which rejects a similar claim with respect to

---

[14] [7] We also reject the contention, advanced by amici, *see, e.g.*, Brief for American Bar Association as Amicus Curiae 20-22, and accepted by some courts considering claims like petitioner's, that a type of "per se" ineffective assistance of counsel results — due to the particular complexity of RICO or drug-enterprise cases — when a defendant is not permitted to use assets in his possession to retain counsel of choice, and instead must rely on appointed counsel. If such an argument were accepted, it would bar the trial of indigents charged with such offenses, because those persons would have to rely on appointed counsel — which this view considers per se ineffective.

[15] [10] Petitioner advances three additional reasons for invalidating the forfeiture statute, all of which concern possible ethical conflicts created for lawyers defending persons facing forfeiture of assets in their possession.

Petitioner first notes the statute's exemption from forfeiture of property transferred to a bona fide purchaser who was "reasonably without cause to believe that the property was subject to forfeiture." 21 U.S.C. § 853(n)(6)(B). This provision, it is said, might give an attorney an incentive not to investigate a defendant's case as fully as possible, so that the lawyer can invoke it to protect from forfeiture any fees he has received. Yet given the requirement that any assets which the Government wishes to have forfeited must be specified in the indictment, see Fed. Rule Crim. Proc. 7(c)(2), the only way a lawyer could be a beneficiary of § 853(n)(6)(B) would be to fail to read the indictment of his client. In this light, the prospect that a lawyer might find himself in conflict with his client, by seeking to take advantage of

pretrial orders and assets not yet judged forfeitable.

*   *   *

IV

For the reasons given above, we find that petitioner's statutory and constitutional challenges to the forfeiture imposed here are without merit. The judgment of the Court of Appeals is therefore

Affirmed.

JUSTICE BLACKMUN, WITH WHOM JUSTICE BRENNAN, JUSTICE MARSHALL, and JUSTICE STEVENS join, dissenting. [This opinion applies also to No. 88-454, *United States v. Monsanto, ante.*]

Those jurists who have held forth against the result the majority reaches in these cases have been guided by one core insight: that it is unseemly and unjust for the Government to beggar those it prosecutes in order to disable their defense at trial. The majority trivializes "the burden the forfeiture law imposes on a criminal defendant." *Caplin & Drysdale, Chartered v. United States.* Instead, it should heed the warnings of our District Court judges, whose day-to-day exposure to the criminal trial process enables them to understand, perhaps far better than we, the devastating consequences of attorney's fee forfeiture for the integrity of our adversarial system of justice.

The criminal-forfeiture statute we consider today could have been interpreted to avoid depriving defendants of the ability to retain private counsel — and should

---

§ 853(n)(6)(B), amounts to very little. Petitioner itself concedes that such a conflict will, as a practical matter, never arise: a defendant's "lawyer . . . could not demonstrate that he was 'reasonably without cause to believe that the property was subject to forfeiture,' " petitioner concludes at one point.

The second possible conflict arises in plea bargaining: petitioner posits that a lawyer may advise a client to accept an agreement entailing a more harsh prison sentence but no forfeiture — even where contrary to the client's interests — in an effort to preserve the lawyer's fee. Following such a strategy, however, would surely constitute ineffective assistance of counsel. We see no reason why our cases such as Strickland v. Washington, 466 U.S. 668 (1984), are inadequate to deal with any such ineffectiveness where it arises. In any event, there is no claim that such conduct occurred here, nor could there be, as Reckmeyer's plea agreement included forfeiture of virtually every asset in his possession. Moreover, we rejected a claim similar to this one in *Evans v. Jeff D.*, 475 U.S. 717, 727-728 (1986).

Finally, petitioner argues that the forfeiture statute, in operation, will create a system akin to "contingency fees" for defense lawyers: only a defense lawyer who wins acquittal for his client will be able to collect his fees, and contingent fees in criminal cases are generally considered unethical. See ABA Model Rule of Professional Conduct 1.5(d)(2) (1983); ABA Model Code of Professional Responsibility DR 2-106(C) (1979). But there is no indication here that petitioner, or any other firm, has actually sought to charge a defendant on a contingency basis; rather the claim is that a law firm's prospect of collecting its fee may turn on the outcome at trial. This, however, may often be the case in criminal defense work. Nor is it clear why permitting contingent fees in criminal cases — if that is what the forfeiture statute does — violates a criminal defendant's Sixth Amendment rights. The fact that a federal statutory scheme authorizing contingency fees — again, if that is what Congress has created in § 853 (a premise we doubt) — is at odds with model disciplinary rules or state disciplinary codes hardly renders the federal statute invalid.

have been so interpreted, given the grave "constitutional and ethical problems" raised by the forfeiture of funds used to pay legitimate counsel fees. But even if Congress in fact required this substantial incursion on the defendant's choice of counsel, the Court should have recognized that the Framers stripped Congress of the power to do so when they added the Sixth Amendment to our Constitution.

I

The majority acknowledges, as it must, that no language in the Comprehensive Forfeiture Act of 1984 (Act) expressly provides for the forfeiture of attorney's fees, and that the legislative history contains no substantive discussion of the question.[16] The fact that "the legislative history and congressional debates are similarly silent on the use of forfeitable assets to pay stockbroker's fees, laundry bills, or country club memberships" means nothing, for one cannot believe that Congress was unaware that interference with the payment of attorney's fees, unlike interference with these other expenditures, would raise Sixth Amendment concerns.

Despite the absence of any indication that Congress intended to use the forfeiture weapon against legitimate attorney's fees, the majority — all the while purporting to "respect" the established practice of construing a statute to avoid constitutional problems contends that it is constrained to conclude that the Act reaches attorney's fees. The Court cannot follow its usual practice here, we are told, because this is not a "close cas[e]" in which "statutory language is ambiguous." The majority finds unambiguous language in 21 U.S.C. § 853(a), which provides that when a defendant is convicted of certain crimes, the defendant "shall forfeit to the United States" any property derived from proceeds of the crime or used to facilitate the crime. I agree that § 853(a) is broad in language and is cast in mandatory terms. But I do not agree with the majority's conclusion that the lack of an express exemption for attorney's fees in § 853(a) makes the Act as a whole unambiguous.

* * *

II

The majority has decided otherwise, however, and for that reason is compelled to reach the constitutional issue it could have avoided. But the majority pauses hardly long enough to acknowledge "the Sixth Amendment's protection of one's right to retain counsel of his choosing," let alone to explore its "full extent." Instead, it moves rapidly from the observation that " '[a] defendant may not insist on representation by an attorney he cannot afford,' " quoting *Wheat v. United States*, 486 U.S. 153, 159 (1988), to the conclusion that the Government is free to deem the defendant indigent by declaring his assets "tainted" by criminal activity the Government has yet to prove. That the majority implicitly finds the Sixth Amendment right to counsel of

---

[16] [2] Indeed, the strongest statement on the question is the comment in the House Report: "Nothing in this section is intended to interfere with a person's Sixth Amendment right to counsel." H. R. Rep. No. 98-845, pt. 1, p. 19, n.1 (1984). Even if the majority were correct that this statement is "nothing more than an exhortation for the courts to tread carefully in this delicate area," *United States v. Monsanto, ante,* at 609, n.8, the majority does not explain why it proceeds to ignore Congress' exhortation to construe the statute to avoid implicating Sixth Amendment concerns.

choice so insubstantial that it can be outweighed by a legal fiction demonstrates, still once again, its " ' apparent unawareness of the function of the independent lawyer as a guardian of our freedom.' " *Walters v. National Assn. of Radiation Survivors*, 473 U.S. 305, 371 (1985) (Stevens, J., dissenting).

* * *

B

Had it been Congress' express aim to undermine the adversary system as we know it, it could hardly have found a better engine of destruction than attorney's-fee forfeiture. The main effect of forfeitures under the Act, of course, will be to deny the defendant the right to retain counsel, and therefore the right to have his defense designed and presented by an attorney he has chosen and trusts. If the Government restrains the defendant's assets before trial, private counsel will be unwilling to continue, or to take on, the defense. Even if no restraining order is entered, the possibility of forfeiture after conviction will itself substantially diminish the likelihood that private counsel will agree to take the case. The "message [to private counsel] is 'Do not represent this defendant or you will lose your fee.' That being the kind of message lawyers are likely to take seriously, the defendant will find it difficult or impossible to secure representation." *United States v. Badalamenti*, 614 F. Supp. at 196.

Perhaps most troubling is the fact that forfeiture statutes place the Government in the position to exercise an intolerable degree of power over any private attorney who takes on the task of representing a defendant in a forfeiture case. The decision whether to seek a restraining order rests with the prosecution, as does the decision whether to waive forfeiture upon a plea of guilty or a conviction at trial. The Government will be ever tempted to use the forfeiture weapon against a defense attorney who is particularly talented or aggressive on the client's behalf — the attorney who is better than what, in the Government's view, the defendant deserves. The specter of the Government's selectively excluding only the most talented defense counsel is a serious threat to the equality of forces necessary for the adversarial system to perform at its best. An attorney whose fees are potentially subject to forfeiture will be forced to operate in an environment in which the Government is not only the defendant's adversary, but also his own.

The long-term effects of the fee-forfeiture practice will be to decimate the private criminal-defense bar. As the use of the forfeiture mechanism expands to new categories of federal crimes and spreads to the States, only one class of defendants will be free routinely to retain private counsel: the affluent defendant accused of a crime that generates no economic gain. As the number of private clients diminishes, only the most idealistic and the least skilled of young lawyers will be attracted to the field, while the remainder seek greener pastures elsewhere. In short, attorney's-fee forfeiture substantially undermines every interest served by the Sixth Amendment right to chosen counsel, on the individual and institutional levels, over the short term and the long haul.

* * *

III

In my view, the Act as interpreted by the majority is inconsistent with the intent of Congress, and seriously undermines the basic fairness of our criminal-justice system. That a majority of this Court has upheld the constitutionality of the Act as so interpreted will not deter Congress, I hope, from amending the Act to make clear that Congress did not intend this result. This Court has the power to declare the Act constitutional, but it cannot thereby make it wise.

I dissent.

C. FIDUCIARY DUTIES

In addition to contractual duties and tort duties, lawyers owe their clients fiduciary duties. A fiduciary is one in whom a special trust in placed. A fiduciary has special obligations to care for the interests of the beneficiary (in the lawyer-client context, the client), even when those interests are not aligned with the fiduciary's own interests. A fiduciary owes to the beneficiary scrupulous good faith, candor, and care in the management of the beneficiary's interests.

A lawyer must keep client property separate from the lawyer's property. In the trust account context, this means that, except for depositing the lawyer's own funds in a client trust account to cover bank service charges, MR 1.15(b), only client money may be in the trust account; the lawyer must maintain a separate office operating account. When a lawyer commingles his funds with a client's, the lawyer is subject to discipline. MR 1.15(a). The cases of disbarment for this violation are legion.

[Recall the excerpt from *In re Warhaftig*, 524 A.2d 398 (N.J. 1987), Chapter II.]

IN RE ROSELLINI
646 P.2d 122 (Wash. 1982)

This is an attorney discipline proceeding involving the misuse of trust funds. The hearing panel officer and the Disciplinary Board recommended that attorney John M. Rosellini be disbarred. [Rosellini was a candidate for State Attorney General when these charges came to light. —Ed.] We concur. The complaint of the bar association alleged 21 violations of the Discipline Rules for Attorneys and the Code of Professional Responsibility. The hearing panel officer found 14 violations and recommended disbarment. The Board, by a 3- to-2 vote, adopted the hearing panel officer's findings, conclusions, and recommendations. Other members of the Board were either absent or disqualified themselves. The two dissenting members disagreed with the majority only on the issue of the proper sanction. The dissenters believed a 1-year suspension was appropriate.

The respondent admits that he violated the rules governing trust funds. He argues only that he should be suspended, not disbarred.

These charges arise from the following facts. Respondent John Rosellini was employed to probate the estate of Voyena Brandt. On May 31, 1977, he received and placed in his trust account $10,000 which was to be paid to the decedent's two *waited 16 mos. to distribute funds.* children. Those funds were not disbursed to the Brandt children until September 11, 1978, more than 16 months later.

In the meantime respondent attorney drew the following checks on his trust account for the stated purposes:

Date	Payee	Amount	Purpose
(1) 7-29-77	Seattle 1st Nat Bank	$1,968.00	office rent
(2) 8-8-77	Seattle 1st Nat Bank	1,968.00	office rent
(3) 9-20-77	Equitable Savings & Loan Ass'n	1,275.77	residence mortgage payment
(4) 10-4-77	John M. Rosellini	800.00	personal expenses
(5) 10-5-77	Cash	546.03	office telephone
(6) 10-17-77	Pacific NW Bell	427.86	office telephone
(7) 10-21-77	John M. Rosellini	750.00	personal expenses
(8) 10-28-77	Pacific Nat Bank	300.00	residence mortgage payment
(9) 11-4-77	John M. Rosellini	750.00	personal expenses
11-8-77	Equitable Savings & Loan Ass'n	92.68	residence mortgage payment
11-8-77	Cash	225.00	personal expenses
11-8-77	Equitable Savings & Loan Ass'n	636.77	residence mortgage payment
11-16-77	John M. Rosellini	700.00	personal expenses
3-23-78	Seattle Seahawks	200.00	personal expenses

These withdrawals totaled $10,640.11.

Mr. Brandt made numerous inquiries as to when the $10,000 would be disbursed. Eventually, he filed a complaint with the bar association and an investigation was started. Respondent then disbursed the funds, explaining that he was waiving fees and costs because of unanticipated delays in processing the estate. *didn't give out money until complaint filed*

The payment to the Brandt heirs was made possible by the following transaction. Three days before disbursing the money respondent received $22,063.94. These funds were from the estate of an Italian national and were delivered to respondent in his capacity as Honorary Vice Consul for Italy. After deducting a fee, respondent put the balance in his consular account. He then transferred $10,000 to his trust account. With these funds he was then able to disburse the amount owed to the Brandt heirs. *where he got the money.*

On March 21, 1978, after making 13 withdrawals from his trust account for personal use, respondent signed an affidavit required by DRA 13.3, swearing under oath that all clients' funds were kept in his trust account in the manner specified in CPR DR 9-102. That section prohibits the commingling of personal and client funds, and requires that an attorney promptly pay or deliver to the client upon demand all funds in the attorney's possession to which the client is entitled. *Swore the funds were kept safe.*

Respondent admits that he knew at the time he filed the affidavit that the

answers were not true and the trust account was not maintained in the manner specified in CPR DR 9-102 nor were all clients' funds to the extent required by CPR DR 9-102 kept therein. Respondent admits also that at the time he was taking money from the trust account he knew it was wrong, but "it was easy to do."

We are faced with a disciplinary matter where an attorney over a period of 8 months intentionally invaded a trust fund containing his clients' funds.

This court has long disbarred attorneys for such flagrant violation of their professional and fiduciary duties. We have said: "[t]hose few lawyers who mishandle trust funds, who fail to maintain complete records of trust funds and who fail to account and deliver funds as requested are reminded that disbarment is the usual result." *In re Deschane*, 84 Wn.2d 514, 516-17, 527 P.2d 683 (1974).

Over the years trust account violations have led to disbarment in these cases. *In re Gowan*, 104 Wash. 166, 176 P. 7 (1918); *In re Ward*, 104 Wash. 170, 176 P. 2 (1918); *In re Martin*, 107 Wash. 372, 181 P. 880 (1919); *In re Gwynn*, 179 Wash. 389, 37 P.2d 1114 (1934); *In re Grant*, 4 Wn.2d 617, 104 P.2d 602 (1940); *In re Moran*, 5 Wn.2d 679, 106 P.2d 571 (1940); *In re Beakley*, 6 Wn.2d 410, 107 P.2d 1097 (1940); *In re Scott*, 12 Wn.2d 736, 737, 121 P.2d 953 (1942); *In re McCoy*, 20 Wn.2d 884, 146 P.2d 818 (1944); *In re Grimm*, 29 Wn.2d 147, 185 P.2d 990 (1947); *In re Walsh*, 40 Wn.2d 593, 244 P.2d 868 (1952); *In re King*, 42 Wn.2d 617, 257 P.2d 219 (1953); *In re Park*, 45 Wn.2d 383, 274 P.2d 1006 (1954); *In re Dillard*, 48 Wn.2d 376, 293 P.2d 761 (1956); *In re Ward*, 54 Wn.2d 593, 343 P.2d 872 (1959); *In re Carroll*, 54 Wn.2d 633, 343 P.2d 1023 (1959); *In re Peterson*, 56 Wn.2d 187, 351 P.2d 533 (1960); *In re Griffin*, 58 Wn.2d 149, 361 P.2d 569 (1961); *In re Timothy*, 58 Wn.2d 153, 361 P.2d 642 (1961); *In re McDole*, 63 Wn.2d 962, 390 P.2d 9 (1964); *In re Marsh*, 65 Wn.2d 390, 397 P.2d 828 (1964); *In re Chantry*, 67 Wn.2d 190, 407 P.2d 160 (1965); *In re Moody*, 69 Wn.2d 808, 420 P.2d 374 (1966); *In re Warnock*, 70 Wn.2d 457, 423 P.2d 929 (1967); *In re Randall*, 72 Wn.2d 676, 435 P.2d 26 (1967); *In re Hall*, 73 Wn.2d 401, 438 P.2d 874 (1968); *In re Anderson*, 73 Wn.2d 587, 439 P.2d 981 (1968); *In re Johnson*, 74 Wn.2d 21, 442 P.2d 948 (1968); *In re Stromberg*, 75 Wn.2d 955, 452 P.2d 547 (1969); *In re Soderquist*, 78 Wn.2d 227, 472 P.2d 395 (1970); *In re Garvin*, 78 Wn.2d 832, 479 P.2d 930 (1971); *In re Slater*, 78 Wn.2d 958, 481 P.2d 564 (1971); *In re Johnson*, 81 Wn.2d 46, 499 P.2d 879 (1972); *In re Espedal*, 82 Wn.2d 834, 514 P.2d 518 (1973); *In re England*, 82 Wn.2d 121, 508 P.2d 611 (1973); *In re Delaney*, 83 Wn.2d 415, 518 P.2d 713 (1974); *In re Kirchen*, 83 Wn.2d 727, 522 P.2d 188 (1974); *In re Deschane*, 84 Wn.2d 514, 527 P.2d 683 (1974); *In re Batali*, 85 Wn.2d 246, 533 P.2d 843 (1975); *In re Smith*, 85 Wn.2d 738, 539 P.2d 83 (1975); *In re Robinson*, 89 Wn.2d 519, 573 P.2d 784 (1978); *In re Gibson*, 90 Wn.2d 440, 442, 583 P.2d 633 (1978); *In re Cary*, 90 Wn.2d 762, 585 P.2d 1161 (1978); *In re Hawkins*, 91 Wn.2d 497, 589 P.2d 247 (1979); *In re Zderic*, 92 Wn.2d 777, 600 P.2d 1297 (1979); *In re Allper*, 94 Wn.2d 456, 617 P.2d 982 (1980).

Despite these strong precedential statements that disbarment results from misuse of trust funds, there have been instances where this court has imposed less severe discipline. [W]e will look to other acts of misconduct and the presence or absence of mitigating circumstances. For instance, lack of cooperation with the bar investigation may be an aggravating circumstance. But lack of prior discipline and

full cooperation will not excuse the conduct. Furthermore, restitution and repentance do not constitute a defense.

Given this historical pattern of dealing with trust account violations, we reiterate the considerations inherent in determining the appropriate sanction:

> The two basic purposes of attorney discipline are to protect the public from future misconduct of an attorney and to preserve public confidence in the legal system.

In an individual case, however, recitation of disciplinary purposes does not resolve the issue of appropriate discipline, which must be determined by the facts and circumstances of each case. This court has reiterated several considerations in making this determination: (1) the seriousness and circumstances of the offense; (2) avoidance of repetition; (3) deterrent effect upon others; (4) maintaining respect for the legal profession; (5) assurance that those who seek legal services will be insulated from unprofessional conduct.

There is no question that respondent's violations were serious and intentional. Only when faced with a bar investigation did respondent disburse the Brandts' funds. But at that time he took other trust funds to cover his earlier defalcations. Finally, respondent compounded his violations of his duty to the public and the bar by falsely and knowingly alleging that his trust account was properly maintained.

Admittedly respondent is now remorseful and contrite. Nothing less would be expected. His remorse is not impressive, however, when viewed in light of his attempts at concealment.

Public confidence in the legal system would hardly be maintained and furthered by merely suspending a lawyer for 14 intentional violations of his clients' funds followed by attempts to cover up the violation by filing a knowingly false affidavit.

In conclusion, there are no mitigating circumstances that justify not applying the usual sanction of disbarment for intentional use of clients' funds.

Respondent John M. Rosellini is hereby disbarred and his name is stricken from the roll of attorneys in this state. Since we have not been furnished a statement of costs and expenses, none are awarded.

DOLLIVER, J. (dissenting).

John M. Rosellini is guilty. There can be no mistake in that. The record is clear as to his violation of the Discipline Rules for Attorneys and the Code of Professional Responsibility. As Mr. Rosellini states, he did a "terrible thing." He brought disgrace to himself, shame to his family name, and public outcry against himself and his profession.

In addition to the two traditional purposes given by this court for attorney discipline, there is another purpose which is inherent in all of the discipline cases. It is perhaps the major purpose of discipline although the court has consistently denied it exists. That purpose is punishment. A wrong has been committed; the court determines the attorney will pay the penalty. The penalty received is the penalty deserved.

Although the court is loath to say so, it is punishment in the sense of penalty that provides the real engine for lawyer discipline. The moral sensibilities of the bar — and perhaps the public — have been outraged. There has been a violation and an appropriate punishment will be meted out to the offender. Once the court forthrightly faces up to the punishment function of bar discipline and does not disguise it under a variety of high-sounding and self-serving phrases, I believe it will be able to administer discipline more logically.

* * *

There remains the question of punishment. A grave offense was committed. It was an affront to the bar and to the moral standards of society. It cannot be condoned; the offender must be punished. What should the punishment be? Against the egregious nature of his offense I believe must be balanced the nature of the punishment John Rosellini already has received. As the record shows, his offenses were for days the major topic of interest in the media. The words of counsel in respondent's brief eloquently describe the situation:

Certain it is, however, that right at the height of the 1980 final election campaign for State Attorney General, after respondent had been nominated by the Democratic Party, the [Seattle Post-Intelligencer] commenced publication of the series of front-page articles about respondent, which articles are in this record as part of Exhibits 7-44, inclusive. And of course the information was picked up and used by other newspapers across the State — it was too sensational to be ignored. The P-I's articles are masterpieces of that genre of journalistic work. They even appeared serially, thus exciting the maximum of curiosity. Buy tomorrow's paper and we'll tell you more of this evil man. Watch him hanging there, turning slowly in the withering winds of our questions and our further disclosures.

Well, I mean no invidious criticism of the P-I. Its conduct was in the course of the nature of the press institution. As well be indignant with the crow who eats the robin's eggs or the weasel who runs the rabbit to earth.

* * *

I would suspend John M. Rosellini for 2 years and, thus, I dissent.

NOTES, QUESTIONS, AND EXAMPLES

To clarify a few technical difficulties that lawyers have had with client trust accounts, a few modest changes were made to Model Rule 1.15 in the February 2002 amendments.

First, a new subsection (b) was added to allow lawyers to put the lawyer's own funds in a trust account for the sole purpose of covering bank service charges.

Second, a new subsection (c) was added to make clear that when a client pays fees or expenses in advance of the lawyer earning those fees or incurring those expenses, the lawyer must place those funds in a client account, withdrawing them as the fees are earned or the expenses incurred.

Third, old subsection (c), now subsection (e), was amended to instruct lawyers in possession of disputed funds that they must distribute the portions of those funds about which there is no dispute.

D. COMPETENCE AND DILIGENCE

Competence and diligence are core lawyer duties. MR 1.1 and 1.3. Together, they form the Model Rules' analog to the Model Code's duty to provide the client with zealous representation within the bounds of the law and its basic competence standard. *See* Canons 6 and 7; DR 6-101, 7-101, 7-102.

Competence requires that the lawyer possess and exercise on the client's behalf "the legal knowledge, skill, thoroughness, and preparation reasonably necessary for the representation." MR 1.1.

COMMITTEE ON PROFESSIONAL ETHICS AND CONDUCT OF THE IOWA STATE BAR ASSOCIATION v. NADLER
467 N.W.2d 250 (Iowa 1991)

In May 1990, the Committee on Professional Ethics and Conduct of the Iowa State Bar Association (committee) charged Isadore Nadler with three counts of unethical and unprofessional conduct. Following hearing, a division of the Grievance Commission of the Supreme Court of Iowa (commission) found Nadler had violated provisions of the Iowa Code of Professional Responsibility for Lawyers. The commission recommended Nadler's license to practice law be suspended for a period of three years.

Isadore Nadler was admitted to practice law in Iowa in 1950. He maintained a law practice in Waterloo, Iowa, from 1953 until his license was suspended by us in August of 1989. He also secured a real estate license in 1989.

I. GREER MATTER

The commission found Nadler violated DR 6-101 (failure to act competently) in his handling of a legal matter entrusted to him. The commission also found he violated DR 6-102 (attempt to limit liability to client) when he offered to pay his clients the sum of $1900 after discovering the statute of limitations had run out on the personal injury claim he was handling.

David Greer, Jr., a seventeen-year-old high school senior, was injured in a collision on February 8, 1985. He was a passenger on a school bus that was struck by an automobile driven by Leland Sommerfelt and owned by Ronald Sommerfelt. David's mother retained Nadler to represent David and his parents in connection with their claims against the Waterloo Independent School District and the Sommerfelts.

Nadler secured a patient's waiver and obtained medical records relating to David's injuries. He contacted the insurance carriers of both the school district and the Sommerfelts advising them of his employment as legal counsel for the Greers.

In January of 1986, Nadler obtained a partial settlement of his clients' claims.

The school district insurance carrier paid $2,000 to David and his parents for a covenant not to sue and a limited release. Nadler retained $500 as legal fees and $100 as advance costs from the cash settlement. He told the Greers he was going to bring suit against the Sommerfelts.

The two-year statute of limitations ran on the personal injury claims without Nadler having filed suit. In March 1987, the Greers contacted Nadler to find out what was going on. Nadler told them the lawsuit had not been filed and that the statute of limitations had run. Nadler offered to pay the Greers the sum of $1,900, this being the amount he considered their claim was worth less his one-third contingent fee and less $100 for expenses advanced. The offer was not accepted. Rather, the Greers brought an action for legal malpractice against Nadler. The action was tried to the court, and on November 8, 1988, the court entered judgment against Nadler for $35,500 ($35,000 for David and $500 for his parents). The judgment has not been satisfied. The Greers have foreclosed on two parcels of real estate and garnished attorney fees to secure partial satisfaction of the judgment.

Based on these facts, the commission found Nadler had violated two disciplinary rules. In addition to the transcript of the proceedings before the commission, we review the exhibits offered and received at the hearing. Here, a transcript of the evidence in the legal malpractice action was received as an exhibit. In our de novo review, we agree with the commission's findings but make additional findings and conclusions.

Although Nadler, in September of 1985, secured from Dr. Crouse, an orthopedic specialist, a written medical evaluation suggesting David had no long-term disability, Nadler was aware David continued to have back and knee problems after the evaluation. After securing the partial settlement in January of 1986, Nadler suggested David get a second opinion from Dr. Delbridge, an orthopedic surgeon. On April 25, 1986, Greer was examined by Dr. Delbridge. Greer continued to experience back and knee problems. He was again seen by Dr. Delbridge on December 24, 1986. In the opinion of Dr. Delbridge, Greer's injury to his back and knee would continue, and he would have future pain and problems. In his opinion, these injuries were related to the accident on February 8, 1985. Although he was aware of Dr. Delbridge's examination of his client, Nadler did not talk to the surgeon or secure a written report from him.

In August and October of 1986 the claims representative of Sommerfelt's insurance carrier wrote letters to Nadler requesting the opportunity to sit down and discuss possible settlement of the Greers' claim and also requesting Nadler furnish an update of the medical condition of his client. Nadler did not respond to these requests.

Although Nadler advised Greers of his failure to timely file suit, he did not alert them of their possible malpractice claim nor did he advise them to seek the advice of another attorney. Contrary to Nadler's explanation, we do not find his offer of $1,900 was intended as a gift.

Nadler acted pro se in defense of the legal malpractice suit. The district court found Nadler's handling of the Greers' legal matter was negligent in (1) attempting to negotiate a settlement of the claim without having appropriate medical information upon which to value the claim, (2) attempting to negotiate a settlement at a level that was not authorized by his clients, and (3) allowing the statute of limitations to run without filing a suit.

The court also found Nadler displayed the same lack of professional care and competence in defending the legal malpractice case as he did in representing the Greers. He failed to respond to requests for admissions. He responded untimely and improperly to the plaintiffs' motion for partial summary judgment. He filed an untimely request to designate additional expert witnesses. He was late for the beginning of the trial, and he was late in returning from several recesses during the trial. After the completion of the plaintiffs' case, Nadler's request for a recess was granted. However, Nadler failed to return to court following the recess, and the trial was completed in Nadler's absence with no additional evidence presented on his behalf. No appeal was taken from the district court judgment.

Nadler was incomp. even for himself.

While the legal malpractice action was pending, Nadler conveyed two parcels of real estate to his wife without consideration. On November 10, 1988, one day after judgment was entered, the Greers filed an action to set aside the Nadler conveyance as fraudulent. Following hearing, the court on February 21, 1989, granted the Greers' motion for summary judgment and set aside the Nadler deed. No appeal was taken. Nadler acknowledged he "goofed" by not preparing a proper resistance to the motion for summary judgment. The two parcels of real estate held by Nadler were sold at sheriff's sale, and the proceeds of approximately $22,000 were applied as partial satisfaction of the judgment.

shady transfer.

While an honest mistake made by a lawyer in handling a client's legal matter does not ordinarily afford a basis for disciplinary action, incompetence is grounds for disciplinary action. There is a convincing preponderance of evidence of Nadler's neglect and indifference in handling legal work. We find the acts and conduct of Nadler, as charged in count I of the complaint, violated DR 6-101 and DR 6-102(A) as found by the commission and, in addition, violated EC 1-5 (requires high standards of professional conduct), EC 6-1 (requires competent and proper care in representing clients), EC 6-4 (requires adequate preparation for and appropriate attention to legal work), EC 9-2 (requires lawyers fully and promptly to inform clients of developments in matters being handled for the client), EC 9-6 (requires lawyers to uphold the integrity of the profession and to inspire confidence of clients and public), and DR 1-102(A) (prohibits lawyer misconduct).

harsh but he was particularly bad

* * *

IV. FAILURE TO RESPOND

Nadler received from the committee six letters advising him that the committee had received complaints regarding three separate matters that later were identified in the three counts of the complaint filed with the commission. The notices were received by Nadler between November 1988 and May 1989. They advised him that his failure to respond could result in a separate complaint. The commission found Nadler's failure to respond was misconduct.

We find the failure to cooperate and to answer inquiries from the committee violates EC 1-4 (requires lawyers to assist committee having responsibility for administration of disciplinary rules). DR 1-102(A)(1) (prohibits violation of disciplinary rule), DR 1-102(A)(5) (prohibits conduct prejudicial to the administration of justice) and DR 1-102(A)(6) (prohibits any other conduct that adversely reflects on the fitness to practice law). An attorney commits a separate ethical violation by failing to answer the committee's request for a reply. *See also* Annotation, *Failure to Co-Operate with or Obey Disciplinary Authorities as Ground for Disciplining Attorney — Modern Cases*, 37 A.L.R. 4th 646 (1985).

V. DISPOSITION

*   *   *

Under the circumstances, we find the commission's recommendation of a three year suspension appropriate, but we do not believe it is appropriate to have the suspension date back to August 16, 1989. We do not consider the delay between the date of the events prompting the filing of the complaint and the actual filing of the complaint by the committee in May of 1990 as a mitigating factor. Nothing that has occurred during the delay mitigates the seriousness of Nadler's action and conduct.

Accordingly, we extend the suspension of Nadler's license to practice law indefinitely, with no possibility of reinstatement for three years from the filing of this decision and order. The requirements for reinstatement set forth in our prior opinion filed August 16, 1989, shall remain.

We further order that the costs of this action be assessed against Nadler. Iowa Sup. Ct. R. 118.22.

License Suspended.

NOTES, QUESTIONS, AND EXAMPLES

1.   How is Nadler's "goof" different from Neale's voluntary dismissal-statute of limitations mistake? (*See Florida Bar v. Neale*, Chapter II.)

2.   Diligence is the timeliness aspect of competence. Lawyers are obligated to be diligent in their clients' behalf. Perhaps the most commonly filed complaint about lawyer conduct is that of delay and neglect. Diligence requires a persistent pursuit of the client's matter. MR 1.3. The duty of diligence is related to the lawyer's duty to expedite matters consistent with client interests. MR 3.2. The most common pattern in a diligence duty violation involves a lawyer who begins work on a client's matter, perhaps even by filing a civil complaint, but then does little or nothing to pursue the matter to a conclusion.

3.   How do the Model Rules' combination of competence and diligence differ from the Model Code's "zealous advocacy within the bounds of the law"?

E.   COMMUNICATION AND SHARED DECISION-MAKING

Lawyers owe clients a duty to communicate with clients and to meaningfully share decision-making responsibilities with them. MR 1.2 and 1.4. These two duties work together, neither one being particularly meaningful without the other.

The communication duty is critical to maintaining a quality lawyer-client relationship. It is related to the duties regarding shared decision-making, competence and diligence, and it forms the underpinning of every duty that requires client consent and consultation. MR 1.4. A lawyer must keep a client informed of the status of the client's matter and must respond to a client's reasonable requests for information. MR 1.4(a). In order for the client to be an effective partner of the lawyer in the decision-making process, and in order for the client to intelligently manage his own affairs, the lawyer must explain matters to the client sufficiently to allow the client to function and make informed decisions. MR 1.4(b).

Lawyers and clients must share decision-making responsibility. The law governing such sharing is established generally by agency law: As the client's agent, the lawyer must abide by the client's choices with various exceptions and within various constraints. Further, the lawyer lacks authority to make and implement certain decisions on the client's behalf.

Because the scope of their relationship is generally set by contract, lawyers and their clients may negotiate and settle upon the lawyer's scope of representation. Lawyer and client can negotiate over the lengths to which the lawyer is committed to proceed in the matter. The lawyer and client, for example, may agree that the lawyer will undertake representation short of litigation or through the first appeal. The lawyer and client may negotiate the breadth of the lawyer's service. They may agree, for example, that the lawyer will be responsible for legal matters relating to the client's sale of his ongoing business, but not the tax aspects of the transaction.

As a general proposition, clients set the goals or ends of the representation while lawyers generally are empowered to determine the best means to use to achieve those ends. MR 1.2(a), Comment. As a general rule, this division of decision-making responsibility serves well because it matches the relative strengths of the lawyer and client and the client's more direct relative interest in the matter. Lawyers are trained to determine and execute the means; clients have the greater interest and stake in the goals of the representation and therefore ought to retain decision-making authority in such matters.

JONES v. BARNES
463 U.S. 745 (1983)

CHIEF JUSTICE BURGER delivered the opinion of the Court.

We granted certiorari to consider whether defense counsel assigned to prosecute an appeal from a criminal conviction has a constitutional duty to raise every nonfrivolous issue requested by the defendant.

I

The jury convicted respondent of first-and second-degree robbery and second degree assault.

The Appellate Division of the Supreme Court of New York, Second Department, assigned Michael Melinger to represent respondent on appeal. Respondent sent Melinger a letter listing several claims that he felt should be raised. Included were claims that [the victim's] identification testimony should have been suppressed, that the trial judge improperly excluded psychiatric evidence, and that respondent's trial counsel was ineffective. Respondent also enclosed a copy of a pro se brief he had written.

In a return letter, Melinger accepted some but rejected most of the suggested claims, stating that they would not aid respondent in obtaining a new trial and that they could not be raised on appeal because they were not based on evidence in the record. Melinger then listed seven potential claims of error that he was considering including in his brief, and invited respondent's "reflections and suggestions" with regard to those seven issues. The record does not reveal any response to this letter.

Melinger's brief to the Appellate Division concentrated on three of the seven points he had raised in his letter to respondent: improper exclusion of psychiatric evidence, failure to suppress Butts' identification testimony, and improper cross-examination of respondent by the trial judge. In addition, Melinger submitted respondent's own pro se brief. Thereafter, respondent filed two more pro se briefs, raising three more of the seven issues Melinger had identified.

At oral argument, Melinger argued the three points presented in his own brief, but not the arguments raised in the pro se briefs. On May 22, 1978, the Appellate Division affirmed by summary order. The New York Court of Appeals denied leave to appeal.

[The Court explains that Mr. Barnes raised a claim that appellate counsel was ineffective because counsel failed to raise the issues that Barnes had suggested. —Ed.]

This Court, in holding that a state must provide counsel for an indigent appellant on his first appeal as of right, recognized the superior ability of trained counsel in the "examination into the record, research of the law, and marshaling of arguments on [the appellant's] behalf," *Douglas v. California, supra,* at 358. Yet a per se rule that the client, not the professional advocate, must be allowed to decide what issues are to be pressed [would] seriously undermine the ability of counsel to present the client's case in accord with counsel's professional evaluation.

Experienced advocates since time beyond memory have emphasized the importance of winnowing out weaker arguments on appeal and focusing on one central issue if possible, or at most on a few key issues. Justice Jackson, after observing appellate advocates for many years, stated:

> One of the first tests of a discriminating advocate is to select the question, or questions, that he will present orally. Legal contentions, like the currency, depreciate through over-issue. The mind of an appellate judge is habitually receptive to the suggestion that a lower court committed an

error. But receptiveness declines as the number of assigned errors increases. Multiplicity hints at lack of confidence in any one. . . . [Experience] on the bench convinces me that multiplying assignments of error will dilute and weaken a good case and will not save a bad one.

Jackson, *Advocacy Before the United States Supreme Court*, 25 TEMPLE L.Q. 115, 119 (1951).

A brief that raises every colorable issue runs the risk of burying good arguments — those that, in the words of the great advocate John W. Davis, "go for the jugular," Davis, *The Argument of an Appeal*, 26 A.B.A. J. 895, 897 (1940) — in a verbal mound made up of strong and weak contentions. *See generally, e.g.*, Godbold, *Twenty Pages and Twenty Minutes — Effective Advocacy on Appeal*, 30 SW. L.J. 801 (1976).[17]

Respondent points to the ABA Standards for Criminal Appeals, which appear to indicate that counsel should accede to a client's insistence on pressing a particular contention on appeal. The ABA Defense Function Standards provide, however, that, with the exceptions specified above, strategic and tactical decisions are the exclusive province of the defense counsel, after consultation with the client. In any event, the fact that the ABA may have chosen to recognize a given practice as desirable or appropriate does not mean that that practice is required by the Constitution.

This Court's decision in *Anders*, far from giving support to the new per se rule announced by the Court of Appeals, is to the contrary. *Anders* recognized that the role of the advocate "requires that he support his client's appeal to the best of his ability." Here the appointed counsel did just that. For judges to second-guess reasonable professional judgments and impose on appointed counsel a duty to raise every "colorable" claim suggested by a client would disserve the very goal of vigorous and effective advocacy that underlies *Anders*. Nothing in the Constitution or our interpretation of that document requires such a standard. The judgment of the Court of Appeals is accordingly

Reversed.

JUSTICE BLACKMUN, concurring in the judgment.

I do not join the Court's opinion, because I need not decide in this case whether there is or is not a constitutional right to a first appeal of a criminal conviction, and because I agree with Justice Brennan, and the American Bar Association, ABA Standards for Criminal Justice 21-3.2, Comment, p. 21.42 (2d ed. 1980), that, as an ethical matter, an attorney should argue on appeal all nonfrivolous claims upon

[handwritten margin note: not a Const. Issue]

---

[17] [6] The ABA Model Rules of Professional Conduct provide:

A lawyer shall abide by a client's decisions concerning the objectives of representation . . . and shall consult with the client as to the means by which they are to be pursued. . . . In a criminal case, the lawyer shall abide by the client's decision, . . . as to a plea to be entered, whether to waive jury trial and whether the client will testify.

Model Rules of Professional Conduct, Proposed Rule 1.2(a) (Final Draft 1982).

With the exception of these specified fundamental decisions, an attorney's duty is to take professional responsibility for the conduct of the case, after consulting with his client.

which his client insists. Whether or not one agrees with the Court's view of legal strategy, it seems to me that the lawyer, after giving his client his best opinion as to the course most likely to succeed, should acquiesce in the client's choice of which nonfrivolous claims to pursue.

Certainly, *Anders v. California*, 386 U.S. 738 (1967), and *Faretta v. California*, 422 U.S. 806 (1975), indicate that the attorney's usurpation of certain fundamental decisions can violate the Constitution. I agree with the Court, however, that neither my view, nor the ABA's view, of the ideal allocation of decisionmaking authority between client and lawyer necessarily assumes constitutional status where counsel's performance is "within the range of competence demanded of attorneys in criminal cases," *McMann v. Richardson*, 397 U.S. 759, 771 (1970), and "[assures] the indigent defendant an adequate opportunity to present his claims fairly in the context of the State's appellate process," *Ross v. Moffitt*, 417 U.S. 600, 616 (1974). I agree that both these requirements were met here.

NOTES, QUESTIONS, AND EXAMPLES

1.   The law is fairly clear regarding who has the decision-making authority on certain matters. Clients and not lawyers have final authority to settle matters. A lawyer is obliged to communicate to the client all bona fide offers of settlement from an opposing party, and the ultimate decision about whether or not to accept an offer of settlement is the client's.

2.   Other issues on which the client is expected to make the decision include entry of a criminal plea, whether to request a judge or jury trial, and whether or not the client will testify. Lawyers are expected to make decisions about various procedural aspects of litigation.

3.   When a lawyer represents a client whose capacity to make decisions regarding the representation is impaired, the lawyer must attempt to maintain an ordinary lawyer-client relationship to the extent possible. MR 1.14(a). Such an impairment may derive from minority or mental disability. MR 1.14(a). A lawyer may seek to have a guardian appointed to represent the interests of the client when the lawyer reasonably believes that the client cannot act in his own interest. MR 1.14(b).

4.   Congress has in some controversial ways limited lawyers communications to clients. For example, the Intelligence Reform and Terrorism Prevention Act, Pub. L. No. 108-458, 118 Stat. 3638 (2004), criminalizes "expert advice or assistance" given to groups designated as "a foreign terrorist organization." This prohibition was attacked by lawyers wanting to provide legal assistance to the Kurdistan Workers Party and the Liberation Tigers of Tamil Eelam regarding non-violent and lawful peace-making activities of the organizations. The Supreme Court upheld the ban on lawyer assistance. *Holder v. Humanitarian Law Project*, 130 S. Ct. 2705 (2010). In addition, the Bankruptcy Abuse Prevention and Consumer Protection Act of 2005, Pub. L. No. 109-8, 119 Stat. 23, prohibits certain advice to bankruptcy clients and requires lawyers to make certain statements in their advertising of bankruptcy services. The Supreme Court has also upheld these speech obligations and limitations. *Milavetz, Gallop & Milavetz v. United States*, 130 S. Ct. 1324

(2010). See a discussion of these and other similar cases in Renee Newman Knake, *Attorney Advice and the First Amendment*, 68 WASH. & LEE L. REV. 639 (2011).

A lawyer's representation of a client does not implicate the lawyer's sharing of, or responsibility for, the client's cause or views regarding matters relevant to the representation. Lawyers operate under the principle that they are independent of their clients' politics or moral views. MR 1.2(b).

As an underpinning to the scope of decision-making between lawyer and client, lawyers are prohibited from counseling or assisting their clients in the commission of crimes or frauds. MR 1.2(d). When a lawyer does so advise or assist, the lawyer is not only subject to discipline but is liable criminally or civilly as the case may be. This prohibition does not prevent a lawyer from either discussing proposed courses of action with a client nor assisting a client in the pursuit of a test case. Clients may at times wish to test the application of current law. When they do so in good faith, a lawyer is permitted to assist. Indeed, without the assistance of lawyers in such cases, little would change in the law. Model Rule 1.2(d)'s prohibition is not intended to prevent a lawyer from discussing various proposed courses of action with a client. If a client proposes a course of action, the lawyer is permitted to investigate the lawfulness of the client's proposal and advise the client of the results of the lawyer's research and analysis. To require otherwise would prohibit the lawyer from engaging in the process of counseling a client against engaging in unlawful conduct.

William H. Simon,[18] *Should Lawyers Obey The Law?*
Symposium: W.M. Keck Foundation Forum on the
Teaching of Legal Ethics
38 WM. & MARY L. REV. 217 (1996)[19]

At the same time that it denies authority to nonlegal norms, the dominant view of legal ethics (the "Dominant View") insists on deference to legal ones. "Zealous advocacy" stops at the "bounds of the law."

* * *

The basic difficulty is that the plausibility of a duty of obedience to law depends on how we define law. If we define law in narrow Positivist terms, then we cannot provide plausible reasons why someone should obey a norm just because it is "law." In order to give substance to the idea that law entails respect and obligation, we have to resort to broader, more substantive notions of law. These broader notions of law, however, are hostile to both the narrowness and the categorical quality of the Dominant View's idea of legal obligation. I and others have argued elsewhere that these broader notions often require advocacy to stop short of the limits prescribed by the Dominant View.

* * *

------

[18] Kenneth and Harle Montgomery Professor of Public Interest Law, Stanford University.

[19] Copyright © 1996 by the William & Mary Law Review; William H. Simon. Reprinted with permission.

Suppose we are in a jurisdiction with an old-fashioned divorce statute that conditions divorce upon proof of one of a small number of grounds, such as adultery or abuse. A childless husband and wife have agreed that they want a divorce and on reasonable arrangements for separating their financial affairs. The lawyer believes that the proposed divorce and financial arrangements are in the interests of each of them. They cannot honestly prove, however, any of the grounds the statute requires. Suppose further, as was true in some of the jurisdictions that used to have such statutes, that it is possible, at little risk to either lawyer or clients, for the lawyer to help the couple get a divorce by coaching and presenting perjured testimony about, say, adultery. The Dominant View forbids the lawyer to help clients in this way, no matter how strongly she believes that the couple is entitled to a divorce. If the lawyer believes the divorce statute is unjust, it says, she should work to induce the legislature to change it. This view condemns coaching and presenting perjury as a transgression of the "bounds of the law."

The Dominant View, however, is considerably less clear about lawyer activities that bear a less direct relation to client illegality, in particular, advice that it is likely to encourage or facilitate illegal conduct. Some advice — for example, information about the core terms of a statute — is clearly both a right of the client and a core function of lawyering. Other forms of advice — say, about where to hide from the police or how to build a bomb — clearly represent improper participation in illegal conduct.

However, at least one form of advice that clients often seek is harder to classify. This is advice about the enforcement practices of officials. Suppose I say to a tax client that, while the aggressive position she wants to take is unlikely to survive an audit, less than five percent of returns in her class are in fact audited. Or suppose, knowing my client's expenses are considerably lower than seventy percent of revenues, I tell her that the IRS's practice is not to question returns for businesses like hers unless they show expenses above seventy percent. Such advice is probably not unlawful, but since its only effect is to impede the enforcement process, it is troubling.

The Dominant View has yet to produce a clear answer to the question of whether such advice is improper. It hesitates between, on the one hand, defining it as legal advice and thus categorically appropriate, and on the other hand, defining it as assisting illegal conduct and thus categorically improper.

In fact, neither answer is plausible. The only satisfactory answer calls for contextual judgment. Most lawyers will readily concede this in the case of enforcement advice, for this is one area where the commitment of the Dominant View to categorical judgment is out of step with mainstream views and practices. The conclusion may be harder to accept in the case of direct participation, such as the Divorce Perjury story, but the same considerations that support contextual judgment in the indirect cases apply here as well.

* * *

Positivism has a strong affinity with the commitment of the Dominant View to categorical judgment. The Positivist perspective facilitates categorical judgment by banishing a broad range of potentially relevant factors (the putatively nonlegal ones) and by providing for the rigid priority of jurisdictional over substantive norms.

The Dominant View conjoins the Positivist notion of law with a commitment to obedience to law (and only law). The narrow way in which it defines law, however, makes it hard to explain why law should be regarded as binding.

*   *   *

We now return to the problems of divorce perjury and enforcement advice discussed above as illustrations of the treatment in the Dominant View of direct and indirect participation in illegality.

Begin with the latter problem, because the inadequacy of categorical approaches is most obvious here. In at least some cases, enforcement advice would be unacceptable to nearly everyone. For example, the client is a serial rapist who wants information about the schedules and routes of police patrols in the area where he plans to strike next. Giving such information might constitute unlawful assistance under the criminal law, but that is far from clear. If it is not itself illegal, then it is not unethical under the Dominant View, and that surely is an objection to the Dominant View.

On the other hand, hardly anyone is going to support a categorical ban on such information either. Many feel strongly that clients are entitled to know the extent to which the laws against fornication, sodomy, misprision of felony (failing to report someone else's criminal activity), small stakes gambling, marijuana possession, and nonpayment of employment taxes for part-time domestic workers are unenforced or underenforced.

Health and safety and environmental regulatory enforcement also resist categorical treatment. Where evasive behavior threatens serious harm that the regulatory scheme is designed to protect against, advice that facilitates evasion seems wrong. On the other hand, sometimes evasion seems not only not to threaten major harm, but to be acceptable to the enforcement authorities and perhaps even the legislature. Maybe the agency underenforces because it thinks the statutory standards are too strict. Maybe it underenforces because the legislature, divided on the efficacy of the statute, has cut the agency's enforcement budget, intending to limit enforcement.

Of course, there are objections to this type of administrative and legislative behavior. There is no doubt, however, that it occurs, and given that it occurs, it seems both unfair and inefficient to preclude lawyers from providing relevant information about enforcement practices.

Any plausible assessment of the propriety of enforcement advice requires a willingness to distinguish the relative weights of different substantive norms. This requires an at least moderately Substantive approach and contextual judgment.

Some cases are easy. (Although not everyone will have the same list of easy cases, each person will have some list of cases she finds easy, and some cases will appear on most people's lists). Advice that facilitates violence and largescale property crime will usually seem clearly inappropriate. Advice that facilitates moderate speeding, misprision of felony, and consensual fornication will usually seem proper, or at least tolerable.

Other cases are harder. For example, playing the "tax lottery" by submitting a weakly grounded tax claim, knowing it is unlikely to be audited. The case is potentially hard because of the possibility that, while the claim may be weak in terms of the narrow positive law, it may be stronger when viewed more broadly and substantively. Playing the "tax lottery" might then be viewed as an appropriate form of nullification of a normatively weak positive law. This may seem unlikely — it does to me — but the point is that a plausible defense of advice that has little function other than to facilitate evasion requires the type of principled Substantive justification associated with nullification.

Although it may seem more radical in the context of direct lawyer illegality, the same analysis applies there. We have already noted the broad variety of circumstances in which the culture accepts, and occasionally exalts, direct violation of the positive law. Most of these examples, however, involve citizens in general rather than lawyers, and some lawyers believe that their duties differ in this regard. These lawyers feel that they have a stronger obligation to the law than lay people because they publicly profess commitment to it, have a strong exemplary influence on the lay public, or acquire special privileges through participation in a regulated monopoly. Thus, a categorical prohibition of direct participation in illegality makes more sense for lawyers than lay people.

Of course, this argument is yet another variation on the jurisprudential mistake we have noted repeatedly. It does not follow from the fact that lawyers have a stronger obligation to the "law" that the type of conduct we are considering is less appropriate for them. For the conceptions of law most compatible with strong obligations are Substantive, and on a Substantive conception, obligation to "law" may require violation of some legal norms in order to vindicate more basic ones.

The argument comes close to making explicit the effect I noted above regarding the Dominant View's jurisprudential commitments. By adopting a Positivist notion of law, it characterizes the considerations favoring compliance as legal and those weighing against it as nonlegal, perhaps "moral." If we accept the definitional premise, unless we are prepared to reject the appealing proposition that lawyers have an exceptionally strong obligation to law, we will find it very hard to support lawyer noncompliance.

However, there is no reason why we should accept the premise. Many of the most important reasons weighing toward noncompliance can be aptly expressed in legal — especially nullification — terms. For example, perhaps the strongest case for lawyer participation in the Divorce Perjury example would be to portray it as an instance of Calabresian nullification. First, the statute is an old one. Second, it is out of harmony with more recent legal developments that imply that, where there are no children, the social interest in preserving marriage is much weaker and the individual interests in structuring one's own intimate relations are much stronger than the statute presupposes. Third, there are apparent institutional dysfunctions that provide more likely explanations for the failure to repeal the statute than current popular support. Perhaps the statute is supported by only a small minority. This group would not be able to secure the enactment of the statute today, but it can block repeal because it is well-organized; because most who oppose the statute feel less intensely; and because those who are tangibly harmed by the statute, such as the clients in question here, are not able to organize (because their status is hard to anticipate and episodic) and relatively poor (because affluent people can avoid its effects by taking advantage of the more accommodating laws of other states).

Of course, we should consider why, if there is a strong case for nullification, it has to be accomplished by the lawyer rather than, as Calabresi proposed, the court. Why not have the lawyer bring an action on the true facts urging the court to nullify and grant the divorce? One answer is that most states reject judicial nullification except on constitutional grounds, which might not be available. Even if judges could nullify, they might refuse to do so because, for example, they are unwilling to take the heat from the small but passionate minority that intensely supports the statute. Or perhaps the judges would think that the existence of such a minority would make nullification illegitimate. It might be, however, that the statute is of largely symbolic importance to this group, and it has no stake in low visibility enforcement decisions. Thus, while public judicial nullification would not be feasible, low visibility ad hoc lawyer nullification would be.

F. TERMINATING REPRESENTATION

The formal lawyer-client relationship ends when representation terminates. Despite termination, many lawyer duties to clients continue, such as confidentiality and a limited conflict avoidance duty (see Chapters IV and V). Clients have an absolute right to discharge counsel. From the lawyer side, withdrawal from representation is a critically important device for the lawyer who is faced with the prospect that continued representation of the client will result in a violation of the ethics code or other law.

1. Mandatory Withdrawal

Under some circumstances, lawyers are required to withdraw from representation, thereby terminating the lawyer-client relationship. Failure to withdraw under these circumstances subjects the lawyer to discipline. MR 1.16(a).

MARICOPA COUNTY PUBLIC DEFENDER'S OFFICE v. SUPERIOR COURT
927 P.2d 822 (Ariz. Ct. App. 1996)

NOYES, JUDGE.

These special actions arise from two unrelated cases in which the Maricopa County Public Defender's Office ("the public defender") moved to withdraw on grounds that an ethical conflict existed between its duty to zealously represent a current client (the defendant) and its duty of loyalty to a former client (an adverse witness). In each case, the trial court denied the motion because counsel failed to disclose confidential information about the former client. The public defender then filed petitions for special action, arguing that the trial court abused its discretion and that we should accept jurisdiction and remand with directions to grant the motion to withdraw. We consolidated the actions, accepted jurisdiction, and granted the requested relief.

* * *

II

On November 27, 1995, the superior court appointed the public defender to represent Clarence Charles Nelson on a burglary charge. The case was assigned to Deputy Public Defender Diane Enos, who soon interviewed Shawna Debus, who had been arrested with Nelson, and determined that she was a potential unindicted coconspirator and had given the police inculpatory statements about Nelson.

On December 7, Enos learned from her conflicts check that the public defender represented Debus on charges "similar" to Nelson's, and that Debus was to be sentenced on December 15. Enos filed a "Motion to Determine Counsel" and requested a hearing. At the ex parte hearing, Deputy Public Defender Christopher Johns appeared with Enos and, after stating the facts, avowed that an ethical conflict existed requiring withdrawal as Nelson's counsel because the public defender's file on Debus contained confidential information that should be used to impeach her.

Judge Rogers advised that avowals were not sufficient; that counsel needed to show "something that another — that an attorney wouldn't come across, or to put it another way, that you learned because of looking through the client's file. . . . [Y]ou're going to have to give me what I'll call some meat rather than just talking in these broad generalities as to why I should allow you to withdraw." The court advised that it would seal any confidential information counsel disclosed and would recuse itself if the information affected its impartiality. Counsel declined to disclose any confidential information and the court denied the motion to withdraw.

Also on November 27, 1995, the public defender was appointed to represent Frank Rangel on a burglary charge. The case was assigned to Deputy Public Defender Chelli Wallace, who conducted a conflicts check and learned that two people with Rangel at relevant times were former clients of the public defender. Wallace reviewed the office files and discovered confidential information to impeach Juan Salas, whom the public defender had represented in various juvenile court proceedings, one of which was a burglary charge.

Rangel's defense was that he was sitting in the car, unaware that Salas was committing a burglary. Salas did not support this defense, but the victim arguably did: the victim identified Salas as the one who came out of the backyard and shot him, and he identified Rangel as the one sitting in the car. Salas, however, had told police that he, Salas, was not in the backyard, and he did not shoot the victim; he was sitting in the back seat of the car when the victim was shot. Salas also stated to police that he had told Rangel not to do a burglary because he, Salas, did not want to get in trouble. (The other former client told police that he, himself, was sitting in the car and knew nothing about a burglary, but he did honk the horn to alert Rangel, who was in the backyard.)

Wallace filed a motion to withdraw, supported by a confidential memorandum containing the above-related facts. Judge Seidel denied the motion, explaining in a minute entry that:

> [T]here is nothing in the confidential memorandum which sets forth or describes what, if any, confidential information was obtained from either witness in the course of the prior representation which could be used in this case if the person was called as a witness and if counsel had to cross-examine the person. This Court is therefore unable to find a conflict, and accordingly, the motion to withdraw is denied.

After Wallace received a telephonic, informal ethics opinion from the State Bar advising that continued representation of Rangel would be an ethical violation, she moved for reconsideration of the motion to withdraw. At the ensuing open-court hearing, the court said it assumed that the public defender's file on Salas contained information that would benefit Rangel, but "my understanding is that you [Wallace] have to make a showing that you have got some kind of information that you can use to cross-examine [Salas] . . . that nobody else can get at, such as an attorney/client conversation." The court stated its presumption that what Wallace knew about Salas was available in the juvenile court file, and that new counsel could access that file with a court order. Wallace did not disclose any confidential information to overcome the court's presumption, and the court denied the motion for reconsideration.

III

The State advises that "the gist of this action is whether defense counsel or the trial court is going to decide if there is a conflict of interest necessitating disqualification of counsel," but we disagree with this "either-or" proposition.

Defense counsel and the trial court each decide something here: counsel decides whether to file a motion to withdraw, and the court decides whether to grant it. As we see it, the issue has to do with disclosure: the question is whether the trial court should require defense counsel to disclose confidential information when counsel avows that counsel has an ethical conflict requiring withdrawal. We conclude that ordinarily the trial court should not do that.

*   *   *

In the State's view, the ultimate decision on those [withdrawal] matters must remain with the trial judge; otherwise unscrupulous defense attorneys might abuse their "authority," presumably for purposes of delay or obstruction of the orderly conduct of the trial.

The State has an obvious interest in avoiding such abuses. But our holding does not undermine that interest. When an untimely motion for separate counsel is made for dilatory purposes, our holding does not impair the trial court's ability to deal with counsel who resort to such tactics. Nor does our holding preclude a trial court from exploring the adequacy of the basis of defense counsel's representations regarding a conflict of interests without improperly requiring disclosure of the confidential communications of the client.

We also note the Comment to ER 1.16, which concerns motions to withdraw based on client demands that counsel engage in unprofessional conduct: "The court may wish an explanation for the withdrawal, while the lawyer may be bound to keep confidential the facts that would constitute such an explanation. The lawyer's statement that professional considerations require termination of the representation ordinarily should be accepted as sufficient."

IV

In each of these special actions, we conclude that the trial court abused its discretion in denying the motion to withdraw, given what defense counsel had timely shown: facts establishing an apparent conflict of interest, compliance with the public defender's conflicts policy, an understanding of the applicable rules and cases, an avowal that counsel had an ethical conflict requiring withdrawal, and no reason to reject that avowal.

Relief has already been granted by separate orders directing the trial court to grant the public defender's motions to withdraw.

2.   Permissive Withdrawal

In some instances lawyers are permitted but not required to withdraw. The practical effect of this rule is to allow lawyers to withdraw from representation in the enumerated circumstances without breaching a duty of continued representation to the client. MR 1.16(b).

Without regard to any cause for withdrawal, a lawyer may withdraw if it can be done without material adverse effect to the client. MR 1.16(b).

Even if some harm may come to the client from the withdrawal, a lawyer may withdraw when any of the following causes exist. A lawyer is required to withdraw when the lawyer knows that the client is using the lawyer's services to perpetrate crimes or frauds. MR 1.16(a)(1). When there is somewhat less certainty that the lawyer's services will result in crimes or frauds, but the lawyer nonetheless reasonably believes that the client is engaging in conduct that is criminal or fraudulent, the lawyer may withdraw. MR 1.16(b)(1). When the lawyer learns that past services of the lawyer have been used by the client to perpetrate a crime or fraud, the lawyer may withdraw even if it does not appear that the lawyer's current services for the client are being so used. MR 1.16(b)(2). This rule permits a lawyer to withdraw from a client's representation and distance herself from the client's crimes or frauds at the earliest possible opportunity to do so.

When, after the lawyer has advised to the contrary, a client intends to continue with a course of conduct that the lawyer finds morally repugnant or imprudent, even though lawful, the lawyer may withdraw. MR 1.16(b)(3). When a client has failed to meet the client's obligations, most often to pay the lawyer's reasonable fee, the lawyer must first warn the client that the lawyer intends to withdraw if the client does not meet his obligations. If the client persists in failing to meet obligations after the warning, the lawyer may withdraw. MR 1.16(b)(4). If the representation will result in unreasonable financial burden to the lawyer, the lawyer may withdraw. This financial burden is not a mere loss, but is on the same order as the sort of financial burden that would permit a lawyer to decline a court appointment. MR 1.16(b)(5).

If a client has made the representation unreasonably difficult for the lawyer, the lawyer may withdraw. MR 1.16(b)(5). If good cause exists of a kind not enumerated by the rule, the lawyer may withdraw. MR 1.16(b)(6).

INTERNATIONAL NOTES

1.   The umbrella European standards for ending lawyer-client relationships are much more explicit. The CCBE says that withdrawal is not allowed by default. If the lawyer can show that the client can find alternative representation in time to avoid prejudice, he can then withdraw according to the CCBE. CCBE Rule 3.1.4. Individual countries allow withdrawal in a variety of circumstances. Italian lawyers, for example, have a right to withdraw that is so broad, that there are no explicit rules. As long as the lawyer gives the client adequate notice and adequate information, the lawyer can withdraw. ETHICAL CODE FOR ITALIAN LAWYERS, art. 47.

2.   In China, the Lawyers Law provides that, "Once they have accepted an appointment, lawyers may not refuse to defend or represent a client without proper reason." Proper reasons include that the subject matter of the appointment violates the law, the client uses the services provided by the lawyer to engage in illegal activities or the client conceals facts. When a proper reason exists, lawyers have the right to refuse to defend or represent such client. LAWYERS LAW, art. 29 (P.R.C.).

3.   Duties upon Termination of the Lawyer-Client Relationship

Even when a lawyer has good cause to withdraw, a court may order the lawyer to continue the representation. MR 1.16(c). When ordered to continue, a lawyer must continue the representation. Such an order will often come during or on the eve of trial and be issued by a judge who is trying to thwart a client's attempt to delay the proceedings by switching lawyers at the eleventh hour.

Although a client may discharge a lawyer without cause, the client will continue to have an obligation to pay fees to the lawyer that have already been earned. MR 1.16(d).

ROSENBERG v. LEVIN
409 So. 2d 1016 (Fla. 1982)

This is a petition to review a decision of the Third District Court of Appeal. The issue to be decided concerns the proper basis for compensating an attorney discharged without cause by his client after he has performed substantial legal services under a valid contract of employment. We find conflict with our decision in *Goodkind v. Wolkowsky*, 132 Fla. 63, 180 So. 538 (1938).

We hold that a lawyer discharged without cause is entitled to the reasonable value of his services on the basis of quantum meruit, but recovery is limited to the maximum fee set in the contract entered into for those services. We have concluded that without this limitation, the client would be penalized for the discharge and the lawyer would receive more than he bargained for in his initial contract. In the instant case, we reject the contention of the respondent lawyer that he is entitled to $55,000 as the reasonable value of his services when his contract fee was $10,000. We affirm the decision of the district court and recede from our prior decision in *Goodkind*.

The facts of this case reflect the following. Levin hired Rosenberg and Pomerantz to perform legal services pursuant to a letter agreement which provided for a $10,000 fixed fee, plus a contingent fee equal to fifty percent of all amounts recovered in excess of $600,000. Levin later discharged Rosenberg and Pomerantz without cause before the legal controversy was resolved and subsequently settled the matter for a net recovery of $500,000. Rosenberg and Pomerantz sued for fees based on a "quantum meruit" evaluation of their services. After lengthy testimony, the trial judge concluded that quantum meruit was indeed the appropriate basis for compensation and awarded Rosenberg and Pomerantz $55,000. The district court also agreed that quantum meruit was the appropriate basis for recovery but lowered the amount awarded to $10,000, stating that recovery could in no event exceed the amount which the attorneys would have received under their contract if not prematurely discharged.

The issue submitted to us for resolution is whether the terms of an attorney employment contract limit the attorney's quantum meruit recovery to the fee set out in the contract. This issue requires, however, that we answer the broader underlying question of whether in Florida quantum meruit is an appropriate basis for compensation of attorneys discharged by their clients without cause where there is a specific employment contract.

There are two conflicting interests involved in the determination of the issue presented in this type of attorney-client dispute. The first is the need of the client to have confidence in the integrity and ability of his attorney and, therefore, the need for the client to have the ability to discharge his attorney when he loses that necessary confidence in the attorney. The second is the attorney's right to adequate compensation for work performed. To address these conflicting interests, we must consider three distinct rules.

Contract Rule

The traditional contract rule adopted by a number of jurisdictions holds that an attorney discharged without cause may recover damages for breach of contract under traditional contract principles. The measure of damages is usually the full contract price, although some courts deduct a fair allowance for services and expenses not expended by the discharged attorney in performing the balance of the contract. e.g., *Bockman v. Rorex*, 212 Ark. 948, 208 S.W.2d 991 (1948) (fixed fee contract); *Tonn v. Reuter*, 6 Wis. 2d 498, 95 N.W.2d 261 (1959) (contingency fee contract); *see generally* 1 S. Speiser, Attorneys' Fees §§ 4:24-:36 (1973). Some jurisdictions following the contract rule also permit an alternative recovery based on quantum meruit so that an attorney can elect between recovery based on the contract or the reasonable value of the performed services. e.g., *In re Downs*, 363 S.W.2d 679 (Mo.1963); *French v. Cunningham*, 149 Ind. 632, 49 N.E. 797 (1898).

See 1 S. Speiser, Attorneys' Fees § 4:36 (1973).

Support for the traditional contract theory is based on: (1) the full contract price is arguably the most rational measure of damages since it reflects the value that the parties placed on the services; (2) charging the full fee prevents the client from profiting from his own breach of contract; and (3) the contract rule is said to avoid the difficult problem of setting a value on an attorney's partially completed legal work.

Quantum Meruit Rule

To avoid restricting a client's freedom to discharge his attorney, a number of jurisdictions in recent years have held that an attorney discharged without cause can recover only the reasonable value of services rendered prior to discharge. *See, e.g., Covington v. Rhodes*, 38 N.C. App. 61, 247 S.E.2d 305 (1978), cert. denied, 296 N.C. 410, 251 S.E.2d 468 (1979); *Johnson v. Long*, 15 Ill. App. 3d 506, 305 N.E.2d 30 (1973); *State Farm Mutual Insurance Co. v. St. Joseph's Hospital*, 107 Ariz. 498, 489 P.2d 837 (1971). *See generally* 1 S. Speiser, §§ 4:28, :35-:36.

Quantum Meruit Rule Limited by the Contract Price

The third rule is an extension of the second that limits quantum meruit recovery to the maximum fee set in the contract. This limitation is believed necessary to provide client freedom to substitute attorneys without economic penalty. Without such a limitation, a client's right to discharge an attorney may be illusory and the client may in effect be penalized for exercising a right.

Conclusion

We have carefully considered all the matters presented, both on the original argument on the merits and on rehearing. It is our opinion that it is in the best interest of clients and the legal profession as a whole that we adopt the modified quantum meruit rule which limits recovery to the maximum amount of the contract fee in all premature discharge cases involving both fixed and contingency employment contracts. The attorney-client relationship is one of special trust and confidence. The client must rely entirely on the good faith efforts of the attorney in representing his interests. This reliance requires that the client have complete confidence in the integrity and ability of the attorney and that absolute fairness and candor characterize all dealings between them. These considerations dictate that clients be given greater freedom to change legal representatives than might be tolerated in other employment relationships.

Accordingly, we hold that an attorney employed under a valid contract who is discharged without cause before the contingency has occurred or before the client's matters have concluded can recover only the reasonable value of his services rendered prior to discharge, limited by the maximum contract fee. We reject both the traditional contract rule and the quantum meruit rule that allow recovery in excess of the maximum contract price because both have a chilling effect on the client's power to discharge an attorney. Under the contract rule in a contingent fee situation, both the discharged attorney and the second attorney may receive a substantial percentage of the client's final recovery. Under the unlimited quantum meruit rule, it is possible, as the instant case illustrates, for the attorney to receive a fee greater than he bargained for under the terms of his contract. Both these results are unacceptable to us.

We further follow the California view that in contingency fee cases, the cause of action for quantum meruit arises only upon the successful occurrence of the contingency. If the client fails in his recovery, the discharged attorney will similarly fail and recover nothing.

In computing the reasonable value of the discharged attorney's services, the trial court can consider the totality of the circumstances surrounding the professional relationship between the attorney and client. Factors such as time, the recovery sought, the skill demanded, the results obtained, and the attorney-client contract itself will necessarily be relevant considerations.

We conclude that this approach creates the best balance between the desirable right of the client to discharge his attorney and the right of an attorney to reasonable compensation for his services. We find the district court of appeal was correct in limiting the quantum meruit award to the contract price, and its decision is approved. It is so ordered.

NOTES, QUESTIONS, AND EXAMPLES

The ABA rejected proposals from the Ethics 2000 Commission that would have created exceptions to the duty of confidentiality permitting lawyers to reveal client confidences to prevent clients from committing future frauds and to prevent, mitigate, or rectify financial losses occasioned by a client's use of the lawyer's services to commit crimes or frauds. The "answer" at the time was the concept of "noisy withdrawal," which allowed a lawyer to withdraw and to disaffirm any communications she had made to another upon discovery that the client had used the lawyer's services to commit a fraud. This slight-of-hand approach to revealing confidential information without the necessity of an exception to the confidentiality rule was often criticized. A year after rejecting a confidentiality exception for client frauds, the Enron financial fiascos occurred and the ABA reversed itself, adopting the exceptions. A majority of states have some form of such rules currently in force. More on this in Chapter IV.

Chapter IV

CONFIDENTIALITY

Confidentiality is among the core duties that lawyers owe clients. It is, therefore, a topic that pervades the study of professional responsibility. The applicability of the duty of confidentiality is a part of the analysis in a wide range of professional responsibility rules in addition to the central confidentiality rule, Model Rule 1.6. *See, e.g.*, MR 1.2, 1.17, 4.1, 8.1(b), 8.3(c). The duty of confidentiality furthers a number of important policies. By encouraging a full sharing of information from client to lawyer, it permits sounder, better representation of the client. It permits the lawyer to know enough about the client's future actions and plans to enable the lawyer to act in the role of counsel, advising the client of lawful courses of action and discouraging unlawful or immoral courses of action.

policy

Once established, and in the absence of an exception, the duty of confidentiality prohibits the lawyer from communicating protected information at all times and in all contexts: The duty lives with the lawyer when he is at work, when he is at the PTA potluck dinner, and at all times in between.

The duty of confidentiality and the evidentiary attorney-client privilege overlap in important respects. This overlap creates confusion. A basic understanding of the evidentiary privilege is a necessary ingredient to an understanding of the ethical duty of confidentiality. While the ethical duty of confidentiality is substantially broader in scope than the evidentiary privilege, because the ethical duty has an exception for those occasions when a court orders a lawyer to communicate otherwise protected client information, the effectiveness of the privilege is often controlling. For example, if a lawyer's files about a client are subpoenaed, the lawyer might well resist the subpoena with a claim that the materials are protected by the evidentiary privilege. A court reviewing this claim will determine the applicability of the privilege. If the court determines that the evidentiary privilege does not protect the material, the lawyer will be ordered to comply with the subpoena, effectively triggering the operation of the confidentiality duty's exception for court orders. Thus, no matter how broad the coverage of the duty of confidentiality, the application of the evidentiary privilege controls the issue of the material's revelation in such an instance.

can overlap w/ evidentiary priv.

A. THE DUTY OF CONFIDENTIALITY AND THE ATTORNEY-CLIENT EVIDENTIARY PRIVILEGE

PROBLEM 4-1

Sam McDowell represented Don Hoak in a criminal matter that is now completed. Hoak has requested that McDowell not reveal Hoak's whereabouts. Jim Perry represents Bob Clements in an unrelated civil case against Hoak. Perry has requested that McDowell reveal Hoak's whereabouts. May (must) McDowell do so?

PROBLEM 4-2

Lauren D'Amiga had represented dozens of criminal defendants charged with violent felonies including eight capital murder cases. But nothing could have prepared her for her representation of Thomas Damascus. D'Amiga was appointed to represent Damascus, who was charged with the murder of Terrence Johnson. Johnson had been shot once in the head. When Damascus was arrested, Johnson's two children were missing and police suspected that Damascus had been responsible for their disappearance. Damascus had told the police nothing about the children. But he did tell D'Amiga something. Damascus told D'Amiga, "The Devil killed Johnson. Jesus saved the kids." Damascus then drew a detailed map of a forested area that he said would show where the children could be found.

Fearing for the children's safety in the forest, D'Amiga made an anonymous phone call to the police from a pay telephone, explaining where they might find the Johnson children. Unknown to D'Amiga at the time, the children were dead, shot by Damascus.

Has D'Amiga behaved properly? What options did she have?

This section is about the overlap between the evidentiary privilege and the duty of confidentiality. The Model Code duty of confidentiality provision (DR 4-101) defined the scope of the duty as the sum of the material protected by the evidentiary attorney-client privilege (called "confidences" in DR 4-101) and material that, while not included in the attorney-client evidentiary privilege would be embarrassing or detrimental to the client if revealed or that the client has expressly requested be held in confidence (called "secrets" in DR 4-101). The Model Rules provision abandons the "confidences" + "secrets" = duty of confidentiality formula in favor of a more general and inclusive definition, "information relating to representation of a client." MR 1.6(a). The D.C. bar and some states, when adopting their versions of the Model Rules, retained the Model Code's secrets + confidences formula.

Despite the change of terminology from the Code to the Rules, the scope of the attorney-client evidentiary privilege remains critical to defining what is ultimately protected by the duty of confidentiality. When information is within the ethical duty of confidentiality, but outside the protection of the evidentiary privilege, a judge may order the lawyer to speak in the form of testimony or otherwise. Thus, although the lawyer would not be free to speak absent court compulsion, the coverage of the evidentiary privilege largely determines whether compulsion will be well founded.

1. Generally

The parameters of the evidentiary privilege vary to some extent from jurisdiction to jurisdiction. It is a creature of the evidence law rather than professional responsibility law. It is meant to further many of the same interests as the duty of confidentiality. In general, the evidentiary privilege is created when a client or prospective client communicates in confidence to a lawyer or a person the client reasonably believes to be a lawyer who is being consulted as a lawyer.

PEOPLE v. FENTRESS
425 N.Y.S.2d 485 (N.Y. Cty. Ct. 1980)

Opinion of the Court.

What are the statutory and ethical obligations of an attorney who receives a telephone call from a friend who states that he has just killed someone and is about to take his own life? May the divulgence, under any circumstances, be disclosed, and if so, to whom, and with what consequences? The defendant argues that attorney-client confidentiality in this instance is absolute, and that any disclosure which, directly or indirectly, leads to a discovery of the body and evidence, mandates dismissal of an indictment.

client calls: killed someone and abt. to kill himself.

The defendant stands indicted for intentional murder. While the facts adduced before the Grand Jury are sufficient to establish the crime, the defendant avers that the indictment must be dismissed because it is the product of tainted and inadmissible evidence, presented in violation of the attorney-client privilege, as codified in CPLR 4503.

D says tainted evidence

The attorneys for both sides have asserted that the case is unprecedented in American legal annals. This court's research has not uncovered any opinion involving the confluence of an alleged breach of confidence by one's own attorney and the applicability of an exclusionary statute as a proposed remedy.

FACTS

The defendant asserts that he contacted Wallace Schwartz, and in quest of legal advice, confided to him the facts regarding the event, and that the attorney called his own mother, who, in turn, called the defendant and then the police, as a result of which the defendant was arrested, and the body of the victim discovered in his home. He maintains that the disclosures were unauthorized, that the evidence presented to the Grand Jury flowed from the breach of confidentiality which he never waived, and that CPLR 4503 precludes the use, directly or derivatively, of any evidence obtained in violation of the attorney-client privilege. In short, he contends that the alleged breach of confidentiality immunizes him from criminal responsibility.

D says breach of Confid.

The case presents issues at the root of the attorney-client relationship, the professional duty of confidentiality, the concept of waiver, the statutory prohibitions, and the vexing ethical and moral dilemmas which marked the episode itself.

CPLR 4503 reads as follows:

> § 4503. Attorney. (a) Confidential communication privileged; nonjudicial proceedings. Unless the client waives the privilege, an attorney or his employee, or any person who obtains without the knowledge of the client evidence of a confidential communication made between the attorney or his employee and the client in the course of professional employment, shall not disclose, or be allowed to disclose such communication, nor shall the client be compelled to disclose such communication, in any action, disciplinary trial or hearing, or administrative action, proceeding or hearing conducted by or on behalf of any state, municipal or local governmental agency or by the legislature or any committee or body thereof. Evidence of any such communication obtained by any such person, *and evidence resulting therefrom*, shall not be disclosed by any state, municipal or local governmental agency or by the legislature or any committee or body thereof. (Emphasis added.)

Upon the italicized language, the defendant bases his contention that the indictment rests on proof "resulting" from the breach, but for which there would have been no arrest, discovery of evidence, or indictment.

Because the motion is addressed to the sufficiency of legal proof before the Grand Jury, it has been necessary to hear witnesses, in order to factually determine whether an attorney-client relationship was born, whether the utterances were made within its lifetime and parameters, and if so, whether a seal of contemplated secrecy was broken by Wallace Schwartz, or by the defendant's own acts, thereby constituting a waiver.

I

FINDINGS OF FACT

Albert Fentress was a schoolteacher in the City of Poughkeepsie school system.

Among his colleagues there for more than a decade was Enid Schwartz, a fellow teacher and personal friend, whom Fentress visited at her home once or twice yearly. Her friendship with Fentress was substantial, and was based on his having taught two of her children, as well as on the independent basis of their relationships as colleagues over the years.

One of these sons, Wallace, had been taught by Fentress in the ninth grade, and through the years had developed an independent personal friendship with him. After graduating, Wallace Schwartz and Fentress visited at each others' homes and had engaged in sports together.

After Wallace graduated from law school, and joined a civil firm in New York City, he gave Fentress his card and told him that he could call him at any time. On August 20, 1979, the court finds the following to have occurred:

2:12 a.m. Fentress, from his home in Poughkeepsie, called Wallace Schwartz at the latter's home in Hartsdale, Westchester County. The first thing that Fentress said was that he was about to kill himself. Fentress spoke in a low monotone, and was distraught, but coherent. He told Schwartz that he had just killed someone, that a terrible thing had happened, which he could not square with God, and that he was going to kill himself.

Incredulous, Wallace Schwartz said it must have been an accident, but was told it was not, and that there had been a sexual mutilation as well.

In continuing attempts to dissuade his valued friend from suicide, Wallace Schwartz told Fentress that suicide would not square anything with God, and that whatever had happened, Fentress could get help. Wallace Schwartz invited Fentress to his house, and offered to go to Fentress' house, but Fentress refused.

Wallace Schwartz then suggested various persons he might be able to call and stay with Fentress, all of whom were rejected. However, later in the conversation Fentress said he would like the local rabbi, Rabbi Zimet, to come to his house, and asked Wallace Schwartz to call the rabbi for him, which Wallace Schwartz agreed to do immediately. Fentress said he would leave the door open, and wait for the rabbi. It was also agreed that the police be summoned. (*See* point IV, *infra.*)

Schwartz testified that it was his "legal" advice to Fentress that the police be called.

At this point, of course, Schwartz did not have firsthand knowledge of the facts, but, recognizing the urgent need for immediate action (he could not fully conclude that any victim was actually dead) and because he was some 50 miles away, he immediately attempted to arrange to contact the rabbi.

2:40 a.m. Wallace Schwartz called his mother, Enid Schwartz, who lived in Poughkeepsie, to enlist her aid in calling the rabbi and arranging for him to go to Fentress' house.

Wallace Schwartz told Enid of the call he had just received, and of his extreme anxiety about Fentress having said that there had been a killing, or that he had killed someone, and that he was going to kill himself, and wanted Rabbi Zimet to come to see him. Enid, herself a close friend of Fentress, agreed to call the rabbi but said she was going to call Albert Fentress first to verify that there was a real problem there.

2:45 a.m. As soon as Enid hung up, she called and asked Fentress what had happened. He told her either that he had killed someone, or that there had been a killing.

Notably, she never told Fentress that Wallace Schwartz had revealed to her any of the substance of the conversation between Fentress and Wallace Schwartz.

When Enid telephoned Fentress she did not state or imply, nor could she have concluded, that Fentress had committed a crime. She knew, from Wallace, that Fentress may have killed someone, but she could not have concluded whether it was self-defense or the justifiable killing of an intruder, or willful murder. Her overriding concern was for the preservation of the life of her friend, Albert Fentress.

During the 2:45 a.m. conversation, Enid told Fentress that the police must be called, saying either "You must call the police" or "I am going to call the police." Fentress' response was that he would like Rabbi Zimet there waiting until the police came. She got the understanding that Albert Fentress acknowledged that it was proper for the police to come. (*See* point V, *infra.*)

Notably, Fentress did not state that he wanted his attorney there, only the rabbi. This is important, in that Fentress recognized that the presence of an attorney in the case would not (or should not) stem the arrival of the police. The court thus finds that Fentress agreed that the police be called, and further, that he did not attempt to place any condition, as to the presence of an attorney, on their being called. His wish for a rabbi, while understandable for purposes of spiritual comfort, has no legal implications whatever.

2:50 a.m. After Enid spoke to Fentress, she immediately called Rabbi Zimet but there was no answer.

While Fentress had asked her to let him know if she reached the rabbi, she was fearful that if she informed him of her failure, he might carry out his suicide threat.

It was because she could not reach the rabbi that she decided to call the police, to protect Fentress from harming himself.

2:59 a.m. Enid Schwartz called her son Wallace, to tell him of her unsuccessful attempts to reach the rabbi, and her intention to call the police. The court finds that the decision to call the police was made by Enid alone, although Wallace Schwartz concurred in it, principally because they both wished to prevent the defendant's suicide. Because of Wallace Schwartz' concern for Fentress' (legal) position, he cautioned his mother to be discreet in what she told the police, and to limit her remarks to the effect that there may have been a shooting at Fentress' house, and that there was fear that Fentress might commit suicide.

3:05 a.m. Enid called the police and told Officer Thomas Ghee that it was reported to her by her son, and then by Fentress, that there had been a shooting or killing at his home. She warned the police that because of Fentress' alleged suicidal intentions, it would be unwise to approach with sirens.

3:15 a.m. The police, dispatched by Sgt. Krauer, arrived at defendant's house. The lights were on and the door open. Fentress was seated next to an open window, and beckoned: "Officer, please come in and take the gun."

3:19 a.m. The defendant was given his Miranda warnings, according to Officer Perkins. The defendant declined to speak, stating that he was "waiting for his attorney," whom "he had already contacted," and whom he was expecting shortly. The police desisted questioning.

3:30 a.m. Fentress was driven to the police station, and told the police that his attorney was Wallace Schwartz. After arriving at the police station, Fentress, on three or four occasions, asked for "his attorney, Wallace Schwartz."

5:09 a.m. Wallace Schwartz arrived in Poughkeepsie, and advised the police that he was not a criminal lawyer and would not be able to properly represent the defendant. By that time Wallace Schwartz had decided to recommend Peter L. Maroulis to the defendant.

5:30 a.m. Peter L. Maroulis telephoned the police, and instructed them not to question the defendant. They had not; they did not.

As additional findings of facts, the court further concludes that:

(1) At no time before the arrest did Wallace Schwartz ever tell Fentress that he was representing him or that he was not representing him in the matter. The conversation, understandably, dealt with more immediate affairs.

(2) Wallace Schwartz never told the police how he wanted them to deal with Fentress regarding questioning, procedures, or the like.

(3) Although Wallace Schwartz never for a moment envisioned himself as being Fentress' attorney of record in this case, Fentress, in speaking to Wallace Schwartz during the 2:10 a.m. phone call, spoke to him as a friend and as an attorney, and the disclosures to Wallace Schwartz are within the attorney-client privilege.

(4) When Enid made the decision to call Fentress at 2:45 a.m., she did so on her own, independently, and, in calling, did not act as the agent of Wallace Schwartz.

(5) Fentress' disclosures to Enid during the 2:45 a.m. conversation, were voluntarily and independently made, without duress, pressure, or exploitation of any kind. Fentress made those disclosures without any knowledge that Enid already knew (through her conversation with Wallace Schwartz) what had occurred, and absent any subjective thoughts that disclosure to Enid was on constraint of or a necessary concomitant of his earlier statements to Wallace Schwartz. These disclosures to Enid were totally attenuated from those earlier disclosures to Wallace Schwartz. Wallace Schwartz never told Fentress that he was going to communicate with Enid. This is a significant omission, supportive of the factual conclusion that Fentress, when responding to Enid's inquiry as to "what happened," removed the conversation from the ambit of any pre-existing attorney-client confidentiality which had been formed at his 2:12 a.m. conversation with Wallace Schwartz. The omission, among other things, eviscerates

defendant's claim that for purposes of the attorney-client relationship, Enid was Wallace's agent.

(6) The disclosures by Fentress to Enid Schwartz were not within the scope of the attorney-client privilege.

(7) During the 2:45 a.m. conversation with Enid, Fentress voluntarily consented that the police be called.

Conclusions of Law

It is useful to begin with a general discussion of the attorney-client privilege, its origins, purposes, and application to the case at bar.

The basis for the preservation of attorney-client confidentiality dates back to at least the Roman era (Radin, *The Privilege of Confidential Communication Between Lawyer and Client*, 16 Cal L. Rev. 487). In England, by the time of Elizabeth I, the evidentiary privilege against disclosure appears to have been unquestioned. It evolved from a concept assuring the sanctity of the attorney's honor, into a highly functional concern for the encouragement of unrestrained communication by laymen, so that they might, without fear of betrayal, conduct their affairs through the hands of skilled practitioners. By the last quarter of the 18th century, this rationale became the exclusive justification for the preservation of confidentiality, although, to be sure, the earlier underpinnings remain, particularly where the attorney's obligation rests on the ethical duty[1] as opposed to the privilege against compelled disclosure.

We may take it that if an attorney-client relationship was created, the right to insist on any confidentiality belonged not to Wallace Schwartz, as it once might have, but to Albert Fentress.

The primary issues to be decided are, therefore, whether the requisites for confidentiality were established, and if so, whether they were waived by Fentress.

Wigmore, as usual, is an apt starting place, and provides the most orderly formulation of the rule (8 Wigmore, Evidence, [McNaughton rev], § 2292):

(1) Where legal advice of any kind is sought

(2) from a professional legal adviser in his capacity as such,

(3) the communications relating to that purpose,

(4) made in confidence

(5) by the client,

(6) are at his instance permanently protected

(7) from disclosure by himself or by the legal adviser,

(8) except the protection be waived.

---

[1] [2] The "privilege" is codified in CPLR 4503. For the ethical duty to preserve secrets of a client, see Disciplinary Rule 4-101 of the Code of Professional Responsibility.

II

Wallace Schwartz' Professional Capacity

If Wallace Schwartz was not being consulted in a professional capacity for legal advice, the inquiry is at an end. Fentress' contention would fail because a prime component of the statutory (and Wigmorian) relationship is lacking. The District Attorney argues that Wallace Schwartz was predominantly a friend, who never handled a criminal case, and was neither retained nor gave any appreciable amount of legal advice to the defendant. To be sure, he "withdrew" in favor of Mr. Maroulis at the earliest time, and made no secret of his discomfort in the unfamiliar surroundings of the criminal law.

It is well settled, however, that the professional relationship may exist in a financial vacuum, and that the absence of a fee or retainer does not alone destroy it.

Under any view, the defendant and Wallace Schwartz were friends. And while there would be no privilege if Wallace Schwartz was acting solely as a friend, abjuring professional involvement, it may be inferred that the defendant communicated with Wallace Schwartz because he was not only a friend but an attorney, from whom he was seeking support, advice, and guidance. That Wallace Schwartz was in effect called upon to serve as psychologist, therapist, counselor, and friend, does not derogate from his role as lawyer.

ok to be friend.

Fentress told the police on several occasions that he had an attorney, Wallace Schwartz, and was eagerly awaiting his arrival. It is indicative of his own subjective and articulated belief that he contacted his friend, Wallace Schwartz, qua attorney, but did not, and could not have concluded that their conversation was to be kept confidential in all respects.

III

The Legal Advice

Fentress urges, as he must to fit within CPLR 4503, that his call was for "legal advice." Ironically, the only "legal advice" which he can identify — and the court adopts it as such — is the advice that the police must be called, the very advice which Fentress is now trying to disown. He cannot have it both ways.

Wallace Schwartz' advice was not the least bit unprofessional. Even the most seasoned criminal lawyers often "legally advise" their clients to turn themselves in for reasons which are strategic, if not moral. An experienced criminal practitioner might, of course, refrain from making that suggestion and still be on arguably stable grounds (both legally and ethically, despite the existence of an undetected body),[2] but he would have to weigh the risk of its ultimate discovery, and the disdain

---

[2] [3] *People v. Belge*, 83 Misc. 2d 186, *aff'd*, 50 A.D.2d 1088, *aff'd*, 41 N.Y.2d 60; NY State Bar Opn. No. 479 (1978). [This case is excerpted in Section D.3. of this chapter. —Ed.]

of a jury for any defense interposed by someone who had the cunning to suppress the corpus delicti. Duplicity is not tactically sound "legal advice." What other "legal advice" could Wallace Schwartz have given?

Had Schwartz affirmatively advised Fentress to conceal or dispose of the body, he would have been counseling the commission of a crime which involves professional actions beyond those found endurable in *Belge*. They are violative of Disciplinary Rule 1-102 (subd [A], pars [4], [5]) of the Code of Professional Responsibility, and may thus demolish the attorney-client privilege itself.[3]

IV

Nonconfidentiality

Not every communication made to a lawyer in his professional capacity is confidential or intended to be so. As a general rule the question of privileged confidentiality depends on the circumstances. Fentress' intentions and his reasonable expectations of confidentiality or disclosure, as expressed and inferred from his conversations are of critical importance. Fentress, when he spoke to Wallace Schwartz at 2:12 a.m., imparted the killing, and his suicidal intentions. Wallace Schwartz told him, and he agreed, that the police would have to be called.

The conclusion is inescapable, and the court has found as a fact, that Fentress did not intend to keep the corpus of the crime from the police.

While he may have wanted the rabbi there first, that desire relates merely to chronology and does not affect its inevitable disclosure. By suggesting a sequence of events, Fentress did not revoke his plainly stated agreement that the fact of the homicide was to be divulged to the police.

* * *

When Fentress concurred in the decision to call the police, he waived confidentiality of the corpus. Both to Wallace Schwartz and Enid Schwartz, he knew that disclosure to the police was inevitable both from his viewpoint and from the advice he received from his attorney, and later, from his friend, Enid Schwartz. His express eschewal of confidentiality is controlling.

There is more here than mere waiver by implication.[4] Here we have the converse, the avowed intention, on the client's part, to have the fact of homicide revealed to the police.

---

[3] [4] The privilege may not be asserted when the communication relates to the commission of a future crime, or to advise the client to suppress or destroy evidence, or to conceal wrong doing. The same result would follow, of course, if the attorney were to aid in impeding discovery of evidence. Lastly, there is the actual entrustment of evidence to the lawyer.

[4] [5] There is no need to go so far as to hold that the client bears the duty of taking precautions to protect the privilege. It would, indeed, devitalize the privilege and render it too fragile if the client had to repeatedly preface his statements with admonitions of confidentiality.

V

Agency and Waiver

After the 2:12 a.m. conversation between Fentress and Wallace Schwartz, and the 2:40 a.m. conversation between Wallace Schwartz and Enid, Fentress received a telephone call from Enid at 2:45 a.m. She did not tell Fentress that Wallace Schwartz had related to her any admissions that Fentress made to Wallace Schwartz. She began immediately by asking Fentress what happened, and he then told her that there had been a killing. They both then agreed that the police would have to be summoned (*see* point IV, *supra*), with Fentress stating that he wanted her to call Rabbi Zimet.

At this point, for reasons which are expanded upon below, the court finds that the conversation between Fentress and Enid, in which he divulged the killing, was a communication made independently freely by Fentress to Enid, a friend and teaching colleague whom he had known for 10 years. He did not make the disclosure on the belief or expectation that Enid was an extension of Wallace Schwartz, qua attorney, or under the impression that she was Wallace Schwartz' agent for purposes of any attorney-client confidentiality.

The advice later given by Wallace Schwartz to his mother, Enid, at 2:59 a.m., that she should be discreet in what she tells the police because there "may" be an attorney-client privilege, did not and does not alter the relationship between Fentress and Enid. To the extent that there was an attorneyclient relationship between Fentress and Wallace Schwartz, Enid was no part of it, nor was she in any manner acting as her son's agent, qua attorney. After her conversation with Fentress at 2:40 a.m., she was entirely free to call the police on her own for the reasons given. It is hard to conceive of anyone doing otherwise.

The defendant recognizes that the presence of an unnecessary third party will destroy confidentiality. The waiver doctrine, however, is applied not only when a third nonindispensable person is present, but when such a person is let in on the secret before or after the attorney-client consultation. Thus, when the client, after consultation, reveals the contents of the consultation to someone else a waiver is effectuated. This is not new, and represents the unswerving application of the waiver doctrine on the basis of voluntary disclosures made by clients to third persons after the initial consultation.

Enid was not a person whose participation was necessary for furtherance of the professional relationship. Had she been present during the 2:12 a.m. conversation, her role as a friend could not be transmuted into that of an attorney's agent or be perceived as essential to or in furtherance of the attorney-client conference.

VI

SUICIDE

The defendant's announced suicidal intentions pervade the case. Wallace Schwartz was burdened with a trilemma. He had just been told of a frightful homicide and an undiscovered victim. Secondly, Fentress said he was about to take a second life, his own. Given the desperation of the call, it would not have been possible for Wallace Schwartz, or anyone else, to determine whether the victim was still alive or beyond all hope. Fentress had mentioned drinking and a sexual mutilation as well. Schwartz could not possibly travel quickly enough to save anyone's life, but he knew that lives were in serious jeopardy at the very least. The implication of Fentress' motion is that Wallace Schwartz somehow broke a confidence by telephoning his parents, who lived moments away from Fentress, who was their friend as well, for the express purpose of complying with Fentress' request that Rabbi Zimet be summoned to the scene, and to avert a suicide.

The ethical oath of secrecy must be measured by common sense. It is one thing to act as did Francis Belge (*People v. Belge*, 83 Misc. 2d 186) and to withhold knowledge of the whereabouts of victims' remains. There, the agonizing silence, held in the name of privilege, was finally pierced to the shock and outrage of many who would substitute pragmatism for ethical abstractionism. At least there it could be said that in hiding bodies behind a privilege, no life was endangered, although the anguish of the victims' family must have been excruciating. Here, Wallace Schwartz was confronted not only with the vexing moral and ethical predicament which faced Belge, but with one, and possibly two lives, still hanging, literally, in the balance.

To exalt the oath of silence, in the face of imminent death, would, under these circumstances, be not only morally reprehensible, but ethically unsound. As Professor Monroe Freedman reminds us, "At one extreme, it seems clear that the lawyer should reveal information necessary to save a life." If the ethical duty exists primarily to protect the client's interests, what interest can there be superior to the client's life itself?

The issue was addressed in New York State Bar Opinion 486. Posing the question "May a lawyer disclose his client's expressed intention to commit suicide?" the New York State Bar Association, in interpreting Ethical Consideration 4-2 and Disciplinary Rule 4-101 (subd C, par [3]) of the Code of Professional Responsibility answered in the affirmative, despite the repeal of suicide as a crime.[5]

Thus, even if the defendant flatly forbade Wallace Schwartz from calling the police, the ethical duty of silence would be of dubious operability. We need not decide the legal consequences of such an interdiction, having rejected the defendant's contention that he did not acquiesce in the call to the police, and having found waiver by repetition to Enid Schwartz.

It seems safe to say, however, that Wallace Schwartz acted with exemplary fidelity to his client, and to his moral responsibilities to society, by doing as he did.

---

[5] [The February 2002 amendment to MR 1.6, effectively creating a "future harm" exception to the duty of confidentiality, brings MR 1.6 to a position consistent with this opinion —Ed.]

Had he acted any differently, he would have blindly and unpardonably converted a valued ethical duty into a caricature, a mockery of justice and life itself.

In conclusion, the court holds that the indictment is based on legally sufficient and competent evidence within the meaning of CPL 190.65, 210.20, 210.25 and 210.30, and CPLR 4503. Accordingly, the motion to dismiss the indictment is denied.

Lastly, the court expresses its gratitude to both attorneys for their excellent briefs and presentations.

Rules of Evidence for United States Courts and Magistrates
Article V. Privileges

Rule 501. General Rule

Except as otherwise required by the Constitution of the United States or provided by Act of Congress or in rules prescribed by the Supreme Court pursuant to statutory authority, the privilege of a witness, person, government, State, or political subdivision thereof shall be governed by the principles of the common law as they may be interpreted by the courts of the United States in the light of reason and experience. However, in civil actions and proceedings, with respect to an element of a claim or defense as to which State law supplies the rule of decision, the privilege of a witness, person, government, State, or political subdivision thereof shall be determined in accordance with State law.

Rule 503. Lawyer-Client Privilege [not enacted]

(a) **Definitions.** As used in this rule:

(1) A "client" is a person, public officer, or corporation, association, or other organization or entity, either public or private, who is rendered professional legal services by a lawyer, or who consults a lawyer with a view to obtain professional legal services from him.

(2) A "lawyer" is a person authorized, or reasonably believed by the client to be authorized, to practice law in any state or nation.

(3) A "representative of the lawyer" is one employed to assist the lawyer in the rendition of professional legal services.

(4) A communication is "confidential" if not intended to be disclosed to third persons other than those to whom disclosure is in furtherance of the rendition of professional legal services tot he client or those reasonably necessary for the transmission of the communication.

(b) **General rule of privilege.** A client has the privilege to refuse to disclose and to prevent any other person from disclosing confidential communications made for the purpose of facilitating the rendition of professional legal services to the client, (1) between himself or his representative and his lawyer or his lawyer's representative, or (2) between his lawyer and the lawyer's representative, or (3) by him or his lawyer to a lawyer representing another in a matter of common interest, or (4) between representatives of the client or between the client and a representative of the client, or (5) between lawyers representing the client.

(c) Who may claim the privilege. The privilege may be claimed by the client, his guardian or conservator, the personal representative of a deceased client, or the successor, trustee, or similar representative of a corporation, association, or other organization, whether or not in existence. The person who was the lawyer at the time of the communication may claim the privilege but only on behalf of the client. His authority to do so is presumed in the absence of evidence to the contrary.

(d) Exceptions. There is no privilege under this rule:

(1) Furtherance of crime or fraud. If the services of the lawyer were sought or obtained to enable or aid anyone to commit or plan to commit what the client knew or reasonably should have known to be a crime or fraud; or

(2) Claimants through same deceased client. As to a communication relevant to an issue between parties who claim through the same deceased client, regardless of whether the claims are by testate or intestate succession or by *inter vivos* transaction; or

(3) Breach of duty by lawyer or client. As to a communication relevant to an issue of breach of duty by the lawyer to his client or by the client to his lawyer; or

(4) Document attested by lawyer. As to a communication relevant to an issue concerning an attested document to which the lawyer is an attesting witness; or

(5) Joint clients. As to a communication relevant to a matter of common interest between two or more clients if the communication was made by any of them to a lawyer retained or consulted in common, when offered in an action between any of the clients.

INTERNATIONAL NOTES

1. In most civil law countries, confidentiality and privilege are conceived less as duties to the client and more as public obligations necessary to maintain trust in the legal system and profession. Typical of civil law countries, Article 2.1 of the harmonized Practice Rules of the French Bar provides that:

[T]he lawyer's duty to respect confidentiality is an obligation imposed by law. It is general, absolute and unlimited in time. Since clients must necessarily confide in their lawyers, this duty of confidentiality is established in the public interest. Lawyers may not be released from this obligation by their clients, by any authority or, more generally, by any other person.

NATIONAL COUNCIL OF FRANCE, HARMONISED PRACTICE RULES, art. 2.1. The professional secrets doctrine, like the U.S. attorney-client privilege and work product doctrine, provides protection against compelled disclosure. Because it is not limited to communications with the client, or to information obtained in anticipation of litigation, its protection is even broader. *See* GEOFFREY HAZARD, JR. & ANGELO DONDI, LEGAL ETHICS: A COMPREHENSIVE STUDY 208–09 (2004).

2. The Japanese Code of Ethics for Practicing Attorneys provides broadly that, "[a]n attorney shall not disclose or utilize, without due reason, confidential information of a client which is obtained in the course of his or her practice." JAPANESE FEDERATION OF BAR ASSOCIATIONS, BASIC RULES ON THE DUTIES OF PRACTICING ATTORNEYS, art. 23. Japanese lawyers who divulge confidential information without "due reason" face criminal sanctions. *See* JAPANESE PENAL CODE, art. 134. The Japanese duty of confidentiality may create a dilemma for Japanese lawyers who represent companies subject to securities regulation in the United States. The Securities and Exchange Commission proposed regulations under the Sarbanes-Oxley Act that would have required a covered lawyer to disaffirm documents and withdraw from representation if the lawyer discovered that documents she had prepared on behalf of a publicly traded corporation were materially false or misleading. *See* IMPLEMENTATION OF PROFESSIONAL CONDUCT FOR ATTORNEYS, 67 Fed. Reg. 71,670 (proposed Dec. 2, 2002) (codified, in part, at C.F.R. pt. 205). Several Japanese law firms argued that the rule conflicted with the Japanese rule of confidentiality.

2. The Privilege Applies to What?

PROBLEM 4-3

Defendant is charged with burglary. He is accused of breaking into a home and stealing valuable coins. He tells Lawyer that he threw several of the coins into a river that was adjacent to the home as he fled the scene. Lawyer's investigator searches the river bank and sees five coins partially embedded in the mud of the river bank. He returns one of the five to Lawyer and leaves the other four in place. Lawyer determines that the coin is one of those stolen from the home and turns it in to the prosecutor. The police never find any of the other four coins. Can the prosecutor get evidence regarding the coin's original *location*?

The privilege is not created when the communication is made in circumstances that do not indicate a desire for confidentiality by the client. For example, when a client meets with the lawyer in the presence of third parties who are not necessary to the lawyer-client relationship, the privilege is not created.

The privilege covers the client's communication, not the client's knowledge that was communicated. In ordinary civil discovery, for example, clients must answer proper questions truthfully, even when the answers to those questions will reveal the substance of what the client has communicated in confidence to his lawyer. For example, when it applies, the privilege prevents the lawyer from being required to say, "My client told me that he ran the red light," and prevents the client from being required to say, "I told my lawyer that I ran the red light." It does not prevent the client from being required to say, "I ran the red light" in answer to a proper question from an opposing party. Such proper questions may come, for example, in interrogatories, in a deposition, or at trial.

The privilege may also protect lawyer observations that result directly from the client's protected communications, as long as the lawyer does nothing to prevent other interested parties from making the same observation.

Although the observations of a lawyer that result directly from client communication may sometimes be privileged, items collected by the lawyer are not privileged.

PEOPLE v. MEREDITH
631 P.2d 46 (Cal. 1981)

Defendants Frank Earl Scott and Michael Meredith appeal from convictions for the first degree murder and first degree robbery of David Wade. Meredith's conviction rests on eyewitness testimony that he shot and killed Wade. Scott's conviction, however, depends on the theory that Scott conspired with Meredith and a third defendant, Jacqueline Otis, to bring about the killing and robbery. To support the theory of conspiracy the prosecution sought to show the place where the victim's wallet was found, and, in the course of the case this piece of evidence became crucial. The admissibility of that evidence comprises the principal issue on this appeal.

At trial the prosecution called Steven Frick, who testified that he observed the victim's partially burnt wallet in a trash can behind Scott's residence. Scott's trial counsel then adduced that Frick served as a defense investigator. Scott himself had told his former counsel that he had taken the victim's wallet, divided the money with Meredith, attempted to burn the wallet, and finally put it in the trash can. At counsel's request, Frick then retrieved the wallet from the trash can. Counsel examined the wallet and then turned it over to the police.

The defense acknowledges that the wallet itself was properly admitted into evidence. The prosecution in turn acknowledges that the attorney-client privilege protected the conversations between Scott, his former counsel, and counsel's investigator. Indeed the prosecution did not attempt to introduce those conversations at trial. The issue before us, consequently, focuses upon a narrow point: whether under the circumstances of this case Frick's observation of the location of the wallet, the product of a privileged communication, finds protection under the attorney-client privilege.

This issue, one of first impression in California, presents the court with competing policy considerations. On the one hand, to deny protection to observations arising from confidential communications might chill free and open communication between attorney and client and might also inhibit counsel's investigation of his client's case. On the other hand, we cannot extend the attorney-client privilege so far that it renders evidence immune from discovery and admission merely because the defense seizes it first.

Balancing these considerations, we conclude that an observation by defense counsel or his investigator, which is the product of a privileged communication, may not be admitted unless the defense by altering or removing physical evidence has precluded the prosecution from making that same observation. In the present case the defense investigator, by removing the wallet, frustrated any possibility that the police might later discover it in the trash can. The conduct of the defense thus precluded the prosecution from ascertaining the crucial fact of the location of the wallet. Under these circumstances, the prosecution was entitled to present evidence to show the location of the wallet in the trash can; the trial court did not err in admitting the investigator's testimony.

*   *   *

In the criminal context, as we have recently observed, these policies assume particular significance: "As a practical matter, if the client knows that damaging information could more readily be obtained from the attorney following disclosure than from himself in the absence of disclosure, the client would be reluctant to confide in his lawyer and it would be difficult to obtain fully informed legal advice.' . . . Thus, if an accused is to derive the full benefits of his right to counsel, he must have the assurance of confidentiality and privacy of communication with his attorney."

Judicial decisions have recognized that the implementation of these important policies may require that the privilege extend not only to the initial communication between client and attorney but also to any information which the attorney or his investigator may subsequently acquire as a direct result of that communication. In a venerable decision involving facts analogous to those in the instant case, the Supreme Court of West Virginia held that the trial court erred in admitting an attorney's testimony as to the location of a pistol which he had discovered as the result of a privileged communication from his client. That the attorney had observed the pistol, the court pointed out, did not nullify the privilege: "All that the said attorney knew about this pistol, or where it was to be found, he knew only from the communications which had been made to him by his client confidentially and professionally, as counsel in this case. And it ought therefore, to have been entirely excluded from the jury. It may be, that in this particular case this evidence tended to the promotion of right and justice, but as was well said in *Pearce v. Pearce*, 11 Jar. 52, in page 55, and 2 De Gex & Smale 25-27: 'Truth like all other good things may be loved unwisely, may be pursued too keenly, may cost too much.' " (*State of West Virginia v. Douglass* (1882) 20 W. Va. 770, 783.)

More recent decisions reach similar conclusions. In *State v. Olwell* (1964) 64 Wash. 2d 828, the court reviewed contempt charges against an attorney who refused to produce a knife he obtained from his client. The court first observed that "[to] be protected as a privileged communication . . . the securing of the knife . . . must have been the direct result of information given to Mr. Olwell by his client." The court concluded that defense counsel, after examining the physical evidence, should deliver it to the prosecution, but should not reveal the source of the evidence; "[by] thus allowing the prosecution to recover such evidence, the public interest is served, and by refusing the prosecution an opportunity to disclose the source of the evidence, the client's privilege is preserved and a balance reached between these conflicting interests."

*   *   *

Finally, we note the decisions of the New York courts in *People v. Belge* (1975) 83 Misc. 2d 186 [372 N.Y.S.2d 798], affirmed in *People v. Belge* (1975) 50 App. Div. 2d

1088 [376 N.Y.S.2d 771]. Defendant, charged with one murder, revealed to counsel that he had committed three others. Counsel, following defendant's directions, located one of the bodies. Counsel did not reveal the location of the body until trial, 10 months later, when he exposed the other murders to support an insanity defense.

Counsel was then indicted for violating two sections of the New York Public Health Law for failing to report the existence of the body to proper authorities in order that they could give it a decent burial. The trial court dismissed the indictment; the appellate division affirmed, holding that the attorney-client privilege shielded counsel from prosecution for actions which would otherwise violate the Public Health Law.

The foregoing decisions demonstrate that the attorney-client privilege is not strictly limited to communications, but extends to protect observations made as a consequence of protected communications. We turn therefore to the question whether that privilege encompasses a case in which the defense, by removing or altering evidence, interferes with the prosecution's opportunity to discover that evidence.[6]

We therefore conclude that whenever defense counsel removes or alters evidence, the statutory privilege does not bar revelation of the original location or condition of the evidence in question.[7] We thus view the defense decision to remove evidence as a tactical choice. If defense counsel leaves the evidence where he discovers it, his observations derived from privileged communications are insulated from revelation. If, however, counsel chooses to remove evidence to examine or test it, the original location and condition of that evidence loses the protection of the privilege. Applying this analysis to the present case, we hold that the trial court did not err in admitting the investigator's testimony concerning the location of the wallet.

In other circumstances, when it is not possible to elicit such testimony without identifying the witness as the defendant's attorney or investigator, the defendant may be willing to enter a stipulation which will simply inform the jury as to the relevant location or condition of the evidence in question.

When such a stipulation is proffered, the prosecution should not be permitted to

---

[6] [7] We agree with the parties' suggestion that an attorney in Schenk's position often may best fulfill conflicting obligations to preserve the confidentiality of client confidences, investigate his case, and act as an officer of the court if he does not remove evidence located as the result of a privileged communication. We must recognize, however, that in some cases an examination of evidence may reveal information critical to the defense of a client accused of crime. If the usefulness of the evidence cannot be gauged without taking possession of it, as, for example, when a ballistics or fingerprint test is required, the attorney may properly take it for a reasonable time before turning it over to the prosecution. Similarly, in the present case the defense counsel could not be certain the burnt wallet belonged in fact to the victim: in taking the wallet to examine it for identification, he violated no ethical duty to his client or to the prosecution. (*See generally Legal Ethics and the Destruction of Evidence* (1979) 88 YALE L.J. 1665.)

[7] [8] In offering the evidence, the prosecution should present the information in a manner which avoids revealing the content of attorney-client communications or the original source of the information. In the present case, for example, the prosecutor simply asked Frick where he found the wallet; he did not identify Frick as a defense investigator or trace the discovery of the wallet to an attorney-client communication.

reject the stipulation in the hope that by requiring defense counsel personally to testify to such facts, the jury might infer that counsel learned those facts from defendant.

*   *   *

The judgment, as modified, is affirmed.

BUNTROCK v. BUNTROCK
419 So. 2d 402 (Fla. Dist. Ct. App. 1982)

DELL, JUDGE.

The petitioner seeks review by writ of certiorari under Rule 9.030(b)(2)(A), Florida Rules of Appellate Procedure, of a trial court's denial of his motion to have foreign attorneys admitted to practice as co-counsel.

Petitioner/husband moved to admit three members of an Illinois law firm as co-counsel in the divorce suit sub judice. The firm has represented the husband for many years. These attorneys are familiar with the facts and circumstances of the divorce suit, the husband's business, and his financial affairs. Respondent/wife objected to their admission to practice in Florida as co-counsel on the grounds that the firm and at least one of the attorneys, Peer Pedersen, also represented her during the marriage, thus raising a conflict of interest. Respondent demonstrated that Pedersen prepared a will for her in 1981 and that the law firm engaged in tax planning for the couple earlier this year. She also presented evidence that Pedersen is one of petitioner's partners in certain businesses which may constitute marital property; that Pedersen is a member of the Board of Directors of Waste Management, Inc., her family's business; and that the principle asset in contention is 600,000 shares of Waste Management stock.

*   *   *

In the hearing on petitioner's motion, respondent testified that Pedersen had been her father's attorney and that she has known him since she was young. When asked if she told Pedersen all her little financial secrets for purposes of estate planning, respondent replied, "Well, most of the things Mr. Pedersen already knew there because he had been there since I was young." Petitioner contends that respondent has failed to show that she made confidential communications to Pedersen, therefore she cannot establish the appearance of impropriety. The Code of Professional Responsibility protects more than confidential communications, it protects confidences and secrets of a client. Fla. Bar Code Prof. Resp., D.R. 4-101(A) & (B). This protection is broader than the evidentiary attorney-client privilege, and applies even though the same information is discoverable from other sources. Additionally, Pedersen is personally involved in certain business enterprises, including Waste Management, Inc., in which respondent claims an interest. A lawyer shall not use a confidence or secret of his client for the advantage of himself or of a third person. Fla. Bar Code Prof. Resp. D.R. 4-101(B)(3). Although respondent makes no allegation of impropriety, we agree that the situation is fraught with the potential for abuse, and thus raises the appearance of impropriety.

*   *   *

3. Exceptions

PROBLEM 4-4

Elaine Alexander took a job in-house at Gamma Industries because she preferred 50-hour-weeks to the 70-hour-weeks she was putting in at her former law firm. Little did she expect to find herself in the middle of a corporate life and death controversy. Gamma distributes medical equipment including kidney dialysis equipment. Alexander examines production quality reports to monitor compliance with FDA regulations. One such report indicates that a recently manufactured batch of dialysis filters are below industry standards. Patients will receive somewhat less than the full advantage of treatment when the defective filters are used. The difference is subtle and, although over a series of treatments patients will suffer potentially life-threatening consequences, the cause is unlikely to be attributed to the faulty filters.

Alexander reports to the Gamma CEO that these filters should not be distributed. The CEO agrees and Alexander leaves for the day, satisfied at her good work. Two weeks later, Alexander checks distribution records and learns to her dismay that the filters have been sold and are in use. She approaches the CEO and explains that a mistake must have occurred resulting in the distribution of the filters. "No, no mistake, Elaine," the CEO responds. "The filter defects were minor and I authorized their sale. I thought it was best for you not to know. I wanted to spare you from a professionally uncomfortable position. I trust you'll leave this alone."

What is Alexander to do?

Many of the exceptions to the duty of confidentiality are paralleled by exceptions to the evidentiary privilege. The client holds (controls the assertion of) the evidentiary privilege; client waiver eviscerates the privilege. Communications that further future crimes or frauds are excepted from protection by the evidentiary privilege.

UNITED STATES v. JACOBS
117 F.3d 82 (2d Cir. 1997)

CUDAHY, CIRCUIT JUDGE.

Donald E. Jacobs appeals his convictions and sentences for conspiracy, bank fraud and mail fraud. After a jury trial Jacobs was sentenced to 51 months on each count, to be served concurrently. He now argues that letters from his attorney were admitted into evidence in violation of his attorney-client privilege. . . . We affirm.

I. Factual Background

Donald Jacobs apparently had a penchant for activities on the edge of legality. Jacobs was engaged in efforts to avoid taxes through the use of off-shore banking and by ownership of off-shore corporations. His involvement in these off-shore activities began at various seminars, where he met the other participants in the somewhat different scheme that has led him to his present straits. Jacobs was involved in a so-titled "Debt Elimination Program," in which unwitting debtors were enticed to purchase "certified drafts" drawn on non-existent financial entities in Mexico. First, the targeted debtor would obtain an exact accounting from the creditor to whom the debtor owed money. Then the debtor would give this information to one of Jacobs' "downline" distributors along with a fee of about 15% of the total debt owed. In return, the debtor would receive an official-looking, but worthless, piece of paper purporting to be a "certified draft," drawn on a fictitious financial institution, with a face value equal to the debt owed. Along with this, the debtor received instructions to submit the draft to the creditor, together with a demand for the return of any collateral or evidence of indebtedness. Banks would accept the draft, but following sound banking practice, would decline to release the collateral until the draft cleared, which, of course, never happened. Thus, the debtor was out the 15% of face value paid for the draft, and the bank was out whatever expenses it incurred attempting to collect on the draft. The debtor would often be responsible for late fees and accrued interest as well as for the original balance.

Jacobs was convicted of one count of conspiracy to create fraudulent certified drafts with the intent to market the drafts to customers in the Debt Elimination Program (DEP). Jacobs was also convicted of 30 counts of bank fraud for his attempt to defraud federally insured financial institutions through the DEP. Each count of bank fraud reflected the submission of one certified draft to a financial institution. Jacobs was also convicted of mail fraud, each of these eighteen counts arising from the mailing of one certified draft to be handled by the United States Postal Service.

Jacobs now appeals his conviction, alleging that privileged communications between his attorney and himself were improperly and prejudicially admitted into evidence, depriving him of a fair trial.

Jacobs became associated with the DEP while attending an off-shore investment seminar in Acapulco, Mexico, in March of 1987. This seminar, which focused on offshore banking, was hosted by Happy Dutton and attended by Paul Robinson. Paul Robinson, who also went by the names "Walter Martin," "Ed Lee," "Paul Martin" and "Leandro," was invited to the seminar after Dori Dutton (Happy's daughter) found his name on a tax protestor mailing list. Paul Robinson appears to be the "brains" behind the DEP; he introduced the scheme to Happy Dutton, who in turn hand-picked various individuals from the seminar to be "leaders." At the same time that the DEP scheme was getting off the ground, Happy Dutton continued her business running seminars on off-shore banking and off-shore corporations. In order to be a "leader" in the DEP, Jacobs was required to hold a seminar, which he scheduled for June 1987, in Cincinnati.

By April of 1987 Jacobs was well on his way to registering people to attend his

Cincinnati seminar and was attempting to entice people to purchase certified drafts. Testimony also showed that the DEP was discussed at Jacobs' seminar. About this time Jacobs requested that his attorney, Jay Swob, investigate the DEP and give him his opinion of its merits. Attorney Swob wrote Jacobs two letters, one on May 28, 1987, and one on July 12, 1987. Each of these letters discussed the many potential problems associated with the DEP, explained the legal liabilities that could flow from them, and strongly advised Jacobs to have nothing to do with the DEP.

By October of 1987, Jacobs was recognized as the number one producer in the DEP scheme. He received an award for his productivity. He was also involved in developing variations on the scheme, including a plan to purchase gold with the drafts.

By November of 1987, Jacobs had been told by one customer that he had been visited by the FBI and that a local prosecutor had warned him that the drafts were a "fraudulent . . . scam . . . ." Jacobs also saw a television news story that focused on the certified drafts and alleged that Jacobs had sold Frank Patton a fraudulent draft. In response to these events, Jacobs admitted to Frank Patton that the drafts were worthless. Yet he continued to process draft requests from his downline sellers. These actions resulted in Jacobs' indictment on June 11, 1993 and his conviction after a five week jury trial.

II. ATTORNEY-CLIENT PRIVILEGE

The attorney-client privilege is "the oldest of the privileges for confidential communications known to the common law." *Upjohn Co. v. United States*, 449 U.S. 383, 389 (1981). The purpose of the attorney-client privilege is to foster open communication between attorneys and their clients, so that fully informed legal advice may be obtained. However, because invocation of the attorney-client privilege will necessarily exclude relevant evidence from consideration, its application must be limited in some circumstances. One such circumstance involves a waiver by the client; a second involves use of the communication in furtherance of a crime or fraud. The district court found that the crime-fraud exception applied to the two letters from Attorney Swob and therefore admitted the letters as evidence. The district court then declined to reach the issue of waiver.

A. Crime-Fraud Exception

The crime-fraud exception removes the privilege from those attorney-client communications that are "relate[d] to client communications in furtherance of contemplated or ongoing criminal or fraudulent conduct." *In re John Doe, Inc.*, 13 F.3d 633, 636 (2d Cir. 1994) (quoting *In re Grand Jury Subpoena Duces Tecum Dated September 15, 1983*, 731 F.2d 1032, 1038 (2d Cir. 1984)). "It is the purpose of the crime-fraud exception to the attorney-client privilege to assure that the 'seal of secrecy' between lawyer and client does not extend to communications 'made for the purpose of getting advice for the commission of a fraud' or crime." *United States v. Zolin*, 491 U.S. 554, 563 (1989).

A party wishing to invoke the crime-fraud exception must demonstrate that there is a factual basis for a showing of probable cause to believe that a fraud or crime has been committed and that the communications in question were in furtherance of the fraud or crime. This is a two-step process. First, the proposed factual basis must strike "a prudent person" as constituting "a reasonable basis to suspect the perpetration or attempted perpetration of a crime or fraud, and that the communications were in furtherance thereof." *In re John Doe*, 13 F.3d at 637. Once there is a showing of a factual basis, the decision whether to engage in an in camera review of the evidence lies in the discretion of the district court. Second, if and when there has been an in camera review, the district court exercises its discretion again to determine whether the facts are such that the exception applies. These factual determinations are governed by the clearly erroneous standard.

The district court here admitted as evidence two letters written by Attorney Swob to Jacobs.[8] Jacobs argues vociferously against the application of the crime-fraud exception to these letters. The letters were seized pursuant to a search warrant for Jacobs' residence. Since the letters were from Jacobs' attorney, the government appropriately turned the letters over to the district court. The government requested that the district court review the letters in camera and determine whether they were privileged, and if so, whether the crimefraud exception applied.

The government was required to present a sufficient factual basis for a showing of probable cause to believe that a fraud had been committed by Jacobs and that the communications from his attorney were in furtherance of the fraud. The government did this to the district court's satisfaction by submitting tape recordings of statements made by Jacobs to an undercover FBI agent. At the government's request, the district court found that:

> The government has provided a sufficient factual basis. Defendant told [an undercover FBI agent] that his attorney started "lookin' into this" and gave his opinion that "if, they would honor those drafts in an acceptable manner, there was absolutely nothing about the program that was illegal." Defendant stated that his attorney spent time with certain individuals apparently in connection with matters charged in the indictment and actually attended one of the seminars. Defendant also said that his attorney told him "they were kiting the drafts that ah, he didn't know how long it would be." These statements by defendant do support a good faith belief by a reasonable person that in camera review of the letters from the attorney to defendant may reveal evidence to establish the claim that the crime-fraud exception applies.

While providing only the minimum showing required before an in camera review is authorized, this decision was not clearly erroneous. After review of the letters allegedly protected by the attorney-client privilege, the district court found in addition that a prudent person would have a reasonable basis to suspect the

---

[8] [1] The two letters were written by Attorney Swob and addressed to Jacobs and his wife. Attached to the letters were copies of portions of the Uniform Commercial Code, case law and legal encyclopedic excerpts.

perpetration of a crime or fraud and that defendant's communications to his attorney were in furtherance thereof.

Unfortunately, the critical element necessary for application of the exception is somewhat obscure in the district court's cursory conclusion. For the crime-fraud exception has a narrow and precise application:

> It applies only when the communications between the client and his lawyer further a crime, fraud or other misconduct. It does not suffice that the communications may be related to a crime. To subject the attorney-client communications to disclosure, they must actually have been made with an intent to further an unlawful act.

United States v. White, 887 F.2d 267, 271 (D.C. Cir. 1989).

A wrongdoer's failure to heed the advice of his or her lawyer does not remove the privilege. The attorney-client privilege is strongest where a client seeks counsel's advice to determine the legality of conduct before taking action. With strong emphasis on intent, the crime-fraud exception applies "only when there is probable cause to believe that the communications with counsel were intended in some way to facilitate or to conceal the criminal activity." *In re Grand Jury Subpoena Duces Tecum*, 798 F.2d 32, 34 (2d Cir. 1986). It is therefore relevant to show that the wrong-doer had set upon a criminal course before consulting counsel. The district court carefully addressed the issue of intent when it reexamined the applicability of the crime-fraud exception in connection with a motion for reconsideration.

Before Attorney Swob wrote the May 28, 1987, letter to Jacobs, Jacobs had already agreed to host a seminar in Cincinnati and obtained a false driver's license, social security card and juristic identification in Mexico. These facts, the district court held, indicated that Jacobs had formed an intent to become involved in the Debt Elimination Program before he received his attorney's advice. More inculpatory still, the evidence presented indicated that Jacobs had been picked to be a leader in the scheme and knew about the commission structure. Since the 15% purchase price was being split three ways — 5% to Jacobs and helpers, 5% to Happy Dutton and 5% to Paul Robinson — a reasonable person would recognize that nothing remained to back the "certified drafts." A reasonable person would also have noticed, and questioned the fact, that the address for the juristic identities and each of the several banks "backing" the certified drafts was the same post office box in Mexico. Jacobs had this information before he sought Attorney Swob's advice. Thus there was evidence that Jacobs had set upon an illegal course before seeking advice about the scheme's legality; then, in the words of the district court: "What then were those communications?"

Lending more weight to the reasonable belief that Jacobs intended to utilize the communications from Attorney Swob to further his fraudulent scheme is the fact that he did so. On several occasions Jacobs used the communications to lend credibility to the scheme, by telling prospective customers that his attorney declared the program legal. Thus, it is reasonable to believe (although there was some evidence to the contrary) that Jacobs' intent in securing Attorney Swob's opinion was to further his Debt Elimination Program fraud. Accordingly, the attorney-client privilege cannot protect those communications, and the admission of the letters was not an abuse of the district court's discretion.

B. Waiver

The district court declined to reach the issue of waiver of the attorney-client privilege. Since the issue of waiver is in the first instance for the district court's discretion, we reach the matter here only because the parties have extensively argued the governing principles and they stand in need of clarification.

Essentially, it seems to be the case here that Jacobs publicly disclosed a "summary" of the two letters from his lawyer — but a summary that inverted the analysis and conclusion. Attorney Swob's letters actually told Jacobs that the scheme was of dubious legality and that he should steer clear of it. The bulk of the letters was a more detailed explication of this general theme. Jacobs, on the other hand, reported that his attorney had approved of his participation. Jacobs accomplished this deception essentially by quoting a sentence of one of the letters out of context. The problem here is that this was a disclosure that we must treat as extrajudicial and therefore one which, under the case law, may not generally be used as a basis for invoking the "fairness doctrine." *See In re von Bulow*, 828 F.2d 94, 102 (2d Cir. 1987).

In re von Bulow was a civil suit against *von Bulow* following his acquittal in a criminal trial, *State v. von Bulow*, 475 A.2d 995 (R.I. 1984). After the criminal trial, the defendant "knew of, consented to, and actually encouraged attorney Dershowitz's plans to write a book providing an 'insider look' into his case." *In re von Bulow*, 828 F.2d at 100. Thus, even though the actual disclosures were made by attorney Dershowitz in the book, von Bulow impliedly waived his privilege by consenting to them. The district court held that it would be unfair to allow von Bulow to use privileged information as a sword in public, and then invoke the privilege as a shield in the courtroom.

An inaccurate statement of a privileged communication waives the privilege with respect to that communication. *United States v. Mendelsohn*, 896 F.2d 1183, 1188-89 (9th Cir. 1990). Mendelsohn was selling an illegal bookmaking computer program through the U.S. mails, and in the course of a sale told a potential customer (actually an undercover federal agent) that his attorney had said that selling the program was legal. Mendelsohn then argued that "there was no waiver because he did not truthfully disclose the advice his attorney gave him and he did not disclose a significant portion of attorneyclient communication." The Ninth Circuit found, and we agree, that the privilege is waived even if the defendant misstated what his attorney told him. Of course, in such a case the waiver extends only to the specific communication involved and not generally to other communications on the same subject. For Jacobs, this seems to mean that the waiver of his attorney-client privilege extends to the two letters written by Attorney Swob, the gist of which Jacobs purported to convey while selling the DEP. There thus appears to have been a waiver as to the two letters, and they may be introduced to indicate their true import.[9]

---

[9] [6] Testimony showed that Jacobs had represented to customers that his attorney had told Jacobs

*   *   *

that the DEP was legal. For example, witnesses testified that "[Jacobs] told us that he had an attorney on retainer, that he had run all the trust papers and talked to him and showed him the drafts and we were under the impression that everything was legal. . . . Don told us that he had, Mr. Attorney Swob had said that the paperwork was legal." Further, at a Miami seminar, Jacobs was tape-recorded giving a DEP sales pitch where he stated:

> Our attorney . . . I can give you his background . . . and we used him . . . he checked out this program for legality and I can share with you what he said. Basically, was that there is virtually nothing at all anywhere that can cause us any problem if the draft is honored when it is presented.

The reality, however, is that Attorney Swob's letter to Jacobs read (in part) as follows:

> Will the financial instruments used to pay off your client's debt obligations, be properly honored and paid in acceptable monetary form when processed thru the banking system for presentment and collection of funds?

> If "YES," then I see no significant legal roadblock toward the implementation of the programs. However, since you will in all likelihood be dealing with offshore entities who will provide the financial pay-off instrument, you will have no control over the process, and very little, if any recourse should payment ever be dishonored. . . .

> Therefore, I would advise your participation in such programs only if all down payment monies, application fees, deed conveyances, etc., are done in an extended escrow within the jurisdiction of Ohio courts.

>   . . . .

> If "NO," then I would suggest that you refrain from participating in the program in all respects. . . . Now, how do you know if a dishonor will occur? Answer: you don't! Therefore, I must advise that you proceed on the assumption that a dishonor may occur; and because of that possibility, I must advise that you do not involve yourself in the programs. . . .

However, the criminal liability could be horrendous:

(1)   State fraud
(2)   State conspiracy
(3)   State RICO (Racketeering and Influenced Corrupt Organizations Act)
(4)   State securities violation
(5)   Federal bank fraud
(6)   Federal conspiracy
(7)   Federal RICO
(8)   Federal securities violation
(9)   Federal foreign corrupt practices act

> . . . your participation (overall) in the program would, in my opinion, be more than sufficient to give rise to criminal liability.

> On balance, I cannot in good conscience recommend your participation in these programs. [Specific concerns:]

> The draft has the notation of "certified" on it; certified by whom? — and in what capacity? Frankly, I have never heard of a certified draft; the customary notation is an "accepted draft."

> —In a draft, you generally have a 3-party document: Drawer, Drawee, and Payee. In a note, you have Maker (also called a Payor) and a Payee. Yet, in the draft which you presented to me, the Drawer is referred to as a "Payor" — this is confusing and not standard.

> —The Drawee's address is the same as Servicio Bustos!

> —The wording of the draft says that it is "redeemable in 'current funds (credit)' when presented. . . ." The use of 'current funds' under ORC 1303.06 (UCC 3-107) means payable in money (currency); yet the parenthetical calls for "(credit)," an obvious inconsistency with Ohio UCC law.

> —"Protest" will be required upon dishonor of this draft since it is payable outside of the U.S. (ORC 1303.56 (UCC 3-501)[)]. This is a clear "time-delayer."

>   . . . .

> . . . let me reiterate my overall recommendation to you: Don't do it!

V. Conclusion

Donald Jacobs was engaged in a fraudulent scheme to defraud individual debtors, banks and other creditors. After being convicted of conspiracy, bank fraud and mail fraud, Jacobs appealed on several points.

Key pieces of evidence included two letters written to Jacobs by his attorney. After evaluating Jacobs' knowledge and actions before receipt of the letters and his use of certain portions of the letters during the course of the DEP, we affirm as not clearly erroneous the district court's application of the crimefraud exception to the attorney-client privilege with regard to these letters. We also conclude, though not required to do so, that Jacobs waived the attorney-client privilege as to the letters by disclosing their substance (incorrectly and dishonestly) on a number of occasions.

Affirmed.

NOTES, QUESTIONS, AND EXAMPLES

1.   What, if any, implications does the application of the crime-fraud exception to the evidentiary privilege have on the ethical duty of confidentiality?

2.   What difficulties are created by the difference in scope of the crime-fraud exception and the future harms exception to the ethical duty?

3.   What aspects of the ethical duty of confidentiality are analogous to the evidentiary privilege waiver concept?

4.   When a trial court rejects a claim of privilege, it orders revelation of the subject information. Because the privilege is meant to prevent the revelation itself and not only its use in court, a reversal of such an order on appeal is of little value to the party whose private communications have now been revealed. Some thought that this anomaly should require courts to entertain immediate, interlocutory appeals of such trial court orders to have a final determination of the privilege claim before the revelation. But the Supreme Court has held there is no such right to interlocutory review. *Mohawk Industries v. Carpenter*, 130 S. Ct. 599 (2009).

5.   Should there be an exception to the duty of confidentiality allowing a lawyer to reveal client confidences to rectify the wrongful conviction of another? For example, what if during the course of a criminal defense representation, a lawyer's client tells the lawyer that the client committed a different crime for which an innocent person is in prison. Should the lawyer be permitted to reveal the client's information? *See State v. Macumber*, 582 P.2d 162 (Ariz. 1978) (answering "no"); Mass. R. Prof. C. 1.6 (2006) and Alaska R. Prof. Conduct 1.6(b)(1)(B) (2010) (creating such exceptions to confidentiality in Massachusetts and Alaska); James E. Moliterno, *Rectifying Wrongful Convictions: May a Lawyer Reveal Her Client's Confidences to Rectify the Wrongful Conviction of Another?*, 38 Hastings Const. L.Q. 811 (2011) (arguing there should be such an exception generally).

B. TO WHOM IS THE DUTY OWED?

The duty of confidentiality is owed to current clients, former clients, and prospective clients. Prospective clients are owed a measure of confidentiality. As soon as the lawyer and prospective client begin talking with each other as such, the duty of confidentiality attaches to the protected information that the client conveys. If it did not, then the client and lawyer would have to decide whether the client was going to retain the lawyer's services without the candor that the duty of confidentiality is meant to encourage.

Ethics 2000 Commission, February 2002 ABA Amendment to Model Rules

Model Rule 1.18, Prospective Clients

MR 1.18, defines and identifies duties owed to prospective clients.

By reference to Model Rule 1.9, MR 1.18(b) equates the confidentiality duty owed to prospective clients with that owed to former clients. MR 1.18(c) states the terms on which a lawyer who possesses information received from a prospective client is prohibited from representing clients with interests materially adverse to the prospective client. This restriction only applies when the matters are the same or substantially related and when the possessed information could be "significantly harmful" to the prospective client. The latter standard is considerably higher than that which would disqualify a lawyer from representing concurrent clients.

Subject to exception, disqualification of a lawyer under MR 1.18(c) imputes to the firm. The disqualification does not impute when either "both the affected client and the prospective client have given informed consent, confirmed in writing," or the disqualified lawyer acted reasonably in receiving no more information from the prospective client than was necessary, the disqualified lawyer is effectively screened, and written notice is sent to the prospective client. The former of these two exceptions to imputation (the dual client waiver) might in fact allow the affected lawyer, and not just the lawyer's firm, to proceed with the matter if that is what the two clients waive. A more limited waiver of the disqualification of the firm would allow the firm but not the affected lawyer to proceed.

Former clients are owed the duty because the duty would be worth little, would encourage communication little, if its time ran out when the representation ceased. Lawyers take the duty of confidentiality, and the clients' protected information, to the grave.

SWIDLER & BERLIN v. UNITED STATES
524 U.S. 399 (1998)

Chief Justice Rehnquist delivered the opinion of the Court.

Petitioner, an attorney, made notes of an initial interview with a client shortly before the client's death. The Government, represented by the Office of

Independent Counsel, now seeks his notes for use in a criminal investigation. We hold that the notes are protected by the attorney-client privilege.

This dispute arises out of an investigation conducted by the Office of the Independent Counsel into whether various individuals made false statements, obstructed justice, or committed other crimes during investigations of the 1993 dismissal of employees from the White House Travel Office. Vincent W. Foster, Jr., was Deputy White House Counsel when the firings occurred. In July, 1993, Foster met with petitioner James Hamilton, an attorney at petitioner Swidler & Berlin, to seek legal representation concerning possible congressional or other investigations of the firings. During a 2-hour meeting, Hamilton took three pages of handwritten notes. One of the first entries in the notes is the word "Privileged." Nine days later, Foster committed suicide.

In December 1995, a federal grand jury, at the request of the Independent Counsel, issued subpoenas to petitioners Hamilton and Swidler & Berlin for, inter alia, Hamilton's handwritten notes of his meeting with Foster. Petitioners filed a motion to quash, arguing that the notes were protected by the attorney-client privilege and by the work product privilege. The District Court, after examining the notes in camera, concluded they were protected from disclosure by both doctrines and denied enforcement of the subpoenas.

The Court of Appeals for the District of Columbia Circuit reversed.

The dissenting judge would have affirmed the District Court's judgment that the attorney client privilege protected the notes. He concluded that the common-law rule was that the privilege survived death. He found no persuasive reason to depart from this accepted rule, particularly given the importance of the privilege to full and frank client communication.

Petitioners sought review in this Court on both the attorney-client privilege and the work product privilege. We granted certiorari, and we now reverse.

The attorney-client privilege is one of the oldest recognized privileges for confidential communications. *Upjohn Co. v. United States*, 449 U.S. 383, 389 (1981); *Hunt v. Blackburn*, 128 U.S. 464, 470 (1888). The issue presented here is the scope of that privilege; more particularly, the extent to which the privilege survives the death of the client. Our interpretation of the privilege's scope is guided by "the principles of the common law . . . as interpreted by the courts . . . in the light of reason and experience." Fed. Rule Evid. 501.

The Independent Counsel argues that the attorney-client privilege should not prevent disclosure of confidential communications where the client has died and the information is relevant to a criminal proceeding. There is some authority for this position. One state appellate court, *Cohen v. Jenkintown Cab Co.*, 238 Pa. Super. 456, 357 A.2d 689 (1976), and the Court of Appeals below have held the privilege may be subject to posthumous exceptions in certain circumstances. In *Cohen*, a civil case, the court recognized that the privilege generally survives death, but concluded that it could make an exception where the interest of justice was compelling and the interest of the client in preserving the confidence was insignificant.

But other than these two decisions, cases addressing the existence of the privilege after death — most involving the testamentary exception — uniformly presume the privilege survives, even if they do not so hold. *See, e.g., Mayberry v. Indiana*, 670 N.E.2d 1262 (Ind. 1996); *Morris v. Cain*, 39 La. Ann. 712, 1 So. 797 (1887); *People v. Modzelewski*, 203 A.D.2d 594, 611 N.Y.S.2d 22 (1994). Several State Supreme Court decisions expressly hold that the attorney-client privilege extends beyond the death of the client, even in the criminal context. *See In re John Doe Grand Jury Investigation*, 408 Mass. 480, 481-483, 562 N.E.2d 69, 70 (1990); *State v. Doster*, 276 S.C. 647, 650-651, 284 S.E.2d 218, 219 (1981); *State v. Macumber*, 112 Ariz. 569, 571, 544 P.2d 1084, 1086 (1976). In *John Doe Grand Jury Investigation*, for example, the Massachusetts Supreme Court concluded that survival of the privilege was "the clear implication" of its early pronouncements that communications subject to the privilege could not be disclosed at any time. The court further noted that survival of the privilege was "necessarily implied" by cases allowing waiver of the privilege in testamentary disputes.

Such testamentary exception cases consistently presume the privilege survives. *See, e.g., United States v. Osborn*, 561 F.2d 1334, 1340 (9th Cir. 1977). They view testamentary disclosure of communications as an exception to the privilege: "[T]he general rule with respect to confidential communications . . . is that such communications are privileged during the testator's lifetime and, also, after the testator's death unless sought to be disclosed in litigation between the testator's heirs." *Osborn*, 561 F.2d at 1340. The rationale for such disclosure is that it furthers the client's intent.[10]

The Independent Counsel contends that the testamentary exception supports the posthumous termination of the privilege because in practice most cases have refused to apply the privilege posthumously. He further argues that the exception reflects a policy judgment that the interest in settling estates outweighs any posthumous interest in confidentiality. He then reasons by analogy that in criminal proceedings, the interest in determining whether a crime has been committed should trump client confidentiality, particularly since the financial interests of the estate are not at stake.

But the Independent Counsel's interpretation simply does not square with the Case law's implicit acceptance of the privilege's survival and with the treatment of testamentary disclosure as an "exception" or an implied "waiver." And the premise of his analogy is incorrect, since cases consistently recognize that the rationale for the testamentary exception is that it furthers the client's intent. There is no reason to suppose as a general matter that grand jury testimony about confidential

---

[10] [2] About half the States have codified the testamentary exception by providing that a personal representative of the deceased can waive the privilege when heirs or devisees claim through the deceased client (as opposed to parties claiming against the estate, for whom the privilege is not waived). These statutes do not address expressly the continuation of the privilege outside the context of testamentary disputes, although many allow the attorney to assert the privilege on behalf of the client apparently without temporal limit. They thus do not refute or affirm the general presumption in the case law that the privilege survives. California's statute is exceptional in that it apparently allows the attorney to assert the privilege only so long as a holder of the privilege (the estate's personal representative) exists, suggesting the privilege terminates when the estate is wound up. But no other State has followed California's lead in this regard.

communications furthers the client's intent.

Commentators on the law also recognize that the general rule is that the attorney-client privilege continues after death. *See, e.g.*, 8 Wigmore, Evidence § 2323 (McNaughton rev. 1961); Frankel, *The Attorney-Client Privilege After the Death of the Client*, 6 Geo. J. Legal Ethics 45, 78-79 (1992); 1 J. Strong, McCormick on Evidence § 94, at 348 (4th ed. 1992). Undoubtedly, as the Independent Counsel emphasizes, various commentators have criticized this rule, urging that the privilege should be abrogated after the client's death where extreme injustice would result, as long as disclosure would not seriously undermine the privilege by deterring client communication. *See, e.g.*, C. Mueller & L. Kirkpatrick, 2 Federal Evidence § 199, at 380-381 (2d ed. 1994); Restatement (Third) of the Law Governing Lawyers § 127, Comment d (Proposed Final Draft No. 1, Mar. 29, 1996). But even these critics clearly recognize that established law supports the continuation of the privilege and that a contrary rule would be a modification of the common law.

Despite the scholarly criticism, we think there are weighty reasons that counsel in favor of posthumous application. Knowing that communications will remain confidential even after death encourages the client to communicate fully and frankly with counsel. While the fear of disclosure, and the consequent withholding of information from counsel, may be reduced if disclosure is limited to posthumous disclosure in a criminal context, it seems unreasonable to assume that it vanishes altogether. Clients may be concerned about reputation, civil liability, or possible harm to friends or family. Posthumous disclosure of such communications may be as feared as disclosure during the client's lifetime.

The Independent Counsel assumes, incorrectly we believe, that the privilege is analogous to the Fifth Amendment's protection against self-incrimination. But as suggested above, the privilege serves much broader purposes. Clients consult attorneys for a wide variety of reasons, only one of which involves possible criminal liability. Many attorneys act as counselors on personal and family matters, where, in the course of obtaining the desired advice, confidences about family members or financial problems must be revealed in order to assure sound legal advice. The same is true of owners of small businesses who may regularly consult their attorneys about a variety of problems arising in the course of the business. These confidences may not come close to any sort of admission of criminal wrongdoing, but nonetheless be matters which the client would not wish divulged.

The contention that the attorney is being required to disclose only what the client could have been required to disclose is at odds with the basis for the privilege even during the client's lifetime. In related cases, we have said that the loss of evidence admittedly caused by the privilege is justified in part by the fact that without the privilege, the client may not have made such communications in the first place. This is true of disclosure before and after the client's death. Without assurance of the privilege's posthumous application, the client may very well not have made disclosures to his attorney at all, so the loss of evidence is more apparent than real. In the case at hand, it seems quite plausible that Foster, perhaps already contemplating suicide, may not have sought legal advice from Hamilton if he had not been assured the conversation was privileged.

Finally, the Independent Counsel, relying on cases such as *United States v. Nixon*, 418 U.S. 683, 710 (1974), and *Branzburg v. Hayes*, 408 U.S. 665 (1972), urges that privileges be strictly construed because they are inconsistent with the paramount judicial goal of truth seeking. But both *Nixon* and *Branzburg* dealt with the creation of privileges not recognized by the common law, whereas here we deal with one of the oldest recognized privileges in the law. And we are asked, not simply to "construe" the privilege, but to narrow it, contrary to the weight of the existing body of case law.

It has been generally, if not universally, accepted, for well over a century, that the attorney-client privilege survives the death of the client in a case such as this. While the arguments against the survival of the privilege are by no means frivolous, they are based in large part on speculation — thoughtful speculation, but speculation nonetheless — as to whether posthumous termination of the privilege would diminish a client's willingness to confide in an attorney. In an area where empirical information would be useful, it is scant and inconclusive.

Rule 501's direction to look to "the principles of the common law as they may be interpreted by the courts of the United States in the light of reason and experience" does not mandate that a rule, once established, should endure for all time. But here the Independent Counsel has simply not made a sufficient showing to overturn the common law rule embodied in the prevailing case law. Interpreted in the light of reason and experience, that body of law requires that the attorney client privilege prevent disclosure of the notes at issue in this case.

The judgment of the Court of Appeals is

Reversed.

JUSTICE O'CONNOR, with whom JUSTICE SCALIA and JUSTICE THOMAS join, dissenting.

Although the attorney-client privilege ordinarily will survive the death of the client, I do not agree with the Court that it inevitably precludes disclosure of a deceased client's communications in criminal proceedings. In my view, a criminal defendant's right to exculpatory evidence or a compelling law enforcement need for information may, where the testimony is not available from other sources, override a client's posthumous interest in confidentiality.

We have long recognized that "[t]he fundamental basis upon which all rules of evidence must rest — if they are to rest upon reason — is their adaptation to the successful development of the truth." *Funk v. United States*, 290 U.S. 371, 381 (1933). In light of the heavy burden that they place on the search for truth, "[e]videntiary privileges in litigation are not favored, and even those rooted in the Constitution must give way in proper circumstances," *Herbert v. Lando*, 441 U.S. 153, 175 (1979). Consequently, we construe the scope of privileges narrowly. We are reluctant to recognize a privilege or read an existing one expansively unless to do so will serve a "public good transcending the normally predominant principle of utilizing all rational means for ascertaining truth." *Trammel v. United States*, 445 U.S. 40, 50 (1980).

The attorney-client privilege promotes trust in the representational relationship, thereby facilitating the provision of legal services and ultimately the administration of justice. The systemic benefits of the privilege are commonly understood to outweigh the harm caused by excluding critical evidence. A privilege should operate, however, only where "necessary to achieve its purpose," *see Fisher v. United States*, 425 U.S. 391, 403 (1976), and an invocation of the attorney-client privilege should not go unexamined "when it is shown that the interests of the administration of justice can only be frustrated by [its] exercise," *Cohen v. Jenkintown Cab Co.*, 238 Pa. Super. 456, 464, 357 A.2d 689, 693-694 (1976).

I agree that a deceased client may retain a personal, reputational, and economic interest in confidentiality. But, after death, the potential that disclosure will harm the client's interests has been greatly diminished, and the risk that the client will be held criminally liable has abated altogether. Thus, some commentators suggest that terminating the privilege upon the client's death "could not to any substantial degree lessen the encouragement for free disclosure which is [its] purpose." 1 J. Strong, MCCORMICK ON EVIDENCE § 94, at 350 (4th ed. 1992); *see also* RESTATEMENT (THIRD) OF THE LAW GOVERNING LAWYERS § 127, Comment d (Proposed Final Draft No. 1, Mar. 29, 1996). This diminished risk is coupled with a heightened urgency for discovery of a deceased client's communications in the criminal context.

As the Court of Appeals observed, the costs of recognizing an absolute posthumous privilege can be inordinately high. Extreme injustice may occur, for example, where a criminal defendant seeks disclosure of a deceased client's confession to the offense. In my view, the paramount value that our criminal justice system places on protecting an innocent defendant should outweigh a deceased client's interest in preserving confidences. Indeed, even petitioner acknowledges that an exception may be appropriate where the constitutional rights of a criminal defendant are at stake. An exception may likewise be warranted in the face of a compelling law enforcement need for the information.

* * *

Where the exoneration of an innocent criminal defendant or a compelling law enforcement interest is at stake, the harm of precluding critical evidence that is unavailable by any other means outweighs the potential disincentive to forthright communication. In my view, the cost of silence warrants a narrow exception to the rule that the attorney-client privilege survives the death of the client.

Accordingly, I would affirm the judgment of the Court of Appeals. Although the District Court examined the documents in camera, it has not had an opportunity to balance these competing considerations and decide whether the privilege should be trumped in the particular circumstances of this case. Thus, I agree with the Court of Appeals' decision to remand for a determination whether any portion of the notes must be disclosed.

With respect, I dissent.

In addition to representing people, lawyers represent all manner of organizations as clients. The duty of confidentiality is owed to the lawyer's client whether that client is a person or an organization, such as a corporation, a labor union, a public interest group, or a government agency. *See* MR 1.13, Comments 3 and 6.

UPJOHN CO. v. UNITED STATES
449 U.S. 383 (1981)

JUSTICE REHNQUIST delivered the opinion of the Court.

We granted certiorari in this case to address important questions concerning the scope of the attorney-client privilege in the corporate context. . . . With respect to the privilege question the parties and various *amici* have described our task as one of choosing between two "tests" which have gained adherents in the courts of appeals. We are acutely aware, however, that we sit to decide concrete cases and not abstract propositions of law. We decline to lay down a broad rule or series of rules to govern all conceivable future questions in this area, even were we able to do so. We can and do, however, conclude that the attorney-client privilege protects the communications involved in this case from compelled disclosure. . . .

I

Petitioner Upjohn Co. manufactures and sells pharmaceuticals here and abroad. In January 1976 independent accountants conducting an audit of one of Upjohn's foreign subsidiaries discovered that the subsidiary made payments to or for the benefit of foreign government officials in order to secure government business. The accountants so informed petitioner Mr. Gerard Thomas, Upjohn's Vice President, Secretary, and General Counsel. Thomas is a member of the Michigan and New York Bars, and has been Upjohn's General Counsel for 20 years. He consulted with outside counsel and R.T. Parfet, Jr., Upjohn's Chairman of the Board. It was decided that the company would conduct an internal investigation of what were termed "questionable payments." As part of this investigation the attorneys prepared a letter containing a questionnaire which was sent to "All Foreign General and Area Managers" over the Chairman's signature. The letter began by noting recent disclosures that several American companies made "possibly illegal" payments to foreign government officials and emphasized that the management needed full information concerning any such payments made by Upjohn. The letter indicated that the Chairman had asked Thomas, identified as "the company's General Counsel," "to conduct an investigation for the purpose of determining the nature and magnitude of any payments made by the Upjohn Company or any of its subsidiaries to any employee or official of a foreign government." The questionnaire sought detailed information concerning such payments. Managers were instructed to treat the investigation as "highly confidential" and not to discuss it with anyone other than Upjohn employees who might be helpful in providing the requested information. Responses were to be sent directly to Thomas. Thomas and outside counsel also interviewed the recipients of the questionnaire and some 33 other Upjohn officers or employees as part of the investigation.

On March 26, 1976, the company voluntarily submitted a preliminary report to the Securities and Exchange Commission on Form 8-K disclosing certain

questionable payments. A copy of the report was simultaneously submitted to the
Internal Revenue Service, which immediately began an investigation to determine
the tax consequences of the payments. Special agents conducting the investigation
were given lists by Upjohn of all those interviewed and all who had responded to
the questionnaire. On November 23, 1976, the Service issued a summons pursuant
to 26 U.S.C. § 7602 demanding production of:

> All files relative to the investigation conducted under the supervision of
> Gerard Thomas to identify payments to employees of foreign governments
> and any political contributions made by the Upjohn Company or any of its
> affiliates since January 1, 1971 and to determine whether any funds of the
> Upjohn Company had been improperly accounted for on the corporate
> books during the same period.

> The records should include but not be limited to written questionnaires
> sent to managers of the Upjohn Company's foreign affiliates, and memo-
> randums or notes of the interviews conducted in the United States and
> abroad with officers and employees of the Upjohn Company and its
> subsidiaries.

The company declined to produce the documents specified in the second
paragraph on the grounds that they were protected from disclosure by the
attorney-client privilege . . . . On August 31, 1977, the United States filed a petition
seeking enforcement of the summons in the United States District Court for the
Western District of Michigan. That court adopted the recommendation of a
Magistrate who concluded that the summons should be enforced. Petitioners
appealed to the Court of Appeals for the Sixth Circuit which rejected the
Magistrate's finding of a waiver of the attorney-client privilege, but agreed that the
privilege did not apply "[to] the extent that the communications were made by
officers and agents not responsible for directing Upjohn's actions in response to
legal advice . . . for the simple reason that the communications were not the
'client's.'" The court reasoned that accepting petitioners' claim for a broader
application of the privilege would encourage upper-echelon management to ignore
unpleasant facts and create too broad a "zone of silence." Noting that Upjohn's
counsel had interviewed officials such as the Chairman and President, the Court of
Appeals remanded to the District Court so that a determination of who was within
the "control group" could be made. In a concluding footnote the court stated that
the work-product doctrine "is not applicable to administrative summonses issued
under 26 U.S.C. § 7602."

II

Federal Rule of Evidence 501 provides that "the privilege of a witness . . . shall
be governed by the principles of the common law as they may be interpreted by the
courts of the United States in light of reason and experience."

. . . Admittedly complications in the application of the privilege arise when the
client is a corporation, which in theory is an artificial creature of the law, and not an
individual; but this Court has assumed that the privilege applies when the client is
a corporation and the Government does not contest the general proposition.

The Court of Appeals, however, considered the application of the privilege in the corporate context to present a "different problem," since the client was an inanimate entity and "only the senior management, guiding and integrating the several operations, . . . can be said to possess an identity analogous to the corporation as a whole." The first case to articulate the so-called "control group test" adopted by the court below, *Philadelphia v. Westinghouse Electric Corp.*, 210 F. Supp. 483, 485 (E.D. Pa.), *petition for mandamus and prohibition denied sub nom.*, *General Electric Co. v. Kirkpatrick*, 312 F.2d 742 (3d Cir. 1962), *cert. denied*, 372 U.S. 943 (1963), reflected a similar conceptual approach:

> Keeping in mind that the question is, Is it the corporation which is seeking the lawyer's advice when the asserted privileged communication is made?, the most satisfactory solution, I think, is that if the employee making the communication, of whatever rank he may be, is in a position to control or even to take a substantial part in a decision about any action which the corporation may take upon the advice of the attorney, . . . then, in effect, he is (or personifies) the corporation when he makes his disclosure to the lawyer and the privilege would apply.

Such a view, we think, overlooks the fact that the privilege exists to protect not only the giving of professional advice to those who can act on it but also the giving of information to the lawyer to enable him to give sound and informed advice. The first step in the resolution of any legal problem is ascertaining the factual background and sifting through the facts with an eye to the legally relevant. . . .

In the case of the individual client the provider of information and the person who acts on the lawyer's advice are one and the same. In the corporate context, however, it will frequently be employees beyond the control group who will possess the information needed by the corporation's lawyers. Middle-level — and indeed lower-level — employees can, by actions within the scope of their employment, embroil the corporation in serious legal difficulties, and it is only natural that these employees would have the relevant information needed by corporate counsel if he is adequately to advise the client with respect to such actual or potential difficulties.

* * *

The control group test adopted by the court below thus frustrates the very purpose of the privilege by discouraging the communication of relevant information by employees of the client to attorneys seeking to render legal advice to the client corporation. The attorney's advice will also frequently be more significant to noncontrol group members than to those who officially sanction the advice, and the control group test makes it more difficult to convey full and frank legal advice to the employees who will put into effect the client corporation's policy.

The narrow scope given the attorney-client privilege by the court below not only makes it difficult for corporate attorneys to formulate sound advice when their client is faced with a specific legal problem but also threatens to limit the valuable efforts of corporate counsel to ensure their client's compliance with the law. In light of the vast and complicated array of regulatory legislation confronting the modern corporation, corporations, unlike most individuals, "constantly go to lawyers to find out how to obey the law," Burnham, *The Attorney-Client Privilege in the Corporate*

Arena, 24 Bus. Law. 901, 913 (1969), particularly since compliance with the law in this area is hardly an instinctive matter.

The communications at issue were made by Upjohn employees[11] to counsel for Upjohn acting as such, at the direction of corporate superiors in order to secure legal advice from counsel. As the Magistrate found, "Mr. Thomas consulted with the Chairman of the Board and outside counsel and thereafter conducted a factual investigation to determine the nature and extent of the questionable payments and to be in a position to give legal advice to the company with respect to the payments." Information, not available from upper-echelon management, was needed to supply a basis for legal advice concerning compliance with securities and tax laws, foreign laws, currency regulations, duties to shareholders, and potential litigation in each of these areas. The communications concerned matters within the scope of the employees' corporate duties, and the employees themselves were sufficiently aware that they were being questioned in order that the corporation could obtain legal advice. The questionnaire identified Thomas as "the company's General Counsel" and referred in its opening sentence to the possible illegality of payments such as the ones on which information was sought. A statement of policy accompanying the questionnaire clearly indicated the legal implications of the investigation. The policy statement was issued "in order that there be no uncertainty in the future as to the policy with respect to the practices which are the subject of this investigation." It began "Upjohn will comply with all laws and regulations," and stated that commissions or payments "will not be used as a subterfuge for bribes or illegal payments" and that all payments must be "proper and legal." Any future agreements with foreign distributors or agents were to be approved "by a company attorney" and any questions concerning the policy were to be referred "to the company's General Counsel." This statement was issued to Upjohn employees worldwide, so that even those interviewees not receiving a questionnaire were aware of the legal implications of the interviews. Pursuant to explicit instructions from the Chairman of the Board, the communications were considered "highly confidential" when made, and have been kept confidential by the company. Consistent with the underlying purposes of the attorney-client privilege, these communications must be protected against compelled disclosure.

*   *   *

Needless to say, we decide only the case before us, and do not undertake to draft a set of rules which should govern challenges to investigatory subpoenas. Any such approach would violate the spirit of Federal Rule of Evidence 501. *See* S. Rep. No. 93-1277, p. 13 (1974) ("the recognition of a privilege based on a confidential relationship . . . should be determined on a case-by-case basis"). While such a "case-by-case" basis may to some slight extent undermine desirable certainty in the boundaries of the attorney-client privilege, it obeys the spirit of the Rules. At the same time we conclude that the narrow "control group test" sanctioned by the

---

[11] [3] Seven of the eighty-six employees interviewed by counsel had terminated their employment with Upjohn at the time of the interview. Petitioners argues that the privilege should nonetheless apply to communications by these former employees concerning activities during their period of employment. Neither the District Court nor the Court of Appeals had occasion to address this issue, and we decline to decide it without the benefit of treatment below.

Court of Appeals in this case cannot, consistent with "the principles of the common law as . . . interpreted . . . in the light of reason and experience," Fed. Rule Evid. 501, govern the development of the law in this area.

* * *

Accordingly, the judgment of the Court of Appeals is reversed, and the case remanded for further proceedings.

It is so ordered.

NOTES, QUESTIONS, AND EXAMPLES

1. What must the government do to obtain the information it wants after the Court's decision in *Upjohn*? What if this had instead been a criminal investigation against one of the officers and the government sought that officer's response to counsel? What if it had been the officer's private counsel? Who or what holds the privilege in an organization? Who or what decides to waive it?

2. A government agency-organizational client presents special problems for the duty of confidentiality. Because of the special public responsibilities of government agencies, government lawyers may strike a confidentiality balance somewhat more toward the public interest in disclosure of government wrongdoing. *See* Moliterno, *The Federal Government Lawyer's Duty to Breach Confidentiality*, 14 TEMP. POL. & CIV. RTS. L. REV. 633 (2005).

INTERNATIONAL NOTES

1. One of the most striking differences with U.S. confidentiality conventions is the doctrine in civil law systems that correspondence between a lawyer and his opposing counsel is protected as confidential even from the client, unless the document bears a stamp with contrary indication. The official commentary on the CCBE Code provides this explanation, "In certain member states, communication between lawyers (written or by word of mouth) are normally regarded as confidential." This means that lawyers accept that those communications may not be disclosed to others and copies may not be sent to the lawyer's own client. This principle is recognized in Belgium, France, Greece, Italy, Luxemburg, Portugal, and Spain. Such communications if in writing are marked as "confidential" or "sous la foi du Palais." CCBE Explanatory Memorandum, Commentary on art. 5.3 (adopted in May 1989, superseded in May, 2006). This material is quoted from the old version of the Explanatory Memorandum as the newer version omits reference to specific countries.

2. In 2010, in *Akzo Nobel Chemicals Ltd. v. EU*, the European Court of Justice (ECJ) unanimously decided that communications between in-house counsel and company executives are not subject to the attorney client-privilege, which is called the professional privilege in Europe. This ruling reaffirmed earlier decisions to the same effect.

3. In its articulation of a lawyer's duty of confidentiality, the Lawyers Law of the People's Republic of China emphasizes the protection of "state secrets" as well as the secrets of clients. It provides that, "lawyers shall maintain the confidentiality of any State secrets and commercial secrets of the parties concerned that they learn in the course of their practice. Lawyers may not reveal the private affairs of the parties concerned." LAWYERS LAW, art. 33 (P.R.C.). The need to protect the confidentiality of state secrets may inhibit a Chinese lawyer's ability to represent the interests of a client. In cases involving state secrets, a suspect may be denied counsel in the investigation phase of a case. When access is allowed to a client, authorities may insist on remaining within hearing distance or record attorney-client conversations, thus breaching attorney-client confidentiality. *See* Ping Yu, *Glittery Promise vs. Dismal Reality: The Role of a Criminal Lawyer in the People's Republic of China After the 1996 Revision of the Criminal Procedure Law,* 35 VAND. J. TRANSNAT'L L. 827, 836 (2002).

IN RE GRAND JURY SUBPOENA DUCES TECUM
112 F.3d 910 (8th Cir. 1997)

BOWMAN, CIRCUIT JUDGE.

The Office of Independent Counsel (OIC) appeals from an order of the District Court denying the OIC's motion to compel the production of documents subpoenaed by a federal grand jury. We reverse and remand.

I.

The task assigned to Independent Counsel Kenneth W. Starr is to investigate and prosecute matters "relating in any way to James B. McDougal's, President William Jefferson Clinton's, or Mrs. Hillary Rodham Clinton's relationships with Madison Guaranty Savings & Loan Association, Whitewater Development Corporation, or Capital Management Services, Inc." Mr. Starr also is charged with the duty of pursuing evidence of other violations of the law developed during and connected with or arising out of his primary investigation, known generally as "Whitewater."

On June 21, 1996, as part of its investigation, the OIC directed to the White House a grand jury subpoena that required production of "[a]ll documents created during meetings attended by any attorney from the Office of Counsel to the President and Hillary Rodham Clinton (regardless whether any other person was present)" pertaining to several Whitewater-related subjects. The White House identified nine sets of notes responsive to the subpoena but refused to produce them, citing executive privilege, attorney-client privilege, and the attorney work product doctrine.

On August 19, 1996, the OIC filed a motion before the District Court to compel production of two of the nine sets of documents identified by the White House. The first set of documents comprises notes taken by Associate Counsel to the President Miriam Nemetz on July 11, 1995, at a meeting attended by Mrs. Clinton, Special Counsel to the President Jane Sherburne, and Mrs. Clinton's personal attorney,

David Kendall. The subject of this meeting was Mrs. Clinton's activities following the death of Deputy Counsel to the President Vincent W. Foster, Jr. The documents in the second collection are notes taken by Ms. Sherburne on January 26, 1996, during meetings attended by Mrs. Clinton, Mr. Kendall, Nicole Seligman (a partner of Mr. Kendall's), and, at times, John Quinn, Counsel to the President. These meetings, which took place during breaks in and immediately after Mrs. Clinton's testimony before a federal grand jury in Washington, D.C., concerned primarily the discovery of certain billing records from the Rose Law Firm in the residence area of the White House.

The White House abandoned its claim of executive privilege before the District Court, relying solely on the attorney-client privilege and the work product doctrine. Mrs. Clinton also entered a personal appearance through counsel in the District Court and asserted her personal attorney-client privilege. The District Court found it unnecessary to reach the broadest question presented by the OIC, whether a federal governmental entity may assert the attorney-client privilege or the work product doctrine in response to a subpoena by a federal grand jury. Instead, the court concluded that because Mrs. Clinton and the White House had a "genuine and reasonable (whether or not mistaken)" belief that the conversations at issue were privileged, the attorney-client privilege applied. In addition, the court held that the work product doctrine prevented disclosure of the notes to the grand jury.

The OIC appealed, and we granted expedited review. Mrs. Clinton moved to intervene formally, and we granted her motion. The case was submitted following oral arguments in a closed session.

*   *   *

III.

We will address first the issue that the District Court found it unnecessary to decide: whether an entity of the federal government may use the attorney-client privilege to avoid complying with a subpoena by a federal grand jury. Before we confront the merits of this question, however, we believe it is important to identify what is not at issue in this case. The OIC does not seek to invade the attorney-client relationship existing between Mrs. Clinton, in her personal capacity, and Mr. Kendall, her personal lawyer. The privilege set up by the White House is strictly a governmental privilege, with the White House (or the Office of the President, alternatively) as client and Ms. Sherburne and Ms. Nemetz as attorneys. Accordingly, the White House is the real party in interest in this case, although Mrs. Clinton presents arguments similar to those of the White House in her capacity as an intervenor.

The discussion that follows can be summed up rather simply. We need not decide whether a governmental attorney-client privilege exists in other contexts, for it is enough to conclude that even if it does, the White House may not use the privilege to withhold potentially relevant information from a federal grand jury.

A.

"[T]he privilege of a witness, person, government, State, or political subdivision thereof [is] governed by the principles of the common law as they may be interpreted by the courts of the United States in the light of reason and experience." Fed. R. Evid. 501. We must therefore apply the federal common law of attorney-client privilege to the situation presented by this case.

[The court explained that for purposes of the privilege, a government entity may be a client.]

The White House has located only two cases involving a clash between a grand jury and a claim of governmental attorney-client privilege, [one of which is clearly inapposite.] In *In re Grand Jury Subpoena (Doe)*, 886 F.2d 135 (6th Cir. 1989), the Sixth Circuit considered a subpoena issued by a federal grand jury to the city of Detroit. The court vacated the district court's finding that the city council was not the client of the city's corporation counsel but concluded that the application of the attorney-client privilege depended on the confidentiality of the communications, which in turn depended on the proper application of the state open-meetings law. The court remanded the case to allow the district court to resolve that issue.

For several reasons, we do not find this case particularly persuasive. The Sixth Circuit case, involving a standoff between a federal grand jury and a city government, implicates potentially serious federalism concerns not present in the case before us. The court's brief opinion is also rather unpersuasive legally, as it contains no acknowledgment that to extend the privilege to a governmental body where individuals within the government are being scrutinized by a grand jury for criminal activity poses anything but a routine concern. (The court cited only two privilege cases, neither of which had anything to do with government lawyers.)

Moving somewhat further afield, the White House cites a number of cases in which courts have applied a governmental attorney-client privilege in civil actions. These cases, all of which involved either the sui generis jurisprudence of the Freedom of Information Act or a situation in which the party seeking information was a private litigant adversarial to the government, are not particularly persuasive in the circumstances of this case. Even if we were to conclude that the governmental attorney-client privilege ordinarily applies in civil litigation pitting the federal government against private parties, a question that we need not and do not decide, we believe the criminal context of the instant case, in which an entity of the federal government seeks to withhold information from a federal criminal investigation, presents a rather different issue.

Lacking persuasive direction in the case law, we turn to general principles.

> For more than three centuries it has now been recognized as a fundamental maxim that the public (in the words sanctioned by Lord Hardwicke) has a right to every man's evidence. When we come to examine the various claims of exemption, we start with the primary assumption that there is a general duty to give what testimony one is capable of giving, and that any exemptions which may exist are distinctly exceptional, being so many derogations from a positive general rule.

general rule

United States v. Bryan, 339 U.S. 323, 331 (1950) (quoting 8 J. WIGMORE, EVIDENCE § 2192 (3d ed. 1940)). Privileges, as exceptions to the general rule, "are not lightly created nor expansively construed, for they are in derogation of the search for truth." *Nixon*, 418 U.S. at 710. It is appropriate to recognize a privilege " 'only to the very limited extent that permitting a refusal to testify or excluding relevant evidence has a public good transcending the normally predominant principle of utilizing all rational means for ascertaining truth.' "

Federal common law recognizes a privilege only in rare situations.

The White House does not dispute that a grand jury has broad investigatory powers. As the Supreme Court has recognized, the principle that the public is entitled to "every man's evidence" is "particularly applicable to grand jury proceedings." *Branzburg*, 408 U.S. at 688. . . .

In essence, the parties' arguments center on two cases, neither of which is directly analogous to this case, but each of which has relevance to our decision: *Nixon* and *Upjohn*. In *Nixon*, a special prosecutor directed a subpoena duces tecum to President Nixon, seeking tapes and other materials for use in the criminal trial of seven defendants, including former White House officials. The President refused to comply with the subpoena, claiming executive privilege. The Court recognized that the need for confidential presidential communication "can be said to derive from the supremacy of each branch within its own assigned area of constitutional duties," and that the privilege for presidential communications "is fundamental to the operation of Government and inextricably rooted in the separation of powers under the Constitution." Despite the strong constitutional foundations of the privilege, however, the Court concluded that it had to give way to the special prosecutor's subpoena . . . .

The OIC argues that under the logic of Nixon, the White House's claim of privilege must give way here, for if the governmental attorney-client privilege exists at all, it is certainly not constitutionally based. It is true, as the White House responds, that the President did not assert an attorney-client privilege in *Nixon*, and so the case is not directly controlling. We agree with the OIC, however, that *Nixon* is indicative of the general principle that the government's need for confidentiality may be subordinated to the needs of the government's own criminal justice processes.

The White House counters by pointing out that *Nixon* itself recognized the importance of common-law privileges, including the attorney-client privilege. No one, the White House argues, would suppose that the special prosecutor could compel the production of notes made by a private lawyer concerning a conversation with a private client about even the most routine traffic ticket. Why then, the argument continues, should the benefit of this important privilege not be available to the White House?

Our discussion of the White House's primary argument, revolving around *Upjohn*, should demonstrate why we believe the private-attorney analogy is inapposite. The White House proffers *Upjohn* as emblematic of the wide sweep of the attorney-client privilege, and we agree with that characterization, to a point. . . .

As the White House points out, *Upjohn* contains strong language about the importance of the attorney-client privilege in encouraging the full and frank presentation of legal advice to corporations, which helps to insure that corporations will act within the law. And the Court recognized that "if the purpose of the attorney-client privilege is to be served, the attorney and client must be able to predict with some degree of certainty whether particular discussions will be protected." Nevertheless, we believe that important differences between the government and nongovernmental organizations such as business corporations weigh against the application of the principles of *Upjohn* in this case. First, the actions of White House personnel, whatever their capacity, cannot expose the White House as an entity to criminal liability. (No one suggests that any of the conduct under investigation by the OIC could expose the White House to civil liability.) A corporation, in contrast, may be subject to both civil and criminal liability for the actions of its agents, and corporate attorneys therefore have a compelling interest in ferreting out any misconduct by employees. The White House simply has no such interest with respect to the actions of Mrs. Clinton.

We also find it significant that executive branch employees, including attorneys, are under a statutory duty to report criminal wrongdoing by other employees to the Attorney General. *See* 28 U.S.C. § 535(b) (1994). Even more importantly, however, the general duty of public service calls upon government employees and agencies to favor disclosure over concealment. The difference between the public interest and the private interest is perhaps, by itself, reason enough to find *Upjohn* unpersuasive in this case.

*   *   *

We believe the strong public interest in honest government and in exposing wrongdoing by public officials would be ill-served by recognition of a governmental attorney-client privilege applicable in criminal proceedings inquiring into the actions of public officials. We also believe that to allow any part of the federal government to use its in-house attorneys as a shield against the production of information relevant to a federal criminal investigation would represent a gross misuse of public assets. *See also Jupiter Painting*, 87 F.R.D. at 598 (recognizing the "pernicious potential" of a governmental attorney-client privilege "in a government top-heavy with lawyers").[13]

We recognize the White House's concern that "[a]n uncertain privilege, or one which purports to be certain but results in widely varying applications by the courts,

---

[13] [10] Judge Kopf cites several opinions of the Office of Legal Counsel for support. We find each of these opinions unpersuasive in the context of this case. Theodore Olson's 1982 opinion concerning the confidentiality of communications between the President and the Attorney General relies significantly on Freedom of Information Act cases and *Upjohn*, which we believe are not helpful to the White House in this case, and does not purport to address the viability of the privilege in the face of a grand jury subpoena. *See* Memorandum for the Attorney General re: Confidentiality of the Attorney General's Communications in Counseling the President, 6 Op. Off. Legal Counsel 481, 490-97 (1982). Each of the other opinions cited by the White House involves a government attorney representing a government official sued in his or her individual capacity in a *Bivens* action. In such a case, the government attorney enters into a personal attorney-client relationship with the individual defendant, and the usual privilege applies. No such personal attorney-client relationship exists between Mrs. Clinton and the White House attorneys.

is little better than no privilege at all." *Upjohn*, 449 U.S. at 393. Our first response is that the White House assumes that the attorney-client privilege is more predictable ex ante than it actually is. A client discussing an issue with a lawyer cannot know, for example, whether a bankruptcy trustee will later waive the privilege, or whether the lawyer's assistance will later become an issue in a proceeding, or whether the lawyer and client will later become involved in a dispute, any of which may result in disclosure of the conversation. Even so, we believe our holding in this case does not make the duties of government attorneys significantly more difficult. Assuming arguendo that there is a governmental attorney-client privilege in other circumstances, confidentiality will suffer only in those situations that a grand jury might later see fit to investigate. Because agencies and entities of the government are not themselves subject to criminal liability, a government attorney is free to discuss anything with a government official — except for potential criminal wrongdoing by that official — without fearing later revelation of the conversation. An official who fears he or she may have violated the criminal law and wishes to speak with an attorney in confidence should speak with a private attorney, not a government attorney.

Nor do we foresee any likely effect of our decision on the ability of a government lawyer to advise an official who is contemplating a future course of conduct. If the attorney explains the law accurately and the official follows that advice, no harm can come from later disclosure of the advice, which would be unlikely anyway. Like the *Nixon* Court, "we cannot conclude that advisers will be moved to temper the candor of their remarks by the infrequent occasions of disclosure because of the possibility that such conversations will be called for in the context of a criminal prosecution." *Nixon*, 418 U.S. at 712. The White House's "chilling effect" argument is no more persuasive in this case than it was in Nixon.

*   *   *

D

For the reasons stated, we conclude that the White House may not use the attorney-client privilege to avoid complying with the subpoena issued in this case by a federal grand jury calling for the notes in question of Ms. Nemetz and Ms. Sherburne.

*   *   *

VI.

To sum up, we hold that neither the attorney-client privilege nor the attorney work product doctrine is available to the White House in the circumstances of this case. Accordingly, the order of the District Court is reversed, and the case is remanded for the entry of an order granting the OIC's motion to compel.

KOPF, DISTRICT JUDGE, dissenting.

I. INTRODUCTION

I respectfully dissent. This case involves the institutional capacity of the President of the United States to function with the advice of legal counsel. The clarity of this point is made evident by the subpoena, which demands notes taken by "the Office of Counsel to the President." Because of this important fact, I would apply *United States v. Nixon*, 418 U.S. 683 (1974), rather than the position urged by the Independent Counsel (IC). I would not follow *Nixon* for some purposes, and disregard it for others.

Federal Rule of Evidence 501 requires that we decide whether federal common law extends the attorney-client privilege to the White House.

*   *   *

There is no reason to deny the well-recognized principle that the government, including the White House, is legitimately entitled to the attorney-client privilege (and the work-product doctrine). The White House, no less than a state government or a corporation, is entitled to the privilege in all types of cases, including criminal cases, so that the White House can comply with the law. The privilege advances the public interest by assuring that the White House will receive well-founded, fact-specific legal advice based upon candid responses from White House officials. Accordingly, I disagree with the IC's position that the White House lacks the attorney-client privilege.

However, the Supreme Court's decision in *Nixon* persuades me that the White House privilege gives way to a grand jury subpoena duces tecum issued under the direction of the IC provided the procedural protections of *Nixon* have been observed.

Unlike the IC, I believe *Nixon* overcomes, but does not erase, the privilege. *Nixon* requires us to conclude that the President's general need for confidentiality, expressed here by the attorney-client privilege, is overshadowed by the grand jury's general need for evidence of the truth. Still, *Nixon* does not, as the IC urges and the majority finds, permit us to assume that the White House lacks the privilege in the first instance.

In particular, I would require, as *Nixon* did in the context of a trial subpoena, that before documents are revealed to the grand jury:

> (1) the special prosecutor must make an initial threshold showing before the district court that the documents are: (a) specifically needed; (b) relevant; and (c) admissible;

> (2) assuming such a showing has been made, the documents are first delivered to the district judge, who will examine the documents in chambers, to decide if in fact the documents are relevant and admissible, and irrelevant documents will be returned under seal to the White House.

I do not agree that a grand jury subpoena directed at the White House is more important than the trial subpoena directed at the White House in *Nixon*. The President's justifiable need for confidentiality is, as *Nixon* recognized, ever present no matter what other governmental interests are asserted by a prosecutor. The public purpose served by a grand jury is no more important than the public purpose served by a criminal trial. Thus, I disagree with the court's failure to require the IC to make the same type of showing on a motion to compel a response to a grand jury subpoena directed at the White House as would be required by *Nixon* for a trial subpoena.

Finally, because we should now declare for the first time that *Nixon* overcomes the White House privilege if a proper showing is made, Mrs. Clinton would consult with White House lawyers at her peril in the future. She would be informed from our opinion that such consultations might no longer be protected since the other party to her conversations (the White House and its lawyers) could be obligated to respond to a grand jury subpoena if the prosecutor made the showing required by *Nixon*. Consequently, in the future, and to the extent of a grand jury subpoena, any such communications could not legally be "intended" by Mrs. Clinton as "confidential" under Rule 503(a)(4) because she would know and understand that her communications could be "disclosed to third persons."

Accordingly, I would affirm the district court's properly cautious decision refusing to enforce the subpoena. Yet I would make it clear that the White House attorney-client privilege gives way to a grand jury subpoena issued under the supervision of the IC if the procedural protections afforded the White House by *Nixon* are satisfied.

* * *

I would affirm the district court's prudent refusal to enforce the subpoena.

NOTES, QUESTIONS, AND EXAMPLES

1. The court says that White House and other government lawyers are under a "duty to report criminal wrongdoing by other employees to the Attorney General" pursuant to 28 U.S.C. § 535(b). Is § 535(b) an "other law" exception to Model Rule 1.6 for government lawyers? If so, may government lawyers ever maintain a confidence for an individual government employee client regarding a past crime? Or is it that the government employee client is not the government lawyer's client at all? What about the whistleblower laws? Are they "other law"? See, for example, Whistleblower Protection Act of 1989 (WPA), Pub. L. No. 101-12, 103 Stat. 16 (Apr. 10, 1989), whose purpose is stated to be to "encourage" revelation of government employee misconduct. 5 U.S.C. § 2302(b)(8) (2000).

2. Both lawyers and clients routinely use agents for communicating with each other. Both lawyers and clients employ agents for various functions. These agents' communications on behalf of either lawyer or client are within the evidentiary privilege.

C.   TO WHAT DOES THE DUTY APPLY?

The duty of confidentiality applies to "information relating to representation of a client." MR 1.6(a). For some purposes, it is important to distinguish between what is protected by both the evidentiary privilege and the duty of confidentiality and what is protected by the duty of confidentiality alone. In general, to be protected by the evidentiary privilege, the information must come from the client or a client's agent. Information that the lawyer learns from third parties is protected by the duty of confidentiality but not the privilege. Remember, to be protected by the duty of confidentiality, the information need merely "relat[e] to representation of a client." MR 1.6(a).

The duty of confidentiality applies to all information relating to the representation, not merely communications from client to lawyer. Lawyer observations are protected by the duty of confidentiality. Communications from third parties about the representation are protected by the duty of confidentiality.

NOTES, QUESTIONS, AND EXAMPLES

1.   Lawyer represents Client in an auto accident case. Lawyer goes to Joe's AllStar Café, a bar outside Client's place of employment. Bartender Joe tells Lawyer that Client is a regular customer who consumes several shots of bourbon whiskey each day at the end of Client's shift. Joe's statement to Lawyer is protected by the duty of confidentiality but not by the evidentiary privilege. It is not a communication from the client.

2.   Lawyer represents Client in a property dispute. Lawyer searches the property records at the county courthouse and discovers that Client does not have a sound claim to the disputed property. This information is protected by the duty of confidentiality but not by the evidentiary privilege.

3.   Lawyer represents Client in a contract dispute. Client is a manufacturer of wing-nuts. Client sold defective wing-nuts to Careless Buyer. Client tells Lawyer that he intentionally defrauded Careless Buyer. This information is protected by both the evidentiary privilege and the duty of confidentiality.

D.   EXCEPTIONS TO THE DUTY OF CONFIDENTIALITY

1.   Consent

The client is the holder of the evidentiary privilege and the party whose communication is being protected. After consultation, a client may consent to disclosure of information that would otherwise be protected by the duty of confidentiality. MR 1.6(a). In order to carry out the purposes of the representation, some information that would be subject to the duty of confidentiality must be disclosed.

2. Self-Defense and Fees

A lawyer is permitted to reveal (and use for her own benefit) information that would be protected by the duty of confidentiality in three self-defense type situations. The three self-defense type situations are:

> [T]o establish a claim or defense on behalf of the lawyer in a controversy between the lawyer and the client, to establish a defense to a criminal charge or a civil claim against the lawyer based upon conduct in which the client was involved, or to respond to allegations in any proceeding concerning the lawyer's representation of the client.

MR 1.6(b)(2).

SQUIRE, SANDERS & DEMPSEY, L.L.P. v. GIVAUDAN FLAVORS CORPORATION
127 Ohio St. 3d 161, 937 N.E.2d 533 (2010)

O'DONNELL, J.

Squire, Sanders & Dempsey, L.L.P., appeals from a judgment of the Eighth District Court of Appeals reversing a discovery order that had compelled Givaudan Flavors Corporation to produce documents related to Squire Sanders' representation of Givaudan and that had directed Givaudan's former and current general counsel to testify regarding attorney-client communications in connection with litigation over the amount of Squire Sanders' legal fees and the adequacy of the legal services it rendered.

The issue in this case is whether the common-law self-protection exception to the attorney-client privilege, permitting an attorney to reveal attorney-client communications when necessary to establish a claim or defense on the behalf of the attorney, applies as an exception to R.C. 2317.02(A), which provides that an attorney "shall not testify . . . concerning a communication made to the attorney by a client in that relation or the attorney's advice to a client."

Ohio recognizes other common-law exceptions to the attorney-client privilege. For example, as detailed below, Ohio recognizes the crime-fraud exception to prevent concealment of attorney or client wrongdoing. Similarly, in this case, recognition of the common-law self-protection exception to the attorney-client privilege as part of Ohio law aids the administration of justice and is supported by decisions of other jurisdictions addressing this issue.

Pursuant to the common-law self-protection exception to the attorney-client privilege, an attorney should be permitted to testify concerning attorney-client communications when necessary to collect a legal fee or to defend against a charge of malpractice or other wrongdoing in litigation against a client or former client. Ohio recognizes this exception. As a result, we reverse the judgment of the court of appeals and remand the cause for further proceedings consistent with this opinion.

Facts and Procedural History

In 2003, the law firm of Squire, Sanders & Dempsey, L.L.P., began to represent Givaudan Flavors Corporation in connection with litigation filed by employees and others who allegedly became ill after inhaling the butter flavoring that Givaudan produced for use on popcorn. At that time, Frederick King, then Givaudan's vice president for legal affairs, selected Squire Sanders to handle the litigation and generally approved payment of invoices submitted by the firm.

In January 2007, Givaudan replaced King with Jane Garfinkel, naming her senior vice president and general counsel. She determined that the litigation attorneys defending the "butter flavor" litigation lacked sufficient qualification, experience, or expertise in pulmonary toxic tort litigation, and she thought that Squire Sanders had inadequately handled the defense, prolonging the litigation and generating excessive legal fees. Her deposition testimony revealed that she decided not to submit Squire Sanders' invoices for payment out of her concern that they showed a pattern of dishonesty, inaccuracy, and incompleteness. In May 2007, she terminated Squire Sanders without paying any of the outstanding invoices for legal services rendered by Squire Sanders.

Squire Sanders filed this action for breach of contract and money due on account, alleging that Givaudan owed $1,801,204.37 in legal fees as a result of work it had performed up to the date of its termination. Givaudan denied liability and counterclaimed for breach of contract, legal malpractice, breach of fiduciary duty, fraud, and unjust enrichment. It asserted that Squire Sanders had charged unreasonably excessive, and unnecessary legal fees while failing to provide competent and adequate legal services.

Through discovery, Squire Sanders sought production of documents related to its representation of Givaudan, including its budgeting and staffing of the litigation, trial strategy, handling of witnesses, and Givaudan's allegation that it failed to pursue opportunities for settlement; it also requested documents concerning Givaudan's decision to terminate its representation. Givaudan objected, asserting that the law firm sought documents protected by the attorney-client privilege and the work-product doctrine.

Further, when Squire Sanders deposed King and Garfinkel, Givaudan asserted attorney-client privilege and the work-product doctrine to prevent either King or Garfinkel from answering questions. Givaudan objected when counsel for Squire Sanders asked King about the firm's staffing of the case, the resources the firm committed to the litigation, the strategy it pursued in defending Givaudan, and the adequacy of the firm's trial preparation. Givaudan similarly asserted attorney-client privilege to prohibit Garfinkel from answering questions about how she had formed her view that the Squire Sanders litigation team lacked qualified leadership and experienced attorneys, that it had inadequately prepared for trial and performed unauthorized work, and that Givaudan should retain different outside counsel. Givaudan further invoked the attorney-client privilege and the work-product doctrine to prevent Squire Sanders from having an independent expert review its billing invoices and other documents in its effort to establish the reasonable value of the legal services it rendered to Givaudan.

Squire Sanders moved to compel the production of documents and testimony from both King and Garfinkel, relying on the self-protection exception to the attorney-client privilege and the work-product doctrine. The trial court granted the motion, compelling Givaudan to produce the documents that Squire Sanders had requested and directing King and Garfinkel to answer questions related to the Givaudan/Squire Sanders relationship. The court also permitted Squire Sanders to use documents already in its possession relative to the billing dispute.

Givaudan appealed the trial court's discovery order to the Eighth District Court of Appeals. The appellate court reversed the trial court, holding that R.C. 2317.02(A) provides the exclusive means for a client to waive the attorney-client privilege for *testimonial* statements and that the implied waiver test articulated in *Hearn v. Rhay* (E.D.Wash.1975), 68 F.R.D. 574, applies to *nontestimonial* statements.

Squire Sanders appealed that decision to this court, contending that the common-law self-protection exception to the attorney-client privilege is recognized both in American jurisprudence and in Ohio law and is incorporated into the attorney-client privilege codified in R.C. 2317.02(A). According to Squire Sanders, when the exception applies, there is no privilege for the client to assert or waive, and the "good cause" requirement for obtaining attorney work product is satisfied. It also contends that the court of appeals erred in relying on cases dealing with waiver of the attorney-client privilege, which would be relevant only if no exception applied. And it further asserts that the trial court correctly concluded that the communications it sought fell outside the attorney-client privilege and the work-product doctrine.

By contrast, Givaudan argues that the attorney-client privilege provided in R.C. 2317.02(A) is unambiguous and does not create an exception for attorney self-protection.

Thus, the central issue in this case is whether Ohio recognizes the self-protection exception to the attorney-client privilege permitting an attorney to testify concerning attorney-client communications to establish a claim or defense on behalf of the attorney in connection with litigation against a client or a former client.

The Attorney-Client Privilege

"[I]n Ohio, the attorney-client privilege is governed by statute, R.C. 2317.02(A), and in cases that are not addressed in R.C. 2317.02(A), by common law." *Leslie*, 105 Ohio St.3d 261, 2005-Ohio-1508, 824 N.E.2d 990, ¶ 18.

Codification of the Privilege

Central to the issue in this case is R.C. 2317.02(A):

"The following persons shall not testify in certain respects:

"(A)(1) An attorney, concerning a communication made to the attorney by a client in that relation or the attorney's advice to a client, except that the attorney may testify by express consent of the client or, if the client is deceased, by the express consent of the surviving spouse or the executor or administrator of the estate of the deceased client. However, if the client voluntarily testifies or is deemed by section 2151.421 of the Revised Code to have waived any testimonial privilege under this division, the attorney may be compelled to testify on the same subject.

"* * *

"(2) An attorney, concerning a communication made to the attorney by a client in that relationship or the attorney's advice to a client, except that if the client is an insurance company, the attorney may be compelled to testify, subject to an in camera inspection by a court, about communications made by the client to the attorney or by the attorney to the client that are related to the attorney's aiding or furthering an ongoing or future commission of bad faith by the client, if the party seeking disclosure of the communications has made a prima facie showing of bad faith, fraud, or criminal misconduct by the client."

Exceptions to the Attorney-Client Privilege

We have previously recognized several exceptions to the attorney-client privilege codified by R.C. 2317.02(A) notwithstanding their absence from the statutory text.

Cooperation with Wrongdoing (Crime-Fraud) Exception

In *Lemley v. Kaiser* (1983), 6 Ohio St.3d 258, 266, 452 N.E.2d 1304, 6 OBR 324, the court explained that the attorney-client privilege may not be asserted to conceal the attorney's cooperation with the client's wrongdoing.

Lack-of- Good-Faith Exception

The court discussed a second type of exception to the attorney-client privilege in *Moskovitz v. Mt. Sinai Med. Ctr.*, 69 Ohio St.3d 638, 635 N.E.2d 331. Because the attorney-client privilege does not apply when the client seeks to abuse the attorney-client relationship, the court in *Moskovitz* held that "[d]ocuments and other things showing the lack of a good faith effort to settle by a party or the attorneys acting on his or her behalf are wholly unworthy of the protections afforded by any claimed privilege

In *Boone v. Vanliner Ins. Co.* (2001), 91 Ohio St.3d 209, 212, 744 N.E.2d 154, the court extended the exception recognized in *Moskovitz* to attorney-client communications furthering an insurance company's lack of good faith in denying coverage, holding such communications to be "unworthy of protection" by the attorney-client privilege.

Joint-Representation Exception

In addition, Ohio courts have applied the common-law joint-representation exception to the attorney-client privilege, which provides that a client of an attorney cannot invoke the privilege in litigation against a co-client.

Although the crime-fraud, lack-of-good-faith, and joint-representation exceptions to the attorney-client privilege are not expressly codified in R.C. 2317.02(A), they nonetheless "exist within the body of common-law principles governing privilege." Weissenberger's Ohio Evidence at 246 (noting the crime-fraud, fee-dispute, malpractice, and co-client exceptions. These exceptions define the scope of the protections afforded to attorney-client communications by R.C. 2317.02(A), because, as the court explained in *Moskovitz*, "the privilege does not attach" when an exception applies. 69 Ohio St.3d at 661, 635 N.E.2d 331.

The Self-Protection Exception

At common-law, "[a]n exception to the attorney-client privilege permits an attorney to reveal otherwise protected confidences when necessary to protect his own interest." Levine, Self-Interest or Self-Defense: Lawyer Disregard of the Attorney-Client Privilege for Profit and Protection (1977), 5 Hofstra L. Rev. 783. This exception provides that "when an attorney becomes involved in a legal controversy with a client or former client, the attorney may reveal any confidences necessary to defend himself or herself or to vindicate his or her rights with regard to the disputed issues." 1 Stone & Taylor, Testimonial Privileges (2d Ed.1995) 1–177, Section 1.66.

The self-protection exception dates back over 150 years to its articulation by Justice Selden in *Rochester City Bank v. Suydam, Sage & Co.* (N.Y.Sup.Ct.1851), 5 How. Pr. 254, 262. There he wrote, "Where the attorney or counsel has *an interest in the facts communicated* to him, and when their disclosure becomes necessary *to protect his own personal rights*, he must of necessity and in reason be *exempted* from the obligation of secresy [sic]." (Emphasis added in part.)

Since that time, this exception has become firmly rooted in American jurisprudence. The Supreme Court of the United States recognized it in 1888 in *Hunt v. Blackburn* (1888), 128 U.S. 464, 470–471, 9 S.Ct. 125, 32 L.Ed. 488, and courts and commentators have accepted the self-protection exception as black-letter law defining which communications are subject to the attorney-client privilege. Restatement (Third) of the Law Governing Lawyers (2000), Section 83.

[O]ur caselaw recognizes that the attorney-client privilege does not prevent an attorney from testifying to the correctness, amount, and value of the legal services rendered to the client in an action calling those fees into question.

Further, the self-protection exception to the attorney-client privilege permitting the attorney to testify also applies when the client puts the representation at issue by charging the attorney with a breach of duty or other wrongdoing. Thus, a client may not rely on attorney-client communications to establish a claim against the attorney while asserting the attorney-client privilege to prevent the attorney from rebutting that claim.

Rather, "the attorney-client privilege exists to aid in the administration of justice and must yield in circumstances where justice so requires," *Moskovitz v. Mt. Sinai Med. Ctr.*, 69 Ohio St.3d at 661, 635 N.E.2d 331. The same considerations of justice and fairness that undergird the attorney client privilege prevent a client from employing it in litigation against a lawyer to the lawyer's disadvantage.

Wolfram, Modern Legal Ethics (1986) 308, Section 6.7.8; Wright & Miller, Federal Practice & Procedure (1997, Supp.2010), Section 5503; Restatement (Third) of the Law Governing Lawyers, Section 83, Comment b.

Givaudan, however, relies on *Jackson v. Greger*, 110 Ohio St.3d 488, 2006-Ohio-4968, 854 N.E.2d 487, ¶ 13, for the proposition that this court has "consistently rejected the adoption of judicially created waivers, exceptions, and limitations for testimonial privilege statutes." *Jackson* dealt with the question of whether to recognize the doctrine of implied waiver of the attorney-client privilege as articulated in *Hearn v. Rhay*, 68 F.R.D. 574. Applying *State v. McDermott* (1995), 72 Ohio St.3d 570, 651 N.E.2d 985, the court explained that R.C. 2317.02(A) provides the exclusive means by which privileged communications directly between an attorney and a client can be waived. *Jackson* at ¶ 11. *Jackson* is distinguishable on its facts because it dealt only with a *waiver* of the attorney-client privilege; we concern ourselves in the instant case with a common-law *exception* to the privilege, the self-protection exception.

In deciding *Jackson* and *McDermott*, we did not cast aside the well-established common-law exceptions to the attorney-client privilege. Unlike *waiver*, which involves the client's relinquishment of the protections of R.C. 2713.02(A) once they have attached, an *exception* to the attorney-client privilege falls into the category of situations in which the privilege does not attach to the communications in the first instance and is therefore excluded from the operation of the statute.

Our decision today also comports with Prof. Cond. R. 1.6(b)(5), which provides:

"A lawyer may reveal information relating to the representation of a client, including information protected by the attorney-client privilege under applicable law, to the extent the lawyer *reasonably believes* necessary . . .

"(5) to establish a claim or defense on behalf of the lawyer in a controversy between the lawyer and the client . . . (Emphasis sic.)

Further, Comment [10] to Prof.Cond.R. 1.6 explains that an attorney has a right to respond to the allegations of a client in a lawsuit that the attorney committed a wrong against the client. Comment [11] also specifies that an attorney may prove the legal services rendered to a client in an action to collect a fee, noting that this aspect of Prof.Cond.R. 1.6(b) "expresses the principle that the beneficiary of a fiduciary relationship may not exploit it to the detriment of the fiduciary."

Ohio recognizes the self-protection exception to the attorney-client privilege, and that exception applies in this situation. Therefore, R.C. 2317.02(A) does not prevent an attorney from responding to allegations that the attorney wronged a client or from establishing the reasonable value of the legal services rendered to a client to the extent that such evidence is necessary to establish a claim or defense on behalf of the attorney in litigation between the attorney and the client.

Accordingly, the judgment of the court of appeals is reversed, and the cause is remanded to the trial court, which has already made a finding of good cause requiring Givaudan to produce the requested documents, testimony, and other evidence. Therefore, the trial court is instructed to conduct further proceedings consistent with this opinion and its earlier journalized orders.

Judgment reversed and cause remanded.

PFEIFER, LUNDBERG STRATTON, O'CONNOR, and CUPP, JJ., concur.

LANZINGER, J., concurs in judgment only.

BROWN, C.J., not participating.

NOTES, QUESTIONS, AND EXAMPLES

1.   Lawyer represented Client in a financial matter. Client became dissatisfied with Lawyer's representation, and discharged him. After Client discharged Lawyer, Client filed suit seeking to enjoin Lawyer from harassing her. In Lawyer's Answer, Lawyer avers, "Client was constantly worried about everything, including an affair that her husband supposedly had eight years ago with Client's sister." Is Lawyer subject to discipline? *See Dixon v. State Bar of California*, 32 Cal. 3d 728 (1982).

2.   Lawyer represented Adoptive Parents in their efforts to adopt a child. After Adoptive Parents received custody of the child, but before the final hearing on the matter, a fee dispute between Adoptive Parents and Lawyer arose. Lawyer wrote to Social Worker, suggesting that Adoptive Parents may not be fit parents because of their financial irresponsibility in failing to pay Lawyer's fee. Is lawyer subject to discipline? *See Florida Bar v. Ball*, 406 So. 2d 459 (Fla. 1981).

3.   Future Crimes, Frauds, and Harms

In certain circumstances, lawyers may reveal confidential information to prevent future crimes or frauds by clients.

The states, in their adoption and modification of the Model Rules, have been active tinkerers with respect to the future crimes exception.

Ethics 2000 Commission, February 2002 ABA Amendment to Model Rules

Model Rule 1.6(b)(1), Future Crime Exception

Following the amendment to MR 1.6(b)(1), this exception to the confidentiality duty might better be referred to as the "future harm" exception rather than the future crime exception. The new language permits lawyer revelation of client confidences "to prevent reasonably certain death or substantial bodily harm." The removed language narrowed the exception to client criminal acts that the lawyer believed would cause the same order of harm.

The new exception does not require as a trigger any criminal act by the client. It is focused on preventing serious, imminent harms, and authorizes the revelation of client information when necessary to accomplish its ends. The example chosen by the drafters involves a negligent, not necessarily criminal, discharge of pollutants into a water supply that presents a "substantial risk" of "life-threatening or debilitating disease" to the water drinkers. In such an instance, the lawyer is permitted to reveal the information necessary to prevent the harm. *See* MR 1.6, comment 6.

In some ways, this change reflects a debate that bedeviled the RESTATEMENT drafters. There, the inclusion of an example about revealing a client's guilt when necessary to prevent the execution of a wrongly convicted person created controversy. In the February 2002 amendment to MR 1.6, the "future harm" exception, by removing any future act of the client as a trigger, arguably means that the lawyer in the controversial RESTATEMENT hypothetical may reveal the information necessary to prevent the wrongful execution.

Texas Disciplinary Rules of Professional Conduct Rule

1.05. Confidentiality of Information

*   *   *

(c) A lawyer may reveal confidential information:

(1) When the lawyer has been expressly authorized to do so in order to carry out the representation.

(2) When the client consents after consultation.

(3) To the client, the client's representatives, or the members, associates, and employees of the lawyer's firm, except when otherwise instructed by the client.

(4) When the lawyer has reason to believe it is necessary to do so in order to comply with a court order, a Texas Disciplinary Rules of Professional Conduct, or other law.

(5) To the extent reasonably necessary to enforce a claim or establish a defense on behalf of the lawyer in a controversy between the lawyer and the client.

(6) To establish a defense to a criminal charge, civil claim or disciplinary complaint against the lawyer or the lawyer's associates based upon conduct involving the client or the representation of the client.

(7) *When the lawyer has reason to believe it is necessary to do so in order to prevent the client from committing a criminal or fraudulent act.*

(8) *To the extent revelation reasonably appears necessary to rectify the consequences of a client's criminal or fraudulent act in the commission of which the lawyer's services had been used.* (emphasis added)

(d) A lawyer also may reveal unprivileged client information:

(1) When impliedly authorized to do so in order to carry out the representation.

(2) When the lawyer has reason to believe it is necessary to do so in order to:

(i) carry out the representation effectively;

(ii) defend the lawyer or the lawyer's employees or associates against a claim of wrongful conduct;

(iii) respond to allegations in any proceeding concerning the lawyer's representation of the client; or

(iv) prove the services rendered to a client, or the reasonable value thereof, or both, in an action against another person or organization responsible for the payment of the fee for services rendered to the client.

(e) *When a lawyer has confidential information clearly establishing that a client is likely to commit a criminal or fraudulent act that is likely to result in death or substantial bodily harm to a person, the lawyer shall reveal confidential information to the extent revelation reasonably appears necessary to prevent the client from committing the criminal or fraudulent act. (emphasis added)*

(f) *A lawyer shall reveal confidential information when required to do so by Rule 3.03(a)(2), 3.03(b), or by Rule 4.01(b). (emphasis added)*

Michigan Rules of Professional Conduct
Client-Lawyer Relationship

Rule 1.6. Confidentiality of Information

*   *   *

(c) A lawyer may reveal:

(1) confidences or secrets with the consent of the client or clients affected, but only after full disclosure to them;

(2) confidences or secrets when permitted or required by these rules, or when required by law or by court order;

(3) *confidences and secrets to the extent reasonably necessary to rectify the consequences of a client's illegal or fraudulent act in the furtherance of which the lawyer's services have been used;*

(4) *the intention of a client to commit a crime and the information necessary to prevent the crime;* (emphasis added) and

(5) confidences or secrets necessary to establish or collect a fee, or to defend the lawyer or the lawyer's employees or associates against an accusation of wrongful conduct.

*   *   *

Illinois Rules of Professional Conduct

Rule 1.6. Confidentiality of Information

*   *   *

(b) A lawyer shall reveal information about a client to the extent it appears necessary to prevent the client from committing an act that would result in death or serious bodily harm. (emphasis added)

(c) A lawyer may use or reveal:

(1) confidences or secrets when permitted under these Rules or required by law or court order;

(2) *the intention of a client to commit a crime in circumstances other than those enumerated in Rule 1.6(b)*; (emphasis added) or

(3) confidences or secrets necessary to establish or collect the lawyer's fee or to defend the lawyer or the lawyer's employees or associates against an accusation of wrongful conduct.

*   *   *

Rules Regulating the Florida Bar
Chapter 4. Rules of Professional Conduct
4-1. Client-Lawyer Relationship

Rule 4-1.6. Confidentiality of Information

(a) Consent Required to Reveal Information. A lawyer shall not reveal information relating to representation of a client except as stated in subdivisions (b), (c), and (d), unless the client consents after disclosure to the client.

(b) When Lawyer Must Reveal Information. *A lawyer shall reveal such information to the extent the lawyer reasonably believes necessary*:

(1) to prevent a client from committing a crime; or

(2) to prevent a death or substantial bodily harm to another. (emphasis added)

(c) When Lawyer May Reveal Information. A lawyer may reveal such information to the extent the lawyer reasonably believes necessary:

(1) to serve the client's interest unless it is information the client specifically requires not to be disclosed;

(2) to establish a claim or defense on behalf of the lawyer in a controversy between the lawyer and client;

(3) to establish a defense to a criminal charge or civil claim against the lawyer based upon conduct in which the client was involved;

(4) to respond to allegations in any proceeding concerning the lawyer's representation of the client; or

(5) to comply with the Rules of Professional Conduct.

(d) Exhaustion of Appellate Remedies. When required by a tribunal to reveal such information, a lawyer may first exhaust all appellate remedies.

(e) Limitation on Amount of Disclosure. When disclosure is mandated or permitted, the lawyer shall disclose no more information than is required to meet the requirements or accomplish the purposes of this rule.

Minnesota Rules of Professional Conduct
Client-Lawyer Relationship

Rule 1.6. Confidentiality of Information

*   *   *

(b) A lawyer may reveal:

(1) confidences or secrets with the consent of the client or clients affected, but only after consultation with them;

(2) confidences or secrets when permitted under the Rules of Professional Conduct or required by law or court order;

(3) *the intention of a client to commit a crime and the information necessary to prevent a crime*;

(4) *confidences and secrets necessary to rectify the consequences of a client's criminal or fraudulent act in the furtherance of which the lawyer's services were used*; (emphasis added)

(5) confidences or secrets necessary to establish or collect a fee or to defend the lawyers or employees or associates against an accusation of wrongful conduct;

(6) secrets necessary to inform the Office of Lawyers Professional Responsibility of knowledge of another lawyer's violation of the Rules of Professional Conduct that raises a substantial question as to that lawyer's honesty, trustworthiness or fitness as a lawyer in other respects. See Rule 8.3.

PEOPLE v. BELGE
372 N.Y.S.2d 798 (N.Y. Cty. Ct. 1975)

In the summer of 1973 Robert F. Garrow, Jr., stood charged in Hamilton County with the crime of murder. The defendant was assigned two attorneys, Frank H. Armani and Francis R. Belge. A defense of insanity had been interposed by counsel for Mr. Garrow. During the course of the discussions between Garrow and his two counsel, three other murders were admitted by Garrow, one being in Onondaga County. On or about September of 1973 Mr. Belge conducted his own investigation based upon what his client had told him and with the assistance of a friend the location of the body of Alicia Hauck was found in Oakwood Cemetery in

Syracuse. Mr. Belge personally inspected the body and was satisfied, presumably, that this was the Alicia Hauck that his client had told him that he murdered.

This discovery was not disclosed to the authorities, but became public during the trial of Mr. Garrow in June of 1974, when to affirmatively establish the defense of insanity, these three other murders were brought before the jury by the defense in the Hamilton County trial. Public indignation reached the fever pitch, statements were made by the District Attorney of Onondaga County relative to the situation and he caused the Grand Jury of Onondaga County, then sitting, to conduct a thorough investigation. As a result of this investigation Frank Armani was no-billed by the Grand Jury but Indictment No. 75-55 was returned as against Francis R. Belge, Esq., accusing him of having violated subdivision 1 of section 4200 of the Public Health Law, which, in essence, requires that a decent burial be accorded the dead, and section 4143 of the Public Health Law, which, in essence, requires anyone knowing of the death of a person without medical attendance, to report the same to the proper authorities. Defense counsel moves for a dismissal of the indictment on the grounds that a confidential, privileged communication existed between him and Mr. Garrow, which should excuse the attorney from making full disclosure to the authorities.

The National Association of Criminal Defense Lawyers, as amicus curiae, succinctly state the issue in the following language: If this indictment stands, "The attorney-client privilege will be effectively destroyed. No defendant will be able to freely discuss the facts of his case with his attorney. No attorney will be able to listen to those facts without being faced with the Hobson's choice of violating the law or violating his professional code of Ethics."

*   *   *

In the most recent issue of the New York State Bar Journal (June, 1975) there is an article by Jack B. Weinstein, entitled "Educating Ethical Lawyers." In a subcaption to this article is the following language which is pertinent: "The most difficult ethical dilemmas result from the frequent conflicts between the obligation to one's client and those to the legal system and to society. It is in this area that legal education has its greatest responsibility, and can have its greatest effects." In the course of his article Mr. Weinstein states that there are three major types of pressure facing a practicing lawyer. He uses the following language to describe these: "First, there are those that originate in the attorney's search for his own well-being. Second, pressures arise from the attorney's obligation to his client. Third, the lawyer has certain obligations to the courts, the legal system, and society in general."

Our system of criminal justice is an adversary system and the interests of the State are not absolute, or even paramount. "The dignity of the individual is respected to the point that even when the citizen is known by the state to have committed a heinous offense, the individual is nevertheless accorded such rights as counsel, trial by jury, due process, and the privilege against self incrimination." Freedman, Criminal Law Bulletin (Dec, 1974).

A trial is in part a search for truth, but it is only partly a search for truth. The mantle of innocence is flung over the defendant to such an extent that he is safeguarded by rules of evidence which frequently keep out absolute truth, much to the chagrin of juries. Nevertheless, this has been a part of our system since our laws were taken from the laws of England and over these many years has been found to best protect a balance between the rights of the individual and the rights of society.

* * *

The effectiveness of counsel is only as great as the confidentiality of its client-attorney relationship. If the lawyer cannot get all the facts about the case, he can only give his client half of a defense. This, of necessity, involves the client telling his attorney everything remotely connected with the crime.

Apparently, in the instant case, after analyzing all the evidence, and after hearing of the bizarre episodes in the life of their client, they decided that the only possibility of salvation was in a defense of insanity. For the client to disclose not only everything about this particular crime but also everything about other crimes which might have a bearing upon his defense, requires the strictest confidence in, and on the part of, the attorney.

When the facts of the other homicides became public, as a result of the defendant's testimony to substantiate his claim of insanity, "Members of the public were shocked at the apparent callousness of these lawyers, whose conduct was seen as typifying the unhealthy lack of concern of most lawyers with the public interest and with simple decency." Freedman, Criminal Law Bulletin (Dec, 1974). A hue and cry went up from the press and other news media suggesting that the attorneys should be found guilty of such crimes as obstruction of justice or becoming an accomplice after the fact. From a layman's standpoint, this certainly was a logical conclusion. However, the Constitution of the United States of America attempts to preserve the dignity of the individual and to do that guarantees him the services of an attorney who will bring to the Bar and to the Bench every conceivable protection from the inroads of the State against such rights as are vested in the Constitution for one accused of crime. Among those substantial constitutional rights is that a defendant does not have to incriminate himself. His attorneys were bound to uphold that concept and maintain what has been called a sacred trust of confidentiality.

* * *

In the case at bar we must weigh the importance of the general privilege of confidentiality in the performance of the defendant's duties as an attorney, against the inroads of such a privilege on the fair administration of criminal justice as well as the heart tearing that went on in the victim's family by reason of their uncertainty as to the whereabouts of Alicia Hauck. In this type situation the court must balance the rights of the individual against the rights of society as a whole. There is no question but Attorney Belge's failure to bring to the attention of the authorities the whereabouts of Alicia Hauck when he first verified it, prevented bringing Garrow to the immediate bar of justice for this particular murder. This was in a sense, obstruction of justice. This duty, I am sure, loomed large in the mind of Attorney Belge. However, against this was the Fifth Amendment right of his client, Garrow, not to incriminate himself. If the Grand Jury had returned an indictment charging Mr. Belge with obstruction of justice under a proper statute, the work of this court would have been much more difficult than it is.

There must always be a conflict between the obstruction of the administration of criminal justice and the preservation of the right against self incrimination which permeates the mind of the attorney as the alter ego of his client. But that is not the situation before this court. We have the Fifth Amendment right, derived from the Constitution, on the one hand, as against the trivia of a pseudo-criminal statute on the other, which has seldom been brought into play. Clearly the latter is completely out of focus when placed alongside the client-attorney privilege. An examination of the Grand Jury testimony sheds little light on their reasoning. The testimony of Mr. Armani added nothing new to the facts as already presented to the Grand Jury. He and Mr. Belge were co-counsel. Both were answerable to the Canons of professional ethics. The Grand Jury chose to indict one and not the other. It appears as if that body were grasping at straws.

It is the decision of this court that Francis R. Belge conducted himself as an officer of the court with all the zeal at his command to protect the constitutional rights of his client. Both on the grounds of a privileged communication and in the interests of justice the indictment is dismissed.

PEOPLE v. BELGE
376 N.Y.S.2d 771 (N.Y. Sup. Ct. App. Div. 1975)

Order affirmed. All concur, except Del Vecchio, J. not participating. Memorandum: We affirm the order of the trial court which properly dismissed the indictments laid against defendant for alleged violations of section 4200 (duty of a decent burial) and section 4143 (requirement to report death occurring without medical attendance) of the Public Health Law. We believe that the attorney-client privilege attached insofar as the communications were to advance a client's interests, and that the privilege effectively shielded the defendant attorney from his actions which would otherwise have violated the Public Health Law. In view of the fact that the claim of absolute privilege was proffered, we note that the privilege is not all encompassing and that in a given case there may be conflicting considerations. We believe that an attorney must protect his client's interests, but also must observe basic human standards of decency, having due regard to the need that the legal system accord justice to the interests of society and its individual members. We write to emphasize our serious concern regarding the consequences which emanate from a claim of an absolute attorney-client privilege. Because the only question presented, briefed and argued on this appeal was a legal one with respect to the sufficiency of the indictments, we limit our determination to that issue and do not reach the ethical questions underlying this case.

4.   "Other Law" or Orders of Court

Lawyers may reveal confidences when required to do so by other law or by order of court. When a court orders a lawyer to speak about matters that will reveal protected client information, usually after an unsuccessful assertion of the attorney-client evidentiary privilege, the lawyer may reveal the information without risking disciplinary liability. MR 1.6, Comment 11. Despite a presumption against other provisions of law superseding the duty of confidentiality (*see* MR 1.6, Comment 10), in several circumstances, provisions of law outside the professional responsibility rules require or permit lawyers to disclose information that would otherwise be protected by the duty of confidentiality.

NOTES, QUESTIONS, AND EXAMPLES

1. Could the Health Code provision under which Belge was charged be regarded as an "other law" requiring disclosure of confidential information? See MR 1.6, Comment 10.

2. What if Belge had revealed the information about the bodies to the authorities upon discovering them? Would he have been subject to discipline?

What if Belge had disturbed the bodies when he examined them? For example, what if he had further obstructed their view? Reconsider the Meredith case in this context.

E.   USE OF CONFIDENTIAL INFORMATION FOR THE LAWYER'S BENEFIT

As a client's agent, a lawyer is generally restricted from using confidential information of the client either for the lawyer's benefit or to the client's detriment. Even if some scenario of lawyer gain without client opportunity loss is imaginable, as a matter of general agency law, a lawyer's (agent's) gain that is attributable to his duty to a client (principal) is the property of the client and not the lawyer. Although the client may, of course, consent to the lawyer's use and retention of the gain, in such a case the lawyer would no longer be making use of protected client confidences.

RESTATEMENT (THIRD) OF AGENCY[14]
Chapter 8. Duties of Agent and Principal to Each Other
Topic 1. Agent's Duties to Principal
Title B. Duties of Loyalty

§ 8.02 **Material Benefit Arising Out of Position.** An agent has a duty not to acquire a material benefit from a third party in connection with transactions conducted or other actions taken on behalf of the principal or otherwise through the agent's use of the agent's position.

* * *

§ 8.05 **Use of Principal's Property; Use of Confidential Information.** An agent has a duty (1) not to use property of the principal for the agent's own purposes or those of a third party; and (2) not to use or communicate confidential information of the principal for the agent's own purposes or those of a third party.

§ 8.06 **Principal's Consent.** (1) Conduct by an agent that would otherwise constitute a breach of duty as stated in §§ 8.01, 8.02, 8.03, 8.04, and 8.05 does not constitute a breach of duty if the principal consents to the conduct, provided that (a)

---

[14] Copyright © 2006 by the American Law Institute. Reprinted with permission.

in obtaining the principal's consent, the agent (i) acts in good faith, (ii) discloses all material facts that the agent knows, has reason to know, or should know would reasonably affect the principal's judgment unless the principal has manifested that such facts are already known by the principal or that the principal does not wish to know them, and (iii) otherwise deals fairly with the principal; and (b) the principal's consent concerns either a specific act or transaction, or acts or transactions of a specified type that could reasonably be expected to occur in the ordinary course of the agency relationship.

* * *

Chapter V

CONFLICTS OF INTEREST

Conflicts of interest issues are among those most central, most pervasive, most complex, and most important to practicing lawyers in the professional responsibility field. Conflicts of interest concepts have become increasingly important for several reasons:

• Lawyers change jobs during a career with much greater frequency today than did lawyers of even 30 years ago. Because conflicts between former clients and current clients must be analyzed, the moving lawyer carries potential conflicts with all of his former clients with him into the new job.

• Corporate mergers, acquisitions, dissolutions, and divestitures occur at a much greater pace today than they did even 30 years ago. When corporate clients and opponents buy each other, sell off parts, and split up, potential conflicts occur.

• Law firms are bigger today than they were 30 years ago. Because many kinds of conflicts are presumed to affect the entire firm rather than the individual conflicted lawyer in the firm, conflicts affecting a two hundred lawyer firm are far more numerous and likely than conflicts affecting a 20-lawyer firm.

• The job changing's effect on conflicts is magnified by the reality that many large firm lawyers move to other large firms and they move to do work within their particular specialties. The result is that when lawyers change jobs, they are likely to move from one firm that works on a matter to another firm working on the same or a substantially related matter for a different client.

In part because of the increased frequency of conflicts issues, litigating lawyers now move to disqualify opposing counsel when they believe that a conflict exists. Filing a motion gets the matter before a court and affects strategies and outcomes of pending litigation. Therefore, conflicts issues are analyzed with much greater frequency than other professional responsibility issues that are chiefly raised through the infrequently operative bar disciplinary machinery.

When you analyze conflicts problems, ask yourself these questions:

• What is the source of the conflict? (third-party interference? multiple client conflict? lawyer interests?)

• Does the conflict meet its particular rule's threshold requirements?

• Is the conflict one that imputes to the entire law organization?

• If so, can the affected lawyer be effectively screened or isolated from the organization?

• Is the conflict of a type that allows client waiver?

- If so, what has to occur for the waiver to be effective?

A. LOYALTY AND OTHER GENERAL PRINCIPLES

A variety of central principles are at play in analyzing conflicts of interest questions. Basic to the lawyer-client relationship is the premise that lawyers owe clients a duty of loyalty. Lawyers owe clients a duty of independent professional judgment. When the independence is threatened by some interest other than the client's, a conflicts question is present and requires analysis. Many conflicts questions are primarily about breaches of confidentiality. When a lawyer who is serving multiple clients has confidences of one that would benefit the other, a conflict of interest problem exists. Such a lawyer must either breach the confidences of one client or serve the other's interests less well than would be possible through the breach of the first client's confidence. Either choice is a breach of lawyer duty, hence, the conflict of interest problem.

The application of many of the conflicts rules is triggered by a determination of whether the conflict creates "a significant risk that the representation . . . will be materially limited by the [conflict]." MR 1.7(a)(2). This standard is objective. It requires an examination to determine whether the lawyer's options on behalf of the client will be limited in ways of consequence by interests other than the client's.

Ethics 2000 Commission, February 2002 ABA Amendment to Model Rules

Model Rule 1.7 Concurrent Client Conflicts

Model Rule 1.7 has been refocused on "current" clients and "concurrent" conflicts. Model Rule 1.9 continues as it has been, focused on former clients, and Model Rule 1.18 addresses prospective clients for the first time in a specific rule.

No change was made in the language regarding directly adverse representations. But Model Rule 1.7 raises the threshold somewhat for what constitutes a conflict outside the context of direct adversity. The former MR 1.7 identified a conflict when the lawyer's representation of a client "*may be* materially limited" by third parties, the lawyer's interests or another client. The amended MR 1.7 identifies a conflict when "there is a *significant risk* that the representation of [a client] *will be* materially limited" by third parties, the lawyer's interests or another client. The new language substitutes "will" for "may," raising the threshold, but also adds the "significant risk" standard. The result is a change from a "may be materially limited" standard to a "significant risk" of material limitation standard.

The waiver standard was also changed in two ways of consequence. First, the threshold objective judgment that the lawyer must make changed focus. The former 1.7 focused on "adverse" effect, requiring the lawyer to "reasonably believe" that the representation would not be "adversely affected" by the conflict before an effective client waiver could occur. The 2002 amendment focuses on the quality of the representation, requiring the lawyer to "reasonably believe that the lawyer will be able to provide competent and diligent representation [despite the conflict]." Competence and diligence are, of course, fundamental attributes of ethical representation. MR 1.1, 1.3. The new waiver threshold thus keys itself to the lawyer's ability, despite the existence of the conflict, to render fundamentally ethical service to the affected client.

Second, the rule requires that the client give "informed consent," consistent with the change made throughout the Model Rules in the February 2002 amendments. The rule also increased the requirements for consent by adding a requirement that the consent be "confirmed in writing." Confirming consent in writing has always been the better practice, but before the February 2002 amendments was not required by rule.

The 2002 comments to MR 1.7 provide particular examples of various concurrent conflict situations. Comment 22 (consent to future conflicts); comment 24 (positional conflicts); comment 25 (class actions); and comment 34 (representation of corporate subparts).

INTERNATIONAL NOTES

1.   In some European jurisdictions, the term "independence" can take on an alternative meaning that refers to the client's own demands. This occurs when a client's own demands are unreasonable or harmful to the public interest and the lawyer must remain independent of the client's wishes. In France, the term independence reflects an especially radical idea. Traditionally, a lawyer (avocat) was an independent person who lent his eloquence and credibility to someone in whose cause he believed and who needed his help. An avocat was not an agent of the client, and thus the client had no control over the avocat. The avocat was free to accept or reject a client, and even after accepting, to withdraw after giving proper notice.

2.   In the United Kingdom, the makeup of the legal profession has specific implications on the concept of legal independence. In the United Kingdom, the legal profession is divided into two branches: barristers and solicitors. Barristers are governed by the Bar Code of Conduct which contains no provisions concerning conflicts of interest. This is because barristers can only be instructed by solicitors and have no direct clients except for solicitors. For the barrister, the primary duty of loyalty is to the lay client (the solicitor's client) and not to the professional client (the solicitor). If a barrister should become aware of a conflict between his lay client and his professional client, he should advise the lay client to seek another professional advisor. Solicitors, on the other hand, are governed by the Solicitor's practice rules which do include provisions prohibiting conflicts of interest. The substance of these rules is similar to those in the United States.

B.   WAIVER OF CONFLICTS

Because most conflicts put client interests at risk and because client autonomy and decision-making are values worthy of respect, clients are empowered to waive most conflicts of interest. By doing so, a client may then be represented by counsel of the client's choice in spite of the existence of a conflict of interest concern. As you consider the various conflicts rules covered in section C, note the presence or absence of waiver language.

Restatement (Third) of The Law Governing Lawyers[1]
Rules and Principles
Chapter 8 — Conflicts of Interest
Topic 1 — Conflicts of Interest in General

§ 122. Client Consent to a Conflict of Interest

(1) A lawyer may represent a client notwithstanding a conflict of interest prohibited by § 121 if each affected client or former client gives informed consent to the lawyer's representation. Informed consent requires that the client or former client have reasonably adequate information about the material risks of such representation to that client or former client.

(2) Notwithstanding the informed consent of each affected client or former client, a lawyer may not represent a client if:

(a) the representation is prohibited by law;

(b) one client will assert a claim against the other in the same litigation; or

(c) in the circumstances, it is not reasonably likely that the lawyer will be able to provide adequate representation to one or more of the clients.

Comments & Illustrations:

Comment:

* * *

b. Rationale. The prohibition against lawyer conflicts of interest is intended to assure clients that a lawyer's work will be characterized by loyalty, vigor, and confidentiality (*see* § 121, Comment b). The conflict rules are subject to waiver through informed consent by a client who elects less than the full measure of protection that the law otherwise provides. For example, a client in a multiple representation might wish to avoid the added costs that separate representation often entails. Similarly, a client might consent to a conflict where that is necessary in order to obtain the services of a particular law firm.

Other considerations, however, limit the scope of a client's power to consent to a conflicted representation. A client's consent will not be effective if it is based on an inadequate understanding of the nature and severity of the lawyer's conflict (Comment c hereto), violates law (Comment g(i)), or if the client lacks capacity to consent (Comment c). Client consent must also, of course, be free of coercion. Consent will also be insufficient to permit conflicted representation if it is not

---

[1] Copyright © 2000 by the American Law Institute. Reprinted with permission.

reasonably likely that the lawyer will be able to provide adequate representation to the affected clients, or when a lawyer undertakes to represent clients who oppose each other in the same litigation (Comment g(iii)).

In effect, the consent requirement means that each affected client or former client has the power to preclude the representation by withholding consent. When a client withholds consent, a lawyer's power to withdraw from representation of that client and proceed with the representation of the other client is determined under § 121, Comment e.

While a lawyer may elect to proceed with a conflicted representation after effective client consent as stated in this Section, a lawyer is not required to do so (*compare* § 14, Comment g (required representation by order of court)). A lawyer might be unwilling to accept the risk that a consenting client will later become disappointed with the representation and contend that the consent was defective, or the lawyer might conclude for other reasons that the lawyer's own interests do not warrant proceeding.

In such an instance, the lawyer also may elect to withdraw if grounds permitting withdrawal are present under § 32. After withdrawal, a lawyer's ability to represent other clients is as described in § 121, Comment e.

c(i). The requirement of informed consent — adequate information. Informed consent requires that each affected client be aware of the material respects in which the representation could have adverse effects on the interests of that client. The information required depends on the nature of the conflict and the nature of the risks of the conflicted representation. The client must be aware of information reasonably adequate to make an informed decision.   *info for informed consent*

Information relevant to particular kinds of conflicts is considered in several of the Sections hereafter. In a multiple-client situation, the information normally should address the interests of the lawyer and other client giving rise to the conflict; contingent, optional, and tactical considerations and alternative courses of action that would be foreclosed or made less readily available by the conflict; the effect of the representation or the process of obtaining other clients' informed consent upon confidential information of the client; any material reservations that a disinterested lawyer might reasonably harbor about the arrangement if such a lawyer were representing only the client being advised; and the consequences and effects of a future withdrawal of consent by any client, including, if relevant, the fact that the lawyer would withdraw from representing all clients (*see* § 121, Comment e). Where the conflict arises solely because a proposed representation will be adverse to an existing client in an unrelated matter, knowledge of the general nature and scope of the work being performed for each client normally suffices to enable the clients to decide whether or not to consent.

When the consent relates to a former-client conflict (*see* § 132), it is necessary that the former client be aware that the consent will allow the former lawyer to proceed adversely to the former client. Beyond that, the former client must have adequate information about the implications (if not readily apparent) of the adverse representation, the fact that the lawyer possesses the former client's confidential information, the measures that the former lawyer might undertake to protect against unwarranted disclosures, and the right of the former client to refuse consent. The former client will often be independently represented by counsel. If so, communication with the former client ordinarily must be through successor counsel (*see* § 99 and following).

The lawyer is responsible for assuring that each client has the necessary information. A lawyer who does not personally inform the client assumes the risk that the client is inadequately informed and that the consent is invalid. A lawyer's failure to inform the clients might also bear on the motives and good faith of the lawyer. On the other hand, clients differ as to their sophistication and experience, and situations differ in terms of their complexity and the subtlety of the conflicts presented. The requirements of this Section are satisfied if the client already knows the necessary information or learns it from other sources. A client independently represented — for example by inside legal counsel or by other outside counsel — will need less information about the consequences of a conflict but nevertheless may have need of information adequate to reveal its scope and severity. When several lawyers represent the same client, responsibility to make disclosure and obtain informed consent may be delegated to one or more of the lawyers who appears reasonably capable of providing adequate information.

Disclosing information about one client or prospective client to another is precluded if information necessary to be conveyed is confidential (*see* § 60). The affected clients may consent to disclosure (*see* § 62), but it also might be possible for the lawyer to explain the nature of undisclosed information in a manner that nonetheless provides an adequate basis for informed consent. If means of adequate disclosure are unavailable, consent to the conflict may not be obtained.

The requirement of consent generally requires an affirmative response by each client. Ambiguities in a client's purported expression of consent should be construed against the lawyer seeking the protection of the consent (*cf.* § 18). In general, a lawyer may not assume consent from a client's silent acquiescence. However, consent may be inferred from active participation in a representation by a client who has reasonably adequate information about the material risks of the representation after a lawyer's request for consent. Even in the absence of consent, a tribunal applying remedies such as disqualification (*see* § 121, Comment f) will apply concepts of estoppel and waiver when an objecting party has either induced reasonable reliance on the absence of objection or delayed an unreasonable period of time in making objection.

Effective client consent to one conflict is not necessarily effective with respect to other conflicts or other matters. A client's informed consent to simultaneous representation of another client in the same matter despite a conflict of interest (*see* Topic 3) does not constitute consent to the lawyer's later representation of the other client in a manner that would violate the former-client conflict rule (*see* § 132; *see also* § 121, Comment e(i)).

Illustration:

1. Client A and Client B give informed consent to a joint representation by Lawyer to prepare a commercial contract. Lawyer's bill for legal services is paid by

both clients and the matter is terminated. Client B then retains Lawyer to file a lawsuit against former Client A on the asserted ground that A breached the contract. Lawyer may not represent Client B against Client A in the lawsuit without A's informed consent (*see* § 132). Client A's earlier consent to Lawyer's joint representation to draft the contract does not itself permit Lawyer's later adversarial representation.

c(ii). The requirement of informed consent — the capacity of the consenting person. Each client whose consent is required must have the legal capacity to give informed consent. Consent purportedly given by a client who lacks legal capacity to do so is ineffective. Consent of a person under a legal disability normally must be obtained from a guardian or conservator appointed for the person. Consent of a minor normally is effective when given by a parent or guardian of the minor. In class actions certification of the class, determination that the interests of its members are congruent, and assessment of the adequacy of representation are typically made by a tribunal.

In some jurisdictions, a governmental unit might lack legal authority under applicable law to give consent to some conflicts of interest (*see* Comment g(ii) below).

When the person who normally would make the decision whether or not to give consent — members of a corporate board of directors, for example — is another interested client of the lawyer, or is otherwise self-interested in the decision whether to consent, special requirements apply to consent (*see* §§ 131 & 135, Comment d). Similarly, an officer of a government agency capable of consenting might be disabled from giving consent when that officer is a lawyer personally interested in consenting to the conflict.

d. Consent to future conflicts. Client consent to conflicts that might arise in the future is subject to special scrutiny, particularly if the consent is general. A client's open-ended agreement to consent to all conflicts normally should be ineffective unless the client possesses sophistication in the matter in question and has had the opportunity to receive independent legal advice about the consent. A client's informed consent to a gift to a lawyer (*see* § 127) ordinarily should be given contemporaneously with the gift.

On the other hand, particularly in a continuing client-lawyer relationship in which the lawyer is expected to act on behalf of the client without a new engagement for each matter, the gains to both lawyer and client from a system of advance consent to defined future conflicts might be substantial. A client might, for example, give informed consent in advance to types of conflicts that are familiar to the client. Such an agreement could effectively protect the client's interest while assuring that the lawyer did not undertake a potentially disqualifying representation.

Illustrations:

2. Law Firm has represented Client in collecting commercial claims through Law Firm's New York office for many years. Client is a long-established and sizable business corporation that is sophisticated in commercial matters generally and specifically in dealing with lawyers. Law Firm also has a Chicago office that gives

tax advice to many companies with which Client has commercial dealings. Law Firm asks for advance consent from Client with respect to conflicts that otherwise would prevent Law Firm from filing commercial claims on behalf of Client against the tax clients of Law Firm's Chicago office (*see* § 128). If Client gives informed consent the consent should be held to be proper as to Client. Law Firm would also be required to obtain informed consent from any tax client of its Chicago office against whom Client wishes to file a commercial claim, should Law Firm decide to undertake such a representation.

3. The facts being otherwise as stated in Illustration 2, Law Firm seeks advance consent from each of its Chicago-office corporate-tax clients to its representation of any of its other clients in matters involving collection of commercial claims adverse to such tax clients if the matters do not involve information that Law Firm might have learned in the tax representation. To provide further assurance concerning the protection of confidential information, the consent provides that, should Law Firm represent any client in a collection matter adverse to a tax client, a procedure to protect confidential information of the tax client will be established (*compare* § 124, Comment d). Unless such a tax client is shown to be unsophisticated about legal matters and relationships with lawyers, informed consent to the arrangement should be held to be proper.

If a material change occurs in the reasonable expectations that formed the basis of a client's informed consent, the new conditions must be brought to the attention of the client and new informed consent obtained (*see also* Comment f hereto (client revocation of consent)). If the new conflict is not consentable (*see* Comment g hereto), the lawyer may not proceed.

e. Partial or conditional consent. A client's informed consent to a conflict can be qualified or conditional. A client might consent, for example, to joint representation with one co-party but not another. Similarly, the client might condition consent on particular action being taken by the lawyer or law firm. For example, a former client might consent that the conflict of one individually prohibited lawyer should not be imputed (*see* § 123) to the rest of the firm, but only if the firm takes steps to assure that the prohibited lawyer is not involved in the representation (*see* § 124; *see also* Illustration 3 hereto). Such a partial or conditional consent can be valid even if an unconditional consent in the same situation would be invalid. For example, a client might give informed consent to a lawyer serving only in the role of mediator between clients (*see* § 130, Comment d), but not to the lawyer representing those clients opposing each other in litigation if mediation is unavailing (*see* Comment g(iii) hereto).

f. Revocation of consent through client action or a material change of circumstances. A client who has given informed consent to an otherwise conflicted representation may at any time revoke the consent (*see* § 21(2)). Revoking consent to the client's own representation, however, does not necessarily prevent the lawyer from continuing to represent other clients who had been jointly represented along with the revoking client. Whether the lawyer may continue the other representation depends on whether the client was justified in revoking the consent (such as because of a material change in the factual basis on which the client originally gave informed consent) and whether material detriment to the other client or lawyer would result.

In addition, if the client had reserved the prerogative of revoking consent, that agreement controls the lawyer's subsequent ability to continue representation of other clients.

A material change in the factual basis on which the client originally gave informed consent can justify a client in withdrawing consent. For example, in the absence of an agreement to the contrary, the consent of a client to be represented concurrently with another (*see* Topic 3) normally presupposes that the co-clients will not develop seriously antagonistic positions. If such antagonism develops, it might warrant revoking consent. If the conflict is subject to informed consent (*see* Comment g(iii) hereto), the lawyer must thereupon obtain renewed informed consent of the clients, now adequately informed of the change of circumstances. If the conflict is not consentable, or the lawyer cannot obtain informed consent from the other client or decides not to proceed with the representation, the lawyer must withdraw from representing all affected clients adverse to any former client in the matter (*see* § 121, Comment e).

A client who has given informed consent to be represented as a joint client with another would be justified in revoking the consent if the common lawyer failed to represent that client with reasonable loyalty (*see* Comment h hereto). The client would also be justified in revoking consent if a co-client materially violated the express or implied terms of the consent, such as by abusing the first client's confidential information through disclosing important information to third persons without justification. Improper behavior of the other client or the lawyer might indicate that one or both of them cannot be trusted to respect the legitimate interests of the consenting client.

* * *

The terms of the consent itself can control the effects of revocation of consent. A client's consent could state that it is conditioned on the client's right to revoke consent at any time for any reason. If so conditioned, the consent would cease to be effective if the client exercised that right.

g. Nonconsentable conflicts. Some conflicts of interest preclude adverse representation even if informed consent is obtained.

g(i). Representations prohibited by law. As stated in Subsection (2)(a), informed consent is unavailing when prohibited by applicable law. In some states, for example, the law provides that the same lawyer may not represent more than one defendant in a capital case and that informed consent does not cure the conflict (*see* § 129, Comment c). Under federal criminal statutes, certain representations by a former government lawyer (*cf.* § 133) are prohibited, and informed consent by the former client is not recognized as a defense.

* * *

g(iii). Conflicts between adversaries in litigation. When clients are aligned directly against each other in the same litigation, the institutional interest in vigorous development of each client's position renders the conflict nonconsentable (*see* § 128, Comment c, & § 129). The rule applies even if the parties themselves believe that the common interests are more significant in the matter than the interests dividing them. While the parties might give informed consent to joint representation for purposes of negotiating their differences (*see* § 130, Comment d), the joint representation may not continue if the parties become opposed to each other in litigation.

GREENE v. GREENE
391 N.E.2d 1355 (N.Y. 1979)

OPINION OF THE COURT

The issue presented for review is whether plaintiff's counsel, the law firm of Eaton, Van Winkle, Greenspoon & Grutman, should be disqualified because two of the members of the firm were formerly partners in defendant law firm, Finley, Kumble, Wagner, Heine & Underberg. For diverse reasons the Eaton firm should be disqualified.

In the action underlying this controversy, plaintiff, Helen Greene, alleges that the firm of Finley, Kumble and one of its partners, Theodore Greene, committed a breach of fiduciary duties, fraud, and a host of other wrongs in connection with the creation and management of an inter vivos trust established in 1969. Plaintiff was the settlor, sole beneficiary, and co-trustee of the trust. The two third-party defendants, Grutman and Bjork, are former members of the Finley, Kumble law firm. Grutman was affiliated with defendant firm from 1970 to 1976, during which time he acted as a managing partner of the firm and directed its litigation department. Bjork, Grutman's wife, joined Finley, Kumble as an associate in 1974, and became a member of the firm in 1975. She departed with her husband in 1976. Apparently, both joined the Eaton firm soon after leaving Finley, Kumble.

In August, 1977 plaintiff retained the Eaton firm to represent her and this action was instituted some four months later. According to plaintiff, she was fully advised that Grutman and Bjork, as former members of defendant firm, might be jointly and severally liable for any wrongdoing. She was further informed that since Grutman and Bjork had become members of Eaton, there might be "at least the appearance of a conflict of interest between [their] position as members of the firm representing [her] and their possible liability." Nonetheless, plaintiff expressed her desire that the Eaton firm represent her.

Defendants moved at Special Term for the disqualification of plaintiff's counsel on conflict of interest grounds. Special Term denied the motion, and the Appellate Division affirmed, with two Justices dissenting. That court subsequently granted leave to appeal, certifying the following question for our review: "Was the order of Supreme Court, as affirmed by this Court, properly made?" We now modify the order of the Appellate Division and grant defendants' motion insofar as it sought to disqualify Eaton, Van Winkle, Greenspoon and Grutman from acting as plaintiff's counsel.

It is a long-standing precept of the legal profession that an attorney is duty bound to pursue his client's interests diligently and vigorously within the limits of the law. For this reason, a lawyer may not undertake representation where his independent professional judgment is likely to be impaired by extraneous considerations. Thus, attorneys historically have been strictly forbidden from placing themselves in a position where they must advance, or even appear to advance, conflicting interests. This prohibition was designed to safeguard against not only violation of the duty of loyalty owed the client, but also against abuse of the adversary system and resulting harm to the public at large.

Perhaps the clearest instance of impermissible conflict occurs when a lawyer represents two adverse parties in a legal proceeding. In such a case, the lawyer owes a duty to each client to advocate the client's interests zealously. Yet, to properly represent either one of the parties, he must forsake his obligation to the other. Because dual representation is fraught with the potential for irreconcilable conflict, it will rarely be sanctioned even after full disclosure has been made and the consent of the clients obtained. Particularly is this so when the public interest is implicated, or where the conflict extends to the very subject matter of the litigation.

By the same token, where it is the lawyer who possesses a personal, business or financial interest at odds with that of his client, these prohibitions apply with equal force. Viewed from the standpoint of a client, as well as that of society, it would be egregious to permit an attorney to act on behalf of the client in an action where the attorney has a direct interest in the subject matter of the suit. As in the dual representation situation, the conflict is too substantial, and the possibility of adverse impact upon the client and the adversary system too great, to allow the representation. In short, a lawyer who possesses a financial interest in a lawsuit akin to that of a defendant may not, as a general rule, represent the plaintiff in the same action.

Aptly illustrating these problems are the circumstances of the present case. Plaintiff's counsel, the Eaton firm, has strong interests on both sides of the litigation. It has undertaken to represent plaintiff, owing her the highest duty of loyalty and professional skill in carrying on the legal action. At the same time, Grutman and Bjork, members of the firm, are manifestly liable, jointly and severally, for all tortious conduct which might have occurred during their tenure with defendant, Finley, Kumble (Partnership Law, §§ 24-26). That a possibility of their being cast in damages exists is demonstrated by their status as third-party defendants in this lawsuit. Hence, the firm representing plaintiff has a direct and substantial stake in the outcome of the litigation.[2] Whether this conflict may be effectively waived by the client need not now be addressed, as there are additional considerations which dictate disqualification.

*   *   *

As former partners in defendant law firm, Grutman and Bjork owe a fiduciary obligation similar to that owed by an attorney to his client. This is especially so with respect to Grutman, a former managing partner of the firm. Defendant relates, in its affidavits, that Grutman and Bjork gained confidential information in their capacity as members of the firm. Indeed, it is alleged that one or both of them were privy to partnership discussions concerning the firm's potential liability for its

---

[2] [3] Of course, we apply here the familiar principle that a conflict of interest involving even one lawyer in a firm taints the entire firm. [See section D in this chapter on imputed disqualification. —Ed.]

management of plaintiff's trust. In view of these allegations, we cannot discount the possibility that information obtained by Grutman and Bjork in their role as fiduciaries will be used in the pending lawsuit.

Although it is usually recognized that a party to litigation may select an attorney of his or her choosing, this general right is not limitless. The attorney may not accept employment in violation of a fiduciary relationship and may not allow his own interests to conflict with those of his client. To hold otherwise would be to ignore the overriding public interest in the integrity of our adversary system.

For these reasons, the Eaton firm should be disqualified from representing plaintiff in this matter. Accordingly, the order of the Appellate Division should be modified in accordance with this opinion, with costs to appellants, and, as so modified, affirmed. The certified question is answered in the negative.

* * *

Some of the conflicts rules that allow waiver require more than informed consent. *See, e.g.*, MR 1.7, 1.8(a), 1.8(g), 1.9, 1.11, and 1.12.

INTERNATIONAL NOTE

Most European civil law countries follow the European Union's rules in regards to the client's ability to waive a potential conflict of interest. In other countries, the client often has no say in the decision whatsoever. For example, Article 37(1) of the Ethical Code for Italian lawyers states that, "if conflict is potential, the client has no say in the matter. Lawyers must decline new business that potentially creates a conflict with the interests of existing clients." In France, the Law Decree Article 155 states that, "if the conflict is potential, a client may waive. If it is actual, the client may not. If the potential is not apparent when the lawyer begins representation but subsequently manifests, the lawyer must advise the client to seek alternative representation." In Germany, a lawyer cannot participate in a matter where he or she has previously given advice or represented the opponent. Conflicts of interest amount to criminal activity.

C. SOURCES OF CONFLICTS

There are three primary sources of conflicts of interest: third-party interference, lawyer interests, and multiple client interests. Identifying the conflict's source tracks the lawyer into the applicable rules and analytical modes.

1. Third-Party Interference

PROBLEM 5-1

Twenty-three-year-old Arthur approaches Lawyer for representation in a divorce action. Arthur is between employment, and Lawyer agrees to represent Arthur for $50 per hour, one-half of Lawyer's usual fee. The next day, Lawyer receives a telephone call from Arthur's Mother. She tells Lawyer that

Arthur has told her of their arrangement and that she wants to pay the balance of Lawyer's usual fee. She further indicates that because Arthur is "foolishly proud," she prefers to pay this fee without informing Arthur. How should Lawyer respond? What alternatives exist?

Third-party interference conflicts occur when someone who is not a party to the lawyer-client relationship seeks to affect or becomes positioned to affect the independence of the lawyer's judgment on behalf of the client. *See* MR 1.7(b) for the general rule. Such conflicts may be waived if the client consents after consultation.

The most common third-party interference example occurs when a third party pays the lawyer's fee for the lawyer's representation of a client. MR 1.8(f). Some practice settings place the lawyer in a position of guarding against inappropriate third-party influence as a regular, daily part of practice. Some of these involve third parties who pay the lawyer; others are less direct but no less real. Consider, for example, the lawyer selected and paid by an insurer to represent the insured; or the legal aid lawyer who is paid by a non-profit service corporation to represent eligible clients; or the military lawyer who represents an accused but is paid by her military branch.

PARSONS v. CONTINENTAL NATIONAL AMERICAN GROUP
550 P.2d 94 (Ariz. 1976)

OPINION: Appellants Ruth, Dawn and Gail Parsons obtained a judgment against appellant Michael Smithey, and then had issued and served a writ of garnishment on appellee, Continental National American Group (hereinafter referred to as CNA).

We accepted this petition for review because of the importance of the question presented. We are asked to determine whether an insurance carrier in a garnishment action is estopped from denying coverage under its policy when its defense in that action is based upon confidential information obtained by the carrier's attorney from an insured as a result of representing him in the original tort action.

Appellant, Michael Smithey, age 14, brutally assaulted his neighbors, appellants Ruth, Dawn and Gail Parsons, on the night of March 26, 1967.

During April, 1967 Frank Candelaria, CNA claims representative, began an investigation of the incident. On June 6, 1967 he wrote to Howard Watt the private counsel retained by the Smitheys advising him that CNA was "now in the final stages of our investigation," and to contact the Parsons' attorney to ascertain what type of settlement they would accept. Watt did contact the Parsons' attorney and requested that a formal demand settlement be tendered and the medical bills be forwarded to Candelaria. On August 11, 1967 Candelaria wrote a detailed letter to his company on his investigation of Michael's background in regards to his school experiences. He concluded the letter with the following:

> In view of this information gathered and in discussion with the boy's father's attorney, Mr. Howard Watts, and with the boy's parents, I am

reasonably convinced that the boy was not in control of his senses at the time of this incident.

It is, therefore, my suggestion that, and unless instructed otherwise, I will proceed to commence settlement negotiations with the claimant's attorney so that this matter may be disposed of as soon as possible.

Prior to the following dates: August 15, 1967, August 28, 1967, and October 23, 1967, Candelaria tried to settle with the Parsons for the medical expenses and was unsuccessful.

On October 13, 1967, the Parsons filed a complaint alleging that Michael Smithey assaulted the Parsons and that Michael's parents were negligent in their failure to restrain Michael and obtain the necessary medical and psychological attention for him. At the time that the Parsons filed suit they tendered a demand settlement offer of $22,500 which was refused by CNA as "completely unrealistic."

CNA's retained counsel undertook the Smithey's defense and also continued to communicate with CNA and advised him on November 10, 1967:

I have secured a rather complete and confidential file on the minor insured who is now in the Paso Robles School for Boys, a maximum security institution with facilities for psychiatric treatment, and he will be kept there indefinitely and certainly for at least six months. . . .

The above referred-to confidential file shows that the boy is fully aware of his acts and that he knew what he was doing was wrong. It follows, therefore, that the assault he committed on claimants can only be a deliberate act on his part.

After CNA had been so advised they sent a reservation of rights letter to the Smitheys stating that the insurance company, as a courtesy to the insureds, would investigate and defend the Parsons' claim, but would do so without waiving any of the rights under the policy. The letter further stated that it was possible the act involved might be found to be an intentional act, and that the policy specifically excludes liability for bodily injury caused by an intentional act. This letter was addressed only to the parents and not to Michael.

In preparing for trial the CNA attorney retained to undertake the defense of the Smitheys interviewed Michael and received a narrative statement from him in regards to the events of March 26, 1967, and then wrote to CNA: "His own story makes it obvious that his acts were willful and criminal."

CNA also requested an evaluation of the tort case and the same attorney advised CNA: "Assuming liability and coverage, the injury is worth the full amount of the policy or $25,000.00."

On the issue of liability the trial court directed a verdict for Michael's parents on the grounds that there was no evidence of the parents being negligent. This Court affirmed. On the question of Michael's liability the trial court granted plaintiff's motion for a directed verdict after the defense presented no evidence and there was no opposition to the motion. Judgment was entered against Michael in the amount of $50,000.

The Parsons then garnished CNA, and moved for a guardian ad litem to be appointed for Michael which was granted by the trial court. On November 23, 1970, appellee Parsons offered to settle with CNA in the amount of its policy limits, $25,000. This offer was not accepted.

CNA successfully defended the garnishment action by claiming that the intentional act exclusion applied. The same law firm and attorney that had previously represented Michael represented the carrier in the garnishment action.

Appellants contend that CNA should be estopped to deny coverage and have waived the intentional act exclusion because the company took advantage of the fiduciary relationship between its agent (the attorney) and Michael Smithey. We agree.

The attorneys, retained by CNA, represented Michael Smithey at the personal liability trial, and, as a result, obtained privileged and confidential information from Michael's confidential file at the Paso Robles School for Boys, during the discovery process and, more importantly, from the attorney-client relationship. Both the A.B.A. Committee on Ethics and Professional Responsibility and the State Bar of Arizona, Committee on Rules of Professional Conduct have held that an attorney that represented the insured at the request of the insurer owes undivided fidelity to the insured, and, therefore, may not reveal any information or conclusions derived therefrom to the insurer that may be detrimental to the insured in any subsequent action.

The attorney who represents an insured owes him "undeviating and single allegiance" whether the attorney is compensated by the insurer or the insured.

The attorney in the instant case should have notified CNA that he could no longer represent them when he obtained any information (as a result of his attorney-client relationship with Michael) that could possibly be detrimental to Michael's interests under the coverage of the policy.

The attorney representing Michael Smithey in the personal injury suit instituted by the Parsons had to be sure at all times that the fact he was compensated by the insurance company did not "adversely affect his judgment on behalf of or dilute his loyalty to [his] client, [Michael Smithey]."

*   *   *

The attorney in the present case continued to act as Michael's attorney while he was actively working against Michael's interests. When an attorney who is an insurance company's agent uses the confidential relationship between an attorney and a client to gather information so as to deny the insured coverage under the policy in the garnishment proceeding we hold that such conduct constitutes a waiver of any policy defense, and is so contrary to public policy that the insurance company is estopped as a matter of law from disclaiming liability under an exclusionary clause in the policy. *Employers Casualty Company v. Tilley*, 496 S.W.2d 552 (Tex. 1973). . . .

Appellee urges that the personal liability matter was defended under a reservation of rights agreement and this agreement had the effect of allowing the insurance company to investigate and defend the claim and still not waive any defenses. We hold that the reservation of rights agreement is not material to this case because the same attorney was representing conflicting clients. Appellee further urges that the procedure followed in the instant case is provided for by statute in Arizona. A.R.S. § 20-1130 states inter alia:

> Without limitation of any right or defense of an insurer otherwise, none of the following acts by or on behalf of an insurer shall be deemed to constitute a waiver of any provision of a policy or of any defense of the insurer thereunder:

*   *   *

> 3. Investigating any loss or claim under any policy or engaging in negotiations looking toward a possible settlement of any such loss or claim.

Appellee misconstrues the protection offered to the carrier under A.R.S. § 20-1130. This statute does not grant to a carrier the right to engage an attorney to act on behalf of the insured to defend a claim against the insured while at the same time build a defense against the insured on behalf of the insurer. This conflict of interest constitutes a source of prejudice upon which the insured may invoke the doctrine of estoppel.

. . . Opinion of the Court of Appeals vacated; judgment of the trial court reversed and judgment entered in favor of appellants Parsons in the sum of $50,000.

NOTES, QUESTIONS, AND EXAMPLES

1.   Conduct similar to that in *Parsons* by insurers through lawyers selected to represent insureds has been condemned by the highest courts of several other jurisdictions. In *Tiedtke v. Fidelity & Casualty Company of New York*, 222 So. 2d 206 (Fla. 1969); *Bogle v. Conway*, 433 P.2d 407 (Kan. 1967); *Crum v. Anchor Casualty Co.*, 119 N.W.2d 703 (Minn. 1963); *Merchants Indemnity Corp. v. Eggleston*, 179 A.2d 505 (N.J. 1962); *Van Dyke v. White*, 349 P.2d 430 (Wash. 1960); and *Perkoski v. Wilson*, 92 A.2d 189 (Pa. 1952), analogous conduct was held to preclude or estop the insurer from denying coverage or liability.

2.   Is it also possible to see an insurer-insured conflict as a lawyer's personal interest vs. a client's interest conflict? As a multiple client conflict?

INTERNATIONAL NOTE

The relevant conflict of interest rules for lawyers in the European Union are controlled by the Council of the Bars and Law Societies of Europe and found in the Code of Conduct for Lawyers in the European Union § 3.2. The general rule regarding conflicts of interest greatly resembles the American rules discussed above. Rule 3.2.1 states that "a lawyer may not advise, represent or act on behalf of two or more clients in the same matter if there is a conflict, or a significant risk of a conflict, between the interests of those clients." However, there are several rules dealing with the lawyer's procedure once a conflict of interest has been established that are in stark contrast to the American rules. First, once a conflict has been recognized, Code of Conduct for Lawyers in the European Union § 3.2.2 states that, "a lawyer must cease to act for both client when a conflict of interests arises between those clients and also whenever there is a risk of a breach of confidence or where his independence may be impaired." Furthermore, the Code of Conduct for Lawyers in the European Union § 3.2.3 deals with new clients that potentially have conflicts of interest. In those situations, the code dictates that:

> [A] lawyer must also refrain from acting for a new client if there is a risk of a breach of confidence entrusted to the lawyer by a former client or if the knowledge which the lawyer possesses of the affairs of the former client would give an undue advantage to the new client.

PFEIFER v. SENTRY INSURANCE
745 F. Supp. 1434 (E.D. Wis. 1990)

[This case is further excerpted at Chapter III, Section [B][1].]

On October 13, 1988, Western World wrote a letter to the City reserving its rights under the policy and authorizing von Briesen & Purtell to continue to act as defense counsel for the City. In another letter sent directly to von Briesen & Purtell on October 18, 1988, Western World requested that the firm defend the City of Brookfield. In the same letter Western World included a list of the following eight guidelines for defense counsel:

GUIDELINE 1:

Preliminary workup should be restricted to a review of the Summons and Complaint, Appearance, investigative material, Answer, Demands for Answers to Interrogatories, requests for admission, requests for production of documents and filing of Cross-Complaints, if applicable. No further workup is to be done without express authorization from the Company.

GUIDELINE 2:

Attorneys should not engage in investigation or lengthy and repeated interviews with witnesses or insureds if those procedures can be properly performed by independent adjusters or investigators. If extenuating circumstances cause a deviation from this instruction, authorization must be obtained from the Company.

GUIDELINE 3:

Legal research requirements should be promptly reported to the Company. You are requested to provide a summary of the reasons necessitating research requiring more than two hours, and not undertake same without authorization from the Company.

GUIDELINE 4:

Six-month interim billing is encouraged; however, other arrangements will be entertained. In no case will billing be considered on less than a quarterly basis. Time sheets and details of the services performed are required.

GUIDELINE 5:

If depositions are authorized, we request a "brief" narrative report covering the highlights of the testimony as they refer to the liability and damages. If the testimony simply confirms our prior knowledge of the claim, it is not necessary to highlight that testimony. In no case do we require copies of depositions unless specifically requested.

GUIDELINE 6:

The Company must be promptly advised of court appearances, settlement conferences, pre-trial depositions, and trial. It is required that counsel report twice daily when on trial. If reporting should have to take place after Company local hours, arrangements may be made to report to the handling examiner at home.

GUIDELINE 7:

The Company requests that attorney reports be concise and brief.

GUIDELINE 8:

Reports are to be forwarded directly to the examiner in charge of the file, addressing your correspondence to their individual attention. Single copies of your reports are all that is needed.

In conclusion, Western World stated that:

This letter sets forth guidelines only. It is not expected that it will be possible to follow these guidelines to the letter in every lawsuit that we refer to you. If, as you proceed with the defense, the exercise of your professional responsibility to your client, our insured, you believe a deviation from these guidelines is necessary, please advise us immediately and we will provide you with the necessary authorization.

On behalf of von Briesen & Purtell, Attorney James Reiher wrote to Western World to object to some of the guidelines. In his November 9, 1988 letter, Reiher took issue with the two-hour limit on legal research and with the semiannual billing policy. Reiher asked that his firm be allowed to send monthly statements. He explained that: "In this way, if a client has a question about the services or the fees, the issue can be raised, discussed, and resolved contemporaneously with the events as they occur and any disputes can be finalized while the case is immediate and in progress." Reiher also asked that the firm's bills be paid quarterly. In the same letter Reiher informed Western World that three von Briesen & Purtell attorneys would be working on the case.

In a reply dated December 6, 1988, Western World stated that it preferred that the case be handled by one attorney and insisted that only one attorney be in attendance at discovery and court proceedings.

*   *   *

————————

The lawyer who represents an organization (e.g., a corporation, a labor union) represents the organization, not the individual directors or managers of the organization. MR 1.13. Nonetheless, the organization's lawyer talks and interacts with the directors and managers; indeed, the primary way in which the organization's legal needs and interests can be made known to the lawyer is through the communications of the directors and managers. To the extent that the managers and directors articulate the organization's interests, the lawyer is hearing from her client. But when the directors and managers interpose their personal interests between the lawyer and the organization-client, a third-party interference conflict of interest occurs.

2. Lawyer-Client Conflicts

The second major source of conflicts are lawyer interests that conflict with client interests. As a general matter, a conflict of interest exists when there is a "substantial risk" that "representation of [a client] will be materially limited . . . by a personal interest of the lawyer." MR 1.7(a)(2). Waiver of this general lawyer vs. client conflict is permissible when the "lawyer reasonably believes that the lawyer will be able to provide competent and diligent representation to [the client]" and the "client gives informed consent, confirmed in writing." MR 1.7(b).

A variety of particular transactions between lawyers and clients are governed by specific conflicts rules, some of which are less about normal conflicts of interest analysis than they are about the common law prohibitions (abolished in most jurisdictions) against champerty, barratry, and maintenance.

a. Business Transactions with Clients

GOLDMAN v. KANE
329 N.E.2d 770 (Mass. App. Ct. 1975)

OPINION: The defendants, Barry Kane and Higley Hill, Inc., appeal from a judgment of a Probate Court ordering them to pay $50,806, plus interest, to the plaintiff Goldman, as the executor of the estate of Lawrence E. Hill.

Lawrence Hill, a fifty-three year old law school graduate, and his wife moved to Cape Cod in October, 1967. At that time Hill was the income beneficiary of two trusts. He received weekly income from one trust of about $200, and from the other he received approximately $30,000 a year, which was divided into two semi-annual payments. In 1968 Hill was introduced to Barry Kane, a practicing attorney with offices in Chatham and Yarmouth, after Hill had decided to purchase a parcel of real estate in Chatham (Kent Road property). As Hill's attorney, Kane set up a corporation, Lawrence Properties, Inc. (the other plaintiff in this suit and of which Hill owned all the outstanding shares), drew up a purchase and sale agreement for the Kent Road property whereby title to the parcel was to be taken by Lawrence Properties, Inc., and arranged for and obtained a mortgage loan on Hill's behalf. Between 1968 and 1970 Kane acted as Hill's attorney on a number of matters, including matters arising from the death of Hill's wife. During that period he received fees for legal services performed by him. It also appears that at various times throughout their relationship Hill paid money to Kane, who in turn paid Hill's bills.

In October, 1970, Hill decided to "change his lifestyle and live aboard a boat";

whereupon he left for Florida in the "Alas II," a twenty-two foot sloop which he owned. At about this time, Hill decided that he needed a larger vessel. While he was in the process of looking for an appropriate vessel to buy, Hill continuously sought advice from Kane both by telephone and letter. On April 17, 1971, Hill signed an agreement to purchase a forty-three foot ketch called the "Sea Chase" for $31,500, towards which he paid a deposit of $3,150, agreeing to pay the balance on or before May 17, 1971. Prior to Hill's signing the agreement Kane advised him on matters such as negotiations for the transfer of the "Sea Chase," the registration thereof, and technical nautical requirements of the vessel. Hill also asked Kane to arrange for the financing of the balance of $28,350 which would have to be paid by May 17.

In early May, 1971, Kane informed Hill that he was unable to arrange a loan with a bank, whereupon Hill instructed Kane to sell the Kent Road property. That property was put on the market at an offering price of $85,000, but Kane was unable to effect a sale. On May 30, Hill telephoned Kane on two or three occasions and told him he was in dire need of the money because he stood to lose the $3,150 deposit if he should be unable to raise the balance of the purchase price of the "Sea Chase" by the next day. In one of those conversations Kane told Hill that "it was virtually impossible" to get a loan in view of Hill's financial predicament and in view of the time limitation. In a subsequent conversation Kane told Hill that Kane's corporation[3] would loan him $30,000 but that, in consideration of making the loan, Hill would have to convey to the corporation absolute title to (1) the Kent Road property, (2) all of the personal property located therein, and (3) the "Alas II." In addition, Hill and Lawrence Properties, Inc. would have to execute a note to Kane's corporation for the repayment of the $30,000, and to secure the performance of the note, Hill would have to convey to Kane's corporation title to the "Sea Chase," which would be reconveyed upon full repayment of the note. After Hill agreed to the terms of the loan, Kane obtained the $30,000, prepared some of the necessary documents, and left for Florida, arriving there shortly after midnight on June 2. During that day he advised Hill not to enter into the agreement and to "walk away" from his deposit. However, Hill insisted on going forward, and the transaction was consummated on June 2, when Hill signed the following documents prepared by Kane: (1) a quitclaim deed transferring the title of the Kent Road property from Lawrence Properties, Inc. to Kane's corporation, subject to two outstanding mortgages; (2) a bill of sale transferring the "Alas II" from Hill to Kane's corporation; (3) a bill of sale transferring all of the personal property located in the Kent Road property from Lawrence Properties, Inc. to Kane's corporation; and (4) a non-interest bearing note for $30,000 requiring payment in two installments of $15,000 each on September 15, 1971, and March 1, 1972. Hill also signed an agreement, prepared by Kane, which recited the terms of the loan and which indicated that Hill was aware of the drawbacks of the agreement and that Kane had advised him against entering into it.[4] Shortly thereafter, by arrangement of

loan agreement

---

[3] [2] Kane's corporation is the defendant, Higley Hill, Inc., of which Kane owned ninety-five per cent of the outstanding stock.

[4] [3] The agreement stated in part: "I fully understand that Barry Kane, Esq., my attorney, is a major stockholder of Higley Hill, Inc., the transferee named herein. As my attorney, he has strongly advised me that this transfer is adverse to my financial welfare and has recommended that I not make said

the parties, title to the "Sea Chase" was taken in the name of Kane's corporation.

In July, 1971, Kane's corporation sold the Kent Road property with furnishings for $86,000. In September, 1971, Hill defaulted on the first payment of the $30,000 note, whereupon Kane, without notice to Hill, took possession of the "Sea Chase."

The judge concluded that at the time of the transaction the relationship of attorney and client existed between Kane and Hill and that Kane breached his fiduciary obligations to Hill by taking unfair advantage of that relationship. As a result the judge ordered that the defendants pay to Hill's executor $50,806, plus interest.

*   *   *

The defendants argue that even if an attorney-client relationship existed the record does not support the conclusion that there was a breach of that relationship. We disagree. The relationship of attorney and client is highly fiduciary in nature. "Unflinching fidelity to their genuine interests is the duty of every attorney to his clients. Public policy hardly can touch matters of more general concern than the maintenance of an untarnished standard of conduct by the attorney at law toward his client." *Berman v. Coakley, supra*, at 354.

The law looks with great disfavor upon an attorney who has business dealings with his client which result in gains to the attorney at the expense of the client. "The attorney is not permitted by the law to take any advantage of his client. The principles holding the attorney to a conspicuous degree of faithfulness and forbidding him to take personal advantage of his client are thoroughly established." *Berman v. Coakley, supra*, at 355. *See* Canon DR 5- 104 of the A.B.A. Code of Professional Responsibility (1970). When an attorney bargains with his client in a business transaction in a manner which is advantageous to himself, and if that transaction is later called into question, the court will subject it to close scrutiny. In such a case, the attorney has the burden of showing that the transaction "was in all respects fairly and equitably conducted; that he fully and faithfully discharged all his duties to his client, not only by refraining from any misrepresentation or concealment of any material fact, but by active diligence to see that his client was fully informed of the nature and effect of the transaction proposed and of his own rights and interests in the subject matter involved, and by seeing to it that his client either has independent advice in the matter or else receives from the attorney such advice as the latter would have been expected to give had the transaction been one between his client and a stranger." *Hill v. Hall*, 191 Mass. 253, 262 (1906).

Applying these principles to the case at bar, it is clear that the judge was correct in concluding that Kane, by entering into the transaction, breached his fiduciary duty to Hill. While the defendants contend that Kane's conduct did not constitute a breach of his fiduciary duty because Hill fully understood the nature and effect of the transaction and because Kane advised Hill against it,[5] in the circumstances of

---

transfer. My only expectations from this said transfer are that I shall receive legal title to the aforesaid Bluenose ketch upon having completed repayment of the $30,000 loan to Higley Hill, Inc., in accordance with the terms of the note."

[5] [5] It is important to note that after Hill agreed to the loan arrangement on the telephone and prior

this case, Kane's full disclosure and his advice were not sufficient to immunize him from liability. The fundamental unfairness of the transaction and the egregious overreaching by Kane in his dealings with Hill are self-evident. In light of the nature of the transaction, Kane, at a bare minimum, was under a duty not to proceed with the loan until he was satisfied that Hill had obtained independent advice on the matter. The purpose of such a requirement is to be certain that in a situation where an attorney deals with a client in a business relationship to the attorney's advantage, the "presumed influence resulting from the relationship has been neutralized." *Israel v. Sommer, supra,* at 123.

*　*　*

Judgment affirmed.

NOTES, QUESTIONS, AND EXAMPLES

1.　How does Model Rule 1.8(a)'s waiver provision differ from Model Rule 1.7's?

2.　The Goldman client was sophisticated and mature. Is Model Rule 1.8(a) unnecessarily paternalistic?

3.　Would additional acts by Kane have satisfied Model Rule 1.8(a)'s requirements?

b.　Literary Rights

UNITED STATES v. HEARST
638 F.2d 1190 (9th Cir. 1980)

Choy, Circuit Judge.

Hearst appeals the district court's denial, without discovery or a hearing, of her motion for "habeas corpus," 28 U.S.C. § 2255. We affirm in part and vacate in part, and remand for further proceedings.

I. Introduction

Hearst was arrested in September 1975 for bank robbery. Soon after, she made incriminating statements, which were captured by jail officials on the "Tobin tape," in a jailhouse interview with her friend Tobin. F. Lee Bailey and his associate J. Albert Johnson entered the case on October 2 as Hearst's counsel and prepared a defense based on a coercion theory. They did not move for a change of venue or for a continuance on the ground of pretrial publicity, choosing instead to rely on the voir dire of the prospective jurors. Their motion to suppress the Tobin tape was denied. Trial began in February 1976. Bailey put Hearst on the witness stand; she

---

to any negative advice given by Kane, Kane prepared some of the documents necessary to consummate the agreement. Two days later Kane went to Florida where he advised Hill not to go through with the loan. However, this advice was given only a short time before the transaction was consummated.

took the Fifth Amendment in the presence of the jury. Hearst was convicted on March 20. Her motions for a new trial were denied. She took an unsuccessful appeal, and certiorari was denied. Bailey and Johnson were fired, and through present counsel Hearst filed a § 2255 motion, which Judge Orrick denied without a hearing. While the appeal from this ruling was pending, President Carter commuted Hearst's sentence.

Most of the above is well known, for Hearst's case was a cause celebre. We now know, in addition, that during the course of the proceedings Bailey contracted to write a book about the trial, thus raising questions of potential or actual conflict of interest.

Bailey has admitted by affidavit that

> In February of 1976, I had received several offers to publish a book concerning the Hearst trial. A contract was eventually signed with G.P. Putnam, however, that contract was made contingent upon Ms. Hearst agreeing not to write about her experiences for a period of eighteen months subsequent to the publication. I indicated to Putnam that I would not submit any agreement on this subject to Ms. Hearst while the matter was still being litigated and the contract thus remained contingent upon Ms. Hearst's approval.

On March 22, 1976, Hearst signed the following covenant:

> March 22, 1976

> Putnam/Berkley Publishing Corp.

> New York, New York

Gentlemen:

> I understand that F. Lee Bailey is writing a book about my trial and life story as it pertains to the trial for which he will contract with you for publication in the United States and Canada.

> As an inducement for you to publish this book, I hereby agree not to publish any account of my experiences in book, magazine, or any other form, prior to 18 months from your initial (hardcover) publication of Mr. Bailey's book, and I further agree to cooperate fully and exclusively with Mr. Bailey in his preparation and writing of the book in any manner he requires.

Very truly yours,

/s/ Patricia C. Hearst

Patricia Campbell Hearst

PCH.sm

Randolph Hearst, appellant's father, declared by affidavit that in September 1975 he discussed with Bailey the possibility of a book, and did not rule out the possibility. Mr. Hearst declared that he did not consider book rights to be part of the fee arrangement for the trial. He declared further that "after . . . trial"

Johnson told him that Bailey wanted to write a book about Ms. Hearst's trial, that this would be part of the fee arrangement for the appeal, and that Ms. Hearst would have to sign a covenant not to publish anything for eighteen months after the trial. Mr. Hearst, not knowing that Bailey had negotiated or contracted during the trial to write a book, told Johnson to tell Ms. Hearst that he had no objection to the arrangement Johnson had described.

Ms. Hearst declared by affidavit that before trial Johnson told her that Bailey would write a book about her, that the book rights were part of the fee arrangement her parents had made, that she had to agree to the arrangement but was not to discuss it, and that Johnson would someday ask her to sign a paper relating to it. She further declared that on March 22, two days after her conviction, Johnson brought her the covenant and said, "Remember the paper I would be bringing you to sign one day; well this is it"; that she did not have independent counsel, feel a sense of free will, or understand the effect of the covenant; and that it was never her desire that Bailey write a book about her or the trial.[6]

II. HEARST'S CONTENTIONS

*   *   *

A. Conflict of Interest

Hearst claims that Bailey's book contract created a conflict of interest that deprived her of her Sixth Amendment right to the assistance of counsel. This alleged conflict was not total, for surely the salability of Bailey's book would have been enhanced had he gained an acquittal for Hearst. Nonetheless, Hearst charges that Bailey (1) failed to seek a continuance, so public interest would not cool and competing authors would not get the jump on him; (2) failed to seek a change of venue, because publicity would be maximized by a trial in San Francisco, a media center and the home of the Hearst family; and (3) put her on the witness stand, so her story would go on the public record and he would not be constrained by the attorney-client confidentiality rules. These decisions prejudiced Hearst, she says, because the case came to trial in the full heat of prejudicial publicity, and she was forced to plead the Fifth forty-two times in the presence of the jury.

The Government and Bailey denied that Bailey's book interest played any role in these tactical decisions, and advanced plausible reasons why he made those decisions.

The district court denied relief, on the grounds that counsel's reasonable tactical decisions could not be challenged, and that Hearst had not shown actual prejudice.

We hold that the district court erred in denying Hearst a hearing on these issues.

---

[6] [2] Hearst alleged that Bailey's book contract called for a $70,000 advance and a total of $225,000; that the advance was paid; that Bailey had a ghostwriter write "The Trial of Patty Hearst"; and that the publisher rejected the manuscript. Hearst declared by affidavit that on August 1, 1977, Bailey wrote her that since the book had not been published yet, there was no need for the covenant and she could consider it null and void.

On remand, the district court should conduct a hearing and apply to the facts the law recently laid down by the Supreme Court in *Cuyler v. Sullivan*, 446 U.S. 335 (1980).

1. The *Cuyler v. Sullivan* Test

In *Cuyler v. Sullivan*, a decision of which the district court did not have the benefit, the Supreme Court considered a claim that retained counsel's conflict of interest violated the client's Sixth Amendment right to the assistance of counsel. Sullivan sought federal habeas corpus relief from a state conviction, whereas Hearst's conviction was federal; Sullivan's lawyer's conflict was based on multiple representation, whereas Hearst's was based on private financial interests. These differences are immaterial. We consider the rules laid down in Sullivan to be directly applicable to the present case, and they should govern the case on remand.

*   *   *

Once Hearst established an actual conflict of interest with adverse effect on her counsel's performance, she would be entitled to relief on contentions (A)(1) and (2) even if no prejudice to her chance of acquittal at trial appeared. Therefore, if Hearst is entitled to relief on contentions (A)(1) and (2) she will gain the relief she seeks through contention (E); yet if she is not entitled to relief on the former contentions, she could not be entitled to relief on the later contention (because she would not have established "cause"). Since the district court's decision on contentions (A)(1) and (2), which we have remanded for a hearing, will effectively moot contention (E), we see no reason to disturb the district court's decision on that issue.

III. ATTORNEY DISCIPLINE

A. Standards of Conduct

Under Federal Rule of Appellate Procedure 46, a Court of Appeals can discipline any attorney who practices before it for "conduct unbecoming a member of the bar." This language is not unconstitutionally vague. It refers to the legal profession's "code of behavior" and "lore," of which all attorneys are charged with knowledge and of which the American Bar Association Code of Professional Responsibility (ABA CPR) is an illustration.

B. Bailey's Conduct

The allegations and admissions in the record of the present case raise serious questions as to whether Bailey and, to the extent of his participation, Johnson have been guilty of conduct unbecoming members of the bar.

1. The Book Contract

Bailey's book contract created a potential conflict of interest; this case tests whether it ripened into an actual conflict of interest. Therefore, Bailey may have violated ABA CPR Disciplinary Rule 5-101(A), which reads:

> Except with the consent of his client after full disclosure, a lawyer shall not accept employment if the exercise of his professional judgment on behalf of his client will be or reasonably may be affected by his own financial, business, property, or personal interests.

The obvious reason for this rule is well expressed in ABA CPR Ethical Consideration 5-1:

> The professional judgment of a lawyer should be exercised, within the bounds of the law, solely for the benefit of his client and free of compromising influences and loyalties. Neither his personal interests, the interests of other clients, nor the desires of third persons should be permitted to dilute his loyalty to his client.

Bailey's book contract might not fall within ABA CPR Disciplinary Rule 5-104(B), because the contract itself was not an acquisition from the client of an interest in publication rights. Nonetheless, Rule 5-104(B) recognizes the dangers inherent in simultaneous lawyering and authoring.[7] Moreover, all courts before which the issue has been raised have disapproved the practice of attorneys arranging to benefit from the publication of their clients' stories. . . .

In light of Rule 5-101(A), Bailey's decision to enter into a book contract during the course of the trial was most unfortunate. Potential and actual conflicts of interest always bring disrepute upon the bar, the court, and the law. They do so to an even greater degree when the case is a cause celebre and the attorney has the reputation of being an outstanding lawyer. Moreover, Bailey is in no position to claim that the book contract was necessary to finance his fee.

2. The Covenant

ABA CPR Disciplinary Rule 5-104(B) reads:

> Prior to conclusion of all aspects of the matter giving rise to his employment, a lawyer shall not enter into any arrangement or understanding with a client or a prospective client by which he acquires an interest in publication rights with respect to the subject matter of his employment or proposed employment.

---

[7] [6] This recognition becomes even more explicit in Rule 1.9(d) [eventually adopted as Model Rule 1.8(d). —Ed.] of the Discussion Draft of the ABA Model Rules of Professional Conduct, Reprinted in 48 U.S.L.W., No. 32, at 8 (Feb. 19, 1980):

> Prior to the conclusion of representation of a client, a lawyer shall not make or negotiate an agreement giving the lawyer literary rights to a matter arising from the representation.

The Comment to that proposed Rule reads in part:

> An agreement by which a lawyer acquires literary rights concerning the subject matter of the representation involves incompatible standards for the lawyer's performance, one being effectiveness in representing the client and the other being performance that has literary value. Even after conclusion of representation, a lawyer may make use of information about a client in an account of professional experience only to the extent permitted by Rule 1.7. [Eventually Model Rule 1.6. — Ed.]

The proposed Rule, if in effect at the time, would explicitly have prohibited Bailey's book contract.

Even though Bailey's book contract itself technically might not violate this Rule, Hearst's March 22 covenant to cooperate exclusively with Bailey and not to publish on her own was obtained pursuant to his representation and, we believe, constituted an "interest in publication rights." Although Hearst's trial had ended on March 22, Bailey's representation of Hearst had not. He continued to represent her through a motion for new trial, a second motion for new trial, sentencing, a direct appeal to this Court, a petition for rehearing en banc, a petition for certiorari, a motion to vacate a concurrent sentence, and a Rule 35 motion to reduce sentence. Thus, Bailey was apparently in violation of ABA CPR Disciplinary Rule 5-104(B) from March 22, 1976, onward.

* * *

C. Disciplinary Proceedings

We suggest that the district court, on remand, might find it advisable to issue to Bailey (and perhaps to Johnson as well) an order to show cause why he should not be disciplined, on the grounds noted above, in his capacity as a member pro hac vice of the bar of the United States District Court for the Northern District of California.

IV. CONCLUSION

As to Hearst's contentions that Bailey suffered from an actual conflict of interest that adversely affected his performance, in that it caused him to fail to seek a continuance, to fail to seek a change of venue, and to put Hearst on the witness stand, the district court's denial of the motion for relief is VACATED, and the case REMANDED for reconsideration of Hearst's discovery request, and for a hearing.

As to all other matters, the judgment of the district court is AFFIRMED.

NOTES, QUESTIONS, AND EXAMPLES

1. What does it mean to enter a contract for literary rights with a client?

2. Why does Model Rule 1.8(d) lack a waiver provision?

c. Drafting Instruments That Benefit the Lawyer

A lawyer is prohibited from drafting a document that makes a substantial gift to the lawyer or the lawyer's close relatives. This restriction does not apply when the donee is related to the donor. MR 1.8(c). Amended in February 2002, this rule applies now to donor-clients only and the prohibition extends beyond preparing instruments to the act of soliciting the gift by the lawyer. The amendment also provides a definition of persons related to the lawyer.

d.   Sexual or Amorous Relations with Clients

Ethics 2000 Commission, February 2002 ABA Amendment to Model Rules

Model Rule 1.8(j), Sexual Relationships with Clients

MR 1.8(j), prohibits most sexual relationships between lawyers and clients. The rule does not prohibit sexual relationships that predated the beginning of the lawyer-client relationship.

A few states had already addressed this issue either through adoption of rules [*see, e.g.*, Minn. PRC 1.8(k), California Rule 3-120, Florida RPC 4-8.4(i), and New York CPR DR 1-102(A)(7)] or through case-law [*see, e.g.*, *In re Heard*, 963 P.2d 818 (Wash. 1998); *In re Hawkins*, 695 N.E.2d 109 (Ind. 1998), below]. Two rationales have presented themselves for these rules: a conflicts rationale and a moral turpitude rationale.

IN RE HEARD
963 P.2d 818 (Wash. 1998) (en banc)

TALMADGE, JUSTICE.

In this case we review the Washington State Bar Association (WSBA) Disciplinary Board's (the Board) unanimous recommendation of a two-year suspension of an attorney's license to practice law. The recommendation is based on two principal areas of misconduct — the attorney's mishandling of a client's personal injury settlement and his sexual exploitation of that client.

James Heard negotiated a settlement on behalf of his client during the handling of a personal injury matter. He evaluated the case at more than $150,000, and retained the only cash in the settlement — $50,000 in insurance proceeds. However, much of the settlement's "value" ultimately proved to be illusory. During the process, Heard failed to apprise his client of the problematic quality of the settlement or that he was retaining the only cash in the settlement.

Heard also committed an act of moral turpitude by exploiting his professional relationship with the client to give her alcohol and have sexual relations with her, knowing she had a history of alcohol and drug problems and had sustained severe head injuries in an accident.

We affirm the Board's determination Heard violated the Rules of Professional Conduct (RPC) in handling the settlement and the Rules of Lawyer Discipline (RLD) by engaging in an act of moral turpitude. We suspend him for two years from the practice of law and order him to pay restitution and costs.

*   *   *

2. Does an attorney commit an act of moral turpitude within the meaning of the RLD if he exploits his professional relationship with a vulnerable client by providing her alcohol and having sexual relations with her?

Issue

FACTS

In 1989, 23-year-old Katrina Menz was seriously injured in an accident while a passenger on a motorcycle. Menz sustained severe head injuries from the accident, was comatose for a week, and remained in the hospital for several weeks thereafter. Menz's mother retained attorney James A. Heard, then 43-years-old, to represent Menz in her action to recover damages for her injuries.

*   *   *

Prior to the conclusion of the settlement, Heard went to Menz's house and asked her if she would like to discuss the case. Heard knew of Menz's vulnerability, having had access to her medical history. He had successfully secured a guardian ad litem for her in the lawsuit and had instituted a separate guardianship proceeding, which was later dropped. He also knew she had prior problems with drug and alcohol abuse. Moreover, he knew she was scheduled for further surgery, a cranio-plasty, in February 1990. Nevertheless, they went to a local lounge to "discuss her case" where they started drinking. They then decided to visit another local lounge. Heard told Menz to drive his car despite her protests that she should not drive due to her status as a habitual traffic offender. After more drinking at a second lounge, they returned to Heard's apartment where they had consensual sexual relations.

*   *   *

On December 14 and 15, 1995, a formal disciplinary hearing was held pursuant to RLD 4.10 before a hearing examiner. In a written opinion, the hearing examiner concluded the WSBA failed to meet its burden of proof on each count. WSBA disciplinary counsel appealed this decision to the Board. . . .

In a written opinion, the Board reversed the hearing examiner on seven of the eight counts, finding the hearing examiner's conclusions were not supported by the evidence or by the law. The Board found no violation as to Heard's alleged failure to obtain Menz's signature on the retainer, but sustained the other seven charges against Heard.

As to sanctions, the Board recommended a two-year suspension of Heard's license to practice and ordered him to pay restitution in the amount of $28,334.34 plus interest and costs. The Board based its sanctions recommendation on a finding of numerous aggravating circumstances including dishonest or selfish motives, vulnerability of victim, refusal to acknowledge wrongdoing, and indifference in making restitution. Heard appealed the Board's decision and sanctions recommendation to us.

*   *   *

The Board's findings and recommendations essentially involve three issues: Heard's alleged misconduct involving the settlement agreement and his fee, Heard's alleged act of moral turpitude, and the sanction to be imposed against Heard, if any. We address each of these issues in order.

*   *   *

B. Moral Turpitude

Count VIII alleges Heard committed an act of "moral turpitude" in violation of the Rules of Lawyer Discipline 1.1(a) by having sex with his client. RLD 1.1 provides:

> A lawyer may be subjected to the disciplinary sanctions or actions set forth in these rules for any of the following:

> (a) The commission of any act involving moral turpitude, dishonesty, or corruption, or any unjustified act of assault or other act which reflects disregard for the rule of law. . . .

The RLD does not specifically define the term "moral turpitude," although we have previously sustained attorney discipline based on findings of moral turpitude. In *In re Disciplinary Proceeding Against McGrath*, 98 Wash. 2d 337, 655 P.2d 232 (1982), *reinstatement granted*, 112 Wash. 2d 481, 772 P.2d 502 (1989), we recognized the general nature of "moral turpitude":

> This definition of moral turpitude is necessarily general. In the setting of attorney discipline, its application depends upon the collective conscience and judgment of the members of this court. It is as meaningful as other phrases adopted by other courts. *See Searcy v. State Bar of Texas*, 604 S.W.2d 256, 258 (Tex. Civ. App. 1980) which sets forth the various definitions. "Its definition does not gain in clarity by prolixity of statement." *In re Jacoby*, 74 Ohio App. 147, 155, 57 N.E.2d 932 (1943). *See also* 58 C.J.S. Moral 1200-07 (1948).

Id. at 342, 655 P.2d 232. We essentially look to the inherent nature of the act committed by the attorney to answer the following question:

> [D]o the acts found against the appellant, and for which he was convicted . . . , violate the commonly accepted standard of good morals, honesty, and justice? Suppose we measure his conduct in this regard, not by any puritanical standard, but by the standard of right conduct generally prevailing among our people, uninfluenced by the fact that the statute law also punishes such conduct as a crime. What, then, is the answer to the question whether or not such acts involve moral turpitude?

In re Disciplinary Proceeding Against Hopkins, 54 Wash. 569, 572, 103 P. 805 (1909). *See also In re Disciplinary Proceeding Against Stroh*, 97 Wash. 2d 289, 644 P.2d 1161 (1982) (attorney's crime of tampering with a witness strikes at the very core of the judicial system and therefore necessarily involves moral turpitude), *cert. denied*, 459 U.S. 1202 (1983); *McGrath*, 98 Wash. 2d at 340-43, 655 P.2d 232 (attorney's assault in the second degree involving a deadly weapon constituted moral turpitude).

Although seven states have adopted explicit limitations on attorney-client sexual relations,[8] Washington has not adopted such a rule. The WSBA recently proposed such a rule to this Court which stated: "[i]t is professional misconduct for a lawyer to . . . have sexual relations with a current client of the lawyer unless a consensual sexual relationship existed between them before the lawyer/client relationship commenced." RPC Proposed Rule 8.4. However, we did not adopt it.

Despite the absence of an express rule banning attorney-client sexual relations, an attorney's sexual relations with a client can constitute "moral turpitude," justifying the imposition of disciplinary sanctions. *See, e.g., In re Disciplinary Proceeding Against Rinella*, 175 Ill. 2d 504, 222 Ill. Dec. 375, 677 N.E.2d 909, *cert. denied*, 522 U.S. 951, 118 S. Ct. 371, 139 L. Ed. 2d 288 (1997), therein the Supreme Court of Illinois suspended an attorney from practice for three years, rejected his argument that he could not be sanctioned for engaging in sexual relations with his clients because no disciplinary rule specifically proscribes such conduct. The *Rinella* Court noted:

> Initially, we reject respondent's contention that attorney misconduct is sanctionable only when it is specifically proscribed by a disciplinary rule. On the contrary, the standards of professional conduct enunciated by this court are not a manual designed to instruct attorneys what to do in every conceivable situation. . . .

> [W]e do not believe that respondent, or any other member of the bar, could reasonably have considered the conduct involved here to be acceptable behavior under the rules governing the legal profession.

In *People v. Good*, 893 P.2d 101 (Colo. 1995), the court recognized that no rule explicitly prohibits a sexual relationship between attorney and client, but found Good had violated the state's ethical rules and suspended him for one year, noting:

> Because the lawyer stands in a fiduciary relationship with the client, an unsolicited sexual advance by the lawyer debases the essence of the lawyer-client relationship. Often the lawyer-client relationship is characterized by the dependence of the client on the lawyer's professional judgment, and a sexual relationship may well result from the lawyer's exploitation of the lawyer's dominant position. *See* ABA Comm. on Ethics and Professional Responsibility, Formal Op. 92-364 at 2.

* * *

. . . Heard used his professional relationship with Menz to initiate the social

---

[8] [8] Iowa Code of Professional Responsibility for Lawyers EC 5-25 (1998); Minnesota Rules of Professional Conduct Rule 1.8(k) (1997); Oregon Code of Professional Responsibility DR 5-110(A) (1998); Wisconsin Rules of Professional Conduct SCR 20: 1.8(k)(2) (1998); Rules of Professional Conduct of the State Bar of California Rule 3-120 (1998); Florida Rules of Professional Conduct Rule 4-8.4(I) (1998); New York Code of Professional Responsibility DR1-102(A)(7) (1994).

relationship (he went to her home and invited her to "go out" to discuss her case). As Menz's attorney, Heard had intimate knowledge of her vulnerabilities. Heard knew Menz had sustained a significant head injury for which she required multiple surgeries, and she was psychologically and physically impaired, undergoing a period of prolonged rehabilitation. Through access to her medical records, Heard knew Menz had an extensive history of alcohol and drug problems, and had been sexually abused. He further knew that as a result of her brain injury Menz continued to have memory, reading comprehension, auditory processing, attention, speech, problem solving and other cognitive deficits. He also knew her medical providers were concerned about her judgment, safety and ability to live independently. Despite this knowledge, Heard took Menz to two cocktail lounges and gave her alcoholic beverages at both. When Menz informed Heard she should not be drinking, he assured her that everything would be all right. Heard then took Menz to his apartment where they engaged in sexual relations. Heard sexually exploited a client with alcohol problems and who suffered the effects of serious head injuries. Heard's use of his professional position to exploit a vulnerable young woman constituted moral turpitude within the meaning of RLD 1.1.

Conclusion

James Heard engaged in numerous instances of misconduct involving the negotiation of a settlement agreement and the fee he earned for his work. He made matters worse by exploiting his authority as an attorney and taking advantage of an exceedingly vulnerable client to have sexual relations with her. We do not condone such exploitative behavior. The Board properly found Heard to have violated the RPC and the RLD and appropriately sanctioned him by suspending his license for two years, and ordering him to pay restitution to Menz. We also award costs on appeal to the WSBA.

Sanders, Justice, dissenting.

The majority's affirmation of discipline against Attorney James A. Heard rests on two doubtful propositions: (1) we review factual findings of the Disciplinary Board rather than findings made by the hearing examiner who actually received the evidence and had the opportunity to judge the credibility of the witnesses before him; and (2) an attorney may be disciplined for an act of "moral turpitude" without necessity to prove that the act also "reflects disregard for the rule of law." RLD 1.1(a).

* * *

Moral Turpitude

[I]f required for disposition, I would also disagree with the majority's legal conclusion that the Bar's allegation of sexual contact, even if proved on its face, constitutes a clear violation of the rules governing attorney discipline, as we rejected just such a bright-line rule several years ago and it is legally erroneous, if not patently unfair, to apply a rule without first adopting it.

At most under the current rules attorney-client sex is prohibited only if it violates some other rule set out in our Rules of Professional Conduct or the Rules for Lawyer Discipline; however, there is no violation under these facts.

Other jurisdictions are in accord. [citing *Musick v. Musick*, 192 W. Va. 527, 453 S.E.2d 361 (1994); *Edwards v. Edwards*, 165 A.D.2d 362, 567 N.Y.S.2d 645 (1991)]

In contrast are a few cases where attorney-client sex may involve alleged violation of some other rule. Compare, for example, *In re McBratney*, 320 S.C. 416, 465 S.E.2d 733 (1996), in which attorney sexual relations with client prejudiced terms of divorce settlement; however, here there is no allegation, nor even suggestion, this alleged act affected the representation. In fact by the time the single sexual act allegedly occurred the settlement had been finalized and further professional services were unnecessary.

The only rule arguably applicable is RLD 1.1 which provides:

> A lawyer may be subjected to the disciplinary sanctions or actions set forth in these rules for any of the following:

> (a) The commission of any act involving moral turpitude, dishonesty, or corruption, or any unjustified act of assault or other act which reflects disregard for the rule of law, whether the same be committed in the course of his or her conduct as a lawyer, or otherwise. . . .

While the majority looks to itself, the practitioner must look to the rule. RLD 1.1(a) is qualified in two important respects: first, in pertinent part, it applies to acts of moral turpitude; second, it references acts which "reflect[] disregard for the rule of law."

> [A]cts of moral turpitude usually involve evil intent. But none was found here. Moreover "moral turpitude" is vague and overly broad absent at least some nexus to the practice of law which is the only justification for any of these rules in the first place.

That nexus is also required by the very text of the rule which requires us to connect the act of moral turpitude with a finding that it "reflect[ ] disregard for the rule of law." RLD 1.1(a). Requiring such a link serves a rational purpose because, arguably, an attorney who acts with disregard for the rule of law may to that extent demonstrate unfitness to uphold the law which he practices. "RLD 1.1(a) speaks to the standards governing discipline in order to encourage obedience to the law. We decline to interpret this rule as speaking to conduct tending to embarrass the bar." Thus, for example, in *In re Discipline of Kerr*, 86 Wash. 2d 655, 548 P.2d 297 (1976) an attorney was disciplined for attempted subornation of perjury as an act of moral turpitude, which indeed reflects a disregard for the rule of law.

The majority, however, ignores that part of the text of RLD 1.1 which expressly references "disregard for the rule of law." . . .

However much one may frown on Heard's alleged act of attorney-client sex under these circumstances, it simply does not "reflect[ ] disregard for the rule of law," and there is no claim to the contrary. The alleged sex was consensual between adults and completely lawful. If the complainant was marginally mentally impaired due to her injuries, there is no finding that impairment rendered her incompetent to consent to sexual intercourse. As a matter of fact the examiner specifically found "no guardian was ever appointed for Katrina Menz," whereas, the guardian ad litem was appointed narrowly for the litigation, not generally for the person.

*   *   *

If, as many believe, any sex outside marriage is evidence of "moral turpitude," as are many deviations from the heterosexual norm also so considered, the majority lacks any principled basis to limit its moral insight to sex merely with clients. Indeed, the clear language of the rule ("whether the same be committed in the course of his or her conduct as a lawyer . . . .") dispels any such limitation by its text, and I can see no practical reason to limit this holding in practice beyond those objections I previously stated. If it is our duty to uplift the moral character of our fellow practitioners in all respects, we certainly have our work cut out. This rule, as the majority construes it, has no limits. Nor has it rudder or anchor, but plenty of sail to get us out to sea.

IN RE HAWKINS
695 N.E.2d 109 (Ind. 1998)

PER CURIAM.

The respondent and the Disciplinary Commission agree that the respondent violated the Rules of Professional Conduct for Attorneys at Law and that he should be suspended from the practice of law for a period of ninety days for that misconduct. This opinion sets forth the facts and circumstances of this case.

The respondent was admitted to the bar of this state in 1971. The respondent and the Commission agree that in August of 1994, a client retained him to represent her in two cases in which the client was charged with operating a motor vehicle while intoxicated. She paid him a total of $400 as a retainer for his representation. On September 8, 1994, the respondent met his client for a hearing in the City-County Building in Indianapolis and obtained a continuance on her behalf. Following the hearing, the respondent asked his client to go with him to his private law office to discuss the pending actions. The client rode with the respondent to his office, where after arrival each consumed an alcoholic beverage. Following the drinks, the respondent and his client engaged in sexual intercourse on a couch located in the respondent's office. Thereafter, the respondent drove his client back to her car at the City-County Building. On September 30, 1994, at the suggestion of his attorney, the respondent filed a motion to withdraw his appearance on behalf of his client. The court granted the motion that day.

Indiana Professional Conduct Rule 1.7(b) provides, in relevant part:

> A lawyer shall not represent a client if the representation of that client may be materially limited by the lawyer's responsibilities to another client or to a third person, or by the lawyer's own interests, unless:
>
> (1) the lawyer reasonably believes the representation will not be adversely affected; and

(2) the client consents after consultation.

By having sexual relations with his client, the respondent promoted and served his own interests and thereby threatened material limitation of his representation of her. We therefore conclude that he violated Ind. Professional Conduct Rule 1.7(b).

Professional Conduct Rule 8.4(d) provides that it is professional misconduct for a lawyer to engage in conduct prejudicial to the administration of justice. By engaging in sexual intercourse with his client during the course of his representation of her, the respondent violated Prof. Cond. R. 8.4(d).

The parties agree that the respondent should be suspended from the practice of law for a period of ninety days for his misconduct. We find that the agreed sanction is acceptable. Lawyers who choose to engage in sexual relations with clients during the period of representation threaten damage to their ability effectively to represent the client. Objective detachment, essential for clear and reasoned analysis of issues and independent legal judgment, may be lost.

It is, therefore, ordered that the respondent, William M. Hawkins, be suspended from the practice of law for a period of ninety (90) days, beginning July 1, 1998, at the conclusion of which he shall be automatically reinstated to the practice of law.

The Clerk of this Court is directed to provide notice of this order in accordance with Admis. Disc. R. 23(3)(d) and to provide the clerk of the United States Court of Appeals for the Seventh Circuit, the clerk of each of the Federal District Courts in this state, and the clerk of the United States Bankruptcy Court in this state with the last known address of respondent as reflected in the records of the Clerk.

Costs of this proceeding are assessed against the respondent.

NOTES, QUESTIONS AND EXAMPLES

1.   How do the Washington and Indiana courts' approaches to the issue differ? Which is based on the clearer and more defensible set of policies?

2.   Agreements limiting the lawyer's liability: A lawyer is prohibited from entering into a contract with a client that prospectively limits the lawyer's liability for malpractice unless state law permits and the client is represented by independent counsel with respect to the agreement. MR 1.8(h).

3.   Settling claims with unrepresented clients: A lawyer is prohibited from settling malpractice claims with unrepresented clients or former clients unless the lawyer first advises the client or former client that independent counsel is advisable. MR 1.8(h).

e.   Lawyer-Client Conflicts and Champerty, Barratry, and Maintenance

Various restrictions on lawyer conduct, often interrelated with lawyer-client conflicts issues, are based on the doctrines of champerty, barratry, and maintenance. These three doctrines together were concerned with prohibiting the malicious stirring up and maintaining of litigation. They were crimes of general application (they applied to anyone, not just lawyers) in many jurisdictions until they faded from application. They were abolished in England in the 1960s. Champerty is the malicious purchase or investment in litigation. The Model Rules incarnation of champerty is Rule 1.8(j), prohibiting lawyers from acquiring an interest in the subject matter of a client's claim. Barratry is the malicious encouragement of claim-bringing. Persuading your neighbor to sue another because of your ill-will toward that other is barratry. There is an overlap between barratry and the client-getting restrictions on solicitation. (*See* MR 7.3 and Chapter IX.) Maintenance is the malicious supporting of one in litigation because of your ill-will toward their opponent in litigation. The spirit of maintenance is found in Model Rule 1.8(e), prohibiting lawyers from providing financial assistance to clients when litigation is pending or contemplated. Significantly, no client waiver of these "conflicts" is permitted.

Although the doctrines date back at least to 13th century England, they also have an unfavorable history in connection to regulation of the American bar. Especially in the late 19th and early 20th centuries, these rules were used to exclude and persecute urban, ethnic lawyers, many of whom represented injured people in actions against the corporate clients of the powerful lawyers of the time who controlled the American Bar Association and many state bar associations and their disciplinary mechanisms. In this regard, these conflicts rules are much more oriented to restrictions on client-getting activities than they are toward restrictions on conflicts of interest.

A lawyer is prohibited from acquiring an interest in litigation or its subject matter, whether that interest is consistent or inconsistent with the client's interests. This prohibition is not a restriction on the lawyer's contract with a client for a reasonable contingent fee.

IOWA STATE BAR ASSOCIATION v. BITTER
279 N.W.2d 521 (Iowa 1979)

LARSON, JUSTICE.

This is [an en banc] proceeding under Court Rule 118.10 to make a final determination upon findings and recommendations of the Grievance Commission. No appeal or statement of exceptions under Court Rule 118.11 were filed by respondent. However, an *amicus curiae* brief was presented to this court by the Committee on Professional Ethics and Conduct of the Iowa State Bar Association, as complainant, in support of the findings and recommendations, and written responses to the recommendation of the Commission were presented by the respondent. Upon our review, we conclude the respondent shall be suspended from the practice of law for a period of two months.

* * *

The specific charges now before us include the following: (1) that respondent advanced or guaranteed financial assistance, other than expenses of litigation, in violation of Ethical Consideration (EC) 5-8 and Disciplinary Rule (DR) 5- 103(A);

(2) that he neglected legal matters entrusted to him in violation of DR 6-101(A)(3); and (3) that he was guilty of "misconduct" under DR 1- 102(A)(4), (5) and (6). The Grievance Commission, having found that the evidence supported these complaints, recommended that the respondents license be suspended for a period of four months. Respondent asks for disposition in the form of probation.

*   *   *

I. The specific facts alleged in support of the first ground are that Bitter advanced money to three clients, during pending litigation, for purposes other than for the cost of litigation. The respondent does not contest the facts in regard to this charge but seeks by his response to mitigate their effects by showing that he was unaware of the impropriety of the acts, that he did not advance the money to acquire legal business or to collect interest and that the loans were made solely for humanitarian reasons.

*   *   *

The incident occurring after the date of adoption of the Code and rules under it involves clients named Arnie and Judy Bunkofske, and an advance to them admittedly made by Bitter. The record shows the advance was made in the amount of $986.70, sometime after Bitter had been retained by them in a matter arising out of an accident in which they and their son had been involved. No interest was charged on the advance and there was no evidence that the advance was made in order to obtain employment by the Bunkofskes. Respondent contends he was not aware that his conduct was unethical, and claimed that "[t]he act was done entirely for charitable and humanitarian reasons" to assist his clients who "were in extremely dire financial need."

The rule proscribing such acts, however, makes no exceptions for these factors. It provides that the rule is intended to prevent an attorney's procuring an interest in a legal matter by advancements of money or the like. The rule does not require proof of such intent or effect, only that the conditions exist where such results might reasonably be expected to occur. The attorney must not, by his actions, give rise to reasonable speculation that he has thus asserted himself into the legal affairs of his potential clients.

*   *   *

IV. We conclude the evidence has established these violations by the respondent: (a) violation of EC 5-8 and DR 5-103(A) by making advancements for his clients Bunkofskes at a time when litigation was pending and for purposes other than costs of litigation; (b) violation of DR 6-101(A)(3) by neglecting legal matters entrusted to him by failing to complete the replatting matter in a timely manner and maintaining an unreasonably large number of probate delinquencies despite notices and court warnings; (c) violation of DR 1-102(A)(6) (engaging in conduct that adversely reflects on his fitness to practice law) in regard to the addition of his name as payee on the Bechen check.

*   *   *

Respondent's license to practice law is hereby suspended for two months and thereafter until such time as his application for reinstatement is approved. Respondent shall [notify] clients and counsel of his suspension. This suspension shall apply to and include all facets of the practice of law, including but not limited to examination of abstracts, consummation of real estate transactions, preparation of deeds, buy and sell agreements, contracts, wills, and tax returns. Upon any application for reinstatement respondent shall also prove that he has not performed any of such services during the suspension period and that he has provided the necessary notifications. . . .

License Suspended.

NOTES, QUESTIONS, AND EXAMPLES

1. Although the financial assistance rule has in some respects ancient roots dating back to maintenance and champerty doctrines of early English law and Roman and Greek law before that, the nature and breadth of the financial assistance restrictions have expanded in recent times. Prior to the adoption of the Model Code in 1969, American courts disciplined lawyers who made loans to their clients only when the loan or other financial assistance was a means used by the lawyer to induce the client to retain the lawyer. Thus, the rule against financial assistance was an adjunct to the rules against client solicitation. *See* Chapter IX, *Advertising and Solicitation.*

2. Following the lead of several states, the ABA has slightly relaxed the Model Rule 1.8(f) restriction when the client is indigent. These variations permit very limited financial assistance without the requirement that the assistance be repaid.

3. Miscellaneous lawyer-client conflicts rules: Using confidential information to the client's detriment — A lawyer is prohibited from using information learned in the lawyer-client relationship to the detriment of the client. In most instances, a lawyer is also prohibited from using such information to the lawyer's benefit on the theory that such use is also detrimental to the client. MR 1.8(b). Prospective limitation of malpractice liability: Lawyers may not prospectively, for example, by a term in a retainer agreement, limit their liability to a client for malpractice. MR 1.8(h). The ABA has opined that inclusion of a binding arbitration term in a retainer agreement does not violate this prohibition. ABA Formal Op. 02-425 (2002). This opinion stands in contrast to an ABA policy statement disapproving of such terms when used by health care professionals. ABA/AMA/AAA Health Care Due Process Protocol, adopted as Report 114 at ABA Midyear meeting, 1999.

3. Multiple Client Conflicts

The third major source of conflicts is the interaction of multiple client interests. Largely because lawyers owe a duty of confidentiality (and to a limited extent loyalty) to both prospective and former clients, multiple client conflicts can implicate not only concurrent representation of multiple clients but also conflicts between former and current clients, or prospective and current clients, or prospective and former clients.

a. Concurrent Clients

The easiest cases involve multiple representation of clients whose interest are in direct conflict. Simply put, lawyers may not represent clients on opposite sides of the same matter, especially when litigation is involved. Such a direct conflict cannot be effectively waived by the clients on the theory that it is too gross a conflict. MR 1.7(b)(3). More general forms of adversity among concurrent clients' interests may be permitted if the clients consent, and still more limited adversity of interests may be permitted even in the absence of client consent. For example, Lawyer represents Criminal Defendant against burglary charges. Lawyer also represents Grocery Store Owner as a regular matter in filing small claims to collect on bad checks and unpaid credit charges. Grocery Store Owner has such a claim against Criminal Defendant and wants Lawyer to file it. Lawyer may only engage in these two representations if both clients consent after consultation. MR 1.7, Comment. Lawyer regularly represents Bank 1 and Bank 2 in a variety of matters. Bank 1 and Bank 2 are generally competitors in the marketplace, but Lawyer's work for Banks does not implicate conflicting legal positions between them. This generally adverse simultaneous representation should be permitted without the necessity of client waiver. MR 1.7, Comment.

JPMORGAN CHASE BANK v. LIBERTY MUTUAL INSURANCE COMPANY
189 F. Supp. 2d 20 (S.D.N.Y. 2002)

RAKOFF, J.

Even in an age of convenience, for a law firm to bring a multi-million dollar claim on behalf of one corporate client against the primary subsidiary of another of that law firm's corporate clients might be expected to raise some eyebrows. In this case, it also requires the law firm's disqualification.

The law firm in question is the well regarded New York firm of Davis Polk & Wardwell ("Davis Polk"). The party seeking Davis Polk's disqualification is Federal Insurance Company ("Federal"), a large insurance company and one of the defendants here. In 1967, Davis Polk, acting as counsel for Federal, helped organize and incorporate The Chubb Corporation ("Chubb") a holding company, the primary holding of which was Federal. Since that time Davis Polk has represented Chubb in a wide variety of matters, including, *inter alia*, capital market transactions, securities filings, bank financings, and ERISA work; and Davis Polk's representation of Chubb continues to the present. In addition, Davis Polk has periodically represented Federal on discrete projects, though none since 1996.

[T]he relationship [between Chubb and Federal] is extremely close and interdependent, both financially and in terms of direction. Financially, Federal accounts for over 95% of Chubb's total revenue and over 90% of Chubb's total net income. In terms of direction, Chubb and Federal operate from the same New Jersey headquarters and, since 1967, have shared the same Board of Directors. They also share certain common officers; of particular relevance here, the General

Counsel (and a Senior Vice President) of Chubb, Joanne L. Bober, is also the General Counsel (and a Senior Vice President) of Federal.

DP retained by JPMorgan!

In October 2001, Davis Polk was retained by JPMorgan Chase Bank ("JPM Chase"), the plaintiff here, to represent that bank in connection with matters arising from the burgeoning difficulties of the Enron Corporation ("Enron") and its affiliates. By late November, Davis Polk, notwithstanding its representation of Chubb (and without Chubb's knowledge or consent), had begun examining, *inter alia*, the obligation to JPM Chase (acting for and on behalf of Mahonia Limited and Mahonia Natural Gas Limited, collectively "Mahonia") of Chubb's primary subsidiary, Federal, on no less than $183 million in surety bonds guaranteeing Enron obligations.

DP examining what Chubb owed JPMorgan in association w/ Enron

Davis Polk did not seek Chubb's or Federal's consent to undertake this inquiry. When, on December 7, 2001, Ms. Bober learned of the representation, she telephonically informed Frank S. Moseley, the Davis Polk partner working on the matter, that she thought that Davis Polk needed Chubb's consent to undertake representation adverse to Federal and that, at least until she learned more of the relationship between JPM Chase and Mahonia, she would not waive the conflict. Davis Polk nonetheless continued the representation and began preparing the instant lawsuit against Federal.

Meanwhile, as part of its ongoing representation of Chubb, Davis Polk was also preparing an SEC Form S-3, a disclosure form related to a so-called "shelf registration." On December 11, 2001, Davis Polk filed the S-3. Under the heading "Recent Developments" the S-3 stated that "Chubb has obligations under outstanding surety bonds relating to Enron affiliates [of] approximately $220 million," Bober Dec. Ex. C, Form S-3 Registration Statement Under the Securities Act of 1933, The Chubb Corporation, filed on December 11, 2001, at 4. Although the bulk of this obligation consisted of the very surety bonds on which Chubb's subsidiary, Federal, allegedly was obligated to Mahonia, Davis Polk did not reveal to Chubb that it was preparing, on behalf of Davis Polk's other client, JPM Chase, a lawsuit demanding payment of $183 million from Federal. Rather, without Chubb's prior knowledge or consent, Davis Polk, acting for JPM Chase, filed the instant lawsuit on the very same day (Dec. 11) that, acting for Chubb, it filed the S-3.

The next day, December 12, 2001, Ms. Bober wrote to Mr. Moseley, demanding that Davis Polk either withdraw as counsel for JPM Chase or provide legal justification for its dual representation. Moseley responded on December 14, 2001, contending that because Davis Polk only represented Chubb and not Federal, New York law did not preclude its representing JPM Chase against Federal. In turn, Gary L. Leshko, the outside counsel hired to represent Federal in the instant lawsuit, wrote to Davis Polk on January 2, 2002, advising it that Federal intended to file a motion to disqualify Davis Polk in this action. On January 7, 2002, Federal filed such a motion. Following review of papers from both sides, the Court heard oral argument (and conducted a brief evidentiary inquiry) on January 23, 2002.

The parties agree that the issue of disqualification is essentially governed by New York law. *See* Local Rules of the United States District Courts for the Southern and Eastern Districts of New York, Local Civil Rules 1.3(a)(6); 1.5(b)(5) (adopting New York law for this purpose). In particular, DR 5-105(B) of the New York Code of Professional Responsibility provides in pertinent part that "A lawyer shall not continue multiple employment . . . if it would be likely to involve the lawyer in representing differing interests." Even if one views Davis Polk's current representations as only involving JPM Chase and Chubb, one need look no further than the aforementioned S-3 to see how Davis Polk has already entangled itself in conflicts of interest; for while it is clearly to JPM Chase's interest that Chubb has already acknowledged that the Federal security bonds are obligations of Chubb, it is doubtful that Chubb would have approved such wording, drafted with the aid of Davis Polk, if it had known that Davis Polk would simultaneously bring suit on these bonds against Federal.

Furthermore, it is wholly artificial to separate Chubb and Federal for purposes of analyzing Davis Polk's responsibilities in this context. Just from the fact that Federal accounts for more than 90% of Chubb's business and that Chubb and Federal share identical corporate headquarters, an identical board, and an identical general counsel, it is obvious that the two share a wealth of common interests adversely impacted by the lawsuit in question. Thus, this case is patently unlike *Brooklyn Navy Yard Cogeneration Partners L.P. v. PMNC*, 174 Misc.2d 216, 663 N.Y.S.2d 499 (Sup. Ct. Kings Cty. 1997), *aff'd*, 254 A.D.2d 447, 679 N.Y.S.2d 312 (2d Dep't 1998) — the case principally relied upon by Davis Polk to support their argument that representation of Chubb is not here tantamount to representation of Federal — for in that case, the court held that the fact that a law firm advised a defendant's remote subsidiary based in Moscow on Russian law matters that had "absolutely nothing in common with the subject matter" of the controversy did not preclude the same firm from suing the parent. Given the practical realities of the situation, then, the doctrine of concurrent representation applies and the burden of avoiding disqualification then shifts to Davis Polk to "show, at the very least, that there will be no actual or apparent conflict in loyalties or diminution in the vigor of his representation." *Cinema 5 Ltd. v. Cinerama, Inc.*, 528 F.2d 1384, 1387 (2d Cir. 1976). Davis Polk would minimize and shift back this burden by arguing that, in light of subsequent Second Circuit cases, disqualification of Davis Polk is not required unless Federal, the movant, can show that Davis Polk's representation of JPM Chase would adversely affect Federal at trial. But in all of the circuit cases relied on by plaintiff for this proposition, the underlying conflict of interest was *not* based on concurrent, ongoing representation of two clients. *See Armstrong v. McAlpin*, 625 F.2d 433 (2d Cir. 1980), *overruled on other grounds*, 449 U.S. 1106 (1981) (alleged conflict arose from use by plaintiff of a law firm whose members included a former SEC assistant director who had been involved in SEC's action against movant defendant); *Board of Educ. v. Nyquist*, 590 F.2d 1241 (2d Cir. 1979) (alleged conflict arose from lawyer for an association representing one set of members of a union that provided financial support for that association in a dispute against another set of members of the union).

By contrast, where, as here, there is in effect concurrent representation of two adverse clients, the potential for conflict is hardly limited to the trial context but can infect, actually or potentially, a broad spectrum of activities, as the aforementioned S-3 demonstrates. Moreover, in contrast to most (if not all) of the "trial taint" cases, the Court here confronts the issue of disqualification near the very outset of the litigation when, on the one hand, determining the potential for "trial taint" is difficult, and where, on the other hand, the prejudice to plaintiff in having to substitute new counsel is relatively modest.

Most fundamentally, Davis Polk's attempt to apply to the instant situation lesser standards of disqualification drawn from other contexts overlooks both the stark realities of the instant situation and the interests it implicates. For most practical purposes, including those materially affected by this lawsuit, Chubb and Federal are inextricably intertwined, and for most practical purposes Davis Polk functions as Chubb's ongoing outside counsel. To permit Davis Polk in such circumstances to prosecute a major lawsuit against Chubb's primary subsidiary, Federal, would be not only to undercut a lawyer's duty of loyalty to his client and cast considerable doubt on the independence of his professional judgment, *see* Canon 5 and EC 5-14, but also to provide support for the public's increasingly cynical view of the legal profession. *See* Canon 9 and EC 9-1.

For the forgoing reasons, Davis Polk is disqualified from representing JPM Chase against Federal in this matter. Since there is no good reason to sever Federal from the other defendants, the effect is to remove Davis Polk from the case altogether. The Court will, however, stay all proceedings in this case for two weeks, to enable plaintiff to obtain new counsel and/or for plaintiff to seek a stay of this Order if it wishes to appeal.

So Ordered.

b. Positional Conflicts of Interest

Lawyers are trained to be able to argue either side of a legal issue. When a lawyer represents two clients in unrelated matters for whom the lawyer must argue opposite sides of the same legal issue, a potential positional conflict of interest exists. Although "[o]rdinarily a lawyer may take inconsistent legal positions in different tribunals at different times on behalf of different clients," a conflict of interest exists "[when] there is a significant risk that the lawyer's action on behalf of one client will materially limit the lawyer's effectiveness in representing another client in a different case." MR 1.7, Comment 24. Especially when these opposite positions are argued before the same court, however, the lawyer is effectively arguing for a precedent in one case that harms the client in the other case, something that would "adversely affect" one of the clients while benefiting the other. This situation ought to be regarded as a multiple client conflict under Model Rule 1.7 that requires client consent for the lawyer to continue with both representations or that should require a lawyer to withdraw from one or the other of the matters. *See, e.g., Williams v. State*, 805 A.2d 880 (Del. 2002).

John S. Dzienkowski, *Positional Conflicts of Interest*
71 Tex. L. Rev. 457 (1993)[9]

I. Introduction

* * *

A positional conflict of interest occurs when a law firm adopts a legal position for one client seeking a particular legal result that is directly contrary to the position taken on behalf of another present or former client, seeking an opposite legal result, in a completely unrelated matter. The classic positional conflict of interest arises in litigation when a lawyer or law firm argues for one interpretation of the law on behalf of one client and for a contrary interpretation on behalf of another client. Such conflicts may also arise in the lobbying context when the lawyer or law firm is arguing for a particular change in the law for one client and in another representation is making a legal argument inconsistent with the position advanced for the first client. These conflicts may further arise in the transaction context when the lawyer or law firm drafts a particular arrangement for one client and for another client attacks the propriety of a similar arrangement.

* * *

The comment to the general conflict of interest rule states that "it is ordinarily not improper to assert such [antagonistic legal] positions in cases pending in different trial courts, but it may be improper to do so in cases pending at the same time in an appellate court." This comment and the general conflict of interest provisions do not adequately address the question of when a positional conflict requires an independent determination of propriety by the lawyer and client consent to the representation after disclosure.

The inadequacy of the Model Rules provision is illustrated by the several state ethics committee opinions that have directly addressed positional conflicts. In 1987, the Arizona State Bar Committee on the Rules of Professional Conduct examined a hypothetical situation involving two lawyers in one law firm who were representing an employee and an employer in two unrelated employment cases, which involved the same legal issues, before two different panels of the Ninth Circuit Court of Appeals. The only issue before the appellate court was the interpretation of the same law; if the law firm prevailed in one case, the other client would lose its case. In the only type of situation that the Model Rules seem to directly prohibit, the ethics committee allowed the law firm to continue to represent both clients as long as the firm had notified the clients of the conflict and the clients had consented after consulting with independent counsel.

In 1989, the California State Bar Standing Committee on Professional Responsibility and Conduct addressed the question of a positional conflict on behalf of two clients before the same federal district court judge. Although the opinion identified the conflict of interest that may arise from an attorney creating adverse precedent

---

and from a possible credibility problem before the same court, it refused to apply conflict of interest law to positional conflicts. Based upon several "jurisprudential and practical reasons," the committee found that it should not delineate any restrictions on positional conflicts. Although other recent opinions have found positional conflicts problems more troublesome than the California committee did, they similarly have failed to provide a coherent approach to resolving such problems in practice.

The reason the legal profession has sought to limit the effect of positional conflicts of interest is clear. The regulation of conflicts based upon legal arguments made by lawyers within a particular firm poses many difficult problems for the practice of law. A very broad approach to positional conflicts of interest may force practitioners and firms to become associated with particular legal positions. From a practical perspective, this may create a nightmare for law firms that seek to avoid positions they may be currently arguing or may have argued in the past. However, a narrow response to this very specialized conflict of interest problem ignores the reality that positional conflicts may affect a client's representation. No lawyer with only one client would argue both sides of the same legal issue to the same judge, nor urge another court to publish an opinion hostile to his client's interests. How can this become permissible when the positional conflict involves two or more clients? Further, such an approach discounts my perception that clients' expectations of loyalty go beyond the lawyer's agreement not to accept representations in the "same or a substantially related matter."

* * *

II. An Overview of the Positional Conflict of Interest Problem

* * *

A. Types of Positional Conflicts

This Article classifies positional conflicts into three types: (1) litigational positional conflicts, (2) lobbying positional conflicts, and (3) transactional positional conflicts. Although the litigational conflict is the most common and can serve as a model for analyzing all positional conflicts of interest, conflicts that involve a lobbying or a transaction representation can sometimes implicate other important interests. Some of these interests arise from the potentially different role that a lawyer may adopt outside of the courtroom. Other interests may focus on the fact that, in the lobbying context, the legislature is not usually presiding over an adjudicative proceeding, and in the transaction context, no judge or jury scrutinizes the lawyer's conduct. The nature of the positional conflict may determine the type of potential injury to the lawyer's other present or former clients. By considering both the circumstances under which the positional conflict arises and the appropriate role of the attorney, it is possible to address the nature of the positional conflicts problem and its possible resolution.

1. Litigational Positional Conflicts. — A litigational positional conflict is defined as a positional conflict of interest involving two litigation matters. In other words,

the lawyer or law firm represents two unrelated clients in litigation before a court or administrative agency on opposing sides of the same legal issue. Litigational positional conflicts may occur whenever a flurry of disputes arises regarding an issue of law and a lawyer or law firm represents clients on both sides of the issue. An example of a litigational positional conflict can be found in the recent litigation over the breach of take-or-pay contracts in the natural gas industry. In the late 1970s, natural gas pipelines entered into long-term contracts with natural gas producers to purchase gas at prices usually tied to escalator clauses. The pipelines agreed to take a certain quantity each year or to pay for it at the agreed price with a right to take the natural gas at a future time. By 1983, an overabundance of natural gas existed in the marketplace. This oversupply, combined with the move of the Federal Energy Regulatory Commission to deregulate the natural gas industry, caused natural gas pipelines to breach their take-or-pay obligations. The take-or-pay litigation explosion began in 1985 and involves billions of dollars worth of promised payments. Oil and gas law firms in the Southwest that had drafted such contracts found themselves with both pipelines and producers seeking their services for litigation. In the take-or-pay example, many law firms have represented both natural gas producers and pipelines in the past; thus, the lawyers found themselves in the situation of arguing for producer clients that the take-or-pay contracts were enforceable and for the pipeline clients that the take-or-pay contracts were unenforceable.

The take-or-pay example presents an interesting litigational positional conflict of interest. Because most take-or-pay contracts are similar, the pipelines have developed several broad arguments that call into question the enforceability of all take-or-pay contracts. These defenses include arguments that take-or-pay contracts are preempted by federal law, that their performance is excused by force majeure created by unexpected events in the marketplace, and that such contracts are unconscionable. The law firm on both sides of the take-or-pay issue will probably need to raise such issues on behalf of the pipeline client and defend against such issues on behalf of the producer client. The breadth of the legal defenses and the federal nature of this type of litigation enhance the danger of the positional conflict of interest. Also, both sets of clients — pipelines and producers — may be repeat litigators and thus may have a long-term interest in the legal issues developed from the case.

2. Lobbying Positional Conflicts. — A lobbying positional conflict is defined as a positional conflict of interest involving at least one lobbying matter. In other words, the lawyer or law firm represents one client before a legislative body on a particular legal issue while representing another client in a litigation or transaction matter. A classic example of a hybrid lobbying positional conflict arose in an often-discussed conflicts of interest case. In 1976, Westinghouse Electric Corporation retained the law firm of Kirkland & Ellis to file an antitrust action against numerous domestic and foreign entities involved in the uranium industry, alleging anticompetitive practices that made it difficult for Westinghouse to meet its own uranium supply contracts. In the same year, the American Petroleum Institute (API) hired Kirkland's Washington, D.C. office to oppose congressional legislation designed to divest energy companies from their holdings in energy resources other than oil and gas in order to encourage competition in such industries. The API requested that

Kirkland serve as independent counsel to the lobbying group and make an independent study of the oil companies' involvement in other energy industries.

The Kirkland example illustrates a case in which the position taken by the law firm lobbying in Washington was different from the position taken by the law firm in federal district court. If the court in the antitrust case had adopted the findings in Kirkland's report to the API, then the client, Westinghouse, would have lost its lawsuit. This case contains both a legal and a factual positional conflict. The Kirkland lobbying effort examined the facts surrounding the oil industry's involvement in solid minerals to determine if the API members had violated any existing law. Lobbying may involve two different types of representations. The first may involve only the presentation of facts to the legislature. Although a factual presentation may seem outside the realm of a positional conflict, such presentations usually are implicit efforts to show that the law should remain the same or that the existing law should be changed. To the extent that such factual presentations involve an effort to influence the legislature's decision, they should be treated as positional conflicts of interest. A second type of representation may involve a presentation of a legal conclusion to the legislature about a particular area of the law. This raises issues similar to the ones found in the litigational positional conflict.

3. Transactional Positional Conflicts. — A transactional positional conflict is defined as including at least one transaction matter involving a positional conflict of interest. In other words, the lawyer or law firm represents at least one client in a transaction matter and another client in either the litigation, lobbying, or transaction context. Transactional positional conflicts include some of the least troublesome and most difficult conflicts to analyze. In the positional conflict involving two transaction matters, lawyers and law firms usually can explain the risks of contrary legal positions, and the clients can evaluate whether they wish to assume a particular position. Thus, disclosure to the client often resolves this type of positional conflict. However, in a hybrid transactional positional conflict, when one of the other representations involves either lobbying or litigation, the lawyer or law firm is often undercutting the transaction client's position with the arguments made in the other representation. An example is presented when a law firm advises its corporate clients to adopt poison pill arrangements while filing a case on behalf of a plaintiff to invalidate a poison pill arrangement. This example is based upon the actual conduct of the law firm of Skadden, Arps, Slate, Meagher & Flom (Skadden Arps).

Skadden Arps is well known for its expertise in corporate takeover matters; over the years, the firm has represented both targets and aggressors. Before 1985, Skadden Arps argued that poison pill arrangements were improper. In 1985, lawyers in the firm began to draft poison pill arrangements and to recommend that boards of directors adopt them to make clients less attractive in takeover attempts. In 1986, Skadden Arps, along with two other law firms, filed a brief in a federal district court in California on behalf of an aggressor corporation, Dart, which sought to invalidate a poison pill arrangement adopted by the board of directors and shareholders of Safeway, a takeover target. The brief argued that the Safeway poison pill was illegal under state law; moreover, it maintained that if state law allowed such an arrangement, it would excessively burden tender offers made in interstate commerce and thus violate the United States Constitution. By making this argument, Skadden Arps was attempting to create authority adverse to clients that it may have been advising to adopt similar poison pill arrangements, as well as past clients who had in fact taken Skadden's advice.

The poison pill example illustrates the difficult questions that must be addressed in drafting rules to resolve the positional conflict of interest problem. On one hand, it is easy to understand the expectations of clients who have paid significant fees to a law firm for its expertise in drafting a particular arrangement. These clients may very well expect the firm not to attack similar arrangements currently or in the future, which would jeopardize the very structures that it had created. On the other hand, one can quickly begin to see the practical problems that firms face in identifying positional conflicts and the claims that present clients may make upon the law firm's ability to represent future clients.

*   *   *

C. The Interests at Stake in a Positional Conflict of Interest

The positional conflict of interest raises four distinct problems that the law of professional responsibility seeks to control. First, when a lawyer or law firm is involved in a positional conflict, one or both of the representations may be adversely affected by the fact that the lawyer or firm is advancing opposing arguments on the same legal issue. The law of professional responsibility addresses this type of injury to a representation through the conflict of interest rules that are based upon instrumental justifications. Instrumental justifications explain the following conflicts rules: (1) a lawyer should not represent two clients concurrently when the representation of one client will cause the lawyer's representation of the other client to be materially limited; and (2) a lawyer should not represent a client when the interests of the lawyer or a third party will limit the lawyer's representation. Without these rules, conflicting interests may affect the effectiveness and vigor of the lawyer's representation. In positional conflicts, the inquiry based upon the effectiveness concern must examine all of the potential effects on the two representations.

Second, lawyers or law firms who are representing different sides of the same legal issues are likely to share information between the two representations. To the extent that such information is confidential, positional conflicts of interest may lead to the violation of the rules of confidentiality in the attorney-client relationship that give clients control of most confidential information acquired by the lawyer or law firm. When confidential information is shared between the two representations on the same legal issues, the lawyer or law firm may be violating this entitlement and may be damaging the representations of one or both clients.

Third, positional conflicts of interest are likely to be contrary to clients' expectations about the loyalty of the lawyer to the client's cause. To the extent that positional conflicts affect the integrity of the client or the client's expectations, they may undercut the intrinsic justifications behind certain conflict of interest rules. The intrinsic justification of "concern for the moral integrity of the client" primarily explains the following conflicts rules: (1) a lawyer should not in most cases accept a representation against a present client in an unrelated matter; and (2) a lawyer shall not engage in certain transactions with a client (e.g., business arrangements, the purchase of portrayal rights, the settlement of malpractice liability, or the acceptance of a gift through will or bequest) without certain procedural and substantive safeguards. Each of these conflict of interest rules illustrates a situation in which society protects an aspect of the client's interest by providing the client with an entitlement. These rules that guard the integrity of the client may require that the client be informed of the positional conflict or that the lawyer obtain the client's consent.

Finally, intrinsic justifications may also rest upon the protection of the rights of third parties or the goals of the legal system. The intrinsic justification of protecting the integrity of the legal and judicial system explains the provisions that lawyers should avoid (1) the appearance of impropriety and (2) conduct prejudicial to the administration of justice. These rules protect the legal system's image without regard to the effect on the advancement of the individual client's legal interests. To the extent that positional conflicts of interest affect such societal objectives, our proposals may wish to address such concerns.

*　　*　　*

c. Same-Side Multiple Client Representation

PROBLEM 5-2

Richard Carro is a thoughtful, reflective lawyer whose practice specializes in estate planning. He has an appointment with John and Helen Thompson, an elderly couple, and their adult son Frank. The four of them sit in Carro's office and get acquainted.

After taking the time to get a good sense of the Thompsons as a family, Carro asks what he can do for them. They explain, with Frank doing most of the talking, that Helen has been diagnosed as being in the early stages of Alzheimer's disease, that significant assets of the Thompsons are in Helen's name alone, that some important documents have been lost or misplaced (probably through Helen's oversight), that some internal disputes exist between John and Helen about which of their respective siblings should receive certain family items, that Frank is financially stable and has no immediate needs for his parents' assets, that John and Helen's age and health have made it difficult for them to care for themselves in their home, and that if Helen's condition deteriorates, John will be quickly overwhelmed by any effort to maintain their home and care for Helen.

Carro listens well, asks several insightful questions, and explains the potential areas of conflict among the three that might develop. The Thompsons indicate their understanding and ask Carro to proceed on their joint behalf. Carro tells the Thompsons that he will have an outline of a plan for their situation in a week. The Thompsons leave feeling contented and comforted, making an appointment for the following week with Carro's staff.

Does Carro's conduct comply with the ethics rules? If not, should the rules or Carro's conduct change?

Even multiple representation of clients who are at least initially on the same side of litigation or a transaction implicates conflicts analysis. Joint representation on civil claims brought simultaneously by multiple clients is permitted if the clients consent after consultation and if both the objective and subjective elements of the waiver test are met. When such representation is permissible, withdrawal from all representation may be the only adequate remedy if nonwaivable conflicts later develop. When that is the case, the lawyer may represent none of the multiple clients.

STATE FARM MUTUAL AUTOMOBILE INSURANCE CO. v. K.A.W.
575 So. 2d 630 (Fla. 1991)

OPINION: . . . .

David Wilkerson was driving a rental car in which his wife and infant daughter were passengers when it was struck by another car. The Wilkersons retained the law firm of Sheldon J. Schlesinger, P.A. (Schlesinger firm) and filed suit against the driver and owner of the other vehicle and others for injuries suffered by the three of them in the accident. The action included a count against petitioner State Farm Mutual Automobile Insurance Company (State Farm), the Wilkersons' insurer, for uninsured motorist coverage. The Wilkersons also filed a separate malpractice action against various health care providers for alleged negligent treatment of their daughter after the accident. The Schlesinger firm represented the Wilkersons in the malpractice action.

After the personal injury action had proceeded for approximately one year, the Wilkersons added new defendants, including petitioners Interstate Fire and Casualty Company and Continental Casualty Company, which had issued uninsured motorist insurance to Wilkerson's employer. The following year, the Wilkersons' attorneys determined that David Wilkerson's negligence may have contributed to the automobile accident. Thereupon, Mr. Wilkerson discharged the Schlesinger firm as his counsel in the personal injury action and retained a former member of the Schlesinger firm as new counsel. Shortly thereafter, Mrs. Wilkerson and her daughter filed a second amended complaint in that action, adding David Wilkerson as a defendant. The Schlesinger firm continued to represent Mrs. Wilkerson and the daughter in that action, and Mr. Wilkerson consented to be sued up to the limits of his insurance coverage. The firm also continued to represent all three Wilkersons in the medical malpractice action.

Asserting their exposure as liability insurers of Mr. Wilkerson, each of the petitioners filed motions seeking the disqualification of the Schlesinger firm in the personal injury action. Petitioners objected to the potential for the Schlesinger firm to use confidential information gained during the course of the prior representation of Mr. Wilkerson in this action against him. In opposition to the motion, David Wilkerson filed an affidavit stating that he did not consider anything he discussed with Sheldon Schlesinger privileged because he had disclosed everything in his deposition and he did not feel that Mr. Schlesinger's representation of his wife and daughter disadvantaged him in any way. Mrs. Wilkerson also submitted an affidavit in which she stated that she and her daughter would be prejudiced if the Schlesinger firm were required to withdraw.

The trial court refused to disqualify the Schlesinger firm, finding that the petitioners lacked standing to request disqualification in the face of Mr. Wilkerson's consent to the firm's representation of his wife and child. In addition, the court found that the petitioners failed to show clearly and convincingly that they would be prejudiced or that the continued representation would interfere with the fair and impartial administration of justice. The Fourth District Court of Appeal denied the insurers' petitions for writ of certiorari, finding no proof of substantial prejudice or circumstances calling into question the fair and efficient administration of justice.

*   *   *

The ethical principle at issue is an attorney's duty to maintain the confidences of his client. That principle is embodied in two rules of professional conduct. Rule Regulating The Florida Bar 4-1.6(a) provides that "[a] lawyer shall not reveal information relating to representation of a client . . . unless the client consents after disclosure to the client." The duty of confidentiality continues after termination of the attorney-client relationship.

Rule Regulating The Florida Bar 4-1.9 provides:

> A lawyer who has formerly represented a client in a matter shall not thereafter:
>
> (a) Represent another person in the same or a substantially related matter in which that person's interests are materially adverse to the interests of the former client unless the former client consents after consultation; or
>
> (b) Use information relating to the representation to the disadvantage of the former client except as rule 4-1.6 would permit with respect to a client or when the information has become generally known.[10]

Mr. Wilkerson is, in effect, both a former client of the Schlesinger firm for purposes of rule 4-1.9 (in the personal injury action) and a current client for purposes of rule 4-1.7 (in the medical malpractice action). The duty of confidentiality is present regardless of whether Mr. Wilkerson is viewed as the firm's former or current client.

The purpose of the requirement that an attorney maintain client confidences is twofold. It advances the interests of the client by encouraging a free flow of

---

[10] [1] Rule Regulating The Florida Bar 4-1.7 is also pertinent here. That rule provides:

> (a) A lawyer shall not represent a client if the representation of that client will be directly adverse to the interests of another client, unless:
>
> (1) The lawyer reasonably believes the representation will not adversely affect the lawyer's responsibilities to and relationship with the other client; and
>
> (2) Each client consents after consultation.

information and the development of trust essential to an attorney-client relationship. However, it also serves a second purpose fundamental to a fair adversary system. Our legal system cannot function fairly or effectively if an attorney has an informational advantage in the form of confidences gained during a former representation of his client's current opponent.

The question then is whether the insurers may "stand in the shoes" of their insured for purposes of seeking disqualification of the Schlesinger firm on grounds of conflict of interest. Comments to the Rules of Professional Conduct indicate that under certain circumstances someone other than the client may request disqualification. Thus, where a conflict "is such as clearly to call in question the fair or efficient administration of justice, opposing counsel may properly raise the question." Comment to Rule Regulating The Florida Bar 4-1.7.

We find that the facts of this case call into question the fair administration of justice. Mr. Wilkerson is not exposed to any personal liability because he may be sued only up to the amount of any available insurance coverage. This is, in reality, not an action between Mr. Wilkerson and his child, but an action by the mother and child against the parent's insurance carriers. Mr. Wilkerson is in a position adverse to his daughter in theory only. He reasonably hopes to enhance his daughter's chance of recovery. The petitioners, on the other hand, will be acting in Mr. Wilkerson's defense, attempting to persuade the fact finder that he was not negligent in the automobile accident in order that they may avoid liability. Because of this situation, Wilkerson's consent to the firm's representation of his wife and daughter does not end the inquiry. Information disclosed by Mr. Wilkerson to his attorneys during the course of the attorney-client relationship could be used to prove that Mr. Wilkerson was negligent. This is adverse to the petitioners who are obligated to act in his defense. The unfairness of the situation results from the fact that Mrs. Wilkerson and her daughter have a potential informational advantage over those who must defend Mr. Wilkerson which was gained as a result of her law firm's former representation of Mr. Wilkerson in this action. It defies logic to suggest that the petitioners do not have a legitimate interest in seeking to prevent the opposing parties from using confidential information obtained from their insured through a prior attorney-client relationship. We conclude that the petitioners have standing to request the law firm's disqualification.

We next address the issue of the appropriate standard to apply to determine whether the Schlesinger firm should be disqualified. In conflict-of-interest cases such as this arising under the former Code of Professional Responsibility,[11] one seeking to disqualify opposing counsel was required to show that (1) an attorney-client relationship existed, thereby giving rise to an irrefutable presumption that confidences were disclosed during the relationship, and (2) the matter in which the law firm subsequently represented the interest adverse to the former client was the same or substantially related to the matter in which it represented the former client. This standard was based on the Code of Professional Responsibility, Canon 4, which provided that an attorney should preserve the confidences and secrets of a client.

---

[11] [2] The Code of Professional Responsibility was replaced by the Rules of Professional Conduct, effective January 1, 1987.

In *Junger Utility & Paving Co. v. Myers*, 14 F.L.W. 2650, 578 So. 2d 1117 (Fla. 1st DCA, Nov. 15, 1989), the court applied the same standard to a question of disqualification arising under the new Rules of Professional Conduct.[12] Like the *Junger* court, we do not believe that a different standard now applies because the specific admonition to avoid the appearance of impropriety does not appear in the Rules of Professional Conduct.

Accordingly, we disagree with the court below that actual proof of prejudice is a prerequisite to disqualification under these circumstances. The Schlesinger firm represented Mr. Wilkerson in the personal injury action for more than two years, and the existence of this relationship raised the irrefutable presumption that confidences were disclosed. Moreover, the firm continues to represent Mr. Wilkerson in the medical malpractice action. Under Florida law, Mr. Wilkerson could be found liable in the instant case not only for those injuries which were sustained by his daughter in the automobile accident but also for any injuries she received as a result of any subsequent medical malpractice. Thus, even now Mr. Wilkerson may be disclosing confidences to the Schlesinger firm as his counsel in the medical malpractice action which could be used against him by the Schlesinger firm in the instant case.

In reaching our decision, we do not imply any misconduct on the part of the Schlesinger firm. In this respect, we find the statement in *Rotante v. Lawrence Hospital*, 46 A.D.2d 199, 200, 361 N.Y.S.2d 372, 373 (App. Div. 1974), apropos:

> While these facts neither indicate nor imply any departure from professional conduct or breach of any ethical canon, we cannot escape the conclusion that this is a situation rife with the possibility of discredit to the bar and the administration of justice. Obviously Mr. Turkewitz cannot erase from his mind the confidences he received from his former client or the plan of defense he envisaged. Though we do not dispute his good faith or the good faith of the firm representing plaintiff, both the possibility of conflict of interest and the appearance of it are too strong to ignore.

We quash the decision below and direct that the Schlesinger firm be disqualified from further representation of Mrs. Wilkerson and her minor child in this action.

It is so ordered.

CUYLER v. SULLIVAN
446 U.S. 335 (1980)

JUSTICE POWELL delivered the opinion of the Court.

The question presented is whether a state prisoner may obtain a federal writ of habeas corpus by showing that his retained defense counsel represented

---

[12] [3] Even though the *Junger* court found that the law firm should have been disqualified, the party seeking disqualification was required to show actual prejudice to reverse the final judgment because the case had already proceeded to final judgment. The instant case has not proceeded to final judgment. The insurers sought interlocutory review of the trial court's denial of their motions for disqualification by way of petitions for writ of certiorari in the district court of appeal.

potentially conflicting interests.

I

Respondent John Sullivan was indicted with Gregory Carchidi and Anthony DiPasquale for the first-degree murders of John Gorey and Rita Janda. The victims, a labor official and his companion, were shot to death in Gorey's second-story office at the Philadelphia headquarters of Teamsters' Local 107. Francis McGrath, a janitor, saw the three defendants in the building just before the shooting. They appeared to be awaiting someone, and they encouraged McGrath to do his work on another day. McGrath ignored their suggestions. Shortly afterward, Gorey arrived and went to his office. McGrath then heard what sounded like firecrackers exploding in rapid succession. Carchidi, who was in the room where McGrath was working, abruptly directed McGrath to leave the building and to say nothing. McGrath hastily complied. When he returned to the building about 15 minutes later, the defendants were gone. The victims' bodies were discovered the next morning.

Two privately retained lawyers, G. Fred DiBona and A. Charles Peruto, represented all three defendants throughout the state proceedings that followed the indictment. Sullivan had different counsel at the medical examiner's inquest, but he thereafter accepted representation from the two lawyers retained by his codefendants because he could not afford to pay his own lawyer.[13] At no time did Sullivan or his lawyers object to the multiple representation. Sullivan was the first defendant to come to trial. The evidence against him was entirely circumstantial, consisting primarily of McGrath's testimony. At the close of the Commonwealth's case, the defense rested without presenting any evidence. The jury found Sullivan guilty and fixed his penalty at life imprisonment. Sullivan's post-trial motions failed, and the Pennsylvania Supreme Court affirmed his conviction by an equally divided vote. Sullivan's codefendants, Carchidi and DiPasquale, were acquitted at separate trials.

Sullivan then petitioned for collateral relief under the Pennsylvania Post Conviction Hearing Act. He alleged, among other claims, that he had been denied effective assistance of counsel because his defense lawyers represented conflicting interests. In five days of hearings, the Court of Common Pleas heard evidence from Sullivan, Carchidi, Sullivan's lawyers, and the judge who presided at Sullivan's trial.

DiBona and Peruto had different recollections of their roles at the trials of the three defendants. DiBona testified that he and Peruto had been "associate counsel" at each trial. Peruto recalled that he had been chief counsel for Carchidi and DiPasquale, but that he merely had assisted DiBona in Sullivan's trial. DiBona and Peruto also gave conflicting accounts of the decision to rest Sullivan's defense. DiBona said he had encouraged Sullivan to testify even though the Commonwealth had presented a very weak case. Peruto remembered that he had not "want[ed] the defense to go on because I thought we would only be exposing the [defense]

---

[13] [1] DiBona and Peruto were paid in part with funds raised by friends of the three defendants. The record does not disclose the source of the balance of their fee, but no part of the money came from either Sullivan or his family.

witnesses for the other two trials that were coming up." Sullivan testified that he had deferred to his lawyers' decision not to present evidence for the defense. But other testimony suggested that Sullivan preferred not to take the stand because cross-examination might have disclosed an extramarital affair. Finally, Carchidi claimed he would have appeared at Sullivan's trial to rebut McGrath's testimony about Carchidi's statement at the time of the murders.

The Pennsylvania Supreme Court affirmed both Sullivan's original conviction and the denial of collateral relief. The court saw no basis for Sullivan's claim that he had been denied effective assistance of counsel at trial. It found that Peruto merely assisted DiBona in the Sullivan trial and that DiBona merely assisted Peruto in the trials of the other two defendants. Thus, the court concluded, there was "no dual representation in the true sense of the term."

Having exhausted his state remedies, Sullivan sought habeas corpus relief in the United States District Court for the Eastern District of Pennsylvania. The petition was referred to a Magistrate, who found that Sullivan's defense counsel had represented conflicting interests. The District Court, however, accepted the Pennsylvania Supreme Court's conclusion that there had been no multiple representation. The court also found that, assuming there had been multiple representation, the evidence adduced in the state post conviction proceeding revealed no conflict of interest.

The Court of Appeals for the Third Circuit reversed. It first held that the participation by DiBona and Peruto in the trials of Sullivan and his codefendants established, as a matter of law, that both lawyers had represented all three defendants. The court recognized that multiple representation " 'is not tantamount to the denial of effective assistance of counsel . . . .' " But it held that a criminal defendant is entitled to reversal of his conviction whenever he makes " 'some showing of a possible conflict of interest or prejudice, however remote . . . .' " The court acknowledged that resting at the close of the prosecutor's case "would have been a legitimate tactical decision if made by independent counsel." Nevertheless, the court thought that action alone raised a possibility of conflict sufficient to prove a violation of Sullivan's Sixth Amendment rights. The court found support for its conclusion in Peruto's admission that concern for Sullivan's codefendants had affected his judgment that Sullivan should not present a defense. To give weight to DiBona's contrary testimony, the court held, "would be to . . . require a showing of actual prejudice."

We granted certiorari to consider recurring issues left unresolved by *Holloway v. Arkansas*, 435 U.S. 475 (1978). We now vacate and remand.

*　　*　　*

IV

We come . . . to Sullivan's claim that he was denied the effective assistance of counsel guaranteed by the Sixth Amendment because his lawyers had a conflict of interest. The claim raises two issues expressly reserved in *Holloway v. Arkansas*, 435 U.S. at 483-484. The first is whether a state trial judge must inquire into the propriety of multiple representation even though no party lodges an objection. The second is whether the mere possibility of a conflict of interest warrants the conclusion that the defendant was deprived of his right to counsel.

A

In *Holloway*, a single public defender represented three defendants at the same trial. The trial court refused to consider the appointment of separate counsel despite the defense lawyer's timely and repeated assertions that the interests of his clients conflicted. This Court recognized that a lawyer forced to represent codefendants whose interests conflict cannot provide the adequate legal assistance required by the Sixth Amendment. Given the trial court's failure to respond to timely objections, however, the Court did not consider whether the alleged conflict actually existed. It simply held that the trial court's error unconstitutionally endangered the right to counsel.

Holloway requires state trial courts to investigate timely objections to multiple representation. But nothing in our precedents suggests that the Sixth Amendment requires state courts themselves to initiate inquiries into the propriety of multiple representation in every case. Defense counsel have an ethical obligation to avoid conflicting representations and to advise the court promptly when a conflict of interest arises during the course of trial. Absent special circumstances, therefore, trial courts may assume either that multiple representation entails no conflict or that the lawyer and his clients knowingly accept such risk of conflict as may exist. Indeed, as the Court noted in *Holloway*, trial courts necessarily rely in large measure upon the good faith and good judgment of defense counsel. "An 'attorney representing two defendants in a criminal matter is in the best position professionally and ethically to determine when a conflict of interest exists or will probably develop in the course of a trial.' " Unless the trial court knows or reasonably should know that a particular conflict exists, the court need not initiate an inquiry.

Although some Circuits have said explicitly that the Sixth Amendment does not require an inquiry into the possibility of conflicts, *United States v. Steele*, 576 F.2d 111 (6th Cir.) (per curiam), *cert. denied*, 439 U.S. 928 (1978); *United States v. Mavrick*, 601 F.2d 921, 929 (7th Cir. 1979), a recent opinion in the Second Circuit held otherwise, *Colon v. Fogg*, 603 F.2d 403, 407 (2d Cir. 1979).

Seventy percent of the public defender offices responding to a recent survey reported a strong policy against undertaking multiple representation in criminal cases. Forty-nine percent of the offices responding never undertake such representation. Lowenthal, *Joint Representation in Criminal Cases: A Critical Appraisal*, 64 VA. L. REV. 939, 950, and n.40 (1978). The private bar may be less alert to the importance of avoiding multiple representation in criminal cases. *See* Geer, *Representation of Multiple Criminal Defendants: Conflicts of Interest and the Professional Responsibilities of the Defense Attorney*, 62 MINN. L. REV. 119, 152-157 (1978); Lowenthal, *supra*, at 961-963.

Nothing in the circumstances of this case indicates that the trial court had a duty to inquire whether there was a conflict of interest. The provision of separate trials for Sullivan and his codefendants significantly reduced the potential for a divergence in their interests. No participant in Sullivan's trial ever objected to the multiple representation. DiBona's opening argument for Sullivan outlined a defense compatible with the view that none of the defendants was connected with the murders. The opening argument also suggested that counsel was not afraid to call witnesses whose testimony might be needed at the trials of Sullivan's codefendants. Finally, as the Court of Appeals noted, counsel's critical decision to rest Sullivan's defense was on its face a reasonable tactical response to the weakness of the circumstantial evidence presented by the prosecutor. On these facts, we conclude that the Sixth Amendment imposed upon the trial court no affirmative duty to inquire into the propriety of multiple representation.

B

Holloway reaffirmed that multiple representation does not violate the Sixth Amendment unless it gives rise to a conflict of interest. Since a possible conflict inheres in almost every instance of multiple representation, a defendant who objects to multiple representation must have the opportunity to show that potential conflicts impermissibly imperil his right to a fair trial. But unless the trial court fails to afford such an opportunity, a reviewing court cannot presume that the possibility for conflict has resulted in ineffective assistance of counsel. Such a presumption would preclude multiple representation even in cases where " '[a] common defense . . . gives strength against a common attack.' "

In order to establish a violation of the Sixth Amendment, a defendant who raised no objection at trial must demonstrate that an actual conflict of interest adversely affected his lawyer's performance. In *Glasser v. United States*, for example, the record showed that defense counsel failed to cross-examine a prosecution witness whose testimony linked Glasser with the crime and failed to resist the presentation of arguably inadmissible evidence. The Court found that both omissions resulted from counsel's desire to diminish the jury's perception of a codefendant's guilt. Indeed, the evidence of counsel's "struggle to serve two masters [could not] seriously be doubted." Since this actual conflict of interest impaired Glasser's defense, the Court reversed his conviction.

Dukes v. Warden, 406 U.S. 250 (1972), presented a contrasting situation. Dukes pleaded guilty on the advice of two lawyers, one of whom also represented Dukes' codefendants on an unrelated charge. Dukes later learned that this lawyer had sought leniency for the codefendants by arguing that their cooperation with the police induced Dukes to plead guilty. Dukes argued in this Court that his lawyer's conflict of interest had infected his plea. We found " 'nothing in the record . . . which would indicate that the alleged conflict resulted in ineffective assistance of counsel and did in fact render the plea in question involuntary and unintelligent.' " Since Dukes did not identify an actual lapse in representation, we affirmed the denial of habeas corpus relief.

Glasser established that unconstitutional multiple representation is never harmless error. Once the Court concluded that Glasser's lawyer had an actual conflict of interest, it refused "to indulge in nice calculations as to the amount of prejudice" attributable to the conflict. The conflict itself demonstrated a denial of the "right to have the effective assistance of counsel." Thus, a defendant who shows that a conflict of interest actually affected the adequacy of his representation need not demon strate prejudice in order to obtain relief. But until a defendant shows that his counsel actively represented conflicting interests, he has not established the constitutional predicate for his claim of ineffective assistance.

C

The Court of Appeals granted Sullivan relief because he had shown that the multiple representation in this case involved a possible conflict of interest. We hold that the possibility of conflict is insufficient to impugn a criminal conviction. In order to demonstrate a violation of his Sixth Amendment rights, a defendant must establish that an actual conflict of interest adversely affected his lawyer's performance. Sullivan believes he should prevail even under this standard. He emphasizes Peruto's admission that the decision to rest Sullivan's defense reflected a reluctance to expose witnesses who later might have testified for the other defendants. The petitioner, on the other hand, points to DiBona's contrary testimony and to evidence that Sullivan himself wished to avoid taking the stand. Since the Court of Appeals did not weigh these conflicting contentions under the proper legal standard, its judgment is vacated and the case is remanded for further proceedings consistent with this opinion.

So ordered.

JUSTICE BRENNAN, concurring in Part III of the opinion of the Court and in the result.

Holloway v. Arkansas, 435 U.S. 475 (1978), settled that the Sixth Amendment right to effective assistance of counsel encompasses the right to representation by an attorney who does not owe conflicting duties to other defendants. While *Holloway* also established that defendants usually have the right to share a lawyer if they so choose, that choice must always be knowing and intelligent. The trial judge, therefore, must play a positive role in ensuring that the choice was made intelligently. The court cannot delay until a defendant or an attorney raises a problem, for the Constitution also protects defendants whose attorneys fail to consider, or choose to ignore, potential conflict problems. "Upon the trial judge rests the duty of seeing that the trial is conducted with solicitude for the essential rights of the accused. . . . The trial court should protect the right of an accused to have the assistance of counsel." *Glasser v. United States*, 315 U.S. 60, 71 (1942). "While an accused may waive the right to counsel, whether there is a proper waiver should be clearly determined by the trial court, and it would be fitting and appropriate for that determination to appear upon the record." *Johnson v. Zerbst*, 304 U.S. 458, 465 (1938). This principle is honored only if the accused has the active protection of the trial court in assuring that no potential for divergence in interests threatens the adequacy of counsel's representation.

It is no imposition on a trial court to require it to find out whether attorneys are representing "two or more defendants [who] have been jointly charged . . . or have been joined for trial . . . ," to use the language of proposed Federal Rule of Criminal Procedure 44 (c). It is probable as a practical matter that virtually all instances of joint representation will appear from the face of the charging papers and the appearances filed by attorneys. The American Bar Association's standards under the ABA Project on Standards for Criminal Justice, Function of the Trial Judge § 3.4 (b) (App. Draft 1972), are framed on the premise that judges will be readily able to ascertain instances of joint representation.

"[A] possible conflict inheres in almost every instance of multiple representation." *Ante,* at 348. Therefore, upon discovery of joint representation, the duty of the trial court is to ensure that the defendants have not unwittingly given up their constitutional right to effective counsel. This is necessary since it is usually the case that defendants will not know what their rights are or how to raise them. This is surely true of the defendant who may not be receiving the effective assistance of counsel as a result of conflicting duties owed to other defendants. Therefore, the trial court cannot safely assume that silence indicates a knowledgeable choice to proceed jointly. The court must at least affirmatively advise the defendants that joint representation creates potential hazards which the defendants should consider before proceeding with the representation.[14]

d. Aggregate Settlements

In both civil and criminal matters, a lawyer is prohibited from engaging in aggregate settlements of multiple clients' claims or charges unless all clients give informed consent. MR 1.8(g).

Ethics 2000 Commission, February 2002 ABA Amendment to Model Rules

Model Rule 1.8(g), Aggregate Settlements, Consent in Writing

The prior aggregate settlements rule required that clients consent after consultation to the lawyer's negotiation of multiple clients' claims. The amendment requires that the client consent be in a writing, signed by the client. This change will make the provisions of the aggregate settlement rule much more onerous for mass tort plaintiffs' lawyers.

---

[14] [2] See also ABA Project on Standards for Criminal Justice, Function of the Trial Judge § 3.4(b) (App. Draft 1972), which provides:

> Whenever two or more defendants who have been jointly charged, or whose cases have been consolidated, are represented by the same attorney, the trial judge should inquire into potential conflicts which may jeopardize the right of each defendant to the fidelity of his counsel.

QUINTERO v. JIM WALTER HOMES, INC.

709 S.W.2d 225 (Tex. App. 1985)

OPINION

NYE, CHIEF JUSTICE.

Appellants Louis Quintero and Paula Quintero sued Jim Walter Homes, Inc., for violations of the Deceptive Trade Practices Act and the Consumer Credit Code. The Quinteros alleged that, during contractual negotiations for the purchase and construction of a new home, the salesman for Jim Walter Homes made misrepresentations about the quality of the home to their damage. A judgment for over $78,000 was initially entered in favor of the Quinteros. This was later set aside by the trial court and replaced by a take nothing judgment. The Quinteros appeal the trial court's decision to set aside the judgment in their favor and seek to have the initial judgment reinstated.

In 1976, Jim Walter Homes contracted to build a home for Louis and Paula Quintero in a "good, substantial, and workmanlike manner." Dissatisfied with their new home, the Quinteros retained attorney Hector Gonzalez, who filed a lawsuit on their behalf in 1978. Because he had several hundred similar lawsuits pending against Jim Walter Homes, Gonzalez arranged for another attorney, the Honorable Francis Gandy, to actually try the Quintero case, with the Quinteros' consent. Attorney Gandy successfully recovered a jury verdict in favor of the Quinteros on April 20, 1981. A judgment on the verdict was entered on May 27, 1981, for $78,385.65. The judgment also released the Quinteros from their installment note debt to Jim Walter Homes in the principal sum of $38,424.40.

In the meantime, attorney Gonzalez negotiated an aggregate settlement with Jim Walter Homes on behalf of 349 of his clients for $1.8 million dollars. This was to be divided among his clients according to a formula devised by attorney Gonzalez and overseen by Jim Walter Homes' legal staff. On June 11, two weeks after the judgment had been signed, attorney Gonzalez called the Quinteros to his office to discuss settling their case with Jim Walter Homes. Neither the Quinteros, nor Gonzalez, nor the attorneys for Jim Walter Homes were aware at that time that attorney Gandy had obtained the May 27 judgment. Only attorney Gandy, who had taken the time to check the file at the Courthouse, knew that the trial court had finally entered the judgment. He was unaware of and was not involved with the settlement negotiations between Jim Walter Homes and attorney Gonzalez.

As a result of a conversation with the office manager for attorney Gonzalez, the Quinteros decided to go ahead and settle their claim against Jim Walter Homes. They agreed to join with all the other clients of Gonzalez and share in the settlement and signed a release of their claims against Jim Walter Homes. A joint motion to dismiss the Quinteros' suit was signed by attorney Gonzalez and by Jim Walter Homes' attorney on June 11, 1981. Under the terms of this settlement agreement, the Quinteros were to receive about $3900.00 cash and certain deductions on their note payable to Jim Walter Homes. The total value of their part of the settlement was $13,687.00.

On June 22, 1981, Gandy informed the Quinteros of the May 27, 1981, judgment in their favor. The Quinteros immediately notified the trial court that they disapproved of the settlement and release and were revoking Gonzalez' authority to represent them any further.

Although the attorneys for Jim Walter Homes knew that the Quinteros no longer consented to the joint motion to dismiss, they nonetheless filed the consent dismissal motion with the trial court. Pursuant to the motion, the trial court (impliedly) set aside its first judgment, favorable to the Quinteros, and entered a new judgment on August 18, 1981, which dismissed their suit against Jim Walter Homes.

* * *

In their first four points of error, the Quinteros allege that the release and settlement agreement were invalid because they were made in contravention of Disciplinary Rule 5-106 of the Texas Code of Professional Responsibility. To this we agree.

The Quinteros contend that their attorney, Hector Gonzalez, violated Disciplinary Rule 5-106 of the Code, which provides:

> (a) A lawyer who represents two or more clients shall not make or participate in the making of an aggregate settlement of the claims of or against his clients, unless each client has consented to the settlement after being advised of the existence and nature of all the claims involved in the proposed settlement, of the total amount of the settlement, and of the participation of each person in the settlement.

The trial court was correct in finding that Hector Gonzalez violated this rule. The Quinteros were not informed of the nature and settlement amounts of all the claims involved in the aggregate settlement, nor were they given a list showing the names and amounts to be received by the other settling plaintiffs.

It is noteworthy, too, that the Supreme Court in its earlier opinion in this case referred to DR 5-106 when discussing the aggregate settlement agreement. The Quinteros contend that since Gonzalez violated the Code of Professional Responsibility in the method by which he acquired their consent, the release and settlement agreement are void and unenforceable.

* * *

The policy expressed in DR 5-106 is clearly to ensure that people such as the Quinteros do not give up their rights except with full knowledge of the other settlements involved. That policy was violated when Gonzalez did not inform the Quinteros of the matters required by DR 5-106.

Courts will not enforce contracts made in contravention of the law or public policy of this State. We therefore hold that the contract for the release and settlement of the Quinteros' cause of action is void and unenforceable. In so holding, we are well aware that the Court of Criminal Appeals has adopted a different approach to violations of the Code of Professional Responsibility as the Code relates to criminal matters. *See Pannell v. State,* 666 S.W.2d 96 (Tex. Crim. App. 1984) (holding that the Disciplinary Rules of the Code of Professional Responsibility "are not laws of the State of Texas" for purposes of statute which excludes the admission of evidence obtained in violation of law). However, such holding is inapplicable to civil cases where, as a matter of public policy, the ethics of attorneys and their clients must exist on a very high plane. We sustain the Quinteros' first four points of error. The initial judgment of May 27, 1981, should not have been set aside.

*   *   *

We REVERSE the judgment of the trial court and REMAND the cause with instructions to reinstate the initial judgment of May 24, 1981, including the prejudgment interest award, consistent with this opinion.

IN RE MAL DE MER FISHERIES, INC.
884 F. Supp. 635 (D. Mass. 1995)

MEMORANDUM AND ORDER ON PETITIONER'S MOTION TO ENFORCE SETTLEMENT

SARIS, DISTRICT JUDGE.

Petitioner Mal de Mer Fisheries, Inc. moves the Court to enforce a settlement negotiated between claimant Cheryl S. Costa and petitioner Mal de Mer Fisheries, Inc. in the amount of $115,000.00 (Docket No. 75). For the reasons herein stated, the motion is ALLOWED.

FACTUAL BACKGROUND

The Court treats the following facts as undisputed for purposes of this motion. On January 31, 1994, the F/V SHANNON III sank off the coast of Massachusetts while engaged in a fishing operation. As a result of the sinking two crewmembers, Robert DeJesus and Wayne Costa, were lost and presumed drowned. A third crewmember, Victor Pereira, was the sole survivor of the incident.

On February 2, 1994, the vessel's owner, Mal de Mer Fisheries, Inc., filed a petition for Exoneration from or Limitation of Liability. Cheryl Costa and Susan DeJesus, both represented by attorney Edward White of the law firm of Hunt & White, opposed the petition and filed claims on behalf of the estates of Wayne Costa and Robert DeJesus respectively. Victor Pereira, represented by attorneys Michael B. Latti and David F. Anderson of the law firm of Latti Associates, also filed a claim opposing the petition.

The matter was scheduled to commence a non-jury trial before Senior Circuit Judge Bailey Aldrich on December 19, 1994. On December 13, 1994, however, petitioner's counsel, Thomas J. Muzyka and Robert E. Collins, twice met with attorney White to discuss the possibility of settlement. On December 14, 1994, petitioner's counsel received authority to settle both the Costa and DeJesus death claims for an aggregate amount of $485,000.00 and notified attorney White of the same. That afternoon claimant Costa met with attorneys White and Hunt to discuss settlement. Her attorneys did not inform her of petitioner's offer at this time.

Claimant Costa, accompanied by her two brother-in-laws, again met with her attorney on December 15, 1994 at approximately 5:00 p.m. At this meeting, attorney White informed Costa that the insurance company offered $115,000.00 to settle her claim, but did not disclose that petitioner's offer was in the aggregate. In fact, Costa claims that attorney White stated that her settlement offer "had nothing to do with the DeJesus settlement." However, Costa also states: "At this meeting (5:00 p.m. 12/15/94) Attorney White did inform me that the offer on the DeJesus claim was three times the offer on my claim." Costa refused to settle for $115,000.00 at this meeting, but later that evening returned alone to her attorneys' offices to continue discussions.

During this later meeting, Costa contends that attorney White was heavyhanded in pressuring her into consenting to the settlement. Specifically, Costa claims attorney White told her that she had to accept the offer, she could not get a jury trial, she could not get anything more for her claim, and that she could not go to trial. After about thirty minutes, Costa told attorney White to "go ahead" with the settlement. That same evening, attorney White contacted petitioner's counsel and apprised counsel that Costa had agreed to settle for $115,000.00.

At a lobby conference on December 19, 1994, counsel reported to the court that the Costa and DeJesus had settled. As a result of the reported settlement, Judge Aldrich continued the matter until March 6, 1995.

Thereafter, attorney White sought to have claimant Costa sign releases but to no avail. However, claimant Susan DeJesus executed a release to obtain the settlement draft. On January 10, 1995, Costa discharged attorney White and hired present counsel.

Petitioner now moves to enforce the settlement agreement with claimant Costa in the amount of $115,000.00. Claiming that a factual dispute exists as to the formation and terms of the alleged settlement agreement, Costa requests an evidentiary hearing on the petitioner's motion to enforce. In the event that the court enforces the settlement agreement, Costa argues that because attorney White unilaterally divided the aggregate settlement offer between Costa and DeJesus, the court should hold a separate hearing to determine the relative strengths and weaknesses of each claim.

CONCLUSIONS OF LAW

*   *   *

3. An Attorney's Settlement Authority

Here there is no need for an evidentiary hearing as the court concludes that even if all inferences are drawn in favor of claimant, she does not prevail. It is undisputed that attorney White represented claimant Costa, and that as her counsel, White accepted petitioner's settlement offer in the amount of $115,000.00. Thus, the resolution of this controversy hinges on whether attorney White had authority to bind his client Cheryl Costa.

The authority of an attorney to consummate settlement agreements does not derive by virtue of his employment as counsel. *Interstate Commerce Comm'n v. Holmes Transportation, Inc.*, 983 F.2d 1122, 1129 (1st Cir. 1993) (general powers of an attorney to represent a client do not encompass the authority to settle a case). Where an attorney is merely an agent for his client with respect to negotiation and settlement, the client's approval is essential to completing a settlement. *See Hayes v. Eagle-Picher Industries, Inc.*, 513 F.2d 892, 894 (10th Cir. 1975) (majority agreement to settlement held insufficient to bind nonconsenting parties). Rather, an attorney may only bind his client to a compromise where the client has authorized him to do so. Thus, if Costa authorized attorney White to settle her claim in the amount of $115,000.00, the settlement agreement would be binding and any later repudiation by Costa would be ineffective.

In the instant case, claimant Costa alleges that a factual dispute exists as to the formation and terms of the alleged settlement agreement. Nevertheless, Costa admits in her affidavit that she told attorney White to "go ahead" with the settlement in the amount of $115,000.00. Costa also concedes that "as to the Petitioner, Attorney White had apparent authority." Finally, and most importantly, she concedes that White told her the offer on the DeJesus claim was three times the offer on hers. Although he did not inform Costa that the $485,000 was a package deal, that is not material in light of Costa's knowledge of the approximate amounts which she and the other widow would receive in the settlement. Acting on this authorization, attorney White informed petitioner's counsel that his client accepted its offer. Accordingly, this is not a case where a former attorney and client dispute the giving of authority thereby necessitating an evidentiary hearing. Costa cannot now complain that her attorney lacked authority to bind her to the very agreement to which she consented. 4. D.R. 5-106

Costa contends, however, that because attorney White violated Disciplinary Rule 5-106 by failing to disclose that the settlement offer was an aggregate and by affirmatively representing that the DeJesus' settlement had nothing to do with her offer, he did not have actual authority to settle her claim.

In support of this contention, Costa cites *Hayes v. Eagle-Picher Industries, Inc.*, 513 F.2d 892 (10th Cir. 1975), in which the court reversed the enforcement of a settlement agreement on the ground the attorney had violated the ethical rule prohibiting an attorney from participating a settlement on behalf of two or more clients without their consent.

Costa's reliance on Hayes is misplaced. Although the attorney in Hayes violated an ethical rule, the court based its reversal on the fact that not all clients had agreed to the settlement. The court held "that the arrangement . . . allowing the majority to govern the rights of the minority is violative of the basic tenets of the attorney-client relationship in that it delegates to the attorney powers which allow him to act not only contrary to the wishes of his client, but to act in a manner disloyal to his client and to his client's interests. Because of this, it is essential that the final settlement be subject to the client's ratification particularly in a non-class action case such as the present one." *Hayes v. Eagle-Picher Industries, Inc.*, 513 F.2d 892, 894-95 (10th Cir. 1975). Next, Costa argues that because she was not fully informed as to the terms of the offer as required by Disciplinary Rule 5-106, she could not give informed consent to the settlement. *Cf. Brooks v. Walker*, 82 F.R.D. 95, 97 (D. Mass. 1979) ("[A]lthough some authority exists for the proposition that an attorney's misrepresentations to his client or his gross negligence, of which a diligent client is unaware, may be considered exceptional circumstances which fall within Rule 60(b)(6), [citations omitted], whether relief from judgment should be granted remains a matter of discretion for the district court."). Costa, through counsel, however, admits that she "grudgingly" agreed to settle her claim for $115,000.00, the amount which petitioner now seeks to enforce. While White may have inadequately represented her, that does not defeat the settlement.

> "When a litigant voluntarily accepts an offer of settlement, either directly or indirectly through the duly authorized actions of his attorney, the integrity of the settlement cannot be attacked on the basis of inadequate representation by the litigant's attorney. In such cases, any remaining dispute is purely between the party and his attorney. Unless the resulting settlement is unfair, judicial economy commands that a party be held to the terms of a voluntary agreement."

Petty v. Timken Corp., 849 F.2d 130, 133 (4th Cir. 1988). "A litigant who enters the judicial process through the agency of a freely chosen counsel always assumes a certain risk that the result achieved will not be satisfactory. Defeated expectations do not, therefore, entitle the litigant to repudiate commitments made to opposing parties or to the court." Moreover, even if there were an actual misrepresentation as to the nature of the settlement, that is not material because Costa knew how much both the other widow and she were getting.

5. Fairness of Settlement

*   *   *

Accordingly, Costa cannot be allowed to nullify the agreement to the prejudice of the petitioners who at all times acted in good faith. Rather, Costa's sole recourse is an action against attorney White for malpractice. . . .

*   *   *

ORDER

For the foregoing reasons, petitioner's motion to enforce the settlement agreement between Mal de Mer Fisheries, Inc. and Cheryl Costa (Docket 75) is ALLOWED. By April 28, 1995, the claimant is required to execute releases in the Petitioner's favor and, upon receipt, the Petitioner is required to pay the agreed upon settlement amount of $115,000.00.

e. Prospective and Current Clients

Lawyers owe prospective clients a limited loyalty duty and the duty of confidentiality. Because confidentiality breaches are a primary consideration in multiple client conflicts analysis, conflicts analysis must be done on potential conflicts between prospective and current or former clients.

Ethics 2000 Commission, February 2002 ABA
Amendment to Model Rules

Model Rule 1.18, Prospective Clients

MR 1.18, defines and identifies duties owed to prospective clients. By reference to Model Rule 1.9, MR 1.18(b) equates the confidentiality duty owed to prospective clients with that owed to former clients. MR 1.18(c) states the terms on which a lawyer who possesses information received from a prospective client is prohibited from representing clients with interests materially adverse to the prospective client. This restriction only applies when the matters are the same or substantially related and when the possessed information could be "significantly harmful" to the prospective client. The latter standard is considerably higher than that which would disqualify a lawyer from representing concurrent clients.

Subject to exception, disqualification of a lawyer under MR 1.18(c) imputes to the firm. The disqualification does not impute when either "both the affected client and the prospective client have given informed consent, confirmed in writing," or the disqualified lawyer acted reasonably in receiving no more information from the prospective client than was necessary, the disqualified lawyer is effectively screened, and written notice is sent to the prospective client. The former of these two exceptions to imputation (the dual client waiver) might in fact allow the affected lawyer, and not just the lawyer's firm, to proceed with the matter if that is what the two clients waive. A more limited waiver of the disqualification of the firm would allow the firm but not the affected lawyer to proceed. This exception was meant to prevent prospective clients, especially large institutional clients, from spreading disqualification seeds too broadly by communicating about legal work with many law firms against whom they would prefer not to litigate. The amendment followed repeated instances of institutional clients "interviewing" multiple major law firms in their cities to prevent those law firms from representing opponents of the institutional client.

f.   Former and Current Clients, the Substantial Relationship Test

Because lawyers owe clients a continued measure of loyalty and confidentiality after representation ends, conflicts between former and current clients arise when their interests are directly adverse or when there is a substantial relationship between the two representations. Such a conflict may be waived by both clients by consent after consultation. MR 1.9.

IN RE JOHN J. CAREY

In Re Joseph P. Danis

89 S.W.3d 477 (Mo. 2002)

WILLIAM RAY PRICE, JR.

ORIGINAL DISCIPLINARY PROCEEDING

It is a fair characterization of the lawyer's responsibility in our society that he stands "as a shield," to quote Devlin, J., in defense of right and to ward off wrong. From a profession charged with such responsibilities there must be exacted those qualities of truth-speaking, of a high sense of honor, of granite discretion, of the strictest observance of fiduciary responsibility, that have, throughout the centuries been compendiously described as "moral character."

The Chief Disciplinary Counsel (CDC) filed a three count information against attorneys John J. Carey and Joseph P. Danis based upon their alleged professional misconduct in prosecuting product liability class action suits against a former client, the Chrysler Corporation, and in making misrepresentations in discovery in the subsequent lawsuit for breach of fiduciary duty brought by Chrysler against them. We find that both John Carey and Joseph Danis engaged in professional misconduct by representing another person in a substantially related matter adverse to the interest of a former client in violation of Rule 4-1.9(a),[15] Rule 4-8.4(a), and by making false discovery responses in violation of Rule 4-3.3(a)(1), Rule 4-8.4(c), Rule 4-8.4(d), Rule 4- 3.4(a) and Rule 4-3.4(d). John J. Carey and Joseph P. Danis are indefinitely suspended from the practice of law, with leave to apply for reinstatement not sooner than one year from the date of this opinion.

I. FACTUAL BACKGROUND

We find the following facts:

A. Representation of Chrysler by John Carey and Joseph Danis

John Carey joined Thompson & Mitchell in 1987, after being admitted to practice law in Missouri. While at Thompson & Mitchell, Carey worked under Charles Newman as part of a "team" of partners and associates that defended Chrysler against product liability and consumer class action cases brought against it nationwide. From January 1992 through December 1995, Carey billed 1,314.6 hours to Chrysler. As part of the Chrysler team, Carey was privy to all aspects of the Chrysler representation and directly participated in nearly all aspects of the Chrysler litigation. In addition, Carey assessed Chrysler's potential liability in pending litigation and helped draft a "blueprint" for Chrysler to follow in

---

[15] [1] A lawyer who has formerly represented a client in a matter shall not thereafter represent another person in the same or a substantially related matter in which that person's interests are materially adverse to the interests of the former client unless the former client consents after consultation. Rule 4-1.9(a).

defending class action product defect suits pending concurrently with a National Highway Traffic Safety Administration ("NHTSA") investigation.

Joseph Danis was licensed to practice law in Missouri in 1993 and began work as an associate for Thompson & Mitchell that year. Carey acted as Danis' mentor while Danis was a summer associate and again when Danis was a new associate. Danis joined Carey as a member of Charles Newman's Chrysler team. As a new associate, Danis' involvement with the Chrysler class action litigation was less extensive than Carey's. However, as a member of the team, Danis was privy to all aspects of the Chrysler representation. Danis billed 513.5 hours to Chrysler from January 1992 through December 1995.

Newman would circulate information on the widest possible basis to every member of the Thompson & Mitchell team involved in representation of Chrysler. Carey was the primary associate on four different Chrysler class action cases.[16] Charles Newman testified:

John [Carey] was totally immersed in that case [Osley], along with me, and played the same role that I played in many respects. And that obviously involved . . . determining the legal issues that the case presented. It also involved analyzing the jurisdiction . . . .

. . . .

He was also involved with me and others in massing the facts relevant to the claims that were asserted, and that involved contacting and principally working with the personnel in the office of the general counsel at Chrysler Corporation.

Newman further testified that in the other three cases, Carey had "a similar role with a few additional aspects."

Danis was not involved in *Osley*, but did participate in the other three cases. Danis was involved in the lower level associate functions, but worked extensively with both Newman and Carey. Danis worked principally on drafting discovery responses and obtaining information from Chrysler to respond to discovery requests.

The component parts involved in the class action lawsuits Carey and Danis defended while with Thompson & Mitchell were Renault heater coils and Chrysler minivan door latches. Charles Newman and other Chrysler attorneys, William McLellan and Lewis Goldfarb, each stressed, however, that the actual defective component was not materially important in this type of class action lawsuit. Goldfarb testified:

The products at issue in class actions are almost irrelevant to how we go about defending class actions. There's almost an identity of process in terms of how we defend class actions, regardless of the nature of the component involved.

. . . .

Product-related class actions, particularly those that follow on the heels of a

---

[16] [8] These cases are referred to as *Osley, Larpenteur, Peterson* and *Drake. Osley* involved heater cores while the other three cases each involved Chrysler minivan gate latches.

government investigation, are virtually identical in the way the company handles them. The nature of the component involved is almost irrelevant to these cases because they never go to trial. We're always dealing with the government, that investigation relates to the ongoing class action case. And the class action strategy is almost independent in some respects of the nature of the component involved.

These three Chrysler attorneys also testified that respondents Carey and Danis were privy to a wealth of information that would be useful to them in prosecuting a product-related class action against Chrysler. Newman testified that Carey and Danis learned Chrysler's strategy in defending minivan product liability class action suits:

Respondents [were] present during meetings with in-house Chrysler counsel when there was a discussion of the strengths and weaknesses of various Chrysler employees . . . [and] with non-lawyer Chrysler employees; for example, expert witnesses.

. . . .

We would talk with the client about other pending litigation alleging a similar product or defect . . . . So we would talk to the attorneys at Chrysler about their defense of those cases, what factual defenses were being developed and implemented, what expert witnesses, if any, they were working with there. The legal strategies in those cases, the legal defenses in those cases. Determine their applicability, determine their usefulness, determine whether they could be implemented in the class action . . . .

Newman also said that Carey and Danis knew that Chrysler was very hesitant to interplead or sue a critical supplier because of the way its supply lines were managed.

If somebody was thinking of suing Chrysler and knew . . . that Chrysler had a predisposition against bringing in third parties, you would know in contemplating a suit against Chrysler that it would be relatively efficient in that Chrysler wouldn't bring in everybody else in the world that might be involved or had a bearing with that particular component or product and that you could tailor your claims accordingly to focus just on Chrysler and not have to worry about suppliers and the like.

Newman testified that, although the component parts differed, there were many similarities in available defenses, such as statute of limitations, improper certification of the class, improper class representatives, and improper assertion of claims. Finally, Newman indicated that many expert witnesses overlap: economists, automotive repair experts and human factor engineers.

Newman testified that "the Respondents . . . learned which experts Chrysler chose to use and not use." He stressed that Carey and Danis helped formulate Chrysler's defense strategy in class action product liability cases involving Chrysler minivans.

Lewis Goldfarb also discussed respondents' work for Chrysler. Goldfarb testified that Carey and Danis had access to "detailed, internal information and analysis done by the in-house legal department, as well as [Chrysler] engineers and other

personnel, regarding the status of a confidential government investigation . . . ."
He emphasized that Carey and Danis had a "road map as to how we [Chrysler]
look at and analyze alleged defects concerning our products."

The "road map" Goldfarb spoke of referred to a "matrix" or "blueprint" that the
Chrysler team — including John Carey and Joseph Danis — developed to
formulate Chrysler's defense to class action product liability cases involving
Chrysler minivans. The team prepared a matrix of all considerations that Chrysler
should consider in deciding whether or not to settle the minivan latch cases. This
matrix listed relevant criteria and matched those criteria with a factual scenario.
For each scenario, the team gave thoughts about the applicability of the criteria
and its impact on the company. The matrix also included a form of a decision tree.
The decision tree visually described the different scenarios and their implication on
important areas of the company like marketing, public and consumer relations,
dealer relations, and the recall itself.

B. Carey & Danis, L.L.C. — The Chrysler ABS Class Action

In January 1995, Carey and Danis left Thompson & Mitchell and formed their
own firm, Carey & Danis, L.L.C. Carey & Danis shared office space with the firm
of David Danis — Joseph Danis' father — Danis, Cooper, Cavanagh & Hartweger,
L.L.C. The two firms shared staff, a bookkeeper, a fax machine, and unlocked (but
separate) filing cabinets.

In August 1995, a Thompson & Mitchell secretary referred her brother-in-law,
Dennis Beam, to Carey & Danis after he experienced problems with the anti-lock
brake system on his Chrysler minivan. Carey discussed the potential case with
Beam. Carey, obviously aware that he and Danis had represented Chrysler,
researched Rule 1.9 of the Model Rules of Professional Conduct for an hour or two
to determine if a conflict existed. Carey testified that he "made the determination
that since Joey [Danis] and I had no knowledge or information at all concerning
anti-lock brakes . . . that those were not substantially related under my review of
the case law and reading those rules." Carey determined there was not a conflict.
However, Carey & Danis did not file suit because Thompson & Mitchell had been
referring business to them and they did not want to embarrass their former firm
by filing suit against a former client.

Carey & Danis arranged for the Danis, Cooper firm to represent Beam and a
class of plaintiffs against Chrysler. Danis, Cooper was to get help on the case from
another St. Louis law firm, Blumenfeld, Kaplan & Sandweiss. Carey and Danis met
with attorneys from Danis, Cooper and the Blumenfeld firm to discuss the *Beam*
class action suit over lunch at a restaurant. According to Evan Buxner, who was
working for Blumenfeld at the time, the "purpose of the meeting was to discuss
generally if Blumenfeld, Kaplan & Sandweiss participated in the litigation what
our role was and what we might expect representing a plaintiff in a proposed class
in a plaintiffs' class action case." Carey & Danis was the only firm with any
significant class action litigation experience among the three firms. The firms
discussed a number of topics relating to the class action against Chrysler: attorney
time and cost, the fact that NHTSA was conducting an investigation into the brake
system, that a proposed class action could ride the government coattails and let the

government agency do most of the work, the effect of a recall on a potential class action, the necessity (or lack thereof) of hiring experts, and that they could expect a barrage of motions from Chrysler.

Shortly after their involvement began, Blumenfeld was informed that Carey & Danis' involvement in *Beam* was being investigated for conflict of interest. Blumenfeld then withdrew from the *Beam* litigation. Carey explained:

Once they withdrew David [Danis] and Richard [Cooper] approached Joey [Danis] and I and asked us if we would be interested in getting involved in the case, we knew that there was no conflict of interest, and they needed help because . . . there was a motion to transfer that was pending in St. Louis City. They needed help. There wasn't time to try and go out and find another co-counsel.

Carey & Danis entered their appearance on behalf of the *Beam* plaintiffs. However, neither Carey nor Danis sought or received Chrysler's consent to act as plaintiffs' counsel against Chrysler.

In December 1995, Joseph and David Danis met in New York with Stanley Grossman, an attorney who had a similar ABS class action suit against Chrysler in New Jersey. At the meeting they discussed joining -and later did join -the two class actions as well as a third group of plaintiffs from Mississippi represented by John Deakle. Following the meeting, Joseph Danis wrote Grossman to confirm the discussion regarding the ABS cases. Danis also inquired as to allocation of attorneys' fees if the cases were consolidated, saying there was "plenty of money for all . . . . Consequently, we will all be better served working together against Chrysler . . . ." This correspondence has been termed "the Grossman letter."

While Danis and his father were in New York meeting with Grossman, Carey received a letter from Charles Newman accusing Carey & Danis of having a conflict of interest in the *Beam* case. Carey was "very upset" upon reading Newman's letter and immediately called Newman to tell him that he believed "in the strongest terms that [Carey & Danis] did not have a conflict of interest," but that he did not want to cause any trouble with Newman, Thompson & Mitchell, or Chrysler. Carey inquired if they could put an end to "all this ugliness and nastiness" if he and Danis withdrew from the *Beam* case. Newman did not make any promises, but thought that might appease Chrysler.

Thereafter, the *Beam* case was voluntarily dismissed and then joined with Grossman's case in New York. Carey & Danis withdrew from *Beam*, but the Danis, Cooper firm and John Deakle were among the attorneys listed for the plaintiffs. Carey & Danis associated with a group of class action attorneys -David Danis and John Deakle, among others-that often worked together on cases and shared information. A number of these attorneys were involved in Chrysler ABS litigation. Members of this group would forward correspondence regarding the ABS litigation to each other and many of these communications would find their way to Carey & Danis.

C. Chrysler v. Carey & Danis — False and Misleading Statements

[The court recounted facts relating to the Respondents' misrepresentations in Chrysler's lawsuit against them for breach of fiduciary duty. —Ed.]

As a result of their answer being struck, a default judgment was entered against Carey & Danis in the amount of $ 850,000. The judgment was affirmed against Carey & Danis by the Eighth Circuit Court of Appeals in *Chrysler Corp. v. Carey*, 186 F.3d 1016 (8th Cir. 1999).

II. DISCUSSION

A. Count I: Conflict of Interest

Count I alleges professional misconduct by violating Rule 4-1.9(a), which governs conflict of interest with former clients. Rule 4-1.9(a) states:

> A lawyer who has formerly represented a client in a matter shall not thereafter: (a) represent another person in the same or a substantially related matter in which that person's interests are materially adverse to the interests of the former client unless the former client consents after consultation . . . .

It is not disputed that respondents Carey and Danis formerly represented the Chrysler Corporation, nor is it disputed that respondents' representation of the plaintiffs against Chrysler in *Beam* was materially adverse to Chrysler. The only issue presented is whether the *Beam* case was "substantially related" to Carey's and Danis' previous defense work for Chrysler.

"Gallons of ink" have been consumed by those trying to articulate or explain the test for deciding whether a substantial relationship exists between two representations. ABA/BNA Lawyer's Manual on Professional Conduct, 51:215. *See also Chrispens v. Coastal Ref. & Mktg., Inc.*, 257 Kan. 745, 897 P.2d 104, 111 (Kan. 1995). The "substantially related" test was first announced in *T.C. Theatre Corp. v. Warner Brothers Pictures, Inc.*, 113 F. Supp. 265 (S.D.N.Y. 1953). In announcing the rule, the court was primarily concerned with preserving client confidences and avoiding conflicts of interest.[17] *T.C. Theatre*, 113 F. Supp. at 268-69. The court said:

> It would defeat an important purpose of the rule of secrecy — to encourage clients fully and freely to make known to their attorneys all facts pertinent to their cause. Considerations of public policy, no less than the client's private interest, require rigid enforcement of the rule against disclosure. No client should ever be concerned with the possible use against him in future litigation of what he may have revealed to his attorney.

policy

---

[17] [14] The primary "concern is the possibility, or appearance of the possibility, that the attorney may have received confidential information during the prior representation . . . . The test does not require the former client to show that actual confidences were disclosed. That inquiry would be improper as requiring the very disclosure" that the rule is intended to protect. *Chrispens*, 897 P.2d at 112. When a substantial relationship is found, this Court will presume that confidences were disclosed for conflict of interest purposes.

Matters disclosed by clients under the protective seal of the attorney-client relationship and intended in their defense should not be used as weapons of offense. The rule prevents a lawyer from placing himself in an anomalous position. Were he permitted to represent a client whose cause is related and adverse to that of his former client he would be called upon to decide what is confidential and what is not, and, perhaps, unintentionally to make use of confidential information received from the former client while espousing his cause. Lawyers should not put themselves in the position "where, even unconsciously, they might take, in the interests of a new client, an advantage derived or traceable to, confidences reposed under the cloak of a prior, privileged relationship." In cases of this sort the Court must ask whether it can reasonably be said that in the course of the former representation the attorney might have acquired information related to the subject of his subsequent representation. If so, then the relationship between the two matters is sufficiently close to bring the later representation within the prohibition . . . .

Id. at 269. (Citation omitted).

There are three primary tests for substantial relationship used throughout the country. The first approach compares the facts of the former and current representations. The second approach, which has not been widely adopted, insists that the issues involved in the two representations be identical or essentially the same. The third approach, developed by the Seventh Circuit Court of Appeals, blends the fact and issue comparisons into a three-step test. The Seventh Circuit test states:

Disqualification questions require three levels of inquiry. Initially, the trial judge must make a factual reconstruction of the scope of the prior legal representation. Second, it must be determined whether it is reasonable to infer that the confidential information allegedly given would have been given to a lawyer representing a client in those matters. Finally, it must be determined whether that information is relevant to the issues raised in the litigation pending against the former client.

The test "does not require the former client to show that actual confidences were disclosed. That inquiry would be improper as requiring the very disclosure that [MRPC 1.9(a)] is intended to protect."

Chrispens, 897 P.2d at 112.

The fact that a lawyer has previously represented a client does not automatically preclude the lawyer from opposing that client in a later representation. The court must determine whether confidential information acquired in the course of representing the former client is relevant to the issues raised in the current litigation.

Chrispens offers a short, non-exclusive list of six factors that courts following the Seventh Circuit approach have considered in determining whether a substantial relationship exists The factors include:

(1) the case involved the same client and the matters or transactions in question are relatively interconnected or reveal the client's pattern of conduct; (2) the lawyer had interviewed a witness who was key in both cases; (3) the lawyer's knowledge of

a former client's negotiation strategies was relevant; (4) the commonality of witnesses, legal theories, business practices of the client, and location of the client were significant; (5) a common subject matter, issues and causes of action existed; and (6) information existed on the former client's ability to satisfy debts and its possible defense and negotiation strategies.

In some cases, one factor, if significant enough, can establish that the subsequent case is substantially related. Careful review of the facts at hand in relation to these six factors provides a specific framework for resolution of this case. First, when compared to the prior representation, the ABS cases involve the same client, Chrysler. Because the cases all involve the Chrysler minivan in the same "type" of case, Chrysler's pattern of conduct is applicable despite the different specific component parts involved. It is undisputed that Carey and Danis defended the Chrysler Corporation on product liability class action lawsuits involving Chrysler minivan components and then later prosecuted a product liability class action lawsuit involving another minivan component against Chrysler. The subject matter of the lawsuits was components of Chrysler's minivan. Carey and Danis also knew how important the minivan was to Chrysler and had access to "detailed, internal information and analysis done by the in-house legal department . . . ." In fact, both Carey and Danis helped formulate the "blueprint" Chrysler used when defending a product liability class action suit involving the minivan.

Second, respondents interviewed or deposed a number of expert witnesses while working for Chrysler that could have been called to testify in the *Beam* lawsuit. Carey and Danis were present during meetings with in-house Chrysler counsel when there was a discussion of the strengths and weaknesses of various Chrysler employees and expert witnesses. Carey and Danis had personal contact with a . number of expert witnesses that could be used in both cases and had learned which experts Chrysler chose to use and not use.

Third, Carey's and Danis' knowledge of Chrysler's negotiation strategies were particularly relevant. Respondents helped formulate the decision matrix used by Chrysler when defending suits precisely like *Beam*. The matrix listed criteria Chrysler deemed relevant and matched those criteria with a factual scenario. For each scenario, the team gave thoughts about the applicability of the criteria and the impact on the company.

Fourth and Fifth, the commonality of witnesses, legal theories, and business practices of the client were significant, and there was a common subject matter as well as common issues and causes of action. This case involved the Chrysler minivan. Although the particular minivan parts at issue may have been different, in this case, testimony indicated that the actual components at issue in this type of product liability class action suit are almost irrelevant to how Chrysler defended the case. Lewis Goldfarb testified:

Product-related class actions, particularly those that follow on the heels of a government investigation, are virtually identical in the way the company handles them. The nature of the component involved is almost irrelevant to these cases because they never go to trial. We're always dealing with the government, that investigation relates to the ongoing class action case. And the class action strategy is almost independent in some respects of the nature of the component involved.

Finally, information existed on Chrysler's possible defense and negotiation strategies. As previously discussed, Carey and Danis knew of and actually helped formulate Chrysler's defense and negotiation strategies.

Respondents' justification for prosecuting a consumer class action lawsuit involving Chrysler minivans, within one year after having represented Chrysler, was that the component parts were different. Carey and Danis defended Chrysler on Chrysler minivan door latch cases while *Beam* involved Chrysler minivan anti-lock brake systems.

Certainly, a client does not own a lawyer for all time. In appropriate circumstances our rules allow lawyers to take positions adverse to former clients and even to bring suit against them. *See* Rule 4-1.9. The similarity of each case and its facts and issues is the determinative factor. Rule 4-1.9, however, simply does not allow respondents to cut such a sharp corner here. This is why the rule is not limited to "the same" matter but also extends to "a substantially related" matter.

B. False and Misleading Statements During Discovery

[The court determined that the Respondents were subject to discipline for their misleading statements and actions in the breach of fiduciary duty case. —Ed.]

Respondents are attorneys with a background in litigation. Each was responsible for vast amounts of contentious discovery while defending Chrysler in products liability class actions suits and later when representing plaintiffs. The federal court found, and the evidence supports, that by denying the existence of the documents and information requested in Interrogatory No. 2 and Requests for Production Nos. 8, 12, and 25, respondents purposefully withheld evidence from opposing counsel in violation of Rule 4-3.4 (a) and Rule 4-3.4(d), and made misstatements of material fact to the court in violation of Rule 4-3.3(a)(1), Rule 4-8.4(c) and Rule 4-8.4(d).

III. DISCIPLINE

The purpose of discipline is not to punish the attorney, but to protect the public and maintain the integrity of the legal profession. Those twin purposes may be achieved both directly, by removing a person from the practice of law, and indirectly, by imposing a sanction which serves to deter other members of the Bar from engaging in similar conduct.

Assessing discipline in cases such as this is always difficult. Here, two talented young lawyers, full of promise, lost their way among the economic temptations of modern practice and then again lost their way while struggling to defend themselves. In doing so, they violated two of the most fundamental principles of our profession, loyalty to the client and honesty to the bench. Significant discipline must follow to maintain the public's trust and confidence in our ability to police ourselves. A "slap on the wrist" will not suffice.

While disbarment would ordinarily be expected in a case such as this, the mitigating factors warrant some degree of leniency and offer hope that respondents can return to the responsible practice of law having learned a very hard lesson.

John J. Carey and Joseph P. Danis are indefinitely suspended from the practice of law, with leave to apply for reinstatement not sooner than one year from the date of this opinion.

HAAGEN-DAZS CO. v. PERCHE NO! GELATO, INC.
639 F. Supp. 282 (N.D. Cal. 1986)

Opinion and Order Re: Disqualification of Counsel

I.

This is a motion by the Pillsbury Company, Inc., ("Pillsbury"), the parent company of Haagen-Dazs Company, Inc. ("Haagen-Dazs"), for the disqualification of counsel for Double Rainbow Gourmet Ice Cream, Inc. ("Double Rainbow") in this antitrust litigation.

Double Rainbow is engaged in the manufacture and sale of super premium ice cream. Pillsbury entered the super premium ice cream market when it purchased Haagen-Dazs in 1983. Haagen-Dazs and Double Rainbow are competitors. The main issue presently raised by this litigation is whether Haagen-Dazs' distribution policies violate the antitrust laws.

Pillsbury and Haagen-Dazs filed this motion to disqualify both San Francisco and Minneapolis counsel from representing Double Rainbow in this series of actions, as well as "any other party . . . [in] substantially related litigation."

II.

The basis for this motion is the past and present employment of Mr. Franklin C. Jesse, Esq., an attorney formerly employed as in-house counsel in the Pillsbury Company legal department, and currently associated with Double Rainbow's Minneapolis counsel, Gray, Plant, Mooty, Mooty & Bennett ("the Gray firm"). Haagen-Dazs and Pillsbury contend that Mr. Jesse's former employment with Pillsbury and current employment with the Gray firm require disqualification of Mr. Jesse. They assert that, as a Pillsbury attorney for ten years, Mr. Jesse was aware of Haagen-Dazs' distribution policies, and had access to confidential information relating to the issues underlying this litigation. . . .

The record discloses that Mr. Jesse went to work in the Pillsbury legal department in 1974 and remained until October 1984. During that period, Mr. Jesse held various positions, including general attorney, senior attorney, international group counsel, and senior corporate counsel. From 1980 until October 1984, Mr. Jesse was also a member of the legal department's administration committee.

It appears that Mr. Jesse worked primarily on international business and legal matters while employed by Pillsbury. After Pillsbury acquired Haagen-Dazs in 1983, Mr. Jesse worked on a joint venture with a Japanese dairy through which Haagen-Dazs sought to introduce its super premium ice cream into the Japanese

[handwritten margin note top: Jesse worked on a few international things for HD]

market. Other legal projects for Haagen-Dazs which were handled by Mr. Jesse included an Australian trademark registration and a sales arrangement in Singapore. Haagen-Dazs contends that the international matters handled by Mr. Jesse, particularly the Japanese venture, required a working knowledge of Haagen-Dazs' franchise and distribution policies, including the domestic policies at issue here. Moreover, Haagen-Dazs alleges that Mr. Jesse has knowledge of Pillsbury's acquisition and marketing strategy, since he was a member of the legal department at the time the policy for entering the super premium ice cream market was adopted. Finally, Mr. Jesse was in the legal department in 1984 at the time that office defended a claim brought by Ben & Jerry's Homemade, Inc., which involved issues identical or similar to those raised in this series of cases.

[handwritten margin note left: HD says he knows abt dom. stuff from int. stuff.]

[handwritten margin note left: this same as B&J case]

At the present time, Mr. Jesse is an associate "international counsel" with the Gray firm. Since joining that firm on November 1, 1984, his practice has involved primarily international business matters. Mr. Jesse has stated in a declaration and in a deposition that he has no present knowledge of the distribution policies which are challenged here, and that he was not privy to confidences concerning the issues raised by this litigation. Furthermore, Mr. Jesse states that he has not worked on these cases, or on any of the related cases, and that his only connection with this litigation has been in response to this motion made by Pillsbury and Haagen-Dazs.

III.

Northern District of California Local Rule 110-3 provides that lawyers shall "comply with the standards of professional conduct required of members of the State Bar of California and contained in the State Bar Act, the Rules of Professional Conduct of the State Bar of California, and decisions of any court applicable thereto." Rule 1.9(a) of the American Bar Association Model Rules of Professional Conduct (1983) provides that:

> A lawyer who has formerly represented a client in a matter shall not thereafter:
>
> (a) represent another person in the same or a substantially related matter in which that person's interests are materially adverse to the interests of the former client unless the former client consents after consultation.

[handwritten margin note left: 9th Cir factual adopts Relation test.]

The Ninth Circuit has specifically adopted this "substantial relationship" test, and in *Trone v. Smith*, 621 F.2d 994 (9th Cir. 1980), the court elaborated on the standard by stating that the test is met if the factual contexts of the two representations are similar or related, regardless of "whether confidences were in fact imparted to the lawyer by the client" in the prior representation.

A court faced with a disqualification motion need not determine that actual confidences were disclosed to the lawyer.[18] Elaborating further on the showing required for disqualification, the *Trone* court stated:

---

[18] [1] To the contrary, the courts have held that such a requirement would, in many instances, involve revelation of the confidences the rule was designed to protect.

If there is a reasonable probability that confidences were disclosed which could be used against the client in a later, adverse representation, a substantial relation between the two cases is presumed.

Acknowledging the "potential harshness" of this standard, the Ninth Circuit test for disqualification provides that the lawyer may attempt to rebut the presumption by showing that he "had no personal involvement in such substantially related matters and did not actually receive any confidential information relevant to the matter in which disqualification is sought."

Thus, to make the showing necessary for disqualification of Double Rainbow's counsel, Haagen-Dazs and Pillsbury must establish that Mr. Jesse, while at Pillsbury, worked on matters substantially related to this litigation, or that there is a reasonable probability that Mr. Jesse received confidential information. If there is a showing that Mr. Jesse was privy to client confidences substantially related to this litigation, Double Rainbow may then attempt to show that Mr. Jesse had no personal involvement in the substantially related matters.

Regardless of the particular language used by the courts and the rules of professional conduct to define the standards, a common principle underlies all of them: the interests of the clients are primary, and the interests of the lawyers are secondary.

IV.

The record here discloses substantial similarities in the legal employments of Mr. Jesse and the legal and business matters involved in those employments. While Mr. Jesse and the Gray firm have attempted to show that his distribution-related work was limited to international matters, it appears that Mr. Jesse had information concerning Haagen-Dazs' domestic distribution strategies as well. Mr. Jesse worked for a lengthy period of time in the Pillsbury legal department, and it is reasonable to conclude that, as a senior attorney in that office, he also had significant contact with Pillsbury management during the formulation of its super premium ice cream acquisition and marketing strategy. While Mr. Jesse states that he was not aware of Haagen-Dazs' distribution policies, his presence in the legal department at the time Pillsbury entered the super premium ice cream market suggests that he was at least exposed to management's and the legal department's consideration of distribution policies. In addition, his employment during the Ben & Jerry's litigation raises an inference that he was privy to information about that litigation which is, in itself, substantially related to this litigation.

In reaching these conclusions, the court has taken into consideration the unique role that access to business thinking plays in the context of antitrust litigation.

The court further finds that the presumptions in favor of Pillsbury's and Haagen-Dazs' position have not been rebutted. The record demonstrates that Mr. Jesse did have personal involvement in legal matters which the court finds are substantially related to the issues in this case, and that he did receive certain relevant confidential information.

The court concludes that disqualification of Mr. Jesse is necessary to protect

Haagen-Dazs' and Pillsbury's confidences and to avoid the appearance of impropriety.

* * *

VII.

THEREFORE, IT IS ORDERED that:

(1) Mr. Franklin Jesse is disqualified from further representation of any party to this litigation.

* * *

[The court's treatment of the imputed disqualification issues is excerpted later in this chapter. —Ed.]

MICKENS v. TAYLOR
535 U.S. 162 (2002)

JUSTICE SCALIA delivered the opinion of the Court.

The question presented in this case is what a defendant must show in order to demonstrate a Sixth Amendment violation where the trial court fails to inquire into a potential conflict of interest about which it knew or reasonably should have known.

I

In 1993, a Virginia jury convicted petitioner Mickens of the premeditated murder of Timothy Hall during or following the commission of an attempted forcible sodomy. Finding the murder outrageously and wantonly vile, it sentenced petitioner to death. In June 1998, Mickens filed a petition for writ of habeas corpus in the United States District Court for the Eastern District of Virginia, alleging, inter alia, that he was denied effective assistance of counsel because one of his court-appointed attorneys had a conflict of interest at trial. Federal habeas counsel had discovered that petitioner's lead trial attorney, Bryan Saunders, was representing Hall (the victim) on assault and concealed-weapons charges at the time of the murder. Saunders had been appointed to represent Hall, a juvenile, on March 20, 1992, and had met with him once for 15 to 30 minutes some time the following week. Hall's body was discovered on March 30, 1992, and four days later a juvenile court judge dismissed the charges against him, noting on the docket sheet that Hall was deceased. The one-page docket sheet also listed Saunders as Hall's counsel. On April 6, 1992, the same judge appointed Saunders to represent petitioner. Saunders did not disclose to the court, his co-counsel, or petitioner that he had previously represented Hall. Under Virginia law, juvenile case files are confidential and may not generally be disclosed without a court order, but petitioner learned about Saunders' prior representation when a clerk mistakenly produced Hall's file to federal habeas counsel.

The District Court held an evidentiary hearing and denied petitioner's habeas petition. A divided panel of the Court of Appeals for the Fourth Circuit reversed, and the Court of Appeals granted rehearing en banc. [T]he Court of Appeals assumed that the juvenile court judge had neglected a duty to inquire into a potential conflict, but rejected petitioner's argument that this failure either mandated automatic reversal of his conviction or relieved him of the burden of showing that a conflict of interest adversely affected his representation. Relying on *Cuyler v. Sullivan*, 446 U.S. 335 (1980), the court held that a defendant must show "both an actual conflict of interest and an adverse effect even if the trial court failed to inquire into a potential conflict about which it reasonably should have known." Concluding that petitioner had not demonstrated adverse effect, it affirmed the District Court's denial of habeas relief. We granted a stay of execution of petitioner's sentence and granted *certiorari*.

II

The Sixth Amendment provides that a criminal defendant shall have the right to "the assistance of counsel for his defence." This right has been accorded, we have said, "not for its own sake, but because of the effect it has on the ability of the accused to receive a fair trial." *United States v. Cronic*, 466 U.S. 648, 658 (1984). It follows from this that assistance which is ineffective in preserving fairness does not meet the constitutional mandate, *see Strickland v. Washington*, 466 U.S. 668, 685-686 (1984); and it also follows that defects in assistance that have no probable effect upon the trial's outcome do not establish a constitutional violation. As a general matter, a defendant alleging a Sixth Amendment violation must demonstrate "a reasonable probability that, but for counsel's unprofessional errors, the result of the proceeding would have been different."

There is an exception to this general rule. We have spared the defendant the need of showing probable effect upon the outcome, and have simply presumed such effect, where assistance of counsel has been denied entirely or during a critical stage of the proceeding. When that has occurred, the likelihood that the verdict is unreliable is so high that a case-by-case inquiry is unnecessary. But only in "circumstances of that magnitude" do we forgo individual inquiry into whether counsel's inadequate performance undermined the reliability of the verdict.

We have held in several cases that "circumstances of that magnitude" may also arise when the defendant's attorney actively represented conflicting interests. The nub of the question before us is whether the principle established by these cases provides an exception to the general rule of *Strickland* under the circumstances of the present case. To answer that question, we must examine those cases in some detail. In *Holloway v. Arkansas*, 435 U.S. 475 (1978), defense counsel had objected that he could not adequately represent the divergent interests of three codefendants. Without inquiry, the trial court had denied counsel's motions for the appointment of separate counsel and had refused to allow counsel to cross-examine any of the defendants on behalf of the other two. The *Holloway* Court deferred to the judgment of counsel regarding the existence of a disabling conflict, recognizing that a defense attorney is in the best position to determine when a conflict exists, that he has an ethical obligation to advise the court of any problem, and that his declarations to the court are "virtually made under oath." *Holloway* presumed, moreover, that the conflict, "which [the defendant] and his counsel tried to avoid by timely objections to the joint representation," undermined the adversarial process. The presumption was justified because joint representation of conflicting interests is inherently suspect, and because counsel's conflicting obligations to multiple defendants "effectively seal his lips on crucial matters" and make it difficult to measure the precise harm arising from counsel's errors. *Holloway* thus creates an automatic reversal rule only where defense counsel is forced to represent codefendants over his timely objection, unless the trial court has determined that there is no conflict. ("Whenever a trial court improperly requires joint representation over timely objection reversal is automatic.")

In *Cuyler v. Sullivan*, 446 U.S. 335 (1980), the respondent was one of three defendants accused of murder who were tried separately, represented by the same counsel. Neither counsel nor anyone else objected to the multiple representation, and counsel's opening argument at Sullivan's trial suggested that the interests of the defendants were aligned. We declined to extend *Holloway*'s automatic reversal rule to this situation and held that, absent objection, a defendant must demonstrate that "a conflict of interest actually affected the adequacy of his representation." In addition to describing the defendant's burden of proof, *Sullivan* addressed separately a trial court's duty to inquire into the propriety of a multiple representation, construing *Holloway* to require inquiry only when "the trial court knows or reasonably should know that a particular conflict exists,"[19] — which is not to be confused with when the trial court is aware of a vague, unspecified possibility of conflict, such as that which "inheres in almost every instance of multiple representation." In *Sullivan*, no "special circumstances" triggered the trial court's duty to inquire.

Finally, in *Wood v. Georgia*, 450 U.S. 261 (1981), three indigent defendants convicted of distributing obscene materials had their probation revoked for failure to make the requisite $500 monthly payments on their $5,000 fines. We granted *certiorari* to consider whether this violated the Equal Protection Clause, but during the course of our consideration certain disturbing circumstances came to our attention: At the probation-revocation hearing (as at all times since their arrest) the defendants had been represented by the lawyer for their employer (the owner of the business that purveyed the obscenity), and their employer paid the attorney's fees. The employer had promised his employees he would pay their fines, and had generally kept that promise but had not done so in these defendants' case. This record suggested that the employer's interest in establishing a favorable equal-protection precedent (reducing the fines he would have to pay for his indigent employees in the future) diverged from the defendants' interest in

---

[19] [2] In order to circumvent *Sullivan*'s clear language, Justice Stevens suggests that a trial court must scrutinize representation by appointed counsel more closely than representation by retained counsel. But we have already rejected the notion that the Sixth Amendment draws such a distinction. "A proper respect for the Sixth Amendment disarms [the] contention that defendants who retain their own lawyers are entitled to less protection than defendants for whom the State appoints counsel . . . . The vital guarantee of the Sixth Amendment would stand for little if the often uninformed decision to retain a particular lawyer could reduce or forfeit the defendant's entitlement to constitutional protection." *Cuyler v. Sullivan*, 446 U.S. 335, 344 (1980).

[handwritten margin note at top: employer's interests diff. than Ds]

obtaining leniency or paying lesser fines to avoid imprisonment. Moreover, the possibility that counsel was actively representing the conflicting interests of employer and defendants "was sufficiently apparent at the time of the revocation hearing to impose upon the court a duty to inquire further." Because "on the record before us, we [could not] be sure whether counsel was influenced in his basic strategic decisions by the interests of the employer who hired him," we remanded for the trial court "to determine whether the conflict of interest that this record strongly suggests actually existed."

Petitioner argues that the remand instruction in *Wood* established an "unambiguous rule" that where the trial judge neglects a duty to inquire into a potential conflict, the defendant, to obtain reversal of the judgment, need only show that his lawyer was subject to a conflict of interest, and need not show that the conflict adversely affected counsel's performance. He relies upon the language in the remand instruction directing the trial court to grant a new revocation hearing if it determines that "an actual conflict of interest existed," without requiring a further determination that the conflict adversely affected counsel's performance. As used in the remand instruction, however, we think "an actual conflict of interest" meant precisely a conflict *that affected counsel's performance* — as opposed to a mere theoretical division of loyalties.

[handwritten margin note: D argues Wood created new rule that only conflict is necc.]

It was shorthand for the statement in *Sullivan* that "a defendant who shows that a conflict of interest *actually affected the adequacy of his representation* need not demonstrate prejudice in order to obtain relief."[20] This is the only interpretation consistent with the *Wood* Court's earlier description of why it could not decide the case without a remand: "On the record before us, we cannot be sure whether counsel *was influenced in his basic strategic decisions* by the interests of the employer who hired him. *If this was the case*, the due process rights of petitioners were not respected . . . ." The notion that *Wood* created a new rule *sub silentio* — and in a case where *certiorari* had been granted on an entirely different question, and the parties had neither briefed nor argued the conflict-of-interest issue — is implausible.[21]

[handwritten margin note: Court says no - it must still have affected the outcome; shorthand]

---

[20] [4] Justice Stevens asserts that this reading (and presumably Justice Souter's reading as well), is wrong; that *Wood* only requires petitioner to show that a real conflict existed, not that it affected counsel's performance. This is so because we "unambiguously stated" that a conviction must be reversed whenever the trial court fails to investigate a potential conflict (citing *Wood* footnote). As we have explained earlier this dictum simply contradicts the remand order in Wood.

[21] [5] We have used "actual conflict of interest" elsewhere to mean what was required to be shown in *Sullivan. See United States v. Cronic*, 466 U.S. 648, 662, n. 31 (1984) ("We have presumed prejudice when counsel labors under an actual conflict of interest . . . . *See Cuyler v. Sullivan*, 446 U.S. 335 (1980)"). And we have used "conflict of interest" to mean a division of loyalties *that affected counsel's performance.* In *Holloway*, 435 U.S. at 482, we described our earlier opinion in *Glasser v. United States*, 315 U.S. 60 (1942), as follows:

> The record disclosed that Stewart failed to cross-examine a Government witness whose testimony linked Glasser with the conspiracy and failed to object to the admission of arguably inadmissible evidence. This failure was viewed by the Court as a result of Stewart's desire to protect Kretske's interests, and was thus "indicative of Stewart's struggle to serve two masters . . . ." After identifying *this conflict of interests*, the Court declined to inquire whether the prejudice flowing from it was harmless and instead ordered Glasser's conviction reversed." (Emphasis added.)

Thus, the *Sullivan* standard is not properly read as requiring inquiry into actual conflict as something

Since this was not a case in which (as in *Holloway*) counsel protested his inability simultaneously to represent multiple defendants; and since the trial court's failure to make the *Sullivan*-mandated inquiry does not reduce the petitioner's burden of proof; it was at least necessary, to void the conviction, for petitioner to establish that the conflict of interest adversely affected his counsel's performance. The Court of Appeals having found no such effect, the denial of habeas relief must be affirmed.

III

Lest today's holding be misconstrued, we note that the only question presented was the effect of a trial court's failure to inquire into a potential conflict upon the *Sullivan* rule that deficient performance of counsel must be shown. The case was presented and argued on the assumption that (absent some exception for failure to inquire) *Sullivan* would be applicable — requiring a showing of defective performance, but *not* requiring in addition (as *Strickland* does in other ineffectiveness-of-counsel cases), a showing of probable effect upon the outcome of trial. That assumption was not unreasonable in light of the holdings of Courts of Appeals, which have applied *Sullivan* "unblinkingly" to "all kinds of alleged attorney ethical conflicts." They have invoked the *Sullivan* standard not only when (as here) there is a conflict rooted in counsel's obligations to *former* clients, but even when representation of the defendant somehow implicates counsel's personal or financial interests, including a book deal, a job with the prosecutor's office, the teaching of classes to Internal Revenue Service agents, a romantic "entanglement" with the prosecutor, or fear of antagonizing the trial judge.

This is not to suggest that one ethical duty is more or less important than another. The purpose of our *Holloway* and *Sullivan* exceptions from the ordinary requirements of *Strickland*, however, is not to enforce the Canons of Legal Ethics, but to apply needed prophylaxis in situations where *Strickland* itself is evidently inadequate to assure vindication of the defendant's Sixth Amendment right to counsel. *See Nix v. Whiteside*, 475 U.S. 157, 165 (1986) ("Breach of an ethical standard does not necessarily make out a denial of the Sixth Amendment guarantee of assistance of counsel"). In resolving this case on the grounds on which it was presented to us, we do not rule upon the need for the *Sullivan* prophylaxis in cases of successive representation. Whether *Sullivan* should be extended to such cases remains, as far as the jurisprudence of this Court is concerned, an open question.

For the reasons stated, the judgment of the Court of Appeals is

Affirmed.

---

separate and apart from adverse effect. An "actual conflict," for Sixth Amendment purposes, is a conflict of interest that adversely affects counsel's performance.

JUSTICE KENNEDY, with whom JUSTICE O'CONNOR joins, concurring. [Omitted. —Ed.]

JUSTICE STEVENS, dissenting.

*   *   *

I

The first critical stage in the defense of a capital case is the series of pretrial meetings between the accused and his counsel when they decide how the case should be defended. A lawyer cannot possibly determine how best to represent a new client unless that client is willing to provide the lawyer with a truthful account of the relevant facts. When an indigent defendant first meets his newly appointed counsel, he will often falsely maintain his complete innocence. Truthful disclosures of embarrassing or incriminating facts are contingent on the development of the client's confidence in the undivided loyalty of the lawyer. Quite obviously, knowledge that the lawyer represented the victim would be a substantial obstacle to the development of such confidence.

It is equally true that a lawyer's decision to conceal such an important fact from his new client would have comparable ramifications. The suppression of communication and truncated investigation that would unavoidably follow from such a decision would also make it difficult, if not altogether impossible, to establish the necessary level of trust that should characterize the "delicacy of relation" between attorney and client.

In this very case, it is likely that Mickens misled his counsel, Bryan Saunders, given the fact that Mickens gave false testimony at his trial denying any involvement in the crime despite the overwhelming evidence that he had killed Timothy Hall after a sexual encounter. In retrospect, it seems obvious that the death penalty might have been avoided by acknowledging Mickens' involvement, but emphasizing the evidence suggesting that their sexual encounter was consensual. Mickens' habeas counsel garnered evidence suggesting that Hall was a male prostitute; that the area where Hall was killed was known for prostitution; and that there was no evidence that Hall was forced to the secluded area where he was ultimately murdered. An unconflicted attorney could have put forward a defense tending to show that Mickens killed Hall only after the two engaged in consensual sex, but Saunders offered no such defense. This was a crucial omission — a finding of forcible sodomy was an absolute prerequisite to Mickens' eligibility for the death penalty. Of course, since that strategy would have led to conviction of a noncapital offense, counsel would have been unable to persuade the defendant to divulge the information necessary to support such a defense and then ultimately to endorse the strategy unless he had earned the complete confidence of his client.

Saunders' concealment of essential information about his prior representation of the victim was a severe lapse in his professional duty. . . .

Mickens' lawyer's violation of this fundamental obligation of disclosure is indefensible. The relevance of Saunders' prior representation of Hall to the new appointment was far too important to be concealed.

II

If the defendant is found guilty of a capital offense, the ensuing proceedings that determine whether he will be put to death are critical in every sense of the word. At those proceedings, testimony about the impact of the crime on the victim, including testimony about the character of the victim, may have a critical effect on the jury's decision. Because a lawyer's fiduciary relationship with his deceased client survives the client's death, Saunders necessarily labored under conflicting obligations that were irreconcilable. He had a duty to protect the reputation and confidences of his deceased client, and a duty to impeach the impact evidence presented by the prosecutor.[22]

Saunders' conflicting obligations to his deceased client, on the one hand, and to his living client, on the other, were unquestionably sufficient to give Mickens the right to insist on different representation.[23] For the "right to counsel guaranteed by the Constitution contemplates the services of an attorney devoted solely to the interests of his client."[24]

* * *

IV

Mickens had a constitutional right to the services of an attorney devoted solely to his interests. That right was violated. The lawyer who did represent him had a duty to disclose his prior representation of the victim to Mickens and to the trial judge. That duty was violated. When Mickens had no counsel, the trial judge had a duty to "make a thorough inquiry and to take all steps necessary to insure the fullest protection of" his right to counsel. Despite knowledge of the lawyer's prior representation, she violated that duty.

We will never know whether Mickens would have received the death penalty if those violations had not occurred nor precisely what effect they had on Saunders' representation of Mickens.[25] We do know that he did not receive the kind of

---

[22] [4] For example, at the time of Hall's death, Saunders was representing Hall in juvenile court for charges arising out of an incident involving Hall's mother. She had sworn out a warrant for Hall's arrest charging him with assault and battery. Despite knowledge of this, Mickens' lawyer offered no rebuttal to the victim-impact statement submitted by Hall's mother that " 'all [she] lived for was that boy.' "

[23] [5] A group of experts in legal ethics, acting as *Amici Curiae*, submit that the conflict in issue in this case would be nonwaivable . . . . Unfortunately, because Mickens was not informed of the fact that his appointed attorney was the lawyer of the alleged victim, the questions whether Mickens would have waived this conflict and consented to the appointment, or whether governing standards of professional responsibility would have precluded him from doing so, remain unanswered.

[24] [6] Although the conflict in this case is plainly intolerable, I, of course, do not suggest that every conflict, or every violation of the code of ethics, is a violation of the Constitution.

[25] [10] I disagree with the Court's assertion that the inquiry mandated by *Cuyler v. Sullivan*, 446 U.S. 335 (1980), will not aid in the determination of conflict and effect. As we have stated, "the evil [of conflict-ridden counsel] is in what the advocate finds himself compelled to *refrain* from doing . . . [making it] difficult to judge intelligently the impact of a conflict on the attorney's representation of a

representation that the Constitution guarantees. If Mickens had been represented by an attorney-impostor who never passed a bar examination, we might also be unable to determine whether the impostor's educational shortcomings " 'actually affected the adequacy of his representation.' " We would, however, surely set aside his conviction if the person who had represented him was not a real lawyer. Four compelling reasons make setting aside the conviction the proper remedy in this case.

First, it is the remedy dictated by our holdings in *Holloway v. Arkansas*, 435 U.S. 475 (1978), *Cuyler v. Sullivan*, 446 U.S. 335 (1980), and *Wood v. Georgia*, 450 U.S. 261 (1981). In this line of precedent, our focus was properly upon the duty of the trial court judge to inquire into a potential conflict. This duty was triggered either via defense counsel's objection, as was the case in *Holloway*, or some other "special circumstances" whereby the serious potential for conflict was brought to the attention of the trial court judge. As we unambiguously stated in *Wood*, "*Sullivan mandates* a reversal when the trial court has failed to make an inquiry even though it 'knows or reasonably should know that a particular conflict exists.' " It is thus wrong for the Court to interpret Justice Powell's language as referring only to a division of loyalties "that affected counsel's performance."[26] *Wood* nowhere hints of this meaning of "actual conflict of interest," nor does it reference *Sullivan* in "shorthand." Rather, *Wood* cites *Sullivan* explicitly in order to make a factual distinction: In a circumstance, such as in *Wood*, in which the judge knows or should know of the conflict, no showing of adverse effect is required. But when, as in *Sullivan*, the judge lacked this knowledge, such a showing is required.[27]

---

client." *Holloway v. Arkansas*, 435 U.S. 475, 490-491 (1978). An adequate inquiry by the appointing or trial court judge will augment the record thereby making it easier to evaluate the impact of the conflict.

[26] [11] The Court concedes that if Mickens' attorney had objected to the appointment based upon the conflict of interest and the trial court judge had failed to inquire, then reversal without inquiry into adverse effect would be required. The Court, in addition to ignoring the mandate of *Wood*, reads *Sullivan* too narrowly. In *Sullivan* we did not ask *only* whether an objection was made in order to ascertain whether the trial court had a duty to inquire. Rather, we stated that nothing in the circumstances of this case indicates that the trial court had a duty to inquire whether there was a conflict of interest. The provision of separate trials for Sullivan and his codefendants significantly reduced the potential for a divergence in their interests. No participant in Sullivan's trial ever objected to the multiple representation . . . . On these facts, we conclude that the Sixth Amendment imposed upon the trial court no affirmative duty to inquire into the propriety of multiple representation.

It is also counter to our precedent to treat all Sixth Amendment challenges involving conflicts of interest categorically, without inquiry into the surrounding factual circumstances. In *Cronic*, we cited *Holloway* as an *example* of a case involving "surrounding circumstances [making] it so unlikely that any lawyer could provide effective assistance that ineffectiveness was properly presumed without inquiry into actual performance at trial." The surrounding circumstances in the present case were far more egregious than those requiring reversal in either *Holloway* or *Wood*.

[27] [12] Because the appointing judge knew of the conflict, there is no need in this case to decide what should be done when the judge neither knows, nor should know, about the existence of an intolerable conflict. Nevertheless the Court argues that it makes little sense to reverse automatically upon a showing of actual conflict when the trial court judge knows (or reasonably should know) of a potential conflict and yet has failed to inquire, but *not* to do so when the trial court judge does not know of the conflict. Although it is true that the defendant faces the same potential for harm as a result of a conflict in either instance, in the former case the court committed the error and in the latter the harm is entirely attributable to the misconduct of defense counsel. A requirement that the defendant show adverse effect when the court committed no error surely does not justify such a requirement when the court did err.

Second, it is the only remedy that responds to the real possibility that Mickens would not have received the death penalty if he had been represented by conflict-free counsel during the critical stage of the proceeding in which he first met with his lawyer. We should presume that the lawyer for the victim of a brutal homicide is incapable of establishing the kind of relationship with the defendant that is essential to effective representation.

Third, it is the only remedy that is consistent with the legal profession's historic and universal condemnation of the representation of conflicting interests without the full disclosure and consent of all interested parties. The Court's novel and naive assumption that a lawyer's divided loyalties are acceptable unless it can be proved that they actually affected counsel's performance is demeaning to the profession.

Finally, "justice must satisfy the appearance of justice." *Offutt v. United States*, 348 U.S. 11, 14 (1954). Setting aside Mickens' conviction is the only remedy that can maintain public confidence in the fairness of the procedures employed in capital cases. Death is a different kind of punishment from any other that may be imposed in this country. "From the point of view of the defendant, it is different in both its severity and its finality. From the point of view of society, the action of the sovereign in taking the life of one of its citizens also differs dramatically from any other legitimate state action. It is of vital importance to the defendant and to the community that any decision to impose the death sentence be, and appear to be, based on reason rather than caprice or emotion." A rule that allows the State to foist a murder victim's lawyer onto his accused is not only capricious; it poisons the integrity of our adversary system of justice.

I respectfully dissent.

JUSTICE SOUTER, dissenting.

[After summarizing prior cases and the majority opinion, JUSTICE SOUTER continued. —Ed.]

II

Since the majority will not leave the law as it is, however, the question is whether there is any merit in the rule it now adopts, of treating breaches of a judge's duty to enquire into prospective conflicts differently depending on whether defense counsel explicitly objected. There is not. The distinction is irrational on its face, it creates a scheme of incentives to judicial vigilance that is weakest in those cases presenting the greatest risk of conflict and unfair trial, and it reduces the so-called judicial duty to enquire into so many empty words.

The most obvious reason to reject the majority's rule starts with the accepted view that a trial judge placed on notice of a risk of prospective conflict has an obligation then and there to do something about it. The majority does not expressly

---

It is the Court's rule that leads to an anomalous result. Under the Court's analysis, if defense counsel objects to the appointment, reversal without inquiry into adverse effect is required. But counsel's failure to object posed a greater — not a lesser — threat to Mickens' Sixth Amendment right. Had Saunders objected to the appointment, Mickens would at least have been apprised of the conflict.

repudiate that duty, which is too clear for cavil. It should go without saying that the best time to deal with a known threat to the basic guarantee of fair trial is before the trial has proceeded to become unfair. It would be absurd, after all, to suggest that a judge should sit quiescent in the face of an apparent risk that a lawyer's conflict will render representation illusory and the formal trial a waste of time, emotion, and a good deal of public money. And as if that were not bad enough, a failure to act early raises the specter, confronted by the *Holloway* Court, that failures on the part of conflicted counsel will elude demonstration after the fact, simply because they so often consist of what did not happen. While a defendant can fairly be saddled with the characteristically difficult burden of proving adverse effects of conflicted decisions after the fact when the judicial system was not to blame in tolerating the risk of conflict, the burden is indefensible when a judge was on notice of the risk but did nothing.

With so much at stake, why should it matter how a judge learns whatever it is that would point out the risk to anyone paying attention? Of course an objection from a conscientious lawyer suffices to put a court on notice, as it did in *Holloway*; and probably in the run of multiple-representation cases nothing short of objection will raise the specter of trouble. But sometimes a wide-awake judge will not need any formal objection to see a risk of conflict, as the federal habeas court's finding in this very case shows. Why, then, pretend contrary to fact that a judge can never perceive a risk unless a lawyer points it out? Why excuse a judge's breach of judicial duty just because a lawyer has fallen down in his own ethics or is short on competence? Transforming the factually sufficient trigger of a formal objection into a legal necessity for responding to any breach of judicial duty is irrational.

Nor is that irrationality mitigated by the Government's effort to analogize the majority's objection requirement to the general rule that in the absence of plain error litigants get no relief from error without objection. The Government as *amicus* argues for making a formal objection crucial because judges are not the only ones obliged to take care for the integrity of the system; defendants and their counsel need inducements to help the courts with timely warnings. The fallacy of the Government's argument, however, has been on the books since *Wood* was decided. *See* 450 U.S. at 265, n. 5 ("It is unlikely that [the lawyer on whom the conflict of interest charge focused] would concede that he had continued improperly to act as counsel"). The objection requirement works elsewhere because the objecting lawyer believes that he sights an error being committed by the judge or opposing counsel. That is hardly the motive to depend on when the risk of error, if there is one, is being created by the lawyer himself in acting subject to a risk of conflict. The law on conflicted counsel has to face the fact that one of our leading cases arose after a trial in which counsel may well have kept silent about conflicts not out of obtuseness or inattention, but for the sake of deliberately favoring a third party's interest over the clients, and this very case comes to us with reason to suspect that Saunders suppressed his conflicts for the sake of a second fee in a case getting public attention. While the perceptive and conscientious lawyer (as in *Holloway*) needs nothing more than ethical duty to induce an objection, the venal lawyer is not apt to be reformed by a general rule that says his client will have an easier time reversing a conviction down the road if the lawyer calls attention to his own venality.

I respectfully dissent.[28]

JUSTICE BREYER, with whom JUSTICE GINSBURG joins, dissenting.

The Commonwealth of Virginia seeks to put the petitioner, Walter Mickens, Jr., to death after having appointed to represent him as his counsel a lawyer who, at the time of the murder, was representing the very person Mickens was accused of killing. I believe that, in a case such as this one, a categorical approach is warranted and automatic reversal is required. To put the matter in language this Court has previously used: By appointing this lawyer to represent Mickens, the Commonwealth created a "structural defect affecting the framework within which the trial [and sentencing] proceeds, rather than simply an error in the trial process itself." *Arizona v. Fulminante*, 499 U.S. 279, 310 (1991).

The parties spend a great deal of time disputing how this Court's precedents of *Holloway v. Arkansas*, 435 U.S. 475 (1978), *Cuyler v. Sullivan*, 446 U.S. 335 (1980), and *Wood v. Georgia*, 450 U.S. 261 (1981), resolve the case. Those precedents involve the significance of a trial judge's "failure to inquire" if that judge "knew or should have known" of a "potential" conflict. The majority and dissenting opinions dispute the meaning of these cases as well. Although I express no view at this time about how our precedents should treat *most* ineffective-assistance-of-counsel claims involving an alleged conflict of interest (or, for that matter, whether *Holloway*, *Sullivan*, and *Wood* provide a sensible or coherent framework for dealing with those cases at all), I am convinced that *this* case is not governed by those precedents, for the following reasons.

First, this is the kind of representational incompatibility that is egregious on its face. Mickens was represented by the murder victim's lawyer; that lawyer had represented the victim on a criminal matter; and that lawyer's representation of the victim had continued until one business day before the lawyer was appointed to represent the defendant.

Second, the conflict is exacerbated by the fact that it occurred in a capital murder case. In a capital case, the evidence submitted by both sides regarding the victim's

---

28 [13] Whether adverse effect was shown was not the question accepted, and I will not address the issue beyond noting that the case for an adverse effect appears compelling in at least two respects. Before trial, Saunders admittedly failed even to discuss with Mickens a trial strategy of reasonable doubt about the forcible sex element, without which death was not a sentencing option. In that vein, Saunders apparently failed to follow leads by looking for evidence that the victim had engaged in prostitution, even though the victim's body was found on a mattress in an area where illicit sex was common. There may be doubt whether these failures were the result of incompetence or litigation strategy rather than a conflicting duty of loyalty to the victim or to self to avoid professional censure for failing to disclose the conflict risk to Mickens (though strategic choice seems unlikely given that Saunders did not even raise the possibility of a consent defense as an option to be considered). But there is little doubt as to the course of the second instance of alleged adverse effect: Saunders knew for a fact that the victim's mother had initiated charges of assault and battery against her son just before he died because Saunders had been appointed to defend him on those very charges. Yet Saunders did nothing to counter the mother's assertion in the post-trial victim-impact statement given to the trial judge that " 'all [she] lived for was that boy.' " Saunders could not have failed to see that the mother's statement should be rebutted, and there is no apparent explanation for his failure to offer the rebuttal he knew, except that he had obtained the information as the victim's counsel and subject to an obligation of confidentiality.

character may easily tip the scale of the jury's choice between life or death. Yet even with extensive investigation in post-trial proceedings, it will often prove difficult, if not impossible, to determine whether the prior representation affected defense counsel's decisions regarding, for example: which avenues to take when investigating the victim's background; which witnesses to call; what type of impeachment to undertake; which arguments to make to the jury; what language to use to characterize the victim; and, as a general matter, what basic strategy to adopt at the sentencing stage. Given the subtle forms that prejudice might take, the consequent difficulty of proving actual prejudice, and the significant likelihood that it will nonetheless occur when the same lawyer represents both accused killer and victim, the cost of litigating the existence of actual prejudice in a particular case cannot be easily justified.

Third, the Commonwealth itself *created* the conflict in the first place. Indeed, it was the *same judge* who dismissed the case against the victim who then appointed the victim's lawyer to represent Mickens one business day later. In light of the judge's active role in bringing about the incompatible representation, I am not sure why the concept of a judge's "duty to inquire" is thought to be central to this case. No "inquiry" by the trial judge could have shed more light on the conflict than was obvious on the face of the matter, namely, that the lawyer who would represent Mickens today is the same lawyer who yesterday represented Mickens' alleged victim in a criminal case.

This kind of breakdown in the criminal justice system creates, at a minimum, the appearance that the proceeding will not " 'reliably serve its function as a vehicle for determination of guilt or innocence,' " and the resulting " 'criminal punishment' " will not " 'be regarded as fundamentally fair.' " This appearance, together with the likelihood of prejudice in the typical case, are serious enough to warrant a categorical rule — a rule that does not require proof of prejudice in the individual case.

The Commonwealth complains that this argument "relies heavily on the immediate visceral impact of learning that a lawyer previously represented the victim of his current client." And that is so. The "visceral impact," however, arises out of the obvious, unusual nature of the conflict. It arises from the fact that the Commonwealth seeks to execute a defendant, having provided that defendant with a lawyer who, only yesterday, represented the victim. In my view, to carry out a death sentence so obtained would invariably "diminish faith" in the fairness and integrity of our criminal justice system. That is to say, it would diminish that public confidence in the criminal justice system upon which the successful functioning of that system continues to depend.

I therefore dissent.

MARICOPA COUNTY PUBLIC DEFENDER'S OFFICE v. SUPERIOR COURT
927 P.2d 822 (Ariz. Ct. App. 1996)

The guarantees of the Sixth Amendment include the right to an attorney with undivided loyalty. *See Holloway v. Arkansas*, 435 U.S. 475, 481-82 (1978); *State v. Davis*, 110 Ariz. 29, 31, 514 P.2d 1025, 1027 (1973). Counsel must be free to zealously defend the accused in a conflict-free environment.

The Maricopa County Public Defender's Office has adopted "Conflict of Interest Guidelines" which we will refer to as its "conflicts policy." The current version of this policy became effective on January 4, 1994, and was followed by the deputy public defenders assigned to represent Nelson and Rangel. The public defender's conflicts policy provides, in part, as follows:

IV. FORMER CLIENTS AS WITNESSES

Former representation of a potential witness against a present client is not, in itself, grounds for disqualification. If representation of the former client has resulted in information that is 1) substantially related to the present case, 2) materially adverse to the interests of the former client, and 3) not contained in easily accessible public records, the office should move to withdraw.

. . . .

VI. PROCEDURES FOR DETERMINING CONFLICT

As soon as possible after assignment, the attorney should review all charging documents, police reports, and other available records for potential conflicts of interest. . . .

If a former client is identified [by an office records check], the attorney should examine the case file to determine whether confidential information exists . . . . If the attorney who previously represented the former client is still with the office, the attorney should be contacted to determine whether the attorney is aware of confidential information.

VII. SUPERIOR COURT CONFLICTS OF INTEREST

When an attorney identifies a conflict of interest in superior court, the attorney must complete the potential conflict of interest portion of the Conflict Check and Supervisor Review Form and submit it to the attorney's supervisor for approval before moving to withdraw. If the supervisor does not approve the request, the attorney may request a review by the Chief Trial Deputy or Juvenile Division Supervisor. If the request is approved, the attorney should immediately move to withdraw. The motion to withdraw must thoroughly state the reasons for withdrawal while protecting confidential client information.

Some may question why the public defender's conflicts policy requires defendant's counsel to talk with the former client's counsel and review the former client's file rather than to "screen" herself from both, but we find this action a prudent exercise of professional responsibility. It is certain that a percentage of cases assigned to the public defender will involve conflicts of interest. Those conflicts should be discovered immediately, for they will come out inevitably. The earlier a conflict of interest is discovered and dealt with, the less damage it can do.

Some law firms have the structure and resources to screen attorneys from conflicts of interest, but the record contains no suggestion that the public defender can do so. In any event, public defender screening of conflicts might cost the criminal justice system more than it would save. The actions and inactions of deputy public defenders are occasionally questioned by clients, and screening of public defender conflicts would be a source of pre-trial and post-trial litigation, with all its attendant costs.

In the interest of clarity and brevity, we focus on just two leading cases, *Holloway* and *Davis*, and we refer those interested in a broader discussion to Gary T. Lowenthal, *Successive Representation by Criminal Lawyers*, 93 YALE L.J. 1 (1983), and Bruce A. Green, *"Through a Glass, Darkly": How the Court Sees Motions to Disqualify Criminal Defense Lawyers*, 89 COLUM. L. REV. 1201 (1989). *Holloway* and *Davis* involved counsel who represented codefendants, but we find them instructive here as well. We apply the following principles from *Davis* to motions to withdraw based on conflicts between the interests of current and former clients:

> An attorney representing two defendants in a criminal matter is in the best position professionally and ethically to determine when a conflict of interest exists or will probably develop in the course of a trial. He has an obligation to bring the fact of this conflict to the attention of the court at the earliest possible time after the conflict is discovered. The trial court should give great weight to a representation by counsel that there is a conflict, particularly in the case where the counsel has been appointed by the court rather than retained by the defendants.

Holloway expanded upon *Davis* and explained why counsel's avowal of an ethical conflict requiring withdrawal is entitled to great weight despite the concern that some might abuse this trust:

> [A]ttorneys are officers of the court, and " 'when they address the judge solemnly upon a matter before the court, their declarations are virtually made under oath.' " . . .

g. Lawyer for an Organization

A lawyer who represents an organization, such as a corporation, a labor union, or a public interest organization, represents the organization, not its officers. At times, the interests of the organization and its officers may converge. Under such circumstances, a lawyer may represent both the organization and its officers, but the lawyer must withdraw if the interests of the organization and the officers diverge. MR 1.13.

Milton C. Regan, Jr., *Professional Responsibility and the Corporate Lawyer*
13 GEO. J. LEGAL ETHICS 197 (2000)[29]

I. THE WORLD OF CORPORATE PRACTICE

*   *   *

Aside from the importance of corporate practice for the ways in which modern legal services are provided, certain features of that practice are notable for the important ethical issues that they raise. First are the complexities of representing an organization rather than an individual. That undertaking can be especially challenging because ethical provisions for the most part implicitly are premised on a relationship between an attorney and an individual client. The lawyer who represents a corporation represents an abstraction: her client is the corporate entity rather than any of the individuals who act on its behalf. Such lawyers deal daily with managers and officials who are authorized to speak for the corporation, yet they must not mistake those individuals for the entity itself. Even in the normal course of events, actors in a large organization may not be in full agreement on various matters. Lines of authority are not always clear; the organization chart may obscure as much as reveal who wields power and influence. The lawyer thus often must become familiar with the dynamics of the bureaucratic milieu in order to discern just which actors speak for the corporation on what issues.

The difficulty is compounded when there is reason to question whether an official is acting in the best interests of the corporation. Ethical provisions, along with the business judgment rule, suggest that the lawyer should defer to the manager in most instances, even when she might have charted a different course under the circumstances. That presumption of deference evaporates, however, when the lawyer knows that a corporate official is violating a duty to the entity or is acting illegally so as to threaten the corporation with serious harm. The problem is that this transformative moment can be quite difficult to recognize. One reason is that knowledge often is fragmented in large modern organizations. Information sufficient to ensure that a lawyer "knows" of misconduct may be scattered among several offices and people, no one of whom has the complete picture. It is tempting in such situations to conclude that one lacks the certitude necessary to challenge the corporate decisionmaker, even when such ignorance is the product of diligent avoidance of unpleasant facts.

Even if a lawyer for the corporation concludes that sufficiently serious misconduct is occurring, ethical rules generally give her little concrete guidance about what to do. Model Rule 1.13, typical of many state provisions, directs the lawyer to "proceed as is reasonably necessary in the best interest of the organization." Comments to the rule state that doing so may involve review of the matter by "a higher authority in the organization." They also caution, however, that there should be "[c]lear justification" for taking such a step, and indicate that only in "an extreme case" should the lawyer bring the matter to the attention of the highest authority

---

[29] Copyright © 2000 by the Georgetown Journal of Legal Ethics; Milton C. Regan, Jr.

only in extreme case should lawyer take to org. Auth.?

in the organization. Such ambiguity not only makes charting a course of action difficult. It also creates the risk that the lawyer ultimately will be accused of negligence in representing the entity. Even if taking certain steps were permissive rather than mandatory under state ethical rules, one may claim with the benefit of hindsight that a reasonable lawyer under the circumstances would have taken them. Indeed, even a lawyer who has been deliberately misled by a client may be found liable in some circumstances for failing to undertake her own independent investigation of the facts notwithstanding the client's repeated assurances.

In sum, it is increasingly the case that lawyers in many kinds of modern practice represent organizations rather than individuals. Such a phenomenon calls for a more sophisticated understanding of the organizational milieu and the distinctive ethical issues that it generates. Corporate lawyers have significant experience with such representation, and often are acutely aware of how little guidance ethical rules can provide in this setting. A focus on corporate practice thus can generate insights that are becoming important for an ever larger proportion of lawyers.

A second disjunction between corporate practice and ethical rules is the fact that the latter traditionally have been formulated primarily with the litigator in mind. Yet transactional work, a staple of corporate practice, raises questions that do not always fit easily within this paradigm. Should a party with whom the lawyer is negotiating a joint venture, for instance, be regarded more as an adversary or as a cooperative partner? The answer may be important in determining the attorney's duty of confidentiality, as well as in identifying conflicts of interest that could arise from simultaneous or successive representation of other clients.

Similarly, should the fact that business negotiations typically take place outside the supervision of a court place a greater or lesser responsibility on lawyer and client to disclose information that other parties might regard as relevant to the negotiations? Litigation is marked by both judicial oversight and relatively stringent disclosure duties because of concern about the integrity of legal proceedings. By contrast, disclosure obligations are relatively relaxed in transactional settings, despite the absence of any constraining judicial involvement. They are based primarily on common law fraud standards, which in turn look to conventional expectations of typical parties engaged in negotiation. Yet reliance solely on such expectations as the touchstone of legality has the potential to create a downward spiral, as aggressive practices provoke even more aggressive responses. The cumulative effect may be to lower expectations of fair dealing, increase bargaining costs, and secure judicial validation of provisions formerly regarded as unenforceable. Corporate lawyers historically have had to navigate the transactional terrain with minimal guidance from ethical rules. This does not mean, however, that the ethical issues that arise in this form of practice are of negligible importance. Rather, it highlights the fact that law practice requires a cultivated sense of judgment that goes beyond mere rule compliance.

A third notable dimension of corporate practice is the fact that many corporate lawyers not only represent organizations, but are employed by them. The widely-noted rise in the visibility and prestige of inside counsel in the last two decades or so has fueled the continuing debate over the meaning of lawyers' professional independence. Here again, corporate lawyers have firsthand experience with a growing phenomenon: the increasing number of lawyers who are employees in various types of organizations. To what extent is it possible to preserve a sense of identification with a distinct professional legal culture while being immersed in an organizational culture as well? Is it easier to invoke ethical constraints on company conduct if the lawyer is familiar with corporate operations and is regarded as a member of the "team?" Or does her dependence on a single client who is her employer tend to make her excessively deferential toward company officials?

Many lawyers and commentators suggest that in-house counsel are in a position to provide a unique combination of business and legal advice that helps the organization plan for, rather than simply react to, a tumultuous global economy. Rather than merely passing judgment on the legality of measures that management proposes, counsel help frame strategy with an eye toward anticipating and preventing legal issues from arising in the first place. This "proactive" approach to practice expands the boundaries of legal practice to include functions not traditionally characterized as strictly legal in nature. It also calls into question the traditional assumption that the client determines the ends of representation and the lawyer selects the means to achieve those ends. This dichotomy generally is an important premise of ethical rules, which conceptualize the lawyer as distant from the substantive objectives of the client. If in-house counsel do indeed become integrally involved in formulating company goals and structuring company operations, it may be unrealistic to insist they nonetheless remain legal technicians morally unaccountable for the consequences of those activities.

* * *

Corporate lawyers also tend to be in the vanguard of another emerging trend in legal practice: the subjection of lawyers to multiple sources of ethical governance. The pervasiveness of government regulation in the modern economy, the vast increase in the scope of corporate enterprise and activities, and an era of relatively modest regulatory enforcement resources have led to demands that lawyers be more attentive to the social impact of their clients' activities. One example of this is the subjection of lawyers to liability to clients under common law theories such as malpractice and breach of fiduciary duty, with ethical rules treated as evidence relevant to the issue of the propriety of an attorney's conduct. In addition, lawyers increasingly are potentially subject to liability to non-clients in actions such as suits for negligent misrepresentation. Given the number and interdependence of parties in modern business transactions, and the often plausible claims of reasonable reliance on the lawyer's work, the circle of those who are able to bring actions against corporate attorneys may well continue to widen.

Furthermore, regulatory agencies have steadfastly insisted that state ethical rules are not the sole set of standards to which attorneys must conform. The Securities and Exchange Commission has brought enforcement actions on the basis of its authority to govern the conduct of lawyers that practice before it. In doing so, it has suggested, for instance, that lawyers may have an obligation to prevent a client from consummating a transaction as to which there has been insufficient disclosure. It also has concluded that a lawyer under some circumstances may be held responsible for failing to take steps to prevent a recurrence of illegal activity by company employees. The Office of Thrift Supervision has brought charges alleging that a law firm assumed the regulatory compliance and disclosure duties of its federally insured thrift institution by interposing itself between the client and the regulatory agency. Tax lawyers are subject to a more stringent standard of good faith in presenting client positions than are other lawyers. Finally, bankruptcy rules may impose stricter disclosure requirements than ethical rules regarding potential conflicts of interest, and failure to comply with them may subject a lawyer to criminal prosecution. The fact that corporate lawyers are strategically placed in positions of influence with respect to regulated activities has led some to maintain that they have an obligation to serve as "gatekeepers" who restrain misconduct or even "whistleblowers" who report it. Such roles are in tension with the notion that the attorney's sole obligation is to the client, and the claim that self-regulation by the legal profession offers the best assurance of ethical legal practice.

*   *   *

III. CONCLUSION

[T]the ethical issues involved in corporate representation often require us to address fundamental questions about the roles that lawyers play and the obligations to which they are held. Indeed, as I have suggested, the tranformative character of corporate enterprise virtually guarantees that corporate lawyers perpetually will be facing dilemmas for which our existing professional responsibility framework provides imperfect guidance.

D.   IMPUTED DISQUALIFICATION

PROBLEM 5-3

Rogers, Rogers, Moore and Rogers has its main office in New York and branch offices in 10 other cities, including Orlando. In Orlando, Perry Morris does routine corporate work for Motofoto, a small entity that owns and operates one-hour photo finishing kiosks in shopping center parking lots. Motofoto is a very modest subsidiary of VeryCorp., a sprawling corporate entity with holdings in a wide variety of industries. Mark Rogers of the New York office is approached by a representative of a major international organization that proposes to make a takeover offer to VeryCorp. Rogers very much wants to undertake this representation. What, if any, options does Rogers have that would allow the representation to go forward?

As a general rule, when a lawyer has a conflict of interest, that conflict imputes to (transfers to, extends to) all of the lawyers in the law organization (usually a law firm) in which the lawyer works. MR 1.10 and 1.8(k). This imputed disqualification rule is mainly based on the notion that confidential information possessed by one lawyer is effectively possessed by all lawyers in the same firm. In addition, loyalty and appearance of impropriety concerns arise when one lawyer in a firm engages in representation from which another lawyer in the firm would be disqualified for conflict of interests reasons.

Ethics 2000 Commission, February 2002 ABA
Amendment to Model Rules

Model Rules 1.8 and 1.10(a), Imputed Disqualification

Some of the imputed disqualification changes in Model Rules 1.8 and 1.10 must be read together. Under former rule 1.10, the only rule 1.8 conflicts that produced imputed disqualification were those under MR 1.8(c), the gifts to lawyers rule. The amended rule 1.10, while continuing to identify conflicts under MR 1.7 and 1.9 as those that produce imputed disqualification, defers to MR 1.8 for determinations regarding imputation of conflicts from MR 1.8 events. See MR 1.10, Comment 8. Amended MR 1.8, in a new section (k), states that all MR 1.8 prohibited transactions, except for the new prohibition on lawyer-client sexual relationships in MR 1.8(j), produce imputed disqualification, not merely those under MR 1.8(c) as was the former rule under MR 1.10. As such, under amended rules 1.8(k) and 1.10(a), prohibited transactions under the following rules now produce imputed disqualification analysis:

   1.8(a), business transactions;

   1.8(b), use of confidential information;

   1.8(d), media rights agreements;

   1.8(e), financial assistance in litigation;

   1.8(f), third party compensation;

   1.8(g), aggregate settlements;

   1.8(h), prospective and other settlement of claims against the lawyer;

   1.8(i), acquisition of interest in litigation.

There may be less change in this reconfiguration than first appears for three reasons. First, several of the MR 1.8 sections in the run of instances regulate more than they prohibit transactions. Before imputed disqualification is to occur, an individual lawyer in the firm or other organization must be disqualified. Some of the MR 1.8 restrictions are quite unlikely to produce the initial disqualification from which the imputed disqualification might emerge. MR 1.8(a) and (h), in particular, seem highly unlikely to produce disqualification in some representation based on what is likely to have been a violation of their terms in some other, former transaction. Second, some of the rules that have a conflicts rationale and might produce disqualification are only modestly or at best partly conflicts based and should not routinely produce disqualification of the initial lawyer. Model Rules 1.8(e) and (i), for example, are only partly based on conflicts rationales. Both rules are predominantly based on the common law champerty and maintenance doctrines and historically were more fundamentally anticompetitive, client-getting prohibitions than they were conflicts rules. Disqualification of the offending lawyer has been held, in a well-reasoned decision, to be an inappropriate remedy for a violation of MR 1.8(e). *Shade v. Great Lakes Dredge & Dock Co.*, 72 F. Supp. 2d 518 (E.D. Pa. 1999). If the initial lawyer is not to be disqualified, no imputed disqualification, issue ever arises. Third, the newly covered MR 1.8 sections that are more arguably largely conflicts based, and that might well result in a disqualification, may always have produced MR 1.7 conflicts as well and thus the events that gave rise to the 1.8 violations have already been producing imputed disqualification analysis under the former MR 1.10 because of the MR 1.7 coverage.

Amended rule 1.10 now states that disqualification of a lawyer does not impute to the firm when the disqualification "is based on a personal interest of the prohibited lawyer and does not present a significant risk of materially limiting the representation of the client by the remaining members of the firm." The Comment uses as illustrations contrasting examples of a lawyer's disqualifying political beliefs, from which imputation should not arise, and a lawyer's ownership of an opposing party, from which imputed disqualification should arise. *See* Comment 3. The examples may be too far apart for guidance to emerge. Both of the illustrated interests are personal to the affected lawyer, one being financial and the other intensely belief-based, producing for such a lawyer an inability to provide competent representation for a client. The financial interest illustrated is so grave that it probably produces a non-consentable conflict for the affected lawyer under MR 1.7. The Comment leaves a wide gap between which states considering adoption of the 2002 amendments and eventually the courts will have considerable work filling.

Finally, in a new Comment 4, the drafters suggest that conflicts of non-lawyer firm personnel and those of law students who have subsequently become licensed and members of the firm, do not produce imputed disqualification. The latter suggestion will undoubtedly cheer law students as well as those who hire them and must be concerned about their varied pre-licensure employment. The Comment reminds, however, that even non-lawyer personnel and lawyers with pre-licensure conflicts must be screened from the matter in order that the conflicts not impute to the firm.

Motions to disqualify counsel, and entire law firms for which the disqualified lawyer works, have become a favored tactical device in litigation, effectively denying an opposing party her counsel of choice and preserving the integrity of the justice system from the threat of conflicts of interest. The increasing movement of lawyers from one practice setting to another, from one law firm to another, has dramatically increased the frequency and impact of imputed disqualification rules. A minority but increasing number of courts, supported by Model Rules 1.10, 1.11, and 1.12, have ruled that effective screening procedures will prevent the application of the imputed disqualification rules. Some courts have labeled these screening procedures the "Chinese Wall" defense, because of the walling off of the affected lawyer. Under such procedures, the conflicted lawyer is isolated from other lawyers in the organization by various devices including, for example, the following.

> *Don't talk*: The firm's lawyers are prohibited from speaking with the conflicted lawyer about the particular matter.

> *No pay*: The conflicted lawyer is denied any remuneration from the firm's profits that are attributable to the particular matter.

Lock it up: The files from the particular matter are kept in locked file cabinets to which the conflicted lawyer has no access.

Move him out: When that matter is significant and long-term, the conflicted lawyer's office may be moved to a location away from the lawyers working on the matter.

Ethics 2000 Commission, February 2002 ABA Amendment to Model Rules

Model Rule 1.0(k), "Screened"

In the context of imputed disqualification, a definition for the term "screened" is now provided in the rules. The focus of the definition is on the protection of confidentiality, leaving no new guidance on imputed conflict questions that involve the conflicted lawyer's personal interests and therefore his use of influence on colleagues. In other respects, the definition is unremarkable and consistent with case-law that has developed in the area. Nonetheless, the inclusion of this definition in the rule language itself may eventually be consequential in states that have yet to recognize the utility of screening in imputed disqualification settings.

HAAGEN-DAZS CO. v. PERCHE NO! GELATO, INC.
639 F. Supp. 282 (N.D. Cal. 1986)

Opinion and Order Re Disqualification of Counsel

[For the facts of this case, review *supra* § [C][3][f].]

*   *   *

[In addition to seeking the disqualification of Mr. Jesse,] they also seek an order disqualifying the Gray firm. In addition, they claim that, due to the longstanding affiliation of the Gray firm with Double Rainbow's San Francisco counsel, Alioto & Alioto ("Alioto"), that firm must also be disqualified from participation in this litigation.

[After determining that Mr. Jesse should be disqualified, the court continued. —Ed.]

V.

The court must then consider whether Mr. Jesse's present employer, the Gray firm, should be disqualified from this litigation.

The Ninth Circuit has ruled that an entire law firm must be disqualified when one of its members was counsel for an adverse party in a substantially related matter. *Trone*, 621 F.2d at 999. Disciplinary Rule 5-105(d) of the Model Code states:

> . . . if a lawyer is required to decline employment or to withdraw from employment under a Disciplinary Rule, no partner, or associate, or any

other lawyer affiliated with him or his firm, may accept or continue such employment.

ABA Model Code of Professional Responsibility, DR 5-105(d)(1979).

Since the court has concluded that Mr. Jesse must be disqualified, it follows under the rule set forth in the *Trone* case and the Model rule that the law firm of Gray, Plant, Mooty, Mooty & Bennett must also be disqualified from further representation in this litigation.

The Gray firm has argued that its disqualification is not mandated because it instituted a screening procedure whereby all files and information relating to this litigation were sealed off from Mr. Jesse. The Ninth Circuit has considered this so-called "Chinese Wall" defense twice, but has left open the question whether such a screening procedure is sufficient to defeat a disqualification motion when a member of the firm has previously worked on matters substantially related to the pending litigation. Other courts have found such screening procedures to be acceptable under certain circumstances. *See, e.g., Armstrong v. McAlpin*, 625 F.2d 433, 442-44 (2d Cir. 1980) (en banc) vacated on other grounds, 449 U.S. 1106 (1981).[30] At the least, the burden is shifted to the law firm to establish the effectiveness of its "Chinese Wall" procedures.

[handwritten margin note: Chinese wall.]

In this case, it appears that the Gray firm did not institute the "Chinese Wall" measures until after the first of these suits had been filed. The record discloses that Mr. Jesse joined the Gray firm in November 1984. The Gray firm was first contacted concerning the litigation in August, 1985. The complaint was filed on August 30, 1985. Haagen-Dazs then requested that the Gray firm disqualify itself on or about October 30, 1985. On November 6, 1985, the Gray firm instituted its screening procedures. In light of the fact that the screening procedures were not instituted until after the litigation commenced, and one year after Mr. Jesse's employment, the court concludes that Double Rainbow's "Chinese Wall" defense will not insulate the firm from disqualification.

[handwritten margin note: only after suit.]

Further, Pillsbury and Haagen-Dazs have demonstrated that the interests of those clients would be adversely affected by Gray's continued representation. However, Double Rainbow has not demonstrated that it will suffer any material adverse consequences as a result of Gray's disqualification.

VI.

Haagen-Dazs and Pillsbury argue that the Gray firm and the Alioto firm have a long-standing relationship "characterized by continuous exchange of information, strategy and advice," and that the Alioto firm must therefore be disqualified on the basis of its affiliation with the Gray firm.

The record discloses that Double Rainbow and Two Count Inc., the distributor

---

[30] [5] The Armstrong court found that screening procedures were effective in the context of a firm employing a former government attorney. There, the court endorsed the "Chinese Wall" defense at least in part because of its concern that the government should maintain its ability to recruit highly qualified lawyers for public service. Such a policy consideration is not applicable in this case.

involved in the related state court action, are clients of the Alioto firm. The Gray firm was retained by Alioto to assist in this litigation, and the Gray firm currently works with Alioto on this and approximately ten other cases. The fee arrangement between the firms is that Alioto compensates the Gray firm for fees it generates, and the clients, Double Rainbow and Two Count, Inc., compensate the Alioto firm.

In evaluating the association of these two firms, the court notes that there is nothing on the record to suggest that Mr. Jesse had any direct contact with the Alioto firm. Rather, Haagen-Dazs seeks to disqualify Alioto by imputing knowledge gained from Mr. Jesse's prior employment, through Gray to the Alioto firm. Additionally, Haagen-Dazs has argued that Mr. Jesse's prior employment has created an appearance of impropriety which may extend to the relationship between the Gray firm and Alioto.

However, on the basis of the record, the court finds that while the two firms have worked together on this and other litigation, the association between Alioto & Alioto and the Gray firm does not warrant disqualification of the Alioto firm. In the court's view, the risk of disclosure of client confidences will be virtually eliminated by the disqualification of the Gray firm. That disqualification should also greatly reduce any appearance of impropriety. The record does not warrant the extension of vicarious disqualification to another level.

In addition, the court will order the Alioto firm to return to the Gray firm all of the documents and information which it has obtained from Gray. The court recognizes that there may be questions regarding the effectiveness of, or the compliance with, this requirement. However, the Alioto firm must undertake good faith compliance, which should result in the purging of most of the "tainted" information, if any. If Haagen-Dazs and Pillsbury question the Alioto firm's compliance, or the effectiveness of this requirement, they can raise the issue by further motion at a later time.

VII.

THEREFORE, IT IS ORDERED that:

(2) Gray, Plant, Mooty, Mooty & Bennett, are disqualified from further representation of any party to this litigation;

(3) The requested disqualification of Alioto & Alioto is denied;

(4) Alioto & Alioto will return to the Gray firm all of the information and documents which it has obtained from that firm . . . .

SWS FINANCIAL FUND v. SALOMON BROTHERS
790 F. Supp. 1392 (N.D. Ill. 1992)

MEMORANDUM OPINION.

Plaintiffs (an interconnected set of limited partnerships and corporations, frequently referred to herein collectively as "Hickey") have filed an eight-count complaint against Defendant Salomon Brothers. The complaint charges that

Salomon Brothers [engaged in various securities and commodity trading violations].

[The court relates the actions of Salomon Brothers that are the subject of the civil action. —Ed.]

Salomon Brothers has moved to disqualify Hickey's attorneys, the law firm of Schiff, Hardin and Waite ("Schiff" or "Schiff Hardin"), on the grounds that Schiff's continued representation of Hickey in this lawsuit would violate either Rule 1.7 (governing conflicts of interest with respect to current clients) or Rule 1.9 of the Rules of Professional Conduct (governing conflicts of interest with respect to former clients). Although the court concludes that Schiff in all likelihood did violate Rule 1.7, disqualification is not the proper remedy. Therefore, defendant's motion to disqualify is denied.

Background

This court permitted the parties to file their briefs and supporting affidavits under seal. The court does not believe that the facts contained in this opinion are of such a confidential nature that this opinion should also be filed under seal. This opinion covers a matter of broad public concern regarding the nature of the lawyer-client relationship.

On November 20, 1991, Hickey, represented by Schiff, Hardin and Waite, filed this suit against Salomon Brothers. Prompting this suit was a press release dated August 9, 1991, in which Salomon admitted to irregularities and rule violations in connection with its submitting bids at certain Treasury auctions. Sometime not long thereafter, plaintiffs sought Schiff's advice and took steps to present their claim to Salomon. Schiff has provided a substantial amount of legal services to various of the plaintiff entities since 1982.

Salomon Brothers' relationship with Schiff traces to October, 1989 when Marcy Engel, Vice-President and Counsel of Salomon Brothers, met Kenneth Rosenzweig, a Schiff partner, at a professional conference. Engel was impressed by Rosenzweig's work experience as a lawyer with the Commodity Futures Trading Commission (CFTC) and his knowledge of commodities law. Rosenzweig had worked for the CFTC for eight years prior to joining Schiff in 1987.

In May, 1990, Salomon authorized Engel to retain Mr. Rosenzweig to assist in putting together a compliance manual for Salomon's commodity futures trading operations. Rosenzweig worked on the project throughout 1990 and on November 20, 1990, he sent Salomon the final draft of Schiff's part of the compliance manual. During the course of the project, Rosenzweig met with a number of Salomon personnel and learned about the futures accounts of Salomon and Salomon's subsidiary, Plaza Clearing Corporation, and about the organization of Salomon's customer and proprietary futures business. According to Mr. Randall, Rosenzweig was also educated in detail about Salomon's management of customer order flow and its reaction to, or management decisions about, trading errors.

In a letter dated November 20, 1990 accompanying the work product on the compliance manual, Rosenzweig wrote:

I have enclosed what I hope will be the final version (subject, as always, to legal and regulatory developments).

The November 20, 1990 letter, addressed to Terry Randall, concluded with Rosenzweig's stating that "I have enjoyed working with you and Marcy [Engel] on this project . . . ."

Salomon states that as far as it was concerned the compliance manual project was never fully completed and is still ongoing. In either July or August, 1991, Randall requested that Mr. Rosenzweig provide Salomon with a computer diskette including all the material that Rosenzweig had prepared for the futures compliance manual. Rosenzweig sent the diskette to Mr. Randall along with a letter dated August 30, 1991, in which he stated, "Best of luck in (finally) completing this project!"

Apart from the compliance manual, Schiff undertook a number of other discrete research projects for Salomon, answering commodity law questions when they cropped up. For example, on May 17, 1990, Ms. Engel asked for advice relating to the use of U.S. Treasury securities in meeting the margin obligations for futures contracts. In particular, she asked whether it was permissible for a customer that has received securities from Salomon in a repurchase transaction to post those securities to satisfy the margin requirement. Mr. Rosenzweig provided an answer in a telephone call to Ms. Engel on May 22, 1990.

It is not clear from the record what the other projects were, exactly when they were performed or what went into them. Ms. Engel refers to Schiff's having worked on "not fewer than six matters involving various compliance and regulatory issues." Schiff apparently researched a variety of discrete legal questions mostly relating to commodity futures trading. These projects are referenced in various bills sent by Schiff to Salomon in 1990 and 1991. A review of the bills makes plain that none of these projects required extensive work on Schiff's part. With the exception of one research project concerning the legality of tape-recording customer telephone orders, Mr. Rosenzweig avers that the assignments Schiff did for Salomon related solely to the permissibility of various practices under the commodity laws.

Schiff most recently worked on a Salomon project on June 24-25, 1991. On June 24, Ms. Engel called Mr. Rosenzweig. During her telephone call, Engel posed a number of questions about the use of customer-owned Treasury securities in meeting futures contract margin requirements. Rosenzweig answered those questions in a letter to Engel dated June 25, 1991. The legal fees billed by Schiff to Salomon amounted to a grand total of 39,149.46 representing 214 hours of service extending over a thirteen month period (May, 1990 to June, 1991). Since June 25, Schiff has not performed any legal work for Salomon. Nonetheless there has been a fair amount of contact between the two. In addition to the diskette request discussed above, Salomon personnel and Rosenzweig have corresponded on a number of matters. Tellingly, on August 13, 1991, Mr. Rosenzweig telephoned John Shinkle, thenGeneral Counsel of Salomon, in order to receive his consent allowing Schiff to represent a commodity trading advisor in negotiations with Salomon. After Rosenzweig assured Shinkle that the matter was wholly unrelated to the work Schiff had done for Salomon in the past, Rosenzweig obtained Salomon's consent. Rosenzweig states in his affidavit that "in making that request, I was proceeding in the mistaken belief that Salomon's consent was required even though my last assignment from Salomon had been completed nearly two months earlier."

Rosenzweig has also sent two billings since June 25. The first of the two billings, sent on July 22, 1991, was accompanied by a letter from Mr. Rosenzweig to Ms. Engel in which he wrote:

> I appreciate the opportunity to provide legal services to you, as do others within our firm who participate in these matters. Please do not hesitate to contact me if you have any questions regarding the enclosed.

[The court recounted various continuing contacts between Schiff and Salomon. —Ed.]

Meanwhile, Schiff attorneys pursued their representation of Hickey, a representation directly adverse to Salomon Brothers. In fact, several meetings were held between the plaintiff, Schiff and Salomon Brothers legal personnel. On September 16, 1991, two months before the complaint was filed, plaintiffs' agent Robert Hickey and his attorney Roger Pascal of Schiff met with Salomon's newly appointed General Counsel, Robert Denham, and William McIntosh, Salomon's Director of New York Sales Management. Following that meeting, lawyers representing Salomon communicated with Schiff in efforts to reach a settlement or to find an alternative dispute resolution mechanism that would obviate the need for civil litigation. Schiff, however, apparently never informed Salomon during those communications that it had ever represented Salomon on any matter. For its part, Salomon's lawyers conducted negotiations with lawyers from Schiff unaware of, or at least without taking note of, Salomon's relationship with Schiff.

Schiff first informed a Salomon officer of the potential conflict in early December, 1991. . . .

* * *

On January 9, 1992, both Mr. Krieger and Mr. Scribner spoke with Robert Denham, Salomon's General Counsel, about the conflict. According to Mr. Denham, he was unaware prior to January 9, 1992 that there was any connection between Schiff and Salomon Brothers outside of the Hickey lawsuit. The following day, January 10, 1992, Salomon notified Schiff and this court of the possibility of the present disqualification motion which was brought on January 30, 1992.

DISCUSSION

A. Salomon Was a Present Client

Salomon Brothers contends that Schiff's adverse representation of Hickey violated Rule 1.7 of the Rules of Professional Conduct for the Northern District of Illinois. Rule 1.7(a) regulates an attorney's ability to undertake representation adverse to a present client. It provides:

> A lawyer shall not represent a client if the representation of that client will be directly adverse to another client, unless:

(1) the lawyer reasonably believes the representation will not adversely affect the relationship with the other client; and

(2) each client consents after disclosure.

In the alternative, Salomon argues that even if its client relationship with Schiff had terminated, Schiff's participation in this lawsuit violates Rule 1.9. Rule 1.9(a) regulates an attorney's ability to undertake representation adverse to a former client.

It provides:

> A lawyer who has formerly represented a client in a matter shall not thereafter represent another person in the same or a substantially related matter in which the person's interests are materially adverse to the interests of the former client unless the former client consents after disclosure.

This court concludes that Salomon Brothers was a current client of Schiff's at the time that Schiff undertook the adverse representation and that therefore Rule 1.7 applies. There is no question that Salomon Brothers was a client of Schiff's on June 25 1991 — the last day on which Schiff performed billable work on Salomon's behalf. The question is whether their lawyer-client relationship ended somehow between then and the time that Schiff undertook its adverse representation. The comment to Rule 1.3 discusses the termination of a lawyer-client relationship. In pertinent part the comment states that:

> Unless the relationship is terminated as provided in Rule 1.16, a lawyer should carry through to conclusion all matters undertaken for a client. If a lawyer's employment is limited to a specific matter, the relationship terminates when the matter has been resolved. If a lawyer has served a client over a substantial period in a variety of matters, the client may assume that the lawyer will continue to serve on a continuing basis unless the lawyer gives notice of withdrawal. Doubt about whether a client-lawyer relationship still exists should be clarified by the lawyer, preferably in writing, so that the client will not mistakenly suppose the lawyer is looking after the client's affairs when the lawyer has ceased to do so.

The undisputed facts demonstrate that Schiff served Salomon Brothers over a thirteen month period, answering Salomon's commodity law questions as they arose. The comment makes clear that Salomon Brothers was entitled to "assume" that Schiff would continue to be its lawyer on a continuing basis Schiff had the and that responsibility for clearing up any doubt as to whether the client-lawyer relationship persisted. . . .

* * *

Thus, the court finds that Schiff's representation of Hickey in this suit violates Rule 1.7 of the Rules of Professional Conduct. The court notes that Schiff has not argued that it obtained consent after disclosure even though Salomon's newly appointed General Counsel, Robert Denham, and other officers were aware from meetings held with a Schiff attorney in September (Roger Pascal) that Schiff was representing Hickey. On the contrary, Schiff has explicitly disclaimed any such line of argumentation. See Plaintiff's Memorandum at 15 n.11 ("There is no dispute that Schiff did not seek Salomon's consent to represent plaintiffs in this suit. . . . Schiff has never contended that Salomon gave implicit consent by negotiating with Schiff."). This court will not make on Schiff's behalf arguments that Schiff has so explicitly waived, although the court would have been receptive to an argument that Salomon's extensive negotiations with Schiff amounted to "implicit" or "constructive" consent or else a waiver of the right to demand disqualification.

B. Disqualification Is Not the Appropriate Sanction

Salomon Brothers has assumed that disqualification automatically follows from a finding that a law firm has violated a conflict of interest rule. That assumption is not correct. "The issues of whether a particular representation should be proscribed because of actual or potential conflicting interests and whether disqualification is the proper remedy for a breach are conceptually distinct." *Developments in the Law — Conflicts of Interest in the Legal Profession*, 94 HARV. L. REV. 1244, 1471 n.9 (1981). The reporter of the ABA Committee that drafted the Code of Professional Responsibility has stated that the Code, including the disciplinary rule governing conflicts of interest with current clients (DR 5-102), was aimed at discipline and was not meant as a guideline for disqualification. *See Sutton, How Vulnerable is the Code of Professional Responsibility?*, 57 N.C. L. REV. 497, 514-16 (1979).

"Although disqualification is ordinarily the result of a finding that a disciplinary rule prohibits an attorney's appearance in a case, disqualification is never automatic." *United States v. Miller*, 624 F.2d 1198, 1201 (3rd Cir. 1980).

This court is unaware of any Seventh Circuit authority which requires disqualification upon a showing that a law firm has violated an ethical rule governing conflicts of interest. On the contrary, in *Freeman v. Chicago Musical Instrument Co.*, 689 F.2d 715 (7th Cir. 1982), a "former client" case, the court acknowledged that disqualification is a harsh sanction that should only be imposed where necessary.

Disqualification is one of three sanctions available to enforce the prophylactic conflicts rules. Disciplinary proceedings and civil remedies (i.e., malpractice suits and defenses for the non-payment of legal fees), can also be effective sanctions. In some ways, these other two sanctions are preferable to disqualification, because unlike disqualification they impose costs only on the attorney who has violated the rules. To the extent that civil and disciplinary penalties accurately reflect the social cost of the risk posed by an attorney's misconduct, these sanctions alone could, in principle, provide sufficient deterrent. Disciplinary sanctions also can provide the necessary solemn denunciation of a violation of a lawyer's ethical duties. Disqualification, by contrast, is a blunt device. The sanction of disqualification foists substantial costs upon innocent third parties. The innocent client (Hickey in this case) may suffer delay, inconvenience and expense and will be deprived of its choice of counsel. When disqualification is granted, sometimes the new attorney may find it difficult to master fully the subtle legal and factual nuances of a complex case (like this one), actually impairing the adversarial process. Of course, the court may also lose the time and labor invested in educating itself in the proceedings prior to disqualification. It is no secret that motions to disqualify are frequently brought as dilatory tactics intended to "divert[] the litigation from attention to the merits."

Bobbitt v. Victorian House, Inc., 545 F. Supp. 1124, 1128 (N.D. Ill. 1982).

Given the costs imposed by disqualification and the theoretical availability of alternative means of enforcement of the disciplinary code, a court should look to the purposes behind the rule violated in order to determine if disqualification is a desirable sanction. There are basically two purposes behind Rule 1.7. First it serves as a prophylactic to protect confidences that a client may have shared with his or her attorney. In that regard, Rule 1.9 shares the same concern as it prohibits an attorney from representing a client against a former client if the matter is "substantially related" to the matter(s) of the former client representation. The second purpose behind Rule 1.7 is to safeguard loyalty as a feature of the lawyer-client relationship. A client should not wake up one morning to discover that his lawyer, whom he had trusted to protect his legal affairs, has sued him — even if the suit is utterly unrelated to any of the work the lawyer had ever done for his client.

In this case, even assuming Salomon's version of the facts, it can not reasonably be said that Schiff's work for Salomon is related to the present litigation. As this court has previously observed, the substantial relationship inquiry requires a three-part analysis.

First, the court must factually reconstruct the scope of the prior legal representations. Second, the court must determine what confidential information may reasonably be inferred to have been provided to a lawyer representing a client in such matters. Third, the court must decide whether that information is relevant to the current litigation.

Schiff's representation of Salomon consisted of researching questions of law relating to the trading of commodities. The most significant project was helping to put together a commodities futures compliance manual. Salomon contends that through its work, Schiff obtained " 'highly confidential' information concerning its compliance practices and policies generally" and that Schiff gained "a fairly intimate understanding of Salomon's . . . compliance and business philosophy." Schiff has not refuted that it received confidential information regarding Salomon's compliance practices.

Schiff contends, however, that Salomon's vague depictions about Schiff's knowledge of Salomon's "compliance practices and philosophy" is insufficient to establish that Schiff's work is related to the present suit. According to Schiff, Mr. Rosenzweig provided advice to Salomon solely on commodity futures compliance matters and did not touch upon Treasury securities trading requirements.

Salomon's alleged misconduct, though perhaps undertaken in part to manipulate the futures market, is more obviously put in the category of "noncompliance with Treasury regulations" rather than in the category of "noncompliance with commodities futures law." Salomon has simply failed to show how Schiff's representation of Salomon is substantially related to this lawsuit.

When disqualification is based on the adverse representation of a current client, rather than a former client, the court must look beyond the issue of "substantial relatedness," however. The fact that the court views Schiff's work as not substan tially related to this litigation does not mean that disqualification is out of the question.

The court must also inquire into whether Salomon's expectations of loyalty were so cavalierly trampled that disqualification is warranted as a sanction. In this case, Salomon's General Counsel, Robert Denham (appointed to his position on August 25, 1991) was completely unaware until January 9, 1992 that Schiff had ever provided any legal services to Salomon Brothers. This case is at the polar extreme from the case in which an individual has a personal relationship with a particular attorney who provides for all or substantially all of that client's legal needs. In such a case, were the attorney to "turn on" his client and sue him, disqualification would be appropriate. Materials filed under seal reflect that Salomon Brothers has engaged a number of other outside legal counsel, apart from Schiff, some of whom were retained to do financial futures work.

A court deciding a motion to disqualify in a case involving mega-firms (like Schiff) and mega-parties (like Salomon Brothers) should not be oblivious to "the way that attorneys and clients actually behave in the latter part of the twentieth century, and what they have come to expect from each other in terms of the continuation or termination of the relationship." Drustar, 134 F.R.D. 226, 229 (S.D. Ohio 1991). As the Drustar court noted:

> The concepts of having a 'personal attorney' or a 'general corporate counsel' are much less meaningful today, especially among sophisticated users of legal services, than in the past. Clients may have numerous attorneys, all of whom have some implicit continuing loyalty obligations. Attorney specialization and marketing have contributed to this fractionalizing of a single client's business.

Were this court to rule that disqualification was mandated by Schiff's breach of Rule 1.7 in this case, the implications would be overwhelming. Clients of enormous size and wealth, and with a large demand for legal services, should not be encouraged to parcel their business among dozens of the best law firms as a means of purposefully creating the potential for conflicts. With simply a minor "investment" of some token business, such clients would in effect be buying an insurance policy against that law firm's adverse representation. Although lawyers should not be encouraged to sue their own clients (hence the sanctions discussed above), the law should not give large companies the incentive to manufacture the potential for conflicts by awarding disqualification automatically.

The foregoing discussion should not be misunderstood to mean that this court does not take very seriously a lawyer's ethical responsibilities to avoid conflicts of interest. Schiff should not have agreed to bring this suit against Salomon Brothers. Rule 1.7 prohibited it from doing so. The court, however, does not believe that the costly sanction of disqualification should be automatic for a breach of even so serious an obligation as that imposed by Rule 1.7. There is no danger in this case that Schiff's advocacy of Hickey will be less than fully zealous, the trial would not be tainted by Schiff's continued representation of Hickey, the subject of this litigation is not substantially related to the work Schiff has done for Salomon, and the disqualification would simply not be the appropriate remedy.

The court is cognizant that this decision may be viewed by some as a departure from the norm. Many courts, having determined that a conflict of interest exists, will automatically disqualify. The legal world is changing, however, and courts must be sensitive to the complexities and multiplicities of interests that come into play when enormous corporations and monster law firms interact in a dynamic legal economy. Accordingly, as discussed, this court does not believe that disqualification should be an automatic sanction and should not be imposed here.

CONCLUSION

Salomon Brothers' motion to disqualify Plaintiffs' attorney, the law firm of Schiff, Hardin and Waite, is denied.

NOTES, QUESTIONS, AND EXAMPLES

1.   Notice that when the bar ethics codes are applied outside the disciplinary process, as is the case in disqualification motions and imputed disqualification, interests other than those implicated by disciplining a lawyer come into play. What are some of the interests that the *Haagen-Dazs* and *Salamon Bros.* courts considered?

2.   What factors should determine when screening devices have been success-ful?

E.   SPECIAL ROLE-RELATED CONFLICTS RULES

When former government lawyers or former judges undertake representation that relates to work they have done in their former capacity, special conflicts of interest rules apply. In this setting (especially with former judges), the interest in avoiding the appearance of impropriety takes a greater role. In the pure lawyer conflict circumstances, the appearance interest takes a minor role that is often little more than a make-weight argument filling space in an opinion when the primary issues are loyalty or confidentiality breaches. But the usual explanation for the appearance interest, maintenance of confidence in the administration of justice, applies with greater force when the activities of judges and government lawyers are questioned.

1.   Former Judge

Former judges' conflicts differ from those of lawyers who move from one practice setting to another, and they require special conflicts rules. MR 1.12. In their judicial role, judges do not represent parties and thus have little of the loyalty-transfer concerns of lawyers representing multiple clients. In addition, judges are not the confidants of clients and thus carry forward into private practice no former client confidences. Although a judge may have become privy to confidential material during in camera review, even then the judge was not confided in by a client. The appearance of impropriety considerations is stronger in the case of many former judge conflicts situations than are the like concerns with lawyers' similar conflicts. *See* Chapter X.

A former judge may not engage in private representation in a matter in which the judge participated personally and substantially as a judge, unless all parties to the matter give informed consent. MR 1.12. Judges in most courts are members of a group of judges who individually hear cases brought before their court. The mere fact that a judge was a member of a group of judges that variously hear cases brought to a particular court does not disqualify the judge from all matters that were in the court while the judge was there. Only when the judge has participated personally and substantially will the conflicts rule apply. Personal participation is just that: The rule does not apply if the judge's court, but not the particular judge, heard the matter.

Judges are prohibited from negotiating for employment with lawyers who are currently representing parties before the judge's court if the judge is personally and substantially participating in the matter before the court. Similar, but waivable, restrictions apply to judicial law clerks. MR 1.12(b).

INTERNATIONAL NOTE

These concerns are almost unique to the U.S. In most of the world, legal training separates at a certain point and law students become lawyers while judge students become judges. Only rarely does a lawyer become a judge or a judge become a lawyer.

Special Imputed Disqualification Rules

In order to prevent a hand-cuffing of former judges' efforts to obtain private law firm employment after judicial service and because former judge conflicts do not implicate the same sort of loyalty and confidentiality abuse as do multiple client lawyer conflicts, special, more relaxed imputed disqualification rules apply to the law firms for which former judges work. Effective screening procedures and notice to the judge's former court permit a former judge's law firm to continue with representation in which the former judge is disqualified from participating. MR 1.12(c).

2.   Former Government Lawyer

Special conflicts rules apply to lawyers who move from government practice to private practice. MR 1.11. At least two facts distinguish former government lawyers who move into private practice from private practice lawyers who have moved from employment in one law firm to employment in another law firm. First, government lawyers represent the government (or the public, or the particular agency within which they worked). As a result, in later private practice, any representation of private parties against the government might be seen as former client conflicts. Because of the breadth of the potential disqualification from representation, this result must be ameliorated. Second, as a government lawyer, the stakes of the appearance of impropriety are raised. The possibility of abuses of either relationships with former colleagues still in government practice or of confidential government information create greater concern regarding private practice subsequent to government practice. Both of these facts have effects on the formulation of the special conflicts rules that apply to former government lawyers.

A former government "lawyer shall not represent a private client in connection with a matter in which the lawyer participated personally and substantially" as a government lawyer. MR 1.11. Notice that this conflict rule applies without regard to whether the lawyer has effectively changed sides in the matter.

Similar to the treatment of former judges, the mere fact that a lawyer was employed in a particular agency while that agency was involved in a matter does not disqualify the lawyer under the conflicts rules. Only when the lawyer has participated personally and substantially will the conflicts rule's disqualification threshold issues be satisfied.

Two exceptions allow the former government lawyer to engage in the later private representation even when his participation in the government employment was personal and substantial. The conflicts rule excepts from its reach cases in which the law otherwise expressly permits the private representation to occur. If, for example, the agency for which the lawyer formerly worked has within its regulations a provision authorizing later private practice in various instances, the conflict rule does not restrict the lawyer.

The rule defines what it means by a "matter." It is only later private representation in connection with a government service "matter" that triggers a conflict of interest analysis. A matter includes a wide variety of instances and actions that engage the agency with a particular party or parties. The definition excludes rule drafting and other agency actions that have more general application. So, for example, a former government lawyer who drafted extensive revisions to the IRS Code that were later enacted as statute or regulation is not prohibited from later in private practice representing clients whose cases implicate the application of the drafted rules. Any other result would ultimately require that many former government lawyers abandon their expertise in order to go into private practice.

Special Imputed Disqualification Rules

Special, more relaxed, imputed disqualification rules apply when former government lawyers have a conflict in later private practice. The government would have a difficult time recruiting qualified lawyers if those lawyers knew that their firms would be disqualified from doing virtually all of the type of work they did in government practice.

ARMSTRONG v. MCALPIN
625 F.2d 433 (2d Cir. 1980)

FEINBERG, CIRCUIT JUDGE (with whom KAUFMAN, CHIEF JUDGE, and MANSFIELD, OAKES and TIMBERS, CIRCUIT JUDGES, concur).

. . . Clovis McAlpin and Capital Growth Real Estate Fund, Inc., two of numerous defendants in a suit seeking over $24 million for violation of federal securities laws, appeal from an order of the United States District Court for the Southern District of New York, Henry F. Werker, J., denying their motion to disqualify the law firm representing plaintiffs. The appeal was first heard by a panel of this court, which concluded that the trial judge had erred in denying defendants' disqualification motion. A majority of this court voted to grant en banc reconsideration of the appeal. . . . Subsequently, the parties and a number of amici filed comprehensive briefs on the issues before the en banc court. After full consideration, we affirm the order of the district court and vacate the earlier decision of the panel. . . .

I. The Facts

Appellants' motion to disqualify is based on the prior participation of Theodore Altman, now a partner in the law firm representing plaintiffs-appellees, in an investigation of and litigation against appellants conducted when he was an Assistant Director of the Division of Enforcement of the Securities and Exchange Commission (the SEC). In September 1974, after a nine-month investigation, the SEC commenced an action in the United States District Court for the Southern District of New York against Clovis McAlpin and various other individual and institutional defendants. The complaint alleged that McAlpin and the other defendants had looted millions of dollars from a group of related investment companies, referred to here collectively as the Capital Growth companies; McAlpin was the top executive officer of these companies. The SEC suit sought, among other things, the appointment of a receiver to protect the interests of shareholders in the Capital Growth companies. When McAlpin fled to Costa Rica and certain other defendants failed to appear, the SEC obtained a default judgment; in September 1974, Judge Charles E. Stewart appointed Michael F. Armstrong, the principal appellee in this appeal, as receiver of the Capital Growth companies.

One of Armstrong's principal tasks as receiver for the Capital Growth companies is to recover all moneys and property misappropriated by defendants; to further this task, Armstrong was authorized to initiate litigation in the United States and abroad. In October 1974, Judge Stewart granted Armstrong's request to retain as his counsel the New York firm of Barrett Smith Schapiro & Simon. Shortly after the appointment of Armstrong, the SEC made its investigatory files available to him, in accordance with its practice, we are informed in its brief, of assisting "the efforts of receivers who have been appointed by the courts in Commission law enforcement actions." The Barrett Smith firm reviewed these files, conducted its own investigation for the receiver, and assisted him in taking possession of various Capital Growth properties in the continental United States and in Puerto Rico. For the next year and a half, we are told, Barrett Smith devoted approximately 2,600 hours to assisting the receiver, which included the services of five partners and eight associates; a little over half of this time was spent preparing for litigation.

In early 1976, however, the receiver and Barrett Smith became aware of a potential conflict of interest involving an institutional client of Barrett Smith that might become a defendant in litigation brought by the receiver. Thus, despite Barrett Smith's substantial investment of time, the receiver concluded that it was necessary to substitute litigation counsel. The task, however, was not an easy one; McAlpin had fled to Costa Rica with most of the assets of the Capital Growth companies and hence the funds available to Armstrong to secure new counsel were quite limited. It was therefore necessary to find a firm that could not only handle difficult litigation in Costa Rica and in the United States, but would also commit itself to conclude the task, even if little or no interim compensation was available. Moreover, it was important to retain a law firm large enough to cope with the immense paper work soon to be generated by the firms that would probably represent the institutional defendants.

Because of these considerations, appellees assert, the receiver focused on firms already involved in litigation against Robert L. Vesco, who, like McAlpin, had fled to Costa Rica rather than face possible prosecution for numerous alleged securities fraud violations. After abortive negotiations with two such firms, the receiver in April 1976 retained the law firm of Gordon Hurwitz Butowsky Baker Weitzen & Shalov, the firm that is the target of appellants' disqualification motion. According to Armstrong, the Gordon firm was chosen in part because one partner, David M. Butowsky, was then Special Counsel to International Controls Corporation and was involved in legal work in Costa Rica relating to the alleged Vesco defalcations, while another partner had specialized experience in prosecuting complex fraud cases. In accepting the representation, the Gordon firm agreed to "conduct all Capital Growth litigation through to a conclusion" even if the receiver could not compensate the firm as the litigation progressed.

In October 1975, some seven months before the receiver obtained substitute counsel for Barrett Smith, Theodore Altman ended his nine-year tenure with the SEC to become an associate with the Gordon firm. At the time of his resignation, Altman had been an Assistant Director of the Division of Enforcement for three years, and had about twenty-five staff attorneys working under him. As a high-ranking enforcement officer of the SEC, Altman had supervisory responsibility over numerous cases, including the Capital Growth investigation and litigation. Although he was not involved on a daily basis, he was generally aware of the facts of the case and the status of the litigation. The SEC's complaint was prepared and filed by the staff of the New York Regional Administrator, and the litigation was handled by the New York office. Altman's name appeared on the SEC complaint, although he did not sign it.

At the time that Altman joined the Gordon firm, the receiver had no reason to know that Altman had left the SEC or to be aware of his new affiliation. Subsequently, during the initial meetings with the Gordon firm, Armstrong first learned that Altman had recently become associated with the firm. Both the Gordon firm and Barrett Smith researched the question of the effect of Altman's prior supervisory role in the SEC suit. The two firms concluded that under applicable ethical standards discussed in Part IV of this opinion, Altman should not participate in the Gordon firm's representation of the receiver, but that the firm would not be disqualified if Altman was properly screened from the case. The matter was brought to the attention of Judge Stewart, who nonetheless authorized the receiver to retain the Gordon firm. Shortly thereafter, the firm asked the SEC if it had any objection to the retention, and was advised in writing that it did not, so long as Altman was screened from participation. Barrett Smith then turned over its litigation files to the Gordon firm, including those received from the SEC; in September 1976, the receiver filed the action by plaintiffs-appellees against defendants-appellants that gave rise to this appeal.

In June 1978, almost two years after the commencement of this action, appellants filed their motion to disqualify the Gordon firm because of Altman's prior activities at the SEC. In December 1978, Judge Werker, to whom the case had been reassigned, denied the motion. In his opinion, the judge concluded that the Gordon firm had carried out the letter and spirit of the relevant bar association ethical rulings, that the firm's representation of the receiver was not unethical and did not threaten the integrity of the trial, and that appellants had suffered no prejudice as a result of the representation. . . . We now turn to the issues before us.

*   *   *

IV. The Merits

In his thorough opinion refusing to disqualify the Gordon firm, Judge Werker reviewed the facts set forth in Part I of this opinion and carefully analyzed the ethical problem defendants had raised. He noted that Altman was concededly disqualified from participating in the litigation under Disciplinary Rule 9-101(B) of the American Bar Association Code of Professional Responsibility.[31] That Rule prohibits an attorney's private employment in any matter in which he has had substantial responsibility during prior public employment. The judge then considered the effect of Disciplinary Rule 5-105(D), which deals with disqualification of an entire law firm if one lawyer in the firm is disqualified.[32]

Judge Werker then carefully examined the screening of Altman by the Gordon firm, noting that:

> Altman is excluded from participation in the action, has no access to relevant files and derives no remuneration from funds obtained by the firm from prosecuting this action. No one at the firm is permitted to discuss the matter in his presence or allow him to view any document related to this litigation, and Altman has not imparted any information concerning Growth Fund to the firm.

> [N]othing before this court indicates that Altman, while employed by the SEC, formed an intent to prosecute a later action involving Growth Fund. Indeed, sworn affidavits reveal that he has never participated in any fashion whatever in the Gordon firm's representation of the Receiver, nor has he shared in the firm's income derived from prosecution of this action. And . . . Altman and his two partners Velie and Butowsky have attested under penalty of perjury that Altman has never discussed the action with other firm members. These statements are uncontradicted by defendants and provide a basis for not imputing Altman's knowledge to other members of the firm.

---

[31] [*See* Model Rule 1.11. —Ed.]

[32] [1] Disciplinary Rule 5-105(D) provides:

> If a lawyer is required to decline employment or to withdraw from employment under a Disciplinary Rule, no partner, or associate, or any other lawyer affiliated with him or his firm, may accept or continue such employment.

On this rehearing en banc, we are favored with briefs not only from the parties but also from the United States,[33] the Securities and Exchange Commission, the Interstate Commerce Commission, the Federal Maritime Commission, the Commodities Futures Trading Commission and twenty-six distinguished former government lawyers now employed as practicing attorneys, corporate officers, or law professors, all attesting to the importance of the issues raised on appeal. Thus, the United States asserts that a "decision to reject screening procedures is certain to have a serious, adverse effect on the ability of Government legal offices to recruit and retain well-qualified attorneys"; this view is seconded by the other government amici. And the former government lawyers, including two former Attorneys General of the United States and two former Solicitors General of the United States, state that they are all "affected at least indirectly, by the panel opinion's underlying assumption that government lawyers cannot be trusted to discharge their public responsibilities faithfully while in office, or to abide fully by screening procedures afterwards." While the tone of these assertions may be overly apocalyptic, it is true that a decision rejecting the efficacy of screening procedures in this context may have significant adverse consequences. Thus, such disapproval may hamper the government's efforts to hire qualified attorneys; the latter may fear that government service will transform them into legal "Typhoid Marys," shunned by prospective private employers because hiring them may result in the disqualification of an entire firm in a possibly wide range of cases. The amici also contend that those already employed by the government may be unwilling to assume positions of greater responsibility within the government that might serve to heighten their undesirability to future private employers. Certainly such trends, if carried to an extreme, may ultimately affect adversely the quality of the services of government attorneys.

Weighing the needs of efficient judicial administration against the potential advantage of immediate preventive measures, we believe that unless an attorney's conduct tends to "taint the underlying trial" . . . by disturbing the balance of the presentations, courts should be quite hesitant to disqualify an attorney. Given the availability of both federal and state comprehensive disciplinary machinery, there is usually no need to deal with all other kinds of ethical violations in the very litigation in which they surface.

We believe that this approach is dispositive here and requires our affirmance of the ruling of the district court. It is apparent from a close reading of Judge Werker's opinion that he saw no threat of taint of the trial by the Gordon firm's continued representation of the receiver. . . . Although appellants assert that the trial will be tainted by the use of information from Altman, we see no basis on the record before us for overruling the district court's rejection of that claim.

We recognize that a rule that concentrates on the threat of taint fails to correct all possible ethical conflicts. In adopting this approach, we do not denigrate the importance of ethical conduct by attorneys practicing in this courthouse or

---

[33] [2] The brief of the United States also states that it presents the views of the Federal Trade Commission, the Civil Aeronautics Board, the Federal Energy Regulatory Commission, and the Federal Legal Council, a committee consisting of the General Counsels of fifteen executive branch agencies and chaired by the Attorney General of the United States.

elsewhere, and we applaud the efforts of the organized bar to educate its members as to their ethical obligations. However, absent a threat of taint to the trial, we continue to believe that possible ethical conflicts surfacing during a litigation are generally better addressed by the "comprehensive disciplinary machinery" of the state and federal bar, or possibly by legislation. While there may be unusual situations where the "appearance of impropriety" alone is sufficient to warrant disqualification, we are satisfied that this is not such a case. Nor do we believe, as Judge Newman asserts, that a failure to disqualify the Gordon firm based on the possible appearance of impropriety will contribute to the "public skepticism about lawyers." While sensitive to the integrity of the bar, the public is also rightly concerned about the fairness and efficiency of the judicial process. We believe those concerns would be disserved by an order of disqualification in a case such as this, where no threat of taint exists and where appellants' motion to disqualify opposing counsel has successfully crippled the efforts of a receiver, appointed at the request of a public agency, to obtain redress for alleged serious frauds on the investing public. Thus, rather than heightening public skepticism, we believe that the restrained approach this court had adopted towards attempts to disqualify opposing counsel on ethical grounds avoids unnecessary and unseemly delay and reinforces public confidence in the fairness of the judicial process.

Accordingly, we vacate the panel opinion in this case and affirm the judgment of the district court.

3. Lawyer as Witness

Special conflict problems are associated with the fairly rare occasion on which a lawyer is to be called as a witness. MR 3.7. The lawyer as witness problem is a conflict problem in the sense that the lawyer as witness has a mixture of roles that may compromise the lawyer's independence of judgment on behalf of the client. The compromising aspects are complex, and the lawyer may be disqualified from representing the client when the combination of interests dictates.

Chapter VI

DUTIES TO THIRD PARTIES

Lawyers owe their primary duties to their clients. (*See* Chapters III, IV, and V.) Lawyers also owe duties to the court, the justice system, the profession, and the public generally. (*See* Chapter VII.) This chapter is about the limited duties lawyers owe to specific categories of third parties, as opposed to the client, the court, the profession, or the public generally.

Third parties are strangers to the lawyer-client relationship. They may or may not be represented by another lawyer. Such third parties are, for example, opposing parties, witnesses, jurors, and unrepresented interested parties. The duties owed to third parties operate as limits on the primary duty the lawyer owes to a client. In other words, they operate to form boundaries around acceptable, client-favoring actions by lawyers.

A. TRUTH-TELLING OUTSIDE THE COURT CONTEXT

Rules governing lawyers' truth-telling duties outside the court context contrast with those that apply inside the court context. (*See* Chapter VII.) The outside the court truth-telling rules apply in a lawyer's dealings with opposing lawyers, opposing parties, witnesses, and anyone else with whom the lawyer communicates as a lawyer. These rules apply in a variety of contexts including investigation, negotiation, third-party neutral activities, and so on.

1. False Statements of Material Law or Fact

For a statement to a third party to subject a lawyer to discipline, it must be both false and material. A false statement is one that does not subjectively conform to the lawyer's knowledge of the facts. A statement is material if it bears on the merits of the discussion or is one upon which the recipient's further action of consequence may be based.

Lawyers are prohibited from making statements that are fraudulent or remaining silent when the statement or silence would amount to fraud under applicable tort principles. For Model Rules purposes, fraud "denotes conduct that is fraudulent under the . . . law of the applicable jurisdiction and has a purpose to deceive and not merely negligent misrepresentation or failure to apprise another of relevant information." MR 1.0(d).

Inevitably, some reliance on general tort concepts must be had in interpreting the Model Rules' definition of fraud. For example, fraud generally requires a reasonableness of reliance on the part of the recipient of the fraudulent statement. The same statement made once to a lawyer and another time to an unrepresented witness may be regarded differently in this respect.

2. The Negotiation Setting

The negotiation setting presents a special circumstance within which the nature and effect of misleading statements must be analyzed. By its nature, an element of misleading is present in the negotiation process. Negotiators legitimately mislead other negotiators about their resolve, about estimates of value, about options available to the negotiator's client, about their time constraints, and a variety of other aspects of the negotiation "dance." Some misleading is inevitable in negotiating. The rules prohibit only certain forms of misleading. MR 4.1, Comment.

James J. White, *Machiavelli and the Bar: Ethical Limitations on Lying in Negotiation*
1980 Am. B. Found. Res. J. 926, 927–28, 931–35[1]

Like the poker player, a negotiator hopes that his opponent will overestimate the value of his hand. Like the poker player, in a variety of ways he must facilitate his opponent's inaccurate assessment. The critical difference between those who are successful negotiators and those who are not lies in this capacity both to mislead and not to be misled.

Some experienced negotiators will deny the accuracy of this assertion, but they will be wrong. I submit that a careful examination of the behavior of even the most forthright, honest, and trustworthy negotiators will show them actively engaged in misleading their opponents about their true positions . . . . To conceal one's true position, to mislead an opponent about one's true settling point, is the essence of negotiation.

*   *   *

[C]onsider five cases. Easiest is the question that arises when one misrepresents his true opinion about the meaning of a case or a statute. Presumably such a misrepresentation is accepted lawyer behavior both in and out of court and is not intended to be precluded by the requirement that the lawyer be "truthful." In writing his briefs, arguing his case, and attempting to persuade the opposing party in negotiation, it is the lawyer's right and probably his responsibility to argue for plausible interpretations of cases and statutes which favor his client's interest, even in circumstances where privately he has advised his client that those are not his true interpretations of the cases and statutes.

A second form of distortion that the Comments plainly envision as permissible is distortion concerning the value of one's case or of the other subject matter involved in the negotiation. Thus the Comments make explicit reference to "puffery." Presumably they are attempting to draw the same line that one draws in commercial law between express warranties and "mere puffing" under section 2-313 of the Uniform Commercial Code. While this line is not easy to draw, it generally

---

[1] Reprinted with permission.

means that the seller of a product has the right to make general statements concerning the value of his product without having the law treat those statements as warranties and without having liability if they turn out to be inaccurate estimates of the value. As the statements descend toward greater and greater particularity, as the ignorance of the person receiving the statements increases, the courts are likely to find them to be not puffing but express warranties. By the same token a lawyer could make assertions about his case or about the subject matter of his negotiation in general terms, and if those proved to be inaccurate, they would not be a violation of the ethical standards. Presumably such statements are not violations of the ethical standards even when they conflict with the lawyer's dispassionate analysis of the value of his case.

A third case is related to puffing but different from it. This is the use of the so-called false demand. It is a standard negotiating technique in collective bargaining negotiation and in some other multiple-issue negotiations for one side to include a series of demands about which it cares little or not at all. The purpose of including these demands is to increase one's supply of negotiating currency. One hopes to convince the other party that one or more of these false demands is important and thus successfully to trade it for some significant concession. The assertion of and argument for a false demand involves the same kind of distortion that is involved in puffing or in arguing the merits of cases or statutes that are not really controlling. The proponent of a false demand implicitly or explicitly states his interest in the demand and his estimation of it. Such behavior is untruthful in the broadest sense; yet at least in collective bargaining negotiation its use is a standard part of the process and is not thought to be inappropriate by any experienced bargainer.

Two final examples may be more troublesome. The first involves the response of a lawyer to a question from the other side. Assume that the defendant has instructed his lawyer to accept any settlement offer under $100,000. Having received that instruction, how does the defendant's lawyer respond to the plaintiff's question, "I think $90,000 will settle this case. Will your client give $90,000?" Do you see the dilemma that question poses for the defense lawyer? It calls for information that would not have to be disclosed. A truthful answer to it concludes the negotiation and dashes any possibility in negotiating a lower settlement even in circumstances in which the plaintiff might be willing to accept half of $90,000. Even a moment's hesitation in response to the question may be a nonverbal communication to a clever plaintiff's lawyer that the defendant has given such authority. Yet a negative response is a lie.

It is no answer that a clever lawyer will answer all such questions about authority by refusing to answer them, nor is it an answer that some lawyers will be clever enough to tell their clients not to grant them authority to accept a given sum until the final stages in negotiation. Most of us are not that careful or that clever. Few will routinely refuse to answer such questions in cases in which the client has granted a much lower limit than that discussed by the other party, for in that case an honest answer about the absence of authority is a quick and effective method of changing the opponent's settling point, and it is one that few of us will forego when our authority is far below that requested by the other party. Thus despite the fact that a clever negotiator can avoid having to lie or to reveal his settling point, many lawyers, perhaps most, will sometime be forced by such a question either to lie or to reveal that they have been granted such authority by saying so or by their silence in response to a direct question. Is it fair to lie in such a case?

Before one examines the possible justifications for a lie in that circumstance, consider a final example recently suggested to me by a lawyer in practice. There the lawyer represented three persons who had been charged with shoplifting. Having satisfied himself that there was no significant conflict of interest, the defense lawyer told the prosecutor that two of the three would plead guilty only if the case was dismissed against the third. Previously those two had told the defense counsel that they would plead guilty irrespective of what the third did, and the third had said that he wished to go to trial unless the charges were dropped. Thus the defense lawyer lied to the prosecutor by stating that the two would plead only if the third were allowed to go free. Can the lie be justified in this case?

How does one distinguish the cases where truthfulness is not required and those where it is required? Why do the first three cases seem easy? I suggest they are easy cases because the rules of the game are explicit and well developed in those areas. Everyone expects a lawyer to distort the value of his own case, of his own facts and arguments, and to deprecate those of his opponent. No one is surprised by that, and the system accepts and expects that behavior. To a lesser extent the same is true of the false demand procedure in labor-management negotiations where the ploy is sufficiently widely used to be explicitly identified in the literature. A layman might say that this behavior falls within the ambit of "exaggeration," a form of behavior that while not necessarily respected is not regarded as morally reprehensible in our society.

The last two cases are more difficult. In one the lawyer lies about his authority; in the other he lies about the intention of his clients. It would be more difficult to justify the lies in those cases by arguing that the rules of the game explicitly permit that sort of behavior. Some might say that the rules of the game provide for such distortion, but I suspect that many lawyers would say that such lies are out of bounds and are not part of the rules of the game. Can the lie about authority be justified on the ground that the question itself was improper? Put another way, if I have a right to keep certain information to myself, and if any behavior but a lie will reveal that information to the other side, am I justified in lying? I think not. Particularly in the case in which there are other avenues open to the respondent, should we not ask him to take those avenues? That is, the careful negotiator here can turn aside all such questions and by doing so avoid any inference from his failure to answer such questions.

What makes the last case a close one? Conceivably it is the idea that one accused by the state is entitled to greater leeway in making his case. Possibly one can argue that there is no injury to the state when such a person, particularly an innocent person, goes free. Is it conceivable that the act can be justified on the ground that it is part of the game in this context, that prosecutors as well as defense lawyers routinely misstate what they, their witnesses, and their clients can and will do? None of these arguments seems persuasive. Justice is not served by freeing a guilty person. The system does not necessarily achieve better results by trading two guilty pleas for a dismissal. Perhaps its justification has its roots in the same idea that formerly held that a misrepresentation of one's state of mind was not actionable for it was not a misrepresentation of fact.

In a sense rules governing these cases may simply arise from a recognition by the law of its limited power to shape human behavior. By tolerating exaggeration and puffing in the sales transaction, by refusing to make misstatement of one's intention actionable, the law may simply have recognized the bounds of its control over human behavior. Having said that, one is still left with the question, Are the lies permissible in the last two cases? My general conclusion is that they are not, but I am not nearly as comfortable with that conclusion as I am about the first three cases.

Taken together, the five foregoing cases show me that we do not and cannot intend that a negotiator be "truthful" in the broadest sense of that term. At the minimum we allow him some deviation from truthfulness in asserting his true opinion about cases, statutes, or the value of the subject of the negotiation in other respects. In addition some of us are likely to allow him to lie in response to certain questions that are regarded as out of bounds, and possibly to lie in circumstances where his interest is great and the injury seems small. It would be unfortunate, therefore, for the rule that requires "fairness" to be interpreted to require that a negotiator be truthful in every respect and in all of his dealings. It should be read to allow at least those kinds of untruthfulness that are implicitly and explicitly recognized as acceptable in his forum, a forum defined both by the subject matter and by the participants.

———————

Others, most notably Judge Alvin Rubin, have argued that it is possible, indeed desirable and required, for a lawyer negotiator to be fully honest, candid, and forthright.[2] A distinction in the rules between either immaterial facts or non-facts (such as opinions) and material facts is really a "rules of the game" rule. Deceptions that are of the expected variety (that comport with the rules of the game) are of either immaterial facts or non-facts and are thus permissible under MR 4.1(a). The Comment to the Rule itself acknowledges as much:

> This Rule refers to statements of fact. Whether a particular statement should be regarded as one of fact can depend on the circumstances. Under generally accepted conventions in negotiation, certain types of statements ordinarily are not taken as statements of material fact. Estimates of price or value placed on the subject of a transaction and a party's intentions as to an acceptable settlement of a claim are in this category . . . .[3]

Non-frivolous assertions about what the law is, at least when made to other lawyers, are treated similarly to "nonfacts." Lawyers know and understand the kind of argument that non-frivolously can be made about the law. A lawyer need not subjectively believe that the non-frivolous assertion will ultimately be the prevailing

---

[2] [1] *See* Alvin B. Rubin, *A Causerie on Lawyers' Ethics in Negotiations*, 35 LA. L. REV. 577 (1975). Judge Rubin suggests that it will be in the lawyer's and client's long-term self interest to be candid *and unswerving* about minimum settlement points.

[3] [2] MR 4.1, Comment.

view of the law for it to be asserted as his view. Such statements about a case's or statute's interpretation will be treated as "nonfacts" or opinions. They are statements within the expectations of players of the negotiation game. Remember, a "rules of the game" rule should only apply when all involved are players (lawyers). A statement that would be treated as immaterial or a nonfact when made to a lawyer might well be regarded as false, material, and perhaps fraudulent when made by a lawyer to a nonlawyer. There can be, of course, direct misstatements about the governing legal rules that would be regarded as fraudulent rather than as nonfacts or as legitimate opinion even though the statement is made to another lawyer (for example, "The Supreme Court has reversed that court of appeals decision," when it had not yet decided the case, or "We have a contributory negligence rule in this state," when the legislature has enacted a comparative negligence statute).

Interpreting a "rules of the game" rule is exceedingly difficult; it has no objectively moral component.[4] The rules will inevitably vary from place to place, legal community to legal community, and type of practice to type of practice.

> Lawyers' standards of fairness are necessarily derived from those of society as a whole, and subcultural variations are enormous. At one extreme lies the "rural God-fearing standard," so exacting and tedious that it often excludes the use of lawyers. At the other extreme stands "New York hardball," now played in most larger cities using the wall-to-wall indenture for a playing surface. Between these extremes are regional and local standards and further variations that depend on the business involved, the identity of the participants, and other circumstances. Against this kaleidoscopic background, it is difficult to specify a single standard that governs the parties and thus a correlative standard that should govern their legal representatives.[5]

Some measure of deception is almost universally countenanced within the negotiator's role. Even the simplest act such as the intentional maintenance of a "poker face" when offers are made by the other side is meant to deceive. Perhaps in a perfect world, every deception should be prohibited, but the Model Rules, at least, acknowledge a compromise between a duty to be truthful in statements about important matters and the need to allow the process of negotiation as practiced in a particular community to occur by permitting the subtle forms of deception that are expected by the game's regular players.

Statements made to other lawyers in negotiations (and arguably to very sophisticated non-lawyers) are regarded much differently from statements made to non-lawyers. Lawyers may not legitimately rely on vague misleading statements to the same extent as may non-lawyers.

---

[4] [3] Though perhaps an extreme example, if the rules of the game in your community countenanced the use of physical force to extract a more favorable settlement, a "rules of the game" rule would have nothing to say about it. The local criminal law might dissuade you from such conduct, but a pure "rules of the game" rule of conduct would simply be defined by accepted practice.

[5] [4] Geoffrey C. Hazard, Jr., *The Lawyer's Obligation to be Trustworthy When Dealing With Opposing Partie s*, 33 S.C. L. Rev. 181, 193 (1981).

3. Reducing Agreements to Writing

PROBLEM 6-1

Ed Zimmerman is a legal aid lawyer representing Martin Daniel in a consumer matter. Zimmerman's client bought an audio system from Dante's Appliance and Audio. Dante's is represented by Gabe Modell. Zimmerman's client responded to a Dante's ad. Once in the store, Dante's personnel performed a "bait and switch," moving Daniel from the $500 advertised system to a $1,500 one. Not having enough money in cash, the customer was assisted in filling out a credit application that imposed a usurious interest rate. The customer, wanting to obtain the credit, gave false information about his income. He made a $500 down payment and left with the audio system and $1,000 of debt.

Zimmerman learned in his interview of his client that he had falsely stated his income on the credit application, a low grade felony. Zimmerman's legal research indicated that Dante's would have clear liability in a statutorily set amount of $1,000 for the usurious interest rate charged in the contract and another $1,000 for the bait and switch. Zimmerman's client is anxious to harm Dante's and would like his matter to result in action against Dante's by the state's consumer protection agency. Zimmerman would like this as well, or some other result that would benefit his other clients.

At the negotiation session, Zimmerman and Modell agreed that Daniel could keep the $500 worth of equipment that he went in to buy, that Dante's would return Daniel's $500 down-payment, that Daniel would return the $1,500 system, that both Daniel and Dante's would release the other from further liability, and that, unless ordered by proper authority to do so, Dante's would not reveal Daniel's fraudulent statement of income on the credit application. During the early moments of the negotiation, Modell had said that his client would be pleased to get this matter behind him without the negative publicity that a lawsuit over usurious interest practices could bring. The topic of publicity never came up again during the negotiation session. Zimmerman offered to draft the agreement and send it on to Modell.

Zimmerman is working on the agreement. Zimmerman is considering including a provision as follows: "Mr. Daniel agrees to make no report to any authority regarding the credit practices of Dante's Appliance and Audio." Such a provision would, Zimmerman thinks, prohibit Daniel from reporting the violations to the prosecutor or the consumer protection agency, and perhaps even the Better Business Bureau, but would clearly not prohibit him from calling the newspaper to see if someone there would be interested in writing a story.

Would it be appropriate at this stage for Zimmerman to include the contemplated reporting provision to the settlement agreement? If he includes it, is he obligated to explain its implications to Modell? Is he obligated to explain its implications to Daniel?

NOTES, QUESTIONS, AND EXAMPLES

What possible actions in response might be taken if a lawyer intentionally alters the agreed-to terms in the process of reducing the agreement to writing?

B.   HARASSMENT AND OTHER ABUSIVE CONDUCT

PROBLEM 6-2

[handwritten: Lawyer] *[handwritten: Client]*

[handwritten margin note: bought stove from Dante's at unfair interest rate]

George Cos represents Marina Voinovic in a consumer matter. Ms. Voinovic, who speaks little English, is a recent Croatian immigrant. She purchased a kitchen stove for an exorbitant price financed at a high rate of interest from Dante's Appliances. Cos has grown enamored with the idea of litigating against what he sees as a blight on the community. He has come to believe that Dante's advertising and credit practices are an abomination, and regards his work on Ms. Voinovic's case as a public service. Cos is about to do some investigating. He speaks a good bit of Croatian (his mother was a Croatian immigrant), and has decided he wants to know what happens when a non-English speaker deals with the sales staff at Dante's Appliance and Audio.

[handwritten margin note: Lawyer fakes like he is Croatian, no Eng]

Upon entering the store, Cos is approached by a salesman. "What can I do for you today?" begins the salesman. "Péc" ("stove" in Croatian), says Cos. "I don't understand, do you speak English?" responds the salesman. Haltingly and in a broken English, Cos responds, "I have no English." Cos then points to the area of the store in which the ovens and stoves are displayed. "Ah, sure, ovens. Let me show you what I have," responds the salesman as he directs Cos to the oven displays. Once there, the salesman takes Cos directly to the top-of-the-line, most extravagant and expensive stove on the display. Cos recognizes the type and model of oven and notes that the price marked on it is $500 more than its price at Sears or other similar retail outlets. After making various motions and demonstrations with the oven, opening and closing doors, lifting burners to show access for cleaning and so forth, the salesman continues, "This is the one you have to have. Do you have money, dollars?" The salesman demonstrates by pulling his wallet out and showing Cos a $100 bill. Cos nods and is led to an office. The salesman pulls a document out of his desk drawer and begins writing. He looks up from his desk at Cos and asks, "Your name. What are you called?" "Antal Voinovic," responds Cos. The salesman prints the name on the form, does some other blank filling, and then turns the paper toward Cos and hands him a pen. "I need some money from you, and you sign your name here," the salesman says using gestures and motions to demonstrate. "This is how we buy things in America." Cos thinks that he has seen enough to know precisely what had happened to his client. He already had the salesman's business card in his pocket. He shakes his head, mutters, and turns and walks slowly out of the store.

[handwritten margin note: is this violation?]

Has Cos violated ethical norms with his investigative technique? Could Cos have learned as much as he did with more candor? Could the civil discovery process have produced this information? Can you square your answer to the previous two questions with our notion of civil justice?

[handwritten: yes. p. 360]

Lawyers may not use unlawful means to achieve a client's goals. As well, lawyers may not use lawful but harassing conduct to achieve a client's goals if there is no legitimate, substantial purpose served by the harassing conduct. Several special harassment rules apply in the context of specific categories of third parties.

IN RE KNIGHT
281 A.2d 46 (Vt. 1971)

Knight - Actor
Harrington - Firm owner

PER CURIAM.

The Attorney General has filed a presentment seeking disciplinary action against the respondent, an attorney. The respondent was an employee of John B. Harrington, a former attorney of this Court, who was convicted of extortion. Harrington was later disbarred by this Court.

The presentment filed by the Attorney General makes no claim that the respondent participated in the extortion attempt by Harrington, but charges him with participating in the planning and the execution of the plan to entrap a libelee in a proposed divorce action in a compromising situation with a young woman hired for the purpose of such entrapment.

This Court appointed a committee, pursuant to 4 V.S.A. § 844, to hear evidence from both the State and the respondent on the matters charged in the presentment, and that committee has made findings of fact for the consideration of this Court.

The findings clearly indicate that the respondent was present when the plans were made for the proposed entrapment, and that he journeyed to New Hampshire where the entrapment took place, and participated in both the electronic eavesdropping and the taking of photographs of the meeting between the possible libelee in the proposed divorce action and the young woman hired by Harrington to effect a compromising situation with the victim. . . .

The respondent had been admitted to practice in Vermont in February, 1967. In July, 1967, he went to work for the Harrington firm as an employee, on a weekly salary basis. The events which led to this presentment occurred on or about March 6, 1968, at a time when the respondent had been engaged in the practice of law for about eight months.

* * *

The Court will take this opportunity to express its strong disapproval that evidence of an adulterous act, obtained by connivance, or by entrapment is in any way proper or acceptable. Participation is any such scheme is unprofessional conduct warranting and justifying disciplinary action. The conduct complained of here is unworthy of the high standards of the Bar and of the honorable profession of law.

* * *

We are of the opinion that the respondent must be disciplined for his unethical conduct, and his inaction, when an opportunity came to disassociate himself from the nefarious plan before its culmination. The State does not ask that the respondent be disbarred, and we agree that considering the mitigating circumstances in the situation of the respondent, such severity would not be justified. However, since the conduct of the respondent cannot be entirely excused or palliated, the following judgment is imposed:

Judgment that the respondent, William J. Knight, is suspended from the office of attorney at law and solicitor in chancery beginning July 1, 1971, with leave to apply for reinstatement on or after October 1, 1971.

NOTES, QUESTIONS, AND EXAMPLES

1. How does routine, police undercover investigation under prosecutorial direction differ from Knight's conduct?

2. How should courts treat the use of litigation "testers"? Plaintiff's lawyers in, for example, housing discrimination or consumer fraud cases sometimes use testers. Testers pose as prospective home purchasers or apartment renters or consumers shopping at a particular store to gather evidence of the conduct of sellers who are suspected of engaging in discrimination or fraud. Are these lawyers engaging in disciplinable conduct?

Model Rule 4.4 prohibits a lawyer from using "means that have no substantial purpose other than to embarrass, delay, or burden a third person." At first reaction, one might guess that the prohibition should be absolute, but reflection says otherwise. Lawyers legitimately do a wide variety of acts that embarrass, delay, and burden others. Merely noticing a deposition creates a possibility of embarrassment, delay, and burden to a third person who is commanded to attend and be a witness. Cross-examination, filing a complaint, sending a demand letter and so on, all create possibilities for third parties to be delayed and burdened. Thus the rule only prohibits actions that serve no substantial, legitimate purpose, but are merely done to embarrass, delay, or burden the third person.

Opposing parties are a special category of third party. Their interests are most directly contrary to those of the lawyer's client. Opposing parties are, therefore, routinely the object of a lawyer's client-favoring activities. Specific limits on those client-favoring activities directed toward opposing parties are found in the assisting client misconduct rule (*see* MR 1.2(d)), the statements to others rule (*see* MR 4.1), the communications limits rules, and in various in-litigation rules (*see* MR 3.1–3.4).

A great deal of lawyer conduct toward witnesses may be perceived by the witness as harassing.

Lawyers are prohibited from engaging in live contact investigations of jurors and from other harassing conduct. (For other, "duty to the justice system" rules that relate to lawyers and jurors, see Chapter VII.) Lawyers may investigate prospective jurors' backgrounds by means of public records such as deeds, judgments, available voting records, and so on. After discharge, lawyers may communicate with jurors within certain constraints. Contact is prohibited if it is prohibited by other law, if the juror has made known to the lawyer the juror's desire not to be contacted or if the communication involves misrepresentation, coercion, or other misconduct.

MR 3.5(c). Lawyers may not engage in conduct that will cause jurors to question the justice system's use of their verdict. Lawyers may contact jurors to inquire about the lawyer's trial performance, provided the lawyer refrains from harassing conduct.

IN RE HANSEN
318 N.W.2d 856 (Minn. 1982)

Per Curiam.

After considering charges of unprofessional conduct brought against respondent, Clifford F. Hansen, a panel of the Lawyers Professional Responsibility Board (LPRB) had recommended that he be indefinitely suspended and instructed the director of LPRB to file a petition for disciplinary action.

Respondent, who practices in Minneapolis as a sole practitioner, was admitted to the Minnesota Bar in 1922. He is 88 years old. One of his clients is Carl Henning, who owns certain residential rental property in Minneapolis. In February of 1978, Eileen Gravening, one of Henning's former tenants, filed a claim in Hennepin County Conciliation Court to recover a $75 damage deposit from Henning. She was awarded the full amount. Respondent, representing Henning, removed the matter to Hennepin County Municipal Court, where Gravening's husband was added as co-plaintiff.

The matter was heard by a jury on March 6, 1979. The jury awarded the Gravenings $427, which was the full amount of their damage deposit plus statutory and punitive damages. A three-judge panel of the Hennepin County District Court affirmed the action of the Municipal Court. Respondent then had Henning and his wife take polygraph tests. The cost of the tests was $350, which respondent advanced to the Hennings. The results of the tests apparently led respondent to believe that the Hennings had told the truth at the trial and that the Gravenings therefore must have lied. He also concluded that the Gravenings' attorney, Thomas Vasaly, must have encouraged them to present perjured testimony. Respondent then wrote a letter to Henning in which he criticized the jury's verdict and sent copies of the letter to each member of the jury. The letter stated in part:

> Obviously, you unfortunately got a Jury (5 female-persons, and 1 male-person), who either lacked good judgment or were in-different to their responsibilities as sworn jurors. It appears that they were out only a very short time to organize and discuss two days of testimony; and then returned a verdict soaking you for $200 — the maximum allowed by statute as punitive damages. — I wonder what they would have done had the statute allowed $500. — If they are ever again called as prospective jurors they should disclose the above.

In August of 1979, Thomas Vasaly filed allegations of unprofessional conduct against respondent with the LPRB.

At about the same time, respondent brought an action in Hennepin County District Court against the Ethics Committee. Shortly thereafter he filed a supplemental complaint naming LPRB as an additional defendant. Respondent's lawsuit was dismissed on February 5, 1980.

In December 1979, the Ethics Committee notified the director of LPRB regarding Vasaly's complaint and respondent's lawsuit, and recommended additional investigation. Respondent was asked by letter to meet with the director. Respondent replied, also by letter, that he would provide additional information only if ordered to do so by the Minnesota Supreme Court. He did not appear for the meeting with the director.

On March 31, 1980, respondent filed on behalf of Henning a lawsuit against the Gravenings; Thomas Vasaly; Vasaly's employer, the Legal Aid Society; and the Honorable Dana Nicholson, the presiding judge at the Municipal Court trial. Respondent sought to have the judgment in the Henning case vacated on the ground that the Gravenings submitted false evidence. The complaint charged that Vasaly had suborned perjury and that Judge Nicholson had "recklessly" misconstrued the law. Respondent also sought a grand jury investigation of the Gravening's allegedly false testimony and Vasaly's part in it, but the county attorney refused to initiate any such investigation. On September 24, 1980, the court granted summary judgment against respondent.

A panel of LPRB held a hearing on October 3, 1980, to consider the matter of respondent's conduct. The panel concluded that respondent had engaged in unprofessional conduct and found that, because respondent did not seem to recognize that his conduct was improper, it was likely to continue. . . .

On November 10, 1981, respondent brought an action in the United States District Court, District of Minnesota, naming as defendants the State of Minnesota, the Minnesota Supreme Court, Michael J. Hoover, Ben Grussendorf, the American Bar Association, and "John Doe and Richard Roe." The complaint alleged that by instituting disciplinary proceedings against respondent, the defendants violated respondent's first and fourteenth amendment rights, giving rise to a cause of action under 42 U.S.C. § 1983 (1976). The court granted the defendants' motion to dismiss on January 19, 1982.

(1) respondent sent the letter to the members of the jury to harass or embarrass them and to influence any future action they might take as jurors; (2) respondent's lawsuit against the Ethics Committee and LPRB was without basis and was intended to harass and injure defendants; . . . and (4) respondent's lawsuit against Thomas Vasaly and Judge Nicholson was also without merit and was intended to harass and injure them

* * *

We do not believe that the severe sanction of indefinite suspension is either appropriate or necessary for the protection of the public in this case. We are instead placing respondent on inactive status; he will remain a member of the bar of this state with the limitation that he may represent only members of his family. He will be required to wind up his practice with respect to all other matters, including that which gave rise to these proceedings.

So ordered.

NOTES, QUESTIONS, AND EXAMPLES

1. What is the relationship between the harassment rules, as applied to opposing parties, and Federal Rule of Civil Procedure 11 and the ethics codes' frivolous claims rule (MR 3.1)?

2. The Model Code included a provision prohibiting threats of criminal prosecution "solely to obtain advantage in a civil matter." DR 7-105. The Model Rule drafters melted this prohibition into the general harassment rule, Model Rule 4.4. The Comment to 4.4 suggests that the prohibition is coextensive with criminal liability for extortion. What threats are or are not appropriate under such rules?

C. COMMUNICATING WITH REPRESENTED PERSONS

Lawyers are prohibited from communicating about the subject matter of a dispute with represented opposing parties without first obtaining permission from the opposing party's lawyer. MR 4.2. The original version of Model Rule 4.2 adopted by the ABA prohibited unauthorized contact with opposing "parties." The rule has been amended to change "parties" to "persons" to make clear that there need not be pending litigation for the rule to have effect.

Particularly in the corporate context, difficulties have arisen in determining who is a person within the meaning of the rule.

NIESIG v. TEAM I
558 N.E.2d 1030 (N.Y. 1990)

OPINION OF THE COURT.

Plaintiff in this personal injury litigation, wishing to have his counsel privately interview a corporate defendant's employees who witnessed the accident, puts before us a question that has generated wide interest: are the employees of a corporate party also considered "parties" under Disciplinary Rule 7-104(A)(1) of the Code of Professional Responsibility, which prohibits a lawyer from communicating directly with a "party" known to have counsel in the matter?[6] The trial court and the Appellate Division both answered that an employee of a counseled corporate party in litigation is by definition also a "party" within the rule, and prohibited the interviews. For reasons of policy, we disagree.

Employees individually named as parties in the litigation, and employees individually represented by counsel, are not within the ambit of the question presented by this appeal. Nor, obviously, are direct interviews on consent of counsel, or those authorized by law, or communications by the client himself (unless instigated by counsel).

---

[6] [1] DR 7-104(A)(1) reads: "During the course of [the] representation of a client a lawyer shall not . . . [c]ommunicate or cause another to communicate with a party [the lawyer] knows to be represented by a lawyer in that matter unless [the lawyer] has the prior consent of the lawyer representing such other party or is authorized by law to do so."

As alleged in the complaint, plaintiff was injured when he fell from scaffolding at a building construction site. At the time of the accident he was employed by DeTrae Enterprises, Inc.; defendant J.M. Frederick was the general contractor, and defendant Team I the property owner. Plaintiff thereafter commenced a damages action against defendants, asserting two causes of action centering on Labor Law § 240, and defendants brought a third-party action against DeTrae.

Plaintiff moved for permission to have his counsel conduct ex parte interviews of all DeTrae employees who were on the site at the time of the accident, arguing that these witnesses to the event were neither managerial nor controlling employees and could not therefore be considered "personal synonyms for DeTrae." DeTrae opposed the application, asserting that the disciplinary rule barred unapproved contact by plaintiff's lawyer with any of its employees. Supreme Court denied plaintiff's request, and the Appellate Division modified by limiting the ban to DeTrae's current employees.

The Appellate Division concluded, for theoretical as well as practical reasons, that current employees of a corporate defendant in litigation "are presumptively within the scope of the representation afforded by the attorneys who appeared [in the litigation] on behalf of that corporation." Citing *Upjohn Co. v. United States*, the court held that DeTrae's attorneys have an attorney-client relationship with every DeTrae employee connected with the subject of the litigation.

In the main we disagree with the Appellate Division's conclusions. However, because we agree with the holding that DR 7-104(A)(1) applies only to current employees, not to former employees, we modify rather than reverse its order, and grant plaintiff's motion to allow the interviews.

DR 7-104(A)(1), which can be traced to the American Bar Association Canons of 1908, fundamentally embodies principles of fairness. The general thrust of the rule is to prevent situations in which a represented party may be taken advantage of by adverse counsel; the presence of the party's attorney theoretically neutralizes the contact. By preventing lawyers from deliberately dodging adversary counsel to reach — and exploit — the client alone, DR 7-104(A)(1) [and MR 4.2 —Ed.] safeguards against clients making improvident settlements, ill-advised disclosures and unwarranted concessions.

There is little problem applying DR 7-104(A)(1) to individuals in civil cases. In that context, the meaning of "party" is ordinarily plain enough: it refers to the individuals, not to their agents and employees. The question, however, becomes more difficult when the parties are corporations — as evidenced by a wealth of commentary, and controversy, on the issue.

The difficulty is not in whether DR 7-104(A)(1) applies to corporations. It unquestionably covers corporate parties, who are as much served by the rule's fundamental principles of fairness as individual parties. But the rule does not define "party," and its reach in this context is unclear. In litigation only the entity, not its employee, is the actual named party; on the other hand, corporations act solely through natural persons, and unless some employees are also considered parties, corporations are effectively read out of the rule. The issue therefore distills to which corporate employees should be deemed parties for purposes of DR 7-

104(A)(1), and that choice is one of policy. The broader the definition of "party" in the interests of fairness to the corporation, the greater the cost in terms of foreclosing vital informal access to facts.

The many courts, bar associations and commentators that have balanced the competing considerations have evolved various tests, each claiming some adherents, each with some imperfection. At one extreme is the blanket rule adopted by the Appellate Division and urged by defendants, and at the other is the "control group" test — both of which we reject. The first is too broad and the second too narrow.

Defendants' principal argument for the blanket rule — correlating the corporate "party" and all of its employees — rests on *Upjohn v. United States*. As the Supreme Court recognized, a corporation's attorney-client privilege includes communications with low-and mid-level employees; defendants argue that the existence of an attorney-client privilege also signifies an attorney-client relationship for purposes of DR 7-104(A)(1).

Upjohn, however, addresses an entirely different subject, with policy objectives that have little relation to the question whether a corporate employee should be considered a "party" for purposes of the disciplinary rule. First, the privilege applies only to confidential communications with counsel, it does not immunize the underlying factual information — which is in issue here — from disclosure to an adversary. Second, the attorney-client privilege serves the societal objective of encouraging open communication between client and counsel, a benefit not present in denying informal access to factual information. Thus, a corporate employee who may be a "client" for purposes of the attorney-client privilege is not necessarily a "party" for purposes of DR 7-104(A)(1).

The single indisputable advantage of a blanket preclusion — as with every absolute rule — is that it is clear.

Most significantly, the Appellate Division's blanket rule closes off avenues of informal discovery of information that may serve both the litigants and the entire justice system by uncovering relevant facts, thus promoting the expeditious resolution of disputes. Foreclosing all direct, informal interviews of employees of the corporate party unnecessarily sacrifices the long recognized potential value of such sessions.

Nor, in our view, is it necessary to shield all employees from informal interviews in order to safeguard the corporation's interest. Informal encounters between a lawyer and an employee-witness are not — as a blanket ban assumes — invariably calculated to elicit unwitting admissions; they serve long-recognized values in the litigation process.

We fully recognize that, as the Appellate Division observed, every rule short of the absolute poses practical difficulties as to where to draw the line, and leaves some uncertainty as to which employees fall on either side of it. Nonetheless, we conclude that the values served by permitting access to relevant information require that an effort be made to strike a balance, and that uncertainty can be minimized if not eliminated by a clear test that will become even clearer in practice.

We are not persuaded, however, that the "control group" test — defining "party" to include only the most senior management exercising substantial control over the corporation — achieves that goal. Unquestionably, that narrow (though still uncertain) definition of corporate "party" better serves the policy of promoting open access to relevant information. But that test gives insufficient regard to the principles motivating DR 7-104(A)(1), and wholly overlooks the fact that corporate employees other than senior management also can bind the corporation. The "control group" test all but "nullifies the benefits of the disciplinary rule to corporations." Given the practical and theoretical problems posed by the "control group" test, it is hardly surprising that few courts or bar associations have ever embraced it.

The test that best balances the competing interests, and incorporates the most desirable elements of the other approaches, is one that defines "party" to include corporate employees whose acts or omissions in the matter under inquiry are binding on the corporation (in effect, the corporation's "alter egos") or imputed to the corporation for purposes of its liability, or employees implementing the advice of counsel. All other employees may be interviewed informally.

Unlike a blanket ban or a "control group" test, this solution is specifically targeted at the problem addressed by DR 7-104(A)(1). The potential unfair advantage of extracting concessions and admissions from those who will bind the corporation is negated when employees with "speaking authority" for the corporation, and employees who are so closely identified with the interests of the corporate party as to be indistinguishable from it, are deemed "parties" for purposes of DR 7-104(A)(1). Concern for the protection of the attorney-client privilege prompts us also to include in the definition of "party" the corporate employees responsible for actually effectuating the advice of counsel in the matter.

In practical application, the test we adopt thus would prohibit direct communication by adversary counsel "with those officials, but only those, who have the legal power to bind the corporation in the matter or who are responsible for implementing the advice of the corporation's lawyer, or any member of the organization whose own interests are directly at stake in a representation." (Wolfram, § 11.6, at 613.) This test would permit direct access to all other employees, and specifically — as in the present case — it would clearly permit direct access to employees who were merely witnesses to an event for which the corporate employer is sued.

Apart from striking the correct balance, this test should also become relatively clear in application. It is rooted in developed concepts of the law of evidence and the law of agency, thereby minimizing the uncertainty facing lawyers about to embark on employee interviews. A similar test, moreover, is the one overwhelmingly adopted by courts and bar associations throughout. the country, whose long practical experience persuades us that — in day-to-day operation — it is workable.

Accordingly, the order of the Appellate Division should be modified, without costs, by reversing so much of the Appellate Division order as denied plaintiff's motion to permit ex parte interviews of current DeTrae employees and, as so modified, the Appellate Division order should be affirmed and the certified question answered in the negative.

*   *   *

Order modified, without costs, in accordance with the opinion herein and, as so modified, affirmed. Certified question answered in the negative.

NOTES, QUESTIONS, AND EXAMPLES

1.   In the context of Model Rule 4.2, all forms of communication are prohibited including in-person, telephone, and written or electronic forms of communication.

2.   Lawyers may not avoid the application of this rule by communicating with opposing parties through a lawyer's agent. MR 5.4(c).

3.   Opposing parties, however, may communicate with one another without offending Model Rule 4.2, provided that the lawyer has not instructed the client to do so as a means of circumventing the rule. *See In re Marietta*, 569 P.2d 921 (Kan. 1977).

4.   The *Niesig* court says when applying Model Rule 4.2 to individuals, "party" (now "person") "plain[ly] enough refers to the individuals, not their agents or employees." Why are an individual's agents and employees such an insignificant analytical problem when agents and employees of a corporation or other organization are so great an analytical problem?

5.   In the February 2002 amendments to Model Rule 4.2, the ABA has taken the position that "consent of the organization's lawyer is not required for communication with a former [employee]." MR 4.2, Comment 7.

Special Criminal Prosecution Concerns

In criminal practice, of course, the opposing party of the prosecutor is a criminal defendant. Two different aspects of this special configuration are worthy of note. Fifth and Fourteenth Amendment due process rights and Sixth Amendment right to counsel protections restrain prosecutors' contact with criminal defendants in ways that go beyond the professional responsibility law constraints of Model Rule 4.2. Although the details of the constitutional constraints are beyond the scope of this book, when a prosecutor intentionally violates the constitutional constraints, the prosecutor is subject to discipline for engaging in conduct that is prejudicial to the administration of justice. MR 8.4(d).

Prosecutors, especially federal prosecutors invoking not only Model Rule 4.2's "authorized by law" language but also the Supremacy Clause of the United States Constitution, have argued that their crime investigation activities are not restricted by Model Rule 4.2's requirements of consent by an opposing party's lawyer prior to communication. In essence, the prosecutors have argued that crime investigation, particularly surreptitious crime investigation, would be unreasonably diminished by a rule that required a prosecutor to contact a criminal investigation target's lawyer prior to any contact by the prosecutor's agents, police investigators.

When prosecutors, through police undercover agents, seek to infiltrate the ranks of organized crime, the prosecutors know as a general matter that some of the investigation's targets are represented by counsel. Strict compliance with Model Rule 4.2 would require the prosecutor to obtain the target's counsel's permission prior to the investigation proceeding to the stage at which the undercover investigators communicate with the target, thwarting any effort to ferret out crime through undercover investigations.

UNITED STATES v. LOPEZ
765 F. Supp. 1433 (N.D. Cal. 1991)

MARILYN HALL PATEL, UNITED STATES DISTRICT JUDGE.

INTRODUCTION

The past decade has witnessed a rapidly growing concern regarding the ethical conduct of lawyers. More and more citizens are lodging complaints alleging misconduct by attorneys, and state bar associations are becoming increasingly active in investigating and addressing such complaints. Even with these efforts, the public remains critical of existing mechanisms for lawyer discipline and has demanded more accountability from the legal profession.

* * *

Rather than evading the new focus on lawyer misconduct, government attorneys and prosecutors often have found themselves at the center of it. The most recent report of the Attorney General's Office of Professional Responsibility indicates that there has been a notable increase in the number of complaints, both substantiated and unsubstantiated, of ethical violations by federal prosecutors. This growth undoubtedly arises from both the swift increase in the number of attorneys employed by the Department of Justice and evolving efforts by the Department to limit the rights of suspects and defendants in certain areas.[7] Many commentators have voiced concern over the increasing frequency of incidents of prosecutorial misconduct and the ineffectiveness or non-existence of sanctions designed to prevent such misdeeds.

In the midst of these developments, the Attorney General has issued a policy directive which purports to exempt Department of Justice attorneys from one of the most widely-accepted and time-honored ethical rules governing the conduct of attorneys involved in litigation. The implementation of the Attorney General's policy in this case has resulted in the motion to dismiss now before the court.

BACKGROUND

[Lopez, Olivas, and Escobedo were indicted for various drug offenses and they were denied bail. Escobedo's brother contacted attorney Twitty regarding repre

---

[7] [6] *See, e.g.*, Memorandum To All Justice Department Litigators From Dick Thornburgh, Attorney General, June 8, 1989 ("Thornburgh Memorandum").

sentation, and Twitty entered appearances on behalf of all three defendants at various preliminary matters. Olivas then retained attorney Rosenthal, and Lopez retained attorney Tarlow.

[Tarlow took the position that Lopez had a viable defense and that he (Tarlow) would not engage in any plea negotiations. Tarlow informed Lopez that he would not participate in any plea negotiations. Disputes developed between the prosecutor, Assistant United States Attorney Lyons, and Tarlow. Tarlow authorized Twitty and Rosenthal to speak with Lopez as necessary. After approximately two months in jail, plea negotiations resumed, at whose initiation Lopez and Twitty disagreed. Without notice to Tarlow, Twitty contacted Lyons to arrange a meeting among Twitty, Lyons, Lopez and Escobedo. Lyons later asserted that he did not inquire about Tarlow's absence from the arrangements because he believed that if Tarlow had learned of the meeting, Lopez's family would be endangered. Lyons claimed that because Lopez was enmeshed in a drug distribution ring and because Lyons believed that Tarlow's fee was being paid by the drug ring, Lyons believed that Lopez was interested in engaging in the negotiations without Tarlow in order to guard his family's safety. Twitty asserted that he specifically told Lyons that Lopez was not concerned about his family's safety and that no one connected to the drug ring was paying Tarlow's fees.

[Lyons approached the court ex parte regarding the possibility of a meeting among Twitty, Lyons, Lopez and Escobedo without notice to Tarlow. Lyons told the court of his belief regarding Lopez's family and of Lyons's belief that that concern was motivating Lopez to seek a meeting without notice to Lopez's lawyer despite having been told by Twitty that these concerns were unfounded. An in camera hearing was held before a magistrate judge with Lyons and Lopez present. At the hearing, Lopez signed a document waiving his right to have counsel present at the upcoming meeting among Twitty, Lyons, Lopez and Escobedo. Thereafter, the meeting was held. No record of the meeting was kept. Following the meeting, Twitty continued his contact with Lopez and Escobedo regarding possible plea arrangements, all without notice to Tarlow.

[After once again clearing the procedure with the magistrate judge, a second meeting among the four was held. Under pressure from Lyons, at the second meeting Lopez for the first time provided Lyons with names of others involved in drug trafficking. After the second meeting, Lyons sent Twitty a proposed plea agreement for Escobedo and informed him that a similar agreement for Lopez would be made available provided Lopez secured counsel. After considering Lyons's proposal, both Lopez and Escobedo rejected it.

[Some time later, Lyons informed Rosenthal of the meetings that had been occurring. Although encouraged by Twitty to keep this information from Tarlow, Rosenthal told Tarlow of the secret meetings that had occurred. Tarlow then withdrew as counsel for Lopez based on the conflict that had been created by the secret meetings. —Ed.]

Defendant Lopez has now filed his motion to dismiss the indictment, alleging that the government violated both his sixth amendment right to counsel and rules of professional conduct, which prohibit an attorney from communicating with an opposing party who is represented without the knowledge and consent of opposing counsel. The court held a series of evidentiary hearings on the motion and took testimony from AUSA Lyons, attorney Twitty, and defendant Lopez.

Discussion

The proceedings in connection with defendant Lopez's motion to dismiss focused primarily on the applicability to this case of ethical rules limiting contact between an attorney and a represented party, and it is to this issue that the court initially turns.

I. Ethical Requirements

Rule 2-100 of the Rules of Professional Conduct of the State Bar of California states as follows:

> (A) While representing a client, a member shall not communicate directly or indirectly about the subject of the representation with a party the member knows to be represented by another lawyer in the matter, unless the member has the consent of the other lawyer . . .

> (C) This rule shall not prohibit:

>> (1) Communications with a public officer, board, committee, or body;

>> (2) Communications initiated by a party seeking advice or representation from an independent lawyer of the party's choice; or

>> (3) Communications authorized by law.

Rule 2-100 tracks the language of American Bar Association Disciplinary Rule ("DR") 7-104(A)(1) and ABA Model Rule of Professional Conduct 4.2. This court, through its Local Rules, has adopted the State Bar's Rules of Professional Conduct as the applicable standards of professional conduct for the Northern District of California.

Because of the shared language and purpose of ABA DR 7-104, ABA Model Rule 4.2, and Rule 2-100 of the State Bar of California, the court will utilize authority and sources concerning all three in this opinion.

In the case at bar, the prosecutor essentially takes the position that he is exempt from Rule 2-100, and therefore, from the rules explicitly adopted by this court to govern the conduct of attorneys who appear before it. In asserting this position, the prosecutor relies primarily on a policy directive issued by Attorney General Richard Thornburgh on June 8, 1989. The Thornburgh Memorandum declares that Department of Justice ("DOJ") attorneys engaged in law enforcement activity are not bound by the strictures of DR 7-104.

While the prosecutor relies primarily on the Thornburgh Memorandum to support his position with regard to the alleged violation of this court's Local Rules, he also advances several other arguments. First, the government posits that the separation of powers doctrine prevents this court from enforcing its Local Rules against DOJ attorneys where, as here, there is a conflict between those Rules and the policies of the Department of Justice. Second, the prosecutor contends that

Rule 2-100 exempts all criminal investigations from coverage. Third, it is argued that the secret meetings between the government and defendant Lopez are akin to pre-indictment contacts and therefore should be considered exempt from Rule 2-100.

Finally, the government suggests that several factors particular to this case counsel against a finding of prosecutorial misconduct. These include the facts that the Magistrate intervened prior to the secret meetings and that defendant Lopez initiated the contact with the government and waived his right to counsel. As the court will explain below, the government's contentions are completely devoid of merit.

A. Thornburgh Memorandum

The Thornburgh Memorandum laments the purported use of DR 7-104 by defense counsel "to prohibit communications by law enforcement personnel with the target of a criminal investigation, whether or not a constitutional right to counsel has attached." The Memorandum identifies two contexts in which the "problem" has most often arisen: (1) where government agents or attorneys seek to covertly or overtly interview a suspect who has retained counsel; and (2) in instances of multiple representation, where the principal target of an investigation pays an attorney to represent several individuals, or where an organization under investigation pays an attorney who claims to represent all employees of the organization.

The Thornburgh Memorandum reflects the Attorney General's perception that enforcement of DR 7-104 represents "a substantial burden on the law enforcement process." As a result, the Memorandum seeks to exempt DOJ attorneys from compliance with the ethical duties created by the rule. Much of the language of the Memorandum suggests that the Attorney General's policy applies primarily in the pre-indictment context.[8] Moreover, the examples provided by the Memorandum suggest that the policy was meant to be applied in organized crime cases and corporate or organizational-type settings.

While the Memorandum thus seems to suggest that the parameters of the Attorney General's policy are limited, it nonetheless closes with the sweeping statement that "the 'authorized by law' exemption in DR 7-104 applies to all communications with represented individuals by Department attorneys or by others acting at their direction." If there were any doubts as to the scope of the policy, they have been dispelled by the brief filed by the Department of Justice in this case, which makes clear the Department's position that the purported exemption exists after indictment and outside the corporate and organized crime contexts.

There are profound flaws in the Attorney General's policy and they are

---

[8] [21] For example, the Memorandum states that "it is the clear policy of the Department that in the course of a criminal investigation, an attorney for the government is authorized to direct and supervise the use of undercover law enforcement agents, informants, and other cooperating individuals to gather evidence by communicating with any person who has not been made the subject of formal federal criminal adversarial proceedings arising from that investigation, regardless of whether the person is known to be represented by counsel."

demonstrated within the four corners of the Thornburgh Memorandum. Even a cursory examination of the authority cited by the Attorney General reveals that the cases do not support the policy articulated in the Memorandum.

[The court describes several cases cited by the Attorney General to demonstrate that they are inapposite. —Ed.]

Finally, the Attorney General's Memorandum cites to numerous cases which purportedly recognize the legitimacy of undercover law enforcement investigations, even when the investigations involve individuals who keep an attorney on retainer. Without exception, however, these cases involve pre-indictment investigations.[9] Several of the decisions cited by the Department of Justice go to great lengths to distinguish the interests at stake in the pre-indictment context from those which must be considered once an individual has been indicted and is in custody.

Indeed, those courts asked to decide whether DR 7-104 applies in the pre-indictment context have assumed, without finding it necessary to discuss, that the Rule applies to government attorneys in the post-indictment context.

This court has attempted without success to locate any authority for the proposition that DR 7-104 does not apply to a government attorney who communicates with a represented individual under indictment. This, of course, is not surprising in light of the tortured logic of the Attorney General's policy.

The Department asserts that government attorneys involved in criminal investigations are "authorized by law" to make contact with represented individuals by virtue of federal statutes which empower the Attorney General to investigate and prosecute criminal violations. The implications of this assertion are alarming, since nearly all conceivable action taken by a prosecutor involve these activities. Indeed, the entire post-indictment conduct of a prosecutor is driven by the goal of completing the prosecution.

The government argues that federal statutes authorize Department attorneys to make contact with represented individuals in criminal investigations. However, these are nothing more than general authorizing statutes; none expressly or impliedly authorize government attorneys either to disregard court-adopted rules or to violate ethical rules regarding contact with represented individuals. For

---

[9] [22] *United States v. Kenny*, 645 F.2d 1323, 1339 (9th Cir.), *cert. denied*, 452 U.S. 920 (1981) ("We again emphasize the factual setting of the tape recording: a non-custodial environment, prior to Kenny's charge, arrest, or indictment. In our view, the Government's use of such investigative techniques at this stage of a criminal matter does not implicate the sorts of ethical problems addressed by the Code."); *United States v. Lemonakis*, 485 F.2d 941, 956, 158 U.S. App. D.C. 162 (D.C. Cir. 1973), *cert. denied*, 415 U.S. 989 (1974) (pre-indictment government recording of meeting between informant and represented individual without attorney present does not violate DR 7- 104); *United States v. Sutton*, 801 F.2d 1346, 1366, 255 U.S. App. D.C. 307 (D.C. Cir. 1986) (pre-indictment taping of represented individual absent counsel does not violate DR 7-104); *United States v. Fitterer*, 710 F.2d 1328, 1333 (8th Cir.), *cert. denied*, 464 U.S. 852 (1983) (DR 7-104 does not apply when represented individual are not indicted or charged and are not in custody); *United States v. Vasquez*, 675 F.2d 16, 17 (2d Cir. 1983) (no violation of DR 7-104 where government informant taped conversation with represented individual in absence of counsel prior to indictment); *United States v. Jamil*, 707 F.2d 638, 646 (2d Cir. 1984), (in pre-indictment context, where government investigators were not acting as alter egos of prosecutor and prosecutor only became aware of recording after it was made, customs agents' action in wiring informant and recording conversation with represented suspect did not violate DR 7-104).

example, section 547 defines the duties of a U.S. Attorney. Courts interpreting section 547 have consistently ruled that this statute does not exempt U.S. Attorneys from their obligations to act fairly and with proper deference to the rights of the accused.

Were this court to accept the Department's argument in this regard, it is not clear that there would be any conduct the prosecutor could not undertake, as long as it was pursuant to his or her responsibility to investigate and prosecute crimes. DOJ attorneys would be exempt from rules adopted by federal courts to govern ethical conduct of attorneys practicing before them. This is, quite simply, an unacceptable result. Local rules are clearly meant to apply to all attorneys practicing in federal court, regardless of the client they represent.

Without an ethical restraint, a prosecutor's authority to communicate with represented individuals would be virtually limitless. The courts have been careful to avoid such a result and have thus held that Department attorneys are authorized to communicate with represented individuals without their attorney only in the pre-indictment context.

The Attorney General's "authorized by law" theory thus has no foundation. Indeed, there are compelling reasons why the ethical prohibition encompassed in Rule 2-100 and analogous ABA rules should apply to DOJ attorneys, at least in the post-indictment context.

Courts have consistently ruled that DR 7-104 applies to prosecutors. Indeed, it can be argued that the prohibition against communication with a represented individual is even more important in the criminal context than in civil cases. A prosecutor "has more direct power over the lives, property and reputations of those in [his] jurisdiction than anyone else in this nation . . . ." In light of the prosecutor's tremendous power and the fundamental individual rights at stake in criminal prosecutions, " 'the character, quality, and efficiency of the whole [criminal justice] system is shaped in great measure by the manner in which the prosecutor exercises his or her broad discretionary powers.' "

It is for this very reason that ABA Prosecution Function Standard 3-1.1(d) makes it the duty of every prosecutor "to know and be guided by the standards of professional conduct as defined in the codes and canons of the legal profession . . . ? This duty has been codified in the Department of Justice Standards of Conduct, which require DOJ attorneys to be guided in their conduct by the Code of Professional Responsibility of the ABA. 28 CFR § 45.735-1.

Given the above discussion, the court finds that DR 7-104 and its equivalent, Rule 2-100 of the State Bar of California, apply to DOJ attorneys, at least in the post-indictment phase of criminal investigations and prosecutions. To the extent that the Thornburgh Memorandum instructs federal prosecutors to the contrary, it is misguided and not premised on sound legal authority. To the extent that the Memorandum purports to authorize DOJ attorneys to disregard an ethical rule which has been adopted by this court pursuant to its Local Rules, the Memorandum instructs federal prosecutors to violate federal law.

B. Factors Specific To This Case

Although the government relies primarily on the Thornburgh Memorandum to justify the actions of the prosecutor in this case, it also points to several factors which it contends remove AUSA Lyons' conduct from the purview of Rule 2-100. First, the government maintains that Rule 2-100 explicitly exempts criminal investigations of all types. Second, the government suggests that Lyons' communication with Lopez was akin to a pre-indictment investigatory contact. Third, the government argues that the rule is irrelevant because defendant Lopez initiated the contact. Finally, the government contends that Lopez waived the rule and that the court, through the actions of the Magistrate Judge, sanctioned this waiver. The court will address each of these arguments in turn.

[The court rejects the first two arguments of the United States.]

* * *

Nor is the prosecutor's conduct excused by the fact that the defendant initiated contact with the government. Courts have consistently ruled that the ethical prohibition bars a prosecutor from communicating with a represented individual without his or her counsel even if it is the individual who makes the first contact. The Discussion text following Rule 2-100 explicitly states that it is irrelevant whether an attorney is contacted by the opposing party. In addition, the Committee on Professional Ethics of the ABA has unanimously ruled that the ethical prohibition is violated even when the defendant initiates contact with the government. Moreover, as the ethical prohibition applies to attorneys and is designed in part to protect their effectiveness, a represented party may not waive it.

* * *

III. Remedy

[The court determined that the appropriate remedy is dismissal of the charges. —Ed.]

* * *

CONCLUSION

Relying on a faulty and tortured reading of existing authority, the Attorney General has issued a policy directive instructing attorneys of the Department of Justice to disregard a fundamental ethical rule embraced by every jurisdiction in this country. In the case at bar, the Attorney General's policy resulted in both the intentional disregard of the court's Local Rules by an Assistant United States Attorney and the loss by defendant of his counsel of choice. The Department of Justice, invoking the separation of powers doctrine, now seeks to render the court powerless to enforce its own rules and to protect the integrity of the criminal justice system.

This court will not allow the Attorney General to make a mockery of the court's constitutionally-granted judicial powers. The title U.S. Attorney does not give the prosecutor a "hunting license exempt from ethical constraints of advocacy." *United*

States v. Bursten, 453 F.2d 605, 610-11 (5th Cir. 1971), cert. denied, 409 U.S. 843 (1974). If anything, government prosecutors owe a higher duty to the court and the criminal justice system. "The U.S. Attorneys are entrusted with a unique role that includes the duty to protect the interests of all people, including, of course, the legitimate rights of those accused of crime in the federal courts." *United States v. Butler*, 567 F.2d 885, 894 (9th Cir. 1978) (Ely, J., concurring). At a minimum, this means that government prosecutors must scrupulously obey ethical rules adopted by the court.

This court, mindful of the public's strong interest in the completion of criminal prosecutions, has carefully considered the factors weighing against dismissal. Indeed, it is only the perilous threat that the Attorney General's policy poses to the court's constitutional powers and to the integrity of the criminal justice system that has moved the court to consider so extreme a remedy. Nonetheless, the court is convinced that no remedy short of dismissal will have any significant deterrent effect on future government misconduct of the type found in this case.

Therefore, the court hereby exercises its supervisory power and DISMISSES the indictment of Jose Orlando Lopez.

It is so Ordered.

NOTES, QUESTIONS, AND EXAMPLES

1.   On appeal, the Ninth Circuit affirmed the District Court on its application of the California version of Model Rule 4.2, but reversed its remedy determination, saying,

> Consequently, even if the district court's finding that Lyons misled the court is correct, we conclude that the district court abused its discretion in dismissing the indictment. We are sensitive to the district court's concerns that none of the alternative sanctions available to it are as certain to impress the government with our resoluteness in holding prosecutors to the ethical standards which regulate the legal profession as a whole. At the same time, we are confident that, when there is no showing of substantial prejudice to the defendant, lesser sanctions, such as holding the prosecutor in contempt or referral to the state bar for disciplinary proceedings, can be adequate to discipline and punish government attorneys who attempt to circumvent the standards of their profession.

United States v. Lopez, 4 F.3d 1455, 1464 (9th Cir. 1993).

2.   The Department of Justice has promulgated through the normal administrative rule-making process regulations to govern federal government lawyers in the no-contact context. 28 C.F.R. § 77.1 *et seq.* The "Reno rule," as it has come to be called, allows federal government lawyers to have direct contact with represented persons if the party signs a knowing waiver of counsel with court approval, if the communication is made in the course of an investigation of additional, different, or ongoing crimes or civil violations, including attempts to obstruct the immediate proceeding, or if the lawyer has a good faith belief that the communication is

necessary to avert a threat to the life or safety of a third person. In 1998, Congress passed the McDade Amendment (28 U.S.C. § 530B) as a part of the federal appropriations bill. The McDade Amendment appears deceptively simple, declaring that federal government lawyers must comply with state ethics rules. Many questions of the implications of the provision remain, however. For example, because of Model Rule 4.2's authorized by law (and after the February 2002 amendments, the authorized by court order) provision, might the Reno rule or other federal regulations themselves be regarded as the authorization to contact represented persons? Might the McDade Amendment refocus attention on the authority of state prosecutors to contact represented persons under Model Rule 4.2? *See* Fred C. Zacharias & Bruce A. Green, *The Uniqueness of Federal Prosecutors*, 88 GEO. L.J. 207 (2000).

3.   Consider the paternalism in Model Rule 4.2's application to *Lopez.* Lopez wanted to meet separately with the AUSA and he wanted to avoid telling Tarlow in order to preserve the prospect of his serving as trial counsel. Lopez seems to have done just what he wanted to do, and yet Model Rule 4.2 and the court's application of it would prevent him from making these choices.

4.   Oregon has adopted a one-of-a-kind provision relating to lawyers' supervision of covert activity that goes beyond the prosecutor's typical use of Model Rule 4.2's "authorized by law" clause. A new DR 1-102(D) reads as follows:

> Notwithstanding DR 1-102(A)(1), (A)(3) and (A)(4) and DR 7-102(A)(5), it shall not be unprofessional misconduct for a lawyer to advise clients or others about or to supervise lawful covert activity in the investigation of violations of civil or criminal law or constitutional rights, provided the lawyer's conduct is otherwise in compliance with these disciplinary rules. "Covert activity," as used in this rule, means an effort to obtain information on unlawful activity through the use of misrepresentations or other subterfuge. "Covert activity" may be commenced by a lawyer or involve a lawyer as an advisor or supervisor only when the lawyer in good faith believes there is a reasonable possibility that unlawful activity has taken place, is taking place, or will take place in the foreseeable future.

INTERNATIONAL NOTE

Some jurisdictions make exceptions to their "no-contact" rules for limited categories of written communications. For example, the Ethical Code for Italian Lawyers makes an exception to correspondence, copied to the opposing party's lawyer, that notifies the opposing party that a specific act must be completed by a certain date or that a stipulated payment is due. ETHICAL CODE FOR ITALIAN LAWYERS, art. 27. The French National Bar Council rules make an exception for written communications regarding settlement before the commencement of court proceedings and phone calls under the same circumstances if initiated by the opposing party. NATIONAL BAR COUNCIL OF FRANCE, HARMONIZED PRACTICE RULES, art. 8.2.

D. COMMUNICATING WITH UNREPRESENTED PERSONS

While not prohibited from communicating with unrepresented persons who are involved in a client's matter, lawyers are restricted in what they may say to such a person. MR 4.3. Lawyers have both affirmative and clarifying duties with respect to the lawyer's role in communicating with an unrepresented person. A lawyer is under an affirmative obligation to refrain from stating or implying that the lawyer is disinterested in the matter about which the lawyer is communicating. Any effort to mislead an unrepresented person about the lawyer's interest subjects the lawyer to discipline. When a lawyer "reasonably should know" that an unrepresented person misunderstands the lawyer's interest in the matter, the lawyer is obliged to make reasonable efforts to clarify his role.

MONSANTO CO. v. AETNA CASUALTY AND SURETY CO.
593 A.2d 1013 (Del. Super. Ct. 1990)

ORDER

[COUNSEL:] [Telling the truth in civil litigation] is, of course, a very attractive proposition. But, I would like to visit with your Honor further examination of that proposition, because while that might be nice in a perfect world, it is not the way the system operates in litigation in this country.

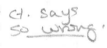

THE COURT: Sad comment [counsel].

Transcript of proceedings, Oral Argument on Temporary Restraining Order at 25 (June 8, 1990).

Upon further reflection, I am compelled in the strongest way possible to reject counsel's observations as being so repugnant and so odious to fair minded people that it can only be considered as anathema to any system of civil justice under law.

1. This matter is presently before the Court on Monsanto Company's ("Monsanto") motion for a protective order pursuant to Rule 26(c) of the Superior Court Civil Rules.[10]

---

[10] [1] Monsanto originally sought a temporary restraining order and in the alternative a Rule 26 protective order. After the oral argument on June 8 on these issues, I decided by written order of the same date, that Monsanto's requests and contentions could more properly be resolved under Rule 26. Monsanto's application comes fast on the heels of a similar application in the case of *National Union Fire Insurance Company of Pittsburgh v. Stauffer Chemical Company*, Del. Super., C.A. No. 87C-SE-11-1-CV (filed September 2, 1987). In that matter, on December 11, 1989, counsel for Stauffer Chemical Company brought to my attention purported irregular conduct on the part of investigators who were, in behalf of counsel for National Union, communicating with Stauffer's former employees. Based on the affirmative representations of counsel of record admitted pro hac vice to the effect that their investigators had always identified themselves and further that they advised the former employees that there was "a controversy among the parties," I did not see the need to do other than provide guidance to the effect that they should ascertain whether the former employees are represented by counsel, should identify who they are, and should advise that a controversy existed among the parties. Having done that and having been advised by counsel admitted hac vice that it was already being done, I then stated:

2. Monsanto contends that investigators, employed by certain defendant insurers, have misled former Monsanto employees in the course of investigating the claims at issue in this lawsuit. Monsanto asserts that such conduct violates Rules 4.2, 4.3 and 5.3 of the Delaware Lawyers' Rules of Professional Conduct.

In support of these contentions, Monsanto has submitted numerous affidavits of former employees of Monsanto who were contacted by investigators hired by the defendants. The affidavits suggest that the investigators have not inquired as to whether the interviewee was represented by counsel, have failed to inform the interviewees that they represented insurance companies involved in litigation adverse to Monsanto, or have misrepresented the scope of their representation. Monsanto requests, inter alia, a protective order to establish a "script," that is, a procedure to be used by investigators in conducting interviews with former Monsanto employees.

3. The defendants respond that interviews with former employees do not violate the Rules of Professional Conduct, that they have no duty to make the disclosures and ask the questions proposed in Monsanto's "script," and that such a "script" violates Rule of Professional Conduct 3.4(f)[11] and would effectively cut-off a very important informal discovery tool.

4. For reasons stated herein and without any compunction whatsoever, I embrace the proposition that in civil litigation in this jurisdiction one who is in search of the truth must tell the truth.

5. The Rules of Professional Conduct implicated in the matter sub judice are Rules 4.2 and 4.3. Rule of Professional Conduct 4.2 generally governs communications with represented persons. Rule 4.2 reads:

RULE 4.2 COMMUNICATION WITH PERSON REPRESENTED BY COUNSEL

> [The court determined that these former employees are not covered by Rule 4.2's restrictions. —Ed.]

At the same time I am satisfied that an attorney has certain ethical obligations

---

I'm glad to hear that's occurring. I think that's all I should say at this point. If it's not occurring, then we may all have a problem, again, with another governing body. And it may be that if that happens, then the friendliness pro hac won't be friendly any more and that's how I get involved. Okay?

On April 26, 1990, by emergency motion, counsel for Stauffer advised that the formerly asserted irregularities were continuing to occur and further advised that certain representations made by counsel admitted pro hac vice were in fact not accurate. Subsequent to a hearing on Stauffer's motion on May 11, 1990, I issued an order dated May 29, 1990, memorializing my ultimate findings that the Rules of Professional Conduct had been violated and directing that certain sanctions issue. The issue in *National Union* is presently before me on National Union's Motion for Reargument of my decision and order. By separate document dated this date, for reasons stated substantially herein, I have denied the Motion for Reargument.

[11] [2] Rule 3.4(f) provides: A lawyer shall not "request a person other than a client to refrain from voluntarily giving relevant information to another party unless: (1) the person is a relative or an employee or other agent of a client; and (2) the lawyer reasonably believes that the persons interests will not be adversely affected by refraining from giving such information."

vis-à-vis an unrepresented non-party witness, such as a former employee, as set forth in Rule 4.3 which provides:

RULE 4.3 DEALING WITH UNREPRESENTED PERSON

In dealing on behalf of a client with a person who is not represented by counsel, a lawyer shall not state or imply that the lawyer is disinterested. When the lawyer knows or reasonably should know that the unrepresented person misunderstands the lawyer's role in the matter, the lawyer shall make reasonable efforts to correct the misunderstanding.

6. The defendants assert that an investigator whose firm has been retained by a lawyer complies with Rule 4.3 by simply stating that he is an investigator seeking information. To support this contention the defendants have submitted the affidavits of two ethics experts, Professor Stephen Gillers and Professor Geoffrey C. Hazard, Jr. The defendants also assert that Rule 4.3 is designed to protect unrepresented persons from receiving legal advice or divulging information to an attorney whose interests are actually or potentially adverse to those of the unrepresented person.[12]

---

[12] [3] I am mindful of additional affidavits filed by Professors Gillers and Hazard in the Motion for Reargument filed in the National Union matter discussed supra at footnote 1. I am simply not persuaded by the analysis of these respected academicians. Indeed, I choose to accept an earlier analysis of Professor Hazard developed in a context removed from the heat of partisan litigation.

Professor Hazard in his treatise, THE LAW OF LAWYERING: A HANDBOOK ON THE MODEL RULES OF PROFESSIONAL CONDUCT, comments on the disclosure required under Rules 4.2 and 4.3. Professor Hazard states:

This short Rule is taken virtually verbatim from DR 7-104(A)(1) of the Code of Professional Responsibility. In tandem with Rule 4.3, it prevents a lawyer from taking advantage of a lay person to secure admissions against interest or to achieve an unconscionable settlement of a dispute. The scheme of the two Rules is that while Rule 4.3 prevents a lawyer from overreaching an unrepresented person, Rule 4.2 prevents a lawyer from nullifying the protection a represented person has achieved by retaining counsel. According to Rule 4.2, therefore, Lawyer A may not speak to Lawyer B's client, except under circumstances controlled by Lawyer B.

Under either Rule, of course, the third party retains ultimate control. An unrepresented person may choose to talk to an opposing lawyer after he has been duly warned, and a represented person may choose not to talk to the opposing side even if his lawyer has consented. Hazard & Hodes, THE LAW OF LAWYERING: A HANDBOOK ON THE MODEL RULES OF PROFESSIONAL CONDUCT, at 434 (Supp. 1989). In the same treatise Professor Hazard illustrates this warning requirement in a hypothetical which is in my view similar to the case sub judice. The "Facts" and "Comment" to that hypothetical read in full and in part as follows:

ILLUSTRATIVE CASE (b)

Facts: Lawyer L is litigating a products liability action against a major producer of home appliances. After considerable discovery has been taken, L sends an investigator to the home of J, one of the company's janitors, to learn information about certain plastic parts the company has claimed were discarded.

Comment: As in Case (a), it makes no difference that L has not gone to interview the janitor himself. If the contact is improper, L will have violated Rule 8.4(a) by procuring a violation of Rule 4.2. Since the investigator is in his employ, L will also have violated Rule 5.3 regarding nonlawyer assistants. The merits of this case are harder to judge than those of Case (a), however.

If the janitor is judged not to be "represented" by the company's lawyer, then he is not represented by anybody, and Rule 4.3 would apply. In that event, L's investigator would have to warn J about their respective positions before pressing ahead, thus giving J a fair

7. In my view Rule 4.3, read in conjunction with Rule 4.2, requires more than a simple disclosure by the investigator of his identity. To hold otherwise would in my judgment violate at least the spirit of the Rules. Rule 4.2 suggests that a relevant inquiry is whether an individual is represented since the Rule is only applicable if the lawyer "knows" that the individual is "represented by another lawyer." The Rules contemplate that former employees, unrepresented by counsel, be warned of the respective positions of the parties to the dispute. Indeed, Professor Hazard recognized that "suitable controls and correctives can be envisioned that would prevent unjust advantage being realized from . . . unfair tactics." Hazard Aff. para. 13.

8. Other courts in construing Rules 4.2 and 4.3, or rules which contain substantially similar language, have implemented procedures to guide the conduct of interviews with both current and former employees. In *Morrison v. Brandeis University*, 125 F.R.D. 14 (D. Mass. 1989) the United States District Court for the District of Massachusetts, interpreting Disciplinary Rule 7-104(A)(1), the counterpart to Rule 4.2, granted the plaintiff's motion to interview current employees/ witnesses of defendant Brandeis University. The court allowed such interviews provided that certain "guidelines" were followed. Those guidelines were:

(1) When plaintiff's counsel initially contacts any person as to which authorization to interview has herein been given (hereinafter, "any person"), she shall immediately disclose her capacity as counsel for the plaintiff in the above-styled litigation and the purpose of the contact, i.e., to request an interview.

(2) Whether or not to grant the request for an interview is completely up to the person, and the person's decision shall be respected.

(3) Any request by any person that the interview take place only in the presence of his or her personal attorney and/or the presence of Brandeis' attorney shall be honored.

(4) Brandeis shall advise all persons within the group which plaintiff's counsel has herein been given authorization to interview that they may, if they wish, agree to be interviewed by plaintiff's counsel to discuss matters which relate to this case and that no disciplinary or other adverse action will be taken by Brandeis against any person who consents to an interview.

9. Applying the foregoing to the case sub judice, I have reviewed the affidavits submitted by Monsanto of former employees who were contacted by investigators hired by the defendants. Therein, a number of the former employees/affiants stated, under oath, that the investigators did not disclose they represented insurance companies. Some stated that the investigators did say they represented Monsanto's

---

opportunity to remain silent or to demand that he be subpoenaed before talking.

Id., Illustrative Case (b). While the above hypothetical involves a current employee, I am satisfied that the analysis is equally applicable to a former employee. This conclusion is supported by the language of Rule 4.3, which does not distinguish between current and former employees but rather broadly refers to "unrepresented persons," and by Professor Hazard's affidavit, wherein he states that "Rule 4.3 precludes an attorney from misrepresenting his interest to [a] former employee." Affidavit of Geoffrey C. Hazard, Jr. [hereinafter Hazard Aff.] para. 12.

insurance companies but did not say that Monsanto was suing the insurance companies. One former employee was told by the investigator that the investigator "worked for a firm in New Orleans which had been commissioned by the chemical industry to look into which companies were polluting." Two former employees were under the impression that the investigators represented Monsanto. One former employee swore that his wife asked one of the investigators whether there was a lawsuit, and the investigator replied "no." One former employee was told that the investigator was "interested in Monsanto's efforts to correct environmental problems." Two former employees were told by investigators that the investigators were "compiling a book" about the plant. Finally, one former employee was told by an investigator that the investigator "worked for the Government, and was checking on pollution."

10. While some of the above statements were contradicted by the counter-affidavits of the investigators filed by the defendants, I am satisfied that there exists prima facie evidence to support the conclusion that some former employees were affirmatively misled. Further, while I am mindful in this case that defense counsel have made efforts to retain the most experienced and professional investigatory companies and that at times some investigators may make improper statements to interviewees in their fervor to gain information, attorneys who are officers of this court must realize that they are accountable and must supervise the investigators in order to assure that the type of misleading conduct that has previously occurred will not happen in the future. I will not countenance this type of conduct and will therefore fashion a protective order to insure that, at least in this litigation in Delaware, the parties and their agents will be guided by truth and honesty, and not by lies and deception.

11. There has been much discussion as to whether I should make a specific finding as to whether there has been a violation of the Rules of Professional Conduct. I am mindful that the Rules of Professional Conduct are "to provide guidance to lawyers and to provide a structure for regulating conduct through disciplinary agencies." Delaware Rules of Professional Conduct preamble. Thus, in general, the "business" of the court is to dispose of "litigation" and not to oversee the ethics of those that practice before it unless the behavior "taints" the trial. At the same time when conduct "taints" the proceedings, and I am convinced that the misleading nature of the conduct of the investigators in this matter has done so, I must take substantial and strong steps to eliminate the taint and protect the process in the future. In order to do so, I am satisfied that it is appropriate to conclude that when the investigators did not determine if former employees were represented by counsel, when the investigators did not clearly identify themselves as working for attorneys who were representing a client which was involved in litigation against their former employer, when investigators did not clearly state the purpose of the interview and where affirmative misrepresentations regarding these matters were made, Rule 4.2 and Rule 4.3 were violated. Further, it is not necessary for me to make a finding that the conduct was intentional in order to find a violation of the Rules of Professional Responsibility or to fashion a protective order under Superior Court Rule 26. At the same time I am quick to state that I am extremely troubled by the referenced conduct and the position taken by the defendants in this regard in light of the guidance I gave to counsel in National Union in December

1989 — knowing full well that guidance of this nature gets immediate and wide dissemination to the members of the bar practicing in the insurance coverage cases pending in this jurisdiction.

12. Having stated the above:

A. Within twenty (20) days from the date of this order, Travelers shall provide Monsanto with the identity and work and home address, to the extent known, of any investigators employed, directly or indirectly, by it who have interviewed any former Monsanto employee.

B. Within twenty (20) days from the date of this order, Travelers shall provide Monsanto with the identity of any former Monsanto employee contacted by investigators (along with an indication of which investigator contacted each individual).

C. Within thirty (30) days from the date of this order, Travelers shall provide to Monsanto any and all statements obtained by Travelers or its investigators from former Monsanto employees and all notes, reports and or documents regarding same.

D. Any evidence obtained as a result of these ex parte communications with former employees of Monsanto shall not be admissible at trial.

E. Monsanto's request for fees and costs of this motion is granted, and the parties are directed to confer as to the amount of those fees and costs, which amount shall be paid directly by counsel, not their clients at an agreed upon schedule or, in the absence of an agreement, forthwith.

F. No interview of any former employee of Monsanto shall be conducted unless the following script is used by the investigator or attorney conducting the interview:

1. I am a (private investigator-attorney) working on behalf of. I want you to understand that and several other insurance companies have sued Monsanto Company. That suit is pending in Delaware Superior Court. The purpose of that lawsuit is to determine whether Monsanto's insurance companies will be required to reimburse Monsanto for any amounts of money Monsanto must pay as a result of alleged environmental property damage and personal injury caused by Monsanto. I have been engaged by to investigate the issues involved in that lawsuit between Monsanto and its insurance companies.

2. Are you represented by an attorney in this litigation between Monsanto and its insurance companies?

If answer is "yes", end questioning.

If answer is "no", ask:

3. May I interview you at this time about the issues in this litigation? If answer is "no", end questioning.

If answer is "yes", substance of interview may commence.

G. Any interview conducted in violation of this order will result in sanctions issued against counsel for the offending party to include, but not be limited to, a fine in the amount of $5,000.00.

H. A copy of this order is being directed to the attention of Charles Slanina, Esquire, Disciplinary Counsel.

In the courts of Delaware, the hallmark of justice under law in civil litigation cannot be expediency marred by deception, but must rather be truth — to accept or require anything less would, in my view, debase the system of justice and belittle all who serve it.

It is so Ordered.

INTERNATIONAL NOTES

1.   In civil law systems, witnesses are examined primarily by the court in the course of its investigatory activities. Because of the fundamental difference in litigation role, civil law lawyers are more restricted in communicating with witnesses than are U.S. lawyers. In some jurisdictions, civil law lawyers are prohibited from any out-of-court contact with witnesses. The Ethical Code for Italian Lawyers lacks specific directions, but provides that "[a] lawyer who speaks to witnesses about circumstances involved in a judicial proceeding must avoid being too forceful or making direct suggestions in an effort to obtain favorable evidence." ETHICAL CODE FOR ITALIAN LAWYERS, art. 52.

2.   Traditionally, it was a violation of professional ethics for an English barrister to have direct contact with witnesses, save her lay client or expert witnesses. U.K. rules continue to prohibit a barrister from interviewing a witness in a criminal case, however, there is no longer any rule which categorically prohibits a barrister from having contact with a witness in a civil case. While contact is no longer forbidden, "[a] barrister must not rehearse, practice, or coach a witness in relation to his evidence" or "encourage a witness to give evidence which is untruthful or which is not the whole truth." BAR COUNCIL OF ENGLAND AND WHALES, CODE OF CONDUCT RULES 705(a)-705(b).

E.   CIVIL LIABILITY TO THIRD PERSONS

In limited circumstances, a lawyer may have civil liability for wrongful or negligent lawyering activity to those outside the lawyer-client relationship. As a general rule, lawyers do not owe a duty to third persons that supports a negligence action. When a lawyer error on behalf of a client harms a third person, that third parson's action against the lawyer will fail because the lawyer generally owes neither a contract nor a tort duty to exercise care on behalf of the third person. In particular, lawyer conduct that harms an opposing party will not support a claim against the lawyer on behalf of the opposing party. In general, lawyers do not owe a duty of care to opposing parties.

RESTATEMENT (THIRD) OF THE LAW GOVERNING LAWYERS[13]

Rules and Principles

Chapter 4 — Lawyer Civil Liability

Topic 1 — Liability For Legal Malpractice[14]

§ 51. Duty of Care to Certain Nonclients

[A] lawyer owes a duty to use care [for purposes of civil liability]:

* * *

(2) to a nonclient when and to the extent that:

 (a) the lawyer or (with the lawyer's acquiescence) the lawyer's client invites the nonclient to rely on the lawyer's opinion or provision of other legal services, and the nonclient so relies; and

 (b) the nonclient is not, under applicable tort law, too remote from the lawyer to be entitled to protection;

(3) to a nonclient when and to the extent that:

 (a) the lawyer knows that a client intends as one of the primary objectives of the representation that the lawyer's services benefit the nonclient;

 (b) such a duty would not significantly impair the lawyer's performance of obligations to the client; and

 (c) the absence of such a duty would make enforcement of those obligations to the client unlikely; and

(4) to a nonclient when and to the extent that:

 (a) the lawyer's client is a trustee, guardian, executor, or fiduciary acting primarily to perform similar functions for the nonclient;

 (b) the lawyer knows that appropriate action by the lawyer is necessary with respect to a matter within the scope of the representation to prevent or rectify the breach of a fiduciary duty owed by the client to the nonclient, where (i) the breach is a crime or fraud or (ii) the lawyer has assisted or is assisting the breach;

 (c) the nonclient is not reasonably able to protect its rights; and

---

[13] Copyright © 2000 by the American Law Institute. Reprinted with permission.

[14] Copyright © 2000 by the American Law Institute. Reprinted with permission.

(d) such a duty would not significantly impair the performance of the lawyer's obligations to the client.

Chapter VII

DUTIES TO THE LEGAL SYSTEM AND SOCIETY

This chapter is about a collection of lawyer duties that are neither duties to clients (see Chapters III, IV, V) nor to third parties (see Chapter VI). Rather, these duties are to the legal system or to the public generally. Many of these duties conflict with duties to clients, and the discussion in this chapter is about rules that set the lines across which client-favoring actions become unacceptably harmful to the legal system or the public.

Many of these duties, particularly those governing litigation conduct, arise from the notion of the lawyer as "officer of the court." A lawyer owes duties to the justice system that create friction with the lawyer's duties to her client.

A. TRUTH-TELLING INSIDE THE COURT CONTEXT

PROBLEM 7-1

Mark Moore is a partner in the firm of Moore & Taylor. At least for now. Moore's former client, a bank president, was charged with various fraudulent statements made in reports to bank regulators. The reports had been prepared by Moore and the bank president. Once charged, the bank president offered to implicate Moore in the frauds in exchange for favorable treatment from the prosecutor. That produced fraud charges against Moore, to which he is about to plead guilty. Moore is represented by his partner, Cheryl Taylor. During her representation of Moore, Cheryl Taylor learned from him that he had, many years ago, been convicted of a low level felony for marijuana possession. Indeed, Cheryl learned that Moore's conviction preceded his law school entrance, had never been reported by Moore on his admission application to law school, his bar application, or on any subsequent licensing documents. Remarkably, it appears that the prosecutor is unaware of Moore's old conviction. A sentencing report has been prepared for use by the district court judge in pronouncing sentence. The sentencing report contains no reference to his marijuana possession conviction. The sentencing hearing has begun, and the formal requirements for the entry of Mark Moore's guilty plea have been satisfied. The judge is about to pronounce the sentence, based as it is on the federal sentencing guidelines.

Is Cheryl Taylor under any obligation to inform the court or the prosecutor of Mark Moore's prior conviction? Should she encourage Mark Moore to disclose the conviction? If she does encourage him to do so and he refuses, what is her obligation?

PROBLEM 7-2

The judge has pronounced sentence on Mark Moore as one year of confinement and a fine of $10,000. Cheryl Taylor knows of a relevant recent opinion of the court of appeals for the circuit to which appeals from district courts sitting in this state are taken. The decision, apparently unknown to both the prosecutor and the district judge, requires that district judges order restitution whenever possible rather than fines. A restitution order would open Mark Moore up to seemingly limitless claims by bank investors and depositors for recoupment of losses that can be attributed to the frauds.

Is Cheryl Taylor under any obligation to disclose this case authority to the prosecutor? Is she under any obligation to disclose this case authority to the district judge? Is the prosecutor subject to discipline for lack of competence for his ignorance of this particular decision?

Truth-telling inside the court context carries implications not present in out-of-court contexts, such as negotiation. When a lawyer misleads in court, both the court and the opposing party are misled. As in the out-of-court context, each side must be zealous in its representation, and in doing so will attempt to persuade the court that the facts and law are favorable to its side. But the reliability, integrity, and neutrality of the judicial system demand a greater level of candor from its participants than that required in out-of-court contexts.

1. Fact Statements to the Court

A lawyer is prohibited from knowingly making false statements of material fact to the court and from otherwise engaging in acts or omissions that amount to fraud. MR 3.3(a). Lawyers must simultaneously serve the interests of their clients and comply with candor obligations to the court. The rules in this area are an attempted balance between these competing responsibilities. Lawyers are prohibited from knowingly making false statements of material fact to the court. MR 3.3(a)(1).

Despite the duty of candor to the court, a lawyer is under no general obligation to reveal unfavorable facts to the court. Although a lawyer is under no general obligation to reveal unfavorable facts to the court, a lawyer must disclose material facts "when disclosure is necessary to avoid assisting a criminal or fraudulent act by the client." MR 3.3(a)(2).

STATE v. CASBY
348 N.W.2d 736 (Minn. 1984)

OPINION: We affirm the misdemeanor conviction of appellant Camelia J. Casby for attorney misconduct in violation of Minn. Stat. § 481.071 (1982).[1] *FACTS*

On June 15, 1980, Peter Spedevick, who was driving after revocation of his driver's license, was arrested for speeding and littering (he had thrown a beer bottle and cigarette pack out of his car while being pursued). Peter falsely identified himself to the arresting officer as Ben Spedevick — Ben being Peter's brother. At his subsequent arraignment on June 30 and his pretrial hearing on September 9, 1980, Peter continued his deception. At the September 9 hearing before the County Court of Rice County, Peter, as Ben, pled guilty and fines were imposed. In late October 1980, Ben discovered the convictions and advised the authorities of his brother's deception.

The State claims that defendant-appellant Camelia J. Casby, as Peter Spedevick's attorney, knew of her client's deceit and, while she did not appear at the court proceedings, she assisted or at least consented to the deception. The trial court heard the case against attorney Casby without a jury, acquitted her of two charges, but found her guilty of attorney misconduct. A three-judge district court panel affirmed the conviction. We granted Ms. Casby's petition for review.

I.

Casby says evid. was insuf. to show that she knew of Peter's use of name

Appellant Casby's first contention is that the evidence is insufficient to support the trial court's finding that she knew Peter Spedevick used a false name with the Rice County authorities. We find the evidence sufficient. *⟹ court disagrees.*

The facts are these. The evening of June 15, 1980, Ms. Casby received a telephone call at her St. Paul home from Peter Spedevick, who was in the jail at Faribault. She had previously done legal work for Peter, knew about his license revocation, and recognized his voice. At the trial, Peter testified he said on the phone, "Hello, doll. This is Ben." Both the jailer and the arresting officer heard this said. Ms. Casby said she did not hear the name Ben. The trial court concluded that "it is reasonably possible that Defendant did not hear Spedevick identify himself as 'Ben.' "

At Peter's urging, Ms. Casby drove to Faribault that evening to arrange for Peter's release, since at the time it appeared he might also have a DWI charge. At the jail, Ms. Casby was given a form entitled "Release on Recognizance Agreement," which had been completed to show that "Spedevick, Benjamin Joseph," declared, among other things, that he resided at a certain St. Paul address (Peter's address), that the offense was "speed & littering," and that his birth date was November 3, 1950 (Ben's birth date). The recognizance was signed "Ben Spedevick." Ms. Casby signed the form, opposite "Ben's" signature, but testified she did not notice the form used the name Ben Spedevick. Ms. Casby gave Peter,

---

[1] [1] Minn. Stat. § 481.071 (1982) provides in part: "Misconduct by Attorneys. Every attorney or counselor at law who shall be guilty of any deceit or collusion, or shall consent thereto, with intent to deceive the court or any party, . . . shall be guilty of a misdemeanor . . . ."

his girlfriend, and other members of his party a ride back to St. Paul. The trial court concluded that "it is certainly likely that that discussion [on the ride back] would include examination of the tickets issued and discussion of what had occurred."

Ms. Casby testified that Peter, on the ride back home, said he would handle the two traffic tickets himself. Ms. Casby said she did not see and was not shown the tickets. She told Peter what her bill was for her evening's work and considered her services ended. Subsequently, on June 30, Peter, as Ben, appeared in court alone for his arraignment. He told the court he had an attorney but gave no name. On September 8, 1980, Peter called Ms. Casby. He said he had to appear in court for a pretrial hearing the next day and asked for her advice, stating he did not want to go to jail. Ms. Casby agreed to call the county attorney. Her telephone call was taken by the secretary of Steven Alpert, the assistant county attorney. Ms. Casby testified she asked to talk about the "Spedevick case." The secretary testified, however, that Ms. Casby specified "Ben Spedevick," and the secretary's telephone message slip, received as an exhibit, reads "Ben Spedevick." Later that day Mr. Alpert returned Ms. Casby's call and negotiated an arrangement whereby Mr. Alpert would recommend a minimal fine and no jail sentence if the defendant pled guilty. During these telephone negotiations, Ms. Casby testified she first referred to her client as Mr. Spedevick, but then "I know I called him Peter throughout the conversation." Mr. Alpert could not recall this. Mr. Alpert did request, however, that Ms. Casby furnish a letter, to be delivered to him the next day by the client, summarizing the negotiations. The telephone conversation ended about 5 p.m. Ms. Casby's secretary having left, Ms. Casby typed the letter herself. Throughout the letter defendant is referred to as "Mr. Spedevick." The next morning, Ms. Casby gave two copies of the letter, signed by her, to Peter, who went to the court hearing in Faribault by himself. Peter gave the copies of the letter to Mr. Alpert, pled guilty as Ben, and received fines for speeding and littering.

Ms. Casby claims that not until September 18, 1980, did she learn, in connection with another matter, that Peter had a brother. On October 23, Mr. Alpert called Ms. Casby on the phone. He said that there was a person in his office who "claims to be Ben Spedevick and he is not the same person you signed out." Ms. Casby replied that she had signed out Peter Spedevick. It developed that Peter and Ben do not get along and each previously has used the other's name in various predicaments. Pointing out that she had no reason to participate in any deceptive scheme of Peter's — indeed, every reason not to — Ms. Casby claims that through her distraction and at most negligence, she, too, was deceived by Peter.

The trial court found "beyond a reasonable doubt that the Defendant had actual knowledge of Spedevick's false use of his brother's name at the time she called Alpert's office to discuss the charges against Spedevick . . . ." The trial court noted that the only direct evidence for this was the testimony of Mr. Alpert's secretary that Ms. Casby asked to discuss the "Ben Spedevick" case, but that this testimony, taken in light of the substantial circumstantial evidence, required a finding that the defendant knew of the deceit. The court pointed to the two discussions defendant had with Peter and the letter she wrote on his behalf as circumstantial evidence tending to show knowledge on her part. The district court panel agreed with the trial court, although it would have given even greater weight to the testimony of Mr. Alpert's secretary.

District Court agreed
Affirmed!

* * *

II.

Appellant next argues, assuming arguendo that she had been aware of her client's deceit, she could not be found guilty of assisting in or consenting to the deceit because she was precluded from disclosing her client's true identity to the authorities by reason of the attorney-client privilege, the code of professional ethics, and her client's fifth and sixth amendment constitutional rights. The district court panel rejected each of these arguments, as do we.

The fact that the person representing himself as Ben was actually Peter was not, for Ms. Casby, information protected by the attorney-client privilege. Ms. Casby knew Peter before she agreed to represent him as a client at the Faribault jail. When she learned her client was perpetrating a fraud on the judicial system, she had a duty, as the district court panel put it, "to advise against the continuation of such action, and if the client persisted, attempt to withdraw from the case. Even if withdrawal had then become impossible, she should have been careful to do nothing which in any way aided her client's deception." ABA Standard, The Defense Function § 7.7. She made no effort, however, to dissuade her client from persisting in his fraud. Indeed, in the circumstances, it is difficult to see how Ms. Casby could have continued to represent Peter, even under the most passive conditions, without the danger of assisting the client's fraudulent conduct and preserving false evidence in violation of DR 7-102(A). But here appellant did more. She knowingly undertook plea negotiations with the authorities based on the deceit including the writing of a letter to the authorities confirming those negotiations. Under DR 4-101(B), an attorney is not to reveal the secrets and confidences of a client, but this rule is tempered by subsection (C)(2) which allows disclosures permitted by other disciplinary rules. There are times when a client places his or her attorney in a situation where the attorney's ethical obligation to withdraw or to disclose is difficult to discern, but in this instance, plainly, the attorney is not excused by the Code of Professional Responsibility for doing what she did.

Lastly, appellant argues that if she had withdrawn she would have violated the client's constitutional right to counsel under the sixth amendment, and that if she had disclosed her client's true identity she would have violated the client's privilege against self-incrimination under the fifth amendment. She argues that the client had already committed the offense of obstructing legal process before he engaged her. True, but it is also true that the client was embarked on a course of continuing deceit. The sixth amendment does not expect an attorney to assist a client in furthering fraud on the court. Nor do we see how Ms. Casby, with no attorney-client privilege to assert, could refuse to divulge Peter Spedevick's true identity on the basis of Peter's fifth amendment privilege not to be a witness against himself.

Affirmed.

VIRZI v. GRAND TRUNK WAREHOUSE AND COLD STORAGE CO.

571 F. Supp. 507 (E.D. Mich. 1983)

OPINION:

This case raises an important issue relating to the ethical obligation of an attorney to inform opposing counsel and the Court, prior to concluding a settlement, of the death of his client. For the reasons set forth in this opinion, the Court holds the attorney has an absolute ethical obligation to do so, and sets aside the settlement ordered in this matter.

I

This is a personal injury diversity action. Pursuant to the authority contained in Rule 32 of the Rules of the United States District Court for the Eastern District of Michigan, the case was referred to a mediation panel for mediation prior to the final pretrial conference.

On June 2, 1983, plaintiff's attorney prepared and filed a mediation statement for plaintiff with the mediation panel. Three days later, plaintiff died unexpectedly from causes unrelated to the lawsuit. On June 14, 1983, the case was mediated, and the mediation panel placed an evaluation of $35,000 on the case. At the time of the mediation hearing, plaintiff's attorney did not know that his client had died.[2]

Several days after the mediation hearing of June 14, plaintiff's attorney learned of his client's death. A personal representative was appointed by the probate court on June 24, 1983 to administer plaintiff's estate, although no suggestion of death was made in this Court, and the representative was not substituted as plaintiff.

On July 5, 1983, counsel for plaintiff and defendants appeared before this Court at a pretrial conference and, after negotiations, entered into a settlement of the lawsuit for the amount of the mediation award — $35,000. At no time, from the time plaintiff's attorney learned of the plaintiff's death until the agreement to settle the case for $35,000 at the pretrial conference, did plaintiff's attorney notify defendants' attorney or the Court of the death of the plaintiff.

After the settlement was agreed upon in chambers and placed upon the record, as both attorneys were walking out of chambers to the elevator together, plaintiff's attorney, for the first time, informed defendants' attorney that plaintiff had died. The facts also show that defendants had learned of plaintiff's death shortly before the settlement was agreed upon, but were unable to convey this information to their attorney before the settlement order was entered. At no time did defendants' attorney ask plaintiff's attorney if plaintiff was still alive and available for trial.

Defendants' counsel claims that his sole reason for recommending acceptance of the mediation award was that plaintiff would have made an excellent witness on his own behalf if the case had gone to trial. Defendants contend that because their

---

[2] [1] It should be noted that attendance of clients is not generally required in mediation hearings.

lawyer did not know of plaintiff's death at the time of the settlement, and because plaintiff's attorney failed to disclose that fact, the settlement is void. . . .

Plaintiff's attorney, on the other hand, contests defendants' motion, claiming that his actions were not unethical or improper. He states that plaintiff was alive at the time the mediation statement was filed and that there was nothing in the statement that was false and misleading. He also points out that he was not aware at the time of the mediation hearing that his client was dead, and did not become aware of that until three days after the award of the mediation panel.

In oral argument, plaintiff's attorney indicated that, had defendants' attorney asked him if his client was still alive at the time of the pretrial hearing before this Court, or had the Court asked the same question, he would have revealed the fact that he was dead. He says, however, that he had no duty to volunteer that information and that the settlement entered into is a fair and reasonable settlement.

* * *

II

The sole issue in the case is whether plaintiff's attorney had an ethical duty to advise this Court and defendants' attorney, who was unaware of the death of plaintiff, that plaintiff had died a few weeks prior to the settlement agreement.

Disciplinary Rule 7-102(A) of the American Bar Association Model Code of Professional Responsibility, which is applicable to lawyers practicing in the United States District Court for the Eastern District of Michigan, provides:

(A) In his representation of a client, a lawyer shall not:

(3) Conceal or knowingly fail to disclose that which he is required by law to reveal.

(5) Knowingly make a false statement of law or fact.

Ethical Consideration 7-27 provides: "Because it interferes with the proper administration of justice, a lawyer should not suppress evidence that he or his client has a legal obligation to reveal or produce. . . ."

Rule 3.3 of the Model Rules of Professional Conduct, adopted by the American Bar Association in August of 1983, provides in pertinent part:[3]

(a) A lawyer shall not knowingly:

(1) make a false statement of material fact or law to a tribunal;

(2) fail to disclose a material fact to a tribunal when disclosure is necessary to avoid assisting a criminal or fraudulent act by the client;

---

[3] [5] The Model Rules of Professional Conduct have not been adopted by the Supreme Court of Michigan or by this Court. Nevertheless, they reflect the most recent thinking on the subject of legal ethics by the American Bar Association.

* * *

(4) offer evidence that the lawyer knows to be false. If a lawyer has offered material evidence and comes to know of its falsity, the lawyer shall take reasonable remedial measures.

* * *

(6) the duties stated in paragraph (a) continue to the conclusion of the proceeding, and apply even if compliance requires disclosure of information otherwise protected by Rule 1.6.

In commenting upon Rule 3.3, the American Bar Association states: "There are circumstances where failure to make a disclosure is the equivalent of an affirmative misrepresentation." The comment, however, does not define or identify such circumstances.

Rule 4.1 of the Model Rules of Professional Conduct provides:

In the course of representing a client a lawyer shall not knowingly:

(a) make a false statement of material fact or law to a third person; or

(b) fail to disclose a material fact to a third person when disclosure is necessary to avoid assisting a criminal or fraudulent act by a client, unless disclosure is prohibited Rule 1.6.

In the commentary on Rule 4.1, the drafters state: "A lawyer is required to be truthful when dealing with others on a client's behalf, but generally has no affirmative duty to inform an opposing party of relevant facts." The drafters also state that: "Misrepresentations can also occur by failure to act." Like the Rules discussed above, this Rule proscribes certain behavior by attorneys in an effort to maintain the integrity of the legal system. It does not, however, define or identify the circumstances in which the Rule is designed to apply.

The Court also cannot rely on case law to define the parameters of these Rules as there is a paucity of case law on the subject. Nonetheless, the following decisions are helpful. In *Spaulding v. Zimmerman*, 263 Minn. 346, 116 N.W.2d 704 (1962), plaintiff was injured in an automobile accident. In addition to plaintiff's physician and two specialists, a fourth physician examined plaintiff at the request of defendants. The defendants' physician found an aneurysm of the aorta, which escaped the notice of the other physicians, and he reported this condition to defendants' lawyers.

Without disclosing this condition to plaintiff or plaintiff's counsel, defendants settled the case. Two years later, plaintiff, at a subsequent physical examination, learned of the aneurysm and brought an action for additional damages against the same defendants. The trial judge vacated the earlier settlement, and his order vacating the settlement was affirmed on appeal.

The Minnesota Court found that there was no duty on defendants to voluntarily disclose this knowledge during the course of negotiations, when the parties were in an adversary relationship, but that a duty to disclose arose once the parties reached a settlement and sought the court's approval.

The Minnesota Court held that defendants' knowing failure to disclose this condition opened the way for the court to later exercise its discretion in vacating the settlement.

In *Toledo Bar Association v. Fell*, 51 Ohio St.2d 33, 364 N.E.2d 872 (1977), an attorney specializing in workman's compensation law, with knowledge of the long-established practice of the Ohio Industrial Commission to deny any claim for permanent total disability benefits upon notice of death of a claimant, deliberately withheld information concerning his client's death prior to a hearing on a motion concerning the claim in order to collect a fee. The Supreme Court of Ohio held that this action violated the Code of Professional Responsibility and justified an indefinite suspension from the practice of law.

Lawyer knew that you had to give notice of death.

* * *

Here, plaintiff's attorney did not make a false statement regarding the death of plaintiff. He was never placed in a position to do so because during the two weeks of settlement negotiations defendants' attorney never thought to ask if plaintiff was still alive. Instead, in hopes of inducing settlement, plaintiff's attorney chose to not disclose plaintiff's death, as he was well aware that defendants believed that plaintiff would make an excellent witness on his own behalf if the case were to proceed to trial by jury. Here, unlike the factual information withheld in Spaulding, above, plaintiff's death was not caused by injuries related to the lawsuit, and did not have any effect on the fairness of the $35,000 mediation award. But the fact of plaintiff's death nevertheless would have had a significant bearing on defendants' willingness to settle.

P knew that D would want to know if he was dead.

There is no question that plaintiff's attorney owed a duty of candor to this Court, and such duty required a disclosure of the fact of the death of a client. Although it presents a more difficult judgment call, this Court is of the opinion that the same duty of candor and fairness required a disclosure to opposing counsel, even though counsel did not ask whether the client was still alive. Although each lawyer has a duty to contend, with zeal, for the rights of his client, he also owes an affirmative duty of candor and frankness to the Court and to opposing counsel when such a major event as the death of the plaintiff has taken place.

disclosure was required.

For the foregoing reasons, the settlement will be set aside and the case reinstated on the docket for trial. Counsel may present an order.

Settlement vacated.

IN RE MORRISSEY
248 Va. 334 (1994)

Opinion by Justice Henry H. Whiting.

This case was heard on an amended complaint filed by the Virginia State Bar charging Joseph Dee Morrissey, then the Commonwealth's Attorney for the City of Richmond, with violations of a number of disciplinary rules in connection with his prosecution of felony charges against Robert William Molyneux, III. Although the trial court dismissed a number of the charges, it found that Morrissey violated the following disciplinary rules:

DR 1-102(A)(4) Misconduct.—

DR 8-101(A)(3) Action as a Public Official.—

Accordingly, the court ordered that Morrissey's license to practice law be suspended for six months. Morrissey appeals. . . .

Molyneux was charged with the abduction and rape of Debra Jean Nuckols in Richmond. Molyneux's father employed James S. Yoffy, a Richmond attorney, to represent Molyneux, who was indigent.

Nuckols and Molyneux each gave inconsistent statements concerning the incident. At first, Nuckols claimed that she did not know Molyneux before he accosted and raped her in an alley as she was walking home from a Richmond night club in the early morning hours of June 9, 1991; however, Nuckols later admitted that she had danced with Molyneux while she was in the night club and had agreed to let him accompany her as she walked home. Molyneux also initially denied having had sexual intercourse with Nuckols, but when DNA tests later indicated the presence of his semen on Nuckol's underpants, he admitted commission of the act, but claimed it was consensual.

Independent DNA tests of Nuckols' clothing, arranged by Yoffy and paid for by Molyneux's father, produced other apparent inconsistencies in Nuckols' version of the incident. Nuckols claimed that she had not had sexual intercourse in the five weeks preceding her alleged rape by Molyneux, yet the DNA tests of semen samples found in her underpants disclosed the presence of semen from Molyneux and another male. Further, Nuckols said that Molyneux had urinated on her during the incident, but chemical tests failed to disclose the presence of urine on Nuckol's clothing.

Recognizing the problems in their respective cases, the two attorneys began to explore the possibility of a plea agreement. After Morrissey alluded to the cost to Molyneux's father of investigating Molyneux's case, Yoffy approached Morrissey about the possibility of settlement of the felony charges on an "accord and satisfaction" basis. In exchange for a nolle prosequi of the abduction charge and a reduction of the rape charge to a charge of sexual battery, a misdemeanor, Molyneux was willing to agree to a 12-month sentence on the misdemeanor. The sentence was to be suspended upon the condition of his payment of court costs and completion of a period of probation, community service, and psychiatric counseling.

Additionally, Yoffy suggested that Molyneux would pay the victim "for her alleged damages," although no specific amount was discussed. According to Yoffy, Morrissey "liked the idea," but told Yoffy that he did not think that Nuckols would settle for less than $25,000. Further, Morrissey said that if Nuckols "was going to get some money then the Commonwealth is going to get something out if it and [Morrissey] wanted $25,000" as partial funding of a television program called "Prosecutor's Corner." Explaining the program to Yoffy, Morrissey said that he "would be the focal point and he would have guests on, [to] explain prosecution oriented issues." Believing that this was an inappropriate use of the money, Yoffy told Morrissey that "perhaps a charity would be a better beneficiary than something more related to him." In a later meeting, Yoffy told Morrissey that "a charity was acceptable to my client and that I had $50,000 to work with." Morrissey then told Yoffy that if the parties agreed to a settlement, Morrissey wanted the Commonwealth's share of the money to be contributed to several charities which he would select.

At Yoffy's request, Morrissey arranged to meet with Nuckols and Yoffy so that Yoffy could offer Nuckols $25,000 as an "accord and satisfaction." Before this meeting, Morrissey asked Yoffy not to tell Nuckols about the additional $25,000 to be paid to the charities.

At the time of the meeting, Nuckols was aware of all the conditions of the proposed plea agreement, except the proposed charitable contributions by Molyneux's father. During the meeting, Morrissey made it clear that if Nuckols accepted the offer, the criminal charges would be disposed of by plea agreement; however, if she rejected the offer, the charges would be prosecuted. After pointing out to Nuckols some of the inconsistencies in her statements, Yoffy "offered her $25,000 to settle the case." Yoffy was asked to leave the room so that Nuckols could discuss the matter with Morrissey.

Upon being asked his opinion of the offer, Morrissey told Nuckols that if she "were his sister that he would strongly suggest to her that she consider the offer." When Nuckols later indicated that she would consider an offer of $100,000, Morrissey replied that "the offer was not up for negotiation." After hearing that Nuckols had rejected his offer, Yoffy suggested a reduction of the charities' share with a corresponding increase of Nuckols' share. Morrissey rejected this idea, insisting that the Commonwealth receive an equal amount of the settlement.

Thereafter, in preparation for the felony trial, Yoffy filed a motion in limine to obtain a ruling regarding the introduction of a psychiatrist's opinion indicating that Nuckols "could very well have made this attack up" because of a mental illness that had occurred five years earlier. Although Morrissey advised Yoffy that he did not plan to have Nuckols testify in the hearing on his motion, Morrissey told Yoffy that he planned to have her there "so she could appreciate what it would be like to be a witness and what evidence might come in against her."

At the hearing on August 18, 1992, Nuckols found the psychiatrist's testimony regarding her psychiatric past "very painful" and she was "devastated at the thought that it could be used at the actual trial." When the Honorable Thomas N. Nance, the judge presiding at the hearing and the subsequent criminal trial, told the lawyers in a side-bar conference that the evidence would not be admitted, Yoffy asked the court to withhold its ruling because the lawyers were negotiating "civil aspects" of the case. Judge Nance withheld a formal ruling and also indicated to the lawyers that he "[did not] want to hear anything about . . . a civil case."

After the hearing, when Nuckols asked Morrissey whether the psychiatric evidence would be admissible, Morrissey responded that he did not know. Nuckols then asked Morrissey if he thought that the offer of settlement was still available. Later, Morrissey called Nuckols and told her that the offer was still available and that he had "basically settled it on [her] behalf." At Morrissey's request, Nuckols wrote him a letter indicating that the Commonwealth was "ready to go forward with the case but I wanted to accept the offer and to thank them for their support."

Shortly thereafter, Molyneux, Yoffy, and Morrissey appeared before Judge

Nance to obtain court acceptance of their plea agreement. Moments before that hearing, Morrissey asked Yoffy not to tell the court about the part of the agreement relating to the proposed contributions of Molyneux's father to charities of Morrissey's choice.

At the hearing, Morrissey proffered the Commonwealth's evidence and advised the court of all the terms of the plea agreement except for the father's $25,000 payments to Nuckols and to the charities. Acting on this information and Molyneux's guilty plea to the misdemeanor of sexual battery, the court found Molyneux guilty, sentenced him, and suspended the sentence upon the conditions disclosed to the court by Morrissey. The court also sustained the Commonwealth's motion to nolle prosequi the abduction charge. Thereafter, Molyneux's father delivered $50,000 to Yoffy in accordance with the agreement.

* * *

I. Morrissey's Violation of DR 1-102(A)(4)

As we have pointed out, "concealment," designed to mislead another, is "conduct involving dishonesty, fraud, [or] deceit" under DR 1-102(A)(4).

* * *

Next, we consider the concealment charge arising out of Morrissey's presentation of the plea agreement to Judge Nance for his acceptance. We conclude that Morrissey concealed an important fact from Judge Nance — the $25,000 charitable contributions to be made by Molyneux's father.[4] Indeed, when the plea agreement was presented, not only did Morrissey deliberately conceal the contributions from the court, he also asked Yoffy not to disclose it to the court.

Although Morrissey concedes he would have been required to disclose the contributions to the court had Molyneux pled guilty to a felony, he contends its disclosure was not required because Molyneux pled guilty to a misdemeanor. We do not agree.

The authorization and procedure for plea agreements in felony and misdemeanor cases is set forth in Rule 3A:8(c). Although misdemeanor plea agreements are not required to be in writing, the Rule requires that counsel make full disclosure to the court of all terms of such agreements. In pertinent part, Rule 3A:8(c)(2) provides that "[t]he court shall require the disclosure of the agreement in open court . . . at the time the plea is offered." Full disclosure of the terms of plea agreements is essential in order that trial courts may properly determine whether to accept or reject such agreements.

Next, Morrissey attempts to justify his intentional concealment by recounting a version of Judge Nance's remark to the effect that he did not want to hear anything about money to be paid in a "civil restitution." Morrissey's interpretation of Judge Nance's remarks is inaccurate.

---

[4] [6] Morrissey also withheld from Judge Nance information of the $25,000 payment to be made to Nuckols. In view of our decision regarding the $25,000 charitable contribution, we need not decide whether Morrissey's nondisclosure of the payment to Nuckols was a violation of DR 1-102(A)(4).

When Yoffy asked the court to withhold its ruling during the August 20 hearing because the lawyers were negotiating "civil aspects" of the case, Judge Nance testified that "I said I didn't want to hear anything about it." Judge Nance concluded his testimony on this issue by stating "[t]he rules are [that] I am not allowed to engage in the negotiating process. That's between the lawyers. If I don't like it I can turn it down." Further, Judge Nance testified that, "[i]f anything had been mentioned about money the antenna would have gone up. I would have looked into it." In our opinion, this evidence indicates that Judge Nance simply refused to be involved in the negotiations, but he gave no indication that he did not want to be advised of all the terms of the plea agreement when it was presented to him for approval.

Nor do we agree with Morrissey's contention that the $25,000 charitable contributions can be considered "civil restitution." Finally, even if, as Morrissey suggests, some prosecutors have engaged in the practice of requiring charitable contributions from accused persons or their families as a condition to plea agreements, we reject Morrissey's contention that a prosecutor is not required to inform the sentencing court of any such condition.

Accordingly we find no merit in Morrissey's contentions that he did not violate DR 1-102(A)(4).

* * *

Therefore, the judgment of the trial court will be Affirmed.

INTERNATIONAL NOTES

1. Ethics codes generally provide rules for a lawyer's conduct with regard to court proceedings. The Japanese Code, for example, provides that "[a]n attorney shall endeavor to realize a fair trial and proper procedure," "shall not cause delay in judicial proceedings by negligence or for illegitimate Purposes," and "shall not use his or her personal relations with a judge, prosecutor or another public servant involved in court proceedings in handling any matter." JAPANESE FEDERATION OF BAR ASSOCIATIONS, BASIC RULES ON THE DUTIES OF PRACTICING ATTORNEYS, art. 74, 76–77.

2. With regard to court demeanor, the CCBE Code notes not only the lawyer's duty to "maintain due respect and courtesy towards the court" but also the lawyer's duty to "defend the interests of his client honourably and fearlessly without regard to his own interests or to any consequences to himself or any other person." CCBE Rule 4.3.

3. English barristers have an even broader duty to "ensure that the Court is informed of all relevant decisions and legislative provisions of which he is aware whether the effect is favourable or unfavourable towards the contention for which he argues." BAR COUNCIL OF ENGLAND AND WALES, CODE OF CONDUCT, Rule 708(c). According to case authority, a barrister must disclose "any authority which might throw light upon matters under debate." *Glebe Sugar Refining Company Ltd. v. Trustees of Port and Harbours and Greenock*, 2 A.C. 66, 68 (1921) (noting that the appeal could succeed on grounds never put forth by the appellants though they should have been).

4. The China Lawyers Law provides that a lawyer shall not "provide false evidence, conceal facts or intimidate or induce another with promise of gain to provide false evidence, conceal facts, or obstruct the opposing part's lawful obtaining of evidence." LAWYERS LAW, art. 35(5) (P.R.C.). A Chinese lawyer who "provid[es] false evidence" or "conceal[s] important facts" is subject to revocation of his practice certificate and criminal prosecution. LAWYERS LAW, art. 45(3) (P.R.C.). These provisions have reportedly been applied in a way that significantly inhibited lawyer's representation of criminal defendants in China. According to one commentator, "lawyers in China can risk their careers and even their personal liberty as a result of confrontations with authorities in the course of representing their clients." Ping Yu, *Glittery Promise vs. Dismal Reality: The Role of a Criminal Lawyer in the People's Republic of China After Revision of the Criminal Procedure Law*, 35 VAND. J. TRANSNAT'L L. 827, 852 (2002).

2. Ex Parte Proceedings

On those occasions when a lawyer is permitted by law to engage in ex parte communications with the court, the lawyer must disclose to the court both favorable and unfavorable material facts. MR 3.3(d).

3. Perjury

Monroe H. Freedman, *Professional Responsibility of the Criminal Defense Lawyer: The Three Hardest Questions*
64 MICH. L. REV. 1469 (1966)[5]

In almost any area of legal counseling and advocacy, the lawyer may be faced with the dilemma of either betraying the confidential communications of his client or participating to some extent in the purposeful deception of the court. This problem is nowhere more acute than in the practice of criminal law, particularly in the representation of the indigent accused. The purpose of this article is to analyze and attempt to resolve three of the most difficult issues in this general area:

* * *

2. Is it proper to put a witness on the stand when you know he will commit perjury?

These questions present serious difficulties with respect to a lawyer's ethical responsibilities. Moreover, if one admits the possibility of an affirmative answer, it is difficult even to discuss them without appearing to some to be unethical.[6] It is not

---

[5] Reprinted with permission. In his latest book with Abbe Smith, UNDERSTANDING LAWYERS' ETHICS (2010), Professor Freedman has updated and expanded his analysis, and has related it to the Model Rules and Model Code.

[6] [2] The substance of this paper was recently presented to a Criminal Trial Institute attended by forty-five members of the District of Columbia Bar. As a consequence, several judges (none of whom had either heard the lecture or read it) complained to the Committee on Admissions and Grievances of the District Court for the District of Columbia, urging the author's disbarment or suspension. Only after four months of proceedings, including a hearing, two meetings, and a de novo review by eleven federal district

surprising, therefore, that reasonable, rational discussion of these issues has been uncommon and that the problems have for so long remained unresolved. In this regard it should be recognized that the Canons of Ethics, which were promulgated in 1908 "as a general guide," are both inadequate and self-contradictory.

I. THE ADVERSARY SYSTEM AND THE NECESSITY FOR CONFIDENTIALITY

At the outset, we should dispose of some common question-begging responses. The attorney is indeed an officer of the court, and he does participate in a search for truth. These two propositions, however, merely serve to state the problem in different words: As an officer of the court, participating in a search for truth, what is the attorney's special responsibility, and how does that responsibility affect his resolution of the questions posed above?

The attorney functions in an adversary system based upon the presupposition that the most effective means of determinate truth is to present to a judge and jury a clash between proponents of conflicting views. It is essential to the effective functioning of this system that each adversary have, in the words of Canon 15, "entire devotion to the interest of the client, warm zeal in the maintenance and defense of his rights and the exertion of his utmost learning and ability." It is also essential to maintain the fullest uninhibited communication between the client and his attorney, so that the attorney can most effectively counsel his client and advocate the latter's cause. This policy is safeguarded by the requirement that the lawyer must, in the words of Canon 37, "preserve his client's confidences." Canon 15 does, of course, qualify these obligations by stating that "the office of attorney does not permit, much less does it demand of him for any client, violations of law or any manner of fraud or chicane." In addition, Canon 22 requires candor toward the court.

The problem presented by these sanitary generalities of the Canons in the context of particular litigation is illustrated by the personal experience of Samuel Williston, which was related in his autobiography. Because of his examination of a client's correspondence file, Williston learned of a fact extremely damaging to his client's case. When the judge announced his decision, it was apparent that a critical factor in the favorable judgment for Williston's client was the judge's ignorance of this fact. Williston remained silent and did not thereafter inform the judge of what he knew. He was convinced, and Charles Curtis agrees with him, that it was his duty to remain silent.

In an opinion by the American Bar Association Committee on Professional Ethics and Grievances, an eminent panel headed by Henry Drinker held that a lawyer should remain silent when his client lies to the judge by saying that he has no prior record, despite the attorney's knowledge to the contrary. The majority of the panel distinguished the situation in which the attorney has learned of the client's prior record from a source other than the client himself. William B. Jones, a distinguished trial lawyer and now a judge in the United States District Court for the District of Columbia, wrote a separate opinion in which he asserted that in neither event should the lawyer expose his client's lie. If these two cases do not constitute "fraud

---

court judges, did the Committee announce its decision to "proceed no further in the matter."

or chicane" or lack of candor within the meaning of the Canons (and I agree with the authorities cited that they do not), it is clear that the meaning of the Canons is ambiguous.

The adversary system has further ramifications in a criminal case. The defendant is presumed to be innocent. The burden is on the prosecution to prove beyond a reasonable doubt that the defendant is guilty. The plea of not guilty does not necessarily mean "not guilty in fact," for the defendant may mean "not legally guilty." Even the accused who knows that he committed the crime is entitled to put the government to its proof. Indeed, the accused who knows that he is guilty has an absolute constitutional right to remain silent. The moralist might quite reasonably understand this to mean that, under these circumstances, the defendant and his lawyer are privileged to "lie" to the court in pleading not guilty. In my judgment, the moralist is right. However, our adversary system and related notions of the proper administration of criminal justice sanction the lie.

Some derive solace from the sophistry of calling the lie a "legal fiction," but this is hardly an adequate answer to the moralist. Moreover, this answer has no particular appeal for the practicing attorney, who knows that the plea of not guilty commits him to the most effective advocacy of which he is capable. Criminal defense lawyers do not win their cases by arguing reasonable doubt. Effective trial advocacy requires that the attorney's every word, action, and attitude be consistent with the conclusion that his client is innocent. As every trial lawyer knows, the jury is certain that the defense attorney knows whether his client is guilty. The jury is therefore alert to, and will be enormously affected by, any indication by the attorney that he believes the defendant to be guilty. Thus, the plea of not guilty commits the advocate to a trial, including a closing argument, in which he must argue that "not guilty" means "not guilty in fact."

There is, of course, a simple way to evade the dilemma raised by the not guilty plea. Some attorneys rationalize the problem by insisting that a lawyer never knows for sure whether his client is guilty. The client who insists upon his guilt may in fact be protecting his wife, or may know that he pulled the trigger and that the victim was killed, but not that his gun was loaded with blanks and that the fatal shot was fired from across the street. For anyone who finds this reasoning satisfactory, there is, of course, no need to think further about the issue.

It is also argued that a defense attorney can remain selectively ignorant. He can insist in his first interview with his client that, if his client is guilty, he simply does not want to know. It is inconceivable, however, that an attorney could give adequate counsel under such circumstances. How is the client to know, for example, precisely which relevant circumstances his lawyer does not want to be told? The lawyer might ask whether his client has a prior record. The client, assuming that this is the kind of knowledge that might present ethical problems for his lawyer, might respond that he has no record. The lawyer would then put the defendant on the stand and, on cross-examination, be appalled to learn that his client has two prior convictions for offenses identical to that for which he is being tried.

Of course, an attorney can guard against this specific problem by telling his client that he must know about the client's past record. However, a lawyer can never anticipate all of the innumerable and potentially critical factors that his client, once cautioned, may decide not to reveal. In one instance, for example, the defendant assumed that his lawyer would prefer to be ignorant of the fact that the client had been having sexual relations with the chief defense witness. The client was innocent of the robbery, with which he was charged, but was found guilty by the jury — probably because he was guilty of fornication, a far less serious offense for which he had not even been charged.

The problem is compounded by the practice of plea bargaining. It is considered improper for a defendant to plead guilty to a lesser offense unless he is in fact guilty. Nevertheless, it is common knowledge that plea bargaining frequently results in improper guilty pleas by innocent people. For example, a defendant falsely accused of robbery may plead guilty to simple assault, rather than risk a robbery conviction and a substantial prison term. If an attorney is to be scrupulous in bargaining pleas, however, he must know in advance that his client is guilty, since the guilty plea is improper if the defendant is innocent. Of course, if the attempt to bargain for a lesser offense should fail, the lawyer would know the truth and thereafter be unable to rationalize that he was uncertain of his client's guilt.

If one recognizes that professional responsibility requires that an advocate have full knowledge of every pertinent fact, it follows that he must seek the truth from his client, not shun it. This means that he will have to dig and pry and cajole, and, even then, he will not be successful unless he can convince the client that full and confidential disclosure to his lawyer will never result in prejudice to the client by any word or action of the lawyer. This is, perhaps, particularly true in the case of the indigent defendant, who meets his lawyer for the first time in the cell block or the rotunda. He did not choose the lawyer, nor does he know him. The lawyer has been sent by the judge and is part of the system that is attempting to punish the defendant. It is no easy task to persuade this client that he can talk freely without fear of prejudice. [T]he truth can be obtained only by persuading the client that it would be a violation of a sacred obligation for the lawyer ever to reveal a client's confidence. Beyond any question, once a lawyer has persuaded his client of the obligation of confidentiality, he must respect that obligation scrupulously.

II. The Specific Questions

* * *

The second question is generally considered to be the hardest of all: Is it proper to put a witness on the stand when you know he will commit perjury? Assume, for example, that the witness in question is the accused himself, and that he has admitted to you, in response to your assurances of confidentiality, that he is guilty. However, he insists upon taking the stand to protest his innocence. There is a clear consensus among prosecutors and defense attorneys that the likelihood of conviction is increased enormously when the defendant does not take the stand. Consequently, the attorney who prevents his client from testifying only because the client has confided his guilt to him is violating that confidence by acting upon the information in a way that will seriously prejudice his client's interest.

Perhaps the most common method for avoiding the ethical problem just posed is for the lawyer to withdraw from the case, at least if there is sufficient time before trial for the client to retain another attorney. The client will then go to the nearest law office, realizing that the obligation of confidentiality is not what it has been represented to be, and withhold incriminating information or the fact of his guilt from his new attorney. On ethical grounds, the practice of withdrawing from a case under such circumstances is indefensible, since the identical perjured testimony will ultimately be presented. More important, perhaps, is the practical consideration that the new attorney will be ignorant of the perjury and therefore will be in no position to attempt to discourage the client from presenting it. Only the original attorney, who knows the truth, has that opportunity, but he loses it in the very act of evading the ethical problem.

The problem is all the more difficult when the client is indigent. He cannot retain other counsel, and in many jurisdictions, including the District of Columbia, it is impossible for appointed counsel to withdraw from a case except for extraordinary reasons. Thus, appointed counsel, unless he lies to the judge, can successfully withdraw only by revealing to the judge that the attorney has received knowledge of his client's guilt. Such a revelation in itself would seem to be a sufficiently serious violation of the obligation of confidentiality to merit severe condemnation. In fact, however, the situation is far worse, since it is entirely possible that the same judge who permits the attorney to withdraw will subsequently hear the case and sentence the defendant. When he does so, of course, he will have had personal knowledge of the defendant's guilt before the trial began. Moreover, this will be knowledge of which the newly appointed counsel for the defendant will probably be ignorant.

The difficulty is further aggravated when the client informs the lawyer for the first time during trial that he intends to take the stand and commit perjury. The perjury in question may not necessarily be a protestation of innocence by a guilty man. Referring to the earlier hypothetical of the defendant wrongly accused of a robbery at 16th and P, the only perjury may be his denial of the truthful, but highly damaging, testimony of the corroborating witness who placed him one block away from the intersection five minutes prior to the crime. Of course, if he tells the truth and thus verifies the corroborating witness, the jury will be far more inclined to accept the inaccurate testimony of the principal witness, who specifically identified him as the criminal.

If a lawyer has discovered his client's intent to perjure himself, one possible solution to this problem is for the lawyer to approach the bench, explain his ethical difficulty to the judge, and ask to be relieved, thereby causing a mistrial. This request is certain to be denied, if only because it would empower the defendant to cause a series of mistrials in the same fashion. At this point, some feel that the lawyer has avoided the ethical problem and can put the defendant on the stand. However, one objection to this solution, apart from the violation of confidentiality, is that the lawyer's ethical problem has not been solved, but has only been transferred to the judge. Moreover, the client in such a case might well have grounds for appeal on the basis of deprivation of due process and denial of the right to counsel, since he will have been tried before, and sentenced by, a judge who has been informed of the client's guilt by his own attorney.

A solution even less satisfactory than informing the judge of the defendant's guilt would be to let the client take the stand without the attorney's participation and to omit reference to the client's testimony in closing argument. The latter solution, of course, would be as damaging as to fail entirely to argue the case to the jury, and failing to argue the case is as improper as though the attorney had told the jury that his client had uttered a falsehood in making the statement.

Therefore, the obligation of confidentiality, in the context of our adversary system, apparently allows the attorney no alternative to putting a perjurious witness on the stand without explicit or implicit disclosure of the attorney's knowledge to either the judge or the jury.

Of course, before the client testifies perjuriously, the lawyer has a duty to attempt to dissuade him on the grounds of both law and morality. In addition, the client should be impressed with the fact that his untruthful alibi is tactically dangerous. There is always a strong possibility that the prosecutor will expose the perjury on cross-examination. However, for the reasons already given, the final decision must necessarily be the client's. The lawyer's best course thereafter would be to avoid any further professional relationship with a client whom he knew to have perjured himself.

The perjury problem presents extraordinary difficulties for the lawyer, especially when the person committing the perjury is the lawyer's client. Perjury's affront to the justice system is great, as is the harm that comes to the client when the lawyer reveals the client's perjury. A lawyer is prohibited from offering evidence the lawyer knows to be false. MR 3.3(a)(3). Further, a lawyer "may refuse to offer evidence other than the testimony of a defendant in a criminal matter, that the lawyer reasonably believes is false." MR 3.3(a)(3). The "reasonably believes" standard is considerably lower than the "knows" standard. A lawyer is given discretion by this rule to decline to present evidence when she "reasonably believes" but does not "know" that the evidence is false. This discretion permits a lawyer to disregard a civil client's preference for offering such evidence without violating the advocacy duty owed the client. Perjury by a witness other than the client is a somewhat easier case. When a lawyer knows that a witness other than the client has offered perjured testimony, the lawyer must promptly reveal the perjury to the court. MR 3.3(a)(3). Even here, however, the lawyer must "know" that the witness's evidence is false.

NIX v. WHITESIDE
475 U.S. 157 (1986)

CHIEF JUSTICE BURGER delivered the opinion of the Court.

We granted certiorari to decide whether the Sixth Amendment right of a criminal defendant to assistance of counsel is violated when an attorney refuses to cooperate with the defendant in presenting perjured testimony at his trial.

Issue

is 6th Am. violated when lawyer refused to present perjured testimony?

I

A

Whiteside was convicted of second-degree murder by a jury verdict which was affirmed by the Iowa courts. The killing took place on February 8, 1977, in Cedar Rapids, Iowa. Whiteside and two others went to one Calvin Love's apartment late that night, seeking marihuana. Love was in bed when Whiteside and his companions arrived; an argument between Whiteside and Love over the marihuana ensued. At one point, Love directed his girlfriend to get his "piece," and at another point got up, then returned to his bed. According to Whiteside's testimony, Love then started to reach under his pillow and moved toward Whiteside. Whiteside stabbed Love in the chest, inflicting a fatal wound.

Whiteside was charged with murder, and when counsel was appointed he objected to the lawyer initially appointed, claiming that he felt uncomfortable with a lawyer who had formerly been a prosecutor. Gary L. Robinson was then appointed and immediately began an investigation. Whiteside gave him a statement that he had stabbed Love as the latter "was pulling a pistol from underneath the pillow on the bed." Upon questioning by Robinson, however, Whiteside indicated that he had not actually seen a gun, but that he was convinced that Love had a gun. No pistol was found on the premises; shortly after the police search following the stabbing, which had revealed no weapon, the victim's family had removed all of the victim's possessions from the apartment. Robinson interviewed Whiteside's companions who were present during the stabbing, and none had seen a gun during the incident. Robinson advised Whiteside that the existence of a gun was not necessary to establish the claim of self-defense, and that only a reasonable belief that the victim had a gun nearby was necessary even though no gun was actually present.

Until shortly before trial, Whiteside consistently stated to Robinson that he had not actually seen a gun, but that he was convinced that Love had a gun in his hand. About a week before trial, during preparation for direct examination, Whiteside for the first time told Robinson and his associate Donna Paulsen that he had seen something "metallic" in Love's hand. When asked about this, Whiteside responded:

> [I]n Howard Cook's case there was a gun. If I don't say I saw a gun, I'm dead.

Robinson told Whiteside that such testimony would be perjury and repeated that it was not necessary to prove that a gun was available but only that Whiteside reasonably believed that he was in danger. On Whiteside's insisting that he would testify that he saw "something metallic" Robinson told him, according to Robinson's testimony:

> [W]e could not allow him to [testify falsely] because that would be perjury, and as officers of the court we would be suborning perjury if we allowed him to do it; . . . I advised him that if he did do that it would be my duty to advise the Court of what he was doing and that I felt he was committing perjury; also, that I probably would be allowed to attempt to impeach that particular testimony.

Robinson also indicated he would seek to withdraw from the representation if Whiteside insisted on committing perjury.

Whiteside testified in his own defense at trial and stated that he "knew" that Love had a gun and that he believed Love was reaching for a gun and he had acted swiftly in self-defense. On cross-examination, he admitted that he had not actually seen a gun in Love's hand. Robinson presented evidence that Love had been seen with a sawed-off shotgun on other occasions, that the police search of the apartment may have been careless, and that the victim's family had removed everything from the apartment shortly after the crime. Robinson presented this evidence to show a basis for Whiteside's asserted fear that Love had a gun.

The jury returned a verdict of second-degree murder, and Whiteside moved for a new trial, claiming that he had been deprived of a fair trial by Robinson's admonitions not to state that he saw a gun or "something metallic." The trial court held a hearing, heard testimony by Whiteside and Robinson, and denied the motion. The trial court made specific findings that the facts were as related by Robinson.

The Supreme Court of Iowa affirmed respondent's conviction. That court held that the right to have counsel present all appropriate defenses does not extend to using perjury, and that an attorney's duty to a client does not extend to assisting a client in committing perjury. Relying on DR 7-102(A)(4) of the Iowa Code of Professional Responsibility for Lawyers, which expressly prohibits an attorney from using perjured testimony, and Iowa Code § 721.2, which criminalizes subornation of perjury, the Iowa court concluded that not only were Robinson's actions permissible, but were required. The court commended "both Mr. Robinson and Ms. Paulsen for the high ethical manner in which this matter was handled."

B

Whiteside then petitioned for a writ of habeas corpus in the United States District Court for the Southern District of Iowa. In that petition Whiteside alleged that he had been denied effective assistance of counsel and of his right to present a defense by Robinson's refusal to allow him to testify as he had proposed. The District Court denied the writ. Accepting the state trial court's factual finding that Whiteside's intended testimony would have been perjurious, it concluded that there could be no grounds for habeas relief since there is no constitutional right to present a perjured defense.

The United States Court of Appeals for the Eighth Circuit reversed and directed that the writ of habeas corpus be granted. . . . We granted certiorari, and we reverse.

II

A

The right of an accused to testify in his defense is of relatively recent origin. Until the latter part of the preceding century, criminal defendants in this country, as at common law, were considered to be disqualified from giving sworn testimony at their own trial by reason of their interest as a party to the case.

By the end of the 19th century, however, the disqualification was finally abolished by statute in most states and in the federal courts. Although this Court has never explicitly held that a criminal defendant has a due process right to testify in his own behalf, cases in several Circuits have so held, and the right has long been assumed. We have also suggested that such a right exists as a corollary to the Fifth Amendment privilege against compelled testimony.

B

In *Strickland v. Washington*, we held that to obtain relief by way of federal habeas corpus on a claim of a deprivation of effective assistance of counsel under the Sixth Amendment, the movant must establish both serious attorney error and prejudice. To show such error, it must be established that the assistance rendered by counsel was constitutionally deficient in that "counsel made errors so serious that counsel was not functioning as 'counsel' guaranteed the defendant by the Sixth Amendment." To show prejudice, it must be established that the claimed lapses in counsel's performance rendered the trial unfair so as to "undermine confidence in the outcome" of the trial.

In Strickland, we acknowledged that the Sixth Amendment does not require any particular response by counsel to a problem that may arise. Rather, the Sixth Amendment inquiry is into whether the attorney's conduct was "reasonably effective." To counteract the natural tendency to fault an unsuccessful defense, a court reviewing a claim of ineffective assistance must "indulge a strong presumption that counsel's conduct falls within the wide range of reasonable professional assistance." In giving shape to the perimeters of this range of reasonable professional assistance, *Strickland* mandates that

> [p]revailing norms of practice as reflected in American Bar Association Standards and the like, . . . are guides to determining what is reasonable, but they are only guides.

Under the Strickland standard, breach of an ethical standard does not necessarily make out a denial of the Sixth Amendment guarantee of assistance of counsel. When examining attorney conduct, a court must be careful not to narrow the wide range of conduct acceptable under the Sixth Amendment so restrictively as to constitutionalize particular standards of professional conduct and thereby intrude into the state's proper authority to define and apply the standards of professional conduct applicable to those it admits to practice in its courts. In some future case challenging attorney conduct in the course of a state-court trial, we may need to define with greater precision the weight to be given to recognized canons of ethics, the standards established by the state in statutes or professional codes, and the Sixth Amendment, in defining the proper scope and limits on that conduct. Here we need not face that question, since virtually all of the sources speak with one voice.

C   *Perjury*

We turn next to the question presented: the definition of the range of "reasonable professional" responses to a criminal defendant client who informs counsel that he will perjure himself on the stand. We must determine whether, in this setting, Robinson's conduct fell within the wide range of professional responses to threatened client perjury acceptable under the Sixth Amendment.

In *Strickland*, we recognized counsel's duty of loyalty and his "overarching duty to advocate the defendant's cause." Plainly, that duty is limited to legitimate, lawful conduct compatible with the very nature of a trial as a search for truth. Although counsel must take all reasonable lawful means to attain the objectives of the client, counsel is precluded from taking steps or in any way assisting the client in presenting false evidence or otherwise violating the law. This principle has consistently been recognized in most unequivocal terms by expositors of the norms of professional conduct.

Both the Model Code of Professional Responsibility and the Model Rules of Professional Conduct also adopt the specific exception from the attorney-client privilege for disclosure of perjury that his client intends to commit or has committed. DR 4-101(C)(3) (intention of client to commit a crime); Rule 3.3 (lawyer has duty to disclose falsity of evidence even if disclosure compromises client confidences). Indeed, both the Model Code and the Model Rules do not merely authorize disclosure by counsel of client perjury; they require such disclosure. See Rule 3.3(a)(4); DR 7-102(B)(1).

These standards confirm that the legal profession has accepted that an attorney's ethical duty to advance the interests of his client is limited by an equally solemn duty to comply with the law and standards of professional conduct; it specifically ensures that the client may not use false evidence. This special duty of an attorney to prevent and disclose frauds upon the court derives from the recognition that perjury is as much a crime as tampering with witnesses or jurors by way of promises and threats, and undermines the administration of justice.

*   *   *

It is universally agreed that at a minimum the attorney's first duty when confronted with a proposal for perjurious testimony is to attempt to dissuade the client from the unlawful course of conduct. [A]n attorney's revelation of his client's perjury to the court is a professionally responsible and acceptable response to the conduct of a client who has actually given perjured testimony. Similarly, the Model Rules and the commentary, as well as the Code of Professional Responsibility adopted in Iowa, expressly permit withdrawal from representation as an appropriate response of an attorney when the client threatens to commit perjury. Model Rules of Professional Conduct, Rule 1.16(a)(1), Rule 1.6, Comment (1983); Code of Professional Responsibility, DR 2-110(B), (C) (1980). Withdrawal of counsel when this situation arises at trial gives rise to many difficult questions including possible mistrial and claims of double jeopardy.[7]

---

[7] [13] In the evolution of the contemporary standards promulgated by the American Bar Association, an early draft reflects a compromise suggesting that when the disclosure of intended perjury is made

The essence of the brief amicus of the American Bar Association reviewing practices long accepted by ethical lawyers is that under no circumstance may a lawyer either advocate or passively tolerate a client's giving false testimony. This, of course, is consistent with the governance of trial conduct in what we have long called "a search for truth." The suggestion sometimes made that "a lawyer must believe his client, not judge him" in no sense means a lawyer can honorably be a party to or in any way give aid to presenting known perjury.

D

Considering Robinson's representation of respondent in light of these accepted norms of professional conduct, we discern no failure to adhere to reasonable professional standards that would in any sense make out a deprivation of the Sixth Amendment right to counsel. Whether Robinson's conduct is seen as a successful attempt to dissuade his client from committing the crime of perjury, or whether seen as a "threat" to withdraw from representation and disclose the illegal scheme, Robinson's representation of Whiteside falls well within accepted standards of professional conduct and the range of reasonable professional conduct acceptable under *Strickland*.

* * *

Reversed.

JUSTICE BRENNAN, concurring in the judgment.

This Court has no constitutional authority to establish rules of ethical conduct for lawyers practicing in the state courts. Nor does the Court enjoy any statutory grant of jurisdiction over legal ethics.

Accordingly, it is not surprising that the Court emphasizes that it "must be careful not to narrow the wide range of conduct acceptable under the Sixth Amendment so restrictively as to constitutionalize particular standards of professional conduct and thereby intrude into the state's proper authority to define and apply the standards of professional conduct applicable to those it admits to practice in its courts." I read this as saying in another way that the Court cannot tell the

---

during the course of trial, when withdrawal of counsel would raise difficult questions of a mistrial holding, counsel had the option to let the defendant take the stand but decline to affirmatively assist the presentation of perjury by traditional direct examination. Instead, counsel would stand mute while the defendant undertook to present the false version in narrative form in his own words unaided by any direct examination. This conduct was thought to be a signal at least to the presiding judge that the attorney considered the testimony to be false and was seeking to disassociate himself from that course. Additionally, counsel would not be permitted to discuss the known false testimony in closing arguments. *See* ABA Standards for Criminal Justice, Proposed Standard 4-7.7 (2d ed. 1980). Most courts treating the subject rejected this approach and insisted on a more rigorous standard. The Eighth Circuit in this case and the Ninth Circuit have expressed approval of the "free narrative" standards.

The Rule finally promulgated in the current Model Rules of Professional Conduct rejects any participation or passive role whatever by counsel in allowing perjury to be presented without challenge.

States or the lawyers in the States how to behave in their courts, unless and until federal rights are violated.

Unfortunately, the Court seems unable to resist the temptation of sharing with the legal community its vision of ethical conduct. But let there be no mistake: the Court's essay regarding what constitutes the correct response to a criminal client's suggestion that he will perjure himself is pure discourse without force of law. As Justice Blackmun observes, that issue is a thorny one, but it is not an issue presented by this case. Lawyers, judges, bar associations, students, and others should understand that the problem has not now been "decided."

I join Justice Blackmun's concurrence because I agree that respondent has failed to prove the kind of prejudice necessary to make out a claim under *Strickland v. Washington*, 466 U.S. 668 (1984).

JUSTICE BLACKMUN, with whom JUSTICE BRENNAN, JUSTICE MARSHALL, and JUSTICE STEVENS join, concurring in the judgment.

How a defense attorney ought to act when faced with a client who intends to commit perjury at trial has long been a controversial issue. But I do not believe that a federal habeas corpus case challenging a state criminal conviction is an appropriate vehicle for attempting to resolve this thorny problem. When a defendant argues that he was denied effective assistance of counsel because his lawyer dissuaded him from committing perjury, the only question properly presented to this Court is whether the lawyer's actions deprived the defendant of the fair trial which the Sixth Amendment is meant to guarantee. Since I believe that the respondent in this case suffered no injury justifying federal habeas relief, I concur in the Court's judgment.

*   *   *

Whiteside had no legitimate interest that conflicted with Robinson's obligations not to suborn perjury and to adhere to the Iowa Code of Professional Responsibility.

In addition, the lawyer's interest in not presenting perjured testimony was entirely consistent with Whiteside's best interest. If Whiteside had lied on the stand, he would have risked a future perjury prosecution. Moreover, his testimony would have been contradicted by the testimony of other eyewitnesses and by the fact that no gun was ever found. In light of that impeachment, the jury might have concluded that Whiteside lied as well about his lack of premeditation and thus might have convicted him of first-degree murder. And if the judge believed that Whiteside had lied, he could have taken Whiteside's perjury into account in setting the sentence. In the face of these dangers, an attorney could reasonably conclude that dissuading his client from committing perjury was in the client's best interest and comported with standards of professional responsibility.[8] In short, Whiteside failed

---

[8] [7] This is not to say that an attorney's ethical obligations will never conflict with a defendant's right to effective assistance. For example, an attorney who has previously represented one of the State's witnesses has a continuing obligation to that former client not to reveal confidential information received during the course of the prior representation. That continuing duty could conflict with his obligation to his present client, the defendant, to cross-examine the State's witnesses zealously. *See Lowenthal,*

to show the kind of conflict that poses a danger to the values of zealous and loyal representation embodied in the Sixth Amendment. A presumption of prejudice is therefore unwarranted.

C

In light of respondent's failure to show any cognizable prejudice, I see no need to "grade counsel's performance." The only federal issue in this case is whether Robinson's behavior deprived Whiteside of the effective assistance of counsel; it is not whether Robinson's behavior conformed to any particular code of legal ethics.

Whether an attorney's response to what he sees as a client's plan to commit perjury violates a defendant's Sixth Amendment rights may depend on many factors: how certain the attorney is that the proposed testimony is false, the stage of the proceedings at which the attorney discovers the plan, or the ways in which the attorney may be able to dissuade his client, to name just three. The complex interaction of factors, which is likely to vary from case to case, makes inappropriate a blanket rule that defense attorneys must reveal, or threaten to reveal, a client's anticipated perjury to the court. Except in the rarest of cases, attorneys who adopt "the role of the judge or jury to determine the facts," *United States ex rel. Wilcox v. Johnson*, 555 F.2d 115, 122 (3d Cir. 1977), pose a danger of depriving their clients of the zealous and loyal advocacy required by the Sixth Amendment.[9]

I therefore am troubled by the Court's implicit adoption of a set of standards of professional responsibility for attorneys in state criminal proceedings. The States, of course, do have a compelling interest in the integrity of their criminal trials that can justify regulating the length to which an attorney may go in seeking his client's acquittal. But the American Bar Association's implicit suggestion in its brief *amicus curiae* that the Court find that the Association's Model Rules of Professional Conduct should govern an attorney's responsibilities is addressed to the wrong audience. It is for the States to decide how attorneys should conduct themselves in state criminal proceedings, and this Court's responsibility extends only to ensuring that the restrictions a State enacts do not infringe a defendant's federal constitutional rights. Thus, I would follow the suggestion made in the joint brief amici curiae filed by 37 States at the certiorari stage that we allow the States to maintain their "differing approaches" to a complex ethical question. The signal merit of asking first whether a defendant has shown any adverse prejudicial effect before inquiring into his attorney's performance is that it avoids unnecessary federal interference in a State's regulation of its bar. Because I conclude that the respondent in this case

---

Successive Representation by Criminal Lawyers, 93 Yale L.J. 1 (1983).

[9] [8] A comparison of this case with *Wilcox* is illustrative. Here, Robinson testified in detail to the factors that led him to conclude that respondent's assertion he had seen a gun was false. The Iowa Supreme Court found "good cause" and "strong support" for Robinson's conclusion. Moreover, Robinson gave credence to those parts of Whiteside's account which, although he found them implausible and unsubstantiated, were not clearly false. By contrast, in *Wilcox*, where defense counsel actually informed the judge that she believed her client intended to lie and where her threat to withdraw in the middle of the trial led the defendant not to take the stand at all, the Court of Appeals found "no evidence on the record of this case indicating that Mr. Wilcox intended to perjure himself," and characterized counsel's beliefs as "private conjectures about the guilt or innocence of [her] client."

failed to show such an effect, I join the Court's judgment that he is not entitled to federal habeas relief.

JUSTICE STEVENS, concurring in the judgment.

Justice Holmes taught us that a word is but the skin of a living thought. A "fact" may also have a life of its own. From the perspective of an appellate judge, after a case has been tried and the evidence has been sifted by another judge, a particular fact may be as clear and certain as a piece of crystal or a small diamond. A trial lawyer, however, must often deal with mixtures of sand and clay. Even a pebble that seems clear enough at first glance may take on a different hue in a handful of gravel.

As we view this case, it appears perfectly clear that respondent intended to commit perjury, that his lawyer knew it, and that the lawyer had a duty — both to the court and to his client, for perjured testimony can ruin an otherwise meritorious case — to take extreme measures to prevent the perjury from occurring. The lawyer was successful and, from our unanimous and remote perspective, it is now pellucidly clear that the client suffered no "legally cognizable prejudice."

Nevertheless, beneath the surface of this case there are areas of uncertainty that cannot be resolved today. A lawyer's certainty that a change in his client's recollection is a harbinger of intended perjury — as well as judicial review of such apparent certainty — should be tempered by the realization that, after reflection, the most honest witness may recall (or sincerely believe he recalls) details that he previously overlooked. Similarly, the post-trial review of a lawyer's pretrial threat to expose perjury that had not yet been committed — and, indeed, may have been prevented by the threat — is by no means the same as review of the way in which such a threat may actually have been carried out. Thus, one can be convinced — as I am — that this lawyer's actions were a proper way to provide his client with effective representation without confronting the much more difficult questions of what a lawyer must, should, or may do after his client has given testimony that the lawyer does not believe. The answer to such questions may well be colored by the particular circumstances attending the actual event and its aftermath.

Because Justice Blackmun has preserved such questions for another day, and because I do not understand him to imply any adverse criticism of this lawyer's representation of his client, I join his opinion concurring in the judgment.

4.   Law Statements to the Court

A lawyer is prohibited from making false statements of law to the court. MR 3.3(a). As an advocate, a lawyer should present the law in the most favorable light for the client. As such, the lawyer need not reveal his objective analysis of the law to the court, but rather may make to the court any non-frivolous, client-favoring arguments regarding the law. Because the law is in large measure indeterminate, significant room for interpretation presents itself. Nonetheless, a lawyer may not make false statements about the law to the court.

Lawyers are obligated to disclose to the court controlling, directly adverse legal authority. MR 3.3(a)(3). Such disclosures may take the form of oral statements in open court during a motion or appellate argument or written statements in briefs or other legal argument papers filed with the court.

Duty to disclose **JORGENSON v. COUNTY OF VOLUSIA**
presedent that
846 F.2d 1350 (11th Cir. 1988)
is even adverse to your client

PER CURIAM.

Lawyer failed to show adverse law

The appellants, attorneys Eric Latinsky and Fred Fendt, were sanctioned by the district court pursuant to Fed. R. Civ. P. 11 for failing to cite adverse, controlling precedent in a memorandum filed in support of an application for a temporary restraining order and a preliminary injunction. In the appellants' initial appeal to this court, the case was remanded to the district court because the court had failed to notify the attorneys in advance that it was considering sanctions, and did not give them an opportunity to respond. On remand, the district court reaffirmed the imposition of sanctions, and the attorneys appeal. We affirm.

Appellants filed an application in the district court for a temporary restraining order and a preliminary injunction on behalf of their clients, who own and operate a lounge known as "Porky's." In support of the application, appellants filed a memorandum of law which challenged the validity of a Volusia County ordinance prohibiting nude or semi-nude entertainment in commercial establishments at which alcoholic beverages are offered for sale or consumption.

Something abt. stripping and alcohol

The memorandum failed to discuss or cite two clearly relevant cases: *City of Daytona Beach v. Del Percio*, 476 So. 2d 197 (Fla. 1985), and *New York State Liquor Authority v. Bellanca*, 452 U.S. 714 (1981). We find that this failure supports the imposition of Rule 11 sanctions in the circumstances of this case.

The field of law concerning the regulation of the sale and consumption of alcohol in connection with nude entertainment is a narrow and somewhat specialized field. Prior to the opinion of the Supreme Court of Florida in *Del Percio*, the critical question of whether the state of Florida had delegated its powers under the Twenty-First Amendment to counties and municipalities had gone unanswered. In some circles, that decision was long-awaited. If the state had delegated the authority, local ordinances regulating the sale or consumption of alcohol would be entitled to a presumption in favor of their validity which is conferred by the Twenty-First Amendment. If the state had not delegated the authority, the ordinances would be subject to the stricter review applicable to exercises of the general police power.

The question regarding Florida's delegation of its powers under the Twenty-First Amendment was answered by the Supreme court of Florida in *Del Percio*, a case in which one of the appellants, Latinsky, participated. The court held that the powers had been delegated. Less than one year later, on or about January 13, 1986, Latinsky and an associate brought the instant suit seeking a declaration that a similar ordinance was unconstitutional and requesting a temporary restraining order and a preliminary injunction. In their presentation to the court, the appellants cited a number of cases describing the limits on the exercise of the general police power. However, they did not advise the court in any way that *Del*

Percio had been decided, despite the fact that *Del Percio* required that the validity of the ordinance be judged in light of powers retained under the Twenty-First Amendment rather than the general police power.

The appellants purported to describe the law to the district court in the hope that the description would guide and inform the court's decision. With apparently studied care, however, they withheld the fact that the long-awaited decision by the Supreme Court of Florida had been handed down. This will not do. The appellants are not redeemed by the fact that opposing counsel subsequently cited the controlling precedent. The appellants had a duty to refrain from affirmatively misleading the court as to the state of the law. They were not relieved of this duty by the possibility that opposing counsel might find and cite the controlling precedent, particularly where, as here, a temporary restraining order might have been issued ex parte.

In this court, appellants argue that the cases were not cited because they are not controlling. We certainly acknowledge that attorneys are legitimately entitled to press their own interpretations of precedent, including interpretations which render particular cases inapplicable. It is clear, however, that appellants' attempts to show that *Del Percio* and *Bellanca* are not controlling are simply post hoc efforts to evade the imposition of sanctions. Neither the original complaint nor the memorandum of law filed by appellants in the district court reflect or support the arguments they now raise. Indeed, it is likely that the arguments were not raised previously because they are completely without merit. In the circumstances of this case, the imposition of Rule 11 sanctions by the district court was warranted. The judgment of the district court is

Affirmed.

B.   WITNESS PAYMENT

A lawyer is limited in the ways in which witnesses may be compensated and in instructing witnesses about whether to make themselves available for testimony or interview by the opposing side. As in all other areas of professional responsibility law, a lawyer may not use a client as an agent to do what the lawyer is prohibited from doing.

Payment of a witness fee to lay witnesses is usually provided for in a state statute. Lawyers may only pay non-expert witnesses that statutory fee and reasonable expenses incurred by the witness in attending the trial or hearing. MR 3.4, Comment 3. Expert witnesses may be paid the professional fee that someone in the expert's field charges for his or her time and reasonable expenses incurred by the witness in attending the trial or hearing. However, an expert may not be paid a fee that is contingent on the outcome of the matter. MR 3.4, Comment 3.

C.   LIMITATIONS ON PRESENTATIONS TO A COURT

In a variety of ways, the ethics rules restrict the ways in which lawyers make their presentations in court.

1.   Frivolous Claims and Litigation Positions

By both ethics code provisions and by litigation sanctions rules, lawyers are prohibited from bringing actions or taking positions in litigation that are frivolous. In several forms, the Model Rules restrict lawyers' behavior regarding frivolous positions. Model Rule 3.1, in most respects tracking Federal Rule of Civil Procedure 11, prohibits lawyers from bringing or defending claims on a frivolous basis.

Frivolous claims or positions may be so because they lack legal or factual merit or because they are taken primarily to harass or maliciously injure a third party. A claim or position is not frivolous merely because it loses the day. To be frivolous, an argument must be one that a reasonable lawyer would regard as having no legal or factual merit. Under the analogous Model Code provision, a claim was frivolous when it was brought merely to harass or injure. DR 7-102(A)(1). That standard is found in the Model Rules in both Model Rule 4.4 and in the Comment to Model Rule 3.1. Such conduct is subject to discipline.

Criminal cases present a special problem for the frivolous claim rule. In a criminal case, unlike a civil case, a defendant has a due process right to plead "not guilty" and require the government to be put to its proof. By contrast, in civil litigation, when an allegation is made in a pleading that requires response or is made through the discovery device called requests for admissions, a responding party must admit allegations that are true. Model Rule 3.1 is not intended to prevent a lawyer from assisting a criminal defendant in the process of putting the government to its proof. Prosecuting lawyers have special obligations regarding the prosecution of charges that lack merit. See Chapter VIII.

Frivolous discovery requests and those intended merely to delay are prohibited. MR 3.4(d).

In general, lawyers are obliged to expedite litigation to the extent that such activity is consistent with the client's interests. MR 3.2. Beyond the ethics code limitations that create disciplinary liability for filing frivolous claims and taking frivolous positions in litigation, Federal Rule of Civil Procedure 11 and its state law counterparts create sanctions liability for similar conduct. A court may consider a motion for sanctions even though the proceedings have ended.

LAWYER DISCIPLINARY BOARD v. NEELY AND HUNTER
528 S.E.2d 468 (W. Va. 1998)

PER CURIAM.

This disciplinary proceeding was instituted by the complainant, Office of Disciplinary Counsel [hereinafter "ODC"] of the West Virginia State Bar against Roger D. Hunter and Richard F. Neely, members of the Bar. Mr. Hunter and Mr. Neely were charged with violating Rule 3.1 of the West Virginia Rules of Professional Conduct. Mr. Neely was also charged with violating Rule 4.4. However, the Lawyer Disciplinary Board [hereinafter "Board"] found that the ODC only proved that Mr. Hunter and Mr. Neely violated Rule 3.1. The Board recommends admonishment. Based upon our review of the recommendation, all matters of record, and the briefs and argument of counsel, we disagree with the Board's recommendation, and we find that the complaint against Mr. Hunter and Mr. Neely should be dismissed.

I

The proceeding against Mr. Hunter and Mr. Neely involved their representation of Linda and Quewanncoii Stephens. Mr. and Mrs. Stephens have a son, Quinton, who is autistic. In September 1990, when Quinton was approximately nine months old, he was enrolled in the Fort Hill Child Development Center [hereinafter Center].

On December 2, 1994, Mrs. Stephens received a phone call from a staff member at the Center asking her to pick up Quinton because the day care employee who was responsible for his supervision was not at work, and Quinton was disrupting the other children during nap time. When Mrs. Stephens arrived at the Center, she found Quinton alone in the director's office strapped to a posture correcting chair, which she had provided, with his hands and face covered with partly-dried fecal material. According to Mrs. Stephens, the room was dark and the blinds were drawn. The employee who had been watching Quinton claimed that she left him alone for about ninety seconds to get a change of diaper for him. Mrs. Stephens immediately removed Quinton from the Center, and shortly thereafter, she and her husband consulted with Mr. Hunter, who was then practicing law with the law firm of Bowles, Rice, McDavid, Graff and Love.

After meeting with the Stephenses, Mr. Hunter wrote a letter to Jean Hawks, the Center's director and owner, and asked that she have her liability carrier contact him promptly. Mr. Hunter also sent letters of complaint to the state Child Protective Services and the federal Office of Civil Rights. Child Protective Services investigated the matter and concluded that Quinton had not been maltreated because he had been watched by an employee of the Center during the forty-five minutes it took Mrs. Stephens to arrive at the Center. The employee had only left Quinton alone for ninety seconds when she went to get a diaper.

Subsequently, Mr. Hunter left the law firm of Bowles, Rice, McDavid, Graff and Love and became a partner of Neely & Hunter. Mr. Hunter took the Stephens' case with him, and Mr. Neely took the lead in preparing the pleadings and handling of the case. On June 12, 1995, Mr. Neely filed a civil action in the name of Linda, Quewanncoii, and Quinton Stephens against the Center and Ms. Hawks.

The complaint alleged that Mr. and Mrs. Stephens and Quinton had suffered intentional infliction of emotional distress based upon the outrageous conduct of the defendants and that Quinton had suffered damages from an intentional battery on December 2, 1994. The complaint further alleged that as a result of interviews with persons associated with the Center, the plaintiffs believed that the December 2, 1994 incident was "but one of many instances in which an autistic child, known to have special needs, in direct contravention of the expressed direction of his parents and of his health care providers, knowingly and willfully and intentionally was strapped to a chair in a dark room for many hours and left alone as a result of his mental and physical handicap." The damages clause asked for $1,500,000.00 in compensatory damages and $1,500,000.00 in punitive damages.

Thereafter, Mr. Hunter submitted answers to interrogatories on behalf of the plaintiffs listing the names of several individuals who served as the basis for the allegation that Quinton had in many instances been left alone in a dark room for many hours. However, none of the individuals testified to such incidents during discovery.

On December 11, 1995, the defendants moved for summary judgment. The court dismissed Mr. and Mrs. Stephens causes of action for intentional infliction of emotional distress. The court also dismissed Quinton's claim for intentional infliction of emotional distress for the "many instances" in which he was allegedly strapped in a chair in a dark room for many hours. This claim was dismissed because the only evidence plaintiffs produced during discovery was the testimony of Mary Ellen Davis, Quinton's special education teacher, that one day she found Quinton in the chair in his classroom when all the other children were up and about in the same room. Finally, the claim for punitive damages was dismissed for being duplicative of the claim for damages from intentional infliction of emotional distress. Only Quinton's claim for intentional infliction of emotional distress was permitted to go forward.

Subsequently, the plaintiffs requested a voluntary dismissal of the remaining claim in order to appeal the summary judgment order. The defendants then filed a motion for sanctions under Rule 11 of the West Virginia Rules of Civil Procedure. Thereafter, the parties reached an agreement whereby the plaintiffs agreed to dismiss the appeal and all claims with prejudice in return for the defendants dismissing the Rule 11 motion and agreeing not to seek attorney sanctions against either Mr. Hunter or Mr. Neely.

On March 17, 1997, the Investigative Panel of the Board filed a Statement of Charges in this matter. Mr. Neely was charged with violating Rule 4.4 of the West Virginia Rules of Professional Conduct based on the settlement demand letters he sent to the Center's insurance company.[10] Mr. Neely and Mr. Hunter were both

---

[10] [2] On May 26, 1995, Mr. Neely wrote a letter to Karen M. Meyd, senior claims representative for The Maryland Insurance Group, informing her that Mr. Hunter had entered law practice with him. The letter stated that he intended to file a civil action asking for "substantial damages, both compensatory and punitive." The letter further stated:

> I understand from my clients that effective next year, your clients are going to be doing a large amount of special care for the handicapped, particularly wheelchair bound special needs students. Since this law firm tends to be extraordinarily high-profile, and since the mere filing of a complaint may cause your clients unnecessary embarrassment, if you would like to discuss the settlement of this claim before the filing of the suit, I shall be more than pleased to do so.

In a subsequent letter which included a copy of the proposed complaint and first set of interrogatories and requests for production of documents, Mr. Neely made a settlement demand of $151,516.00 and further stated:

> Although (as you can see from my immediate preparation of the included paperwork) I have little true expectation that this case will settle until right before trial, if at all, I nonetheless believe that it is in everyone's interest to devote the roughly $40,000 that you would need to spend to defend this lawsuit through a nasty trial to the settlement fund. In addition, of course, your client will be spared substantial embarrassment, as this is obviously a case that will attract substantial press attention because of the profile of my clients.

Neely and Hunter charged w/ 3.1 violation.

charged with violating Rule 3.1[11] in that the complaint filed by Mr. Neely asserted emotional distress counts on behalf of Linda and Quewanncoii Stephens, a count of intentional battery on behalf of Quinton Stephens, and a count of emotional distress based on many alleged instances where Quinton had been left alone in a dark room for many hours.

On October 10, 1997, the Hearing Panel Subcommittee issued a report which dismissed the Rule 4.4 charge and by majority vote, found a violation of Rule 3.1 by both Mr. Hunter and Mr. Neely. The Board recommended admonishment. Thereafter, pursuant to Rules 3.11 and 3.13 of the West Virginia Rules of Lawyer Disciplinary Procedure, Mr. Hunter and Mr. Neely filed a notice of objection to the Hearing Panel Subcommittee Report with this Court.[12]

Board
- dismissed 4.4
found both
violated 3.1
- recomm.
"Admonishment"

II

In this proceeding, the Board found a violation of Rule 3.1 based solely on the allegations set forth in paragraph VII of the complaint.[13] The Board concluded that a reasonable attorney should have known that the allegations set forth in paragraph VII were unwarranted and that Mr. Hunter and Mr. Neely knew they were without basis. In reaching this decision, the Board recognized that the entire lawsuit was not baseless or frivolous because Quinton Stephens' intentional tort claim survived the motion for summary judgment. In effect, the Board seeks to

---

Both of the parents involved in this case are prominent in the Charleston Community. Quewanncoii Stephens is a retired lieutenant colonel in the United States Army; he was a Ranger, Airborne troop who commanded special forces in Vietnam. LTC Stephens has been awarded two bronze stars and one army commendation medal (valor). LTC Stephens is currently a member of the West Virginia Board of Probation and Parole, and he formerly served as executive director of the West Virginia Human Rights Commission.

Stephenses are
upstanding citizens.

[11] [3] Rule 3.1 of the West Virginia Rules of Professional Conduct provides, in pertinent part:

A lawyer shall not bring or defend a proceeding, or assert or controvert an issue therein, unless there is a basis for doing so that is not frivolous, which includes a good faith argument for an extension, modification or reversal of existing law.

frivolous

[12] [4] The ODC did not object to the Board's dismissal of the Rule 4.4 charge against Mr. Neely. Therefore, that issue is not before this Court. However, we are troubled by the threatening content of the letters Mr. Neely sent to the insurance company. While Mr. Neely claims he only intended to facilitate a settlement, his predictions of adverse publicity and a nasty trial were inappropriate and overreaching. The claim that "this law firm tends to be extraordinarily high-profile" and the threat to cause "substantial embarrassment" and "unnecessary embarrassment," along with irrelevant character assertions and claims of high public position (i.e., that one is a member of the West Virginia Board of Probation and Parole and an executive director of the West Virginia Human Rights Commission) are all practices that play no legitimate role in settlement negotiations. We have a large body of law which compels insurance companies to negotiate fairly, and that requirement is a two-edged sword. Simply put, what the lawyer did in this case was unfair and inappropriate.

4.4 dismiss
isn't before this
ct. - but they
still seem to
think he
violated

[13] [5] Paragraph VII of the complaint stated:

Plaintiffs Linda Stephens and Quewanncoii Stephens have diligently investigated the facts and circumstances surrounding this incident. As a result of interviews with persons associated with Fort Hill Child Development Center, Inc., plaintiffs verily believe that the incident described in paragraph III through VI is but one of many instances in which Plaintiff Quinton Stephens, an autistic child, who was known to have special needs, in direct contravention of the express directions of Quinton's parents of his health care providers, was knowingly, willfully and intentionally strapped to a chair in a dark room for many hours and left alone directly as a result of his mental and physical handicap.

↳ based on parents' belief.

admonish Mr. Hunter and Mr. Neely for factual assertions set forth in a single paragraph of a complaint that later proved to be false.

This case illustrates the difficulties in determining what is a frivolous lawsuit. In *Committee on Legal Ethics of the West Virginia State Bar v. Douglas*, 179 W. Va. 490, 370 S.E.2d 325 (1988), this Court set forth a test to determine whether a lawyer had advanced a frivolous claim. However, the Code of Professional Responsibility was in effect at that time. DR 7-102(A)(2) provided that a lawyer shall not "[k]nowingly advance a claim or defense that is unwarranted under existing law, except that he may advance such claim or defense if it can be supported by good faith argument for an extension, modification, or reversal of existing law." Recognizing that DR 7-102(A)(2) was aimed at frivolousness, this Court set forth a twofold inquiry under the rule. The test first required an objective determination of whether the claim or defense was "unwarranted" under the law. A more subjective determination of whether the lawyer asserted the claim or defense with knowledge that it was unwarranted completed the inquiry.

With the adoption of the Rules of Professional Conduct, and more specifically Rule 3.1, an objective standard was established to determine the propriety of pleadings and other court papers.[14] Nonetheless, the term "frivolous," now a part of the rule, remains undefined. However, the Comment to the rule is instructive regarding what conduct is permissible and what constitutes frivolousness. The Comment provides, in pertinent part:

> The filing of an action or defense or similar action taken for a client is not frivolous merely because the facts have not first been fully substantiated or because the lawyer expects to develop vital evidence only by discovery. Such action is not frivolous even though the lawyer believes that the client's position ultimately will not prevail. The action is frivolous, however, if the client desires to have the action taken primarily for the purpose of harassing or maliciously injuring a person or if the lawyer is unable either to make a good faith argument on the merits of the action taken or to support the action taken by a good faith argument for an extension, modification or reversal of existing law.

It is obvious that the drafters of the rules acknowledged that when lawyers prepare and file pleadings in civil actions, they routinely make factual allegations in support of their theories of liability and assert defenses in response thereto, some of which ultimately prove to be unsubstantiated. The Comment suggests that these practices do not warrant discipline under Rule 3.1. In fact, federal courts have been reluctant to impose sanctions for such practices under Rule 11.[15] *See Kamen v. American Telephone & Telegraph Co.*, 791 F.2d 1006, (2d Cir. 1986) (counsel's reliance on his client's assertion that defendant received funding from the United States government making it subject to suit under the Rehabilitation Act of 1973

---

[14] [11] Despite the objective standard, some element of subjectivity remains as a lawyer is not disciplined unless his or her conduct is culpable.

[15] [12] In *Douglas*, this Court also recognized the interrelationship between DR 7-102(A)(2) and Rule 11 of the West Virginia Rules of Civil Procedure. While Rule 11 provides a private remedy, Rule 3.1 is aimed at preventing repeat offenders escaping notice and building confidence in the legal system as a whole.

constituted a reasonable pre-filing inquiry precluding sanctions); *Kraemer v. Grant County*, 892 F.2d 686 (7th Cir. 1990) (sanctions unwarranted where attorney did everything possible to gather information including hiring a private investigator and instituted suit only after hostile attitude of potential defendants made it necessary to use the discovery process to gather additional information).

While we remain concerned about the increasing number of cases that clog our court dockets, we recognize that there are instances where an attorney has exhausted all avenues of pre-suit investigation and needs the tools of discovery to complete factual development of the case. An action or claim is not frivolous if after a reasonable investigation, all the facts have not been first substantiated. A complaint may be filed if evidence is expected to be developed by discovery. A lawyer may not normally be sanctioned for alleging facts in a complaint that are later determined to be untrue.

As previously discussed, the specific allegations in paragraph VII of the Stephens' complaint were not ultimately supported by the facts developed during discovery. Nonetheless, the record indicates that Mr. Hunter and Mr. Neely conducted a reasonable investigation of the case. Because of his autism, Quinton was unable to provide any information about his care at the Center. However, Mrs. Stephens provided the details of what happened on December 2, 1994. In addition, she related at least three other incidents which suggested that the Center may not have been rendering adequate supervision of Quinton. Mrs. Stephens also told Mr. Neely about conversations she had with some of the employees at the Center which caused her to believe that Quinton's posture correcting chair had been used for discipline or management purposes against her specific directions. The record indicates that Mr. Hunter and Mr. Neely received no cooperation from the defendants during their investigation. In the end, they were left with the choice of advising the Stephenses to give up or file the complaint and proceed with discovery. Given these circumstances, we find that Mr. Hunter and Mr. Neely did not violate Rule 3.1

Accordingly, based on all of the above, the complaint filed against Mr. Hunter and Mr. Neely is dismissed.

Charges dismissed.

WORKMAN, J., concurring:

I initially put down for a concurring opinion to say only that although the Lawyer Disciplinary Board dropped the charge involving the letter written to the complainant herein, it should be made clear that the tone and tenor of that letter was threatening and it was wrong. Indeed, it is the kind of thing that can give lawyers a very bad reputation.

The record shows that Mrs. Hawks runs a reputable business that provides a real service to children whose parents must leave them in day care in order to go to work. The letter sent to her by the lawyer here was intimidating and basically threatened to ruin her business and her reputation if she did not meet its demands. This is not a legitimate effort at settlement, but more in the manner of intimidation. As the majority opinion points out, had the charge involving the letter not been dropped by the Lawyer Disciplinary Board, Neely may well have been sanctioned.

After reading the local Charleston newspapers on July 16 and 17, however, I feel it necessary to expand this concurring opinion to say more. If quoted correctly in the newspapers, Mr. Neely and Mr. Hunter had the audacity to once again claim the lawsuit they brought against Mrs. Hawks and the Fort Hill Day Care Center had merit.[16] This is fairly incredible in view of the fact that the lower court dismissed part of the lawsuit as being without merit and in view of the fact that lawyers Neely and Hunter sought a voluntary dismissal of their remaining claims (and agreed not to appeal the lower court's dismissal) in exchange for the defendants agreeing to dismiss a Rule 11 motion seeking monetary sanctions against them.

It is amazing that after getting off by the skin of their teeth for filing a spurious lawsuit and writing a threatening letter, Neely and Hunter would actually again attempt to cast aspersions against this individual and this day care center. These lawyers may never learn their lesson until the time comes when a real sanction is imposed, either through ethical proceedings or in the form of a lawsuit. If they were misquoted, they should immediately demand that a correction be printed. But if they were not misquoted, then shame on them for conducting themselves in this manner. It does not bring respect to the profession.

I am authorized to state that Justice Maynard joins in the concurring opinion.

NOTES, QUESTIONS, AND EXAMPLES

Lawyer makes an argument that seems foreclosed by mandatory authority precedent in the relevant court of appeals. The argument has been accepted in other courts of appeal, whose decisions are persuasive but not mandatory authority. Is Lawyer subject to Rule 11 sanctions? *See Hunter v. Earthgrains Bakery*, 281 F.3d 144 (4th Cir. 2002).

2.   Personal Opinion and Alluding to Matters Outside the Record

Lawyers are prohibited from expressing their personal opinion to jurors about the justness of the client's cause, the credibility of a witness, or the culpability, guilt, or innocence of a party. MR 3.4(e). This rule only applies to personal opinion statements. It does not prohibit vigorous argument that attempts to persuade the jury about any of the prohibited personal opinion subject matters. The rules of evidence are designed to regulate the information that the jury receives at a trial. Lawyers are prohibited from undermining the evidence law policies by alluding to matters that are either irrelevant or will not be supported by admissible evidence. MR 3.4(e).

---

[16] [1] The Charleston Daily Mail on July 16, 1998, and the Charleston Gazette on July 17, 1998, quoted Richard Neely as saying that the charges against him were "silly," and characterized the ethics complaint as an allegation "that I too vigorously went to bat for a black autistic child allegedly abused in a day care center." Roger Hunter is quoted as saying that the lawsuit (against the Center) was "Meritorious."

DARDEN v. WAINWRIGHT
477 U.S. 168 (1986)

Justice Powell delivered the opinion of the Court.

This case presents three questions concerning the validity of petitioner's criminal conviction and death sentence: . . . (ii) whether the prosecution's closing argument during the guilt phase of a bifurcated trial rendered the trial fundamentally unfair and deprived the sentencing determination of the reliability required by the Eighth Amendment. . . .

issue

I

jury verdict for murder

Petitioner was tried and found guilty of murder, robbery, and assault with intent to kill in the Circuit Court for Citrus County, Florida, in January 1974. Pursuant to Florida's capital sentencing statute, the same jury that convicted petitioner heard further testimony and argument in order to make a nonbinding recommendation as to whether a death sentence should be imposed. The jury recommended a death sentence, and the trial judge followed that recommendation. On direct appeal, the Florida Supreme Court affirmed the conviction and the sentence. Petitioner made several of the same arguments in that appeal that he makes here. With respect to the prosecutorial misconduct claim, the court disapproved of the closing argument, but reasoned that the law required a new trial "only in those cases in which it is reasonably evident that the remarks might have influenced the jury to reach a more severe verdict of guilt . . . or in which the comment is unfair." It concluded that the comments had not rendered petitioner's trial unfair. This Court granted certiorari, limited the grant to the claim of prosecutorial misconduct, heard oral argument, and dismissed the writ as improvidently granted.

same jury recom. death

prosecutorial misconduct claim for new trial

court said it wasn't prejudicial.

Petitioner then sought federal habeas corpus relief, raising the same claims he raises here. The District Court denied the petition. A divided panel of the Court of Appeals for the Eleventh Circuit affirmed. The Court of Appeals granted rehearing en banc, and affirmed the District Court by an equally divided court. . . . We now affirm.

II

[The Court recounted at length the facts of the criminal case. —Ed.]

III

[The Court discussed and ruled against Petitioner's juror exclusion issue. —Ed.]

IV

pros. closing at guilt trial

Petitioner next contends that the prosecution's closing argument at the guilt-innocence stage of the trial rendered his conviction fundamentally unfair and deprived the sentencing determination of the reliability that the Eighth

Amendment requires.

It is helpful as an initial matter to place these remarks in context. Closing argument came at the end of several days of trial. Because of a state procedural rule petitioner's counsel had the opportunity to present the initial summation as well as a rebuttal to the prosecutors' closing arguments. The prosecutors' comments must be evaluated in light of the defense argument that preceded it, which blamed the Polk County Sheriff's Office for a lack of evidence,[17] alluded to the death penalty,[18] characterized the perpetrator of the crimes as an "animal,"[19] and contained counsel's personal opinion of the strength of the State's evidence.[20]

The prosecutors then made their closing argument. That argument deserves the condemnation it has received from every court to review it, although no court has held that the argument rendered the trial unfair. Several comments attempted to place some of the blame for the crime on the Division of Corrections, because Darden was on weekend furlough from a prison sentence when the crime occurred.[21] Some comments implied that the death penalty would be the only guarantee against a future similar act.[22] Others incorporated the defense's use of the word "animal."[23] Prosecutor McDaniel made several offensive comments reflecting an emotional reaction to the case.[24] These comments undoubtedly were

---

[17] [5] "The Judge is going to tell you to consider the evidence or the lack of evidence. We have a lack of evidence, almost criminally negligent on the part of the Polk County Sheriff's Office in this case. You could go on and on about it."

[18] [6] "They took a coincidence and magnified that into a capital case. And they are asking you to kill a man on coincidence."

[19] [7] "The first witness you saw was Mrs. Turman, who was a pathetic figure; who worked and struggled all of her life to build what little she had, the little furniture store; and a woman who was robbed, sexually assaulted, and then had her husband slaughtered before her eyes, by what would have to be a vicious animal." "And this murderer ran after him, aimed again, and this poor kid with half his brains blown away. . . . It's the work of an animal, there's no doubt about it."

[20] [8] "So they come on up here and ask Citrus County people to kill the man. You will be instructed on lesser included offenses. . . . The question is, do they have enough evidence to kill that man, enough evidence? And I honestly do not think they do."

[21] [9] "As far as I am concerned, there should be another Defendant in this courtroom, one more, and that is the division of corrections, the prisons. . . . Can't we expect him to stay in a prison when they go there? Can we expect them to stay locked up once they go there? Do we know that they're going to be out on the public with guns, drinking?" "Yes, there is another Defendant, but I regret that I know of no charges to place upon him, except the public condemnation of them, condemn them."

[22] [10] "I will ask you to advise the Court to give him death. That's the only way that I know that he is not going to get out on the public. It's the only way I know. It's the only way I can be sure of it. It's the only way that anybody can be sure of it now, because the people that turned him loose."

[23] [11] "As far as I am concerned, and as Mr. Maloney said as he identified this man this person, as an animal, this animal was on the public for one reason."

[24] [12] "He shouldn't be out of his cell unless he has a leash on him and a prison guard at the other end of that leash." "I wish [Mr. Turman] had had a shotgun in his hand when he walked in the back door and blown his [Darden's] face off. I wish that I could see him sitting here with no face, blown away by a shotgun." "I wish someone had walked in the back door and blown his head off at that point." "He fired in the boy's back, number five, saving one. Didn't get a chance to use it. I wish he had used it on himself." "I wish he had been killed in the accident, but he wasn't. Again, we are unlucky that time." "[D]on't forget what he has done according to those witnesses, to make every attempt to change his appearance from September the 8th, 1973. The hair, the goatee, even the moustache and the weight. The only thing he

improper. But as both the District Court and the original panel of the Court of Appeals (whose opinion on this issue still stands) recognized, it "is not enough that the prosecutors' remarks were undesirable or even universally condemned." The relevant question is whether the prosecutors' comments "so infected the trial with unfairness as to make the resulting conviction a denial of due process." *Donnelly v. DeChristoforo*, 416 U.S. 637 (1974). Moreover, the appropriate standard of review for such a claim on writ of habeas corpus is "the narrow one of due process, and not the broad exercise of supervisory power."

Under this standard of review, we agree with the reasoning of every court to consider these comments that they did not deprive petitioner of a fair trial. The prosecutors' argument did not manipulate or misstate the evidence, nor did it implicate other specific rights of the accused such as the right to counsel or the right to remain silent. Much of the objectionable content was invited by or was responsive to the opening summation of the defense. As we explained in *United States v. Young*, 470 U.S. 1 (1985), the idea of "invited response" is used not to excuse improper comments, but to determine their effect on the trial as a whole. The trial court instructed the jurors several times that their decision was to be made on the basis of the evidence alone, and that the arguments of counsel were not evidence. The weight of the evidence against petitioner was heavy; the "overwhelming eyewitness and circumstantial evidence to support a finding of guilt on all charges," reduced the likelihood that the jury's decision was influenced by argument. Finally, defense counsel made the tactical decision not to present any witness other than petitioner. This decision not only permitted them to give their summation prior to the prosecution's closing argument, but also gave them the opportunity to make a final rebuttal argument. Defense counsel were able to use the opportunity for rebuttal very effectively, turning much of the prosecutors' closing argument against them by placing many of the prosecutors' comments and actions in a light that was more likely to engender strong disapproval than result in inflamed passions against petitioner. For these reasons, we agree with the District Court below that "Darden's trial was not perfect — few are — but neither was it fundamentally unfair."

*   *   *

VI

The judgment of the Court of Appeals is affirmed, and the case is remanded for proceedings consistent with this opinion.

It is so ordered.

Justice Blackmun, with whom Justice Brennan, Justice Marshall, and Justice Stevens join, dissenting.

Although the Constitution guarantees a criminal defendant only "a fair trial [and] not a perfect one," this Court has stressed repeatedly in the decade that the

---

hasn't done that I know of is cut his throat." After this, the last in a series of such comments, defense counsel objected for the first time.

Eighth Amendment requires a heightened degree of reliability in any case where a State seeks to take the defendant's life. Today's opinion, however, reveals a Court willing to tolerate not only imperfection but a level of fairness and reliability so low it should make conscientious prosecutors cringe.

I

A

The Court's discussion of Darden's claim of prosecutorial misconduct is noteworthy for its omissions. Despite the fact that earlier this Term the Court relied heavily on standards governing the professional responsibility of defense counsel in ruling that an attorney's actions did not deprive his client of any constitutional right, *see Nix v. Whiteside*, 475 U.S. 157, 166-171 (1986), today it entirely ignores standards governing the professional responsibility of prosecutors in reaching the conclusion that the summations of Darden's prosecutors did not deprive him of a fair trial.

The prosecutor's remarks in this case reflect behavior as to which "virtually all the sources speak with one voice," *Nix v. Whiteside, supra*, at 166, that is, a voice of strong condemnation.[25] The following brief comparison of established standards of prosecutorial conduct with the prosecutors' behavior in this case merely illustrates, but hardly exhausts, the scope of the misconduct involved:

> 1. "A lawyer shall not . . . state a personal opinion as to . . . the credibility of a witness . . . . or the guilt or innocence of an accused." Model Rules of Professional Conduct, Rule 3.4(e) (1984); see also Code of Professional Responsibility, DR 7-106(C)(4) (1980); ABA Standards for Criminal Justice: 3-5.8(b) (2d ed. 1980). Yet one prosecutor, White, stated: "I am convinced, as convinced as I know I am standing before you today, that Willie Jasper Darden is a murderer, that he murdered Mr. Turman, that he robbed Mrs. Turman and that he shot to kill Phillip Arnold. I will be convinced of that the rest of my life." And the other prosecutor, McDaniel, stated, with respect to Darden's testimony: "Well, let me tell you something: If I am ever over in that chair over there, facing life or death, life imprisonment or death, I guarantee you I will lie until my teeth fall out."
>
> 2. "The prosecutor should refrain from argument which would divert the jury from its duty to decide the case on the evidence, by injecting issues

---

[25] [2] Every judge who has addressed the prosecutors' behavior has condemned it. See *Darden v. State*, 329 So. 2d 287, 290 (Fla. 1976) ("[T]he prosecutor's remarks under ordinary circumstances would constitute a violation of the Code of Professional Responsibility"); id. at 291-95 (dissenting opinion); *Darden v. Wainwright*, 513 F. Supp. 947, 955 (M.D. Fla. 1981) ("Anyone attempting a text-book illustration of a violation of the Code of Professional Responsibility . . . could not possibly improve upon [prosecutor White's final statement]"); *Darden v. Wainwright*, 699 F.2d 1031, 1035-1036 (11th Cir. 1983); id. at 1040-1043 (dissenting opinion). Even the State's Attorney concedes that prosecutor McDaniel's summation was an "unnecessary tirade," that "[n]o one has ever even weakly suggested that McDaniel's closing remarks were anything but improper," Supplemental Answer in *Darden v. Wainwright*, Case No. 79-566-Civ.T.H. (M.D. Fla.) (June 1, 1979), p. 12, and that much of the summation consisted of "inflammatory irrelevancies,"

broader than the guilt or innocence of the accused under the controlling law, or by making predictions of the consequences of the jury's verdict." ABA Standards for Criminal Justice 3-5.8(d) (2d ed. 1980); *cf.* Model Rules of Professional Conduct, Rule 3.4(e); Code of Professional Responsibility, DR 7-106(C)(7); ABA Standards for Criminal Justice 3-6.1(c) (2d ed. 1980). Yet McDaniel's argument was filled with references to Darden's status as a prisoner on furlough who "shouldn't be out of his cell unless he has a leash on him." Again and again, he sought to put on trial an absent "defendant," the State Department of Corrections that had furloughed Darden. He also implied that defense counsel would use improper tricks to deflect the jury from the real issue. Darden's status as a furloughed prisoner, the release policies of the Department of Corrections, and his counsel's anticipated tactics obviously had no legal relevance to the question the jury was being asked to decide: whether he had committed the robbery and murder at the Turmans' furniture store. Indeed, the State argued before this Court that McDaniel's remarks were harmless precisely because he "failed to discuss the issues, the weight of the evidence, or the credibility of the witnesses."

3. "The prosecutor should not use arguments calculated to inflame the passions or prejudices of the jury." ABA Standards for Criminal Justice 3-5.8(c) (2d ed. 1980); *see Berger v. United States*, 295 U.S. 78, 88, 55 S. Ct. 629, 633, 79 L. Ed. 1314 (1935). Yet McDaniel repeatedly expressed a wish "that I could see [Darden] sitting here with no face, blown away by a shotgun." Indeed, I do not think McDaniel's summation, taken as a whole, can accurately be described as anything but a relentless and single-minded attempt to inflame the jury.

B

The Court relies on the standard established in *Donnelly v. DeChristoforo*, 416 U.S. 637, 643 (1974), for deciding when a prosecutor's comments at a state trial render that trial fundamentally unfair. It omits, however, any discussion of the facts, so different from those in this case, that led the Court to conclude in *DeChristoforo* that that defendant had not been deprived of a fair trial.

DeChristoforo concerned "two remarks made by the prosecutor during the course of his rather lengthy closing argument to the jury." One remark was "but one moment of an extended trial." And even the more objectionable remark was so "ambiguous" that it provided no basis for inferring either that the prosecutor "intend[ed] [it] to have its most damaging meaning or that a jury, sitting through lengthy exhortation, [would] draw that meaning from the plethora of less damaging interpretations." Finally, the trial judge in *DeChristoforo* expressly instructed the jury to disregard the improper statements. This Court's holding thus rested on its conclusion that the prosecutor's comments were neither so extensive nor so improper as to violate the Constitution.

Far from involving "ambiguous" statements that "might or might not" affect the jury, the remarks at issue here were "focused, unambiguous, and strong." *Caldwell v. Mississippi*, 472 U.S. 320, 340 (1985). It is impossible to read the transcript of McDaniel's summation without seeing it as a calculated and sustained attempt to

[handwritten margin note: this was pronounced and persistent.]

inflame the jury. Almost every page contains at least one offensive or improper statement; some pages contain little else. The misconduct here was not "slight or confined to a single instance, but . . . was pronounced and persistent, with a probable cumulative effect upon the jury which cannot be disregarded as inconsequential." *Berger v. United States*, 295 U.S. at 89.

* * *

III

Twice during the past year — in *United States v. Young*, 470 U.S. 1 (1985), and again today — this Court has been faced with clearly improper prosecutorial misconduct during summations. Each time, the Court has condemned the behavior but affirmed the conviction. Forty years ago, Judge Jerome N. Frank, in dissent, discussed the Second Circuit's similar approach in language we would do well to remember today:

[handwritten margin note: why condemn but not reverse?]

> This court has several times used vigorous language in denouncing government counsel for such conduct as that of the [prosecutor] here. But, each time, it has said that, nevertheless, it would not reverse. Such an attitude of helpless piety is, I think, undesirable. It means actual condonation of counsel's alleged offense, coupled with verbal disapprobation. If we continue to do nothing practical to prevent such conduct, we should cease to disapprove it. For otherwise it will be as if we declared in effect, 'Government attorneys, without fear of reversal, may say just about what they please in addressing juries, for our rules on the subject are pretend-rules. If prosecutors win verdicts as a result of "disapproved" remarks, we will not deprive them of their victories; we will merely go through the form of expressing displeasure. The deprecatory words we use in our opinions on such occasions are purely ceremonial.' Government counsel, employing such tactics, are the kind who, eager to win victories, will gladly pay the small price of a ritualistic verbal spanking. The practice of this court — recalling the bitter tear shed by the Walrus as he ate the oysters — breeds a deplorably cynical attitude towards the judiciary (footnote omitted).

United States v. Antonelli Fireworks Co., 155 F.2d 631, 661, cert. denied, 329 U.S. 742 (1946).

I believe this Court must do more than wring its hands when a State uses improper legal standards to select juries in capital cases and permits prosecutors to pervert the adversary process. I therefore dissent.

INTERNATIONAL NOTE

A British barrister, while obligated to vigorously defend a client and put the prosecution to its proof, is prohibited from defending on the basis of an affirmative version of events, or inferences from the evidence that are inconsistent with a confession that the defendant has made to counsel. Bar Council of England and Wales, *Written Standards for the Conduct of Professional Work, Standards 12.2–12.5, available at* www.barcouncil.org.uk.

3. Obey Court Orders

[handwritten: Must obey - but can preserve the record for appeal.]

Lawyers must obey court orders. Even when a lawyer knows that a judge is mistaken in making an order or ruling, the lawyer must obey the order, but may make reasonable efforts to preserve the record for later challenge on appeal.

KLEINER v. FIRST NATIONAL BANK OF ATLANTA
751 F.2d 1193 (11th Cir. 1985)

VANCE, CIRCUIT JUDGE.

I. FACTS

This appeal is the closing phase of a ground-breaking class action against the First National Bank of Atlanta filed by Jackie Kleiner, an Atlanta lawyer and real estate investor. The lawsuit, sounding in fraud, RICO and breach of contract, charged the Bank with reneging on its promise to peg the interest it charged smaller customers to the prime rate by undercutting the announced prime rate for the Bank's best commercial customers. Richard M. Kirby, a partner in the Atlanta law firm of Hansell & Post and an attorney experienced at class action litigation, undertook the Bank's defense.

On April 15, 1983, after over two years of discovery, the district judge certified certain of the contract claims for class action treatment. The tripartite plaintiff class, certified under Fed. R. Civ. P. 23(b)(3), numbered approximately 8,600 potential members.

The following month Kirby served notices of deposition and subpoenas duces tecum on twenty-five prospective class members. Plaintiffs moved for a protective order to bar the Bank from badgering class members by taking their depositions. At a May 20 hearing on the motion, the court initially suggested that the Bank confine class member discovery to affidavits. Outspoken protests from plaintiffs, however, caused the court to reconsider its response. Opposing counsel argued that unilateral contacts by the Bank before the close of the exclusion period would intimidate eligible members, many of whom would be very worried about their credit ratings and their ability to borrow in the future. Counsel contended that many would be deterred from participating in the class, which was their right.

After extended discussion, the district judge granted the protective order subject to a proviso allowing the Bank to take depositions of five class members. *[handwritten: Allowed to interview 5 class members]* Both sides were to have the opportunity to interview the deponents before the depositions, and plaintiffs would have the opening interview. The court took the broader question of unsupervised contacts between the Bank and class members under advisement pending further briefing, ruling:

> At this time, I am going to let [defense counsel] take no more than five depositions. Otherwise, I am granting the motion for a protective order. However, if you can get me some law that convinces me that it is right for you to otherwise be able to contact class members, then I will permit you to contact additional people informally.

[handwritten: Judge's orders]

Both Kirby and Richard M. Langway, general counsel for the Bank, attended the hearing.

A month later, on June 29, the district judge approved the class notice required under Fed. R. Civ. P. 23(c)(2). The notice, as approved, informed recipients that they would be included in the class unless they took the affirmative step of opting out by returning an exclusion request to the clerk of the district court within a stated time. The class members were also directed to address any inquiries to their choice of plaintiffs' or defense counsel. After further negotiation, August 13 was set as the date of mailing.

The following day, June 30, the district judge entered a *sua sponte* order amplifying the class notice ruling. According to the addendum, copies of the proposed replies to inquiries, as well as the inquiries themselves, were to be furnished to opposing counsel before being mailed. In addition, the district judge acknowledged the receipt of briefs on the ex parte contact issue and explicitly reiterated that the question of unsupervised Bank contacts with plaintiff class remained under advisement.

By mid-July, the Bank had seized upon the idea of soliciting class exclusion requests as a means to reducing its potential liability and quelling the adverse publicity the lawsuit had spawned. Kirby, alerted of the plan, researched the legality of a solicitation campaign. Meeting with top Bank managers on August 8, Kirby advised that a communications scheme would be lawful under the precepts of *Bernard v. Gulf Oil Co.* as long as the conversations were truthful and noncoercive. The lawyer warned that any such campaign, while legal, would be an extraordinary move likely to provoke the wrath of the court.

Without further hesitation, Thomas R. Williams, chairman of the board, canvassed the potential benefits and costs and resolved to proceed. The remainder of the discussion was devoted to specifics. In response to a question, Kirby opined that phone calls would be better than letters, given the danger that people would disregard letters as more "junk mail." Williams assigned Thomas Chapman, Bank marketing director, responsibility for coordinating all solicitation efforts in close consultation with Kirby and Langway.

Secrecy and haste shrouded the undertaking, which would coincide with the district judge's vacation. Neither the court nor opposing counsel were alerted to the telephone campaign, as was Kirby's intent. Chapman hurriedly organized a force of 175 loan officers to staff the telephones, while lawyers Kirby and Langway lent their assistance by reviewing and revising a briefing letter from Williams to the employees as well as a question-and-answer prompting sheet to be used by the loan officers. Kirby supplied Chapman with the class notice and exclusion request forms for reproduction. He also collaborated with the Bank's computer center to generate lists of potential class members broken down under each of the Bank's cost centers.

On August 11, two days before the scheduled date of class notice mailing, the Bank convened a meeting of the loan officers. Kirby and Langway sat in the front row. Board chairman Williams opened the meeting with brief introductory remarks, the turned the session over to Chapman. Chapman announced that the Bank was going to take "bold, decisive action which had no precedent." He informed the

[handwritten: campaign to tell them they could opt out.]

assembly that the Bank was commencing a "communications program" to insure that the class members in the Kleiner litigation understood the merits of the dispute and their right to opt out.

Chapman went on to say that the officers would be asked to telephone the customers they knew best, and he exhorted them to "do the best selling job they had ever done." The officers were to proceed swiftly since, in Chapman's words, the court might halt the program. The objective, according to Chapman's notes, was to persuade the borrowers to "withdraw from the class."

Chapman repeatedly stressed that the conversations were to proceed on a "factual" plane, without arm-twisting or coercion. The loan officers, however, received "no facts beyond those listed in the Questions and Answers sheet, the letter to employees, and the class action notice. . . . Chapman himself knew little about the lawsuit except what was contained in the materials distributed at the meeting." The loan officers dispersed into smaller groups where they were told to call the most receptive customers first and to avoid phoning antagonistic borrowers altogether. They were handed computer lists of customers marked "Friend" and "Foe" as well as score sheets lined with columns for tallying opt-out commitments and the dollar amounts of the corresponding loans. The telephone campaign began immediately afterward.[26] The Bank eventually succeeded in reaching a little over 3000 customers, nearly 2800 of whom decided to exclude themselves. Many decided to do so before they received the court-approved notice. By August 12 the Bank had reaped opt-out commitments from customers representing a sum total of $694,997,218 in past or present loans.

[handwritten: no arm-twisting]

[handwritten: > opt out]

The district judge, just back from a two-week vacation, held a hearing on August 24 at plaintiffs' request. When apprised of the campaign, she immediately cited Kirby for contempt and restricted communication to class members by all parties and their counsel to approved responses to individual inquiries. She further denied the Bank permission to depose borrowers who had agreed to opt out. Hansell & Post was cited for contempt the following week. An evidentiary hearing was calendared for October 5.

At an in-chambers conference on September 15, the district judge stated that the proceedings were "in the nature of a disciplinary proceeding" rather than for civil or criminal contempt. The contempt citations were later vacated. The district judge explained that the charges against counsel were grounded in violations of the orders dated May 20 and June 30 as well as in Model Rules 4.2 and 8.4(d) of the A.B.A. Model Rules of Professional Conduct (1983).

Following the October hearing, which lasted three days, the court issued an exhaustive order on November 8 declaring the solicitation scheme illegal. The trial court found that Kirby, Hansell & Post, and Langway had rendered advice in bad faith and had knowingly taken part in the illegal opt-out campaign. As a sanction, the court imposed a $50,000 fine on Kirby and Hansell & Post payable to the clerk

---

[26] [9] The Bank tolerated no opposition to the communications program. When James Kilpatrick, a member of the Bar who was then a loan officer, objected to the use of pressure tactics to induce customers to opt out, he was told to follow the program or "find . . . something else to do." He was forced ultimately to resign when he refused to participate.

[handwritten: → refused - forced to quit.]

of the court. Kirby, his firm, and the Bank were additionally assessed attorneys' fees and costs incident to class notice and the subsequent disciplinary proceeding, which totaled $58,577. Both Kirby and Langway were disqualified from further representation in the case. As a final measure, the district court ruled that the exclusion requests would be voidable following entry of judgment. The Bank, Langway, Kirby and Hansell & Post immediately petitioned for review.

II. PRELIMINARY MATTERS: JURISDICTION

Since the date of argument before this court, the underlying litigation proceeded to settlement. Under the terms of the court-approved agreement, all qualifying class members who requested exclusion are entitled to void such requests and participate in the distribution of the settlement on equal footing with the remaining class members. The stipulation awarding attorneys' fees by its terms encompasses the district court's award of fees and costs incident to class notice and the disciplinary proceeding. The parties correctly argue that the settlement has mooted issues of attorneys' fees, costs, and the legality of the voidable exclusion sanction. The issue of the injunction against communication with members of the plaintiff class similarly lapsed into mootness upon conclusion of the litigation.

We remand to the district court with instructions to vacate as moot those portions of the November 8, 1983 order ordering attorneys' fees, costs, voidable opt-out exclusions, and cessation of defense communications with members of the plaintiff class.

A different result must obtain with respect to the fines and disqualification imposed upon counsel. The $50,000 fine assessed against Kirby and Hansell & Post was imposed pursuant to the inherent powers of the district court and is not subject to revocation by the parties. The issue of the fine thus remains alive.

We reach the same conclusion with respect to disqualification of counsel. The unique nature of a class action necessitates participation of counsel even after the settlement is approved by the court. Notice of the settlement must be sent to all class members. Individual claims must be filed, negotiated, and paid. Counsel for both sides bear the primary responsibility for administering the settlement, usually a lengthy process. The Bank can still be hampered, then, by its counsel's inability to appear before the court in this case.[27]

III. DID THE COMMUNICATIONS CAMPAIGN VIOLATE LAW?

Petitioners argue that they cannot be held to account because their actions were not in derogation of law. The district court held otherwise, grounding its order for sanctions in violations of the May 20 protective order, the June 30 class notice order, Local Rule 221.2, and the Model Rules of Professional Conduct. Because we

---

[27] [14] We note further that the brand of disqualification was not lifted at the close of the proceedings. The disciplinary action and consequent disqualification may expose counsel to further sanctions by the bar and portends adverse effects upon counsels' careers and public image. The effects of disqualification will linger long after the closing of the case. The controversy thus remains live and demands consideration.

violated orders.

conclude that the defense campaign violated the protective and class notice orders, we do not reach the question of the constitutional validity of Local Rule 221.2.

We affirm the district court with respect to its rulings predicated on Model Rules 4.2 and 8.4(d).

Kirby acknowledges the existence of the May and June rulings but argues that the orders did not involve and therefore did not ban opt-out solicitations. According to Kirby, the sole effect of the directives was to limit the number of depositions the Bank could take, leaving the Bank free to initiate contacts by other means. In essence Kirby argues that the mandate of the district court cannot exceed the corners of the motion that requested it.

Kirby says that order was not depositions not solicitations.

This appeal is a case in point. The plaintiffs originally moved for a ban on depositions out of concern for harassment. The district judge's suggestions recommending the substitution of affidavits and the pitched debate that followed widened the inquiry to the larger issue of intimidation through all forms of unsupervised contacts. Viewed in context, the import of the resulting order was unmistakable. The decision to take the question of informal contacts with class members under advisement acted as an order which barred opt-out solicitations and similar communications until further notice. With a single narrow exception, defense counsel *were not to contact* prospective class members.

P wanted ban on dep b/c of harassment.

We therefore conclude that the May 20 ruling and the companion June ruling prohibited the Bank's communications campaign. The orders, which were directed to counsel as agents of the Bank, were binding on the Bank in its capacity as principal.

Held: the campaign violated the order

VI. Sanctions for Advice Given by Counsel

The district court twice over issued orders directing counsel for the Bank to refrain from contacting the plaintiff class. Kirby knew of the orders, as the trial court found. Nevertheless he counseled the Bank to disregard them. The question on review is whether Kirby and his firm, as counsel for the Bank, properly face discipline as a consequence of their advice.

Kirby told them to disregard.

Did they get proper discipline?

According to appellants, sanctions must not issue because their advice, however mistaken, was given in good faith. Observing that a lawyer may counsel or assist a client's good faith efforts to test the validity of a law in good conscience, they maintain that a lawyer who counsels disobedience to a standing order of the court stands firmly within ethical bounds.

Kirby argues the advice was in good faith.

The inevitable result of this position would be to cripple orderly processes of trial and appeal on which enforcement of the laws depends. As a fundamental proposition, orders of the court *"must be obeyed"* until reversed by orderly review or disrobed of authority by delay or frustration in the appellate process . . . ." Parties and counsel alike are bound by this admonition. If the order appears to be incorrect, the proper course of action lies in review:

> If the order is believed to be incorrect, the remedy generally is to seek a change in the order — usually by a motion to quash — and, if this is

If party thinks the order is wrong move to change it.

appeal.

denied, then to appeal and, absent a stay, promptly to comply with the order.

except for Const. Right.

Disobedience of a court order unequivocally merits punishment save in instances in which compliance would necessarily result in " '*an irrevocable* and permanent surrender of a constitutional right.' " In *Walker v. City of Birmingham*, 388 U.S. 307 (1967), the Supreme Court "emphatically rejected the suggestion that an individual may disregard a court order simply because [it] interfered with . . . his exercise of First Amendment rights." Obviously, commercial speech commands no greater claim to immunity.

It is essential that lawyers have the liberty to advise their clients of the legal consequences of proposed courses of action free of a Damoclean sword. Otherwise, lawyers would shelve their "zeal for forthrightness and independence," which secures informed compliance with the law.

If not held + the order was rule of law invalid

This case, however, is of an entirely different order. When a court issues a ruling, a lawyer must advise his client to comply and must not counsel disobedience. The opposite result, if sanctioned, could only result in the unraveling of the rule of law. There are few mandates so plain as the command to obey the order of the court.[28] Nevertheless, petitioners gave comfort and counsel to disobedience, in lieu of review. Under such circumstances, we conclude that the imposition of sanctions was an appropriate act by the district court in defense of its authority.

VII. THE NATURE OF THE DISCIPLINARY PROCEEDING AND THE SEVERITY OF SANCTIONS

The vacated citations for contempt and the imposition of a substantial fine payable to the clerk of the district court raise the question of the procedural adequacy of the October 5 proceedings. Petitioners attempt to give the disciplinary proceedings a criminal cast in order to invalidate them for lack of criminal procedural safeguards. The punitive character of the $50,000 fine, in their view, fixes the proceeding as one of criminal contempt, requiring the right to jury trial and analogous criminal procedural rights.

This position was voiced long ago in *Gamble v. Pope & Talbot, Inc.*, 307 F.2d 729 (3d Cir.) (en banc), cert. denied, 371 U.S. 888 (1962), and it is one that has met consistent rejection in this circuit. Courts possess the inherent power to protect the orderly administration of justice and to preserve the dignity of the tribunal. A trial judge possesses the inherent power to discipline counsel for misconduct, short of behavior giving rise to disbarment or criminal censure, without resort to the powers of civil or criminal contempt. The court's power to impose appropriate sanctions on attorneys practicing before it "springs from a different source than does the power to punish for criminal contempt."

The case thus devolves into a question of the severity of the sanctions as opposed to their propriety. . . .

---

28 [31] ABA Model Rule 3.4(c), furthermore, provides that a lawyer shall not "knowingly disobey an obligation under the rules of a tribunal except for an open refusal based on an assertion that no valid obligation exists . . . ."

[The court upheld the district court's imposition of monetary sanctions and disqualification of counsel. —Ed.]

AFFIRMED IN PART, VACATED AS MOOT IN PART, REVERSED IN PART AND REMANDED WITH INSTRUCTIONS.

JAMES C. HILL, CIRCUIT JUDGE, concurring in part and dissenting in part.

I dissent from the majority's affirmance of sanctions against attorney Richard M. Kirby and the law firm of Hansell & Post. I do so not because I approve counsel's action in this case — emphatically, I do not — but because the sanctions here at issue were imposed for the violation of direction by the district court which I believe was unclear. Because I am unwilling in principle to place upon an attorney by hindsight a duty to divine at his peril the import of an unclear directive from the court, I reach a result contrary to the majority on the issue of sanctions.

When a court tells a lawyer that his argument is under advisement that lawyer should, in fairness to the judge, refrain from further action on the contested point or, alternatively, seek clarification from the court. This lawyer acted otherwise and in doing so skated on the thinnest of ice. The issue before us is simply whether the ice broke. The majority concludes it did, and I, that it did not.

4. Intemperate Remarks

Although the First Amendment protects most lawyer expression, lawyers are subject to discipline for intemperate remarks that serve no useful purpose.

IN RE VINCENTI
458 A.2d 1268 (N.J. 1983)

PER CURIAM.

hard to say where lawyer conduct crosses the line

Under some circumstances it might be difficult to determine precisely the point at which forceful, aggressive trial advocacy crosses the line into the forbidden territory of an ethical violation. But no matter where in the spectrum of courtroom behavior we would draw that line, no matter how indulgent our view of acceptable professional conduct might be, it is inconceivable that the instances of respondent's demeanor that we are called upon to review in these proceedings could ever be countenanced. The record lays bare a shameful display of atrocious deportment calling for substantial discipline. *but not in this case.*

I

I. COOLBAUGH V. VINCENTI (V-80-103E)

The respondent represented D.K., the defendant in a child abuse/neglect case involving the defendant's four children. Trial of this matter before the Superior Court, Union County, began on September 16, 1979, and continued to December.

During this proceeding, respondent's in-court conduct, his out of court conduct towards lawyers, witnesses and bystanders in the courthouse, and his written communiques and applications relative to the D.K. proceeding reached a level of impropriety that mandated the filing of a 22 count ethics complaint.

The specific instances of in-court misconduct are fully detailed in the lengthy ethics complaint and, to a lesser degree, in the presentment filed by District V, and need not be fully detailed herein. It is sufficient to note examples of respondent's numerous improprieties here. He was frequently sarcastic, disrespectful and irrational, and accused the Court on numerous occasions of, inter alia, collusion with the prosecution, cronyism, racism, permitting the proceedings to have a "carnival nature," conducting a kangaroo court, prejudging the case, conducting a "cockamamie charade of witnesses" and barring defense counsel from effectively participating in the proceedings, conducting a sham hearing, acting outside the law, being caught up in his "own little dream world," and ex-parte communications with the prosecutor together with other equally outrageous, disrespectful and unsupported charges. These and other comments were made frequently throughout the proceedings and continued at length.

The Committee specifically found that the respondent's conduct exhibited a "constant and deliberate disregard of the minimum standards of conduct expected of a member of the bar" through his repeated discourteous, insulting and degrading verbal attacks on the judge and his rulings, and that these repeated discourses substantially interfered with the orderly process of the trial. The Committee discounted respondent's claim that his conduct was the result of zealously protecting his client's cause as well as the emotional undercurrent of the litigation. To the contrary, the Committee concluded that the pervasiveness of the irrational, intemperate and improper conduct compelled the determination that the respondent's perception of the lawyer's role and his relationship to the court was, at the least, misguided. The Committee concluded that the respondent, in his court appearances, was guilty of unprofessional conduct in violation of DR 1-102(A)(5) and (6), DR 7-106(C)(6), and DR 8-102(B) [prohibiting, respectively, conduct that is prejudicial to the administration of justice, conduct that adversely reflects on one's ability to practice law, undignified or discourteous conduct that is degrading to a tribunal, and the knowing making of false accusations against a judge].

In another instance, the respondent reviewed a witness's files while she was testifying and failed to return them thereafter. The Deputy Attorney General located the files on the counsel table and returned them to the witness, at the witness's request. The respondent, in open court, then accused the Deputy Attorney General of stealing the files, and accused her of being a "bald-faced liar," and "a thief, a liar and a cheat." He also filed an ethics complaint against the Deputy Attorney General for her actions. The Committee concluded that in these two incidents, respondent was in violation of DR 7-102(A)(1) and (5), and DR 7-106(C)(6) [governing the representation of a client within the bounds of the law and proscribing certain trial conduct].

Even more egregious were the respondent's activities with regard to evaluation of respondent's client by a court-appointed psychologist. Respondent's client had paid $300 to Dr. Bennett, the psychologist, at the time of evaluation. Although the trial judge had arranged the appointment, he did not discuss compensation with Dr. Bennett until after respondent objected to his client being charged. The Judge agreed that the State should pay the fee, and on November 26, 1979, so advised the psychologist. When Dr. Bennett appeared to testify on November 29, 1979, he gave respondent a check for $300, thus returning the fee inadvertently received from the respondent. Despite the fact that the misunderstanding regarding payment for the evaluation had been resolved, respondent proceeded to subpoena the trial judge to testify and moved for the Judge's disqualification, stating that the matter involved ". . . a possible collusion between a witness (and) the Court." Additionally, he called Dr. Bennett an "extortionist psychologist", and alleged an appearance of impropriety since ". . . the individual that sits on the stand extorted money from my client on the advice of this Court."

In addition to making these claims in open court, in his appeals to the Appellate Division and the Supreme Court, the respondent further alleged that the trial judge had participated in extortion as well as cronyism, bias, prejudice, racism and religious bigotry during the trial, again without any basis in fact.

The respondent's improprieties continued. The respondent directed the following letter, dated December 13, 1979, to the trial judge, the text of which is set forth below:

I wish to extend my sincerest good wishes for your speedy recovery from the obvious breakdown you suffered in chambers yesterday, Tuesday, December 11, 1979.

Hopefully, with some rest and relaxation from your most taxing schedule, you will be in a position to resume your judicial duties more appropriately than exhibited on the eleventh.

If, however, you feel somehow justified in pressing your demand for written recommendations, I must supply them, if for no other purpose than to demonstrate my client's continuing bona fides herein.

I must admit, with no small degree of trepidation, that we have no confidence in your rationality vis-à-vis this case. Your activities on the eleventh and throughout the trial clearly demonstrate an irrational predisposition to chastise Mr. D. K. and defense counsel. The cronyism I wrote of in our motion for new trial continues unabated.

You have simply closed your mind to our position and have retreated into a dream world not unlike the somnambulist in that early German classic story at the turn of the century.

How do we make any kind of recommendations to you while you sleep-walk through your judicial duties. How does one get through to you.

Regrettably, we have no faith in your ability to preserve your objectivity herein, for whatever reason(s) I don't know.

Mr. D. K.'s recommendations as to disposition are as follows without detailing the charade you are conducting:

1. Give him back his kids forthwith.

2. He, the children, the KXs, T. and B.P., and P.P. ought to agree to have counseling aimed at retrieving their emotional equilibrium which has been so assaulted by this Court and the State for much too long.

3. Re-establish by some appropriately reasonable means the control and authority of Mr. D. K. over his children which you have so blatantly and for too long disregarded.

4. Allow Mr. D. K. to prescribe the mode, method and style of life for his kids, including their religion until their majority.

5. Recognize your own participation in the State's oppression of a member of a bona fide religious minority, the Jehovah's Witnesses, as my people's constitutional right to freedom of religion. I must inform you that I have made an application to the Hon. in response to your attorney's application to quash our subpoena of you to remove you from this case, once again. Parenthetically, your overly strong protest of that subpoena belies your professed inadvertent participation in Bennett's extortion. There is no better proof of your irrational conduct herein than your continued refusal to disqualify yourself and testify under oath as to the extortion episode.

Your refusal to control your people, Ms. Rem, and the Division is only fitting when viewed in light of your refusal to control yourself.

I would respectfully suggest that you await Judge order before adding further insult to the injuries perpetrated upon Mr. D. K. by entering any dispositional order herein. The statements made by respondent in that letter speak for themselves.

In a further display of impropriety, the respondent included the following accusations against the trial judge in his Specification of Trial Errors that accompanied his motion for a new trial following conclusion of the fact-finding phase of the bifurcated child abuse proceeding:

1. Improper coaching of the Deputy Attorney General;

2. Continuous coaching of the Law Guardian;

3. Usurpation of the presentation of the State's case to establish the elements of that entire case;

4. Cross examination of defense witnesses to discredit them;

5. Disregard for the perjury of the State's witnesses;

6. Bias and prejudice in favor of the State;

7. Over-interest, concern, cronyism and improper contact between the Court, Deputy Attorney General, law guardian and legal staff of the trial court;

8. Obvious racism in the Court's application of racial tests with regard to the children's schooling;

9. Perfidy by the Court and State in failing to properly enumerate the bases for allegations of abuse and neglect;

10. Carnival nature of the atmosphere in the courtroom.

The Committee concluded that these various written and oral statements violated DR 1-102(A)(4), (5) and (6) [misconduct]; DR 7-102(A)(1) and (5) [representing a client within the bounds of the law]; and DR 8-102(B) [prohibiting the knowing making of false accusations against a judge]. In addition to respondent's outrageous in-court conduct and equally outrageous written applications and communications, respondent, on numerous occasions, also engaged in reprehensible behavior towards witnesses, potential witnesses, opposing counsel, and other attorneys outside the courtroom but inside the Courthouse. A sampling of the improprieties follows: *outside court improprieties*

1. On September 26, 1979 outside the courtroom, respondent and Assistant Public Defender Eisert were discussing the issues of visitation. Argument ensued, during which, among other obscenities, respondent told Eisert to "go screw himself" and "fuck off," and referred to Eisert as "asshole," "schmuck" and "schmuckface," all in the presence of a number of individuals, some of whom were involved in the case.

2. On October 31, 1979, Deputy Attorney General Rem and Eisert agreed to meet with respondent, at his request, for a settlement conference. The Lawyer's Lounge was selected. In addition to addressing insults at Rem, respondent referred to a female attorney, also in the lounge, as "Miss Wrinkles," "Miss Bags" and "old bag," and stated to her: "Shove it up your ass" and "go fuck yourself." It was following this meeting that respondent addressed his written removal request, discussed *supra*, to opposing counsel and their superiors.

3. Respondent on several occasions either unnecessarily subpoenaed individuals to testify or threatened those under subpoena by opposing counsel.

4. On December 6, 1979, in the Courthouse corridor, after attempting to intimidate a witness by directing her to answer everything he asked, while his secretary wrote down her responses, respondent advised an attorney named Pearson who was standing with the witness but not involved in the proceeding to "just keep your god damn nose out of my business." His conversation thereafter was peppered with the phrase "fuck you." Eisert, who at that point asked respondent's secretary if she was recording the obscene remarks, was charged by respondent, who pressed a Bic pen into Eisert's chest.

About 1/2 hour later, respondent approached Pearson, demanding his card, indicating that it was needed to file an ethics complaint. When Pearson refused to give respondent a card, respondent persisted in his demands in a loud manner, punctuating the demands with questionable phrases, including "shmuckface," "fuckface" and "shit-head." He continued in this manner for sometime, adding to his action by poking his finger in Pearson's chest. Prior to removing himself from the area, respondent intentionally bumped Pearson with his stomach and then his shoulder, and thereafter advised Pearson that he could take his law firm and "shove it up my ass."

Respondent's performance did not conclude there. While Eisert, Pearson and Rem were conversing in the Courthouse, respondent approached, stating loudly that Rem should not be believed since ". . . she's a bald-faced liar." He then called

Rem "fuckface," and while walking away again made the suggestion ". . . shove it up your ass." Within the next several minutes, respondent twice approached the group, each time pushing into Rem, causing her to lurch against a desk in the hallway.

The Committee concluded that these actions of the respondent were designed to ridicule, embarrass and harass the individuals concerned, and in the case of his adversaries, his conduct was designed to intimidate them in the performance of their duties. The Committee therefore found that respondent had violated DR 1-102(A)(5) and (6).

II. BALDASARRE CONTEMPT (V-80-163E)

In March of 1980 the respondent was acting as counsel for the defendant in the case of Baldasarre v. Baldasarre, a matrimonial matter. On March 7th, the respondent was held in contempt by the trial judge and fined $250 for conduct which bears a strong resemblance to respondent's conduct delineated above. In *Baldasarre*, the respondent's belligerent attitude toward the Court led the Judge to advise that he was leaving the bench and would return when respondent had had ". . . an opportunity to collect himself." Respondent replied: "I don't need to collect myself, Judge, you are simply ridiculous, you know."

Respondent appealed the finding of contempt. In affirming the court's action, the Appellate Division found that respondent's conduct interfered with the in-court proceedings and was "insulting."

The Committee found that respondent's conduct "demonstrate(d) a pattern of abuse consistent with that exhibited in the D.K. matter." Therefore, the Committee concluded that respondent had violated DR 1-102(A)(5) and (6) and DR 7-106(C)(6).

CONCLUSION AND RECOMMENDATION

Upon a review of the full record, the Board is satisfied that the conclusions of the Committee in finding unethical conduct on the part of respondent are fully supported by clear and convincing evidence.

III

We would hope, through this opinion, to serve some more salutary purpose than just the distasteful meting out of well-deserved public disciplining to Mr. Vincenti. As pointed out earlier, this ethics proceeding unveils conduct so bizarre, so outrageous, as not to bring us close to what in some other case might be the difficult problem of distinguishing between permissibly vigorous advocacy and an ethical transgression. Although we need not here attempt with exquisite precision to delineate the difference, it may nevertheless be useful to restate, in general terms, the obligation of New Jersey lawyers, that they may readily avoid entanglements of the sort that brings respondent before us.

Unless order is maintained in the courtroom and disruption prevented, reason cannot prevail and constitutional rights to liberty, freedom and equality under law cannot be protected. The dignity, decorum and courtesy [that] have traditionally characterized the courts of civilized nations are not empty formalities. They are essential to an atmosphere in which justice can be done. [Code of Trial Conduct § 17 (American College of Trial Lawyers 1983).]

IV

Respondent is suspended from the practice of law for one year and until the further order of the Court. He is further required to reimburse the Administrative Office of the Courts for appropriate administrative costs, including the cost of producing transcripts.

So ordered.

GRIEVANCE ADMINISTRATOR v. GEOFFREY N. FIEGER
476 Mich. 231, 719 N.W.2d 123 (2006)

Taylor, C.J.

In this case, we conclude that certain remarks by attorney Geoffrey N. Fieger about the appellate judges who were hearing his client's case violated MRPC 3.5(c) (which prohibits undignified or discourteous conduct toward the tribunal) and MRPC 6.5(a) (which requires a lawyer to treat with courtesy and respect all persons involved in the legal process), and that those rules (sometimes referred to as "courtesy" or "civility" rules) are constitutional. Accordingly, we reverse the opinion and order of a divided Attorney Discipline Board (ADB) that incorrectly concluded the rules were unconstitutional and remand for the imposition of the agreed-to professional discipline, a reprimand, on Mr. Fieger.

I. Facts and Proceedings Below

In 1997, a jury in the Oakland Circuit Court returned a $15 million verdict in a medical malpractice action in which Mr. Fieger represented the plaintiff Salvatore Badalamenti. On appeal, the defendants hospital and physician claimed that the verdict was based on insufficient evidence and that they had been denied their constitutional right to a fair trial by Mr. Fieger's intentional misconduct. After hearing argument, a three-judge panel of the Court of Appeals, Jane Markey, Richard Bandstra, and Michael Talbot, unanimously ruled on August 20, 1999, that the defendants were entitled to judgment notwithstanding the verdict because the plaintiff had failed to provide legally sufficient evidence that would justify submitting the case to the jury The panel also held that Mr. Fieger's repeated misconduct by itself would have warranted a new trial. In particular, the Court of Appeals indicated that Mr. Fieger (1) without any basis in fact, accused defendants and their witnesses of engaging in a conspiracy, collusion, and perjury to cover up malpractice, (2) asserted without any basis in fact that defense witnesses had destroyed, altered, or suppressed evidence, and (3) insinuated without any basis in fact that one of the defendants had abandoned the plaintiff's medical care to engage in a sexual tryst with a nurse. The panel described Mr. Fieger's misconduct as "truly egregious" and "pervasive" and concluded that it "completely tainted the proceedings." *Id.* at 289, 290.

Three days later, on August 23, 1999, Mr. Fieger, in a tone similar to that which he had exhibited during the *Badalamenti* trial and on his then-daily radio program in Southeast Michigan, continued by addressing the three appellate judges in that case in the following manner, "Hey Michael Talbot, and Bandstra, and Markey, I declare war on you. You declare it on me, I declare it on you. Kiss my ass, too." Mr. Fieger, referring to his client, then said, "He lost both his hands and both his legs, but according to the Court of Appeals, he lost a finger. Well, the finger he should keep is the one where he should shove it up their asses."

Two days later, on the same radio show, Mr. Fieger called these same judges "three jackass Court of Appeals judges." When another person involved in the broadcast used the word "innuendo," Mr. Fieger stated, "I know the only thing that's in their endo should be a large, you know, plunger about the size of, you know, my fist." Finally, Mr. Fieger said, "They say under their name, 'Court of Appeals Judge,' so anybody that votes for them, they've changed their name from, you know, Adolf Hitler and Goebbels, and I think — what was Hitler's — Eva Braun, I think it was, is now Judge Markey, she's on the Court of Appeals." The three appellate judges did not respond to Mr. Fieger during this period. Code of Judicial Conduct Canon 3(A)(6) states that a judge should abstain from public comments about a pending or impending proceeding in any court. The rationale for this rule is the avoidance of a media war of words that may erode public confidence in the judiciary.

Subsequently, Mr. Fieger filed a motion for reconsideration before the same panel. After that motion was denied, this Court denied Mr. Fieger's application for leave to appeal on March 21, 2003.

On April 16, 2001, the Attorney Grievance Commission (AGC), through its Grievance Administrator, filed a formal complaint with the ADB, alleging that Mr. Fieger's comments on August 23 and 25, 1999, were in violation of several provisions of the Michigan Rules of Professional Conduct, including MRPC 3.5(c), MRPC 6.5(a), and MRPC 8.4(a) and (c). While the complaint was pending, the parties entered into a stipulation. In return for Mr. Fieger's agreement not to contest that his remarks had violated MRPC 3.5(c) and MRPC 6.5(a), the charges alleging a violation of MRPC 8.4(a) and (c) would be dismissed. The parties further stipulated the sanction of a reprimand. The agreement was specifically conditioned on Mr. Fieger's being allowed to argue on appeal, while the discipline was stayed, both the applicability and the constitutionality of MRPC 3.5(c) and MRPC 6.5(a). Mr. Fieger maintained that the rules were inapplicable because his remarks were made after the case was completed and were not made in a courtroom. Further, he maintained that the two rules were unconstitutional because they infringed his First Amendment rights.[29]

---

[29] [5] The First Amendment of the United States Constitution, as applied to the states through the Fourteenth Amendment, provides that the government "shall make no law . . . abridging the freedom of speech . . . ." US Const, Am I.

On appeal to the ADB, with one member recused, the remaining eight members of the ADB issued three opinions. The lead opinion concluded that MRPC 3.5(c) and MRPC 6.5(a) did not apply to Mr. Fieger's comments because they were made outside the courtroom in a case they regarded as completed. They further observed that, if the rules did apply, then they were in violation of the First Amendment. A second opinion agreed that Mr. Fieger's comments were protected by the First Amendment, but dissented from the lead opinion's conclusion that the rules only apply to remarks made within the courtroom. A third opinion, agreeing in part with the second opinion held that Mr. Fieger's remarks, even though made outside the courtroom, were prohibited by the rules, and that the remarks were not protected by the First Amendment.

The sum of all this was that a majority (albeit not the same majority for each issue) concluded that the two rules applied to Mr. Fieger's out-of-court statements, while a different majority concluded that those rules were in violation of the First Amendment.

The AGC, through its Grievance Administrator, sought leave to appeal in this Court. We granted leave to appeal to consider whether the remarks by Mr. Fieger, although uncontestedly discourteous, undignified, and disrespectful, nevertheless did not warrant professional discipline because they were made outside the courtroom and after the Court of Appeals had issued its opinion. We also granted leave to appeal to consider whether the ADB possesses the authority to decide issues of constitutionality and whether the two rules in question are constitutional.

III. Attorney Licensure and Discipline in Michigan

Const. 1963, art. 6, § 5 and MCL 600.904 give this Court the duty and responsibility to regulate and discipline the members of the bar of this state. Most obviously, this responsibility entails concern for the competence, character, and fitness of attorneys, but historically also has included the issuance of rules regulating the manner in which lawyers communicate to the public about other participants in the legal system, primarily judges and other lawyers. While many other professions are regulated with the goal of ensuring competence and fitness, it is only the legal profession that also has imposed upon its members regulations concerning the nature of public comment. The First Amendment implications are easily understood in such a regulatory regime and this Court, like other courts of last resort including the United States Supreme Court, has attempted to appropriately draw the line between robust comment that is protected by the First Amendment and comment that undermines the integrity of the legal system.

Indeed, whether this line can be drawn anywhere to take cognizance of the interests of the legal system is the central issue in this case. The proposition asserted by Mr. Fieger is that, under the First Amendment of the United States Constitution, there can be no courtesy or civility rules at all of this sort and that judges and other lawyers assailed verbally, as public figures, have the same remedies any other public figures have in libel and slander law. As the opinions of the ADB suggest, the absolutism of this argument is not without some allure. Yet, respect for the wisdom of those who have preceded us in the judiciary in this country and the traditions of the legal process counsel that narrow and carefully tailored regulations of the sort set forth in MRPC 3.5(c) and MRPC 6.5(a) are necessary adjuncts to a responsible legal system and are compatible with the First Amendment. It is first necessary to outline why such regulations are necessary at all. That is, what substantial interests are these courtesy and civility rules designed to further? In particular, are there some interests that such rules further beyond merely protecting judges from the robust criticism that is sometimes a part of the give-and-take of the democratic process? Do such rules merely insulate judges from the inconvenience of being held accountable from their public actions? In establishing rules designed to deter and sanction uncivil and discourteous conduct on the part of lawyers, we believe that this Court is doing far more than protecting the sensitivities of judges; rather, we believe that we are upholding the integrity of that which is being carried out by the judicial branch of government.

The performance of these responsibilities requires a process in which the public can have the highest sense of confidence, one in which the fairness and integrity of the process is not routinely called into question, one in which the ability of judges to mete out evenhanded decisions is not undermined by the fear of vulgar characterizations of their actions, one in which the public is not misled by name-calling and vulgarities from lawyers who are held to have special knowledge of the courts, one in which discourse is grounded in the traditional tools of the law — language, precedents, logic, and rational analysis and debate. To disregard such interests in the pursuit of a conception of the First Amendment that has never been a part of our actual Constitution would in a real and practical sense adversely affect our rule of law, a no less indispensable foundation of our constitutional system than the First Amendment.

These interests in a responsible legal process heretofore have been unquestioned and have been thought to justify a lawyer discipline system in this state that encompasses rules on courtesy and civility toward others. In furtherance of this, the law has reposed special stewardship duties on lawyers on the basis of the venerable notion that lawyers are more than merely advocates who happen to carry out their duties in a courtroom environment, they are also officers of the court. In this exclusive role, lawyers have special responsibilities in their relations with other officers of the court.

In discussing the scope of this obligation in the 19th century, the United States Supreme Court stated that attorneys are under an implied "obligation . . . to maintain at all times the respect due to courts of justice and judicial officers. This obligation . . . includes abstaining out of court from all insulting language and offensive conduct toward the judges personally for their judicial acts." *Bradley v. Fisher*, 80 U.S. (13 Wall) 335, 355, 20 L. Ed. 646 (1871).

More recently, the United States Supreme Court elaborated on this unique status:

As an officer of the court, a member of the bar enjoys singular powers that others do not possess; by virtue of admission, members of the bar share a kind of monopoly granted only to lawyers. Admission creates a license not only to advise and counsel clients but also to appear in court and try cases; as an officer of the court, a lawyer can cause persons to drop their private affairs and be called as witnesses in court, and for depositions and other pretrial processes that, while subject to the ultimate control of the court, may be conducted outside courtrooms. The license granted by the court requires members of the bar to conduct themselves in a manner compatible with the role of courts in the administration of justice. [*In re Snyder*, 472 U.S. 634, 644–645, 105 S. Ct. 2874, 86 L. Ed. 2d 504 (1985).]

The license to practice law in Michigan is, among other things, a continuing proclamation by the Supreme Court that the holder is fit to be entrusted with professional and judicial matters and to aid in the administration of justice as an attorney and counselor and as an officer of the court. It is the duty of every attorney to conduct himself or herself at all times in conformity with standards imposed on members of the bar as a condition of the privilege to practice law. These standards include, but are not limited to, the rules of professional responsibility and the rules of judicial conduct that are adopted by the Supreme Court.

As contemplated by this rule, this Court has promulgated the Michigan Rules of Professional Conduct. Of immediate interest is MRPC 3.5(c), which does not preclude criticism by a member of the legal profession, of even the most robust character, but precludes only "undignified or discourteous conduct toward the tribunal." The comment on MRPC 3.5 elaborates:

The advocate's function is to present evidence and argument so that the cause may be decided according to law. Refraining from undignified or discourteous conduct is a corollary of the advocate's right to speak on behalf of litigants. A lawyer may stand firm against abuse by a judge, but should avoid reciprocation; the judge's default is no justification for similar dereliction by an advocate. An advocate can present the cause, protect the record for subsequent review, and preserve professional integrity by patient firmness no less effectively than by belligerence or theatrics.

Similarly, MRPC 6.5(a) provides only that "[a] lawyer shall treat with courtesy and respect all persons involved in the legal process."

As should be clear, these rules are designed to prohibit only "undignified," "discourteous," and "disrespectful" conduct or remarks. The rules are a call to discretion and civility, not to silence or censorship, and they do not even purport to prohibit criticism. The wisdom of such rules was recognized by United Stated Supreme Court Justice Potter Stewart in his concurring opinion in *In re Sawyer*, 360 U.S. 622, 646 (1959), in which he remarked, "A lawyer belongs to a profession with inherited standards of propriety and honor, which experience has shown necessary in a calling dedicated to the accomplishment of justice. He who would follow that calling must conform to those standards."

It is in this historical and professional context that Mr. Fieger's remarks must be reviewed.

IV. Analysis of the Applicability of the Rules

A. Were Mr. Fieger's remarks made after the conclusion of the case?

Mr. Fieger asserts that the remarks in controversy were made after the *Badalamenti* case was concluded. This matter is consequential because greater restraint, if indeed any is constitutionally allowed, is permissible when a case is ongoing than when it is completed. As the United States Supreme Court said in *Gentile, supra* at 1070, 111 S.Ct. 2720 " 'When a case is finished, courts are subject to the same criticism as other people, but the propriety and necessity of preventing interference with the course of justice by premature statement, argument or intimidation hardly can be denied.' " (Citation omitted.) Accordingly, "the speech of lawyers representing clients in pending cases may be regulated under a less demanding standard than that established for regulation of the press . . . ." *Id.* at 1074, 111 S. Ct. 2720.

The obvious question here is whether the *Badalamenti* case was actually "pending" at the time of Mr. Fieger's comments. [Pending means:] Begun, but not yet completed; during; before the conclusion of; prior to the completion of; unsettled; undetermined; in process of settlement or adjustment. Awaiting an occurrence or conclusion of action, period of continuance or indeterminancy. Thus, an action or suit is "pending" from its inception until the rendition of final judgment.

Mr. Fieger made his remarks on August 23 and 25, 1999, three days and five days, respectively, after the Court of Appeals issued its decision, when the time for filing either for rehearing in the Court of Appeals or an application for leave to appeal in this Court had not yet expired. Indeed, Mr. Fieger ultimately did file a timely motion for rehearing in the Court of Appeals on September 10, 1999.

Because the Court of Appeals decision had not yet become effective as of the date of Mr. Fieger's comments, and because the Court of Appeals, by granting a motion for reconsideration or rehearing, could still have affected the substantial rights of his client, we conclude that the *Badalamenti* case was "begun, but not yet completed" and that Mr. Fieger's comments were made "during," "before the conclusion of," and "prior to the completion of" that case. Moreover, the case was "awaiting an occurrence or conclusion of action" — namely, the running of the aforementioned periods for filing. During this interim, then, the case was in a "period of continuance or indeterminancy."

Thus, the *Badalamenti* case was clearly still pending when Mr. Fieger made his remarks.

B. Do the rules only apply to comments made in a courtroom?

Mr. Fieger next asserts that MRPC 3.5(c) and MRPC 6.5(a) only apply to comments within a courtroom or its immediate environs. We disagree.

MRPC 3.5(c) provides that a lawyer shall not "engage in undignified or discourteous conduct *toward* the tribunal." (Emphasis added.) We note that the rule does not provide a definition of the word "toward." It is well established that if a term in a court rule is not defined, we interpret the term in accordance with its everyday, plain meaning.

[W]e disagree with Mr. Fieger's argument that the rule is inapplicable to his statements because those statements were directed toward an audience and outside a courtroom, and, therefore, not toward a tribunal. Mr. Fieger made remarks about (a) the three judges (b) who comprised the panel (c) that ruled against his client (d) with regard to the content and value of that judgment, (e) which remarks aired on a public broadcast. Even though made outside a courtroom, Mr. Fieger's statements attacked the judges in their capacity as judges and in a forum designed to reach both the public and these judges (who were included among the members of the community who could receive this broadcast). Because such comments were "in the direction of" and "with respect to" these judges, they were necessarily comments made "toward the tribunal."

There is nothing in this phrase "toward the tribunal" that limits the applicability of the rule only to remarks made in a courtroom.[30] Mr. Fieger's construction of the rule would effectively insert the requirement that the conduct "actually disrupt the proceeding." Yet this language, which is in the American Bar Association version of this rule, is absent from our rule. Further, if MRPC 3.5(c) applies only when an attorney is in a courtroom, the rule would be largely superfluous, and of little practical utility, given that a court's contempt power, enforceable by fine or incarceration pursuant to MCL 600.1711(1), is always available to restore or maintain order when the offending conduct or remarks occur before the judge in the courtroom.

The construction of the rule asserted by Mr. Fieger fails to accord consideration to the importance the courtesy and civility rules serve as a vehicle for preserving the public's confidence in the integrity of the legal process. Most significantly, however, it is a construction that is not in accord with the actual language of the rule. Thus, we agree with the conclusion of the majority of the ADB that MRPC 3.5(c) applies to Mr. Fieger's remarks.

Therefore, we conclude that the comments made by Mr. Fieger are in violation of both MRPC 3.5(c) and MRPC 6.5(a).

V. Can the ADB Declare a Rule Unconstitutional?

The AGC, through its Grievance Administrator, asserts that the ADB has no authority to declare unconstitutional a rule of professional conduct. We agree.

A disciplinary proceeding in Michigan commences upon the filing of a formal

---

[30] [18] The dissents would limit the phrase "toward the tribunal" to comments made in a courtroom. But there is no warrant for such a limitation in the wording of MRCP 3.5(c), which contemplates a broader prohibition. Moreover, Mr. Fieger called the judges by name. Surely this demonstrates that the remarks were made "toward the tribunal." Notwithstanding Justice Kelly's assertion that this opinion "necessarily chills comment," post at 356, it will only "chill," those comments that are properly "chilled" among members of a profession who are bound to conduct themselves in a courteous and civil manner. In contrast with the dissents, we have no difficulty concluding that the interests of the rule of law, one of the towering achievements of our society, outweighs the interests of an officer of the court in uttering vulgar epithets toward a judge in a pending case.

complaint and is heard before a panel of three lawyers. Appeals are then taken to the ADB. The ADB is an administrative body, comprised of nine individuals appointed by this Court, three of whom are not attorneys. While the ADB, like all other governmental entities, must operate in accord with the Constitution, for example, on questions such as compelled witness self-incrimination, it does not possess the power to hold unconstitutional rules of professional conduct that have been enacted by this Court. Administrative agencies generally do not possess the power to declare statutes unconstitutional because this is a core element of the "judicial power" and does not belong to an agency that is not exercising this constitutional power. The power of judicial review is one that belongs exclusively to the judicial branch of our government.

Should any attorney appearing before the ADB believe a rule itself to be unconstitutional, such as in this case, resort must be made to an appeal to this Court, and, if we concur in this assessment, it is our responsibility to declare such rule unconstitutional.

VI. Are MRPC 3.5(c) and MRPC 6.5(a) Unconstitutionally Vague?

Mr. Fieger next argues that whatever the other constitutional shortcomings of MRPC 3.5(c) and MRPC 6.5(a), they are unconstitutionally vague because a lawyer cannot know ahead of time which of his or her remarks might run afoul of the rules. Such a challenge cannot be successfully advanced here because there is no question that even the most casual reading of these rules would put a person clearly on notice that the kind of language used by Mr. Fieger would violate MRPC 3.5(c) and MRPC 6.5(a). To invite the sodomization of a judge, with a client's finger, a plunger, or his own fist, and to invite a judge to kiss one's ass are statements that do not come close to the margins of the "civility" or "courtesy" rules.[31] While MRPC 3.5(c) and MRPC 6.5(a) are undoubtedly flexible, and the AGC will exercise some discretion in determining whether to charge an attorney with violating them, perfect clarity and precise guidance have never been required even of regulations that restrict expressive activity.

If "civility" and "courtesy" rules can ever satisfy constitutional muster, as we believe they can, it is beyond peradventure that the comments at issue in this case clearly violated such rules.

Mr. Fieger also argues that his remarks are political speech and thus fit within the protection afforded campaign speech in *In re Chmura (After Remand)*, 464 Mich. 58, 72–73, 626 N.W.2d 876 (2001) (*Chmura II*). In *Chmura II* we considered the propriety of a variety of remarks made by an incumbent judge during a reelection campaign that had served as the basis for sanction by the Judicial

---

[31] [124] Justice Kelly's dissent states a concern that our rules of professional conduct might be arbitrarily or discriminatorily enforced by the AGC. Yet, we note that any validly enacted rule, regulation, or statute carries with it the risk of arbitrary or discriminatory enforcement. Such concerns, when they arise, are typically addressed on a case-by-case basis, and Justice Kelly's dissent offers no reason to believe that alleged violations of MRPC 3.5(c) or MRPC 6.5(a) could not be handled in such a manner. Moreover, neither respondent nor Justice Kelly points to a single case in which an attorney was charged with violating our courtesy or civility rules for inconsequential behavior.

Tenure Commission of our state. We concluded in light of the First Amendment that the judge's statements were all constitutionally protected. But, the *Chmura II* political context is entirely missing here. There was no political campaign underway nor was Mr. Fieger attempting by his comments to participate in such a campaign. Thus, *Chmura II* offers no safe harbor for Mr. Fieger.

Not only was Mr. Fieger's speech not campaign speech, it was not political speech of any kind. In discussing political speech, the United States Supreme Court has stated:

> "The freedom of speech and of the press guaranteed by the Constitution embraces at the least the liberty to discuss publicly and truthfully all matters of public concern without previous restraint or fear of subsequent punishment." [*Thornhill v. Alabama*, 310 U.S. 88, 101–102, 60 S. Ct. 736, 84 L. Ed. 1093 (1940).] The First Amendment "was fashioned to assure unfettered interchange of ideas for the bringing about of political and social changes desired by the people." *Roth v. United States*, 354 U.S. 476, 484, [77 S. Ct. 1304, 1 L. Ed. 2d 1498] (1957). [*Meyer v. Grant*, 486 U.S. 414, 421, 108 S. Ct. 1886, 100 L. Ed. 2d 425 (1988).]

To invite the sodomization of a judge, with a client's finger, a plunger, or one's own fist, and to invite a judge to kiss one's ass can hardly be considered an "interchange of ideas for the bringing about of political and social changes." "Resort to epithets or personal abuse is not in any proper sense communication of information or opinion safeguarded by the Constitution . . . ." *Cantwell v. Connecticut*, 310 U.S. 296, 309–310, 60 S. Ct. 900, 84 L. Ed. 1213 (1940). In discussing cases that have given vulgar and offensive speech First Amendment protection, the dissents lose sight of the fact that we are dealing here, not with the general context of the right of citizens to speak freely, but with the very specific context of the right of attorneys, who are licensed in terms of character and fitness and who serve as officers within our legal system, to engage in such speech in the course of their professional responsibilities. In conflating these two contexts, the various dissents lose sight of the governing legal standard. In *Gentile*, the United States Supreme Court supplied the standard for a First Amendment challenge to a professional conduct rule. The Court concluded that the state had an interest in the integrity of its judicial system and that the regulation at issue there was narrowly tailored, viewpoint neutral, and left open alternative avenues for expression.

Mr. Fieger further urges that his remarks should receive the same broad protection the First Amendment was found to provide in *New York Times Co. v. Sullivan*, 376 U.S. 254, 84 S. Ct. 710, 11 L. Ed. 2d 686 (1964). We disagree because this is an attorney discipline matter and more restrictive rules are permissible in such a circumstance. Whereas *Sullivan* was designed to further robust public discussion in the press, and to avoid the chilling effects on the media of defamation or libel lawsuits predicated upon mere mistakes or inaccuracies in reporting, neither of these constitutional concerns is implicated by court rules allowing the sanctioning an attorney for crude or vulgar language directed against a judge in a pending proceeding.

Gentile also held that in analyzing whether an ethics rule violates a lawyer's First Amendment rights, the court must engage "in a balancing process, weighing the

State's interest in the regulation of a specialized profession against a lawyer's First Amendment interest in the kind of speech that was at issue." These state interests include promoting the respect of the courts by the citizenry and maintaining the integrity of the judicial process so as to enhance compliance with adjudications. Further, in a system with hundreds of judges, each of whom is subject to popular election, the state also has an interest in limiting attorney comment that takes the form of personal attacks on judges, because a system in which intimidating attacks are permitted fosters the risk of eventually realizing the intended effect of such attacks: a potentially cowed judiciary.

[T]o assess the constitutionality of a rule of lawyer discipline, a court must weigh the state's interests in support of the rule against an attorney's First Amendment interests in the kind of speech at issue. In this case, we must balance Mr. Fieger's right to criticize judges as he did, using foul and vulgar language, against the state's interest in the maintenance of a system of lawyer discipline that imposes some measure of limitation on such language.

Before undertaking this balancing process, it may be appropriate to consider this Court's demonstrated solicitude for lawyer speech, and in particular this lawyer's freedom of speech, by reviewing how we struck the balance with Mr. Fieger in an earlier professional disciplinary matter. In *Grievance Administrator v. Fieger*, 469 Mich. 1241 (2003), we declined to review a dismissal by the ADB of an AGC claim that Mr. Fieger had violated MRPC 8.2(a) when he accused a county prosecutor of covering up a murder because the ADB arguably had considered Mr. Fieger's accusations to constitute a comment or opinion on the office holder's performance of his duties. As a result, Mr. Fieger was found not to be subject to sanction for his statement. Although Mr. Fieger's comment was an irresponsible and baseless comment, and altogether unfair to the prosecutor, this Court gave every benefit of the doubt to Mr. Fieger in its interpretation of what he had meant to communicate by his statement. However, there can be no similar benefit to any doubt in the current case in which Mr. Fieger has uttered the crudest and most vulgar statements concerning judges in a pending lawsuit.

There is no reasonable construction of Mr. Fieger's remarks that could lead to the conclusion that these were mere comment on the professional performance of these three judges of the Court of Appeals. To call a judge a "jackass," a "Hitler," a "Goebbels," a "Braun" and to suggest that a lawyer is "declar[ing] war" on them and that the judge should "[k]iss [the lawyer's] ass," or should be anally molested by finger, fist, or plunger, is, to say the least, not to communicate information; rather, it is nothing more than personal abuse. We conclude that such coarseness in the context of an officer of the court participating in a legal proceeding warrants no First Amendment protection when balanced against this state's compelling interest in maintaining public respect for the integrity of the legal process.

MRPC 3.5(c) and MRPC 6.5(a) did not preclude Mr. Fieger from expressing disagreement with the judges in his case, and they did not preclude criticism, even strong criticism, from being directed toward these judges; rather, they only precluded him from casting such disagreement and criticism in terms that could only bring disrepute on the legal system. The limited restriction placed by the rules on Mr. Fieger's speech is narrowly drawn and is no greater than is necessary to maintain this state's longstanding and legitimate interests in the integrity of its legal system.

Mr. Fieger's comments then are not protected under his various theories of vagueness, of political speech, or of public-figure comment. It is important, however, to reiterate that we are not now, nor have we ever in the past, suggested that judges are beyond criticism.

It is for all these reasons that we conclude that Mr. Fieger's vulgar and crude attacks on three members of our Court of Appeals were not constitutionally protected and that he is subject to professional discipline for having made them.

VII. Response to Justice Kelly's and Justice Cavanagh's Dissents

In their repudiation of "courtesy" and "civility" rules, the dissents would usher an entirely new legal culture into this state, a Hobbesian legal culture, the repulsiveness of which is only dimly limned by the offensive conduct that we see in this case. It is a legal culture in which, in a state such as Michigan with judicial elections, there would be a permanent political campaign for the bench, pitting lawyers against the judges of whom they disapprove. It is a legal culture in which rational and logical discourse would come increasingly to be replaced by epithets and coarse behavior, in which a profession that is already marked by declining standards of behavior would be subject to further erosion, and in which public regard for the system of law would inevitably be diminished over time.

By allowing a lawyer to say anything short of libel under *New York Times v. Sullivan*, the position of the dissents would also necessarily and inevitably require that judges — persons who are periodically subject to popular reelection under our Constitution — be allowed to engage in the same kind of "free speech" to which attorneys are entitled — if only for the purposes of electoral self-defense. Further, such a required loosening of the canons of judicial conduct would also likely have other lamentable effects that could quickly jeopardize even the freedom of speech lawyers currently enjoy. It is hard to imagine the lawyer who would want to test the proposition of how much effect a judge's retaliatory comment adverting to the lawyer's lack of competence, character, or the like would have on the lawyer's practice. Thus, the newly given lawyer right of speech the dissents would recognize would perversely conduce to a situation where lawyers would be silenced. While surely all would hope judges would not use this new opportunity to intimidate the bar, the history of how authority is eventually used by those empowered is not encouraging. The dissents accord virtually no consideration to these ramifications of their position. To the majority, however, such consequences are of grave concern.

VIII. Conclusion

For the reasons set forth in this opinion, we reverse the opinion and order of the ADB and remand to the ADB for entry of the agreed-to order of reprimand.

MAURA D. CORRIGAN, ROBERT P. YOUNG, JR., and STEPHEN J. MARKMAN, JJ., concur.

[Dissenting opinions of considerable length and complexity are not reprinted here. —Ed.]

NOTES, QUESTIONS, AND EXAMPLES

1. In a subsequent action for declaratory and injunctive relief, the United States District Court for the Eastern District of Michigan ruled in Fieger's favor, holding the courtesy and civility rules to be unconstitutionally vague. The Sixth Circuit reversed on non-substantive grounds, holding that Fieger lacked standing to make a facial challenge on the rules. *Fieger v. Michigan Sup. Ct.*, 553 F.3d 955 (6th Cir. 2009).

2. Sanctions other than discipline have been imposed on unduly vituperative lawyers using profanities to express their frustrations with courts or opposing counsel. *See, e.g., Comuso v. National Railroad Passenger Corp.*, 267 F.3d 331 (3d Cir. 2001) (lawyer disqualified from continuing to represent plaintiff and ordered to pay opposing party's attorney fees); *United States v. Ortlieb*, 274 F.3d 871 (5th Cir. 2001) (contempt power invoked to punish lawyer's profanities uttered in open court).

D. LIMITATIONS ON LITIGATION PUBLICITY

Lawyers generally, and especially prosecutors, are limited in what they may say to the media regarding pending litigation and criminal investigations. The restrictions are meant to protect the integrity of the adversary system by keeping statements about pending matters inside the courtroom where they will get directly to the decision-makers, jurors, and judges, and where they can be challenged by an adversary at the time of their making. MR 3.6; MR 3.8(e) and (g).

GENTILE v. STATE BAR OF NEVADA
501 U.S. 1030 (1991)

JUSTICE KENNEDY announced the judgment of the Court and delivered the opinion of the Court with respect to Parts III and VI, and an opinion with respect to Parts I, II, IV, and V, in which JUSTICE MARSHALL, JUSTICE BLACKMUN, and JUSTICE STEVENS join.

Hours after his client was indicted on criminal charges, petitioner Gentile, who is a member of the Bar of the State of Nevada, held a press conference. He made a prepared statement, which we set forth in Appendix A to this opinion, and then he responded to questions. We refer to most of those questions and responses in the course of our opinion.

Some six months later, the criminal case was tried to a jury and the client was acquitted on all counts. The State Bar of Nevada then filed a complaint against petitioner, alleging a violation of Nevada Supreme Court Rule 177, a rule governing pretrial publicity almost identical to ABA Model Rule of Professional Conduct 3.6. We set forth the full text of Rule 177 in Appendix B. Rule 177(1) prohibits an attorney from making "an extrajudicial statement that a reasonable person would expect to be disseminated by means of public communication if the lawyer knows or reasonably should know that it will have a substantial likelihood of materially prejudicing an adjudicative proceeding." Rule 177(2) lists a number of statements that are "ordinarily . . . likely" to result in material prejudice. Rule 177(3) provides a safe harbor of discipline notwithstanding the other parts of the Rule.

Following a hearing, the Southern Nevada Disciplinary Board of the State Bar found that Gentile had made the statements in question and concluded that he violated Rule 177. The board recommended a private reprimand. Petitioner appealed to the Nevada Supreme Court, waiving the confidentiality of the disciplinary proceeding, and the Nevada court affirmed the decision of the board.

Nevada's application of Rule 177 in this case violates the First Amendment. Petitioner spoke at a time and in a manner that neither in law nor in fact created any threat of real prejudice to his client's right to a fair trial or to the State's interest in the enforcement of its criminal laws. Furthermore, the Rule's safe harbor provision, Rule 177(3), appears to permit the speech in question, and Nevada's decision to discipline petitioner in spite of that provision raises concerns of vagueness and selective enforcement.

I

The matter before us does not call into question the constitutionality of other States' prohibitions upon an attorney's speech that will have a "substantial likelihood of materially prejudicing an adjudicative proceeding," but is limited to Nevada's interpretation of that standard. On the other hand, one central point must dominate the analysis: this case involves classic political speech. The State Bar of Nevada reprimanded petitioner for his assertion, supported by a brief sketch of his client's defense, that the State sought the indictment and conviction of an innocent man as a "scapegoat" and had not "been honest enough to indict the people who did it; the police department, crooked cops." At issue here is the constitutionality of a ban on political speech critical of the government and its officials.

A

Unlike [some] other First Amendment cases in which speech is not the direct target of the regulation or statute in question, this case involves punishment of pure speech in the political forum. Petitioner engaged not in solicitation of clients or advertising for his practice, as in our precedents from which some of our colleagues would discern a standard of diminished First Amendment protection. His words were directed at public officials and their conduct in office.

very protected

the speech was abt public officials and their conduct in office.

There is no question that speech critical of the exercise of the State's power lies at the very center of the First Amendment. Nevada seeks to punish the dissemination of information relating to alleged governmental misconduct.

* * *

B

We are not called upon to determine the constitutionality of the ABA Model Rule of Professional Conduct 3.6 (1981), but only Rule 177 as it has been interpreted and applied by the State of Nevada. Model Rule 3.6's requirement of substantial likelihood of material prejudice is not necessarily flawed. Interpreted in a proper and narrow manner, for instance, to prevent an attorney of record from releasing information of grave prejudice on the eve of jury selection, the phrase substantial likelihood of material prejudice might punish only speech that creates a danger of imminent and substantial harm. A rule governing speech, even speech entitled to full constitutional protection, need not use the words "clear and present danger" in order to pass constitutional muster.

Can prohibit speech that will cause imminent prejudice

*   *   *

The drafters of Model Rule 3.6 apparently thought the substantial likelihood of material prejudice formulation approximated the clear and present danger test. See ABA Annotated Model Rules of Professional Conduct 243 (1984) ("formulation in Model Rule 3.6 incorporates a standard approximating clear and present danger by focusing on the likelihood of injury and its substantiality").

The difference between the requirement of serious and imminent threat found in the disciplinary rules of some States and the more common formulation of substantial likelihood of material prejudice could prove mere semantics.

Each standard requires an assessment of proximity and degree of harm. Each may be capable of valid application. Under those principles, nothing inherent in Nevada's formulation fails First Amendment review; but as this case demonstrates, Rule 177 has not been interpreted in conformance with those principles by the Nevada Supreme Court.

II

Owner- Gary Sanders

A

Pre-Indictment Publicity. On January 31, 1987, undercover police officers with the Las Vegas Metropolitan Police Department (Metro) reported large amounts of cocaine (four kilograms) and travelers' checks (almost $300,000) missing from a safety deposit vault at Western Vault Corporation. The drugs and money had been used as part of an undercover operation conducted by Metro's Intelligence Bureau. Petitioner's client, Grady Sanders, owned Western Vault. John Moran, the Las Vegas sheriff, reported the theft at a press conference on February 2, 1987, naming the police and Western Vault employees as suspects.

used in police operations.
Cocaine & money missing
being stored at Western Vault
Sheriff reported owner of Vault as a suspect

Although two police officers, Detective Steve Scholl and Sargeant Ed Schaub, enjoyed free access to the deposit box throughout the period of the theft, and no log reported comings and goings at the vault, a series of press reports over the following year indicated that investigators did not consider these officers responsible. Instead, investigators focused upon Western Vault and its owner. Newspaper reports quoted the sheriff and other high police officials as saying that they had not

· some officers had access to it & no log of what they did.
· but investigators did not consider them responsible
· they (& press) focused on W. Vault owner & employees.

lost confidence in the "elite" Intelligence Bureau. From the beginning, Sheriff Moran had "complete faith and trust" in his officers.

[Other Western Vault customers then reported missing items from their boxes. —Ed.]

Initial press reports stated that Sanders and Western Vault were being coopera- *press saying they focused on Sanders* tive; but as time went on, the press noted that the police investigation had failed to identify the culprit and through a process of elimination was beginning to point toward Sanders. Reports quoted the affidavit of a detective that the theft was part of an effort to discredit the undercover operation and that business records suggested the existence of a business relation between Sanders and the targets of a Metro undercover probe.

The deputy police chief announced the two detectives with access to the vault had *police cleared as suspects* been "cleared" as possible suspects. According to an unnamed "source close to the investigation," the police shifted from the idea that the thief had planned to discredit the undercover operation to the theory that the thief had unwittingly stolen from the police. The stories noted that Sanders "could not be reached for comment."

The story took a more sensational turn with reports that the two police suspects *lie detector test* had been cleared by police investigators after passing lie detector tests. The tests were administered by one Ray Slaughter. But later, the Federal Bureau of Investigation (FBI) arrested Slaughter for distributing cocaine to an FBI informant, Belinda Antal. . . . [P]ress reports indicated that Sanders had refused to take a police polygraph examination. The press suggested that the FBI suspected *Sanders wouldn't take.* Metro officers were responsible for the theft, and reported that the theft had severely damaged relations between the FBI and Metro.

B

The Press Conference. Petitioner is a Las Vegas criminal defense attorney, an author of articles about criminal law and procedure, and a former associate dean of the National College for Criminal Defense Lawyers and Public Defenders. Through leaks from the police department, he had some advance notice of the date an indictment would be returned and the nature of the charges against Sanders. Petitioner had monitored the publicity surrounding the case, and, prior to the indictment, was personally aware of at least 17 articles in the major local newspapers, the Las Vegas Sun and Las Vegas Review-Journal, and numerous local television news stories which reported on the Western Vault theft and ensuing investigation. Petitioner determined, for the first time in his career, that he would call a formal press conference. He did not blunder into a press conference, but acted with considerable deliberation. *→ Gentile really thought abt. it.*

1

Petitioner's Motivation. As petitioner explained to the disciplinary board, his primary motivation was the concern that, unless some of the weaknesses in the State's case were made public, a potential jury venire would be poisoned by repetition in the press of information being released by the police and prosecutors, in particular the repeated press reports about polygraph tests and the fact that the two police officers were no longer suspects. Respondent distorts Rule 177 when it suggests this explanation admits a purpose to prejudice the venire and so proves a violation of the Rule. Rule 177 only prohibits the dissemination of information that one knows or reasonably should know has a "substantial likelihood of materially prejudicing an adjudicative proceeding." Petitioner did not indicate he thought he could sway the pool of potential jurors to form an opinion in advance of the trial, nor did he seek to discuss evidence that would be inadmissible at trial. He sought only to counter publicity already deemed prejudicial. The Southern Nevada Disciplinary Board so found. It said petitioner attempted

> (i) to counter public opinion which he perceived as adverse to Mr. Sanders, (ii) . . . to refute certain matters regarding his client which had appeared in the media, (iii) to fight back against the perceived efforts of the prosecution to poison the prospective juror pool, and (iv) to publicly present Sanders' side of the case.

Far from an admission that he sought to "materially prejudice an adjudicative proceeding," petitioner sought only to stop a wave of publicity he perceived as prejudicing potential jurors against his client and injuring his client's reputation in the community.

Petitioner gave a second reason for holding the press conference, which demonstrates the additional value of his speech. Petitioner acted in part because the investigation had taken a serious toll on his client. Sanders was "not a man in good health," having suffered multiple open-heart surgeries prior to these events. And prior to indictment, the mere suspicion of wrongdoing had caused the closure of Western Vault and the loss of Sanders' ground lease on an Atlantic City, New Jersey, property. An attorney's duties do not begin inside the courtroom door. He or she cannot ignore the practical implications of a legal proceeding for the client. Just as an attorney may recommend a plea bargain or civil settlement to avoid the adverse consequences of a possible loss after trial, so too an attorney may take reasonable steps to defend a client's reputation and reduce the adverse consequences of indictment, especially in the face of a prosecution deemed unjust or commenced with improper motives. A defense attorney may pursue lawful strategies to obtain dismissal of an indictment or reduction of charges, including an attempt to demonstrate in the court of public opinion that the client does not deserve to be tried.

2

Petitioner's Investigation of Rule 177. Rule 177 is phrased in terms of what an attorney "knows or reasonably should know." On the evening before the press conference, petitioner and two colleagues spent several hours researching the extent of an attorney's obligations under Rule 177. He decided, as we have held, that the timing of a statement was crucial in the assessment of possible prejudice and the Rule's application.

Upon return of the indictment, the court set a trial date for August 1988, some six months in the future. Petitioner knew, at the time of his statement, that a jury

[handwritten: read cases where press conferences were "far worse"]

would not be empaneled for six months at the earliest, if ever. He recalled reported cases finding no prejudice resulting from juror exposure to "far worse" information two and four months before trial, and concluded that his proposed statement was not substantially likely to result in material prejudice.

A statement which reaches the attention of the venire on the eve of voir dire might require a continuance or cause difficulties in securing an impartial jury, and at the very least could complicate the jury selection process. As turned out to be the case here, exposure to the same statement six months prior to trial would not result in prejudice, the content fading from memory long before the trial date. *[handwritten: 6 months before jury called is different]*

In 1988, Clark County, Nevada, had population in excess of 600,000 persons. Given the size of the community from which any potential jury venire would be drawn and the length of time before trial, only the most damaging of information could give rise to any likelihood of prejudice. The innocuous content of petitioner's statements reinforces my conclusion. *[handwritten: w/ this many ppl. and this far in advance only really bad statements would be prejudicial.]*

3

The Content of Petitioner's Statements. Petitioner was disciplined for statements to the effect that (1) the evidence demonstrated his client's innocence, (2) the likely thief was a police detective, Steve Scholl, and (3) the other victims were not credible, as most were drug dealers or convicted money launderers, all but one of whom had only accused Sanders in response to police pressure, in the process of "trying to work themselves out of something." He also strongly implied that Steve Scholl could be observed in a videotape suffering from symptoms of cocaine use. Of course, only a small fraction of petitioner's remarks were disseminated to the public, in two newspaper stories and two television news broadcasts. *[handwritten: what he got in trouble for.]*

The stories mentioned not only Gentile's press conference but also a prosecution response and police press conference. The chief deputy district attorney was quoted as saying that this was a legitimate indictment, and that prosecutors cannot bring an indictment to court unless they can prove the charges in it beyond a reasonable doubt. Deputy Police Chief Sullivan stated for the police department: " 'We in Metro are very satisfied our officers (Scholl and Sgt. Ed Schaub) had nothing to do with this theft or any other. They are both above reproach. Both are veteran police officers who are dedicated to honest law enforcement.' " In the context of general public awareness, these police and prosecution statements were no more likely to result in prejudice than were petitioner's statements, but given the repetitive publicity from the police investigation, it is difficult to come to any conclusion but that the balance remained in favor of the prosecution. *[handwritten: response by police + prosecution; Scholl is beyond reproach; Ct. says their statement was worse; balance still in favor of police.]*

* * *

Petitioner's statements lack any of the more obvious bases for a finding of prejudice. Unlike the police, he refused to comment on polygraph tests except to confirm earlier reports that Sanders had not submitted to the police polygraph; he mentioned no confessions and no evidence from searches or test results; he refused to elaborate upon his charge that the other so-called victims were not credible, except to explain his general theory that they were pressured to testify in an attempt to avoid drug-related legal trouble, and that some of them may have

[handwritten: → just talked abt. general theory. · nothing abt. confessions or evidence or test results.]

asserted claims in an attempt to collect insurance money.

C

Events Following the Press Conference. Petitioner's judgment that no likelihood of material prejudice would result from his comments was vindicated by events at trial. . . .

The trial took place on schedule in August 1988, with no request by either party for a venue change or continuance. The jury was empaneled with no apparent difficulty. The trial judge questioned the jury venire about publicity. Although many had vague recollections of reports that cocaine stored at Western Vault had been stolen from a police undercover operation, and, as petitioner had feared, one remembered that the police had been cleared of suspicion, not a single juror indicated any recollection of petitioner or his press conference.

At trial, all material information disseminated during petitioner's press conference was admitted in evidence before the jury, including information questioning the motives and credibility of supposed victims who testified against Sanders, and Detective Scholl's ingestion of drugs in the course of undercover operations (in order, he testified, to gain the confidence of suspects). The jury acquitted petitioner's client, and, as petitioner explained before the disciplinary board,

> when the trial was over with and the man was acquitted the next week the foreman of the jury phoned me and said to me that if they would have had a verdict form before them with respect to the guilt of Steve Scholl they would have found the man proven guilty beyond a reasonable doubt.

There is no support for the conclusion that petitioner's statements created a likelihood of material prejudice, or indeed of any harm of sufficient magnitude or imminence to support a punishment for speech.

III

As interpreted by the Nevada Supreme Court, the Rule is void for vagueness, in any event, for its safe harbor provision, Rule 177(3), misled petitioner into thinking that he could give his press conference without fear of discipline. Rule 177(3)(a) provides that a lawyer "may state without elaboration . . . the general nature of the . . . defense." Statements under this provision are protected "notwithstanding subsection 1 and 2 (a-f)." By necessary operation of the word "notwithstanding," the Rule contemplates that a lawyer describing the "general nature of the . . . defense" "without elaboration" need fear no discipline, even if he comments on "the character, credibility, reputation or criminal record of a . . . witness," and even if he "knows or reasonably should know that [the statement] will have a substantial likelihood of materially prejudicing an adjudicative proceeding."

Given this grammatical structure, and absent any clarifying interpretation by the state court, the Rule fails to provide " 'fair notice to those to whom [it] is directed.' " *Grayned v. City of Rockford*, 408 U.S. 104, 112 (1972). A lawyer seeking to avail himself of Rule 177(3)'s protection must guess at its contours. The right to explain the "general" nature of the defense without "elaboration" provides insufficient guidance because "general" and "elaboration" are both classic terms of degree. In the context before us, these terms have no settled usage or tradition of interpretation in law. The lawyer has no principle for determining when his remarks pass from the safe harbor of the general to the forbidden sea of the elaborated.

[handwritten: lawyer can't know when his actions are bad.]

Petitioner testified he thought his statements were protected by Rule 177(3). A review of the press conference supports that claim. He gave only a brief opening statement, and on numerous occasions declined to answer reporters' questions seeking more detailed comments. One illustrative exchange shows petitioner's attempt to obey the rule:

[handwritten: support that Gentile thought he was ok.]

[handwritten: example of petitioner's attempt to follow his interpretation of the rule]

"QUESTION FROM THE FLOOR: Dominick, you mention you question the credibility of some of the witnesses, some of the people named as victims in the government indictment.

"Can we go through it and elaborate on their backgrounds, interests

"MR. GENTILE: I can't because ethics prohibit me from doing so.

"Last night before I decided I was going to make a statement, I took a good close look at the rules of professional responsibility. There are things that I can say and there are things that I can't. Okay?

[handwritten: Said he couldn't say things b/c of ethics rules.]

"I can't name which of the people have the drug backgrounds. I'm sure you guys can find that by doing just a little bit of investigative work."[32]

---

[32] [22] Other occasions are as follows:

"QUESTION FROM THE FLOOR: Do you believe any other police officers other than Scholl were involved in the disappearance of the dope and —

"MR. GENTILE: Let me say this: What I believe and what the proof is are two different things. Okay? I'm reluctant to discuss what I believe because I don't want to slander somebody, but I can tell you that the proof shows that Scholl is the guy that is most likely to have taken the cocaine and the American Express traveler's checks.

"QUESTION FROM THE FLOOR: What is that? What is that proof?

"MR. GENTILE: It'll come out; it'll come out. "

"QUESTION FROM THE FLOOR: I have seen reports that the FBI seems to think sort of along the lines that you do.

"MR. GENTILE: Well, I couldn't agree with them more.

"QUESTION FROM THE FLOOR: Do you know anything about it?

"MR. GENTILE: Yes, I do; but again, Dan, I'm not in a position to be able to discuss that now.

"All I can tell you is that you're in for a very interesting six months to a year as this case develops."

"QUESTION FROM THE FLOOR: Did the cops pass the polygraph?

"MR. GENTILE: Well, I would like to give you a comment on that, except that Ray Slaughter's trial is coming up and I don't want to get in the way of anybody being able to defend themselves.

"QUESTION FROM THE FLOOR: Do you think the Slaughter case — that there's a connection?

"MR. GENTILE: Absolutely. I don't think there is any question about it, and —

"QUESTION FROM THE FLOOR: What is that?

"MR. GENTILE: Well, it's intertwined to a great deal, I think.

"I know that what I think the connection is, again, is something I believe to be true. I can't point to it being true and until I can I'm not going to say anything.

Nevertheless, the disciplinary board said only that petitioner's comments "went beyond the scope of the statements permitted by SCR 177(3)," and the Nevada Supreme Court's rejection of petitioner's defense based on Rule 177(3) was just as terse. The fact that Gentile was found in violation of the Rules after studying them and making a conscious effort at compliance demonstrates that Rule 177 creates a trap for the wary as well as the unwary.

The prohibition against vague regulations of speech is based in part on the need to eliminate the impermissible risk of discriminatory enforcement, *Kolender v. Lawson*, for history shows that speech is suppressed when either the speaker or the message is critical of those who enforce the law. The question is not whether discriminatory enforcement occurred here, and we assume it did not, but whether the Rule is so imprecise that discriminatory enforcement is a real possibility. The inquiry is of particular relevance when one of the classes most affected by the regulation is the criminal defense bar, which has the professional mission to challenge actions of the State. Petitioner, for instance, succeeded in preventing the conviction of his client, and the speech in issue involved criticism of the government.

IV

The analysis to this point resolves the case, and in the usual order of things the discussion should end here. Five Members of the Court, however, endorse an extended discussion which concludes that Nevada may interpret its requirement of substantial likelihood of material prejudice under a standard more deferential than is the usual rule where speech is concerned. It appears necessary, therefore, to set forth my objections to that conclusion and to the reasoning which underlies it.

Respondent argues that speech by an attorney is subject to greater regulation than speech by others, and restrictions on an attorney's speech should be assessed under a balancing test that weighs the State's interest in the regulation of a specialized profession against the lawyer's First Amendment interest in the kind of speech that was at issue. The cases cited by our colleagues to support this balancing, *Bates v. State Bar of Arizona*, 433 U.S. 350 (1977); *Peel v. Attorney Registration and Disciplinary Comm'n of Ill.*, 496 U.S. 91 (1990); *Ohralik v. Ohio State Bar Assn.*, 436 U.S. 447 (1978); and *Seattle Times Co. v. Rhinehart*, 467 U.S. 20 (1984), involved either commercial speech by attorneys or restrictions upon release of information

---

"QUESTION FROM THE FLOOR: Do you think the police involved in this passed legitimate — legitimately passed lie detector tests?

"MR. GENTILE: I don't want to comment on that for two reasons:

"Number one, again, Ray Slaughter is coming up for trial and it wouldn't be right to call him a liar if I didn't think that it were true.

"But, secondly, I don't have much faith in polygraph tests.

"QUESTION FROM THE FLOOR: Did [Sanders] ever take one?

"MR. GENTILE: The police polygraph?

"QUESTION FROM THE FLOOR: Yes.

"MR. GENTILE: No, he didn't take a police polygraph.

"QUESTION FROM THE FLOOR: Did he take one with you?

"MR. GENTILE: I'm not going to disclose that now."

that the attorney could gain only by use of the court's discovery process. Neither of those categories, nor the underlying interests which justified their creation, were implicated here. Petitioner was disciplined because he proclaimed to the community what he thought to be a misuse of the prosecutorial and police powers. Wide open balancing of interests is not appropriate in this context. *Court disagrees w/ this balancing.*

B

Resp. says lawyer's speech should be subject to extra regulation to protect crim. proceeding.

Respondent relies upon obiter dicta from *In re Sawyer*, 360 U.S. 622 (1959), *Sheppard v. Maxwell*, 384 U.S. 333 (1966), and *Nebraska Press Assn. v. Stuart*, 427 U.S. 539 (1976), for the proposition that an attorney's speech about ongoing proceedings must be subject to pervasive regulation in order to ensure the impartial adjudication of criminal proceedings. *In re Sawyer* involved general comments about Smith Act prosecutions rather than the particular proceeding in which the attorney was involved, conduct which we held not sanctionable under the applicable ABA Canon of Professional Ethics, quite apart from any resort to First Amendment principles. *Nebraska Press Assn.* considered a challenge to a court order barring the press from reporting matters most prejudicial to the defendant's Sixth Amendment trial right, not information released by defense counsel. In *Sheppard v. Maxwell*, we overturned a conviction after a trial that can only be described as a circus, with the courtroom taken over by the press and jurors turned into media stars. The prejudice to Dr. Sheppard's fair trial right can be traced in principal part to police and prosecutorial irresponsibility and the trial court's failure to control the proceedings and the courthouse environment. Each case suggests restrictions upon information release, but none confronted their permitted scope.

(margin: Abt. press - not defense statements)

(margin: ex - where trial was a circus.)

At the very least, our cases recognize that disciplinary rules governing the legal profession cannot punish activity protected by the First Amendment, and that First Amendment protection survives even when the attorney violates a disciplinary rule he swore to obey when admitted to the practice of law. We have not in recent years accepted our colleagues' apparent theory that the practice of law brings with it comprehensive restrictions, or that we will defer to professional bodies when those restrictions impinge upon First Amendment freedoms. And none of the justifications put forward by respondent suffice to sanction abandonment of our normal First Amendment principles in the case of speech by an attorney regarding pending cases.

(margin: 1st Am. wins.)

V

Even if respondent is correct, and as in *Seattle Times* we must balance "whether the practice in question [furthers] an important or substantial governmental interest unrelated to the suppression of expression and whether the limitation of First Amendment freedoms is no greater than is necessary or essential to the protection of the particular governmental interest involved," the Rule as interpreted by Nevada fails the searching inquiry required by those precedents.

*   *   *

[handwritten marginalia: Resp. Argues that b/c officer of the court — he shouldn't talk to press.]

B

Respondent uses the "officer of the court" label to imply that attorney contact with the press somehow is inimical to the attorney's proper role. Rule 177 posits no such inconsistency between an attorney's role and discussions with the press. It permits all comment to the press absent "a substantial likelihood of materially prejudicing an adjudicative proceeding." Respondent does not articulate the principle that contact with the press cannot be reconciled with the attorney's role or explain how this might be so.

[handwritten marginalia: didn't explain why]

*   *   *

One may concede the proposition that an attorney's speech about pending cases may present dangers that could not arise from statements by a nonparticipant, and that an attorney's duty to cooperate in the judicial process may prevent him or her from taking actions with an intent to frustrate that process. The role of attorneys in the criminal justice system subjects them to fiduciary obligations to the court and the parties. An attorney's position may result in some added ability to obstruct the proceedings through well-timed statements to the press, though one can debate the extent of an attorney's ability to do so without violating other established duties. A court can require an attorney's cooperation to an extent not possible of nonpartici-pants. A proper weighing of dangers might consider the harm that occurs when speech about ongoing proceedings forces the court to take burdensome steps such as sequestration, continuance, or change of venue.

[handwritten marginalia: lawyer does have a duty to the court & proceeding]

[handwritten marginalia: weigh whether they're really bad & you can]

*   *   *

The vigorous advocacy we demand of the legal profession is accepted because it takes place under the neutral, dispassionate control of the judicial system. Though cost and delays undermine it in all too many cases, the American judicial trial remains one of the purest, most rational forums for the lawful determination of disputes. A profession which takes just pride in these traditions may consider them disserved if lawyers use their skills and insight to make untested allegations in the press instead of in the courtroom. But constraints of professional responsibility and societal disapproval will act as sufficient safeguards in most cases. And in some circumstances press comment is necessary to protect the rights of the client and prevent abuse of the courts. It cannot be said that petitioner's conduct demon-strated any real or specific threat to the legal process, and his statements have the full protection of the First Amendment.

VI

The judgment of the Supreme Court of Nevada is

Reversed.

APPENDIX TO OPINION OF KENNEDY, J.

*   *   *

Appendix B

Nevada Supreme Court Rule 177, as in effect prior to January 5, 1991. Trial Publicity

1. A lawyer shall not make an extrajudicial statement that a reasonable person would expect to be disseminated by means of public communication if the lawyer knows or reasonably should know that it will have a substantial likelihood of materially prejudicing an adjudicative proceeding.

2. A statement referred to in subsection 1 ordinarily is likely to have such an effect when it refers to a civil matter triable to a jury, a criminal matter, or any other proceeding that could result in incarceration, and the statement relates to:

(a) the character, credibility, reputation or criminal record of a party, suspect in a criminal investigation or witness, or the identity of a witness, or the expected testimony of a party or witness;

(b) in a criminal case or proceeding that could result in incarceration, the possibility of a plea of guilty to the offense or the existence or contents of any confession, admission, or statement given by a defendant or suspect or that person's refusal or failure to make a statement;

(c) the performance or results of any examination or test or the refusal or failure of a person to submit to an examination or test, or the identity or nature of physical evidence expected to be presented;

(d) any opinion as to the guilt or innocence of a defendant or suspect in a criminal case or proceeding that could result in incarceration;

(e) information the lawyer knows or reasonably should know is likely to be inadmissible as evidence in a trial and would if disclosed create a substantial risk of prejudicing an impartial trial; or

(f) the fact that a defendant has been charged with a crime, unless there is included therein a statement explaining that the charge is merely an accusation and that the defendant is presumed innocent until and unless proven guilty.

3. Notwithstanding subsection 1 and 2(a-f), a lawyer involved in the investigation or litigation of a matter may state without elaboration: *[handwritten margin note: May state w/ elaboration]*

(a) the general nature of the claim or defense;

(b) the information contained in a public record;

(c) that an investigation of the matter is in progress, including the general scope of the investigation, the offense or claim or defense involved and, except when prohibited by law, the identity of the persons involved;

(d) the scheduling or result of any step in litigation;

(e) a request for assistance in obtaining evidence and information necessary thereto;

(f) a warning of danger concerning the behavior of a person involved, when there is reason to believe that there exists the likelihood of substantial harm to an individual or to the public interest; and

(g) in a criminal case:

(i) the identity, residence, occupation and family status of the accused;

(ii) if the accused has not been apprehended, information necessary to aid in apprehension of that person;

(iii) the fact, time and place of arrest; and

(iv) the identity of investigating and arresting officers or agencies and the length of the investigation."

CHIEF JUSTICE REHNQUIST delivered the opinion of the Court with respect to Parts I and II, and delivered a dissenting opinion with respect to Part III, in which JUSTICE WHITE, JUSTICE SCALIA, and JUSTICE SOUTER join.

Petitioner was disciplined for making statements to the press about a pending case in which he represented a criminal defendant. The state bar, and the Supreme Court of Nevada on review, found that petitioner knew or should have known that there was a substantial likelihood that his statements would materially prejudice the trial of his client. Nonetheless, petitioner contends that the First Amendment to the United States Constitution requires a stricter standard to be met before such speech by an attorney may be disciplined: there must be a finding of "actual prejudice or a substantial and imminent threat to fair trial." We conclude that the "substantial likelihood of material prejudice" standard applied by Nevada and most other States satisfies the First Amendment.

I

Petitioner's client was the subject of a highly publicized case, and in response to adverse publicity about his client, Gentile held a press conference on the day after Sanders was indicted. At the press conference, petitioner made, among others, the following statements:

> When this case goes to trial, and as it develops, you're going to see that the evidence will prove not only that Grady Sanders is an innocent person and had nothing to do with any of the charges that are being leveled against him, but that the person that was in the most direct position to have stolen the drugs and the money, the American Express Travelers' checks, is Detective Steve Scholl.

> There is far more evidence that will establish that Detective Scholl took these drugs and took these American Express Travelers' checks than any other living human being.

> . . . .

> . . . the so-called other victims, as I sit here today I can tell you that one, two — four of them are known drug dealers and convicted money

launderers and drug dealers; three of whom didn't say a word about anything until after they were approached by Metro and after they were already in trouble and are trying to work themselves out of something.

Now, up until the moment, of course, that they started going along with what detectives from Metro wanted them to say, these people were being held out as being incredible and liars by the very same people who are going to say now that you can believe them.

The following statements were in response to questions from members of the press:

. . . because of the stigma that attaches to merely being accused — okay — I know I represent an innocent man . . . . The last time I had a conference with you, was with a client and I let him talk to you and I told you that that case would be dismissed and it was. Okay?

I don't take cheap shots like this. I represent an innocent guy. All right?

. . . ?

[The police] were playing very fast and loose. . . . We've got some video tapes that if you take a look at them, I'll tell you what, [Detective Scholl] either had a hell of a cold or he should have seen a better doctor.

Articles appeared in the local newspapers describing the press conference and petitioner's statements. The trial took place approximately six months later, and although the trial court succeeded in empaneling a jury that had not been affected by the media coverage and Sanders was acquitted on all charges, the state bar disciplined petitioner for his statements.

The Southern Nevada Disciplinary Board found that petitioner knew the detective he accused of perpetrating the crime and abusing drugs would be a witness for the prosecution. It also found that petitioner believed others whom he characterized as money launderers and drug dealers would be called as prosecution witnesses.

II

In the United States, the courts have historically regulated admission to the practice of law before them and exercised the authority to discipline and ultimately to disbar lawyers whose conduct departed from prescribed standards. "Membership in the bar is a privilege burdened with conditions," to use the oft-repeated statement of Cardozo, J., in *In re Rouss*, 221 N.Y. 81, 84, 116 N.E. 782, 783 (1917).

When the Model Rules of Professional Conduct were drafted in the early 1980's, the drafters did not go as far as the revised fair trial-free press standards in giving precedence to the lawyer's right to make extrajudicial statements when fair trial rights are implicated, and instead adopted the "substantial likelihood of material prejudice" test. . . .

Petitioner maintains, however, that the First Amendment to the United States Constitution requires a State, such as Nevada in this case, to demonstrate a "clear and present danger" of "actual prejudice or an imminent threat" before any discipline may be imposed on a lawyer who initiates a press conference such as occurred here.

It is unquestionable that in the courtroom itself, during a judicial proceeding, whatever right to "free speech" an attorney has is extremely circumscribed. An attorney may not, by speech or other conduct, resist a ruling of the trial court beyond the point necessary to preserve a claim for appeal. Even outside the courtroom, a majority of the Court in two separate opinions in the case of *In re Sawyer*, 360 U.S. 622 (1959), observed that lawyers in pending cases were subject to ethical restrictions on speech to which an ordinary citizen would not be. There, the Court had before it an order affirming the suspension of an attorney from practice because of her attack on the fairness and impartiality of a judge. The plurality opinion, which found the discipline improper, concluded that the comments had not in fact impugned the judge's integrity. Justice Stewart, who provided the fifth vote for reversal of the sanction, said in his separate opinion that he could not join any possible "intimation that a lawyer can invoke the constitutional right of free speech to immunize himself from evenhanded discipline for proven unethical conduct." He said that "obedience to ethical precepts may require abstention from what in other circumstances might be constitutionally protected speech."

* * *

We expressly contemplated that the speech of those participating before the courts could be limited. This distinction between participants in the litigation and strangers to it is brought into sharp relief by our holding in *Seattle Times Co. v. Rhinehart*, 467 U.S. 20 (1984). There, we unanimously held that a newspaper, which was itself a defendant in a libel action, could be restrained from publishing material about the plaintiffs and their supporters to which it had gained access through court-ordered discovery. In that case we said that "although litigants do not 'surrender their First Amendment rights at the courthouse door,' those rights may be subordinated to other interests that arise in this setting," and noted that "on several occasions [we have] approved restrictions on the communications of trial participants where necessary to ensure a fair trial for a criminal defendant."

Even in an area far from the courtroom and the pendency of a case, our decisions dealing with a lawyer's right under the First Amendment to solicit business and advertise, contrary to promulgated rules of ethics, have not suggested that lawyers are protected by the First Amendment to the same extent as those engaged in other businesses. *See, e.g., Bates v. State Bar of Arizona*, 433 U.S. 350 (1977); *Peel v. Attorney Registration and Disciplinary Comm'n of Ill.*, 496 U.S. 91 (1990); *Ohralik v. Ohio State Bar Assn.*, 436 U.S. 447 (1978). In each of these cases, we engaged in a balancing process, weighing the State's interest in the regulation of a specialized profession against a lawyer's First Amendment interest in the kind of speech that was at issue.

* * *

We think that our opinions in *In re Sawyer*, 360 U.S. 622 (1959), and *Sheppard v. Maxwell, supra* , rather plainly indicate that the speech of lawyers representing clients in pending cases may be regulated under a less demanding standard than

Should be higher standard for 1st Am. violation.

that established for regulation of the press in *Nebraska Press Assn. v. Stuart*, 427
U.S. 539 (1976), and the cases which preceded it. Lawyers representing clients in
pending cases are key participants in the criminal justice system, and the State may
demand some adherence to the precepts of that system in regulating their speech
as well as their conduct.

When a state regulation implicates First Amendment rights, the Court must
balance those interests against the State's legitimate interest in regulating the
activity in question. The "substantial likelihood" test embodied in Rule 177 is
constitutional under this analysis, for it is designed to protect the integrity and
fairness of a State's judicial system, and it imposes only narrow and necessary
limitations on lawyers' speech.

*balancing test
in R. 177 is
const'l.
. . . s/c*

The restraint on speech is narrowly tailored to achieve those objectives. The
regulation of attorneys' speech is limited — it applies only to speech that is
substantially likely to have a materially prejudicial effect; it is neutral as to points
of view, applying equally to all attorneys participating in a pending case; and it
merely postpones the attorneys' comments until after the trial. While supported by
the substantial state interest in preventing prejudice to an adjudicative proceeding
by those who have a duty to protect its integrity, the Rule is limited on its face to
preventing only speech having a substantial likelihood of materially prejudicing that
proceeding.

*narrowly
tailored.*

––––––––

Model Rule 3.6 was amended in 1994 in an effort to remedy the Court's
constitutional objections to it.

INTERNATIONAL NOTE

By contrast, United Kingdom Rules categorically prohibit a barrister from
commenting on the merits of a pending case. Specifically, Rule 709.1 provides "[a]
barrister must not in relation to any anticipated or current proceedings or
mediation in which he is briefed or expects to appear or has appeared as an
advocate, express a personal opinion to the press or other media or in any other
public statement upon the facts or issues arising in the proceedings." BAR COUNCIL
OF ENGLAND AND WALES, CODE OF CONDUCT, Rule 709.1.

E.   EX PARTE CONTACT WITH JUDGES AND JURORS

Our judicial system is built upon the premise that adversaries can make their
best arguments to the judge and the judge can then decide the matter. That premise
requires that the adversaries' arguments be made in the presence of one another so
that each side's response can be heard. Ex parte (without the other party)
communications seriously undermine the prospect of fair process in the justice
system. As such, ex parte communication with decision-makers, both judges and
jurors, is strictly regulated.

1. Judges

If lawyers were permitted to have ex parte (without the other party) communications with judges, then litigated matters would be resolved on the basis of a series of one-at-a-time advocacy episodes rather than the give and take of opposing sides presenting evidence in open court and contesting one another's arguments. The justice system would be seriously undermined. As such, except in very limited circumstances, lawyers are prohibited from communicating ex parte with a judge about the subject of a pending dispute. MR 3.5(b). The subject matter requirement of the rule is important. Judges and lawyers may converse about matters unrelated to pending litigation. Lawyers may also communicate with judges ex parte about ministerial matters, such as inquiring about dates that may be available for a hearing.

2. Jurors

Lawyers are strictly prohibited from communicating with jurors outside the courtroom before and during jurors' duties. This restriction applies to both grand jurors and trial jurors. With some exceptions, lawyers are prohibited from communicating with jurors after the jurors' duty ends. Lawyers are prohibited from harassing jurors at any time. MR 3.5.

FLORIDA BAR v. PETERSON
418 So. 2d 246 (Fla. 1982)

Per Curiam.

This disciplinary proceeding is before us on complaint of The Florida Bar, report of the referee, petition for review filed by the Bar, and request for review by respondent, Glen R. Peterson.

The facts underlying the Bar's complaint against Peterson are that, during the luncheon recess of a case in which Peterson was representing the plaintiffs, he and one of his expert witnesses went to a delicatessen and allowed themselves to be seated at a table then occupied by two jurors serving in the case which he was trying. He acknowledged at the hearing before the referee that he knew that the women seated at the table were jurors. While seated with these jurors, he was observed by two secretaries working in the office of the law firm representing defendant in the case being tried. These secretaries reported what they had seen to the defendant's attorney. After the lunch recess, defendant's counsel moved for mistrial on the basis that Peterson had communicated with the jurors during recess. The trial court granted this motion. Peterson apologized to the court for the incident causing the mistrial which occurred and entered into a stipulation that he would pay the county the jurors' fees including mileage for the two days the jurors served.

*   *   *

The referee in the present proceeding found that Peterson did communicate with the two jurors in violation of the proscription of Florida Bar Code of Professional

Responsibility, Disciplinary Rule 7-108(B)(1).[33] He further found, however, that the nature and extent of the communication are unclear and that the evidence does not demonstrate that Peterson did what he did with intent to gain any unfair advantage in the litigation then pending although his conduct may have had that effect had the mistrial not been declared. For this misconduct, the referee recommends that Peterson be publicly reprimanded, not because he communicated with these jurors with any ulterior purpose in mind but simply because he communicated with them. The referee also recommends that Peterson be required to pass the Multistate Professional Responsibility Examination and that he be required to pay defendant's costs and attorney's fees in the cause upon which the mistrial was declared.

[handwritten margin note: referee recommends.]

The Bar requests a greater discipline, a thirty-day suspension. Peterson, on the other hand, requests a lesser discipline, a private reprimand and no requirement that he pass the Multistate Professional Responsibility Examination or that he pay costs and attorney's fees of the defendants in the cause aborted by mistrial.

We find that under the circumstances a public reprimand and a one-year probation with the condition that Peterson be required to pass the ethics portion of the Florida Bar Examination are warranted. . . .

Accordingly, the publication of this decision in Southern Reporter will serve as a public reprimand. Peterson is further placed on probation for one year with the only condition of probation being that he take and pass the Multistate Professional Responsibility Examination. Costs in the amount of $532.79 are assessed against Peterson.

It is so ordered.

NOTES, QUESTIONS, AND EXAMPLES

1. Lawyers are under a duty to report juror misconduct. What if the opposing lawyers in Peterson had gone immediately to the judge to report Peterson's conduct? What would be the proper course? *[handwritten: not ex parte?]*

2. Peterson sat at the jurors' table. What should a lawyer do when juror contact is unavoidable? For example, Lawyer is on the courthouse elevator when the doors open at a floor other than the lawyer's destination, in walks a juror who says to Lawyer, "Great weather, huh?" or "How 'bout those Mets?'" *[handwritten: Say you can't talk.]*

3. When a lawyer files a paper with a court, the lawyer attaches a Certificate of Service, such as the following:

---

[33] [2] DR 7-108(B)(1) provides:

(B) During the trial of a case:

    (1) A lawyer connected therewith shall not communicate with or cause another to communicate with any member of the jury.

CERTIFICATE OF SERVICE

I certify that I served the attached Motion for Summary Judgment on counsel for Defendant Jones: Bill Davis, Esq., Jan Peterson, Esq. and Richard Gill, Esq., Davis, Peterson & Gill, 143 Middle Road, Richmond Virginia 25749, by placing accurate copies in United States mail with first class postage attached, properly addressed to counsel on this 3rd day of April 1999.

WILLIAMS AND ALLEN

By: _____

Martha Williams, Esquire

700 So. Henry Street

Williamsburg, VA 23185

(804) 555-1111

Attorneys for Plaintiff

In terms of the ex parte contact rules, what is the significance of the certificate?

4. Once proceedings have ended, lawyers may have very limited contact with jurors for benign purposes such as to determine whether the lawyer's presentation manner is effective. Even after proceedings end, however, lawyers must refrain from engaging in harassing contacts with jurors and from conduct that would tend to undermine the jurors' confidence in their verdict and the justice system. See Chapter VI.

F. PRO BONO PUBLICO

The legal profession's history of providing service to the poor is not an entirely happy one. Nonetheless, through organized efforts in bar associations, through public agencies, and through individual lawyers' efforts, considerable free and reduced-fee legal service is provided. The ethics rules encourage lawyers to engage in pro bono activities.

1. Organized Legal Services for the Poor

Through the organized bar and public agencies, legal services are provided for a portion of the population that would otherwise be unable to afford to retain a lawyer. Until the decision in *Gideon v. Wainwright*, 372 U.S. 335 (1963), provision of representation for indigent criminal defendants was a hit and miss matter for which some states had provided and others had not. The Supreme Court, in determining that the Sixth Amendment right to counsel requires counsel be appointed in criminal matters for indigent defendants, generated the impetus for public defender agencies and court appointment systems for criminal representation in places without a public defender agency.

No comparable right to counsel exists for most civil cases. As such, states are not required to provide legal service for the poor in most civil matters. Nonetheless, through the federal funding of the Legal Services Corporation and additional funding by states and localities, legal aid or legal services offices exist to serve a portion of population that would otherwise be unable to afford to retain a lawyer in civil matters. Because the funding is inadequate to the task, the continued unserved public need is substantial.

Roger C. Cramton, *Crisis in Legal Services for the Poor*
26 Vill. L. Rev. 521 (1981)[34]

*   *   *

II. The History of Civil Legal Assistance

For most of our history, the situation with respect to civil legal aid for the poor could well have been summed up in Anatole France's famous gibe that: "The law, in its majestic equality, forbids the rich as well as the poor to sleep under bridges, to beg in the streets, and to steal bread." The courts were open to all, but only the well-to-do could afford the lawyer who was necessary for the vindication of rights.

The legal profession recognized an ethical obligation to provide representation for indigents, and many lawyers devoted substantial portions of their time to unpaid practice, especially on behalf of criminal defendants. Substantial changes did not come about until the Supreme Court, beginning with *Gideon v. Wainwright* in 1963, recognized a constitutional right to appointed counsel in criminal cases. Subsequent decisions have expanded this right to misdemeanor cases and to a very limited category of civil proceedings. The indigent criminal defendant is now provided a defense lawyer at public expense, either through a public defender or assigned-counsel system.

Except in a few special instances, however, there was and is no constitutional right to appointed counsel in civil cases. As a practical matter, however, the contingent-fee system provided representation in cases involving personal injuries and job-related injuries. The enactment of attorney's fees provisions has provided some inducement for private attorneys to assist in the vindication of certain statutory rights such as the prohibition of employment discrimination. But most legal problems of the poor have been left unattended because the responsibility for providing assistance was a collective responsibility of the entire bar. Like many shared responsibilities, no one felt individually responsible and the need went unmet.

Four eras in civil legal aid in the United States may be identified. Prior to 1875, legal aid was left to the unorganized and voluntary activities of individual lawyers. Although occasional representation was provided, the pro bono efforts of American lawyers were directed largely to the defense of indigents charged with crime, in itself no small task.

---

[34] Copyright © 1981 by Villanova Law Review. Reprinted with permission.

The rise of voluntary organizations — a typically American response to a tough social problem characterizes the second era.

The year 1875 marked the beginning of traditional legal aid through private organizations financed by charitable contributions, staffed by a small number of fulltime lawyers, and assisted by the volunteered time of lawyers in private practice. Through the efforts of such pioneers as Reginald Heber Smith, and with the support of the organized bar, legal aid offices were established in most large metropolitan areas by 1962.

Traditional legal aid was oriented toward individual client service, helping individuals with legal problems, such as landlord tenant controversies, family quarrels, and consumer affairs. The implicit assumption was that justice was a civil right, not a commodity to be purchased.

A more controversial approach to legal aid characterized the third era, which began in 1965 with the legal services program of the now defunct Office of Economic Opportunity (OEO). The *Gideon* case had recognized a constitutional right to appointed counsel in criminal cases; a period of destructive urban riots had suggested the desirability of providing more peaceful methods of handling the grievances of the urban poor; and President Johnson, with large congressional support, had embarked on his War on Poverty.

The OEO legal services program did not reject the client service objective of traditional legal aid, but it included an emphasis on two additional objectives: 1) social justice through law reform and income redistribution; and 2) political organization of the poor. It was assumed that legal rules and procedures would have a class bias against the poor. These rules could be reformed by impact litigation which would equalize the treatment of the poor and provide them with a larger share of the social pie. Similarly, the powerlessness of the poor — their lack of clout with elected officials — was attributed to their lack of organization. One major purpose of OEO legal services was to assist groups of poor people in organizing as groups. The formation of voting blocs would exert pressure on governmental institutions; poor people would acquire self-confidence and self-direction by participation in the power struggles of a pluralist society; and they would benefit from more favorable decisions by legislatures, administrative bodies, and the courts.

It is not surprising that a taxpayer-funded program with these objectives quickly became highly controversial. Many "poverty lawyers" funded by grants from OEO were viewed as left-wing agitators, engaged in a political agenda of their own and having little interest in the humdrum legal problems of the poor, with which traditional legal aid was almost exclusively concerned.

Political interference with the program began during the Johnson years and during the early '70's the program was fighting for its life. At one point President Nixon decided to dismantle the program and Howard Phillips, a young political lieutenant, was dispatched to the OEO to carry out the task. A series of bruising battles in Congress and the courts left the program in place but crippled in morale and funding. The American Bar Association, which had committed itself to publicly-funded legal assistance a few years earlier under the leadership of Lewis F. Powell, Jr., later Justice Powell, fought hard for the establishment of a permanent legal services program in a form that would remove it from the immediate supervision of the President and vicissitudes of politics. When President Nixon shifted ground and supported this approach, the Legal Services Corporation Act was signed into law, beginning the fourth era in civil legal aid. It was the last major piece of legislation signed by Nixon before his resignation in the summer of 1974.

The early days of the Legal Services Corporation were exciting ones. Since I had the honor of being appointed by President Ford, with Senate confirmation, as the initial chairman of the Board of Directors of the Corporation, I was, as Dean Acheson has put it in another context, "present at the creation." The Corporation started with no offices, a severe labor dispute with the small and demoralized staff inherited from OEO, and field programs that were starved for funds, low in morale, and suspicious of the new Corporation. We didn't even have a photocopy machine. I recall typing and copying our initial budget submission to Congress in the wee hours of the night in the borrowed offices of a government agency in Washington, assisted by a small band of volunteers from the legal services community. By 3 a.m., a few short hours before the hearing on the appropriation request was to begin, we had produced the necessary sixty copies.

The Legal Services Corporation Act (Act) contained two features that were designed to cure most of the deficiencies of its OEO predecessor. The first was independence, both from political control by politicians and from political use by legal service attorneys; and the second was a strong focus on professionalism — delivering quality legal services in accordance with the best traditions of the profession. The creation of a new quasi-governmental body governed by an independent and non-partisan board of directors was designed to insulate legal service programs from the kind of political intervention that had troubled the OEO program. Statutory prohibitions prevented legal service grantees .from using program funds or personnel for political purposes, organizational activities, or participation in strikes, picketing, and demonstrations.

On the major issue of the nature and scope of representation to be provided to poor clients, the Act smothered quite different perspectives and objectives under a soothing new slogan: access to justice for all. This neutral principle clearly encompassed the individual-client service of traditional legal aid. It also included the law reform objective of the OEO program so long as the significant issues to be litigated arose out of client service in actual cases.

The governing principle was that a lawyer for the poor should do the best he can for his client, just as the lawyer for Exxon or anyone else does. If the zealous and complete representation required by the Code of Professional Responsibility leads the lawyer to believe that framing a test case, pursuing extensive discovery, or participating in administrative or legislative proceedings will best advance the interests of the client, then these activities should be undertaken. The explicit statutory proviso was that the legal services attorney cannot dream up the law suit and then solicit the client; the law suit must emerge out of routine client service. Nor could the legal services attorney organize a client group so that he could litigate its rights. But education of poor clients concerning their legal rights, including their right to organize, was not precluded. These competing principles obviously require making a number of fine distinctions.

Hence the present framework for legal services authorizes the full armory of legal techniques and procedures to be brought to bear on behalf of poor clients, as required in the particular case. Impact litigation and lobbying activities are included insofar as they arise out of client representation. But the more frankly political objectives of the OEO program — to organize the poor or constituent segments as effective pressure groups — are excluded by statute. The Act substitutes more neutral rhetoric of "access to justice" for the more emotionally charged "law reform" and "social change" rhetoric of the OEO program.

IV. Criticisms of the Legal Services Program

Criticisms of the current legal services program fall into three categories: 1) the program is a political instrument of activist lawyers; 2) it is not a poor people's program but a lawyers' program; and 3) it is inefficient both in assisting poor people and in the costs it places on others. Each of these charges deserves examination.

A. Political Activism

The most common criticism of the legal services program is that it embodies or encourages activism by staff attorneys who seek to stir up litigation to force judicial resolution of matters that should be left to elected officials. Even the statement of the criticism raises fundamental questions not limited to legal aid, concerning the appropriate role of courts, legislatures, and the executive in a democratic society, to say nothing of the difficulty of characterizing particular issues as "political" or "activist." The legal services program is attacked because it tempts judges to venture into areas in which critics believe they should not enter.

Howard Phillips, who led the Nixon administration's unsuccessful attempt to dismantle the OEO legal program in 1973, and who now heads the National Defeat Legal Services Committee of the Conservative Caucus says:

> [It] is a violation of the constitutional rights of every American to be required to subsidize activities which are essentially political in nature but are not accountable to the market place or the ballot box. . . . Legal services attorneys have been involved in virtually every liberal cause, and through the Legal Services Corp., Congress has subsidized the liberal faith.

If the facts were as implied by Mr. Phillips, most people would agree that taxpayers' funds should not be devoted to essentially political activities. But no factual support for these charges is supplied. Further, the examples given by Mr. Phillips and others are not convincing. In one recent statement, he cited representation of Iranian student protestors, suits promoting affirmative action in employment and education, and claims of American Indians for tribal lands as typical activities of the program. Although it is arguable that neither college students nor aliens should be represented by the federal legal services, it is not apparent to me why deportation proceedings, the enforcement of nondiscrimination in employment and education, and Indian land claims are not appropriate areas in which the rights of poor people should be enforced. The well-to-do utilize members of the private bar to litigate educational discrimination, deportation, and entitlement to federal land. Those claiming interests in federal lands or in their use frequently litigate those claims against the federal government. Why is it "political activism" when poor people enforce their rights in these areas and not when other private interests do so?

All assertions of rights on behalf of a particular class of persons are "Political" in the sense that they involve the social distribution of benefits and status. Rights that are recent creations of legislatures or administrators, such as rights relating to affirmative action in employment, are especially likely to be viewed as controversial in character and hence as "political." In the labor field, for example, statutory provisions relating to union organization were much more bitterly contested, and hence controversial, in the 1930s than they are today. The passage of time may similarly mute some areas of current controversy. But it is not the enforcement of statutory rights in the courts that is "political," since access to the courts is a neutral principle applicable to all rights. The "political" label attaches to the fact that some people, despite the legislative or judicial creation of rights, continue to view them as controversial.

B. A Lawyers' Program, Not a Poor Peoples' Program

A more fundamental but less common critique of the legal services program is that, despite its noble pretense, its benefits go largely to lawyers instead of poor people. The argument has been most fully stated by Stephen Chapman. Mr. Chapman raises provocative questions concerning the purposes and effects of the legal services program.

Who benefits from the program?, asks Mr. Chapman. He answers that its principal benefits run to its lawyer supporters and proponents, not to the poor people who are its ostensible beneficiaries. The legal services program, according to Mr. Chapman, is a full employment bill for lawyers. The ABA and other bar associations support the program because it provides employment for the current overflow of young lawyers from the law schools, who would otherwise be in competition with the existing private bar. Since legal services programs are prohibited from taking fee generating cases, they do not compete with private lawyers. Even more important, every case handled by a legal services lawyer creates new business for other lawyers, since the opposing parties need the services of a lawyer. Thus the program has a tremendous multiplier effect; it not only relieves the competitive pressures of new lawyers entering the legal market, but also requires additional compensated lawyer time to defend the claims brought by legal services lawyers.

There is an old adage that provides jocular support for this view. In a small town in Vermont one lawyer was struggling along, barely eking out a living. Another lawyer moved to town and now both are doing nicely. The point is obvious: the presence of lawyers increases the demand for their services.

The second wing of Mr. Chapman's argument characterizes the program as paternalistic and doubts the importance of the public provision of legal services in contrast to other possible benefits for the poor, especially money. Mr. Chapman argues that lawyers exaggerate the importance of legal counsel, regarding it, like food, shelter, and medical care, as a basic right, the lack of which makes life practically intolerable. Lawyers, like every other group, tend to "magnify the importance of what they do." This is especially so when public provision of legal services serves lawyers' self interest and relieves them of the duty to provide pro bono services to those who can't afford to pay.

Mr. Chapman notes:

> The legal services program may be the most extreme example of the paternalism of the American welfare state: denying the poor what they explicitly lack — money — in favor of the goods and services the government thinks they should have, in the amount and proportion it deems appropriate. There is much validity in the libertarian argument that this approach denies the poor both the freedom to decide their own needs and the responsibility, essential to individual independence and self-reliance, to accept the consequences of such decisions.

If a negative income tax or other program redistributed income to the poor, some of them might purchase legal services with the money. Chapman guesses that most poor people would not value legal services very highly since food, shelter, clothing, education, or even entertainment are likely to have a higher value to them.

Moreover, Mr. Chapman argues, the subsidized availability of lawyers to the poor . . . turn[s] another ordinary piece of social friction into a legal dispute . . . inevitably [reducing] the areas of social life where people are free to interact without the formalities of legal procedures, and without the assistance of lawyers. . . . Few trends are more depressing than the increasingly litigious character of American society and government. Our growing inclination to handle every dispute through our lawyers brings to mind judge Learned Hand's remark that he feared only death and illness as much as a lawsuit . . . "Thickening layers of legalism seem to surround our lives." . . . [T]he blame for too much law can be laid on too many lawyers and their dogmatic reliance on the adversary process as a solution to all social problems.

Lawyers need to struggle with these arguments. The tendency of every group to identify its interest with that of society is almost universal. Lawyers as a class do benefit in many ways, psychic as well as economic, from the legal services program. And the trends toward litigious formalism and social fragmentation are painfully evident.

The issues presented by these arguments are very broad, far beyond the scope of this discussion, but a brief response is required.

First, the opportunity to enforce legal rights and responsibilities involves more than just economics and efficiency. It is a question of the moral tone of a society and the legitimacy of its institutions.

Although we must be self-critical of our tendency as lawyers to prefer the virtues of law over other things, many laymen share our view of the priority of the rule of law.

Second, the economic arguments in favor of distribution of money rather than legal services assume that substantial amounts of money would be available for distribution and that market imperfections do not prevent rational choices by poor people. Both assumptions are dubious. The current appropriation for the national legal services program amounts to only about ten dollars per eligible poor person. That amount of money will not purchase much in the way of legal services or anything else. And poor people, precisely because they are often uneducated and uninformed, may lack reliable information concerning their need for legal services and how to get them, as well as the ability to pay for them. In using money made available by the state, they may not be able to make informed choices.

Finally, especially in situations in which poor people are affected, but each with respect to a small amount, there is a free-rider problem. No one has an incentive to expend the amount necessary to litigate a $100 claim, but the pooling effect of legal services operates to confer a benefit on all members of the group by supporting litigation based on the aggregated value of the claims, which may be very large.

C. Economic Efficiency

Arguments that the legal services program is paternalistic and lawyer-oriented are closely related to attacks on the program on grounds of economic efficiency.

Professor Posner, for example, states some of the same points made by Chapman in language more familiar to economists. Providing legal services to the poor at no price, he argues, "prevents many poor people from achieving their most efficient pattern of consumption." A poor person will accept free legal services unless their value to him is outweighed by the lost time and other inconvenience of dealing with a lawyer. The demand for free legal services will invariably exceed the available supply, creating a serious rationing problem. Since the value to some recipients will be less than its cost to the taxpayers, the distribution of free services is wasteful. It is better, in his view, to give poor persons $100 and let them decide how to spend it.

Posner also argues that free legal services misallocate resources in other respects. Since legal services are usually employed in a dispute with another, the adverse party must increase its legal expenditures or abandon its stake in the dispute. These costs, if a market for services and products is involved, will inevitably be passed on as costs of production. Thus, for example, enforcement of building codes against landlords will result in a substantial reduction in the supply of low-income housing, and a substantial rise in the price of the remaining supply.

Litigation against governmental agencies has somewhat different effects, Posner argues, since the costs are borne by taxpayers rather than by those purchasing the product or service. In some situations such litigation may redistribute income to the poor who are beneficiaries of the social program under consideration, while in others it may merely redistribute the program's benefits among groups of beneficiaries. In any event, if litigation results in increased taxes, legislative efforts may be made to reduce future eligibility or benefits.

The provision of free legal services also creates opportunities for abuse when particular opponents are singled out for extensive and repetitive litigation. The typical litigant's hunger for justice is moderated by the relationship between what is at stake and the costs of getting it. The appetite for litigation will disappear as legal expenses approach the value of the expected outcome. Because a subsidized litigant does not operate under the same constraint, there is always the possibility that his willingness to devote an indefinite amount of legal resources to a case will extort unjust settlements.

A similar problem arises when the stakes of the parties in a legal controversy are widely disparate. If an injured plaintiff in a mass tort situation has only $1,000 at stake while the defendant is worried about the res judicata effect of an adverse decision on claims of a much larger amount, the willingness of the latter to litigate may force a settlement for an amount well below the value of the claim. Institutional litigants may thus often be able to bring great pressure upon individual litigants because they have more at stake.

Although the philosophical and economic objections of critics such as Chapman and Posner raise serious questions, the political opposition to the legal services program is based on its very success and the erroneous perspective that views its law reform aspect as more dominant than it really is. Lawyers who do a good job representing poor people inevitably will collide with the interests of powerful business groups and government agencies; those who are on the receiving end of these not-sotender ministrations of justice will usually not be pleased.

The claims brought by legal services programs on behalf of poor people are decided by judges, not by legal services lawyers. Approximately 85% of all matters are resolved favorably to the program's clients, a remarkably high success rate. The rub about the legal services program maybe that it is successful, and its very success creates opposition among interests adversely affected. "Political activism" and similar slogans may be code words for another complaint "their just claims have been upheld against us and we resent it."

NOTES, QUESTIONS, AND EXAMPLES

In support of organized public services programs, many states have adopted IOLTA (Interest on Lawyer Trust Accounts) programs. Traditionally, trust accounts were not interest bearing. When competition drove banks to offer interest bearing checking accounts, the idea of producing interest on trust accounts took hold. Since client funds move in and out of trust accounts, often residing in the account for very short periods of time, there was some difficulty in identifying the portion of any interest earned with a particular client's funds. An IOLTA program requires the collection of the interest into a common fund, from which grants are made to public service programs in a particular state. Thus, neither the lawyer, nor the client, nor the bank reaps the interest on the account. Fifth Amendment Takings Clause challenges have been made to IOLTA programs. The Supreme Court has held that the funds belong to the client, but that there is no taking because the cost of identifying the amount of funds belonging to any particular client would exceed the value of the client's property. *Brown v. Legal Foundation of Washington*, 538 U.S. 216 (2003). What should happen when the client's funds are significant and may be held for a significant period of time? The Supreme Court decision followed contrasting results in the courts of appeal. *See, e.g., Washington Legal Foundation v. Texas Equal Access to Justice Foundation*, 270 F.3d 180 (5th Cir. 2001) (Texas IOLTA program violates Fifth Amendment); *Washington Legal Foundation v. Legal Foundation of Washington*, 271 F.3d 835 (9th Cir. 2001) (en banc) (Washington state IOLTA program does not produce a taking of property).

2. Individual Lawyer's Duty

Amendments in 1993 and 2002 to Model Rule 6.1 have come as close as the organized bar has to imposing a requirement on individual lawyers to render pro bono service. Nonetheless, even the 2002 version of MR 6.1 remains aspirational and not mandatory. A lawyer is not subject to discipline for failing to render pro bono service.

Model Rule 6.1 sets a goal for each lawyer of 50 hours of pro bono service per year. Model Rule 6.1 suggests some of the following as appropriate for pro bono service — providing service at no fee or reduced fee for those of limited means; service to religious, civic, governmental, educational, or charitable organizations at no fee or reduced fee; activities to improve the law such as bar committees that draft model legislation; and providing financial support for organizations that provide legal service for those of limited means. Model Rule 6.1 encourages lawyers to spend the bulk of their 50 hours per year doing service at no fee either directly for those of limited means or to organizations that directly serve those of limited means.

NOTES, QUESTIONS, AND EXAMPLES

1. Over the years of the Legal Services Corporation's existence, various restrictions on the use of LSC funds have been adopted, effectively limiting the nature of the work that LSC supported lawyers may do on behalf of their clients. In some respects, these limitations may be seen as a third-party interference conflict of interest, with LSC playing the role of a party outside the lawyer-client relationship directing or limiting the actions of the LSC lawyers on behalf of their clients. Challenges have been brought to many of the restrictions, some of which have succeeded. In *LSC v. Velazquez*, 531 U.S. 533 (2001), the Court struck as violative of the First Amendment an LSC restriction on lawyers challenging existing welfare laws. With the restrictions in place, LSC lawyers were permitted to take welfare cases provided they did not challenge the validity or constitutionality of the welfare laws themselves. The Court ruled that this restriction represented viewpoint discrimination in that LSC had facilitated speech on the part of LSC lawyers but had then sought by the restriction to control the viewpoints expressed in that very speech. Other restrictions were simultaneously upheld, including restrictions on undertaking class actions, seeking attorney fees, or undertaking categories of cases involving abortion, reapportionment, and prisoners.

2. As a means of encouraging law firms to engage in pro bono activities, the California legislature has adopted a statute requiring law firms that have substantial contracts with the state to provide pro bono service or risk non-renewal of their state contracts. CAL. BUS. & PROF. CODE § 6072. Such provisions are familiar features of state and federal law with respect to a wide variety of commands tied to receipt of federal and state funds.

Chapter VIII

SPECIAL ROLE-RELATED DUTIES

Although it may actually be accurate to say that the law governing lawyers is somewhat different for every practice setting (that is, the law of lawyering is slightly different depending on whether the lawyer is in a plaintiff's personal injury practice or a criminal defense practice or an in-house corporate practice and so on), several special lawyer roles have such clearly defined duties or responsibility adjustments that they warrant separate study.

The special roles covered in this chapter are those of prosecutor, supervisory or subordinate lawyer, employee, intermediary, and ancillary businessperson. Each of these special roles carries with it special duties and rules governing lawyer conduct. Lawyers in these special roles remain subject to all of the general rules that govern lawyer behavior. An additional special role, that of judge, is covered in Chapter X.

A. SPECIAL DUTIES OF PROSECUTORS

PROBLEM 8-1

Sam Marcio is an elected Prosecutor. Mr. Marcio has a view of law and politics that tends toward a merger of the two. Law, he believes, is the politically acceptable portion of the legislative enactments and applicable court decisions. By this philosophy he rationalizes decisions he must make about whether to charge in a particular case and about how to try a case. He feels a strong obligation to maintain public safety by securing convictions against violent felons. He is preparing his closing argument in a major violent felony case. At the time of arrest, and after receiving his *Miranda* warnings, the defendant made no statement other than to ask for his lawyer to be contacted. At trial, the defendant did not testify. Marcio knows that Supreme Court decisions have held that comments on the accused's silence either at the time of arrest or trial violate the defendant's Fifth Amendment rights against self-incrimination. He also knows that the Supreme Court and the courts of his state jurisdiction have always held single, isolated prosecutorial comments on silence to be harmless error that do not warrant reversal of a conviction. Marcio is considering making such a single, isolated comment during his closing argument (something like, "You watched him during the trial. And you know he did nothing more than sit there and stare."). Having done the research, he is confident that the appellate courts in his jurisdiction will not reverse a conviction on the basis of such a comment. What should he do?

———

Criminal prosecutors have ethical responsibilities in addition to those of other lawyers. Prosecutors represent no individual client but rather the government, or viewed another way, the people of their jurisdiction. In particular, prosecutors, as a matter of criminal law, do not represent the crime victim or a complaining witness. Charged with representing the public's interests rather than those of an individual litigant, prosecutors are required to seek justice rather than mere victory in their litigation work. There are a variety of remedies for unprofessional conduct by a prosecutor, most of which are substantially more valuable to the victim of the prosecutor's conduct than is bar discipline.

1.   Avoid Conflicts with Private Interests

Prosecutors, often part-time prosecutors, may also represent private clients. Prosecutors must avoid conflicts between the representation of private clients and the prosecutor's duty to seek justice on behalf of the public. As well, prosecutors, as public officials, have different conflict of interest avoidance responsibilities than do other lawyers.

IN RE MORRISSEY
248 Va. 334 (1994)

Opinion by JUSTICE HENRY H. WHITING from the Circuit Court of the City of Richmond

This case was heard on an amended complaint filed by the Virginia State Bar charging Joseph Dee Morrissey, then the Commonwealth's Attorney for the City of Richmond, with violations of a number of disciplinary rules in connection with his prosecution of felony charges against Robert William Molyneux, III. Although the trial court dismissed a number of the charges, it found that Morrissey violated the following disciplinary rules:

DR 1-102(A)(4) Misconduct.—

DR 8-101(A)(3) Action as a Public Official.—

Accordingly, the court ordered that Morrissey's license to practice law be suspended for six months. Morrissey appeals, and the State Bar assigns cross-error.

Molyneux was charged with the abduction and rape of Debra Jean Nuckols in Richmond. Molyneux's father employed James S. Yoffy, a Richmond attorney, to represent Molyneux, who was indigent.

Nuckols and Molyneux each gave inconsistent statements concerning the incident. At first, Nuckols claimed that she did not know Molyneux before he accosted and raped her in an alley as she was walking home from a Richmond night club in the early morning hours of June 9, 1991; however, Nuckols later admitted that she had danced with Molyneux while she was in the night club and had agreed to let him accompany her as she walked home. Molyneux also initially denied having had sexual intercourse with Nuckols, but when DNA tests later indicated the presence of his semen on Nuckol's underpants, he admitted commission of the act, but claimed it was consensual.

Independent DNA tests of Nuckols' clothing, arranged by Yoffy and paid for by Molyneux's father, produced other apparent inconsistencies in Nuckols' version of the incident. Nuckols claimed that she had not had sexual intercourse in the five weeks preceding her alleged rape by Molyneux, yet the DNA tests of semen samples found in her underpants disclosed the presence of semen from Molyneux and another male. Further, Nuckols said that Molyneux had urinated on her during the incident, but chemical tests failed to disclose the presence of urine on Nuckol's clothing.

Recognizing the problems in their respective cases, the two attorneys began to explore the possibility of a plea agreement. After Morrissey alluded to the cost to Molyneux's father of investigating Molyneux's case, Yoffy approached Morrissey about the possibility of settlement of the felony charges on an "accord and satisfaction" basis. In exchange for a nolle prosequi of the abduction charge and a reduction of the rape charge to a charge of sexual battery, a misdemeanor, Molyneux was willing to agree to a 12-month sentence on the misdemeanor. The sentence was to be suspended upon the condition of his payment of court costs and completion of a period of probation, community service, and psychiatric counseling.

Additionally, Yoffy suggested that Molyneux would pay the victim "for her alleged damages," although no specific amount was discussed. According to Yoffy, Morrissey "liked the idea," but told Yoffy that he did not think that Nuckols would settle for less than $25,000. Further, Morrissey said that if Nuckols "was going to get some money then the Commonwealth is going to get something out if it and [Morrissey] wanted $25,000" as partial funding of a television program called "Prosecutor's Corner." Explaining the program to Yoffy, Morrissey said that he "would be the focal point and he would have guests on, [to] explain prosecution oriented issues." Believing that this was an inappropriate use of the money, Yoffy told Morrissey that "perhaps a charity would be a better beneficiary than something more related to him."

In a later meeting, Yoffy told Morrissey that "a charity was acceptable to my client and that I had $50,000 to work with." Morrissey then told Yoffy that if the parties agreed to a settlement, Morrissey wanted the Commonwealth's share of the money to be contributed to several charities which he would select.

At Yoffy's request, Morrissey arranged to meet with Nuckols and Yoffy so that Yoffy could offer Nuckols $25,000 as an "accord and satisfaction." Before this meeting, Morrissey asked Yoffy not to tell Nuckols about the additional $25,000 to be paid to the charities.

At the time of the meeting, Nuckols was aware of all the conditions of the proposed plea agreement, except the proposed charitable contributions by Molyneux's father. During the meeting, Morrissey made it clear that if Nuckols accepted the offer, the criminal charges would be disposed of by plea agreement; however, if she rejected the offer, the charges would be prosecuted. After pointing out to Nuckols some of the inconsistencies in her statements, Yoffy "offered her $25,000 to settle the case." Yoffy was asked to leave the room so that Nuckols could discuss the matter with Morrissey.

Upon being asked his opinion of the offer, Morrissey told Nuckols that if she "were his sister that he would strongly suggest to her that she consider the offer." When Nuckols later indicated that she would consider an offer of $100,000, Morrissey replied that "the offer was not up for negotiation." After hearing that Nuckols had rejected his offer, Yoffy suggested a reduction of the charities' share with a corresponding increase of Nuckols' share. Morrissey rejected this idea, insisting that the Commonwealth receive an equal amount of the settlement.

Thereafter, in preparation for the felony trial, Yoffy filed a motion in limine to obtain a ruling regarding the introduction of a psychiatrist's opinion indicating that Nuckols "could very well have made this attack up" because of a mental illness that had occurred five years earlier. Although Morrissey advised Yoffy that he did not plan to have Nuckols testify in the hearing on his motion, Morrissey told Yoffy that he planned to have her there "so she could appreciate what it would be like to be a witness and what evidence might come in against her."

At the hearing on August 18, 1992, Nuckols found the psychiatrist's testimony regarding her psychiatric past "very painful" and she was "devastated at the thought that it cold be used at the actual trial." When the Honorable Thomas N. Nance, the judge presiding at the hearing and the subsequent criminal trial, told the lawyers in a side-bar conference that the evidence would not be admitted, Yoffy asked the court to withhold its ruling because the lawyers were negotiating "civil aspects" of the case. Judge Nance withheld a formal ruling and also indicated to the lawyers that he "[did not] want to hear anything about . . . a civil case."

After the hearing, when Nuckols asked Morrissey whether the psychiatric evidence would be admissible, Morrissey responded that he did not know. Nuckols then asked Morrissey if he thought that the offer of settlement was still available. Later, Morrissey called Nuckols and told her that the offer was still available and that he had "basically settled it on [her] behalf." At Morrissey's request, Nuckols wrote him a letter indicating that the Commonwealth was "ready to go forward with the case but I wanted to accept the offer and to thank them for their support."

Shortly thereafter, Molyneux, Yoffy, and Morrissey appeared before Judge Nance to obtain court acceptance of their plea agreement. Moments before that hearing, Morrissey asked Yoffy not to tell the court about the part of the agreement relating to the proposed contributions of Molyneux's father to charities of Morrissey's choice.

At the hearing, Morrissey proffered the Commonwealth's evidence and advised the court of all the terms of the plea agreement except for the father's $25,000 payments to Nuckols and to the charities. Acting on this information and Molyneux's guilty plea to the misdemeanor of sexual battery, the court found Molyneux guilty, sentenced him, and suspended the sentence upon the conditions disclosed to the court by Morrissey. The court also sustained the Commonwealth's motion to nolle prosequi the abduction charge. Thereafter, Molyneux's father delivered $50,000 to Yoffy in accordance with the agreement.

*　　*　　*

II. MORRISSEY'S VIOLATION OF DR 8-101(A)(3)

The evidence is clear that the charitable contributions were made to influence Morrissey's action as Commonwealth's Attorney in the plea bargaining process. The issue here is whether these payments constituted something of value to Morrissey in violation of DR 8-101(A)(3).

At the time of the plea bargaining negotiations in the summer of 1992, Morrissey knew that he would face a reelection campaign in 1993. When Yoffy rejected Morrissey's proposal to use the $25,000 for the television program "Prosecutor's Corner" and told Morrissey that "a charity" would be acceptable to his client, Yoffy had planned to have Molyneux's father make the charitable contributions himself in order to qualify for a tax deduction. However, during the negotiations, Yoffy got the impression that Morrissey wanted Yoffy to make the contributions from the father's funds, and that such contributions would be made to several major charities named by Morrissey.

After Molyneux was convicted and the money had been deposited with Yoffy, Morrissey directed Yoffy to make the first disbursement of $7,000 by having cashier's checks prepared to eight local charitable organizations in sums ranging from $250 to $2,000 and delivering those checks to Morrissey's office. When Yoffy expressed his concern that Morrissey was planning to use the checks for political purposes, Morrissey responded, "[w] e've got a deal and you better live up to it." Yoffy took this statement as a threat that Morrissey might have Molyneux re-indicted on the abduction charge that had been nol-prossed pursuant to the plea agreement. Accordingly, at Morrissey's direction, Yoffy issued and delivered to Morrissey 47 checks totaling nearly $25,000 payable to the various charities named by Morrissey. Almost all the charities were located in Richmond.

Morrissey's letters reflected a number of methods by which he delivered these checks and informed each charity that he had chosen it as the recipient of a donation from an anonymous donor. In one instance, Morrissey confirmed by letter to the pastor of one church in Richmond that a $2,000 donation "by an anonymous donor" had been delivered by Morrissey during his visit to the church the preceding Sunday and "[a]s I indicated in my brief remarks, I was given the donation and allowed to make it to the charity of my choice." In other instances, Morrissey mailed the checks following telephone conversations with representatives of the charities, or simply mailed the check with a cover letter, but Morrissey never failed to let the donee charity know that he had selected that charity as the donee of the gift.

In our opinion, Morrissey's carefully orchestrated scheme was designed to secure something of value to Morrissey — the possibility that members of the donee charities would express their gratitude in the form of political support in the forthcoming election. Accordingly, we conclude that the evidence clearly supports the trial court's conclusion that Morrissey violated DR 8-101(A)(3).

*   *   *

Therefore, the judgment of the trial court will be Affirmed.

2. Dismissal of Charges Not Supported by Probable Cause

Paralleling the general lawyer duty to refrain from bringing claims or taking positions that are frivolous (*see* MR 3.1), prosecutors are prohibited from prosecuting charges that the prosecutor knows are not supported by probable cause, the usual standard below which judges will not issue warrants and will dismiss charges at preliminary hearings. MR 3.8(a).

3. Disclosure of Exculpatory Evidence

Prosecutors must timely disclose exculpatory evidence and mitigating circumstances regarding sentencing. MR 3.8(d). This ethics rule obligation parallels the right of the accused under the Due Process Clause to be provided access to such materials.

BRADY v. MARYLAND
373 U.S. 83 (1963)

Opinion of the Court by MR. JUSTICE DOUGLAS, announced by MR. JUSTICE BRENNAN.

Petitioner and a companion, Boblit, were found guilty of murder in the first degree and were sentenced to death, their convictions being affirmed by the Court of Appeals of Maryland. Their trials were separate, petitioner being tried first. At his trial Brady took the stand and admitted his participation in the crime, but he claimed that Boblit did the actual killing. And, in his summation to the jury, Brady's counsel conceded that Brady was guilty of murder in the first degree, asking only that the jury return that verdict "without capital punishment." Prior to the trial petitioner's counsel had requested the prosecution to allow him to examine Boblit's extrajudicial statements. Several of those statements were shown to him; but one dated July 9, 1958, in which Boblit admitted the actual homicide, was withheld by the prosecution and did not come to petitioner's notice until after he had been tried, convicted, and sentenced, and after his conviction had been affirmed.

Petitioner moved the trial court for a new trial based on the newly discovered evidence that had been suppressed by the prosecution. Petitioner's appeal from a denial of that motion was dismissed by the Court of Appeals without prejudice to relief under the Maryland Post Conviction Procedure Act. The petition for post-conviction relief was dismissed by the trial court; and on appeal the Court of Appeals held that suppression of the evidence by the prosecution denied petitioner due process of law and remanded the case for a retrial of the question of punishment, not the question of guilt. The case is here on *certiorari*.

*   *   *

We agree with the Court of Appeals that suppression of this confession was a violation of the Due Process Clause of the Fourteenth Amendment. The Court of Appeals relied in the main on two decisions from the Third Circuit Court of Appeals — *United States ex rel. Almeida v. Baldi*, 195 F.2d 815, and *United States ex rel.*

Thompson v. Dye, 221 F.2d 763 — which, we agree, state the correct constitutional rule.

This ruling is an extension of *Mooney v. Holohan*, 294 U.S. 103, 112, where the Court ruled on what nondisclosure by a prosecutor violates due process:

> It is a requirement that cannot be deemed to be satisfied by mere notice and hearing if a State has contrived a conviction through the pretense of a trial which in truth is but used as a means of depriving a defendant of liberty through a deliberate deception of court and jury by the presentation of testimony known to be perjured. Such a contrivance by a State to procure the conviction and imprisonment of a defendant is as inconsistent with the rudimentary demands of justice as is the obtaining of a like result by intimidation.

The Third Circuit in the *Baldi* case construed that statement in *Pyle v. Kansas* to mean that the "suppression of evidence favorable" to the accused was itself sufficient to amount to a denial of due process. In *Napue v. Illinois*, 360 U.S. 264, 269, we extended the test formulated in *Mooney v. Holohan* when we said: "The same result obtains when the State, although not soliciting false evidence, allows it to go uncorrected when it appears."

We now hold that the suppression by the prosecution of evidence favorable to an accused upon request violates due process where the evidence is material either to guilt or to punishment, irrespective of the good faith or bad faith of the prosecution.

The principle of *Mooney v. Holohan* is not punishment of society for misdeeds of a prosecutor but avoidance of an unfair trial to the accused. Society wins not only when the guilty are convicted but when criminal trials are fair; our system of the administration of justice suffers when any accused is treated unfairly. An inscription on the walls of the Department of Justice states the proposition candidly for the federal domain: "The United States wins its point whenever justice is done its citizens in the courts."[1] A prosecution that withholds evidence on demand of an accused which, if made available, would tend to exculpate him or reduce the penalty helps shape a trial that bears heavily on the defendant. That casts the prosecutor in the role of an architect of a proceeding that does not comport with standards of justice, even though, as in the present case, his action is not "the result of guile," to use the words of the Court of Appeals. 226 Md. at 427, 174 A.2d at 169.

*   *   *

Affirmed.

---

[1] [2] Judge Simon E. Sobeloff when Solicitor General put the idea as follows in an address before the Judicial Conference of the Fourth Circuit on June 29, 1954:

> The Solicitor General is not a neutral, he is an advocate; but an advocate for a client whose business is not merely to prevail in the instant case. My client's chief business is not to achieve victory but to establish justice. We are constantly reminded of the now classic words penned by one of my illustrious predecessors, Frederick William Lehmann, that the Government wins its point when justice is done in its courts.

READ v. VIRGINIA STATE BAR
357 S.E.2d 544 (Va. 1987)

THOMAS, J.

This is an appeal of right from an order of the State Bar Disciplinary Board (the Board) revoking Beverly C. John Read's license to practice law. The Board found that Read violated Disciplinary Rules 1-102(A)(3) and 8-102(A)(4), which provide respectively as follows: "A lawyer shall not . . . [c]ommit a crime or other deliberately wrongful act that reflects adversely on a lawyer's fitness to practice law" and "The prosecutor in a criminal case or a government lawyer shall . . . [d]isclose to a defendant all information required by law." At the time of the conduct complained of, Read was the Commonwealth's Attorney for Rockbridge County. The State Bar contends that in the midst of a criminal trial, Read failed to disclose certain exculpatory evidence. Based on this failing, the Board ordered that Read be disbarred. We reverse.

Read was the prosecutor in the case of *Commonwealth v. Mesner.* The defendant was charged with arson and murder in a fire at a Washington and Lee University fraternity house. The fire occurred in April 1984. The trial was scheduled for December 1984.

On October 2, 1984, Mesner's counsel filed a Motion for Discovery and Inspection in which they requested, among other things, all exculpatory evidence. The motion was never formally granted and no order was ever formally entered. However, the trial court addressed the discovery requests in a letter dated November 8, 1984. That letter was treated by all counsel as the discovery order. It provided in pertinent part as follows:

> The pretrial discovery order in this case . . . must adhere . . . (2) to the limitations of the rule set down in *Brady v. Maryland*; and (3) to Rule 3A:11 of the Virginia Rules.

* * *

> Clearly, the Commonwealth has to prove beyond a reasonable doubt that (1) the fire was incendiary in origin (arson) and (2) the defendant was the agent thereof. Under the Virginia Rules, any scientific report which addresses the first prong of proof is discoverable and I hereby order that it be produced. Secondly, any information that may exculpate the defendant as the agent thereof must be disclosed. Since identification is a key element in this particular case, I direct that the [identity] of any material witness who failed to identify the defendant in a photograph lineup be made known to the defendant.

* * *

> The discovery order shall direct that the duty to disclose exculpatory evidence to the defendant is a continuing duty.

During the investigation into the crimes, the Commonwealth learned that Peter Sils and Jean Dunbar, husband and wife, who lived near the fraternity house, went to the scene during the fire and saw a suspicious acting man near a bicycle. The Commonwealth sought to prove that Mesner was the man near the bicycle. At a pretrial conference, the Commonwealth revealed the names of Dunbar and Sils as witnesses who would testify on the Commonwealth's behalf.

At a lineup the day before trial, Dunbar was unable to make an identification. Sils, however, picked Mesner as the man he had seen at the fire. Defense counsel were present at the lineup and were aware that Dunbar could not make an identification.

Shortly after leaving the lineup, Sils had second thoughts about his identification. Sils expressed his concerns to a clerk in Read's office. An assistant commonwealth's attorney visited Sils at home that night. Sils again expressed his doubts.

The trial began on Wednesday, December 19, 1984. Sils was under subpoena from the Commonwealth. While present at the courthouse, he observed Mesner entering and leaving the courtroom. Sils became convinced that Mesner was not the man Sils had seen at the fire. After the trial recessed for the day, Sils told Read that he was certain Mesner was not the man he had seen at the fire. Read then asked whether Sils could say Mesner looked like the man. Sils said he could but that he would have to add that he was certain Mesner was not the man.

On the next day of trial, Thursday, Sils was again present at the courthouse. At the end of the day Sils was told he would not be called as a witness and that his presence was no longer required.

When Sils returned home, he and his wife became concerned that Sils' changed testimony would never be presented to the jury. They called defense counsel to explain their position. The next morning, before trial resumed for the third day, Sils and Dunbar met with defense counsel. Both explained that they were convinced Mesner was not the man they had seen at the fire. Both agreed to testify on Mesner's behalf.

When the trial resumed, Read rested the Commonwealth's case without calling Sils and without telling defense counsel of Sils' change in testimony. At that point, Eric Sisler, one of defendant's lawyers, turned to an associate and told him to tell Sils and Dunbar to get ready to testify. Immediately thereafter, Read attempted to say something to Sisler. Sisler would not listen. Read then wrote something on a legal pad but Sisler would not accept the paper. The transcript next shows that Read stated, on the record, that Sisler would not permit him to pass along "this information." Read then stated for the record the names of Peter Sils and Jean Dunbar and described them as identification witnesses who had changed their testimony from placing Mesner at the scene of the fire to stating that the person they had seen at the fire was not Mesner. Read further advised the Court that he had tried to give the information to Sisler but Sisler "didn't want to hear it."

After this exchange, defense counsel moved to strike the Commonwealth's case and moved to dismiss for prosecutorial misconduct. The motion to strike was denied. The motion to dismiss was granted for reasons unrelated to the failure of the Commonwealth's Attorney to give defense counsel Sils' name.

Read was first charged with misconduct at the district committee level. The Sixth

District Committee of the Bar found a violation of DR 8-102(A)(4) and DR 1-102(A)(3). According to the district committee, Read failed to disclose that Jean Dunbar and Peter Sils had recanted their previously incriminating identification of the defendant and had told [Read], in the case of Sils, that he was sure the defendant was not the man sought to be identified.

The district committee recommended a private reprimand. Read demanded a redetermination of that private reprimand by the Board.

The Board said that the issue before it was whether Read was "required by law" to disclose to defense counsel Sils' change in position. The Board concluded that Read was required to make the disclosure because Sils' changed testimony was exculpatory. The Board made reference to the trial court's November 8, 1984 letter and to a subsequent pretrial conference where the trial court again admonished Read to disclose exculpatory information. The Board pointed out that Read "made no effort to disclose the exculpatory information before the time the Commonwealth rested." The Board stated that Read made "a conscious decision not to reveal Sils' change in position." The Board then concluded that Read "would have knowingly permitted Mesner to be convicted of arson and murder without permitting the jury to consider Sils' testimony that the man on the bicycle at the scene of the fire was not Mesner." The Board imposed the sanction of revocation.

The State Bar contends that Read violated two portions of the trial court's November 8 letter: the portion concerning *Brady v. Maryland*, 373 U.S. 83 (1963), and the portion concerning Rule 3A:11. According to the State Bar, both factors define what Read was "required by law" to disclose. Read argues that he complied with both *Brady* and Rule 3A:11. We agree with Read.

We hold that there was no *Brady* violation in this case. Defense counsel knew of Sils' change in testimony in sufficient time to make use of his testimony at trial. In *United States v. Darwin*, 757 F.2d 1193 (11th Cir. 1985), the defendant complained that *Brady* was violated because the government failed to reveal certain information about a witness until after the witness had testified even though the government had been aware of the information for four days prior to disclosure. The Eleventh Circuit rejected the *Brady* claim:

> The point in the trial when a disclosure is made . . . is not itself determinative of timeliness. We agree with those circuits holding that a defendant must show that the failure to earlier disclose prejudiced him because it came so late that the information disclosed could not be effectively used at trial.

The United States Court of Appeals for the Tenth Circuit wrote as follows with regard to the timing of disclosures required by *Brady*: "This circuit has previously concluded that *Brady* is not violated when *Brady* material is available to defendants during trial." *United States v. Behrens*, 689 F.2d 154 (10th Cir. 1982). Read did not violate the trial court's letter order with regard to *Brady*. Nor did Read violate the portion of the November 8 letter that rests upon the requirements of Rule 3A:11. That rule does not concern disclosure of the type of information complained of in this case.' Disclosure of the name of a witness who changed his testimony in a way beneficial to the defendant is simply not the subject of Rule 3A:11. Therefore, the

State Bar's reliance upon Rule 3A:11 to establish Read's violation of law is misplaced.

We hold that there was no violation of DR 8-102(A)(4). Further, we are of opinion that the conclusion that Read violated DR 1-102(A)(3) was predicated upon the violation of DR 8-102(A)(4). Consequently, we hold that there was no violation of DR 1-102(A)(3).

In light of the foregoing, we will reverse the order of the Disciplinary Board and dismiss the case.

Reversed and dismissed.

NOTES, QUESTIONS, AND EXAMPLES

Enforcement of *Brady*-type violations by bar discipline authorities and by the Department of Justice's internal disciplinary process for U.S. attorneys has been notoriously lax. The issues have received more prominent attention since the 2009 prosecution of Senator Ted Stevens, which essentially fell apart as a result of uncovered Brady violations by federal prosecutors. The judge in the *Stevens* matter eschewed reliance on the internal DOJ disciplinary process and appointed an investigator in the matter. Subsequent to this case and other high-profile reversals of convictions for *Brady* violations, DOJ launched extensive training programs for federal prosecutors. *See, e.g.*, U.S. Attorney Touts Brady Reforms, http://www.mainjustice.com/2010/11/05/u-s-attorney-touts-brady-reform/   and Holder Pushes Back Against News Reports on Prosecutorial Misconduct, http://www.mainjustice.com/tag/brady-violations/.

4. Investigative Limits

In addition to the controversial application of Model Rule 4.2 (the no-contact rule) to prosecutors (*see* Chapter VI), other limits on the prosecutor's investigative tools exist.

COLORADO v. REICHMAN
819 P.2d 1035 (Colo. 1991)

PER CURIAM.

This is an attorney discipline case. A hearing panel approved the findings and recommendation of a majority of the hearing board that the respondent receive a public censure for conduct involving dishonesty, fraud, deceit or misrepresentation, and conduct prejudicial to the administration of justice. We accept the recommendation of the hearing panel and publicly censure the respondent and order that he be assessed the costs of these proceedings.

I

The respondent was admitted to the bar of this court on October 2, 1973, is registered on the official records of this court, and is subject to the jurisdiction of this court and its grievance committee. At all times relevant to this proceeding, the respondent was the duly appointed or elected District Attorney of the Sixth Judicial District, which includes La Plata County.

The complaint filed by the special assistant disciplinary counsel charged the respondent with violations of DR 1-102(A)(4) (a lawyer shall not engage in conduct involving dishonesty, fraud, deceit, or misrepresentation); DR 1- 102(A)(5) (a lawyer shall not engage in conduct prejudicial to the administration of justice); and DR 1-102(A)(6) (a lawyer shall not engage in any other conduct that adversely reflects on his fitness to practice law).[2] At the hearing, the board heard testimony from witnesses, including the respondent and certain expert witnesses, and received exhibits into evidence by stipulation of the parties. A majority of the hearing board found that the following facts were established by clear and convincing evidence.

In the spring of 1987, the respondent and other members of law enforcement in the Sixth Judicial District formed a de facto task force, or "LEADS committee," to conduct undercover operations to investigate and prosecute drug trafficking in the district. A police officer from outside the judicial district was retained to conduct the undercover investigations, and the officer chose the fictitious identity of one "Colton Young," an unemployed biker. The respondent served as the head of the task force.

After several months undercover, "Young" had developed a list of names of suspected drug traffickers in the judicial district. In addition, two individuals had told "Young" that an attorney, Robin K. Auld, accepted drugs in lieu of fees.[3] Then, in September 1987, "Young" called an emergency meeting of the task force to announce that he believed his undercover identity may have been compromised. The task force decided to rehabilitate "Young's" identity. With the respondent's approval, "Young" was "arrested" for a traffic violation on the main street of Durango outside of the business establishment of a significant target of the task force. Auld was not this target. A search of "Young" was then conducted in such a way that the fruits of the search could be easily suppressed and the charges dismissed. "Young" was instructed to contact Robin Auld and retain him as defense counsel. See *People v. Auld*, 788 P.2d 1275 (Colo. 1990).[4]

---

[2] [1] The complaint did not charge the respondent with violating provisions of DR 7-102 (which prohibit a lawyer from making false statements of law or fact or creating or preserving false evidence, and require a lawyer to promptly disclose to a tribunal the fact that a person has perpetrated a fraud on the tribunal); DR 7-103(A) (a public prosecutor shall not institute criminal charges when he knows that the charges are not supported by probable cause); or DR 7-103(B) (which requires a public prosecutor to timely disclose to counsel for the defendant the existence of evidence known to the prosecutor that tends to negate the guilt of the accused). We therefore do not discuss whether these disciplinary rules apply to the respondent's conduct in this case.

[3] [2] On March 19, 1990, this court suspended Robin K. Auld from the practice of law for six months for his involvement in the occurrences which form the basis for this proceeding.

[4] [3] The actual objective of the "arrest" and the filing of the fictitious charges against "Young" was

As part of the plan, fictitious charges were lodged against "Young" with the respondent's knowledge and approval. The respondent, either personally or through his agents, filed a false criminal complaint against "Young," charging him with the illegal possession of a firearm and of marihuana in the County Court of La Plata County. Other documents filed by or on behalf of the respondent in the "Young" case included a surety bond and an offense report, falsely stating "Young's" name and address, and falsely stating that "Young" had committed certain criminal offenses. In addition, with the respondent's knowledge and approval, "Young" appeared in county court and made false statements to the county judge, who was unaware of the deception.[5]

II

A majority of the hearing board concluded that the respondent's conduct in filing the false documents and the fictitious criminal complaint, and otherwise creating and maintaining the deception of the county court, violated DR 1-102(A)(4) (conduct involving dishonesty or misrepresentation), and DR 1-102(A)(5) (conduct prejudicial to the administration of justice).

The respondent argues that his conduct was not unethical and he points to a number of cases in which prosecutors engaged in deception during "sting" operations, including *United States v. Martino*, 825 F.2d 754 (3d Cir. 1987), and *United States v. Murphy*, 768 F.2d 1518 (7th Cir. 1985), *cert. denied*, 475 U.S. 1012 (1986).

In *United States v. Martino*, 825 F.2d 754 (3d Cir. 1987), the Third Circuit held that the issuance of a grand jury subpoena to an undercover FBI agent in the pseudonym under which the agent was working was not prosecutorial misconduct. Since grand jury subpoenas are widely recognized as instrumentalities of the executive branch for investigatory or prosecutorial purposes, the integrity of the judicial process was not compromised in appearance or actuality by the issuance of the sham subpoena.

United States v. Murphy, 768 F.2d 1518 (7th Cir. 1985), *cert. denied*, 475 U.S. 1012 (1986), discussed the participation of the FBI and federal prosecutors in Operation Greylord. The defendant in Murphy, a former associate judge of the Circuit Court of Cook County, Illinois, was convicted of accepting bribes to fix the outcomes of hundreds of criminal cases that came before him. As part of Operation Greylord, FBI agents posed as corrupt lawyers, and other agents testified in made-up criminal cases heard by Judge Murphy. Murphy argued that his convictions were invalid because the Operation Greylord "cases" were frauds on the court, and the undercover agents committed perjury. The court of appeals disagreed, finding

---

hotly disputed. The special assistant disciplinary counsel sought to establish that the respondent's intention was to coerce Auld into betraying Auld's client or clients. The hearing board did not find that this was the respondent's design by clear and convincing evidence. For the purpose of this opinion, we assume that the respondent's intention was to rehabilitate "Young's" undercover identity.

[5] [4] The respondent makes much of the alleged fact that "Young's" statements to the county judge were not made under oath and thus were not testimony. We find such legal hair-splitting immaterial on the question of whether the respondent violated the Code of Professional Responsibility.

that while the agents' acts appeared criminal, the acts were not crimes because they were performed without the requisite criminal intent. Further, *Murphy* held:

> The FBI and prosecutors behaved honorably in establishing and running Operation Greylord. They assure us that they notified the Presiding Judge of the Circuit Court's Criminal Division, the State's Attorney of Cook County, the Attorney General of Illinois, and the Governor of Illinois. Such notice may not be necessary, and certainly a criminal defendant is in no position to complain of the absence of such notice (for he has no personal right to protect the dignity of the Cook County courts), but the notice dispels any argument that the federal Government has offended some principle requiring respect of the internal operations of the state courts.

Prosecutorial deception may not always constitute prosecutorial misconduct for purposes of determining whether a criminal complaint or indictment must be dismissed. It does not necessarily follow, however, that prosecutorial deception of a type which results in directly misleading a court should be exempted from the proscriptions of the Code of Professional Responsibility simply because the deception is not such as to warrant the dismissal of a criminal case.

In *In re Malone,* 105 A.D.2d 455, 480 N.Y.S.2d 603 (1984), *aff'd,* 65 N.Y.2d 772, 492 N.Y.S.2d 947, 482 N.E.2d 565 (1985), the appellate division publicly censured an attorney for his conduct while serving as Inspector General of the New York State Department of Correctional Facilities. During an investigation into the alleged beating of an inmate by several correction officers, the inspector general instructed a correction officer, who was acting as an informant, to lie under oath during an interview conducted in the course of an internal investigation into the beating. The purpose of the deceit was "to protect [the correctional officer] willing to risk retaliation for breaking the correction officers' 'code of silence'. . . . ." The inspector general argued, inter alia, that his conduct was not unethical because it was in accordance with ethical canons requiring the competent and zealous representation of clients, there was precedent for the use of false testimony in the investigation and prosecution of crimes, and because his motive to protect the witness outweighed any ethical breach. The appellate division rejected each argument.

First, the court reasoned that the ethical canons requiring competent and zealous representation cannot in themselves overcome the disciplinary rule, DR 1-102(A)(4), which prohibits an attorney from directing another to testify falsely. *Malone.* . . . Second, while there may be precedent that the creation of false documents and the use of false testimony in the investigation and prosecution of crime may not be so violative of a criminal defendant's due process rights to warrant dismissal of a criminal indictment, such conduct may still be unethical. Finally, citing Friedman, the appellate division refused to accept the inspector general's third argument — that his conduct was not unethical because he was motivated by the desire to protect the witness and by his public responsibilities. This argument is the equivalent of the contention that the end justifies the means, and "that pernicious doctrine," *Olmstead v. United States,* 277 U.S. 438, 485 (1928) (Brandeis, J., dissenting),[6] is unacceptable in the administration of the criminal law. Noting

---

[6] [5] As Justice Brandeis said in dissent in *Olmstead*: Decency, security and liberty alike demand that

that the purpose of disciplinary sanctions is not punishment but the protection of the public, and also noting that it was a case of first impression in New York and that the inspector general seemingly acted out of laudable motives, the appellate division imposed a public censure.

We agree with the reasoning in Malone, and we conclude, as did the hearing panel and the majority of the hearing board, that the respondent's conduct violated DR 1-102(A)(1), and DR 1-102(A)(5). District attorneys in Colorado owe a very high duty to the public because they are governmental officials holding constitutionally created offices. This court has spoken out strongly against misconduct by public officials who are lawyers. The respondent's responsibility to enforce the laws in his judicial district grants him no license to ignore those laws or the Code of Professional Responsibility. While the respondent's motives and the erroneous belief of other public prosecutors that the respondent's conduct was ethical do not excuse these violations of the Code of Professional Responsibility, they are mitigating factors to be taken into account in assessing the appropriate discipline. The respondent has no prior discipline.

We find, therefore, that the respondent's misconduct warrants discipline consistent with our duties to protect the public and maintain the integrity of the legal profession.

III

Accordingly, we accept the recommendation of the hearing panel and publicly censure the respondent Victor Reichman. While the surrounding circumstances may tend to explain and mitigate the misconduct, they do not excuse the deception imposed on the court. We therefore publicly reprimand Reichman and assess him the costs of these proceedings in the amount of $4,851.28.

NOTES, QUESTIONS, AND EXAMPLES

In *Williams v. Taylor*, 529 U.S. 420 (2000), the Court held that a prosecutor's failure to inform the court of a prospective juror's misleading statements during voir dire warranted an evidentiary hearing regarding juror and prosecutorial misconduct. The Court discussed the issue as follows:

> Petitioner's claims are based on two of the questions posed to the jurors by the trial judge at *voir dire*. First, the judge asked prospective jurors, "Are any of you related to the following people who may be called as witnesses?" Then he read the jurors a list of names, one of which was "Deputy Sheriff Claude Meinhard." Bonnie Stinnett, who would later

government officials shall be subjected to the same rules of conduct that are commands to the citizen. In a government of laws, existence of the government will be imperiled if it fails to observe the law scrupulously. Our Government is the potent, the omnipresent teacher. For good or for ill, it teaches the whole people by its example. Crime is contagious. If the Government becomes a lawbreaker, it breeds contempt for law; it invites every man to become a law unto himself; it invites anarchy. To declare that in the administration of the criminal law the end justifies the means — to declare that the Government may commit crimes in order to secure the conviction of a private criminal — would bring terrible retribution. Against that pernicious doctrine this Court should resolutely set its face.

become the jury foreperson, had divorced Meinhard in 1979, after a 17-year marriage with four children. Stinnett remained silent, indicating the answer was "no." Meinhard, as the officer who investigated the crime scene and interrogated [Williams' co-defendant], would later become the prosecution's lead-off witness at trial.

After reading the names of the attorneys involved in the case, including one of the prosecutors, Robert Woodson, Jr., the judge asked, "Have you or any member of your immediate family ever been represented by any of the aforementioned attorneys?" Stinnett again said nothing, despite the fact Woodson had represented her during her divorce from Meinhard.

In an affidavit she provided in the federal habeas proceedings, Stinnett claimed "[she] did not respond to the judge's [first] question because [she] did not consider [herself] 'related' to Claude Meinhard in 1994 [at *voir dire*] . . . . Once our marriage ended in 1979, I was no longer related to him." As for Woodson's earlier representation of her, Stinnett explained as follows:

> When Claude and I divorced in 1979, the divorce was uncontested and Mr. Woodson drew up the papers so that the divorce could be completed. Since neither Claude nor I was contesting anything, I didn't think Mr. Woodson "represented" either one of us.

Woodson provided an affidavit in which he admitted "[he] was aware that Juror Bonnie Stinnett was the ex-wife of then Deputy Sheriff Claude Meinhard and [he] was aware that they had been divorced for some time." Woodson stated, however, "to [his] mind, people who are related only by marriage are no longer 'related' once the marriage ends in divorce." Woodson also "had no recollection of having been involved as a private attorney in the divorce proceedings between Claude Meinhard and Bonnie Stinnett." He explained that "whatever [his] involvement was in the 1979 divorce, by the time of trial in 1994 [he] had completely forgotten about it." [The district court later noted that Woodson, concerned about any ill-feelings Stinnett might harbor for Meinhard, had approached Meinhard during the voir dire of Stinnett to ask Meinhard about the quality of Meinhard's post-divorce relationship with his ex-wife Stinnett. —Ed.]

Even if Stinnett had been correct in her technical or literal interpretation of the question relating to Meinhard, her silence after the first question was asked could suggest to the finder of fact an unwillingness to be forthcoming; this in turn could bear on the veracity of her explanation for not disclosing that Woodson had been her attorney. Stinnett's failure to divulge material information in response to the second question was misleading as a matter of fact because, under any interpretation, Woodson had acted as counsel to her and Meinhard in their divorce. Coupled with Woodson's own reticence, these omissions as a whole disclose the need for an evidentiary hearing. It may be that petitioner could establish that Stinnett was not impartial, or that Woodson's silence so infected the trial as to deny due process.

Upon remand, and following an evidentiary hearing, the district court granted the habeas petition on both grounds, holding that the prosecutor had violated his duty to report juror misconduct under Virginia's version of DR 7-108(G) (now embedded in MR 4.4). *Williams v. Netherland*, 181 F. Supp. 2d 604 (E.D. Va. 2002), *aff'd as Williams v. Tru e*, 39 F. App'x 830 (4th Cir. 2002).

B.   SPECIAL DUTIES OF SUPERVISING AND SUBORDINATE LAWYERS

More frequently than ever before, lawyers practice in settings that involve employer-employee relationships. Within those relationships, some lawyers supervise the work of other lawyers, and lawyers frequently supervise the work of non-lawyer subordinates. Under certain circumstances, supervising lawyers will be ethically responsible for the acts of their subordinates, both lawyer and nonlawyer. Under certain circumstances, subordinate lawyers will be relieved of ethical responsibility for their actions.

1.   Lawyers Subordinate to Other Lawyers

Subordinate lawyers are not relieved of the duty to follow the rules of professional conduct merely because they are supervised, nor for that matter merely because the misconduct in which they might engage is ordered by the supervising lawyer. MR 5.2. A subordinate lawyer is not subject to discipline when she "acts in accordance with a supervisory lawyer's reasonable resolution of an arguable question of professional duty." MR 5.2(b). When close questions arise about which supervisors and subordinates disagree, someone's view of the matter must ultimately control the actions of the lawyer. Under this provision, subordinate lawyers may safely defer on close questions and close questions alone to the judgment of supervisory, usually senior, lawyers.

DANIELS v. ALANDER
268 Conn. 320, 844 A.2d 182 (2004)

KATZ, J.

This case is before us, pursuant to our grant of certification, from the judgment of the Appellate Court dismissing a writ of error brought by the plaintiff in error Dennis Driscoll (plaintiff), who is a member of the bar of this state. *Daniels v. Alander*, 75 Conn.App. 864, 818 A.2d 106 (2003). On appeal to this court, the plaintiff claims that his failure to correct falsehoods made by another attorney during a court proceeding cannot form the basis of the disciplinary action taken against him. We disagree.

Rule 3.3 of the Rules of Professional Conduct provides in relevant part: "(a) A lawyer shall not knowingly:

"(1) Make a false statement of material fact or law to a tribunal . . . .

"(d) In an ex parte proceeding, a lawyer shall inform the tribunal of all material facts known to the lawyer which will enable the tribunal to make an informed decision, whether or not the facts are adverse."

The following procedural history, as set forth by the Appellate Court, is relevant to the plaintiff's claims on appeal. "On January 16, 2001, [Douglas R. Daniels and the plaintiff], both of whom were practicing law in Daniels' law firm, filed an ex parte application for temporary custody and relief from abuse on behalf of Ines Montalvo. [The trial court] conducted an ex parte hearing on the matter on that same date. The application sought an order awarding Montalvo temporary custody of her two minor children as well as an order restraining the children's father, Felipe Nieves, from threatening or assaulting the children or entering Montalvo's Connecticut residence. The application alleged that the children had been abused physically by Nieves and that they feared returning to his care in New Jersey.

"At the [January 16, 2001] hearing, the [trial] court inquired directly of Montalvo and Daniels as to why it should issue the order. Central to the court's line of inquiry was why Montalvo did not file her application before the Superior Court in New Jersey, which already had conducted a hearing on the issue of the children's custody. Montalvo testified that she did not want to file the emergency application in New Jersey because she feared that it would endanger the immediate physical safety of the children. The [trial] court inquired directly of Daniels as to why he chose to pursue the application in Connecticut rather than to pursue it before the New Jersey trial judge who had presided over the custody trial, the Honorable John A. Peterson, Jr. In response to the [trial] court's questioning, Daniels represented that his colleague, [the plaintiff], 'spoke to [Veronica Davis, Montalvo's] counsel in New Jersey and it was her opinion that we should not [pursue the emergency custody application] in New Jersey for a number of reasons, none of which I think are flattering to the judiciary there, but we were relying on that.'

"[The trial court] recessed the hearing on the application and spoke via telephone with Judge Peterson in New Jersey. Judge Peterson agreed to conduct a hearing on Montalvo's application for temporary emergency custody on January 19, 2001, and [the trial court] issued a temporary emergency order awarding Montalvo custody of the children until that time. [The trial court] noted that both [it] and Judge Peterson believed that New Jersey was the appropriate forum in which to resolve the matter.

"After the [January 16] hearing, [the trial court] received a letter from . . . Davis, the attorney who was representing Montalvo in the custody proceeding in New Jersey. Davis informed the court that she had reviewed the transcript of proceedings of January 16, 2001, and that some of the representations made by Daniels during the hearing were false. By means of a letter dated February 5, 2001, [the trial court] informed Davis, as well as the [plaintiff and Daniels], that [it] wanted to conduct a hearing in regard to Davis' allegations and that such hearing would enable [it] to determine if further action was warranted.

"On March 16, 2001, the [trial] court conducted a hearing related to Davis' allegations. Thereafter, on April 9, 2001, the trial court issued its decision concluding that the plaintiff and Daniels had violated subsections (a)(1) and (d) of rule 3.3 of the Rules of Professional Conduct. Critical to the trial court's decision were several findings of fact relating to representations made at the January 16,

2001 hearing, as well as testimony given at the March 16, 2001 hearing. Specifically, after sifting through the conflicting evidence presented at the latter hearing, the trial court found the following facts: "Davis [had] expressly told [the plaintiff] on January 15, 2001, that she was prepared to file an emergency petition for temporary custody on [Montalvo's] behalf in New Jersey. [The plaintiff] did not take . . . Davis up on her offer because he believed that Connecticut had jurisdiction and because of her reluctance to file an emergency petition. . . . [Daniels'] statement to the court that it was the opinion of [Davis] that an emergency application for temporary custody should not be brought in New Jersey for reasons concerning the judiciary there was false. Both . . . Daniels and [the plaintiff] knew it was false. . . . The statement made to the [trial] court by . . . Daniels that it was the opinion of [Davis] that an emergency petition should not be brought in New Jersey did not provide a complete picture of the opinions of . . . Davis as they related to the appropriate forum for bringing an emergency petition in this case. . . . Daniels failed to tell [the trial court] that . . . Davis believed that New Jersey had jurisdiction in this matter and that New Jersey, not Connecticut, was the appropriate forum for filing such a petition. He also neglected to inform [the trial court] that it was . . . Davis' opinion that no emergency petition should be filed at all. Finally, [Davis] did not tell [the trial court] that, despite her reservations . . . Davis was prepared to file an emergency petition on . . . Montalvo's behalf in New Jersey." (Citations omitted.)

The trial court further stated: "Had I known at the time of the ex parte proceeding the accurate and complete opinions of . . . Davis-that she believed that New Jersey had jurisdiction over any application for temporary custody, that New Jersey was the appropriate forum to file such an application, and that she was prepared to file an emergency custody petition in New Jersey, I would have instructed [Montalvo] to file her application for temporary custody in New Jersey and [would] not have granted the emergency application providing temporary custody of the two minor children to [Montalvo]." The trial court thereafter concluded that Daniels had violated rule 3.3(a)(1) by making the false statement to the court and that the plaintiff had violated the same rule by failing to correct that false statement when it was made to the court in his presence. Finally, the trial court determined that Daniels and the plaintiff had violated rule 3.3(d) by failing to inform the court of all the material facts known to them regarding Davis' opinions and the steps she had taken in preparing to file an emergency petition.

[handwritten margin note: TC said they would have sent it to NJ]

[handwritten margin note: what/why violated.]

Accordingly, the trial court reprimanded both Daniels and the plaintiff for their conduct, and thereafter denied their motion to reargue.

On appeal to this court, the plaintiff challenges the judgment of the Appellate Court affirming the trial court's determination that he had violated his professional obligations under rule 3.3(a)(1) and (d) of the Rules of Professional Conduct. He claims that his failure to correct Daniels' false statements to the court concerning the plaintiff's own conversations with Davis cannot, as a matter of law, form the basis of a violation of rule 3.3(a)(1). Specifically, the plaintiff argues that only the attorney who actually made the misstatement can be held accountable under the rule and that, because he personally made no such misstatements to the trial court, there was no basis upon which to conclude that he had violated rule 3.3(a)(1). The plaintiff also argues that the misstatement was not material to the trial court's determination of the issues at hand and that, therefore, it cannot form the basis of a violation of rule 3.3(d). Finally, he argues that rule 3.3(d) should not be extended to a situation in which an associate, like himself, sitting at counsel table with his employer, remains silent when that employer makes a misstatement of fact to the court.

I

The plaintiff's first challenge is to the propriety of the Appellate Court's judgment affirming the trial court's determination that he violated rule 3.3(a)(1). Essentially, he argues that because Daniels made the misstatements, only Daniels could be held accountable. According to the plaintiff, the rule, as adopted by the judges of the Superior Court, applies only to the attorney who actually makes the misstatement, and not to an attorney who simply fails to correct it. We disagree.

In this case, the words Daniels spoke pertained to a conversation that *the plaintiff* had had with Davis. Daniels made representations to the trial court regarding that conversation that the court concluded were not truthful and that the plaintiff knew from his own personal knowledge to be false. Because the recitation by Daniels pertained to the plaintiff's firsthand knowledge of events that had occurred outside the trial court's presence, which the plaintiff personally had related to Daniels as part of their joint representation of Montalvo, the plaintiff was well situated to remedy the misstatement and thereby uphold his duty of candor to the court. Under the particular circumstances of this case, the plaintiff, as an officer of the court, was duty bound to correct the misstatement.

Instead, during the January 16, 2001 proceeding, the plaintiff introduced himself to the trial court as representing Montalvo, but then sat quietly allowing Daniels to answer questions by recounting the details of a conversation that the plaintiff had had with Davis, details that the trial court later concluded had not been reported accurately. Of even greater significance is the fact that the plaintiff had the opportunity to rectify the situation when he testified during the March 16, 2001 hearing. Rather than correct Daniels' misstatement, the plaintiff instead explicitly attested to the accuracy of the representations that Daniels had made during the January 16 ex parte hearing when the plaintiff related that, in his conversation with Davis, he had "asked if she had intended on going forward with any legal proceedings in New Jersey, based on the allegations that . . . Montalvo was making. And that is when [Davis] told [the plaintiff] that she [did not], that she was afraid any further legal proceedings of this nature would anger the judge and would compromise the outcome of the custody trial that had just taken place." Additionally, the plaintiff testified that he had repeated that conversation to Daniels and that the plaintiff had been at the January 16, 2001 hearing when Daniels made representations to the court regarding the plaintiff's conversation with Davis, representations that the court later determined, based on Davis' testimony, to have been untruthful. During the March 16, 2001 hearing, the plaintiff was under oath and, therefore, his representations to the trial court comprised testimonial evidence so that he was obligated, both as a witness and as an attorney and officer of the court, to make truthful representations to the tribunal. See Rules of Professional Conduct 3.3. Importantly, everything that the plaintiff recounted to the trial court was within his own specific knowledge; unlike Daniels, the plaintiff was not making representations concerning the acts of third parties.

II

[8] The plaintiff next argues that the Appellate Court improperly affirmed the trial court's determination that he had violated rule 3.3(d). Specifically, he contends that he had no duty to disclose Davis' representations to him because they were not material. He also argues that rule 3.3(d) should not be extended to a situation in which an associate, like himself, sitting at counsel table with his employer, remains silent when that employer makes a misstatement of fact to the court. We disagree with both assertions.

[The court discussed and ruled against plaintiff's claim that the statements were not material. —Ed.]

Lastly, the plaintiff claims that rule 3.3(d) should not be extended to him because he was merely an associate, sitting at counsel table with Daniels, his employer, and that therefore, remaining silent when Daniels made a misstatement of fact to the court should not serve as the basis for the reprimand. As we stated previously; see footnote 3 of this opinion; rule 3.3(d) of the Rules of professional Conduct provides: "In an ex parte proceeding, a lawyer shall inform the tribunal of all material facts known to the lawyer which will enable the tribunal to make an informed decision, whether or not the facts are adverse." As we already have concluded, the facts were material and they were known to the plaintiff. Therefore, the only question that remains is whether there is some policy reason why Driscoll should not be held accountable. _issue_

It is apparent that the trial court was examining the issues of jurisdiction, namely, whether Montalvo could obtain relief in New Jersey and whether this was a situation involving potential imminent harm to children. Therefore, the status of the proceedings in New Jersey and Davis' views and intentions were material facts known to the plaintiff that would have enabled the trial court to determine what action, if any, to take. The commentary to rule 3.3 regarding ex parte proceedings provides: "Ordinarily, an advocate has the limited responsibility of presenting one side of the matters that a tribunal should consider in reaching a decision; the conflicting position is expected to be presented by the opposing party. However, in an ex parte proceeding, such as an application for a temporary restraining order, there is no balance of presentation by opposing advocates. The object of an ex parte proceeding is nevertheless to yield a substantially just result. The judge has an affirmative responsibility to accord the absent party just consideration. The lawyer for the represented party has the correlative duty to make disclosures of material facts known to the lawyer and that the lawyer reasonably believes are necessary to an informed decision." This is so even when such disclosures may not benefit the disclosing lawyer's position. Therefore, under the circumstances of this case, the trial court reasonably could have expected the plaintiff to inform it of Davis' views and intentions in the January 16, 2001 ex parte proceeding.

Moreover, when Daniels related Davis' observations and the plaintiff remained silent, the trial court reasonably could have inferred that it possessed all the pertinent information. Indeed, if that had not been the case, the circumstances naturally would have called for a reply. The plaintiff has not presented, nor can we identify, any sound reason to graft an exception onto the rule when an attorney whose conduct is at issue is an associate joined by his employer.

The judgment of the Appellate Court is affirmed. In this opinion the other justices concurred.

2. Providing Supervision

Separate from a supervisor's potential responsibility for the *acts* of lawyer subordinates, supervising lawyers are subject to discipline if they fail to provide adequate supervision. Law firm partners must make reasonable efforts to establish systems that will give reasonable assurance that the firm's lawyers will not engage in conduct that would violate the rules of professional conduct for lawyers. Notice the double use of the word "reasonable." Partners are responsible for taking reasonable efforts to set up systems; if the subordinate lawyers engage in violative conduct despite those systems, the partner is not subject to discipline. MR 5.1(a). Typical systems include file maintenance systems, conflict of interest check procedures, standard forms for fee agreements and engagement letters, and confidentiality requirements systems. Supervising lawyers, whether partners or not, who directly supervise other lawyers must make reasonable efforts to ensure that the subordinate lawyers comply with the rules of professional conduct. MR 5.1(b).

IN RE YACAVINO
494 A.2d 801 (N.J. 1985)

Per Curiam.

This matter arises from a report of the Disciplinary Review Board (DRB) recommending a three-year suspension of respondent. The recommendation is based on its finding that respondent repeatedly misrepresented the status of pending adoption proceedings to his client, and prepared two false court orders to stall the client's discovery of his deficiencies. Based upon our independent review of the record, we are clearly convinced that respondent engaged in the described conduct and that it warrants the recommended suspension.

Respondent was admitted to the Bar in 1974 but did not enter private practice until 1980. After a brief period of practice on his own, he became associated, in February 1981, with a firm of twenty lawyers with an office in Newark and satellite offices in Caldwell and Pompton Plains. He was assigned to the office in Pompton Plains. The firm was taking over the practice of an attorney in that area who was entering retirement. In March 1981, respondent was given the responsibility of representing a client of that retiring attorney in adoption proceedings. [The court explains in detail that respondent did nothing on the matter, then lied to the clients about the matter's progress, then created fictitious adoption orders to deceive the clients. All of this unraveled and was discovered. —Ed.]

In respondent's favor are only the facts accepted by the DRB: that respondent's actions were not taken for the purpose of self-enrichment; that he promptly and fully cooperated with law enforcement and disciplinary authorities; and that the incident is one of isolated or aberrant behavior on his part. Nonetheless, the misconduct is grave. Respondent violated DR 1-102(A)(3) and (4) by engaging in illegal conduct adversely reflecting on his fitness to practice law and by engaging in conduct involving dishonesty and misrepresentation. In addition, the respondent's persistent failure to act was grossly negligent, in violation of DR 6-101(A)(1). It is also beyond doubt that in this matter the respondent violated DR 7-101(A)(2) by failing to carry out the client's contract of employment. (In our disposition, we refer to the Disciplinary Rules that governed the conduct of attorneys at the time of these occurrences. Effective September 10, 1984, the Rules of Professional Conduct of the American Bar Association, as modified by the Court, govern that conduct. R. 1:14. Those Rules contain provisions equivalent to the Disciplinary Rules involved here.)

*   *   *

There remains, however, a disturbing aspect to this case that must be mentioned. Without mitigating respondent's fault, there is evidence of concern to all attorneys involved in the episode. According to his testimony, respondent was left virtually alone and unsupervised in the year that he serviced the firm's Pompton Plains office. The office was lacking in the essential tools of legal practice. Partners rarely attended the office; no member of the firm inquired as to the status of the office matters. We would not credit this version of the events without first hearing from the firm. In the future, however, this attitude of leaving new lawyers to "sink or swim" will not be tolerated. Had this young attorney received the collegial support and guidance expected of supervising attorneys, this incident might never have occurred. These clients were delayed well over a year-and-a-half in the handling of a matter that was of intense personal concern to them. "This sorry episode points up the need for a systematic, organized routine for periodic review of a newly admitted attorney's files."

Our Rules of Professional Conduct now make clear the ethical responsibility of a supervising attorney to take reasonable efforts to ensure "that all lawyers [in the organization] conform to the Rules of Professional Conduct." RPC 5.1(a). Under that Rule it is the supervising attorney's responsibility to assure that each lawyer in the organization diligently carries out the firm's contracts of employment with clients.

In these circumstances, we conclude that the appropriate discipline is to suspend respondent for three years. In addition, after the period of suspension, respondent may be re-admitted to practice only under a form of proctorship. Respondent's inability to advance this routine adoption matter manifests a need for a period of supervision. His present attorney has confirmed that respondent's personal isolation from partners, associates or peers was a major contributing cause to his misconduct. The precise details of that proctorship are to be approved by the Office of Attorney Ethics. The arrangement will be for a period of one year from the date upon which it is implemented, and until further order of this Court dissolving the proctorship. The proctor is to submit to the Office of Attorney Ethics detailed reports on respondent's status, on a basis and in a form acceptable to that office. Further, respondent is to reimburse the Ethics Financial Committee for the administrative costs incurred on account of these proceedings.

So ordered.

3. Responsibility for Lawyer or Non-Lawyer Subordinates' Misconduct

Supervising lawyers are subject to discipline for the conduct of lawyer subordinates that violates the rules of lawyer conduct when any of the following occur:

(1) The lawyer orders the subordinate to engage in the misconduct. MR 5.3(c)(1).

(2) The lawyer ratifies the misconduct. MR 5.3(c)(1).

(3) A lawyer who is either a partner or the subordinate's direct supervisor learns of the misconduct at a time when its effect could be avoided or mitigated and yet fails to take reasonable remedial action. MR 5.3(c)(2).

C. LAWYERS AS EMPLOYEES

The traditional lawyer-client relationship, with lawyer as the special-purpose agent of the client, has meant that lawyers have not often been thought of as employees. But more and more lawyers stand in the relationship of employee to a law firm employer, a government agency employer, or an organizational employer. The efforts of courts to deal with these relationships, often by using strained extrapolations of the lawyer-client relationship, have not always been satisfying.

1. Wrongful Discharge

In general, a lawyer has no protected expectation of continuing employment with a particular client. A client may discharge a lawyer without cause. Therefore, in general, lawyers do not have claims for wrongful discharge against clients. However, more and more lawyers are employees of corporations and other organizations, and more lawyers experience their work in a law firm as an employer-employee relationship. The authority is mixed on the question of whether a lawyer may have a claim for wrongful discharge against such an employer.

BALLA v. GAMBRO, INC.
584 N.E.2d 104 (Ill. 1991)

Justice Clark delivered the opinion of the court: The issue in this case is whether in-house counsel should be allowed the remedy of an action for retaliatory discharge.

Appellee, Roger Balla, formerly in-house counsel for Gambro, Inc. (Gambro), filed a retaliatory discharge action against Gambro. . . . Appellee alleged that he was fired in contravention of Illinois public policy and sought damages for the discharge. The trial court dismissed the action on appellants' motion for summary judgment. The appellate court reversed. We granted appellant's petition for leave to appeal and allowed amicus curiae briefs from the American Corporate Counsel Association and Illinois State Bar Association.

Gambro is a distributor of kidney dialysis equipment manufactured by Gambro Germany. Among the products distributed by Gambro are dialyzers which filter excess fluid and toxic substances from the blood of patients with no or impaired kidney function. The manufacture and sale of dialyzers is regulated by the United States Food and Drug Administration (FDA).

Appellee, Roger J. Balla, is and was at all times throughout this controversy an attorney licensed to practice law in the State of Illinois. On March 17, 1980, appellee executed an employment agreement with Gambro which contained the terms of appellee's employment. Generally, the employment agreement provided that appellee would "be responsible for all legal matters within the company and for personnel within the company's sales office." Appellee held the title of director of administration at Gambro. As director of administration, appellee's specific responsibilities included, inter alia: advising, counseling and representing management on legal matters; establishing and administering personnel policies; coordinating and overseeing corporate activities to assure compliance with applicable laws and regulations, and preventing or minimizing legal or administrative proceedings; and coordinating the activities of the manager of regulatory affairs. Regarding this last responsibility, under Gambro's corporate hierarchy, appellee supervised the manager of regulatory affairs, and the manager reported directly to appellee.

In August 1983, the manager of regulatory affairs for Gambro left the company and appellee assumed the manager's specific duties. Although appellee's original employment agreement was not modified to reflect his new position, his annual compensation was increased and Gambro's corporate organizational chart referred to appellee's positions as "Dir. of Admin./Personnel; General Counsel; Mgr. of Regulatory Affairs." The job description for the position described the manager as an individual "responsible for ensuring awareness of and compliance with federal, state and local laws and regulations affecting the company's operations and products." Requirements for the position were a bachelor of science degree and three to five years in the medical device field plus two years experience in the area of government regulations. The individual in the position prior to appellee was not an attorney.

In July 1985 Gambro Germany informed Gambro in a letter that certain dialyzers it had manufactured, the clearances of which varied from the package insert, were about to be shipped to Gambro. Referring to these dialyzers, Gambro Germany advised Gambro:

> For acute patients risk is that the acute uremic situation will not be improved in spite of the treatment, giving continuous high levels of potassium, phosphate and urea/creatine. The chronic patient may note the effect as a slow progression of the uremic situation and depending on the interval between medical check-ups the medical risk may not be overlooked.

Appellee told the president of Gambro to reject the shipment because the dialyzers did not comply with FDA regulations. The president notified Gambro Germany of its decision to reject the shipment on July 12, 1985.

However, one week later the president informed Gambro Germany that Gambro would accept the dialyzers and "sell [them] to a unit that is not currently our customer but who buys only on price." Appellee contends that he was not informed by the president of the decision to accept the dialyzers but became aware of it through other Gambro employees. Appellee maintains that he spoke with the president in August regarding the company's decision to accept the dialyzers and told the president that he would do whatever necessary to stop the sale of the dialyzers.

On September 4, 1985, appellee was discharged from Gambro's employment by its president. The following day, appellee reported the shipment of the dialyzers to the FDA. The FDA seized the shipment and determined the product to be "adulterated within the meaning of section 501(h) of the [Federal Act].

On March 19, 1986, appellee filed a four-count complaint in tort for retaliatory discharge seeking $22 million in damages. Counts III and IV for emotional distress were dismissed from the action, as was the president in an order entered by the trial court on November 5, 1986.

On July 28, 1987, Gambro filed a motion for summary judgment. Gambro argued that appellee, as an attorney, was precluded from filing a retaliatory discharge action. . . .

On November 30, 1988, the trial court granted appellants' motion for summary judgment. In its opinion, the trial court specifically stated that "the very ground [appellee is] claiming as the basis for retaliatory discharge all [sic] involves the decisions which he made applying law to fact to determine whether these things complied with the federal regulations, and that is clearly legal work." Thus, the trial court concluded that the duties appellee was performing which led to his discharge were "conduct clearly within the attorney-client relationship" and that Gambro had the "absolute right" to discharge its attorney. On appeal, the court below held that an attorney is not barred as a matter of law from bringing an action for retaliatory discharge.

* * *

We agree with the trial court that appellee does not have a cause of action against Gambro for retaliatory discharge under the facts of the case at bar. Generally, this court adheres to the proposition that " 'an employer may discharge an employee-at-will for any reason or for no reason [at all].' " *Barr v. Kelso-Burnett Co.* (1985), 106 Ill. 2d 520, 525, 88 Ill. Dec. 628, 478 N.E.2d 1354. However, in *Kelsay v. Motorola, Inc.* (1978), 74 Ill. 2d 172, 23 Ill. Dec. 559, 384 N.E.2d 353, this court first recognized the limited and narrow tort of retaliatory discharge. In *Kelsay*, an at-will employee was fired for filing a worker's compensation claim against her employer. After examining the history and purpose behind the Workers' Compensation Act to determine the public policy behind its enactment, this court held that the employee should have a cause of action for retaliatory discharge. This court stressed that if employers could fire employees for filing workers' compensation claims, the public policy behind the enactment of the Workers' Compensation Act would be frustrated.

Subsequently, in *Palmateer v. International Harvester Co.* (1981), 85 Ill. 2d 124, 52 Ill. Dec. 13, 421 N.E.2d 876, this court again examined the tort of retaliatory discharge. In *Palmateer*, an employee was discharged for informing the police of suspected criminal activities of a co-employee, and because he agreed to provide assistance in any investigation and trial of the matter. Based on the public policy favoring the investigation and prosecution of crime, this court held that the employee had a cause of action for retaliatory discharge. Further, we stated:

> All that is required [to bring a cause of action for retaliatory discharge] is that the employer discharge the employee in retaliation for the employee's activities, and that the discharge be in contravention of a clearly mandated public policy.

In this case it appears that Gambro discharged appellee, an employee of Gambro, in retaliation for his activities, and this discharge was in contravention of a clearly mandated public policy. Appellee allegedly told the president of Gambro that he would do whatever was necessary to stop the sale of the "misbranded and/or adulterated" dialyzers. In appellee's eyes, the use of these dialyzers could cause death or serious bodily harm to patients. As we have stated before, "[t]here is no public policy more important or more fundamental than the one favoring the effective protection of the lives and property of citizens." However, in this case, appellee was not just an employee of Gambro, but also general counsel for Gambro.

[I]n *Herbster v. North American Co. for Life & Health Insurance* (1986), 150 Ill. App. 3d 21, 103 Ill. Dec. 322, 501 N.E.2d 343, our appellate court held that the plaintiff, an employee and chief legal counsel for the defendant company, did not have a claim for retaliatory discharge against the company due to the presence of the attorney-client relationship. Under the facts of that case, the defendant company allegedly requested the plaintiff to destroy or remove discovery information which had been requested in lawsuits pending against the company. The plaintiff refused arguing that such conduct would constitute fraud and violate several provisions of the Illinois Code of Professional Responsibility. Subsequently, the defendant company discharged the plaintiff.

The appellate court refused to extend the tort of retaliatory discharge to the plaintiff in *Herbster* primarily because of the special relationship between an attorney and client. The court stated:

> The mutual trust, exchanges of confidence, reliance on judgment, and personal nature of the attorney-client relationship demonstrate the unique position attorneys occupy in our society.

We agree with the conclusion reached in *Herbster* that, generally, in-house counsel do not have a claim under the tort of retaliatory discharge. However, we base our decision as much on the nature and purpose of the tort of retaliatory discharge, as on the effect on the attorney-client relationship that extending the tort would have. In addition, at this time, we caution that our holding is confined by the fact that appellee is and was at all times throughout this controversy an attorney licensed to practice law in the State of Illinois. Appellee is and was subject to the Illinois Code of Professional Responsibility (see the Rules of Professional Conduct which replaced the Code of Professional Responsibility, effective August 1, 1990), adopted by this court. The tort of retaliatory discharge is a limited and narrow exception to the general rule of at-will employment. The tort seeks to achieve " 'a proper balance . . . among the employer's interest in operating a business efficiently and profitably, the employee's interest in earning a livelihood, and society's interest in seeing its public policies carried out.' " Further, as stated in *Palmateer*, "[t]he foundation of the tort of retaliatory discharge lies in the protection of public policy . . . ."

In this case, the public policy to be protected, that of protecting the lives and property of citizens, is adequately safeguarded without extending the tort of retaliatory discharge to in-house counsel. Appellee was required under the Rules of Professional Conduct to report Gambro's intention to sell the "misbranded and/or adulterated" dialyzers. Rule 1.6(b) of the Rules of Professional Conduct reads:

> A lawyer shall reveal information about a client to the extent it appears necessary to prevent the client from committing an act that would result in death or serious bodily injury.

Appellee alleges, and the FDA's seizure of the dialyzers indicates, that the use of the dialyzers would cause death or serious bodily injury. Thus, under the above-cited rule, appellee was under the mandate of this court to report the sale of these dialyzers.

In his brief to this court, appellee argues that not extending the tort of retaliatory discharge to in-house counsel would present attorneys with a "Hobson's choice." According to appellee, in-house counsel would face two alternatives: either comply with the client/employer's wishes and risk both the loss of a professional license and exposure to criminal sanctions, or decline to comply with client/ employer's wishes and risk the loss of a full-time job and the attendant benefits. We disagree. Unlike the employees in *Kelsay* which this court recognized would be left with the difficult decision of choosing between whether to file a workers' compensation claim and risk being fired, or retaining their jobs and losing their right to a remedy, in-house counsel plainly are not confronted with such a dilemma. In-house counsel do not have a choice of whether to follow their ethical obligations as attorneys licensed to practice law, or follow the illegal and unethical demands of their clients. In-house counsel must abide by the Rules of Professional Conduct. Appellee had no choice but to report to the FDA Gambro's intention to sell or distribute these dialyzers, and consequently protect the aforementioned public policy.

In addition, we believe that extending the tort of retaliatory discharge to in-house counsel would have an undesirable effect on the attorney-client relationship that exists between these employers and their in-house counsel. Generally, a client may discharge his attorney at any time, with or without cause. This rule applies equally to in-house counsel as it does to outside counsel. Further, this rule "recognizes that the relationship between an attorney and client is based on trust and that the client must have confidence in his attorney in order to ensure that the relationship will function properly." As stated in *Herbster*, "the attorney is placed in the unique position of maintaining a close relationship with a client where the attorney receives secrets, disclosures, and information that otherwise would not be divulged to intimate friends." We believe that if in-house counsel are granted the right to sue their employers for retaliatory discharge, employers might be less willing to be forthright and candid with their in-house counsel. Employers might be hesitant to turn to their in-house counsel for advice regarding potentially questionable corporate conduct knowing that their in-house counsel could use this information in a retaliatory discharge suit.

Our decision not to extend the tort of retaliatory discharge to in-house counsel also is based on other ethical considerations. Under the Rules of Professional Conduct, appellee was required to withdraw from representing Gambro if continued representation would result in the violation of the Rules of Professional Conduct by which appellee was bound, or if Gambro discharged the appellee. (*See* 134 Ill. 2d Rules 1.16(a)(2), (a)(4).) In this case, Gambro did discharge appellee, and according to appellee's claims herein, his continued representation of Gambro would have resulted in a violation of the Rules of Professional Conduct. Appellee argues that such a choice of withdrawal is "simplistic and uncompassionate, and is completely at odds with contemporary realities facing in-house attorneys." These contemporary realities apparently are the economic ramifications of losing his position as in-house counsel. However difficult economically and perhaps emotionally it is for in-house counsel to discontinue representing an employer/client, we refuse to allow in-house counsel to sue their employer/client for damages because they obeyed their ethical obligations. In this case, appellee, in addition to being an employee at Gambro, is first and foremost an attorney bound by the Rules of Professional Conduct. These Rules of Professional Conduct hope to articulate in a concrete fashion certain values and goals such as defending the integrity of the judicial system, promoting the administration of justice and protecting the integrity of the legal profession. (*See* Ill. Const. 1970, Preamble.) An attorney's obligation to follow these Rules of Professional Conduct should not be the foundation for a claim of retaliatory discharge.

We also believe that it would be inappropriate for the employer/client to bear the economic costs and burdens of their in-house counsel's adhering to their ethical obligations under the Rules of Professional Conduct. Presumably, in situations where an in-house counsel obeys his or her ethical obligations and reveals certain information regarding the employer/client, the attorney-client relationship will be irreversibly strained and the client will more than likely discharge its in-house counsel. In this scenario, if we were to grant the in-house counsel the right to sue the client for retaliatory discharge, we would be shifting the burden and costs of obeying the Rules of Professional Conduct from the attorney to the employer/client. The employer/client would be forced to pay damages to its former in-house counsel to essentially mitigate the financial harm the attorney suffered for having to abide by Rules of Professional Conduct. This, we believe, is impermissible for all attorneys know or should know that at certain times in their professional career, they will have to forgo economic gains in order to protect the integrity of the legal profession.

Our review of cases from other jurisdictions dealing with this issue does not persuade us to hold otherwise. In *Willy v. Coastal Corp. (S.D.* Tex. 1986), 647 F. Supp. 116, the district court declined to extend the tort of retaliatory discharge to the wrongful termination of in-house counsel. In that case, the plaintiff, in-house counsel for the defendant company, alleged that he was fired because he required the defendant to comply with environmental laws. The court held that the ethical canons and disciplinary rules set forth the standards for attorneys to follow and that they require an attorney presented with ethical conflicts to withdraw from representation. Further, once the client elects to terminate the relationship, "the attorney is required mandatorily to withdraw from any further representation of that client."

In contrast to the two cases discussed above which specifically held that in-house counsel do not have a right to sue for retaliatory discharge, two other cases have allowed in-house counsel to sue their employer for wrongful termination. However, both cases are distinguishable from our holding. In *Parker v. M & T Chemicals, Inc.* (1989), 236 N.J. Super. 451, 566 A.2d 215, the superior court of New Jersey construed that State's "Whistleblowers Act" as compelling "a retaliating employer to pay damages to an employee-attorney who is wrongfully discharged or mistreated . . . for any reason which is violative of law, fraudulent, criminal, or incompatible with a clear mandate of New Jersey's public policy concerning public health, safety or welfare." The court also noted in distinguishing the aforementioned *Herbster* and *Willy* opinions that they did not involve "whistle-blower" statutes, only the right of in-house counsel to maintain a cause of action for retaliatory discharge at common law.

In *Mourad v. Automobile Club Insurance Association* (1991), 186 Mich. App. 715, 465 N.W.2d 395, the plaintiff, as in-house counsel for the defendant company, sued the defendant for, inter alia, breach of employment contract and retaliatory demotion. The appellate court of Michigan determined that the plaintiff had a cause of action for breach of a just-cause contract, but not for retaliatory demotion. The court distinguished the aforementioned *Herbster, Willy* and *Parker* cases as involving the issue of whether the "state will recognize a public policy exception to the typical employment-at-will contract." In this case, however, the Michigan court stated that the defendant company's policy manual and pamphlets had created a contract to terminate for just cause. Thus, plaintiff's claim for retaliatory demotion was an alternative theory of recovery from a breach of a just cause contract, and could not be sustained as an independent claim for recovery. The Michigan court made no statements regarding the propriety of in-house counsel's bringing claims for retaliatory discharge.

* * *

In this case, as the trial court explained, appellee investigated certain facts, applied the law to those investigated facts and reached certain conclusions as to whether these dialyzers complied with the FDA regulations. In that sense, appellee inescapably engaged in the practice of law. Consequently, although appellee may have been the manager of regulatory affairs for Gambro, his discharge resulted from information he learned as general counsel, and from conduct he performed as general counsel.

For the foregoing reasons, the decision of the appellate court is reversed, and the decision of the trial court is affirmed.

Appellate court reversed; circuit court affirmed.

Justice Freeman, dissenting:

I respectfully dissent from the decision of my colleagues. In concluding that the plaintiff attorney, serving as corporate in-house counsel, should not be allowed a claim for retaliatory discharge, the majority first reasons that the public policy implicated in this case, i.e., protecting the lives and property of Illinois citizens, is adequately safeguarded by the lawyer's ethical obligation to reveal information about a client as necessary to prevent acts that would result in death or serious bodily harm. I find this reasoning fatally flawed.

The majority so reasons because, as a matter of law, an attorney cannot even contemplate ignoring his ethical obligations in favor of continuing in his employment. I agree with this conclusion "as a matter of law." However, to say that the categorical nature of ethical obligations is sufficient to ensure that the ethical obligations will be satisfied simply ignores reality. Specifically, it ignores that, as unfortunate for society as it may be, attorneys are no less human than nonattorneys and, thus, no less given to the temptation to either ignore or rationalize away their ethical obligations when complying therewith may render them unable to feed and support their families.

I would like to believe, as my colleagues apparently conclude, that attorneys will always "do the right thing" because the law says that they must. However, my knowledge of human nature, which is not much greater than the average layman's, and, sadly, the recent scandals involving the bench and bar of Illinois are more than sufficient to dispel such a belief. Just as the ethical obligations of the lawyers and judges involved in those scandals were inadequate to ensure that they would not break the law, I am afraid that the lawyer's ethical obligation to "blow the whistle" is likewise an inadequate safeguard for the public policy of protecting lives and property of Illinois citizens.

As reluctant as I am to concede it, the fact is that this court must take whatever steps it can, within the bounds of the law, to give lawyers incentives to abide by their ethical obligations, beyond the satisfaction inherent in their doing so. We cannot continue to delude ourselves and the people of the State of Illinois that attorneys' ethical duties, alone, are always sufficient to guarantee that lawyers will "do the right thing." In the context of this case, where doing "the right thing" will often result in termination by an employer bent on doing the "wrong thing," I believe that the incentive needed is recognition of a cause of action for retaliatory discharge, in the appropriate case.

I would note that were an employee's desire to obey and follow the law an insufficient basis for a retaliatory discharge claim, *Palmateer* would have been decided differently. In this regard, I do not believe any useful purpose is served by distinguishing attorneys from ordinary citizens. It is incontrovertible that the law binds all men, kings and paupers alike. An attorney should not be punished simply because he has ethical obligations imposed upon him over and above the general obligation to obey the law which all men have. Nor should a corporate employer be protected simply because the employee it has discharged for "blowing the whistle" happens to be an attorney.

Additionally, I cannot share the majority's solicitude for employers who dis charge in-house counsel, who comply with their ethical obligations, by agreeing that they should not bear the economic burden which that compliance imposes upon the attorney. Unlike the majority, I do not believe that it is the attorney's compliance with his ethical obligations which imposes economic burdens upon him. Rather, those burdens are imposed upon him by the employer's persistence in conduct the attorney has advised is illegal and by the employer's wrongful termination of the attorney once he advises the employer that he must comply with those obligations.

Ultimately, the court's decision in the instant case does nothing to encourage respect for the law by corporate employers nor to encourage respect by attorneys for their ethical obligations. Therefore, I must respectfully dissent.

CREWS v. BUCKMAN LABORATORIES INTERNATIONAL, INC.
78 S.W.3d 852 (Tenn. 2002)

Factual Background

We granted permission to appeal to review whether the trial court should have granted a motion to dismiss a complaint under Tennessee Rule of Civil Procedure 12.02(6) for the failure to state a common-law claim for retaliatory discharge. The plaintiff, Ms. Julia Beth Crews, was allegedly discharged from her position as in-house counsel for defendant Buckman Laboratories International, Inc. ("Buckman") for reporting that Buckman's general counsel was engaged in the unauthorized practice of law. . . .

According to the allegations of the complaint, the plaintiff was hired by Buckman in 1995 as associate general counsel in its legal department, and while working in this capacity, she reported to Buckman's General Counsel, Ms. Katherine Buckman Davis. Sometime in 1996, the plaintiff discovered that Ms. Davis, who "held herself out as a licensed attorney," did not possess a license to practice law in the State of Tennessee. The plaintiff became concerned that Ms. Davis was engaged in the unauthorized practice of law, and she discussed her suspicions with a member of Buckman's Board of Directors.[7]

Ms. Davis eventually took and passed the bar exam, but the plaintiff learned some time later that Ms. Davis had yet to complete the requirements for licensure by taking the Muti-State Professional Responsibility Examination. The plaintiff informed Buckman officials of the continuing problem, and she advised them on how best to proceed. On June 17, 1999, Ms. Davis allegedly entered the plaintiff's office, yelling that she was frustrated with the plaintiff's actions. The plaintiff responded that she also was frustrated with the situation, to which Ms. Davis remarked that "maybe [the plaintiff] should just leave." The plaintiff declined to leave, and she later received a below-average raise for the first time during her tenure at Buckman, despite having been told earlier by Ms. Davis that she was

---

[7] [1] This Director then requested an opinion from the Board of Professional Responsibility based on a hypothetical scenario mirroring the situation at Buckman. The Board replied that a person without a Tennessee law license may not be employed as general counsel in this state and that the failure to have such a license constitutes the unauthorized practice of law.

"doing a good job in position of Associate Counsel."

In August, the plaintiff sought legal advice concerning her ethical obligations, and based on this advice, she informed the Board of Law Examiners of Ms. Davis's situation. The Board later issued a show-cause order asking Ms. Davis to clarify certain facts in her bar application. Upon receipt of the order, Ms. Davis demanded to know from the plaintiff what information the Board possessed in its application file.

The plaintiff stated that she knew nothing of the file, and she told Ms. Davis that her actions were threatening and inappropriate. Ms. Davis then apologized, but she immediately proceeded to schedule the plaintiff's performance review. The plaintiff then informed Mr. Buckman and the Vice-President of Human Resources that "the situation [had become] untenable and that she could not function under those circumstances." They agreed that the plaintiff should be immediately transferred to a position away from Ms. Davis's supervision and that she should eventually leave the company altogether within six to nine months. However, while the plaintiff was "in the midst of working out the new arrangement," Ms. Davis informed her that her services would no longer be needed. More specifically, Ms. Davis told her that "since [the plaintiff] had given her notice of resignation, it was logically best to end the Plaintiff's association with Buckman." Although the plaintiff denied that she had resigned, her computer was confiscated; she was placed on personal leave; and she was given a notice of termination.

On April 10, 2000, the plaintiff filed suit against Buckman in the Shelby County Circuit Court, alleging a common-law action for retaliatory discharge in violation of public policy. . . . Buckman then moved to dismiss the complaint under Rule of Civil Procedure 12.02(6) for failure to state a claim upon which relief may be granted. On June 11, 2000, the trial court granted Buckman's motion, though its specific reasoning is not contained in the record before this Court.

The plaintiff then appealed to the Court of Appeals, which affirmed the dismissal of the complaint. . . .

We then granted the plaintiff permission to appeal to decide whether in-house counsel may assert a common-law cause of action for retaliatory discharge when counsel is discharged in retaliation for reporting incidents of unauthorized practice of law. We hold that in-house counsel may indeed bring a common-law action of retaliatory discharge resulting from counsel's compliance with an ethical duty that represents a clear and definitive statement of public policy. Accordingly, the judgment of the Court of Appeals is reversed, and this case is remanded to the trial court for further proceedings.

*   *   *

IN-HOUSE COUNSEL AND THE TORT OF RETALIATORY DISCHARGE

Tennessee has long adhered to the employment-at-will doctrine in employment relationships not established or formalized by a contract for a definite term. Under this "employment at will" doctrine, both the employer and the employee are generally permitted, with certain exceptions, to terminate the employment rela tionship "at any time for good cause, bad cause, or no cause." . . .

However, an employer's ability to discharge at-will employees was significantly tempered by our recognition in *Clanton v. Cain-Sloan Co.*, 677 S.W.2d 441 (Tenn. 1984), of a cause of action for retaliatory discharge. Since that time, we have further recognized that an at-will employee "generally may not be discharged for attempting to exercise a statutory or constitutional right, or for any other reason which violates a clear public policy which is evidenced by an unambiguous constitutional, statutory, or regulatory provision." Therefore, in contrast to the purposes typically justifying the employment-at-will doctrine, an action for retaliatory discharge recognizes "that, in limited circumstances, certain well-defined, unambiguous principles of public policy confer upon employees implicit rights which must not be circumscribed or chilled by the potential of termination."

This Court has not previously addressed the issue of whether a lawyer may pursue a claim of retaliatory discharge against a former employer. At least initially, we must recognize that this case differs significantly from the usual retaliatory discharge case involving non-lawyer employees. When the discharged employee served as in-house counsel, the issue demands an inquiry into the corporation's expectations as the lawyer's sole employer and client, the lawyer's ethical obligations to the corporation, and the interest of the lawyer — in her character as an employee — in having protections available to other employees seeking redress of legal harm. Therefore, because this issue is one of first impression in this state, it is perhaps helpful to examine how other jurisdictions have addressed it.

Decisions of Other States Relating to Discharge in Violation of Public Policy

Several jurisdictions have grappled with how to balance the competing interests involved in these types of cases. Although the rationales often differed, most of the earlier cases on this subject held that a lawyer could not bring a retaliatory discharge action based upon the lawyer's adherence to his or her ethical duties. *See, e.g., Willy v. Coastal Corp.*, 647 F. Supp. 116 (S.D. Tex. 1986); *McGonagle v. Union Fid. Corp.*, 556 A.2d 878 (Pa. Super. Ct. 1989); *Herbster v. North Am. Co. for Life & Health Ins.*, 501 N.E.2d 343 (Ill. App. Ct. 1986). This line of cases culminated in *Balla v. Gambro, Inc.*, 584 N.E.2d 104 (Ill. 1991), in which the Illinois Supreme Court . . . set forth several rationales why in-house counsel should not be permitted to assert an action for retaliatory discharge. . . .

In more recent years, however, other states have permitted a lawyer, under limited circumstances, to pursue a claim of retaliatory discharge based upon termination in violation of public policy. The principal case permitting such an action is *General Dynamics Corp. v. Rose*, 876 P.2d 487 (Cal. 1994), in which the California Supreme Court rejected the views held by *Balla* and others and established an analytical framework permitting a lawyer to sue for retaliatory discharge. According to this framework, a lawyer is generally permitted to assert a retaliatory discharge action if the lawyer is discharged for following a mandatory ethical duty or engaging in conduct that would give rise to an action by a non-lawyer employee. However, the *General Dynamics Court* cautioned that the lawyer bringing the action could not rely upon confidential information to establish the claim and that any unsuccessful lawyer breaching his or her duty of confidentiality was subject to disciplinary sanctions.

Following California's lead, the Supreme Judicial Court of Massachusetts has also permitted in-house counsel to assert a limited retaliatory discharge action. In *GTE Products Corp. v. Stewart*, 653 N.E.2d 161 (Mass. 1995), the court questioned why the employee's status as an attorney should preclude an action. . . . However, while the *Stewart* Court permitted a limited retaliatory discharge action based upon a lawyer's refusal to violate "explicit and unequivocal statutory or ethical norms," it also restricted the scope of such an action to that in which "the claim can be proved without any violation of the attorney's obligation to respect client confidences and secrets."

Finally, and most recently, the Montana Supreme Court also held that in-house counsel should be permitted to bring retaliatory discharge actions when necessary to protect public policy. In *Burkhart v. Semitool, Inc.*, 5 P.3d 1031 (Mont. 2000), the court discussed the rationales in favor of adopting such an action and noted that while clients have a right to discharge counsel at any time and for any reason, this right does not necessarily apply to in-house counsel. Instead, the court reasoned that "by making his or her attorney an employee, [the employer] has avoided the traditional attorney-client relationship and granted the attorney protections that do not apply to independent contractors, but do apply to employees . . . ." Moreover, unlike the previous cases recognizing such an action, the *Burkhart* Court permitted lawyers to disclose the employer's confidential information to the extent necessary to establish a retaliatory discharge claim. *Id.* at 1041 (relying upon Montana Rule of Professional Conduct 1.6(b)(2) adopted from the ABA's Model Rules of Professional Conduct).

Rejection of the Rationales Advanced by *Balla* and Other Cases

Considering these two general approaches to retaliatory discharge actions based upon termination in violation of public policy, we generally agree with the approaches taken by the courts in *General Dynamics*, *Stewart*, and *Burkhart*. The very purpose of recognizing an employee's action for retaliatory discharge in violation of public policy is to encourage the employee to protect the public interest, and it seems anomalous to protect only non-lawyer employees under these circumstances. Indeed, as cases in similar contexts show, in-house counsel do not generally forfeit employment protections provided to other employees merely because of their status or duties as a lawyer.[8]

Moreover, we must reject the rationales typically set forth by *Balla* and the Court of Appeals in this case to generally deny lawyers the ability to pursue

---

[8] [2] For example, courts have permitted in-house lawyers to sue for age and race discrimination in violation of federal law, *Stinneford v. Spiegel Inc.*, 845 F. Supp. 1243, 1245-47 (N.D. Ill. 1994); *Golightly-Howell v. Oil, Chem. & Atomic Workers Int'l Union*, 806 F. Supp. 921, 924 (D. Colo. 1992); to sue for protections under a state "whistleblower" statute, *Parker v. M & T Chems., Inc.*, 566 A.2d 215, 220 (N.J. Super. Ct. App. Div. 1989); to sue for breach of express and implied employment contracts, *Chyten v. Lawrence & Howell Invs.*, 46 Cal. Rptr. 2d 459, 464-65 (Cal. Ct. App. 1993); *Nordling v. Northern State Power Co.*, 478 N.W.2d 498, 502 (Minn. 1991); and to sue based on implied covenants of good faith and fair dealing, *Golightly-Howell*, 806 F. Supp. at 924.

retaliatory discharge actions. *Balla's* principal rationale was that recognition of a retaliatory discharge action was not necessary to protect the public interest so long as lawyers were required to follow a code of ethics. Indeed, relying on *Balla*, the intermediate court in this case specifically concluded that statutory and ethical proscriptions are sufficient to protect the public policy against the unauthorized practice of law and that in-house counsel do not need incentives, by way of a cause of action for retaliatory discharge, to comply with the Disciplinary Rules.

We respectfully disagree that the public interest is adequately served in this context without permitting in-house counsel to sue for retaliatory discharge. It is true that counsel in this case was under a mandatory duty to not aid a non-lawyer in the unauthorized practice of law, *see* Tenn. Sup. Ct. R. 8, DR 3-101(A), and the intermediate court was also correct that lawyers do not have the option of disregarding the commandments of the Disciplinary Rules. This is not to say, however, that lawyers can never *choose* to violate mandatory ethical duties, as evidenced by the number of sanctions, some more severe than others, imposed upon lawyers by this Court and the Board of Professional Responsibility for such violations.

Ultimately, sole reliance on the mere presence of the ethical rules to protect important public policies gives too little weight to the actual presence of economic pressures designed to tempt in-house counsel into subordinating ethical standards to corporate misconduct. Unlike lawyers possessing a multiple client base, in-house counsel are dependent upon only *one* client for their livelihood.

The pressure to conform to corporate misconduct at the expense of one's entire livelihood, therefore, presents some risk that ethical standards could be disregarded. Like other non-lawyer employees, an in-house lawyer is dependent upon the corporation for his or her sole income, benefits, and pensions; the lawyer is often governed by the corporation's personnel policies and employees' handbooks; and the lawyer is subject to raises and promotions as determined by the corporation. In addition, the lawyer's hours of employment and nature of work are usually determined by the corporation. To the extent that these realities are ignored, the analysis here cannot hope to present an accurate picture of modern in-house practice.

*   *   *

In summary, we find unpersuasive the rationales set forth by *Balla* and other cases which equate the employment opportunities of in-house counsel with those of a lawyer possessing a larger client base. While in-house counsel may be a lawyer, we must further recognize that he or she is also an employee of the corporation, with all of the attendant benefits and responsibilities. Therefore, we hold that a lawyer may generally bring a claim for retaliatory discharge when the lawyer is discharged for abiding by the ethics rules as established by this Court.

PROPER STANDARD TO APPLY IN TENNESSEE

*   *   *

[A]s we have noted throughout this opinion, this case does not present the typical retaliatory discharge claim. Consequently, while the special relationship between a lawyer and a client does not categorically prohibit in-house counsel from bringing a retaliatory discharge action, other courts have held that it necessarily shapes the contours of the action when the plaintiff was employed as in-house counsel. For example, the courts in *General Dynamics* and *Stewart* held that a lawyer could pursue a retaliatory discharge claim, but only if the lawyer could do so without breaching the duty of confidentiality.

If we perceive any shortcomings in the holdings of *General Dynamics* and *Stewart*, it is that they largely take away with one hand what they appear to give with the other. Although the courts in these cases gave in-house counsel an important right of action, their respective admonitions about preserving client confidentiality appear to stop just short of halting most of these actions at the courthouse door. With little imagination, one could envision cases involving important issues of public concern being denied relief merely because the wrongdoer is protected by the lawyer's duty of confidentiality. Therefore, given that courts have recognized retaliatory discharge actions in order to protect the public interest, this potentially severe limitation strikes us as a curious, if not largely ineffective, measure to achieve that goal.

However, some courts following versions of the Model Rules of Professional Conduct have reached different conclusions concerning a lawyer's ability to use confidential information in a retaliatory discharge action. Unlike Disciplinary Rule 4-101(C), Model Rule 1.6(b)(2) permits a lawyer to reveal "information relating to the representation of a client" when the lawyer reasonably believes such information is necessary "to establish *a claim or defense* on behalf of the lawyer in a controversy between the lawyer and the client . . . ." (emphasis added). Although some commentators have asserted that this provision merely permits lawyers to use confidential information in fee-collection disputes as under the Model Code, the plain language of the Model Rule is clearly more broad than these authorities would presume. In fact, at least one state supreme court has held that this language permits in-house counsel to reveal confidential information in a retaliatory discharge suit, at least to the extent reasonably necessary to establish the claim. *See Burkhart*, 5 P.3d at 1041 (stating that a lawyer "does not forfeit his rights simply because to prove them he must utilize confidential information. Nor does the client gain a right to cheat the lawyer by imparting confidences to him.").

We agree with the approach taken by the Model Rules, and pursuant to our inherent authority to regulate and govern the practice of law in this state, we hereby expressly adopt a new provision in Disciplinary Rule 4-101(C) to permit in-house counsel to reveal the confidences and secrets of a client when the lawyer reasonably believes that such information is necessary to establish a claim or defense on behalf of the lawyer in a controversy between the lawyer and the client.

ANALYSIS OF THE COMPLAINT IN THIS CASE

*   *   *

The next issue, then, is whether the complaint alleges the existence of a "clear public policy which is evidenced by an unambiguous constitutional, statutory, or regulatory provision." To establish this second element, the plaintiff argues that the ethical rules relating to the unauthorized practice of law — such as Disciplinary Rule 3-101(A), which places upon lawyers a mandatory ethical duty "not [to] aid a nonlawyer in the unauthorized practice of law" — are for the protection of the public interest and may serve as the basis for a retaliatory discharge action. We agree. It cannot seriously be questioned that many of the duties imposed upon lawyers by the Tennessee Code of Professional Responsibility represent a clear and definitive statement of public policy. . . .

* * *

CONCLUSION

In summary, we hold that in-house counsel may bring a common-law action of retaliatory discharge resulting from counsel's compliance with a provision of the Code of Professional Responsibility that represents a clear and definitive statement of public policy. We also hold that the complaint in this case, which alleges discharge for reporting the unauthorized practice of law, states a claim for relief.

Furthermore, in accordance with an Order filed simultaneously with the judgment and opinion in this case, we hold that a lawyer may ethically disclose the employer's confidences or secrets when the lawyer reasonably believes that such information is necessary to establish a claim against the employer. However, the lawyer must make every effort practicable to avoid unnecessary disclosure of the employer's confidences and secrets; to limit disclosure to those having the need to know the information; and to obtain protective orders or make other arrangements minimizing the risk of unnecessary disclosure. Accordingly, we reverse the judgment of the Court of Appeals, and we remand this case to the Shelby County Circuit Court for further proceedings consistent with this opinion.

NOTES, EXAMPLES, AND QUESTIONS

1.   Does the court sufficiently evaluate the weight of the policy underlying the UPL restrictions in this case? What public policy is damaged when a corporation employs an unlicensed J.D. as its counsel?

2.   The ABA has taken a position consistent with the *Crews* court on the use of confidences to prove a wrongful discharge claim by in-house counsel. ABA Op. 01-424 (2001).

WIEDER v. SKALA
609 N.E.2d 105 (N.Y. 1992)

HANCOCK, JR., J.

Plaintiff, a member of the Bar, has sued his former employer, a law firm. He claims he was wrongfully discharged as an associate because of his insistence that the firm comply with the governing disciplinary rules by reporting professional misconduct allegedly committed by another associate. The question presented is whether plaintiff has stated a claim for relief either for breach of contract or for the tort of wrongful discharge in violation of this State's public policy. The lower courts have dismissed both causes of action on motion as legally insufficient under CPLR 3211(a)(7) on the strength of New York's employment-at-will doctrine. For reasons which follow, we modify the order and reinstate plaintiff's cause of action for breach of contract.

I.

In the complaint, which must be accepted as true on a dismissal motion under CPLR 3211(a)(7), plaintiff alleges that he was a commercial litigation attorney associated with defendant law firm from June 16, 1986 until March 18, 1988. In early 1987, plaintiff requested that the law firm represent him in the purchase of a condominium apartment. The firm agreed and assigned a fellow associate (L.L.) "to do 'everything that needs to be done.'" For several months, L.L. neglected plaintiff's real estate transaction and, to conceal his neglect, made several "false and fraudulent material misrepresentations." In September 1987, when plaintiff learned of L.L.'s neglect and false statements, he advised two of the firm's senior partners. They conceded that the firm was aware "that [L.L.] was a pathological liar and that [L.L.] had previously lied to [members of the firm] regarding the status of other pending legal matters." When plaintiff confronted L.L., he acknowledged that he had lied about the real estate transaction and later admitted in writing that he had committed "several acts of legal malpractice and fraud and deceit upon plaintiff and several other clients of the firm."

The complaint further alleges that, after plaintiff asked the firm partners to report L.L.'s misconduct to the Appellate Division Disciplinary Committee as required under DR 1-103(A) of the Code of Professional Responsibility,[9] they declined to act. Later, in an effort to dissuade plaintiff from making the report himself, the partners told him that they would reimburse his losses. Plaintiff nonetheless met with the Committee "to discuss the entire matter." He withdrew his complaint, however, "because the [f]irm had indicated that it would fire plaintiff if he reported [L.L.'s] misconduct." Ultimately, in December 1987 — as a result of plaintiff's insistence — the firm made a report concerning L.L.'s "numerous misrepresentations and [acts of] malpractice against clients of the [f]irm and acts of forgery of checks drawn on the [f]irm's account." Thereafter, two partners "continuously berated plaintiff for having caused them to report [the] misconduct." The firm nevertheless continued to employ plaintiff "because he was in charge of handling the most important litigation in the [f]irm." Plaintiff was fired in March 1988, a few days after he filed motion papers in that important case.

Plaintiff asserts that defendants wrongfully discharged him as a result of his insistence that L.L.'s misconduct be reported as required by DR 1-103(A). In his fourth cause of action, he alleges that the firm's termination constituted a breach of

---

[9] [1] DR 1-103(A) provides: "A lawyer possessing knowledge, not protected as a confidence or secret, of a violation of DR 1-103 that raises a substantial question as to another lawyer's honesty, trustworthiness or fitness in other respects as a lawyer shall report such knowledge to a tribunal or other authority empowered to investigate or act upon such violation."

the employment relationship. In the fifth cause of action, he claims that his discharge was in violation of public policy and constituted a tort for which he seeks compensatory and punitive damages.

Defendants moved to dismiss the fourth and fifth causes of action as legally insufficient pursuant to CPLR 3211(a)(7). Supreme Court granted defendants' motion because his employment relationship was at will.

The Appellate Division affirmed. It also concluded that plaintiff failed to state a cause of action because, as an at-will employee, the firm could terminate him without cause. This Court granted leave to appeal.

II.

We discuss first whether, notwithstanding our firmly established employment-at-will doctrine, plaintiff has stated a legal claim for breach of contract in the fourth cause of action. The answer requires a review of the three cases in which that doctrine is fully explained.

The employment-at-will doctrine is a judicially created common-law rule "that where an employment is for an indefinite term it is presumed to be a hiring at will which may be freely terminated by either party at any time for any reason or even for no reason" *Murphy v American Home Prods. Corp.*, 58 NY2d 293, 300, *supra* [citing *Martin v New York Life Ins. Co.*, 148 NY 117]. In *Murphy*, this Court dismissed the claim of an employee who alleged he had been discharged in bad faith in retaliation for his disclosure of accounting improprieties. In so doing, we expressly declined to follow other jurisdictions in adopting the tort-based abusive discharge cause of action for imposing "liability on employers where employees have been discharged for disclosing illegal activities on the part of their employers," being of the view "that such a significant change in our law is best left to the Legislature."

With respect to the contract cause of action asserted in *Murphy*, the Court held that plaintiff had not shown evidence of any express agreement limiting the employer's unfettered right to fire the employee. For this reason, the Court distinguished *Weiner v McGraw-Hill, Inc.*, where such an express limitation had been found in language in the employer's personnel handbook. Finally, in *Murphy*, the Court rejected the argument that plaintiff's discharge for disclosing improprieties violated a legally implied obligation in the employment contract requiring the employer to deal fairly and in good faith with the employee. . . .

Not surprisingly, defendants' position here with respect to plaintiff's breach of contract cause of action is simple and direct, i.e., that: (1) . . . plaintiff has shown no factual basis for an express limitation on the right to terminate; and (2) [our prior cases] rule out any basis for contractual relief under an obligation implied-in-law. We agree that plaintiff's complaint does not contain allegations that could come within the *Weiner* exception for express contractual limitations. As to an implied-in-law duty, however, a different analysis and other considerations pertain.

As plaintiff points out, his employment as a lawyer to render professional services as an associate with a law firm differs in several respects from the employments in *Murphy* and *Sabetay*. The plaintiffs in those cases were in the financial departments of their employers, both large companies. Although they performed accounting services, they did so in furtherance of their primary line responsibilities as part of corporate management. In contrast, plaintiff's performance of professional services for the firm's clients as a duly admitted member of the Bar was at the very core and, indeed, the only purpose of his association with defendants. Associates are, to be sure, employees of the firm but they remain independent officers of the court responsible in a broader public sense for their professional obligations. Practically speaking, plaintiff's duties and responsibilities as a lawyer and as an associate of the firm were so closely linked as to be incapable of separation. It is in this distinctive relationship between a law firm and a lawyer hired as an associate that plaintiff finds the implied-in-law obligation on which he founds his claim.

We agree with plaintiff that in any hiring of an attorney as an associate to practice law with a firm there is implied an understanding so fundamental to the relationship and essential to its purpose as to require no expression: that both the associate and the firm in conducting the practice will do so in accordance with the ethical standards of the profession. Erecting or countenancing disincentives to compliance with the applicable rules of professional conduct, plaintiff contends, would subvert the central professional purpose of his relationship with the firm — the lawful and ethical practice of law. The particular rule of professional conduct implicated here (DR 1-103[A]), it must be noted, is critical to the unique function of self-regulation belonging to the legal profession. Although the Bar admission requirements provide some safeguards against the enrollment of unethical applicants, the Legislature has delegated the responsibility for maintaining the standards of ethics and competence to the Departments of the Appellate Division. To assure that the legal profession fulfills its responsibility of self-regulation, DR 1-103(A) places upon each lawyer and Judge the duty to report to the Disciplinary Committee of the Appellate Division any potential violations of the Disciplinary Rules that raise a "substantial question as to another lawyer's honesty, trustworthiness or fitness in other respects." Indeed, one commentator has noted that, "[t]he reporting requirement is nothing less than essential to the survival of the profession."

Moreover, as plaintiff points out, failure to comply with the reporting requirement may result in suspension or disbarment. Thus, by insisting that plaintiff disregard DR 1-103(A) defendants were not only making it impossible for plaintiff to fulfill his professional obligations but placing him in the position of having to choose between continued employment and his own potential suspension and disbarment. We agree with plaintiff that these unique characteristics of the legal profession in respect to this core Disciplinary Rule make the relationship of an associate to a law firm employer intrinsically different from that of the financial managers to the corporate employers in *Murphy* and *Sabetay*. The critical question is whether this distinction calls for a different rule regarding the implied obligation of good faith and fair dealing from that applied in *Murphy* and *Sabetay*. We believe that it does in this case, but we, by no means, suggest that each provision of the Code of Professional Responsibility should be deemed incorporated as an implied-in-law term in every contractual relationship between or among lawyers.

*   *   *

III.

Plaintiff argues, moreover, that the dictates of public policy in DR 1-103(A) have such force as to warrant our recognition of the tort of abusive discharge pleaded in the fifth cause of action. While the arguments are persuasive and the circumstances here compelling, we have consistently held that "significant alteration of employment relationships, such as the plaintiff urges, is best left to the Legislature." (*Murphy v American Home Prods. Corp., supra*, at 301-302.) We believe that the same rationale applies here. In 1984, the Legislature enacted a "Whistleblower" statute (Labor Law § 740, added by L. 1984, ch 660, § 2). We have noted that, although the present "statute has been criticized by commentators for not affording sufficient safeguards against retaliatory discharge, any additional protection must come from the Legislature."

Accordingly, the judgment appealed from and the order of the Appellate Division brought up for review should be modified, with costs to plaintiff, by denying defendant's motion to dismiss the fourth cause of action and, as so modified, affirmed.

2. The Partnership Decision as an Employment Action

HISHON v. KING & SPALDING
467 U.S. 69 (1984)

CHIEF JUSTICE BURGER delivered the opinion of the Court.

We granted certiorari to determine whether the District Court properly dismissed a Title VII complaint alleging that a law partnership discriminated against petitioner, a woman lawyer employed as an associate, when it failed to invite her to become a partner.

I

A

In 1972 petitioner Elizabeth Anderson Hishon accepted a position as an associate with respondent, a large Atlanta law firm established as a general partnership. When this suit was filed in 1980, the firm had more than 50 partners and employed approximately 50 attorneys as associates. Up to that time, no woman had ever served as a partner at the firm.

Petitioner alleges that the prospect of partnership was an important factor in her initial decision to accept employment with respondent. She alleges that respondent used the possibility of ultimate partnership as a recruiting device to induce petitioner and other young lawyers to become associates at the firm. According to the complaint, respondent represented that advancement to partnership after five or six years was "a matter of course" for associates "who [received] satisfactory evaluations" and that associates were promoted to partnership "on a fair and equal basis." Petitioner alleges that she relied on these representations when she accepted employment with respondent. The complaint further alleges that respondent's promise to consider her on a "fair and equal basis" created a binding employment contract.

In May 1978 the partnership considered and rejected Hishon for admission to the partnership; one year later, the partners again declined to invite her to become a partner. Once an associate is passed over for partnership at respondent's firm, the associate is notified to begin seeking employment elsewhere. Petitioner's employment as an associate terminated on December 31, 1979.

B

Hishon filed a charge with the Equal Employment Opportunity Commission on November 19, 1979, claiming that respondent had discriminated against her on the basis of her sex in violation of Title VII of the Civil Rights Act of 1964, 78 Stat. 241, as amended, 42 U.S.C. § 2000e et seq. Ten days later the Commission issued a notice of right to sue, and on February 27, 1980, Hishon brought this action in the United States District Court for the Northern District of Georgia. She sought declaratory and injunctive relief, backpay, and compensatory damages "in lieu of reinstatement and promotion to partnership." This, of course, negates any claim for specific performance of the contract alleged.

The District Court dismissed the complaint on the ground that Title VII was inapplicable to the selection of partners by a partnership. A divided panel of the United States Court of Appeals for the Eleventh Circuit affirmed. We granted certiorari, and we reverse.

II

At this stage of the litigation, we must accept petitioner's allegations as true. The issue before us is whether petitioner's allegations state a claim under Title VII, the relevant portion of which provides as follows:

(a) It shall be an unlawful employment practice for an employer—

(1) to fail or refuse to hire or to discharge any individual, or otherwise to discriminate against any individual with respect to his compensation, terms, conditions, or privileges of employment, because of such individual's race, color, religion, sex, or national origin.

42 U.S.C. § 2000e-2(a).

A

Petitioner alleges that respondent is an "employer" to whom Title VII is addressed. She then asserts that consideration for partnership was one of the "terms, conditions, or privileges of employment" as an associate with respondent. *See* § 2000e-2(a)(1). If this is correct, respondent could not base an adverse partnership decision on "race, color, religion, sex, or national origin."

Once a contractual relationship of employment is established, the provisions of Title VII attach and govern certain aspects of that relationship. In the context of Title VII, the contract of employment may be written or oral, formal or informal; an informal contract of employment may arise by the simple act of handing a job applicant a shovel and providing a workplace. The contractual relationship of employment triggers the provision of Title VII governing "terms, conditions, or privileges of employment." Title VII in turn forbids discrimination on the basis of "race, color, religion, sex, or national origin."

Because the underlying employment relationship is contractual, it follows that the "terms, conditions, or privileges of employment" clearly include benefits that are part of an employment contract. Here, petitioner in essence alleges that respondent made a contract to consider her for partnership. Indeed, this promise was allegedly a key contractual provision which induced her to accept employment. If the evidence at trial establishes that the parties contracted to have petitioner considered for partnership, that promise clearly was a term, condition, or privilege of her employment. Title VII would then bind respondent to consider petitioner for partnership as the statute provides, i.e., without regard to petitioner's sex. The contract she alleges would lead to the same result.

* * *

Several allegations in petitioner's complaint would support the conclusion that the opportunity to become a partner was part and parcel of an associate's status as an employee at respondent's firm, independent of any allegation that such an opportunity was included in associates' employment contracts. Indeed, the importance of the partnership decision to a lawyer's status as an associate is underscored by the allegation that associates' employment is terminated if they are not elected to become partners. These allegations, if proved at trial, would suffice to show that partnership consideration was a term, condition, or privilege of an associate's employment at respondent's firm, and accordingly that partnership consideration must be without regard to sex.

B

Respondent contends that advancement to partnership may never qualify as a term, condition, or privilege of employment for purposes of Title VII. First, respondent asserts that elevation to partnership entails a change in status from an "employee" to an "employer." However, even if respondent is correct that a partnership invitation is not itself an offer of employment, Title VII would nonetheless apply and preclude discrimination on the basis of sex. The benefit a plaintiff is denied need not be employment to fall within Title VII's protection; it need only be a term, condition, or privilege of employment. It is also of no consequence that employment as an associate necessarily ends when an associate becomes a partner. A benefit need not accrue before a person's employment is completed to be a term, condition, or privilege of that employment relationship. Pension benefits, for example, qualify as terms, conditions, or privileges of employment even though they are received only after employment terminates. Accordingly, nothing in the change in status that advancement to partnership might entail means that partnership consideration falls outside the terms of the statute.

Second, respondent argues that Title VII categorically exempts partnership decisions from scrutiny. However, respondent points to nothing in the statute or the legislative history that would support such a per se exemption. When Congress wanted to grant an employer complete immunity, it expressly did so.

Third, respondent argues that application of Title VII in this case would infringe constitutional rights of expression or association. Although we have recognized that the activities of lawyers may make a "distinctive contribution . . . to the ideas and beliefs of our society," *NAACP v. Button*, 371 U.S. 415, 431 (1963), respondent has not shown how its ability to fulfill such a function would be inhibited by a requirement that it consider petitioner for partnership on her merits. Moreover, as we have held in another context, "[invidious] private discrimination may be characterized as a form of exercising freedom of association protected by the First Amendment, but it has never been accorded affirmative constitutional protections." *Norwood v. Harrison*, 413 U.S. 455, 470 (1973). There is no constitutional right, for example, to discriminate in the selection of who may attend a private school or join a labor union.

III

We conclude that petitioner's complaint states a claim cognizable under Title VII. Petitioner therefore is entitled to her day in court to prove her allegations. The judgment of the Court of Appeals is reversed, and the case is remanded for further proceedings consistent with this opinion.

It is so ordered.

JUSTICE POWELL, concurring.

I join the Court's opinion holding that petitioner's complaint alleges a violation of Title VII and that the motion to dismiss should not have been granted. Petitioner's complaint avers that the law firm violated its promise that she would be considered for partnership on a "fair and equal basis" within the time span that associates generally are so considered.[10] Petitioner is entitled to the opportunity to prove

---

[10] [2] Law firms normally require a period of associateship as a prerequisite to being eligible to "make" partner. This need not be an inflexible period, as firms may vary from the norm and admit to partnership earlier than, or subsequent to, the customary period of service. Also, as the complaint recognizes, many firms make annual evaluations of the performances of associates, and usually are free to terminate employment on the basis of these evaluations.

these averments.

I write to make clear my understanding that the Court's opinion should not be read as extending Title VII to the management of a law firm by its partners. The reasoning of the Court's opinion does not require that the relationship among partners be characterized as an "employment" relationship to which Title VII would apply. The relationship among law partners differs markedly from that between employer and employee — including that between the partnership and its associates.[11] The judgmental and sensitive decisions that must be made among the partners embrace a wide range of subjects.[12] The essence of the law partnership is the common conduct of a shared enterprise. The relationship among law partners contemplates that decisions important to the partnership normally will be made by common agreement, or consent among the partners.

Respondent contends that for these reasons application of Title VII to the decision whether to admit petitioner to the firm implicates the constitutional right to association. But here it is alleged that respondent as an employer is obligated by contract to consider petitioner for partnership on equal terms without regard to sex. I agree that enforcement of this obligation, voluntarily assumed, would impair no right of association.

With respect to laws that prevent discrimination, much depends upon the standards by which the courts examine private decisions that are an exercise of the right of association. For example, the Courts of Appeals generally have acknowledged that respect for academic freedom requires some deference to the judgment of schools and universities as to the qualifications of professors, particularly those considered for tenured positions. The present case does not present such an issue.

In admission decisions made by law firms, it is now widely recognized — as it should be — that in fact neither race nor sex is relevant. The qualities of mind, capacity to reason logically, ability to work under pressure, leadership, and the like are unrelated to race or sex. This is demonstrated by the success of women and minorities in law schools, in the practice of law, on the bench, and in positions of community, state, and national leadership. Law firms — and, of course, society — are the better for these changes.

---

[11] [3] Of course, an employer may not evade the strictures of Title VII simply by labeling its employees as "partners." Law partnerships usually have many of the characteristics that I describe generally here.

[12] [4] These decisions concern such matters as participation in profits and other types of compensation; work assignments; approval of commitments in bar association, civic, or political activities; questions of billing; acceptance of new clients; questions of conflicts of interest; retirement programs; and expansion policies. Such decisions may affect each partner of the firm. Divisions of partnership profits, unlike shareholders' rights to dividends, involve judgments as to each partner's contribution to the reputation and success of the firm. This is true whether the partner's participation in profits is measured in terms of points or percentages, combinations of salaries and points, salaries and bonuses, and possibly in other ways.

3. And Partners, Too?

EQUAL EMPLOYMENT OPPORTUNITY COMMISSION v. SIDLEY AUSTIN BROWN & WOOD
315 F.3d 696 (7th Cir. 2002)

POSNER, CIRCUIT JUDGE.

In 1999, Sidley & Austin (as it then was) demoted 32 of its equity partners to "counsel' or "senior counsel.' The significance of these terms is unclear, but Sidley does not deny that they signify demotion and constitute adverse personnel action within the meaning of the antidiscrimination laws. The EEOC began an investigation to determine whether the demotions might have violated the Age Discrimination in Employment Act. After failing to obtain all the information it wanted without recourse to process, the Commission issued a subpoena duces tecum to the firm, seeking a variety of documentation bearing on two distinct areas of inquiry: coverage and discrimination. The reason for the inquiry about coverage is that the ADEA protects employees but not employers. *E.g., Simpson v. Ernst & Young*, 100 F.3d 436, 443 (6th Cir. 1996); *see* 29 U.S.C. §§ 623(a)(2), (a)(3), 630(f). To be able to establish that the firm had violated the ADEA, therefore, the Commission would have to show that the 32 partners were employees before their demotion.

Sidley provided most of the information sought in the subpoena that related to coverage (but no information relating to discrimination, though Sidley claims that the demotions were due to shortcomings in performance rather than to age), but not all. It contended that it had given the Commission enough information to show that before their demotion the 32 had been 'real' partners and so there was no basis for the Commission to continue its investigation. The Commission applied to the district court for an order enforcing the subpoena. The court ordered the firm to comply in full, and the firm appeals.

*   *   *

The facts as developed so far reveal the following:

The firm is controlled by a self-perpetuating executive committee. Partners who are not members of the committee have some powers delegated to them by it with respect to the hiring, firing, promotion, and compensation of their subordinates, but so far as their own status is concerned they are at the committee's mercy. It can fire them, promote them, demote them (as it did to the 32), raise their pay, lower their pay, and so forth. The only firm-wide issue on which all partners have voted in the last quarter century was the merger with Brown & Wood and that vote took place after the EEOC began its investigation. Each of the 32 partners at the time of their demotion by the executive committee had a capital account with the firm, averaging about $400,000. Under the firm's rules, each was liable for the firm's liabilities in proportion to his capital in the firm. Their income, however, was determined by the number of percentage points of the firm's overall profits that the executive committee assigned to each of them. Each served on one or more of the firm's committees, but all these committees are subject to control by the executive committee.

* * *

A remarkable feature of the way the case has been argued is that neither party has addressed the question *why* some or all members of partnerships should for purposes of the federal antidiscrimination laws be deemed employers and so placed outside the protection of these laws. That question might be avoidable if the laws contained an exemption for discrimination against partners; we might then simply look to the definition of the term in federal or state law. And if we looked there, we would find that Sidley was indeed a partnership and the 32 demoted partners were indeed partners before their demotion. Sidley has complied with all the formalities required by Illinois law to establish and maintain a partnership; the 32 were partners within the meaning of the applicable partnership law.

Although the EEOC does not concede that the 32 are bona fide partners even under state law, it is emphatic that their classification under state law is not dispositive of their status under federal antidiscrimination law. The antidiscrimination laws do not exempt partnerships from coverage (Sidley concedes that) or deny partners, as such, the protection of the laws. Employers are not protected by discrimination laws such as Title VII and the ADEA, but are partners employers? Always? Always for purposes of Title VII or the ADEA, or the other federal laws that prohibit employment discrimination? Statutory purpose is relevant. When the Supreme Court . . . was faced with the question whether "employee" in Title VII includes a former employee, it looked to "consistency with a primary purpose of anti-retaliation provisions: Maintaining unfettered access to statutory remedial mechanisms. The EEOC quite persuasively maintains that it would be destructive of this purpose of the anti-retaliation provision for an employer to be able to retaliate with impunity against an entire class of acts under Title VII." . . .

An individual who was classified as a partner-employer under state partnership law might be classified as an employee for other purposes, including the purpose for which federal antidiscrimination law extends protection to employees but not employers. Against this conclusion it can be argued that partners should be classified as employers rather than employees for purposes of the age discrimination law because partnership law gives them effective remedies against oppression by their fellow partners, because partnership relations would be poisoned if partners could sue each other for unlawful discrimination, and because the relation among partners is so intimate that they should be allowed to discriminate, just as individuals are allowed to discriminate in their purely personal relations. This is not the occasion on which to come down on one side or the other of the issue, though we note that in *Hishon v. King & Spalding*, 467 U.S. 69, 78 (1984), the Supreme Court rejected the argument that the intimate nature of the partnership relation precludes a challenge under Title VII to a discriminatory refusal to promote an employee to partner.

But we do not understand how Sidley, without addressing the purpose of the employer exemption, can be so certain that it has proved that the 32 are employers within the meaning of the ADEA. They are, or rather were, partners, but it does not follow that they were employers. A firm that under pursuit by the EEOC on suspicion of discrimination redesignated its employees "partners" without changing the preexisting employment relation an iota would not by doing this necessarily buy immunity, even if the redesignation sufficed to make them partners under state law.

This case is not as extreme; it does not involve relabeling. Yet it involves a partnership of more than 500 partners in which all power resides in a small, unelected committee (it has 36 members). The partnership does not elect the members of the executive committee; the committee elects them, like the self-perpetuating board of trustees of a private university or other charitable foundation. It is true that the partners can commit the firm, for example by writing opinion letters; but employees of a corporation, when acting within the scope of their employment, regularly commit the corporation to contractual undertakings, not to mention to tort liability. Partners who are not members of the executive committee share in the profits of the firm; but many corporations base their employees' compensation in part anyway, but sometimes in very large part, on the corporation's profits, without anyone supposing them employers. The participation of the 32 demoted partners in committees that have, so far as appears, merely administrative functions does not distinguish them from executive employees in corporations. Corporations have committees and the members of the committees are employees; this does not make them employers. Nor are the members of the committees on which the 32 served elected; they are appointed by the executive committee. The 32 owned some of the firm's capital, but executive-level employees often own stock in their corporations. We shall see that there is authority that employee shareholders of a professional corporation are still employees, not employers, for purposes of federal antidiscrimination law.

Particularly unconvincing is Sidley's contention that since the executive committee exercises its absolute power by virtue of delegation by the entire partnership in the partnership agreement, we should treat the entire partnership as if it rather than the executive committee were directing the firm. That would be like saying that if the people elect a person to be dictator for life, the government is a democracy rather than a dictatorship. The partners do not even elect the members of the committee. They have no control, direct or indirect, over its composition.

Perhaps the most partneresque feature of the 32 partners' relation to the firm is their personal liability for the firm's debts: not because unlimited liability is a sine qua non of partnership (there can be limited partnerships, and there are other business entities besides partnership that have unlimited liability — a sole proprietorship, for example), but because it is the most salient practical difference between the standard partnership and a corporation. Sidley does not have limited liability, and this means, by the way, that although under the firm's rules each partner is liable for the firm's debts only in proportion to his capital, a creditor of the firm could sue any partner for the entire debt owed it. Is this enough to pin the partner tail on the donkey?

*   *   *

The matter of liability for partnership debts illustrates the importance of referring the question whether a partner in a particular firm is an employer or an employee to statutory purpose. If implicit in the ADEA's exemption for employers is recognition that partners ordinarily have adequate remedies under partnership law to protect themselves against oppression (including age or other forms of invidious discrimination) by the partnership, then exposure to liability can hardly be decisive. These 32 partners were not empowered by virtue of bearing large potential liabilities! The 32 were defenseless; they had no power over their fate. If other partners shirked and as a result imposed liability on the 32, the 32 could not, as partners in a conventional partnership could do, vote to expel them. They had no voting power. What could be argued but is not is that because the *other* partners are potentially liable for the pratfalls of the 32, the partnership should have greater power over their employment than if the firm were a corporation and so had limited liability. To repeat, the issue is not whether the 32 before their demotion were partners, an issue to which their liability for the firm's debts is germane; the issue is whether they were employers. The two classes, partners under state law and employers under federal antidiscrimination law, may not coincide.

* * *

We can get a little help on the question in our case from Justice Powell's concurring opinion in *Hishon v. King & Spalding, supra,* 467 U.S. at 79-81, one of the few discussions of the applicability of Title VII to partnerships. Here is what he said:

> I write to make clear my understanding that the Court's opinion [holding discriminatory refusal to promote an associate to partner actionable] should not be read as extending Title VII to the management of a law firm by its partners. The reasoning of the Court's opinion does not require that the relationship among partners be characterized as an "employment" relationship to which Title VII would apply. The relationship among law partners differs markedly from that between employer and employee — including that between the partnership and its associates. (Of course, an employer may not evade the strictures of Title VII simply by labeling its employees as "partners." Law partnerships usually have many of the characteristics that I describe generally here.) The judgmental and sensitive decisions that must be made among the partners embrace a wide range of subjects. The essence of the law partnership is the common conduct of a shared enterprise. The relationship among law partners contemplates that decisions important to the partnership normally will be made by common agreement or consent among the partners.

Justice Powell was saying that a traditional law partnership, involving "the common conduct of a shared enterprise" and a relationship among the partners that "contemplates that decisions will be made by common agreement or consent among the partners," has a governance structure different from the one contemplated or assumed by Title VII. At the same time he was making clear that labeling an enterprise that does not have the structure, the character, of the traditional partnership will not immunize it from the statute. In a case in which we held that partners were employers for purposes of Title VII, the partnership was, so far as appears, an equal partnership of four partners.

All that is clear amidst this welter of cases is that the coverage issue in the present case remains murky despite Sidley's partial compliance with the subpoena. The Commission is therefore entitled to full compliance, at least with regard to coverage, unless the additional documents the Commission is seeking are obviously irrelevant. What the Commission particularly wants to know is how unevenly the profits are spread across the entire firm. Are profits so concentrated in members of the executive committee, or in some smaller or larger set of partners, in relation to the profits that the executive committee allocated to the 32, that the latter occupied the same position they would have if they had been working at a comparable rank for one of the investment banks that once were partnerships but now are corporations? This might not be decisive but it would bear on the unavoidably multi-factored determination of whether this large law firm — which in recognition that conventional partnership is designed for much smaller and simpler firms has contractually altered the structure of the firm in the direction of the corporate form — should for purposes of antidiscrimination law be deemed the employer of some at least of the individuals whom it designates as partners.

We are not ruling that the 32 demoted partners were in fact employees within the meaning of the age discrimination law. Such a ruling would be premature. Sidley has respectable arguments on its side, not least that the functional test of employer status toward which the EEOC is leaning is too uncertain to enable law firms and other partnerships to determine in advance their exposure to discrimination suits — that it would be better if the courts and the Commission interpreted the employer exclusion to require treating all partners as employers, with perhaps a narrow sham exception. These issues will become ripe when Sidley finishes complying with the coverage part of the subpoena. We hold only that there is enough doubt about whether the 32 demoted partners are covered by the age discrimination law to entitle the EEOC to full compliance with that part, at least, of its subpoena.

Vacated and Remanded with Directions.

EASTERBROOK, CIRCUIT JUDGE, concurring in part and concurring in the judgment.

I join my colleagues' exemplary discussion of the law governing agency subpoenas but otherwise concur only in the judgment. I do not think that the scope of the ADEA's coverage is as unfathomable as the majority makes out, nor do I believe that *if* the law were so ambulatory we should punt the legal question to the district court. Instead we should do our best to reduce uncertainty. Sidley and other large partnerships need to plan their affairs; their members also need to know their legal status. Can large law firms adopt mandatory-retirement rules? It is disappointing that the EEOC should profess, some 30 years after the ADEA's enactment, that it hasn't a clue about the answer. My colleagues' opinion does not help matters, and this is a missed opportunity.

*   *   *

. . . No one believes that a *bona fide* partner is in a master-servant relation with the partnership, or that the partner "is employed by" the partnership. The qualification *"bona fide"* is important; as Justice Powell observed in *Hishon*, an employer may not evade obligations under federal law by plastering the *name* "partner" on someone whose legal and economic characteristics are those of an employee.

Were the 32 lawyers *bona fide* partners? The majority all but concedes that they were. . . . We know that all 32 (i) received a percentage of Sidley's profits and had to pony up if Sidley incurred a loss; (ii) had capital accounts that were at risk if the firm foundered; and (iii) were personally liable for the firm's debts and thus put their entire wealth, not just their capital accounts, on the line. We also know that (iv) no nonpartner has an equity interest in the firm. The most important of these is the first (which implies the third): under the Uniform Partnership Act, it is profit-sharing (coupled with the lack of organization as an entity under some other law) that *defines* a partnership and identifies its partners, all of whom are personally liable for the venture's debts.

*　*　*

We should ask not what the organization, or any given state, *calls* this person; we should ask how this set of attributes is classified under the prevailing law of agency. I think it very likely that the 32 lawyers Sidley demoted would be classified as partners rather than employees under this body of rules, but I do not know how Sidley's other lawyers should be classified, so a remand is in order. Enforcing those aspects of the subpoena that call for information relevant to the merits would be unduly burdensome until this task has been completed, and unless the evidence then shows that Sidley has classified as "partners" some persons who are employees under ordinary agency principles.

NOTE

See David B. Wilkins, *Twenty-Five years of Richard Posner, The Judge: Partner, Shmartner!* EEOC v. Sidley Austin Brown & Wood, 120 Harv. L. Rev. 1264 (2007).

4. Employee or Lawyer?

HULL v. CELANESE CORP.
375 F. Supp. 922 (S.D.N.Y. 1974)

Owen, District Judge.

Miss Donata Delulio, an attorney employed in the law department of defendant Celanese Corporation since 1972, claims that she has been damaged by various forms of sex discrimination by Celanese, particularly with respect to hiring, promotions and transfers, salary and raises, training and education programs, public relations and client good-will activities.

She moves for leave to intervene in this action, commenced in 1973 by Joan Hull, an employee of Celanese Fibers Marketing Company (CFMC) a division of defendant Celanese. Plaintiff Hull, seeking class action designation, alleges that Celanese, CFMC, two officers and three directors violated Title VII of the Civil Rights Act of 1964 by discrimination in employment on the basis of sex. Miss Delulio, however, suffers from an impediment which, in my opinion, is fatal to her motion. Specifically she participated as one of a number of Celanese lawyers in an active and substantial way in early stages of the defense of this very action.[13]

The facts as to her participation are well-summarized in Miss Delulio's own words in her letter to the Committee on Professional and Judicial Ethics of the Association of the Bar of the City of New York seeking guidance:

> During the six months that I worked on [the Hull] case I studied the general regulations of the Equal Employment Opportunities Commission, its procedures and the law on sex discrimination generally. I obtained specific information from the personnel department of the division concerning salaries and hiring practices. I attended on (sic) interview of the employee's superior, and attended one interview of another division employee. I participated in a conference with outside consultants hired by the corporation to prepare statistical information regarding employment within the division. I obtained inter-office memoranda and prepared a memorandum myself regarding the case."[14]

Thus, there is no question that Miss Delulio is possessed of substantial knowledge and information as to the Hull case obtained as a lawyer in defending against it.[15]

To the foregoing, Miss Delulio unequivocally states that although she and Joan Hull and other plaintiffs have become social friends and although she has had conferences with Hull's attorneys (who are now her attorneys) concerning this case, she has never revealed anything learned in confidence. Giving these statements full credit, and passing the requirement that a lawyer avoid even the "appearance of impropriety" in his professional conduct[16] nevertheless, the opportunity for inadvertent disclosure is clearly ever-present.

This seems to be a case of first impression, and research has disclosed no authorities directly on point. However, *Emle Industries, Inc. v. Patentex, Inc.*, 478 F.2d 562 (2d Cir. 1973), *Motor Mart, Inc. v. Saab Motors, Inc.*, 359 F. Supp. 156 (S.D.N.Y. 1973), and *T.C. Theatre Corp. v. Warner Bros. Pictures*, 113 F. Supp. 265 (S.D.N.Y. 1953), provide clear and sufficient guidance mandating a denial of this motion as a matter of law. In *Emle*, the Court stated at p. 570-1:

> Canon 4 implicitly incorporates the admonition, embodied in old Canon 6, that "The [lawyer's] obligation to represent the client with undivided fidelity and not to divulge his secrets or confidences forbids also the subsequent acceptance of retainers or employment from others in matters adversely affecting any interest of the client with respect to which confidence has been reposed." Without strict enforcement of such high

---

[13] [2] It would appear that Miss Delulio's work upon the Hull case terminated prior to any activity on her part to intervene therefor.

[14] [3] The Committee advised Miss Delulio in writing that in its opinion she should neither intervene in the Hull action, nor prosecute her own action.

[15] [4] Miss Delulio concedes "It is possible that I might have evidence that would be protected by the attorney-client privilege . . . ."

[16] [6] Canon 9 of the Canons of Legal Ethics. This Canon alone is, in my opinion, sufficient to require denial of this motion, but given the facts herein I need not decide on "appearances" alone.

ethical standards, a client would hardly be inclined to discuss his problems freely and in depth with his lawyer, for he would justifiably fear that information he reveals to his lawyer on one day may be used against him on the next. A lawyer's good faith, although essential in all his professional activity, is, nevertheless, an inadequate safeguard when standing alone. Even the most rigorous self-discipline might not prevent a lawyer from unconsciously using or manipulating a confidence acquired in the earlier representation and transforming it into a telling advantage in the subsequent litigation. . . . The dynamics of litigation are far too subtle, the attorney's role in that process is far too critical, and the public's interest in the outcome is far too great to leave room for even the slightest doubt concerning the ethical propriety of a lawyer's representation in a given case. These considerations require application of a strict prophylactic rule to prevent any possibility, however slight, that confidential information acquired from a client during a previous relationship may subsequently be used to the client's disadvantage.

As her "ultimate position,"[17] it is urged that Miss Delulio has a constitutionally-protected freedom of association, citing *N.A.A. C.P. v. Button*, 371 U.S. 415 (1963). This position I find to be without merit. Miss Delulio is correct to the extent that *N.A.A.C.P. v. Button*, did strike down certain state regulations of the practice of law in conflict with "the First Amendment as absorbed in the Fourteenth . . ." as "unduly inhibiting protected freedoms of expression and association." However, *N.A.A.C.P. v. Button* specifically excepted from the scope of its ruling a situation in which there has been a "showing of a serious danger of professionally reprehensible conflicts of interest[,]" which situation exists here.

For the foregoing reasons, both on the law and in my discretion, I deny the motion.

HULL v. CELANESE CORP.
513 F.2d 568 (2d Cir. 1975)

TENNEY, J.

This Court today hears the appeal from an order of disqualification of plaintiff's counsel, the law firm of Rabinowitz, Boudin & Standard ("the Rabinowitz firm"). The question at issue is whether a law firm can take on, as a client, a lawyer for the opposing party in the very litigation against the opposing party. Factually, the case is novel and we approach it mindful of the important competing interests present. It is incumbent upon us to preserve, to the greatest extent possible, both the

---

[17] [7] THE COURT: Well, Mr. Rabinowitz, . . . :

Is it your ultimate position that she has a constitutional right to associate with others to seek redress of grievances?

MR. RABINOWITZ: Yes.

THE COURT: And you say that I must draw, I must be the one that balances that right against the provisions binding upon her under the Canons of Ethics . . . ?

MR. RABINOWITZ: Yes, as I see it.

individual's right to be represented by counsel of his or her choice and the public's interest in maintaining the highest standards of professional conduct and the scrupulous administration of justice.

The complaint in this action was brought by plaintiff-appellant Joan Hull ("Hull"), an employee of Celanese Corporation ("Celanese"), against Celanese alleging sex-based discrimination in employment in violation of Title VII of the Civil Rights Act of 1964, 42 U.S.C. § 2000e. In its answer, Celanese denied the material allegations of the complaint. Thereafter, the Rabinowitz firm filed a motion seeking leave for five other women to intervene as plaintiffs in the action. One of the proposed intervenors was Donata A. Delulio, an attorney on the corporate legal staff of Celanese. Celanese opposed the proposed intervention and additionally sought the disqualification of the Rabinowitz firm based on the risk that confidential information received by Delulio as Celanese's attorney might be used by the Rabinowitz firm against Celanese in the prosecution of the joint Hull-Delulio claims.

The trial court denied Delulio's motion to intervene and subsequently ordered the disqualification of the Rabinowitz firm.

Judge Owen premised the denial of intervention on the fact that Delulio had been active in the defense of this very action, thus raising a serious risk of disclosure of confidential information. He found the opportunity for even inadvertent disclosure to be ever-present.

In granting the motion to disqualify the Rabinowitz firm, Judge Owen clearly recognized three competing interests: (1) Hull's interest in freely selecting counsel of her choice, (2) Celanese's interest in the trial free from the risk of even inadvertent disclosures of confidential information, and (3) the public's interest in the scrupulous administration of justice. In balancing these competing interests, the trial court acknowledged the right of Hull to counsel of her choice, but held the interests of Celanese and the public to be predominant. Based upon the relationship between Delulio and the Rabinowitz firm, the preparation by the Rabinowitz firm on the motion to intervene, supporting affidavits, and amended complaint, and the contents of those documents, Judge Owen concluded:

> The foregoing contents of affidavits prepared by Delulio and the Rabinowitz office are some evidence, in my opinion, of the possibility that Delulio, unquestionably possessed of information within the attorney-client privilege, did in fact transmit some of it to the Rabinowitz firm, consciously or unconsciously.

The trial court felt that the continued retention of the Rabinowitz firm would create at least the appearance of impropriety due to the on-going possibility for improper disclosure.[18] For the reasons stated infra, we must affirm.

---

[18] [8] Judge Owen initially considered holding a hearing to determine whether there had been actual disclosures, but decided in the negative. He concluded that "a hearing would be self-defeating since it would be necessary to reveal to the Rabinowitz firm in some specificity the extent of Celanese's disclosures to Miss Delulio in the course of ascertaining to what extent, if any, that information reached them."

The unusual factual situation presented here bears repetition in some detail. Hull's employment by Celanese began in 1963; Delulio's employment there began in July 1972. In September of 1972, Hull filed charges with the Equal Employment Opportunity Commission ("EEOC") against Celanese alleging sex-based discrimination in employment. Delulio was assigned to work on the defense of the Hull case in February of 1973 and her work on the case continued until September 1973. In the interim, the complaint herein was filed.

It was during September of 1973 that Hull and Delulio met socially for the first time. Two months later Delulio approached Hull to ascertain the name of the law firm representing Hull. As a result of this conversation, Delulio contacted the Rabinowitz firm on November 9, and on November 15, 1973 the Rabinowitz firm filed sex discrimination charges on behalf of Delulio with the EEOC. Delulio thereafter consulted with the Association of the Bar of the City of New York regarding, inter alia, the propriety of her intervention in the Hull action. By letter dated March 12, 1974, the Association of the Bar of the City of New York advised Delulio against intervention. Subsequently, the motion herein seeking intervention on behalf of Delulio and four other women was filed. Two weeks later Celanese cross-moved to deny intervention and to disqualify the Rabinowitz firm.

* * *

In the instant case we have a divergence from the more usual situation of the lawyer switching sides to represent an interest adverse to his initial representation. Here, the in-house counsel for Celanese switched sides to become a plaintiff (rather than a lawyer) on the other side. Also, here the matter at issue is not merely "substantially related" to the previous representation, rather, it is exactly the same litigation. Thus, while the cases are factually distinguishable, the admonition of Canon 9 is equally appropriate here. This is, in short, one of those cases in which disqualification is "a necessary and desirable remedy . . . to enforce the lawyer's duty of absolute fidelity and to guard against the danger of inadvertent use of confidential information . . . ." *Ceramco, Inc. v. Lee Pharmaceuticals*, 510 F.2d 268, 271 (2d Cir. 1975).

The Rabinowitz firm argues that they had never worked for Celanese and therefore never had direct access to any confidences of Celanese. They maintain that they carefully cautioned Delulio not to reveal any information received in confidence as an attorney for Celanese, but rather to confine her revelations to them to the facts of her own case. This, they contend would avoid even an indirect transferral of confidential information. They conclude that since they never got any information either directly or indirectly, they could not use the information either consciously or unconsciously.

This argument, somewhat technical in nature, seems to overlook the spirit of Canon 9. We credit the efforts of the Rabinowitz firm to avoid the receipt of any confidence. Nonetheless, "where 'it can reasonably be said that in the course of the former representation the attorney *might* have acquired information related to the subject matter of his subsequent representation,' it is the court's duty to order the attorney disqualified." The breach of confidence would not have to be proved; it is presumed in order to preserve the spirit of the Code.

The Rabinowitz firm had notice that Delulio had worked on the defense of the Hull case and should have declined representation when approached. Had Delulio joined the firm as an assistant counsel in the *Hull* case, they would have been disqualified. Here she joined them, as it were, as a client. The relation is no less damaging.

Our holding herein is distinguishable from the result reached in *Meyerhofer v. Empire Fire and Marine Insurance Co.*, 497 F.2d 1190 (2d Cir.), *cert. denied*, 419 U.S. 998 (1974). There it was held that disqualification was unnecessary since the lawyer had acted properly in defending himself "against 'an accusation of wrongful conduct.' "

The novel factual situation presented here dictates a narrow reading of this opinion. This decision should not be read to imply that either Hull or Delulio cannot pursue her claim of employment discrimination based on sex. The scope of this opinion must, of necessity, be confined to the facts presented and not read as a broad-brush approach to disqualification.

The preservation of public trust both in the scrupulous administration of justice and in the integrity of the bar is paramount. Recognizably important are Hull's right to counsel of her choice and the consideration of the judicial economy which could be achieved by trying these claims in one lawsuit. These considerations must yield, however, to considerations of ethics which run to the very integrity of our judicial process.

Accordingly, the order of the district court is affirmed.

NOTES, QUESTIONS, AND EXAMPLES

1. How can an in-house lawyer in DeLulio's position pursue a claim of discrimination?

2. Why was the appellate court unpersuaded by the suggested use of the "self-defense" exception to the duty of confidentiality?

D.   LAWYERS AS INTERMEDIARIES AND THIRD-PARTY NEUTRALS

Contrary to the ordinary picture of the lawyer as a partisan, representing one party against the interests of another, lawyers may in limited circumstances act in the role of intermediaries and sometimes a third-party neutral, such as a mediator or arbitrator. MR 2.4. As an intermediary, a lawyer attempts to achieve the goals and interests of multiple parties with potentially adverse interests. Such a role is inappropriate when litigation is pending or contemplated. Because the role of intermediary is less commonly engaged in, the lawyer must ensure that all parties understand the nature of the relationship.

In order to pursue a matter for multiple clients as an intermediary, several requirements must be met. Each client must consent to the common representation after consultation with the lawyer. Former MR 2.2(a)(1). The consultation must include a discussion of the risks of common representation and its effect on confidentiality. The evidentiary privilege and the duty of confidentiality do not apply as between the parties commonly represented.

With the February 2002 adoption of new Rule 2.4, the ABA deleted the little-used Rule 2.2.

Model Rule 2.4 defines a role other than that of lawyer, in which a lawyer may serve. The third-party neutral role, such as arbitrator or mediator, is now a common, reasonably well-understood role in various alternative dispute resolution systems. Lawyers sometimes serve in such roles, and new Rule 2.4 makes clear that the third-party neutral role is distinct from that of lawyer. The rule defines the third-party neutral role, distinguishes it from that of lawyer, then requires that lawyers serving in the third-party neutral role inform the parties to the process that the lawyer does not represent the parties and inform them of the role's distinctions with that of lawyer.

The role of intermediary is sometimes but not always the equivalent of the role of mediator. A mediator seeks to be a neutral voice that facilitates the voluntary agreement between disputing parties. Lawyers sometimes fill that role. In many other instances, however, a lawyer acting as intermediary is not a neutral in a dispute at all. Rather, the more general intermediary role may involve joint representation of clients who simply want a project such as a real estate closing, or a partnership agreement to work.

A proposed set of standards for mediators: A set of standards for all mediators, including lawyer mediators, has been proposed by a joint group of ABA sections and the American Arbitration Association and is under consideration. These guidelines are not widely accepted as yet, but they have been adopted by eight states. For a lawyer who acts as mediator, the balance between these mediator standards and their general lawyer standards will be delicate and difficult. One thing, however, is clear. For now, at least, the lawyer standards control where a conflict arises. These proposed standards include requirements that a mediator do the following:

    a. Recognize that mediation is based on self-determination of the parties.

    b. Conduct the mediation impartially.

    c. Disclose conflicts of interest.

    d. Mediate only if qualified to do so.

    e. Maintain the parties' reasonable expectations regarding confidentiality.

    f. Conduct the mediation fairly and diligently.

    g. Be truthful in advertising and solicitation.

    h. Fully disclose and explain fees.

    i. Improve the practice of mediation.

E. ANCILLARY BUSINESSES AND MULTIDISCIPLINARY PRACTICE ISSUES

Many lawyers are in some respects business-people, managing their own law practice. But some lawyers also maintain ancillary, associated businesses along with their law practice. Rules appropriate to govern the lawyer in the ancillary businessperson role have been controversial. MR 5.7. No rule regarding ancillary businesses appeared in the Model Code or in the original Model Rules. In 1991, by a close vote, the ABA adopted a restrictive ancillary business rule. Only one year later, the ABA repealed the restrictive rule. In 1994, the ABA adopted the current version of Model Rule 5.7. The Rule has as yet had little effect on the law beyond its expression of the ABA's current position on the matter.

Lawyers are subject to the rules of professional conduct for lawyers while providing ancillary services when either of the following two conditions is present:

> When the services provided are not distinct from the lawyer's legal services. MR 5.7(a)(1).

> When the services are provided by a separate entity either controlled by the lawyer or by the lawyer with others, and the lawyer fails to communicate clearly to the client that the services are not legal services and are not subject to the normal protections in the lawyer-client relationship. MR 5.7(a)(2).

Ancillary or "law-related" services are services that are related to legal services and are not prohibited as unauthorized practice of law when performed by a non-lawyer. MR 5.7(b). Side businesses of lawyers that are entirely unrelated to their law practice are not ancillary businesses. Common examples of ancillary services are trust management, financial planning, investment banking, and title insurance.

The crux of the ancillary business problem is that clients of the ancillary business may expect that, because the businesses are associated with lawyers, lawyer ethics protections such as confidentiality protection, avoidance of conflicts, and so on, attach to the provision of the ancillary business services as well. The ABA rule attempts to place the burden on the lawyer to either provide the lawyer role protections to the ancillary business client or ensure that the client knows that the protections are not associated with the services.

Pennsylvania Bar Association Committee on Legal Ethics and Professional Responsibility
Informal Opinion Number 98-20 (Mar. 13, 1998)[19]

This letter is in response to your faxes dated March 3 and March 5, 1998, requesting an ethics opinion concerning two questions on the topic on lawyers engaged in ancillary businesses.

I understand that you are an attorney-at-law admitted to practice in the

---

[19] Reprinted with permission.

Commonwealth in Pennsylvania in good standing and that you are working full-time as a salaried Collection Manager for a company engaged in consumer credit bureau services and collection agency services; your employer is affiliated with a national credit reporting bureau. You are not presently practicing law or engaged as counsel for your employer, but you do engage in a part-time practice of law outside of your employer's place of business. You are not an owner or controlling party of your employer. You have inquired about the appropriateness of establishing an in-house legal department at the company where you are employed. You have in mind performing legal services concerning collection of consumer accounts for clients of your employer.

As a related inquiry, you have also asked whether a proposed engagement letter with the clients complies with the applicable Pennsylvania Rules of Professional Conduct. In the letter, you would disclose that you are an employee of the credit bureau, that you do not provide legal services on behalf of your employer, that the legal services to be provided by you to the clients will be kept confidential and separate from your employer's records, that your employer has no monetary or ownership interest in your practice of law and they do not exercise any control over your independent legal judgment and that the clients are advised of their right to utilize the legal services of any attorney.

My conclusion is that you may represent clients who are also customers of your employer in connection with the collection of accounts receivable, provided you strictly comply with the requirements of Rule 5.7 of the Pennsylvania Rules of Professional Conduct and other applicable rules. Your proposed disclosure appears to be reasonable. I assume that the engagement letter will also contain the basis or rate of the fee, as required by Rule 1.5(b).

RESPONSIBILITIES REGARDING NON-LEGAL SERVICES Rule 5.7, adopted effective August 31, 1996, provides as follows:

> (a) A lawyer who provides non-legal services to a recipient that are not distinct from legal services provided to that recipient is subject to the Rules of Professional Conduct with respect to the provision of both legal and non-legal services.

> (b) A lawyer who provides non-legal services to a recipient that are distinct from any legal services provided to the recipient is subject to the Rules of Professional Conduct with respect to the non-legal services if the lawyer knows or reasonably should know that the recipient might believe that the recipient is receiving the protection of a client-lawyer relationship.

> (c) A lawyer who is an owner, controlling party, employee, agent, or is otherwise affiliated with an entity providing non-legal services to a recipient is subject to the Rules of Professional Conduct with respect to the non-legal services if the lawyer knows or reasonably should know that the recipient might believe that the recipient is receiving the protection of a client-lawyer relationship.

> (d) Paragraph (b) or (c) does not apply if the lawyer makes reasonable efforts to avoid any misunderstanding by the recipient receiving non-legal services. Those efforts must include advising the recipient that the services

are not legal services and that the protection of a client-lawyer relationship does not exist with respect to the provision of nonlegal services to the recipient.

Rule 5.7(a) applies to you in your current capacity as Collection Manager if the collection services you provide to clients of your employer are not distinct from the proposed legal services. I understand from you that the collection services you are presently providing to your employers' clients are distinct from any legal services and that you are not presently practicing law at your employer's place of business.

Rule 5.7(b) would apply to your situation if you know or reasonably should know that the clients might believe that they are receiving the protection of a client-lawyer relationship. I understand that your business card as Collection Manager uses the word "Esquire" after your name. Based on this, business customers who receive your card may have the impression that they are establishing a "client-lawyer relationship" with you, even though this may be without substantiation.

Rule 5.7(c) also applies to your situation as an employee of the entity providing non-legal services (collection services). As set forth in Pa. Bar Committee Informal Opinion 97-23, Rule 5.7(d) was drafted to adopt a "safe harbor" provision. The intent of 5.7(d) is to protect both attorneys and the clients. To disabuse any misunderstandings of the scope of the non-legal services, I recommend that you use the written disclaimer for your legal clients in accordance with Rule 5.7(d) and that you do not use the words "Esquire" or "Attorney-at-Law" after your name on your business cards or on correspondence for non-legal services.

Based on the application of Rule 5.7 and the extensive Comments adopted by the Pennsylvania Supreme Court, it is my opinion that you may represent clients of your employer in legal matters relating to the collection of accounts receivable, provided that you strictly comply with the following conditions and otherwise fully comply with the Pennsylvania Rules of Professional Conduct:

(1) All legal fees generated as a result of your work involving the legal aspects of each matter would be paid to you individually and be deposited into the appropriate attorney or individual account. You will open and maintain an attorney escrow account, as needed. Your employer, as a non-legal firm, cannot receive or share any fees for legal services.

(2) All client records and legal correspondence would be kept separate from your employer's records and would be kept confidential.

(3) All clients would be apprised in writing as to your employment as a salaried employee of the company.

(4) All legal correspondence will be on separate letterhead and FAX transmittal sheets bearing your law firm's name.

(5) You will pay for use of office space and secretarial and paralegal services.

(6) You will use separate business cards: one for your position as Collection Manager of your company, on which you will not use the word "Esquire" or "Attorney-at-Law" and another business card for your legal

practice.

You may provide legal services from your office at your employer's place of business which is not devoted exclusively to the practice of law, provided the law practice and the business are segregated and operated separately and that you comply with all provisions of the Pennsylvania Rules of Professional Conduct regarding conflicts of interest and confidentiality. For example, I suggest that you have a separate telephone number and FAX number for your law practice and a separate listing in your building directory for you as an attorney; your legal mail should be opened and messages taken by your legal secretary and/or assistant.

DIRECT CONTACT WITH PROSPECTIVE CLIENTS

The advertising rules, particularly Rule 7.3 regarding direct contact with prospective clients, are also applicable. Rule 7.3(a) prohibits an attorney from soliciting legal business from a prospective client through in-person visits or telephone calls absent a family or prior professional relationship. I agree with Pennsylvania Bar Committee Informal Opinion 93-114, which held that "prior professional relationship" refers to an attorney-client relationship. The Rule also applies to third-parties acting on behalf of an attorney. Thus, whether the legal services offered may be discussed during in-person meetings, presentations or seminars with your employer's clients depends entirely on whether there is a prior professional relationship between the prospective clients and you in your capacity as an attorney. If not, your initial contact with prospective clients must be in writing. You can send a letter to the prospect after the meeting or seminar. Only distinct non-legal services may be directly solicited by an attorney.

Also, I advise you to review and comply with the other relevant Rules of Professional Conduct discussed in Pennsylvania Bar Committee Informal Opinion No. 93-114.

Although not a matter of legal ethics, I know that you are aware of the trend to hold attorneys liable for violations of the Fair Debt Collection Practices Act based on lawyers' collection letters. In that connection, please note the case of *Bartlett v. Heibl*, 128 F.3d 497 (7th Cir. 1997), in which the lawyer's letter was held to violate the Fair Debt Collection Practices Act because it was confusing to the consumer, even though the letter contained all the information required by the statute. The Court upheld statutory damages of $1,000 imposed on the lawyer, even though the consumer admitted that he had not read the letter and was not subjectively mislead by the letter. Chief Judge Posner, the author of the Court's opinion, went on to redraft the lawyer's letter in a way he opined would pass muster under the statute. That letter is appended to the Court's opinion.

NOTES, QUESTIONS, AND EXAMPLES

Should all of the lawyer ethics rules apply to the conduct of a lawyer engaged in an ancillary business? Consider the following example. Lawyer is acting as both a sports agent and a lawyer in her practice. She approaches potential Client-Athlete to propose that she represent him as his sports agent in his upcoming contract negotiation with his team. The protections of the lawyer-client relationship, such as confidentiality, loyalty and attendant conflict avoidance, competence, diligence, and so on, will attach to their relationship if Lawyer provides the services together (as appears to be the situation here) or if Lawyer fails to communicate to Client-Athlete that these protections do not apply to their relationship (i.e., that she is not acting as his lawyer). But the rule does not resolve the question of whether or not the advertising and solicitation rules apply to Lawyer's client-getting activity. If they do, then Lawyer is subject to discipline for the direct solicitation of Client-Athlete.

Laurel S. Terry,[20] *Redefining Lawyers' Work: Multidisciplinary Practice: A Primer on MDPs: Should the "No" Rule Become a New Rule?*[21]
72 TEMP. L. REV. 869 (1999)

* * *

I. The Current U.S. Rules Regarding MDPs

In the U.S., partnerships and fee-sharing arrangements between lawyers and nonlawyers are banned. ABA Model Rule of Professional Conduct 5.4, like its predecessors DR 3-102 and DR 3-103, prohibits a lawyer from forming a partnership with a nonlawyer if the partnership will engage in activities constituting the practice of law or the sharing of legal fees with a nonlawyer.

* * *

Unlike many of the ABA Model Rules, Model Rule 5.4 has been adopted virtually intact in most states. Indeed, the District of Columbia ("D.C.") is the only jurisdiction that has departed in substance on the MDP issue from the ABA Model Rule; D.C.'s rule permits fee sharing and partnerships between lawyers and nonlawyers provided the partnership has as its sole purpose the provisions of legal services to clients. This D.C. rule, however, provides little practical guidance on the regulation of MDPs because it appears to be seldom used. D.C. Ethics Counsel Susan Gilbert has offered two reasons for the infrequent use of D.C. Rule 5.4. First, the requirement that the partnership have the provision of legal services as its "sole purpose" is different than what many of the currently proposed MDPs are interested in. In addition, ABA Ethics Committee Formal Opinion 91-360 narrowed the scope of the rule even further by concluding that a multi-jurisdictional law firm having a D.C. office cannot have a nonlawyer partner in that office. Ms. Gilbert concluded that when the multi-jurisdictional firms are eliminated, the rule is available only to D.C.-based boutique law firms that identify a specific need (*i.e.*, the need for an accountant to do tax work or the need for an office manager). There has been no disciplinary action under D.C. Rule 5.4(b). In short, the D.C. experience on its revision of Rule 5.4 offers little on the difficulty or ease of regulating MDPs.

---

[20] Professor of Law, Penn State Dickinson School of Law; J.D., 1980, UCLA School of Law; B.A., 1977, University of California, San Diego.

[21] Copyright © 1999 Prof. Laurel S. Terry, Penn State Dickinson School of Law. Reprinted with Permission of the author, LTerry@psu.edu.

* * *

II. The MDP Phenomenon

As a result of the spate of publicity during the last eighteen months, many U.S. lawyers have now heard the term "MDP." They have learned that a significant number of lawyers now work in one of the Big Five firms.[22] In November 1999, a leading journal reported that excluding tax lawyers, 6,362 lawyers worked for the Big Five firms. This journal integrated the statistics of the Big Five firms with the statistics from traditional law firms; as a result, the listing of the ten largest law firms worldwide included three of the Big Five. Four of the Big Five ranked within the largest twenty law firms. Two years earlier, this same journal reported that almost 2,500 lawyers worked as tax lawyers for three of the Big Five firms.

* * *

Many of the Big Five lawyers included within this data work outside the U.S. Consequently, some commentators believe that Europe is simply different and that one can avoid the MDP phenomenon in the U.S. I disagree. Although the MDP phenomenon has been visible longer in Europe than in the U.S., the MDP phenomenon appears to have significant momentum in the U.S. In November 1999, for example, several lawyers from King & Spaulding left their firm in order to form the new law firm of McKee Nelson Ernst & Young, which is affiliated with Ernst & Young. According to the press release, the new law firm plans to expand to a full-service law firm, expects to have as many as fifty lawyers within the first year, will not engage in fee or profit sharing with Ernst & Young, will be financed by a loan from Ernst & Young, will lease contiguous space with the accounting firm's D.C. office, and may contract for administrative services.

In August 1999, Big Five firm KPMG announced a strategic alliance for state and local tax work with the West Coast law firm Morrison & Foerster, Chicago firm Horwood Marcus & Berk Chartered, and University of Georgia Professor Walter Hellerstein. On another front, the world's largest law firm was created in 1999 by the merger of U.K. firm Clifford Chance, U.S. firm Rogers & Wells, and Germany's firm Pumunder, Volhard, Axel & Webster. Because Pumunder is an MDP, New York lawyers presumably are now partners with nonlawyer partners in Germany. And in early 1999, the new chair of Pillsbury Madison & Sutro pushed for relaxation of the no-MDP rule, convinced that clients want MDPs.

The increased number of lawyers practicing in Big Five firms has come about not only through mergers with existing firms or practices, but also through recruitment of individual lawyers and law school graduates. Indeed, some recent reports indicate that as many as twenty percent of graduates at some law schools are going to Big Five firms.

---

[22] [31] The term Big Five refers to Arthur Andersen L.L.P. ("Andersen"), Deloitte & Touche L.L.P. ("Deloitte & Touche"), Ernst & Young L.L.P. ("Ernst & Young"), KPMG Peat Marwick L.L.P. ("KPMG"), and PricewaterhouseCoopers L.L.P. ("PricewaterhouseCoopers"). For the sake of neutrality, this Article will refer to these five firms as the "Big Five" firms. Opponents of the MDP phenomenon tend to refer to these firms as the "Big Five accounting firms"; the firms refer to themselves as "professional services" firms.

So what do these lawyers working in a Big Five setting do? In addition to their traditional services of auditing, tax advice, and business management, lawyers in Big Five firms provide: estate planning; litigation support (including dispute resolution efforts and front-end services, such as investigation and discovery); valuation and business planning advice (including issues of environmental and labor law compliance and employee benefits issues); and financial planning.

According to testimony before the ABA Commission on Multidisciplinary Practice, these lawyers are quite careful to tell their customers that they are not providing legal services and that they do not hold themselves out as lawyers. At one conference, for example, a lawyer working in a Big Five firm said that he did not practice tax law, but practiced "tax." This limitation is not surprising; a lawyer who admits sharing fees with a nonlawyer is subject to discipline and possible loss of his law license.

Although Big Five lawyers deny that they practice law, they appear to do the same type of work that they did while working in a traditional law firm. ABA Commission Witness Ward Bower, president of the legal consulting firm Altman, Weil, Pensa, Inc., found conservative the estimate that one-half billion dollars of legal fees are currently included in consulting bills.

There have been a few highly publicized efforts to pursue unauthorized practice of law charges against Big Five lawyers, but to date these efforts have been unsuccessful. Thus, there are a large number of lawyers practicing in Big Five firms doing things that if done in a traditional law firm setting would be considered the practice of law; and this number is only increasing. As a result, the MDP phenomenon is real.

This discussion of MDPs, like much of the public discussion, has focused on lawyers working in Big Five firms. But as the Commission learned, lawyers practicing in smaller communities and smaller firms also are interested in forming MDPs. (Lawyers practicing in smaller communities or small firms will be referred to as Main Street lawyers, in contrast with Wall Street lawyers.) Indeed, some have predicted that if the ABA Model Rules of Professional Conduct were changed to permit MDPs, there would be as many Main Street MDPs as Wall Street MDPs. In analyzing whether the ban on MDPs should be lifted, one must consider the impact of any changes and regulation upon Main Street clients and lawyers as well as Wall Street clients and lawyers. A Main Street MDP phenomenon may not have been what prompted the formation of the Commission; nevertheless, if Model Rule 5.4 is revised to permit MDPs and adopted by individual states, then there likely will be significant development of Main Street MDPs.

III. Global Responses to MDPs

Because the MDP phenomenon is occurring on a global scale, bar association and regulatory responses have occurred not just in the U.S., but globally as well. An extensive analysis of these developments is beyond the scope of this Article, but a brief summary is useful to better understand the issues and to place the U.S. responses in context.

A. Jurisdictions Expressly Permitting MDPs

At least four jurisdictions have regulations that expressly permit some form of MDPs. These jurisdictions are Germany, the Netherlands, the Law Society of Upper Canada, and the territory of New South Wales, Australia.

* * *

IV. Common Regulatory Questions

* * *

A. Perceived Advantages and Disadvantages of MDPs

Throughout the world, the arguments offered in support of and in opposition to MDPs have been similar. Those who favor MDPs argue, inter alia, that MDPs provide one-stop shopping, better service (because of the broader expertise of the service-providers and closer cooperation of an interdisciplinary team), and cost-effectiveness. Steven Bennett, for example, testified that from his perspective as corporate counsel to one of the U.S.'s ten largest banks, clients' problems are not just "legal problems," but instead require an interdisciplinary approach. He warned that if lawyers do not adopt a multidisciplinary approach, they risk becoming a mere footnote in the twenty-first century.

Those opposed to MDPs argue that MDPs would impair a lawyer's independent judgment. Larry Fox perhaps best articulates this argument by stating, "he who pays the piper calls the tune." The concern is that lawyers ultimately would follow the dictates of their employers, who don't understand client needs, rather than following the lawyers' own judgment. A related argument is that because of the loss of independence, MDPs would undermine the rule of law that is important in a democratic country. Additional arguments are that there is a fundamental conflict between a lawyer's duty of confidentiality and an auditor's duty to the public and between the lawyers' and accountants' handling of conflicts of interest. An argument against MDPs, espoused more by European lawyers than U.S. lawyers, is that MDPs are bad because they would reduce the number of lawyers available from whom clients could choose. Opponents also express a concern about the impact of MDPs on the attorney-client privilege, and issues related to protecting clients' funds and providing professional indemnity. Perhaps most fundamentally, many opponents worry that there will be no effective way to enforce any MDP regulations.

[Excerpts from the] Report and Recommendation of the District of Columbia Bar Special Committee on Multidisciplinary Practice
October 23, 2001[23]

The Committee and Its Assignments

The Board of Governors of the D.C. Bar formed this committee in August 1999 to study the recommendation of the American Bar Association Commission on Multidisciplinary Practice that restrictions on multidisciplinary practice be substantially relaxed. We were, first, to consider what position the D.C. Bar should take with respect to the ABA Commission's recommendation. We were also directed to consider whether the rules of this jurisdiction related to multidisciplinary practice should be changed.

In a report dated June 26, 2000, the committee urged that the D.C. Bar support the recommendation of the ABA Commission. Shortly afterward, despite support by the District of Columbia delegation, the ABA House of Delegates rejected the ABA Commissions proposal and disbanded the Commission.

Notwithstanding the action of the ABA House of Delegates, this committee and similar committees in other jurisdictions have continued to study the subject of multidisciplinary practice. . . .

Summary of the Committee's Conclusions

After two years of study, our committee, like the ABA Commission before it, has come to the unanimous conclusion that lawyers and non-lawyers should be permitted to work together and share fees in the delivery of professional services without violating professional conduct rules. We are satisfied that such collaboration can take place within the same organization without sacrificing the core values of the legal profession and that prevention of such collaboration among professions is an unwarranted impediment to delivery of multidisciplinary services to the public.

Many lawyers and other professionals are already engaged in multidisciplinary practice, either on an *ad hoc* basis or, increasingly, in long-term contractual arrangements that enable practitioners of different professions to practice and promote their services in a coordinated manner. Nevertheless, Rule 5.4 of the District of Columbia Rules of Professional Conduct continues to forbid a lawyer to share legal fees with a non-lawyer except in very limited circumstances. By generally forbidding nonlawyers to share in legal fees, D.C. Rule 5.4 presents an obstacle to lawyers and nonlawyers who wish to practice their respective professions together in the same firm. Lawyers and nonlawyers can practice in coordinated and affiliated organizations, but usually not in the same organization. . . .

Background

In August 1999, the ABA Commission issued a report recommending that ABA Model Rule of Professional Conduct 5.4 be revised to permit sharing of legal fees between lawyers and non-lawyers in a newly defined multidisciplinary practice entity called an "MDP." An MDP would not have to be controlled by lawyers, but the report recommended that MDPs not controlled by lawyers be required to register with court authorities and to certify in writing that:

(1) it will not directly or indirectly interfere with a lawyer's exercise of independent professional judgment on behalf of a client;

(2) it will establish, maintain and enforce procedures designed to protect a lawyer's exercise of independent professional judgment on behalf of a client from interference by the MDP, any member of the MDP, or any person or entity associated with the MDP;

(3) it will establish, maintain and enforce procedures to protect a lawyer's professional obligation to segregate client funds;

(4) its members will abide by the rules of professional conduct when they are engaged in the delivery of legal services to a client of the MDP;

(5) it will respect the unique role of the lawyer in society as an officer of the legal system, a representative of clients and a public citizen having special responsibility for the administration of justice. This statement should acknowledge that lawyers in an MDP have the same special obligation to render voluntary *pro bono publico* legal service as lawyers practicing solo or in law firms . . . .

Shortly after the Commission issued its recommendations, the ABA House of Delegates adopted the following resolution:

Resolved, that the American Bar Association make no change, addition or amendment to the Model Rules of Professional Conduct which permits a lawyer to offer legal services through a multidisciplinary practice unless and until additional study demonstrates that such changes will further the public interest without sacrificing or compromising lawyer independence and the legal profession's tradition of loyalty to clients.

The House of Delegates' resolution placed the burden of persuasion on those advocating change to demonstrate that change will be in the "public interest" and will not compromise lawyer independence or loyalty to clients.

Subsequently, the ABA Commission continued to meet and consider the subject.

In its December 1999 Report and in a subsequent February 2000 Postscript, the ABA Commission suggested that other jurisdictions might wish to consider adopting D.C. Rule 5.4 or a variant that would relax the "sole purpose" limitation by permitting non-lawyer partners in firms having the practice of law as "a principal purpose." The ABA Commission also suggested that non-lawyer partners might be limited to "professionals" and that control of the resulting organization might be confined to lawyers. In effect, this variant would permit firms managed by lawyers to offer other professional services but would not allow professional service organizations controlled by members of other professions to practice law. Alternatively, the ABA Commission suggested that organizations controlled by non-lawyers might be permitted to offer legal services, but, if they did, their legal services personnel should be organized into separate units supervised by lawyers.

The ABA Commission also recognized in its December 1999 Report and February 2000 Postscript that, in the District of Columbia and elsewhere, it is possible to create arrangements for multidisciplinary collaboration without revision of current rules. Because the only barrier to the collaborative provision of legal and other professional services is the rule prohibiting non-lawyers' sharing in legal fees, it is possible to create arrangements in which lawyers and non-lawyers share in almost every aspect of their respective practices except in the lawyers' fees. The Commission identified the District of Columbia law firm of McKee Nelson Ernst & Young as sharing part of its name with an accounting firm, although the firm does not provide the accounting firm a share of its legal fees. Another District of Columbia firm, Miller & Chevalier, was identified by the Commission as having entered into a "strategic alliance" with the accounting firm of PricewaterhouseCoopers. The legal trade press has also reported an alliance between the law firm of Morrison & Foerster and KPMG, the merger of the money management practice of Bingham Dana LLP with Legg Mason, an investment firm, and the creation of investment and consulting affiliates by McGuire Woods Consulting and McGuire Woods. Therefore, if, as proponents suggest, there is demand for collaborative provision of legal and nonlegal services, means short of single firm collaboration and fee sharing already exist to meet that demand.

It was in this context that in May 2000 the ABA Commission issued a revised Recommendation and Final Report. The ABA Commission's final Recommendation reads as follows:

> RESOLVED, that the American Bar Association amend the Model Rules of Professional Conduct consistent with the following principles:
>
> 1. Lawyers should be permitted to share fees and join with non-lawyer professionals in a practice that delivers both legal and nonlegal professional services (Multidisciplinary Practice), provided that the lawyers have the control and authority necessary to assure lawyer independence in the rendering of legal services.
>
> "Nonlawyer professionals" means members of recognized professions or other disciplines that are governed by ethical standards.
>
> 2. This Recommendation must be implemented in a manner that protects the public and preserves the core values of the legal profession, including competence, independence of professional judgment, protection of confidential client information, loyalty to the client through the avoidance of conflicts of interest, and pro bono publico obligations.
>
> 3. Regulatory authorities should enforce existing rules and adopt such additional enforcement procedures as are needed to implement these principles and to protect the public interest.

4. The prohibition on nonlawyers delivering legal services and the obligations of all lawyers to observe the rules of professional conduct should not be altered.

5. Passive investment in a Multidisciplinary Practice should not be permitted.

On June 26, 2000, shortly after the final ABA Commission Recommendation became available, this committee issued its first report, recommending, in substance, that the D.C. Bar support the Recommendation of the ABA Commission. Despite that recommendation, and support by D.C. Bar delegates, on July 11, 2000, the ABA House of Delegates, by a vote of 314 to 106, rejected the Recommendation of the ABA Commission, resolved to adhere to the current version of ABA Model Rule 5.4, and disbanded the ABA Commission.

Despite the action taken by the ABA House of Delegates, the issues raised by the ABA Commission did not die. State bar committees continued to study multidisciplinary practice and the barriers to it, and bar committees in several states and in several major cities have recommended, with varying limitations and restrictions, that multidisciplinary practice, including sharing of legal fees, be permitted. Nevertheless, to date, no state of the United States permits pooling the revenues of multidisciplinary practice in a single firm (except to the extent permitted in the District of Columbia), and several state bars have rejected any movement in that direction.

WOUTERS v. ALGEMENE RAAD DE NEDERLANDSE ORDE VAN ADVOCATEN
2002 ECR I-1577 (2002)

Court of Justice of the European Communities

On those grounds, the Court, in answer to the questions referred to it by the Raad van State by judgment of 10 August 1999, hereby rules:

1. A regulation concerning partnerships between members of the Bar and other professionals, such as the Samenwerkingsverordening 1993 (1993 regulation on joint professional activity), adopted by a body such as the Nederlandse Orde van Advocaten (the Bar of the Netherlands), is to be treated as a decision adopted by an association of undertakings within the meaning of Article 85(1) of the Treaty (now Article 81 EC).

2. A national regulation such as the 1993 Regulation adopted by a body such as the Bar of the Netherlands does not infringe Article 85(1) of the Treaty, since that body could reasonably have considered that that regulation, despite effects restrictive of competition, that are inherent in it, is necessary for the proper practice of the legal profession, as organised in the Member State concerned.

3. A body such as the Bar of the Netherlands does not constitute either an undertaking or a group of undertakings for the purposes of Article 86 of the Treaty (now Article 82 EC).

4. It is not contrary to Articles 52 and 59 of the Treaty (now, after amendment, Articles 43 and 49 EC) for a national regulation such as the 1993 Regulation to prohibit any multi-disciplinary partnerships between members of the Bar and accountants, since that regulation could reasonably be considered to be necessary for the proper practice of the legal profession, as organised in the country concerned.

The Court, composed of: G.C. Rodriguez Iglesias, President, P. Jann, F. Macken, N. Colneric, and S. Von Bahr (Presidents of Chambers), C. Gulmann, D.A.O. Edward, A. La Pergola, J.-P. Puissochet, M. Wathelet (Rapporteur), R. Schintgen, V. Skouris and J.N. Cunha Rodrigues, Judges, . . . gives the following Judgment.

1. By judgment of 10 August 1999, received at the Court on 13 August 1999, the Raad van State (Netherlands Council of State) referred to the Court for a preliminary ruling under Article 234 EC nine questions on the interpretation of Articles 3(g) of the EC Treaty (now, after amendment, Article 3(1)(g) EC), 5 of the EC Treaty (now Article 10 EC), 52 and 59 of the EC Treaty (now, after amendment, Articles 43 and 49 EC), and 85, 86 and 90 of the EC Treaty (now Articles 81 EC, 82 EC and 86 EC).

2. Those questions were raised in proceedings brought by members of the Bar, among others, against the refusal of the Arrondissementsrechtbank te Amsterdam (Amsterdam District Court, the "Rechtbank") to set aside the decisions of the Nederlandse Orde van Advocaten (Bar of the Netherlands) refusing to set aside the decisions of the Supervisory Boards of the Amsterdam and Rotterdam Bars prohibiting them from practising as members of the Bar in full partnership with accountants.

The Relevant National Legislation

*   *   *

4. [A] law was adopted on 23 June 1952 establishing the Bar of the Netherlands and laying down the internal regulations and the disciplinary rules applicable to "advocaten" and "procureurs" (the "Advocatenwet", the Law on the Bar).

*   *   *

8. Article 26 of the Advocatenwet states that:

> The General Council and the Supervisory Boards shall ensure the proper practice of the profession and have the power to adopt any measures which may contribute to that end. They shall defend the rights and interests of members of the Bar as such, ensure that the obligations of the latter are fulfilled and discharge the duties imposed on them by regulation.

*   *   *

10. Article 29 of the Advocatenwet states that:

> (1) Regulations shall be binding on the members of the Bar of the Netherlands and on visiting lawyers . . . .

*   *   *

11. According to Article 16b and 16c of the Advocatenwet, the term "visiting lawyers" means persons who are not registered as members of the Bar in the Netherlands but who are authorised to carry on their professional activity in another Member State of the European Union under the title of advocate or an equivalent title.

*   *   *

The Samenwerkingsverordening 1993

13. Pursuant to Article 28 of the Advocatenwet, the College of Delegates adopted the Samenwerkingsverordening 1993 (Regulation on Joint Professional Activity 1993, the "1993 Regulation").

14. Article 1 of the 1993 Regulation defines "professional partnership" (samenwerkingsverband) as being "any joint activity in which the participants practise their respective professions for their joint account and at their joint risk or by sharing control or final responsibility for that purpose."

15. Article 2 of the 1993 Regulation provides:

(1) Members of the Bar shall not be authorised to assume or maintain any obligations which might jeopardise the free and independent exercise of their profession, including the partisan defence of clients' interests and the corresponding relationship of trust between lawyer and client.

*   *   *

16. Under Article 3 of the 1993 Regulation:

Members of the Bar shall not be authorised to enter into or maintain any professional partnership unless the primary purpose of each partner's respective profession is the practice of the law.

17. Article 4 of the 1993 Regulation provides:

Members of the Bar may enter into or maintain professional partnerships only with:

(a) other members of the Bar registered in the Netherlands;

(b) other lawyers not registered in the Netherlands, if the conditions laid down in Article 5 are satisfied;

(c) members of another professional category accredited for that purpose by the General Council in accordance with Article 6.

18. According to Article 6 of the 1993 Regulation:

(1) The authorisation referred to in Article 4(c) may be granted on condition that:

(a) the members of that other professional category practise a profession, and

(b) the exercise of that profession is conditional upon possession of a university degree or an equivalent qualification; and

(c) the members of that professional category are subject to disciplinary rules comparable to those imposed on members of the Bar; and

(d) entering into partnership with members of that other professional partnership is not contrary to Articles 2 or 3.

(2) Accreditation may also be granted to a specific branch of a professional category. In that case, the conditions set out in (a) to (d) above shall be applicable, without prejudice to the General Council's power to lay down further conditions.

(3) The General Council shall consult the College of Delegates before adopting any decision as mentioned in the preceding subparagraphs of this Article.

*   *   *

21. Finally, . . .

Members of the Bar shall not set up, or alter the constitution, of a professional partnership until the Supervisory Board has decided whether the conditions on which that partnership is formed or its constitution is altered, including the way in which it presents itself to other parties, satisfy the requirements imposed by or under this Regulation.

22. According to the recitals of the 1993 Regulation, members of the Bar have already been authorised to enter into partnership with notaries, tax consultants and patent agents and authorisation for those three professional categories remains valid. On the other hand, accountants are mentioned as an example of a professional category with which members of the Bar are not authorised to enter into partnership.

*   *   *

The Disputes in the Main Proceedings

24. Mr Wouters, a member of the Amsterdam Bar, became a partner in the partnership Arthur Andersen & Co. Belastingadviseurs (tax consultants) in 1991. Late in 1994 Mr Wouters informed the Supervisory Board of the Rotterdam Bar of his intention to enrol at the Rotterdam Bar and to practise in that city under the name of "Arthur Andersen & Co., advocaten en belastingadviseurs."

25. By decision of 27 July 1995, that Supervisory Board found that the members of the partnership Arthur Andersen & Co. Belastingadviseurs were in professional partnership, within the meaning of the 1993 Regulation, with the members of the partnership Arthur Andersen & Co. Accountants, that is to say with members of the profession of accountants. Accordingly, Mr Wouters was in breach of Article 4 of the 1993 Regulation. . . .

26. By decision of 29 November 1995 the General Council dismissed as unfounded the administrative appeals brought by Mr Wouters, Arthur Andersen & Co. Belastingadviseurs and Arthur Andersen & Co. Accountants against the decision of

27 July 1995.

27. At the beginning of 1995 Mr Savelbergh, a member of the Amsterdam Bar, informed the Supervisory Board of the Amsterdam Bar of his intention to enter into partnership with the private company Price Waterhouse Belastingadviseurs BV, a subsidiary of the international undertaking Price Waterhouse, which includes both tax consultants and accountants.

28. By decision of 5 July 1995 the Supervisory Board declared that the proposed partnership was contrary to Article 4 of the 1993 Regulation.

29. By decision of 21 November 1995, the General Council dismissed the administrative appeal brought by Mr Savelbergh and Price Waterhouse Belastingadviseurs BV against that decision.

30. Mr Wouters, Arthur Andersen & Co. Belastingadviseurs and Arthur Andersen & Co. Accountants, on the one hand, and Mr Savelbergh and Price Waterhouse Belastingadviseurs BV, on the other, then appealed to the Rechtbank. They claimed, inter alia, that the decisions of the General Council of 21 and 29 November 1995 were incompatible with the Treaty provisions on competition, right of establishment and freedom to provide services.

*   *   *

35. The five appellants appealed against the decision of the Rechtbank to the Raad van State.

*   *   *

39. [T]he Raad van State decided to stay proceedings and to refer the following questions to the Court for a preliminary ruling:

*   *   *

2. If the answers to the first question indicate that a rule such as the 1993 Regulation is to be regarded as a decision of an association of undertakings within the meaning of Article 85(1) of the EC Treaty (now Article 81(1) EC), is such a decision, in so far as it adopts universally binding rules, designed to safeguard the independence and loyalty to the client of members of the Bar who provide legal assistance, on the formation of multi-disciplinary partnerships such as the one in question to be regarded as having as its object or effect the restriction of competition within the common market and in that respect affecting trade between the Member States? What criteria of Community law are relevant to the determination of that issue?

*   *   *

7. Are both the Treaty provisions on the right of establishment and those on the freedom to provide services applicable to a prohibition on cooperation between members of the Bar and accountants such as that in question, or is the EC Treaty to be interpreted as meaning that such a prohibition must comply, depending for example on the way in which those concerned actually wish to model their cooperation, with either the pro-visions on the

right of establishment or with those relating to the freedom to provide services?

8. Does a prohibition on multi-disciplinary partnerships including members of the Bar and accountants such as the one in question constitute a restriction of the right of establishment or the freedom to provide services, or both?

*   *   *

Question 2

73. By its second question the national court seeks, essentially, to ascertain whether a regulation such as the 1993 Regulation which, in order to guarantee the independence and loyalty to the client of members of the Bar who provide legal assistance in conjunction with members of other liberal professions, adopts universally binding rules governing the formation of multi-disciplinary partnerships, has the object or effect of restricting competition within the common market and is likely to affect trade between Member States.

*   *   *

81. They maintain that multi-disciplinary partnerships of members of the Bar and accountants would make it possible to respond better to the needs of clients operating in an ever more complex and international economic environment.

82. Members of the Bar, having a reputation as experts in many fields, would be best placed to offer their clients a wide range of legal services and would, as partners in a multi-disciplinary partnership, be especially attractive to other persons active on the market in legal services.

83. Conversely, accountants would be attractive partners for members of the Bar in a professional partnership. They are experts in fields such as legislation on company accounts, the tax system, the organisation and restructuring of undertakings, and management consultancy. There would be many clients interested in an integrated service, supplied by a single provider and covering the legal as well as financial, tax and accountancy aspects of a particular matter.

84. The prohibition at issue in the main proceedings prohibits all contractual arrangements between members of the Bar and accountants which provide in any way for shared decision-making, profit-sharing or for the use of a common name, and this makes any form of effective partnership difficult.

85. By contrast, the Luxembourg Government claimed at the hearing that a prohibition of multi-disciplinary partnerships such as that laid down in the 1993 Regulation had a positive effect on competition. It pointed out that, by forbidding members of the Bar to enter into partnership with accountants, the national rules in issue in the main proceedings made it possible to prevent the legal services offered by members of the Bar from being concentrated in the hands of a few large international firms and, consequently, to maintain a large number of operators on the market.

86. It appears to the Court that the national legislation in issue in the main proceedings has an adverse effect on competition and may affect trade between Member States.

87. As regards the adverse effect on competition, the areas of expertise of members of the Bar and of accountants may be complementary. Since legal services, especially in business law, more and more frequently require recourse to an accountant, a multi-disciplinary partnership of members of the Bar and accountants would make it possible to offer a wider range of services, and indeed to propose new ones. Clients would thus be able to turn to a single structure for a large part of the services necessary for the organisation, management and operation of their business (the "onestop shop" advantage).

88. Furthermore, a multi-disciplinary partnership of members of the Bar and accountants would be capable of satisfying the needs created by the increasing interpenetration of national markets and the consequent necessity for continuous adaptation to national and international legislation.

89. Nor, finally, is it inconceivable that the economies of scale resulting from such multi-disciplinary partnerships might have positive effects on the cost of services.

90. A prohibition of multi-disciplinary partnerships of members of the Bar and accountants, such as that laid down in the 1993 Regulation, is therefore liable to limit production and technical development within the meaning of Article 85(1)(b) of the Treaty.

91. It is true that the accountancy market is highly concentrated. . . .

92. On the other hand, the prohibition of conflicts of interest with which members of the Bar in all Member States are required to comply may constitute a structural limit to extensive concentration of law-firms and so reduce their opportunities of benefiting from economies of scale or of entering into structural associations with practitioners of highly concentrated professions.

93. In those circumstances, unreserved and unlimited authorisation of multi-disciplinary partnerships between the legal profession, the generally decentralised nature of which is closely linked to some of its fundamental features, and a profession as concentrated as accountancy, could lead to an overall decrease in the degree of competition prevailing on the market in legal services, as a result of the substantial reduction in the number of undertakings present on that market.

94. Nevertheless, in so far as the preservation of a sufficient degree of competition on the market in legal services could be guaranteed by less extreme measures than national rules such as the 1993 Regulation, which prohibits absolutely any form of multi-disciplinary partnership, whatever the respective sizes of the firms of lawyers and accountants concerned, those rules restrict competition.

95. As regards the question whether intra-Community trade is affected, it is sufficient to observe that an agreement, decision or concerted practice extending over the whole of the territory of a Member State has, by its very nature, the effect of reinforcing the partitioning of markets on a national basis. . . .

96. That effect is all the more appreciable in the present case because the 1993

Regulation applies equally to visiting lawyers who are registered members of the Bar of another Member State, because economic and commercial law more and more frequently regulates transnational transactions and, lastly, because the firms of accountants looking for lawyers as partners are generally international groups present in several Member States.

97. However, not every agreement between undertakings or any decision of an association of undertakings which restricts the freedom of action of the parties or of one of them necessarily falls within the prohibition laid down in Article 85(1) of the Treaty. For the purposes of application of that provision to a particular case, account must first of all be taken of the overall context in which the decision of the association of undertakings was taken or produces its effects. More particularly, account must be taken of its objectives, which are here connected with the need to make rules relating to organisation, qualifications, professional ethics, supervision and liability, in order to ensure that the ultimate consumers of legal services and the sound administration of justice are provided with the necessary guarantees in relation to integrity and experience. It has then to be considered whether the consequential effects restrictive of competition are inherent in the pursuit of those objectives.

98. Account must be taken of the legal framework applicable in the Netherlands, on the one hand, to members of the Bar and to the Bar of the Netherlands, which comprises all the registered members of the Bar in that Member State, and on the other hand, to accountants.

99. As regards members of the Bar, it has consistently been held that, in the absence of specific Community rules in the field, each Member State is in principle free to regulate the exercise of the legal profession in its territory. For that reason, the rules applicable to that profession may differ greatly from one Member State to another.

100. The current approach of the Netherlands, where Article 28 of the Advocatenwet entrusts the Bar of the Netherlands with responsibility for adopting regulations designed to ensure the proper practice of the profession, is that the essential rules adopted for that purpose are, in particular, the duty to act for clients in complete independence and in their sole interest, the duty, mentioned above, to avoid all risk of conflict of interest and the duty to observe strict professional secrecy.

101. Those obligations of professional conduct have not inconsiderable implications for the structure of the market in legal services, and more particularly for the possibilities for the practice of law jointly with other liberal professions which are active on that market.

102. Thus, they require of members of the Bar that they should be in a situation of independence vis-à-vis the public authorities, other operators and third parties, by whom they must never be influenced. They must furnish, in that respect, guarantees that all steps taken in a case are taken in the sole interest of the client.

103. By contrast, the profession of accountant is not subject, in general, and more particularly, in the Netherlands, to comparable requirements of professional conduct.

104. As the Advocate General has rightly pointed out in paragraphs 185 and 186 of his Opinion, there may be a degree of incompatibility between the "advisory" activities carried out by a member of the Bar and the "supervisory" activities carried out by an accountant. The written observations submitted by the respondent in the main proceedings show that accountants in the Netherlands perform a task of certification of accounts. They undertake an objective examination and audit of their clients' accounts, so as to be able to impart to interested third parties their personal opinion concerning the reliability of those accounts. It follows that in the Member State concerned accountants are not bound by a rule of professional secrecy comparable to that of members of the Bar, unlike the position under German law, for example.

105. The aim of the 1993 Regulation is therefore to ensure that, in the Member State concerned, the rules of professional conduct for members of the Bar are complied with, having regard to the prevailing perceptions of the profession in that State. The Bar of the Netherlands was entitled to consider that members of the Bar might no longer be in a position to advise and represent their clients independently and in the observance of strict professional secrecy if they belonged to an organisation which is also responsible for producing an account of the financial results of the transactions in respect of which their services were called upon and for certifying those accounts.

*   *   *

107. A regulation such as the 1993 Regulation could therefore reasonably be considered to be necessary in order to ensure the proper practice of the legal profession, as it is organised in the Member State concerned.

108. Furthermore, the fact that different rules may be applicable in another Member State does not mean that the rules in force in the former State are incompatible with Community law. Even if multi-disciplinary partnerships of lawyers and accountants are allowed in some Member States, the Bar of the Netherlands is entitled to consider that the objectives pursued by the 1993 Regulation cannot, having regard in particular to the legal regimes by which members of the Bar and accountants are respectively governed in the Netherlands, be attained by less restrictive means.

109. In light of those considerations, it does not appear that the effects restrictive of competition such as those resulting for members of the Bar practising in the Netherlands from a regulation such as the 1993 Regulation go beyond what is necessary in order to ensure the proper practice of the legal profession.

110. Having regard to all the foregoing considerations, the answer to be given to the second question must be that a national regulation such as the 1993 Regulation adopted by a body such as the Bar of the Netherlands does not infringe Article 85(1) of the Treaty, since that body could reasonably have considered that that regulation, despite the effects restrictive of competition that are inherent in it, is necessary for the proper practice of the legal profession, as organised in the Member State concerned.

*   *   *

Questions 7, 8 and 9

* * *

122. On the assumption that the provisions concerning the right of establishment and/or freedom to provide services are applicable to a prohibition of any multi-disciplinary partnerships between members of the Bar and accountants such as that laid down in the 1993 Regulation and that that regulation constitutes a restriction on one or both of those freedoms, that restriction would in any event appear to be justified for the reasons set out in paragraphs 97 to 109 above.

123. The answer to be given to the seventh, eighth and ninth questions must therefore be that it is not contrary to Articles 52 and 59 of the Treaty for a national regulation such as the 1993 Regulation to prohibit any multi-disciplinary partnership between members of the Bar and accountants, since that regulation could reasonably be considered to be necessary for the proper practice of the legal profession, as organised in the country concerned.

* * *

On those grounds,

THE COURT,

in answer to the questions referred to it by the Raad van State by judgment of 10 August 1999, hereby rules:

* * *

2. A national regulation such as the 1993 Regulation adopted by a body such as the Bar of the Netherlands does not infringe Article 85(1) of the Treaty, since that body could reasonably have considered that that regulation, despite effects restrictive of competition, that are inherent in it, is necessary for the proper practice of the legal profession, as organised in the Member State concerned.

* * *

4. It is not contrary to Articles 52 and 59 of the Treaty (now, after amendment, Articles 43 and 49 EC) for a national regulation such as the 1993 Regulation to prohibit any multi-disciplinary partnerships between members of the Bar and accountants, since that regulation could reasonably be considered to be necessary for the proper practice of the legal profession, as organised in the country concerned.

The push for, and reactive push back against, MDPs has ebbed and flowed at least since the 1970s. Clients have clamored for "one-stop-shopping," where they can get legal, accounting, financial services all from the same entity. The legal profession, with some voices excepted, has mainly resisted formal partnerships with other professions and industries.

The MDP phenomenon has a close relationship with the rules prohibiting corporate ownership of law firms. This prohibition is accomplished by the rule prohibiting lawyers from sharing fees with non-lawyers. There can be no real partnership between lawyers and non-lawyers, and non-lawyers cannot realistically own a law firm unless the lawyers may share their fee income with the non-lawyers.

In the early 1980s, a proposal to allow corporate ownership of law firms made its way to the floor of the ABA House of Delegates for a vote. It was defeated in the "fear of Sears" vote, when delegates were told that approval of this rule would mean that Sears could open a law firm. Thought to be dead, the MDP and corporate ownership concept re-emerged in the 1990s as global services competition heightened. The (then) Big 5 accounting firms staffed up with lawyer "consultants" who provided what could only be seen as legal work for the accounting firms' clients.

Then the Enron defalcations occurred and in some respects, blame was laid at the feet of the combination of lawyers and accountants at Arthur Anderson. Thought dead again, the global economic crisis of the mid-2000s led to cries for more efficient and up-to-date business forms for law firms, including corporate ownership. England and Australia have begun experiments with corporate ownership forms, with Australia now having more experience with its effects. But soon, Tesla, the British version of Sears, will be able to open a law firm.

A post-Enron summary of its effects follows.

Bryant G. Garth, *"From the Trenches and Towers": MDPs after Enron/Andersen*
Introduction
29 Law & Soc. Inquiry 591 (2004)[24]

The three articles that make up this "trenches and towers" symposium address the future of multidisciplinary legal practice (MDP) after the regulatory fallout of the Enron scandal. The fallout brought the Sarbanes-Oxley Act, restricting accountants in providing consulting and legal services, and the demise of Arthur Andersen — which had been a global leader in linking law to the major accounting firms. The focus will be less on subtleties of professional ethics and more on the competition and the forces that drive it.

The starting point is that the situation is in many respects very different from what existed before Enron. At one point, in fact, the MDPs associated with the Big Five accounting firms seemed to represent an irresistible force. Their sizes were comparable to global giants Clifford Chance and Baker and McKenzie. Figures reported in May of 2000 gave Clifford Chance over 3,000 lawyers, including the then-recent merger with Rogers and Wells in New York; Baker and McKenzie, almost 2,800 lawyers; 2,860 for Andersen Legal; 1,500 for PricewaterhouseCoopers' Landwell; and 3,300 for KPMG's Klegal (Rosenberg 2000; Dezalay and Garth 2001). The affiliated firms were not yet major players in the most lucrative areas of practice, such as mergers and acquisitions, but they had succeeded in expanding beyond tax and in securing relationships with many of the leading firms around the globe.

The situation is very different today. Clifford Chance reports some 3,700

---

[24] Copyright © 2004 American Bar Foundation; Bryant G. Garth.

lawyers, and Baker and McKenzie reports 3,200, to lead the numerical competition. But Andersen Legal no longer exists, and as of March 2003 Ernst and Young's legal network numbered 2,600 lawyers, Landwell 2,850, and KLegal some 2,000 (1,650 in Europe) (Jaaniste and Sengupta 2003). Only Landwell, which took over some of the Andersen firms, had grown among the Big Five. But more recently (2003), the Economist reported that "lawyers tied to PwC are leaving in droves." Further, KLegal group is formally separating from KPMG. According to the National Law Journal, KLegal made the decision because of "market decisions, including the U.S. Sarbanes-Oxley Act — which restrict the provision of non-audit services to audit clients, particularly legal services" (Rosenberg 2003, 10). Finally, even if the legal-practice affiliates are still limping along, none of the legal programs associated with the Big Four contemplates expanded activity in the United States.

The playing field has changed globally as well. The Sarbanes-Oxley Act prohibits accounting firms more generally from providing any form of consulting — pointedly including legal services — to auditing clients. This restriction has a global impact on the accounting firms that audit major U.S. businesses. The most recent review of global legal services in the Economist (2004) thus stated that "sobered by their experience . . . [since the late 1990s], all the remaining 'Big Four' accountants are retreating from the legal arena, with KPMG the first to throw in the towel altogether."

It does not appear that the accounting firms have a bright future in the provision of legal services to their auditing clients. They could continue with relatively loose networks of law firms affiliated with one or another of the Big Four, as is the case for Ernst and Young, or in Europe, for example, Landwell could grow within the confines of Sarbanes-Oxley and the European equivalents — but even here the dominance of PwC in the auditing of listed companies makes the combination quite difficult to manage.

The question remains, however, as to whether the MDP has been killed generally. Put another way, has the legal profession itself resisted the professional and ethical challenge that was raised by the Big Five as they moved into legal services? Much of the legal profession would answer yes to the question. The fundamental questions defined in the legal profession's debates were whether lawyers could provide legal services as part of an MDP controlled by nonlawyers (accountants in particular), and whether they could share profits with nonlawyers. The argument from this point of view was that nonlawyers who are not steeped in the values of the bar would under those circumstances put pressure on the lawyers to violate their professional standards in the interests of profit. Lawyers would simply be beholden to their business "masters."

That argument, however, is based mainly on the abstract proposition that — in contrast to lawyers working as in-house counsel or under the control of insurance companies — the lawyers working for accountants would be unable to resist pressures to take ethical shortcuts, in this case meaning abuses such as putting too much pressure on clients to buy the nonlegal services offered by the MDP. Dezalay and I conducted a number of interviews in Europe in 1999 and 2000, and we did not find evidence that these abuses in fact had materialized. Indeed, the evidence was that the affiliated law firms had gained more rather than less professional autonomy over time as the accounting firms moved away from the idea of "one-stop shopping" and the law firms sought professional autonomy. The accountants realized also that lawyers could compete for clients better if they resembled traditional law firms, even if they depended to some extent on referrals from the accounting side of the umbrella organization (Garth and Silver 2002). The evidence for the proposition of pressure on legal ethics was mainly that the accounting firms in other contexts had received consulting fees from their auditing clients, and that these fees dwarfed the auditing fees, leading to the assumption that the audit was done with less scrutiny for fear of losing the fees that came with consulting. Since legal services were analogized to consulting, both according to this perspective had to be separated from the audit.

From my sociological perspective, as the Dezalay and Garth article suggests, the negative assumption directed to accountants was based in large part on a distrust of the ethics of accountants. Dezalay and I also think that the distrust was linked to the lower social status of accountants compared to lawyers in the United States. The other side of the equation is a faith that lawyers, just because they are lawyers (and subjected to the professional discipline of lawyers), will avoid the temptation to put business above professional ethics in any business they control. Both propositions may or may not be true. The Enron debacle at least suggests that Enron's lawyers also felt pressures to give Enron what it sought in order to retain its business and the prestige that came from serving it. The result of the process of assessing blame after Enron was to hold accountants back in the competition for legal/business services. But there are reasons to think that lawyers are likely to move ahead at full steam.

Law is a very competitive business, and over the years, ethical standards have evolved with the dictates of competition. We may not have seen the last word on professional ethics regulating the relationships between lawyers and businesses. The competitive pressures on law firms in many respects are parallel to what the accounting firms faced in the 1970s. Accounting firms then responded to increasing price competition in the audit by searching for new products that were not "commodified" and therefore allowed greater profit margins. This search led them into consulting and ultimately legal services. The same pressures are building on law firms as many corporate clients force prices down for what they consider to be a predetermined professional product. Some law firms can exist on "bet the company" litigation and lucrative mergers and acquisitions and their counterpart, lucrative bankruptcies, but competition increases the gap between the industry leaders and those who are outside "charmed" or "magic" circles. The competition continues to intensify. Law firms are advised extensively by business consultants who provide precisely the same advice they provide to businesses — including how to avoid commodification, how to cross-sell different parts of the firm to existing clients, how to exploit a "brand name," how to invent new products, and how to innovate generally to move up the legal pecking order. This advice in an increasingly competitive world will mean that many ambitious law firms will look for ways consistent with professional ethics to move into new areas that can inject further business profits into the firm (Becker et al. 2001). The accountants may be out of the professional competition for the moment, but that does not mean the competition has ended. The boundary lines found in the codes of professional responsibility will be pushed by other actors, including many within the legal profession.

Some potential pressures for change are easy to specify. I am not sure, for example, how we will decide if MBAs who run law firms or subsidiaries are "sharing profits" if they are paid according to some incentive system. If lawyers want to hire the best talent to run their operations, including their subsidiaries, they will be pressured to share the profits with nonlawyers.

Law firms moving into new areas may also invent arrangements with businesses that create informally or formally the same kind of business relationship that the Big Five sought to have with their affiliated law firms. Ernst and Young in fact has moved to a "network," which suggests a less formal arrangement than it had in the past.

In any event, to conclude the legal profession is still moving very quickly. The victory — at least in the United States — over the version of MDP that emerged through the Big Five eliminates one key player, and the terms of that victory also mean that the framework of legal regulation places some obstacles in the way of others, but we will no doubt hear more about these issues in the future.

Chapter IX

ADVERTISING AND SOLICITATION

Because the practice of law is not, as it once was in England, engaged in exclusively by men of means who have no need of additional income, lawyers have a need for clients. Although it has long been urged that lawyers rely only on their good name and reputation to bring in new clients, lawyers do engage in a wide variety of client-getting activities, from joining clubs and civic organizations to making public service speeches in their areas of expertise to print and broadcast advertising to direct in-person solicitation of prospective clients.

When the law governing lawyers interacts with client-getting, one generally thinks in terms of restrictions on advertising and solicitation, though the distinction between the two is not always clear and not always legally significant.

Long thought to be in poor taste, but neither wrong nor unlawful, advertising and solicitation of clients fell more fully out-of-favor in the late 19th and early 20th centuries. In that time period, the organized bar stepped up its regulation of the client-getting activities of lawyers who represented middle and low income clients with personal injury claims. Undoubtedly, some measure of this increased regulation was self-interested; it suppressed competition and made more difficult the bringing of claims against the corporate clients of the lawyers engaged in the rule making and enforcement.

Although all areas of lawyer regulation are subject to potential constitutional limitation, advertising and solicitation regulation is the area most affected by constitutional limitations because of the status of advertising and solicitation as commercial speech. More than any other area in the law governing lawyers, discussion of advertising and solicitation issues resembles Constitutional Law course discussions.

Lawyers have long been restrained by both ethics rules and by criminal statutes from engaging in barratry, maintenance, and champerty. All three of these are related to both client-getting and conflicts of interest restrictions. *See* MR 1.8(e) and (i). All three, at common law, required a malice element, such as is present in the tort of malicious prosecution. The client-getting connection involves the traditional ban on the use of special competitive advantages by some lawyers to generate clients and thereby stir up litigation. Barratry is a term that refers to stirring up controversy and thereby litigation. Its relationship to client-getting activities is the connection between soliciting clients and generating the prospective clients' interest in pursuing litigation. Lawyers are limited in the ways in which they may maintain, that is, support financially, their clients. In terms of client-getting, a lawyer is prohibited from using offers of financial support of a client to induce the client to retain the lawyer. Champerty restricts lawyers from acquiring an interest in the subject matter of litigation. In terms of client-getting, champerty law restricts lawyers from buying into client claims for the purpose of attracting the client to retain the lawyer.

A. INTRODUCTION

BARTON v. STATE BAR OF CALIFORNIA
289 P. 818 (Cal. 1930)

THE COURT. The petitioner was charged by The State Bar of California with a violation of rule 2 of the Rules of Professional Conduct of The State Bar, approved by the Supreme Court of the state on May 24, 1928. Said rule reads as follows: "A member of The State Bar shall not solicit professional employment by advertisement or otherwise. This rule shall not apply to the publication or use of ordinary professional cards, or to conventional listings in legal directories."

[P]etitioner for a period of six months immediately prior to the filing of said charge against him, and thereafter continuously up to the time of said hearing, had published and caused to be published in a daily newspaper printed and published in the city of San Francisco and in the advertising section of said newspaper an advertisement reading as follows: "D. Barton. Advice free, all cases, all courts. Open eves. Room 907, 704 Market Street, phone Douglas 0932." . . . The matter is now before us upon the application of petitioner to have this court review the action of the Board of Bar Governors and of said Local Administrative Committee No. 4 as set forth herein pursuant to the provisions of section 38 of the State Bar Act.

Petitioner earnestly argues that rule 2 which prohibits the solicitation of professional employment by advertisement is an unreasonable regulation. He argues that inasmuch as advertising is universally regarded as a legitimate activity, an activity indispensable to the success of business concerns, it follows that a rule prohibiting the solicitation of professional employment by advertising is unreasonable. In support of his contention he states that "No amount of preaching can alter the cold, indisputable fact that the law has ceased to be a sacrosanct profession and has become a highly competitive business." It is admitted, of course, that the rule is not arbitrary and discriminatory with reference to the members of the legal profession for it applies to each and every member with equal force. The point made, therefore, is that the rule is discriminatory against the legal profession as a whole in that the members are prohibited from doing that which others in commercial occupations and in business are permitted to do as a matter of course.

In the consideration of the reasonableness of this rule, it should be borne in mind that it is a rule proposed and promulgated by the members of the profession itself, and is not a rule forced upon the profession by a law-making body not in sympathy, perhaps, with the problems of the legal profession. . . . It was approved by the Supreme Court on May 24, 1928, and having been adopted by the representatives of The State Bar may be presumed to represent the ideas and attitude of the legal profession as a whole. It is perhaps by virtue of the fact that the profession of the law has come to be considered by some attorneys solely as "a highly competitive business" that it became necessary to give legal sanction to a rule which had theretofore been enforced merely by public opinion.

It is obvious, we think, that the legal profession does stand in a peculiar relation to the public, and that there exists between the members of the profession and those who seek its services, a relationship which can in nowise be regarded as analogous to the relationship of a merchant to his customer. For instance, it may be pointed out that if a customer discovers that one merchant is unworthy of his patronage and trust, he does not thereby brand all merchants as dishonest and unethical, whereas if a client becomes convinced that the attorney to whom he has entrusted the protection of his interests is unworthy of the trust reposed in him, he is very apt indeed to classify attorneys as a class as unworthy of trust and to feel that they are all scoundrels. For this reason alone, it is important to the legal profession as a whole that nothing shall be done by any member which may tend to lessen in any degree the confidence of the public in the fidelity, honesty and integrity of the profession. And it is by reason of the confidential relationship existing between attorneys and clients that certain rules and regulations are applicable to the profession which are not applicable to a business. And in *State Bar v. Superior Court*, the court said: "the profession and practice of the law . . . is essentially and more largely a matter of public interest and concern, not only from the viewpoint of its relation to the administration of civil and criminal law, but also from that of the contacts of its membership with the constituent membership of society at large, whose interest it is to be safeguarded against the ignorances or evil dispositions of those who may be masquerading beneath the cloak of the legal and supposedly learned and upright profession."

Notwithstanding the declaration of the petitioner, we do not believe that the profession of the law is, or ought to be, merely "a highly competitive business." And because it is not, and because it is necessary that the public should not be given the idea that it is so considered by the members of the profession, the rule against the solicitation of business by advertisement is a reasonable regulation. . . .

It is admitted the only serious infraction of the rule is the insertion of the words "Advice free" and that had these words been omitted, the insertion of his name, his business address, his phone number and that he was engaged in the general practice of the law, would not have merited any disciplinary action. We cannot, however, follow the argument of the petitioner that these objectionable words are not a solicitation for employment. . . .

We are, however, of the opinion that the Board of Governors in recommending as a penalty for the infraction of said rule suspension from the practice of the law for a period of three months was too severe, and we, therefore, accept in lieu of said recommendation, the recommendation of Local Administrative Committee No. 4 that he be reprimanded, and this opinion shall constitute such reprimand.

IN RE SIZER AND GARDNER
267 S.W. 922 (Mo. 1924)

Petition to Disbar Attorneys.

GRAVES, C.J. . . . On the face of the pleadings the case appears to be one in the name of the officers of the Kansas City and Springfield bar associations to disbar

F.P. Sizer and H.A. Gardner, doing business as attorneys at law under the firm name of Sizer & Gardner at Monett, Missouri. At least Monett is the headquarters of the firm, but their business (specializing in cases of tort) seems to have extended over much of Missouri, and several other states. Later representatives of the State and St. Louis bar associations were permitted to appear. That the firm succeeded in their line of work is thoroughly evidenced. . . . In the law, as in other learned professions, there are those who specialize in one class or another of legal work. This is proper so long as the members of the classes conduct themselves as real lawyers. There are black sheep in all flocks, and it is proper that all such should be eliminated. In this case it is said that so called damage-suit lawyers were procuring business, and judgments in their cases, at Kansas City, and other places by unprofessional and other wrongful practices. To stop this the first move was made in Kansas City. An organization composed of some eleven railroads (centering in Kansas City), the city itself, through its legal department, one Kansas City newspaper, two or three indemnity insurance companies, a light company and some other corporations, joined hands to suppress the vice. Mr. I.N. Watson, a respectable and reputable lawyer of the city, chanced to represent the paper and a railroad, both of large proportions. According to his evidence he became the alter ego of the lawyers representing these corporations, and meetings were held at his office. His railroad had in its employ one by the name of Pendell, and this party was agreed upon as the proper man to secure evidence, by way of affidavits, against transgressing lawyers, who were suing all these several corporations for damages. All agreed to "chip in" (pardon the expression, but it fits) their proportionate part of the $300 per month for Pendell to seek the evidence (in the form of affidavits) against said transgressing lawyers, suing such corporations. Mr. Pendell was also allowed an expense account, the exact details of which do not clearly appear. These corporation lawyers were not the bar association, but members of some one of them. Pendell, relieved temporarily from duties with his railroad, began his work for these associated corporations, who were putting up $50 each, per month, to a fund for the work. . . .

While the charges are nominally filed by officers of the bar associations, they were clearly induced by the representatives of the corporations aforesaid. The bar associations took up this case at such suggestions. It does not clearly appear in the record, but it can well be inferred from what does appear, that these corporations are financing this case. That they financed Pendell is openly admitted. That they were contributing to a fund at the rate of $50 each per month is candidly stated. This much more than paid Pendell and his legitimate expenses. How long these payments were to continue does not appear, but we are but humans, and can draw conclusions from admitted facts. The evidence further discloses that feeling ran high in Kansas City, and an attempt was made to organize another bar association in that city on the pretense that the then present association officers were men largely engaged in protecting corporation clients from damage suits. These lawyers were largely engaged by plaintiffs in damage suits, and they proceeded through their investigators to investigate the defending damage-suit lawyers, and from dissatisfied clients the evidence shows many affidavits were obtained against some of them. No action was ever taken upon them, however, and the proposed new association never materialized. Sizer & Gardner had nothing to do with the Kansas City move. It clearly appears that the move first started in Kansas City, as stated above, and finally Sizer & Gardner were made the subjects of investigation before the present action. Let us speak plainly, as courts should speak, and say that every earmark of the evidence in this case shows that it is an effort by corporation lawyers as against what they call damage suit lawyers. All this (true, as it may be, and as we think it is) does not change this case. The motive for preferring the charges is of small consequence, if, in fact, the charges are sufficient in law, and the respondents are guilty. So that, we can concede a contest (upon the one side) by the defending corporation damage suit lawyers and the prosecuting damage-suit lawyers upon the other, and the case yet remains as to the sufficiency of the charges and the sufficiency of the proof. If the bar associations, *sua sponte*, had preferred the charges, we would have one background, but where the corporation lawyers of the associations have induced the associations to act upon evidence procured by a special expert, such as Pendell, the background is different. . . .

The Charges.

*   *   *

VI. *The J.M. Parker Case*: Parker was hurt at Jennings, Oklahoma, by the St. Louis and San Francisco Railroad. He was taken to a hospital at Springfield, Missouri. While there he first met one Gray, a claim-agent from the railroad, who tried to settle with him for $1000, which was refused. Parker was on the witness stand in this case, and his testimony does not sustain the charges of the petitioners. One R.C. Robinson was a hired investigator of Sizer & Gardner. He was on a salary to investigate their prospective cases. Much effort was made to show that he was other than what he claimed to be, and that Sizer & Gardner divided fees with him. On this question there was an utter failure of proof. Counsel for petitioner corresponded with both Robinson and Todd, and both wrote him of their connections with Sizer & Gardner, and Robinson, as per a request from such counsel fixed times and places for them to take the evidence. Petitioner's counsel took the testimony of neither. From other testimony in the record these parties were upon salaries as investigators, and in no case was either promised or paid any part of the fees earned by Sizer & Gardner. They per-formed for Sizer & Gardner the services such as are usually rendered by claim-agents and other non-licensed investigators for railways and other corporations.

But to return more directly to Parker's case. Parker said that while in the hospital at Springfield employees of the Frisco railroad, the short name for the road which had injured Parker, . . . had spoken of Sizer & Gardner, as good lawyers, for him to employ. As he left the hospital he chanced to ride from Springfield to Monett with Warren L. White recently elected one of the judges of the circuit court at Springfield, who also spoke well of Sizer & Gardner. . . . At the time Parker was out of employment and had a wife and two children. Parker signed up a percentage contract, and says himself that he then stated the condition of his family, and that winter was coming on, and that he needed $100 as a loan to tide him over — that he only wanted it as a loan, to be repaid. Robinson drew a second and independent contract, saying that he would see what Sizer & Gardner would do, disclaiming his authority to make loans for them. Later Sizer & Gardner brought suit at Springfield, Missouri, for Parker in the sum of $40,000, which suit was settled without the knowledge of Sizer & Gardner, by claim agent Gray, for $1500. Parker says that Gray was informed of the loan of $100 and agreed with him to settle the attorney's fees of Sizer & Gardner and this loan. He also says that Gray obtained his private paper from his wife by lying to her. These were the papers turned over and used in this prosecution. Sizer & Gardner got neither the loan nor the fees from Gray, and in the face of Parker's evidence (a witness for petitioners), Gray does not appear as a witness, so far as the index to the record shows. We searched to see what he would say. Sizer & Gardner say they made the small loan because of the destitute condition of Parker's family. Parker says the same. This state of affairs does not merit the disbarment of these respondents. A lawyer can loan his client money without violating either ethics or law. Of course the loan should not be the consideration for the employment.[1] It does not so appear here.

VII. *The Ellis Case*: The petition for disbarment is far from pleading the real facts of this particular case. It begins in the middle of the case. Respondent Gardner is not involved in this charge. Ellis was an employee of the Midland Valley Railroad Company. In an accident he had both legs cut off. He entered into a contract with Sizer to prosecute his case for one-third of the recovery. Sizer brought suit at Ft. Smith, Arkansas, and without Sizer's knowledge or consent a claim-agent of the railroad settled with Ellis for $10,000. Sizer intervened in the case to enforce his lien for one-third of the $10,000. At this point the petition in the instant case begins. It is charged that whilst Sizer's case for his fee was being heard, Jos. Johnson, a lawyer, and J.H. Todd, whom we have mentioned, approached Ellis with a proposition that Sizer would put up a certified check for $5000 if Ellis would permit him to bring an action to set aside the settlement. In view of the ultimate facts the exact details are not material. Mr. English wrote to Todd at Tulsa, Oklahoma, and Todd answered his letter. The purpose of Mr. English was to get Mr. Todd's evidence at some time and place, and Mr. Todd's answer, in the record, shows no disposition to evade giving testimony. He said that he had read and heard much of this disbarment proceeding, and had been visited by a man whom he supposed came from Mr. English's office. In the letter Todd tells English that Ellis lies, if he says that he approached Ellis for either Sizer or Joseph Johnson. He further says that he worked a year for Sizer, as an investigator, on a salary and not otherwise. Of course Todd's evidence was not taken. Robinson says he had no such talk with Ellis, and had no authority to talk for Sizer. Ellis himself says Sizer made him no proposition, and Sizer says that he made no such proposition, and did not authorize either Todd or Robinson to make it, and had never heard of it prior to this action. These facts do not meet the requirements of the law for conviction. We should add that the Arkansas Supreme Court sustained the validity of Mr. Sizer's contract with Ellis, and also the lien created thereby.

VIII. *The O'Connor Case*: This is another Arkansas case. O'Connor was the step-father of the McCutcheon children. He contracted with Sizer & Gardner to sue for the children, they having been seriously injured at a crossing by the Arkansas Central Railroad Company. Suit was brought and settled by O'Connor for the trifling sum of $5000, after which O'Connor left their place of abode in Ft. Smith, Arkansas, and went to Oklahoma, where he tried to get a divorce from his wife, the

---

[1] [This was the rule regarding financial assistance to clients prior to the adoption of the Model Code in 1969. Only financial assistance that was offered as a client-getting device was prohibited. —Ed.]?

mother of the three crippled children. It should suffice to say that he was thoroughly impeached for truth and veracity, but in justice to respondents further facts should be detailed. O'Connor swears that Harry Davis and R.C. Robinson solicited the case for Sizer & Gardner, and that they as Sizer & Gardner's agents promised him money to live upon. His charge differs from those just disposed of above, in that there is no loan feature. He tries to make out a straight case of getting the case on the ground of giving him money to live upon. We do not have to pass upon the question whether, if these facts were established, the respondents are guilty. We do or should have to pass upon the truthfulness of this evidence. Harry W. Davis had employed Sizer & Gardner in a suit against the Missouri Pacific Railroad Company, and was well pleased with the result of the case. He says that O'Connor sent word for him to come to see him through his uncle, George Dexter. Upon receiving the word he and his uncle went over and saw O'Connor, who inquired as to what lawyers he had in his case against the Missouri Pacific, and as to whether or not they were satisfactory. He told O'Connor that they were good lawyers and that he was well pleased with them. O'Connor requested him to write or wire them to come down and see him. The uncle, Dexter, confirms all this. Davis got in touch with Sizer & Gardner, but they were trying a case and said that Robinson (their investigator) had work there, and would be down soon, and see O'Connor. Davis says that in two or three days Robinson did come, and he went with him to where O'Connor was at work, and later to the house to see the wife. Davis says that there was no agreement to give O'Connor living expenses or to pay court costs; that what he did was at the request of O'Connor, and he was not soliciting cases for Sizer & Gardner, but did speak a good word for them when asked about lawyers, this, because they had served him well. Davis heard all that passed between Robinson and O'Connor, and he flatly contradicts O'Connor. O'Connor is further contradicted by both Davis and his uncle as to how Davis came to see him. O'Connor testifies that just before the cases were set for trial, he asked Sizer for some loans, but Sizer refused to make them. No court costs were paid by either of the respondents, but attorney Love Grant (who was associated in the cases) testifies that he did pay the filing fees, which was customary in Arkansas where he practiced. Sizer testified that O'Connor did ask him for a loan, which he refused, but at no time ever claimed that either Robinson or Davis promised him money. It should be added there is in the record an affidavit from O'Connor's wife which accords with the evidence of Davis and Robinson, but we do not discover the competency of this affidavit from the record, and hence do not consider it. Upon the facts we cannot convict upon this charge.

IX. *The Holloway Case*: This charge is given in petitioners' statement (which we have quoted in full, but reproduce here) is as follows:

> *The Holloway Case.* That respondents through an agent named Workman solicited one Frank Holloway to employ them as attorneys in an action for personal injuries against a railroad company and represented that they would pay all costs and advance Holloway money if he needed it.

When you read the record you would not recognize the case described in the foregoing short statement. There was a Holloway Case, and this court is familiar with it, because we passed upon the case. To start with there is not a word of evidence in this record to show that Workman in any way represented Sizer in what talks he had with Holloway. The Holloway Case arose in 1914 and had a checkered career. It was brought at Clinton, Missouri, and handled by Sizer in connection with Mr. Pogue of Clinton and Claude Wilkerson of Sedalia. Respondent Gardner was not in the Sizer & Gardner firm until 1917. Old man Workman did visit Holloway at the hospital in Sedalia. Holloway lost a leg at Calhoun, Henry County, in a railroad accident on the M.K. & T. Railroad, and was taken to this hospital. Workman had lived near Holloway at one time, and called at the hospital twice. At first Holloway did not recognize him, but did when Workman recalled to him the fact of having once lived in the same block. Sizer had handled a case for Workman, with the result of which he was much pleased. He told Holloway that if he had to have a lawyer to get Sizer, and explained his own case. Holloway says that the old man may have said something to the effect that Sizer would pay expenses, and loan him some money if he needed it. On the second visit some such talk was had. After Holloway got out of the hospital he tried to settle his case without a lawyer, and then wrote Sizer to come up and see him. Sizer seems to have had considerable business around Sedalia before and during this time. Sizer in a few days called on Holloway, and they discussed the case and terms of a contract, but no contract was made, Holloway having a lingering hope of a settlement. He wrote Sizer again, and at the second visit the written contract was made. Holloway asked that his young friend Claude Wilkerson be taken in, as also Mr. Pogue at Clinton, and that the suit be brought at Clinton. Wilkerson was introduced to Sizer just after contract was made by Holloway and was then taken into the case. Holloway, Sizer and Wilkerson all say that there was no agreement to pay expenses or loan Holloway money. Holloway did say that after the contract was signed, Sizer asked him how he was fixed financially, and when he was informed that he owned his home and had gotten some insurance money for the loss of his leg, Sizer simply replied, "You are all right," or words to that effect. As there is not a word of proof to sustain the charge of petitioner's petition, we should stop at this point. We cannot resist, however, to give a few details of this case. As said it was brought at Clinton, and originally defended by some four or five lawyers, including the late and much-lamented Peyton A. Parks. Judge Calvird sustained a demurrer to the testimony, and plaintiff took an involuntary nonsuit. Later, upon motion, this nonsuit was set aside, and the case reinstated for trial. The railroad appealed to this court, and we ruled that plaintiff's case should go to a jury, and thus affirmed the action of Judge Calvird. Pending the time of this appeal the railroad went into hands of a Federal receiver at St. Louis, and the Hon. James A. Seddon was the referee in bankruptcy. Sizer fought the matter there and got an allowance of $6500. In the Federal court at St. Louis a re-organization plan was submitted and approved, and general creditors such as Holloway were required to assign their claims to named fiscal agents, and were required to take stock at certain rate in the new railroad company. Holloway consulted Sizer, and Sizer and Wilkerson told him to go on and get what he could and they would and did release him of all obligations to them. When Holloway testified in the instant case he had received no stock, but was clinging on to a receipt which some fiscal agent gave him. Sizer spent years of work, and many dollars in expenses in the prosecution, and in the end charged nothing to the unfortunate man.

We should not stop here, because the reason for this particular charge does not occur. Some investigator, either for the railroad, or other interested parties (more probably the railroad, because he showed an M.K. & T. pass), came to Sedalia and sent for Holloway to come to the Hotel Terry. Holloway was shown the pass and told that he wanted him to give a statement as it might help him to get his $6500. Holloway detailed his case, and this fellow wrote out duplicate statements, and Holloway says that he presumed that he had written down what he had said, and never discovered that the fellow had put in things which had not been told, until after he got home and read it over. He also says that he never saw the fellow afterward and could not recall his name. This affidavit, whether procured by an M.K. & T. agent or by Pendell, the selected agent for getting affidavits against lawyers, found its way into the hands of petitioners, and was the basis of this charge. The charge fails for want of proof.

[The court recounted the evidence in four additional matters. —Ed.]

Upon the facts in this case F.P. Sizer and H.A. Gardner should be exonerated and discharged from the charges in this petition contained, and said petition dismissed.

[Ed. Note: The preceding two cases were first excerpted in Elliott Cheatham, Cases and Other Materials on the Legal Profession (1938), the first modern casebook on the law governing lawyers.]

INTERNATIONAL NOTES

1. In November 2004, the Japan Federation of Bar Associations adopted the Basic Regulations for Attorney's Duties (*Bengoshi shokumu kihon kitei*). Kyoko Ishida, *Ethical Standards of Japanese Lawyers: Translation of the Ethics Codes for Six Categories of Legal Service Providers*, 14 Pac. Rim L. & Pol'y J. 383, 385–86 (2005). These regulations govern the conduct of Japanese attorneys (*bengoshi*) much the same way that the Model Rules of Professional Conduct regulate lawyers in the United States. Articles 9, 10, and 13 of this code govern general client-getting activities. Article 9 specifically prohibits an attorney from providing "information that is false or misleading in advertising his or her services" and also states that an attorney "shall not advertise in a manner which would degrade his or her dignity." *Id.*

2. The legal professions in Europe have traditionally looked down upon or prohibited advertising by lawyers. However, the Code of Conduct for Lawyers in the European Union (CCBE) recently adopted by the bars of 18 member states, permits advertising by lawyers. Louise L. Hill, *Publicity Rules of the Legal Professions Within the United Kingdom*, 1 *available at* www.law.arizona.edu/ Journals/AJICL/AJICL2003/Vol202/Hill.pdf. In contrast to the more detailed ABA Model Rules governing advertising and solicitation by lawyers, the CCBE Code offers much simpler and seemingly less restrictive rules governing personal publicity by lawyers. Rules 2.6.1 and 2.6.2 permit personal publicity by a lawyer "in any form of media" so long as the "information is accurate and not misleading, and respectful of the obligation of confidentiality and other core values of the profession." CCBE Code 2.6.1 and 2.6.2.

B. THE BLANKET BAN ON ADVERTISING BREAKS DOWN

BATES v. STATE BAR OF ARIZONA
433 U.S. 350 (1977)

MR. JUSTICE BLACKMUN delivered the opinion of the Court.

As part of its regulation of the Arizona Bar, the Supreme Court of that State has imposed and enforces a disciplinary rule that restricts advertising by attorneys. This case presents two issues: whether §§ 1 and 2 of the Sherman Act, 15 U.S.C. §§ 1 and 2, forbid such state regulation, and whether the operation of the rule violates the First Amendment, made applicable to the States through the Fourteenth.

I

Appellants John R. Bates and Van O'Steen are attorneys licensed to practice law in the State of Arizona. As such, they are members of the appellee, the State Bar of Arizona. After admission to the bar in 1972, appellants worked as attorneys with the Maricopa County Legal Aid Society.

In March 1974, appellants left the Society and opened a law office, which they call a "legal clinic," in Phoenix. Their aim was to provide legal services at modest fees to persons of moderate income who did not qualify for governmental legal aid. In order to achieve this end, they would accept only routine matters, such as uncontested divorces, uncontested adoptions, simple personal bankruptcies, and changes of name, for which costs could be kept down by extensive use of paralegals, automatic typewriting equipment, and standardized forms and office procedures. More complicated cases, such as contested divorces, would not be accepted. Because appellants set their prices so as to have a relatively low return on each case they handled, they depended on substantial volume.

After conducting their practice in this manner for two years, appellants concluded that their practice and clinical concept could not survive unless the availability of legal services at low cost was advertised and, in particular, fees were advertised. Consequently, in order to generate the necessary flow of business, that is, "to attract clients," appellants on February 22, 1976, placed an advertisement in the Arizona Republic, a daily newspaper of general circulation in the Phoenix metropolitan area. As may be seen, the advertisement stated that appellants were offering "legal services at very reasonable fees," and listed their fees for certain services.

Appellants concede that the advertisement constituted a clear violation of Disciplinary Rule 2-101(B), incorporated in Rule 29(a) of the Supreme Court of Arizona.

The disciplinary rule provides in part:

(B) A lawyer shall not publicize himself, or his partner, or associate, or any other lawyer affiliated with him or his firm, as a lawyer through newspaper or magazine advertisements, radio or television announcements, display advertisements in the city or telephone directories or other means of commercial publicity, nor shall he authorize or permit others to do so in his behalf.

Upon the filing of a complaint initiated by the president of the State Bar, a hearing was held before a three-member Special Local Administrative Committee . . . . Although the committee took the position that it could not consider an attack on the validity of the rule, it allowed the parties to develop a record on which such a challenge could be based. The committee recommended that each of the appellants be suspended from the practice of law for not less than six months. Upon further review by the Board of Governors of the State Bar . . . the board recommended only a one-week suspension for each appellant, the weeks to run consecutively.

Appellants . . . then sought review in the Supreme Court of Arizona, arguing, among other things, that the disciplinary rule violated §§ 1 and 2 of the Sherman Act because of its tendency to limit competition, and that the rule infringed their First Amendment rights. The court rejected both claims.

[Regarding] the First Amendment issue, the [state court] plurality noted that restrictions on professional advertising have survived constitutional challenge in the past. . . .

Of particular interest here is the opinion of Mr. Justice Holohan in dissent. In his view, the case should have been framed in terms of "the right of the public as consumers and citizens to know about the activities of the legal profession," rather than as one involving merely the regulation of a profession. Observed in this light, he felt that the rule performed a substantial disservice to the public:

> Obviously the information of what lawyers charge is important for private economic decisions by those in need of legal services. Such information is also helpful, perhaps indispensable, to the formation of an intelligent opinion by the public on how well the legal system is working and whether it should be regulated or even altered. . . . The rule at issue prevents access to such information by the public.

Although the dissenter acknowledged that some types of advertising might cause confusion and deception, he felt that the remedy was to ban that form, rather than all advertising. Thus, despite his "personal dislike of the concept of advertising by attorneys," he found the ban unconstitutional.

We noted probable jurisdiction.

*   *   *

THE FIRST AMENDMENT

A

Last Term, in *Virginia Pharmacy Board v. Virginia Consumer Council*, 425 U.S. 748 (1976), the Court considered the validity under the First Amendment of a Virginia statute declaring that a pharmacist was guilty of "unprofessional conduct" if he advertised prescription drug prices. The pharmacist would then be subject to a monetary penalty or the suspension or revocation of his license. The statute thus effectively prevented the advertising of prescription drug price information. We recognized that the pharmacist who desired to advertise did not wish to report any particularly newsworthy fact or to comment on any cultural, philosophical, or political subject; his desired communication was characterized simply: " 'I will sell you the X prescription drug at the Y price.' " Nonetheless, we held that commercial speech of that kind was entitled to the protection of the First Amendment.

* * *

. . . Because of the possibility, however, that the differences among professions might bring different constitutional considerations into play, we specifically reserved judgment as to other professions.

In the instant case we are confronted with the arguments directed explicitly toward the regulation of advertising by licensed attorneys.

B

The issue presently before us is a narrow one. First, we need not address the peculiar problems associated with advertising claims relating to the *quality* of legal services. Such claims probably are not susceptible of precise measurement or verification and, under some circumstances, might well be deceptive or misleading to the public, or even false. Appellee does not suggest, nor do we perceive, that appellants' advertisement contained claims, extravagant or otherwise, as to the quality of services. Accordingly, we leave that issue for another day. Second, we also need not resolve the problems associated with in-person solicitation of clients — at the hospital room or the accident site, or in any other situation that breeds undue influence — by attorneys or their agents or "runners." Activity of that kind might well pose dangers of overreaching and misrepresentation not encountered in newspaper announcement advertising. Hence, this issue also is not before us. Third, we note that appellee's criticism of advertising by attorneys does not apply with much force to some of the basic factual content of advertising: information as to the attorney's name, address, and telephone number, office hours, and the like. The American Bar Association itself has a provision in its current Code of Professional Responsibility that would allow the disclosure of such information, and more, in the classified section of the telephone directory. DR 2- 102(A)(6) (1976). We recognize, however, that an advertising diet limited to such spartan fare would provide scant nourishment.

The heart of the dispute before us today is whether lawyers also may constitutionally advertise the *prices* at which certain routine services will be performed.

Numerous justifications are proffered for the restriction of such price advertising. We consider each in turn:

1. *The Adverse Effect on Professionalism.* Appellee places particular emphasis on the adverse effects that it feels price advertising will have on the legal profession. The key to professionalism, it is argued, is the sense of pride that involvement in the discipline generates. It is claimed that price advertising will bring about commercialization, which will undermine the attorney's sense of dignity and self-worth. The hustle of the marketplace will adversely affect the profession's service orientation, and irreparably damage the delicate balance between the lawyer's need to earn and his obligation selflessly to serve. Advertising is also said to erode the client's trust in his attorney: Once the client perceives that the lawyer is motivated by profit, his confidence that the attorney is acting out of a commitment to the client's welfare is jeopardized. And advertising is said to tarnish the dignified public image of the profession.

We recognize, of course, and commend the spirit of public service with which the profession of law is practiced and to which it is dedicated. The present Members of this Court, licensed attorneys all, could not feel otherwise. And we would have reason to pause if we felt that our decision today would undercut that spirit. But we find the postulated connection between advertising and the erosion of true professionalism to be severely strained. At its core, the argument presumes that attorneys must conceal from themselves and from their clients the real-life fact that lawyers earn their livelihood at the bar. We suspect that few attorneys engage in such self-deception. And rare is the client, moreover, even one of modest means, who enlists the aid of an attorney with the expectation that his services will be rendered free of charge. In fact, the American Bar Association advises that an attorney should reach "a clear agreement with his client as to the basis of the fee charges to be made," and that this is to be done "[a] s soon as feasible after a lawyer has been employed." Code of Professional Responsibility EC 2-19 (1976). If the commercial basis of the relationship is to be promptly disclosed on ethical grounds, once the client is in the office, it seems inconsistent to condemn the candid revelation of the same information before he arrives at that office.

*   *   *

It appears that the ban on advertising originated as a rule of etiquette and not as a rule of ethics. Early lawyers in Great Britain viewed the law as a form of public service, rather than as a means of earning a living, and they looked down on "trade" as unseemly. Eventually, the attitude toward advertising fostered by this view evolved into an aspect of the ethics of the profession. But habit and tradition are not in themselves an adequate answer to a constitutional challenge. In this day, we do not belittle the person who earns his living by the strength of his arm or the force of his mind. Since the belief that lawyers are somehow "above" trade has become an anachronism, the historical foundation for the advertising restraint has crumbled.

2. *The Inherently Misleading Nature of Attorney Advertising.* It is argued that advertising of legal services inevitably will be misleading (a) because such services are so individualized with regard to content and quality as to prevent informed comparison on the basis of an advertisement, (b) because the consumer of legal services is unable to determine in advance just what services he needs, and (c)

because advertising by attorneys will highlight irrelevant factors and fail to show the relevant factor of skill.

We are not persuaded that restrained professional advertising by lawyers inevitably will be misleading. . . . The argument that legal services are so unique that fixed rates cannot meaningfully be established is refuted by the record in this case: The appellee State Bar itself sponsors a Legal Services Program in which the participating attorneys agree to perform services like those advertised by the appellants at standardized rates. Indeed, until the decision of this Court in *Goldfarb v. Virginia State Bar*, 421 U.S. 773 (1975), the Maricopa County Bar Association apparently had a schedule of suggested minimum fees for standard legal tasks. We thus find of little force the assertion that advertising is misleading because of an inherent lack of standardization in legal services.

The second component of the argument — that advertising ignores the diagnostic role — fares little better. It is unlikely that many people go to an attorney merely to ascertain if they have a clean bill of legal health. Rather, attorneys are likely to be employed to perform specific tasks. Although the client may not know the detail involved in performing the task, he no doubt is able to identify the service he desires at the level of generality to which advertising lends itself.

The third component is not without merit: Advertising does not provide a complete foundation on which to select an attorney. But it seems peculiar to deny the consumer, on the ground that the information is incomplete, at least some of the relevant information needed to reach an informed decision. The alternative — the prohibition of advertising — serves only to restrict the information that flows to consumers. . . . [W]e view as dubious any justification that is based on the benefits of public ignorance. Although, of course, the bar retains the power to correct omissions that have the effect of presenting an inaccurate picture, the preferred remedy is more disclosure, rather than less. . . .

3. *The Adverse Effect on the Administration of Justice.* Advertising is said to have the undesirable effect of stirring up litigation. The judicial machinery is designed to serve those who feel sufficiently aggrieved to bring forward their claims. Advertising, it is argued, serves to encourage the assertion of legal rights in the courts, thereby undesirably unsettling societal repose. There is even a suggestion of barratry.

But advertising by attorneys is not an unmitigated source of harm to the administration of justice. It may offer great benefits. Although advertising might increase the use of the judicial machinery, we cannot accept the notion that it is always better for a person to suffer a wrong silently than to redress it by legal action. As the bar acknowledges, "the middle 70% of our population is not being reached or served adequately by the legal profession." ABA Revised Handbook on Prepaid Legal Services 2 (1972). Among the reasons for this underutilization is fear of the cost, and an inability to locate a suitable lawyer. Advertising can help to solve this acknowledged problem: Advertising is the traditional mechanism in a free-market economy for a supplier to inform a potential purchaser of the availability and terms of exchange. The disciplinary rule at issue likely has served to burden access to legal services, particularly for the not-quite-poor and the unknowledgeable. A rule allowing restrained advertising would be in accord with the bar's obligation to "facilitate the process of intelligent selection of lawyers, and to assist in making legal services fully available." ABA Code of Professional Responsibility EC 2-1 (1976).

4. *The Undesirable Economic Effects of Advertising.* It is claimed that advertising will increase the overhead costs of the profession, and that these costs then will be passed along to consumers in the form of increased fees. Moreover, it is claimed that the additional cost of practice will create a substantial entry barrier, deterring or preventing young attorneys from penetrating the market and entrenching the position of the bar's established members.

These two arguments seem dubious at best. Neither distinguishes lawyers from others, *see Virginia Pharmacy Board v. Virginia Consumer Council*, 425 U.S. at 768, and neither appears relevant to the First Amendment. The ban on advertising serves to increase the difficulty of discovering the lowest cost seller of acceptable ability. As a result, to this extent attorneys are isolated from competition, and the incentive to price competitively is reduced. Although it is true that the effect of advertising on the price of services has not been demonstrated, there is revealing evidence with regard to products; where consumers have the benefit of price advertising, retail prices often are dramatically lower than they would be without advertising. It is entirely possible that advertising will serve to reduce, not advance, the cost of legal services to the consumer.

The entry-barrier argument is equally unpersuasive. In the absence of advertising, an attorney must rely on his contacts with the community to generate a flow of business. In view of the time necessary to develop such contacts, the ban in fact serves to perpetuate the market position of established attorneys. Consideration of entry-barrier problems would urge that advertising be allowed so as to aid the new competitor in penetrating the market.

5. *The Adverse Effect of Advertising on the Quality of Service.* It is argued that the attorney may advertise a given "package" of service at a set price, and will be inclined to provide, by indiscriminate use, the standard package regardless of whether it fits the client's needs.

Restraints on advertising, however, are an ineffective way of deterring shoddy work. An attorney who is inclined to cut quality will do so regardless of the rule on advertising. And the advertisement of a standardized fee does not necessarily mean that the services offered are undesirably standardized. Indeed, the assertion that an attorney who advertises a standard fee will cut quality is substantially undermined by the fixed-fee schedule of appellee's own prepaid Legal Services Program. Even if advertising leads to the creation of "legal clinics" like that of appellants' — clinics that emphasize standardized procedures for routine problems — it is possible that such clinics will improve service by reducing the likelihood of error.

6. *The Difficulties of Enforcement.* Finally, it is argued that the wholesale restriction is justified by the problems of enforcement if any other course is taken. . . .

It is at least somewhat incongruous for the opponents of advertising to extol the virtues and altruism of the legal profession at one point, and, at another, to assert that its members will seize the opportunity to mislead and distort. We suspect that, with advertising, most lawyers will behave as they always have: They will abide by their solemn oaths to uphold the integrity and honor of their profession and of the legal system. For every attorney who overreaches through advertising, there will be thousands of others who will be candid and honest and straightforward. And, of course, it will be in the latter's interest, as in other cases of misconduct at the bar, to assist in weeding out those few who abuse their trust.

In sum, we are not persuaded that any of the proffered justifications rise to the level of an acceptable reason for the suppression of all advertising by attorneys.

* * *

IV

In holding that advertising by attorneys may not be subjected to blanket suppression, and that the advertisement at issue is protected, we, of course, do not hold that advertising by attorneys may not be regulated in any way. We mention some of the clearly permissible limitations on advertising not foreclosed by our holding.

Advertising that is false, deceptive, or misleading of course is subject to restraint. *See Virginia Pharmacy Board v. Virginia Consumer Council*, 425 U.S. at 771-772, and n.24. Since the advertiser knows his product and has a commercial interest in its dissemination, we have little worry that regulation to assure truthfulness will discourage protected speech. And any concern that strict requirements for truthfulness will undesirably inhibit spontaneity seems inapplicable because commercial speech generally is calculated. Indeed, the public and private benefits from commercial speech derive from confidence in its accuracy and reliability. Thus, the leeway for untruthful or misleading expression that has been allowed in other contexts has little force in the commercial arena. In fact, because the public lacks sophistication concerning legal services, misstatements that might be overlooked or deemed unimportant in other advertising may be found quite inappropriate in legal advertising. For example, advertising claims as to the quality of services — a matter we do not address today — are not susceptible of measurement or verification; accordingly, such claims may be so likely to be misleading as to warrant restriction. Similar objections might justify restraints on in-person solicitation. We do not foreclose the possibility that some limited supplementation, by way of warning or disclaimer or the like, might be required of even an advertisement of the kind ruled upon today so as to assure that the consumer is not misled. In sum, we recognize that many of the problems in defining the boundary between deceptive and nondeceptive advertising remain to be resolved, and we expect that the bar will have a special role to play in assuring that advertising by attorneys flows both freely and cleanly.

As with other varieties of speech, it follows as well that there may be reasonable restrictions on the time, place, and manner of advertising. Advertising concerning transactions that are themselves illegal obviously may be suppressed. And the special problems of advertising on the electronic broadcast media will warrant special consideration.

The constitutional issue in this case is only whether the State may prevent the publication in a newspaper of appellants' truthful advertisement concerning the availability and terms of routine legal services. We rule simply that the flow of such information may not be restrained, and we therefore hold the present application of the disciplinary rule against appellants to be violative of the First Amendment.

The judgment of the Supreme Court of Arizona is therefore affirmed in part and reversed in part.

NOTES, QUESTIONS, AND EXAMPLES

A number of specific constraints apply specifically to advertising:

Record keeping: In order to guard against any later dispute over content, a lawyer is required to retain a copy of any advertisement, including the text of any broadcast advertisement, for two years after its last publication. Former MR 7.2(b). This requirement was deleted in February 2002 but continues to exist in most states.

Payment for advertising: Lawyers, of course, may pay reasonable costs associated with advertising. MR 7.2(b). This rule states what may seem to be the obvious because outside of the advertising context, lawyers may not pay others for recommending the lawyer.

Name of the lawyer: All advertisements must include the name and address of at least one lawyer or law firm who is responsible for the advertisement's content. MR 7.2(c).

C. WHAT IS FALSE OR MISLEADING? OR, *DE GUSTIBUS NON DISPUTANDUM EST* (THERE IS NO ACCOUNTING FOR MATTERS OF TASTE)

The *Bates* Court left open the power of states to prohibit advertising that is false or misleading, but not that which is merely in poor taste or undignified. Some examples of what is or is not misleading follow:

1. *In re R.M.J.*, 455 U.S. 191 (1982): In *R.M.J.*, the Missouri Bar charged one of its lawyers with violating its highly detailed, restrictive (yet typical at the time) advertising rules regarding practice concentrations. The lawyer had, for example, listed in ads that he practiced "personal injury" and "real estate" law rather than using the state-approved terms "tort" and "property" law; he mailed announcement cards to persons not on the state-approved list of "lawyers, clients, former clients, personal friends, and relatives"; and he listed the truthful but unapproved information that he was licensed to practice in both Missouri and Illinois. The Court struck down the discipline of the lawyer, finding no deception in the lawyer's advertising material. Interestingly, the Court was "more trouble[d by the lawyer's] listing, in large capital letters that he was a member of the Bar of the United States Supreme Court," an almost meaningless claim that might mislead "the general public unfamiliar with the [minimal] requirements of admission to the [Supreme Court Bar]." The state had not charged the lawyer with wrongdoing based on that particular claim.

2. *Zauderer v. Office of Disciplinary Counsel of Supreme Court of Ohio*, 471 U.S. 626 (1985): In *Zauderer*, a lawyer had placed a newspaper ad indicating that he was available to file suits on behalf of women who had been injured by the Dalkon Shield intrauterine device. His ad included a drawing of the device. Ohio disciplined the lawyer for violating its advertising rules in three ways. First, the ad was directed at a particular legal problem in violation of Ohio's advertising rules of the time (they were based on the ABA Model Code provisions). Second, the ad included a drawing, violating the state's advertising rule that required ads to be presented "in a dignified manner, without the use of drawings, illustrations, animation, . . . music, lyrics, or the use of pictures." Third, his ad, in describing his contingent fee arrangement, said "If there is no recovery, no legal fees are owed . . . ." Only the third of these was upheld by the Court, reasoning that the client will still be liable for various litigation costs as opposed to attorney fees even in the event of litigation failure, and that absent such a disclosure, the ad's language is misleading.

3. *In re Zang*, 154 Ariz. 134 (1987): In *Zang*, the Arizona Supreme Court upheld bar discipline of a lawyer whose ads portrayed the lawyer and his associates engaged in various courtroom scenes and included language about prevailing in court. Neither the advertising lawyer nor any of his associates had ever, however, been in a courtroom in a lawyering capacity. The court determined that the ad was not truthful because it gave the clear impression that the lawyer was an experienced courtroom lawyer, and upheld the discipline.

4. Firm names: Firm names may be misleading when they untruthfully imply a relationship to a government or other institution. MR 7.5. Examples: "The Ohio Law Firm," "Social Security Legal Services," or "New York Legal Aid," when used by a private law firm, would be regarded as false or misleading.

5. Testimonials: Courts in some states have held that lawyer ads that use client testimonials are inherently misleading by focusing the viewer's attention on selected, favorable client examples and excluding unfavorable examples. In particular, client testimonials may mislead the viewer into thinking that case results are a function of the lawyer and not the merits of the particular claim that a prospective client may have. *See, e.g., Office of Disc. Counsel v. Shane*, 692 N.E.2d 571 (Ohio 1998).

Arguments Before the Court: Attorneys Misleading Advertising — Testimonials — Presumptions — First Amendment
57 U.S.L.W. 3465 (Jan. 17, 1989)[2]

A client's recommendation is a precious asset for a lawyer to receive, but it can be a dangerous thing for a lawyer to spread around. On Jan. 10, the U.S. Supreme Court heard oral argument on whether a California lawyer's right to free speech was violated by the disciplinary sanction of "public reproval" he received for using testimonial advertising to promote his legal services. Specifically, the court is being asked to decide the constitutionality of the California State Bar's presumption that testimonial advertising is inherently misleading and thus unethical. (*Oring v.*

---

[2] Reproduced with permission from The United States Law Week, Vol. 57, 3465–3466 (Jan. 17, 1989). Copyright © 1989 by the Bureau of National Affairs, Inc. (800-372-1033), *available at* www.bna.com.

California State Bar, No. 87-1224; argued 1/10/89.)

In 1982, Oring's Los Angeles-area firm, Grey & Oring, ran some radio advertisements that featured an account by a former client named Sharon S. of her satisfaction with the outcome of an insurance dispute the firm handled on her behalf. She described how the insurance company had "constantly harassed" her, how a lawyer recommended her to Grey & Oring, and how that firm "immediately took the case." She stated that the firm "hadn't liked the way the insurance company had treated me and they wanted to take them to trial and suddenly the insurance company offered me a settlement of double the amount of the original trial." The client added that if she had "any legal problem, car accident or anything, I would definitely go back to Grey & Oring."

The California State Bar mounted disciplinary proceedings against both Grey and Oring for violating the state's Rule 2-101, which prohibited false or misleading advertising. Subsection (D) of that rule authorized the bar's board of governors to adopt standards as to the types of communications that presumptively violated the rule. Pursuant to this authorization, the board adopted the following standard, which it relied on in this case: "A communication" which contains testimonials about or endorsements of a member [of the bar] is presumed to violate Rule 2-101 . . . ." The lawyer bears the burden of overcoming the presumption, and neither Oring nor Grey met this burden. After protracted proceedings with disciplinary authorities, Oring received the sanction of public reproval.

Overly Burdensome

In the Supreme Court, Oring's attorney, Theodore Cohen, of Beverly Hills, Calif., argued that the bar's presumption is unconstitutional, while Diane Yu, of San Francisco, took the position for the state bar that the presumption is legal and is justified by the "dangerous" nature of such advertising.

The constitutional principle is "crystal clear," Cohen asserted: Restrictions on commercial speech cannot be broader than is reasonably necessary, and here the presumption effectively bans speech. The bar can achieve its goal of policing legal advertising through less restrictive means, he said.

Cohen noted that the California Supreme Court has amended the rule at issue, so that after May 1989 the presumption that an ad is misleading will not apply if it contains a disclaimer that the testimonial "does not constitute a guarantee, warranty, or prediction regarding the outcome of your legal matter." But when Justice Anthony M. Kennedy asked if the disclaimer requirement itself was constitutional, Cohen hedged. It meets the standards of this court, he responded, but a disclaimer may actually be confusing to the consumer. So, interjected Justice Antonin Scalia, your argument is that the bar cannot make a lawyer "add to the truth" or compel him to say something extra. Cohen agreed that was his contention.

Cohen referred the court to *Speiser v. Randall*, 357 U.S. 513 (1958), for the general proposition that a speaker cannot be forced to bear the burden of proving the lawfulness of his speech. But is it possible that the bar can prohibit advertisements it believes are misleading? Justice Sandra Day O'Connor asked.

Cohen said the bar has an obligation to do so. Don't you think the testimonial advertising in this case was somehow misleading, O'Connor continued, because it didn't explain the nature of the claim that Grey & Oring handled for Sharon S.? Cohen replied that the ad did explain what happened to the client, and he argued that it might have been more misleading to tack onto the testimonial a discussion of the cause of action under California law for bad faith refusal to pay insurance benefits. O'Connor did not sound convinced. "My impression is that [the radio advertisement] may have been quite misleading," she said. I wonder, she added, if the First Amendment may not allow the state bar to just prohibit testimonial ads.

Justices Scalia and Byron R. White focused on the nature of the radio ad. If there was no finding that the ad was misleading, White said, is there some indication that it was not? The parties stipulated that it was truthful, which leads to an inference that the ad was not misleading, Cohen replied. But, said Scalia, isn't it the bar's position that all testimonial advertising is inherently deceptive? There is no basis for that finding, Cohen said. The alleged flaw here, White summarized, is that the burden is on the lawyer to prove his advertisement isn't misleading, and this violates the First Amendment. That is our position, Cohen responded. No ad can completely tell all there is to tell, he added. Once a prospective client consults the lawyer, he can ask questions, and the lawyer is obligated to answer them fully and truthfully.

Special Risks

Yu, on the other hand, emphasized the "special risks" of testimonial advertising that she said justify a higher level of regulation. Advertising that is based on a client's experience must be presumed to be misleading, she argued, because it appeals to the consumer's emotions and depends on the credibility of the speaker. "The danger and power of testimonials," the bar states in its brief, "is that, by their very nature, they deflect attention from the content of the message to the speaker." The presumption that an ad containing a testimonial is misleading is a necessary demand upon the lawyer to produce enough information to prevent the ad from being deceptive, the bar contends.

Should testimonial advertising be presumed misleading even when it contains nothing but easily verifiable or obviously truthful statements, or if the lawyer himself describes the client's case? Justice John Paul Stevens inquired. Yes, Yu said, because the form of the advertisement itself is dangerous. It asserts claims of quality, promises results, contains half-truths.

Is there any way a lawyer can get permission in advance to run testimonial ads? White asked. Not with the number of lawyers we have in California, Yu said; we don't have the resources for that. The needs of the public, she asserted, require a strong stand on this issue. The public demands more, not less, information, as well as ethical candor on the part of attorneys.

Oring v. State Bar of Cal., 4 Laws. Man. on Prof. Conduct (ABA/BNA) No. 12, at 206 (July 6, 1988). The United States Supreme Court heard argument in the *Oring* case, but dismissed the writ as improvidently granted and therefore never addressed the merits of the case.

D.   IN-PERSON SOLICITATION

PROBLEM 9-1

George Cos, sole practitioner, is in the courthouse lobby after having filed some real estate transfer documents. He sees a confused and tired woman holding a crying baby. Cos realizes that she needs help and offers it. She hands him a Summons and Complaint, due to be answered today, demanding judgment for $2,500 based on a contract for the purchase of a refrigerator from a local appliance and audio equipment store. She asks Cos in broken English what she is supposed to do. Cos, whose mother was a Croatian immigrant, recognizes her first language as Croatian and responds to her in it. She smiles. Cos tells her what a Complaint is and asks her if she has a lawyer. She says no, and he offers to represent her and file an Answer on her behalf. Delighted, she agrees. They return to his office where he prepares an Answer to be filed, and she agrees to pay him $400 at $10 per week to represent her in the matter. Ordinarily Cos would charge a good deal more for such representation. He files the Answer the same day.

Should Cos be subject to discipline for violating the solicitation rules?

OHRALIK v. OHIO STATE BAR ASSOCIATION
436 U.S. 447 (1978)

Mr. Justice Powell delivered the opinion of the Court.

In *Bates v. State Bar of Arizona*, 433 U.S. 350 (1977), this Court held that truthful advertising of "routine" legal services is protected by the First and Fourteenth Amendments against blanket prohibition by a State. The Court expressly reserved the question of the permissible scope of regulation of "in-person solicitation of clients — at the hospital room or the accident site, or in any other situation that breeds undue influence — by attorneys or their agents or 'runners.'" *Id.* at 366. Today we answer part of the question so reserved, and hold that the State — or the Bar acting with state authorization — constitutionally may discipline a lawyer for soliciting clients in person, for pecuniary gain, under circumstances likely to pose dangers that the State has a right to prevent.

[Holding]

I

Appellant, a member of the Ohio Bar, lives in Montville, Ohio. Until recently he practiced law in Montville and Cleveland. On February 13, 1974, while picking up his mail at the Montville Post Office, appellant learned from the postmaster's brother about an automobile accident that had taken place on February 2 in which Carol McClintock, a young woman with whom appellant was casually acquainted, had been injured. Appellant made a telephone call to Ms. McClintock's parents, who informed him that their daughter was in the hospital. Appellant suggested that he might visit Carol in the hospital. Mrs. McClintock assented to the idea, but requested that appellant first stop by at her home.

[casual Acquaintance]

During appellant's visit with the McClintocks, they explained that their daughter had been driving the family automobile on a local road when she was hit by an uninsured motorist. Both Carol and her passenger, Wanda Lou Holbert, were injured and hospitalized. In response to the McClintocks' expression of apprehension that they might be sued by Holbert, appellant explained that Ohio's guest statute would preclude such a suit. When appellant suggested to the McClintocks that they hire a lawyer, Mrs. McClintock retorted that such a decision would be up to Carol, who was 18 years old and would be the beneficiary of a successful claim.

Appellant proceeded to the hospital, where he found Carol lying in traction in her room. After a brief conversation about her condition, appellant told Carol he would represent her and asked her to sign an agreement. Carol said she would have to discuss the matter with her parents. She did not sign the agreement, but asked appellant to have her parents come to see her.[3] Appellant also attempted to see Wanda Lou Holbert, but learned that she had just been released from the hospital. He then departed for another visit with the McClintocks.

On his way appellant detoured to the scene of the accident, where he took a set of photographs. He also picked up a tape recorder, which he concealed under his raincoat before arriving at the McClintocks' residence. Once there, he re-examined their automobile insurance policy, discussed with them the law applicable to passengers, and explained the consequences of the fact that the driver who struck Carol's car was an uninsured motorist. Appellant discovered that the McClintocks' insurance policy would provide benefits of up to $12,500 each for Carol and Wanda Lou under an uninsured-motorist clause. Mrs. McClintock acknowledged that both Carol and Wanda Lou could sue for their injuries, but recounted to appellant that "Wanda swore up and down she would not do it." The McClintocks also told appellant that Carol had phoned to say that appellant could "go ahead" with her representation. Two days later appellant returned to Carol's hospital room to have her sign a contract, which provided that he would receive one-third of her recovery.

In the meantime, appellant obtained Wanda Lou's name and address from the McClintocks after telling them he wanted to ask her some questions about the accident. He then visited Wanda Lou at her home, without having been invited. He again concealed his tape recorder and recorded most of the conversation with Wanda Lou.[4] After a brief, unproductive inquiry about the facts of the accident, appellant told Wanda Lou that he was representing Carol and that he had a "little tip" for Wanda Lou: the McClintocks' insurance policy contained an uninsured-motorist clause which might provide her with a recovery of up to $12,500. The young woman, who was 18 years of age and not a high school graduate at the time, replied to appellant's query about whether she was going to file a claim by stating

---

[3] [2] Despite the fact that appellant maintains that he did not secure an agreement to represent Carol while he was at the hospital, he waited for an opportunity when no visitors were present and then took photographs of Carol in traction.

[4] [3] Appellant maintains that the tape is a complete reproduction of everything that was said at the Holbert home. Wanda Lou testified that the tape does not contain appellant's introductory remarks to her about his identity as a lawyer, his agreement to represent Carol McClintock, and his availability and willingness to represent Wanda Lou as well. Appellant disputed Wanda Lou's testimony but agreed that he did not activate the recorder until he had been admitted to the Holbert home and was seated in the living room with Wanda Lou.

that she really did not understand what was going on. Appellant offered to represent her, also, for a contingent fee of one-third of any recovery, and Wanda Lou stated "O.K."[5] In explaining the contingent-fee arrangement, appellant told Wanda Lou that his representation would not "cost [her] anything" because she would receive two-thirds of the recovery if appellant were successful in representing her but would not "have to pay [him] anything" otherwise.

Contingency

Wanda's mother attempted to repudiate her daughter's oral assent the following day, when appellant called on the telephone to speak to Wanda. Mrs. Holbert informed appellant that she and her daughter did not want to sue anyone or to have appellant represent them, and that if they decided to sue they would consult their own lawyer. Appellant insisted that Wanda had entered into a binding agreement. A month later Wanda confirmed in writing that she wanted neither to sue nor to be represented by appellant. She requested that appellant notify the insurance company that he was not her lawyer, as the company would not release a check to her until he did so.[6] Carol also eventually discharged appellant. Although another lawyer represented her in concluding a settlement with the insurance company, she paid appellant one-third of her recovery[7] in settlement of his lawsuit against her for breach of contract.[8]

mom tried to repudiate

Ins. Co was ready to pay but not w/ this discrep.

→ Carol fired him but still paid.

Both Carol McClintock and Wanda Lou Holbert filed complaints against appellant with the Grievance Committee of the Geauga County Bar Association. The County Bar Association referred the grievance to appellee, which filed a formal complaint with the Board of Commissioners on Grievances and Discipline of the Supreme Court of Ohio. After a hearing, the Board found that appellant had violated Disciplinary Rules (DR) 2-103(A) and 2-104(A) of the Ohio Code of Professional Responsibility. The Board rejected appellant's defense that his conduct was protected under the First and Fourteenth Amendments. The Supreme Court of Ohio adopted the findings of the Board,[9] reiterated that appellant's

Bar Complaint

Board said it was protected by first.

---

he told her to say OK

[5] [4] Appellant told Wanda that she should indicate assent by stating "O.K.," which she did. Appellant later testified: "I would say that most of my clients have essentially that much of a communication. . . . I think most of my clients, that's the way I practice law."

[6] [5] The insurance company was willing to pay Wanda Lou for her injuries but would not release the check while appellant claimed, and Wanda Lou denied, that he represented her. Before appellant would "disavow further interest and claim" in Wanda Lou's recovery, he insisted by letter that she first pay him the sum of $2,466.66, which represented one-third of his "conservative" estimate of the worth of her claim.

he wanted his 1/3.

[7] [6] Carol recovered the full $12,500 and paid appellant $4,166.66. She testified that she paid the second lawyer $900 as compensation for his services.

→ only paid other lawyer $900

[8] [7] Appellant represented to the Board of Commissioners at the disciplinary hearing that he would abandon his claim against Wanda Lou Holbert because "the rules say that if a contract has its origin in a controversy, that an ethical question can arise." Yet in fact appellant filed suit against Wanda for $2,466.66 after the disciplinary hearing. Appellant's suit was dismissed with prejudice on January 27, 1977, after the decision of the Supreme Court of Ohio had been filed.

[9] [10] The Board found that Carol and Wanda Lou "were, if anything, casual acquaintances" of appellant; that appellant initiated the contact with Carol and obtained her consent to handle her claim; that he advised Wanda Lou that he represented Carol, had a "tip" for Wanda, and was prepared to represent her, too. The Board also found that appellant would not abide by Mrs. Holbert's request to leave Wanda alone, that both young women attempted to discharge appellant, and that appellant sued Carol McClintock.

conduct was not constitutionally protected, and increased the sanction of a public reprimand recommended by the Board to indefinite suspension.

The decision in *Bates* was handed down after the conclusion of proceedings in the Ohio Supreme Court. We noted probable jurisdiction in this case to consider the scope of protection of a form of commercial speech, and an aspect of the State's authority to regulate and discipline members of the bar, not considered in *Bates*. We now affirm the judgment of the Supreme Court of Ohio.

II

The solicitation of business by a lawyer through direct, in-person communication with the prospective client has long been viewed as inconsistent with the profession's ideal of the attorney-client relationship and as posing a significant potential for harm to the prospective client. It has been proscribed by the organized Bar for many years.[10] Last Term the Court ruled that the justifications for prohibiting truthful, "restrained" advertising concerning "the availability and terms of routine legal services" are insufficient to override society's interest, safeguarded by the First and Fourteenth Amendments, in assuring the free flow of commercial information. The balance struck in Bates does not predetermine the outcome in this case. The entitlement of in-person solicitation of clients to the protection of the First Amendment differs from that of the kind of advertising approved in Bates, as does the strength of the State's countervailing interest in prohibition.

A

Appellant contends that his solicitation of the two young women as clients is indistinguishable, for purposes of constitutional analysis, from the advertisement in *Bates*. Like that advertisement, his meetings with the prospective clients apprised them of their legal rights and of the availability of a lawyer to pursue their claims. According to appellant, such conduct is "presumptively an exercise of his free speech rights" which cannot be curtailed in the absence of proof that it actually caused a specific harm that the State has a compelling interest in preventing. But in-person solicitation of professional employment by a lawyer does not stand on a par with truthful advertising about the availability and terms of routine legal services, let alone with forms of speech more traditionally within the concern of the First Amendment.

*   *   *

---

[10] [11] An informal ban on solicitation, like that on advertising, historically was linked to the goals of preventing barratry, champerty, and maintenance. "The first Code of Professional Ethics in the United States was that formulated and adopted by the Alabama State Bar Association in 1887." H. Drinker, Legal Ethics 23 (1953). The "more stringent prohibitions which form the basis of the current rules" were adopted by the American Bar Association in 1908. The present Code of Professional Responsibility, containing DR 2-103(A) and 2-104(A), was adopted by the American Bar Association in 1969 after more than four years of study by a special committee of the Association. It is a complete revision of the 1908 Canons, although many of its provisions proscribe conduct traditionally deemed unprofessional and detrimental to the public.

Moreover, "it has never been deemed an abridgment of freedom of speech or press to make a course of conduct illegal merely because the conduct was in part initiated, evidenced, or carried out by means of language, either spoken, written, or printed." Numerous examples could be cited of communications that are regulated without offending the First Amendment. . . . [T]he State does not lose its power to regulate commercial activity deemed harmful to the public whenever speech is a component of that activity. . . .

In-person solicitation by a lawyer of remunerative employment is a business transaction in which speech is an essential but subordinate component. While this does not remove the speech from the protection of the First Amendment, as was held in *Bates* and *Virginia Pharmacy*, it lowers the level of appropriate judicial scrutiny.

As applied in this case, the Disciplinary Rules are said to have limited the communication of two kinds of information. First, appellant's solicitation imparted to Carol McClintock and Wanda Lou Holbert certain information about his availability and the terms of his proposed legal services. In this respect, in-person solicitation serves much the same function as the advertisement at issue in *Bates*. But there are significant differences as well. Unlike a public advertisement, which simply provides information and leaves the recipient free to act upon it or not, in-person solicitation may exert pressure and often demands an immediate response, without providing an opportunity for comparison or reflection.[11] The aim and effect of in-person solicitation may be to provide a one-sided presentation and to encourage speedy and perhaps uninformed decisionmaking; there is no opportunity for intervention or counter-education by agencies of the Bar, supervisory authorities, or persons close to the solicited individual. . . .

It also is argued that in-person solicitation may provide the solicited individual with information about his or her legal rights and remedies. In this case, appellant gave Wanda Lou a "tip" about the prospect of recovery based on the uninsured-motorist clause in the McClintocks' insurance policy, and he explained that clause and Ohio's guest statute to Carol McClintock's parents. But neither of the Disciplinary Rules here at issue prohibited appellant from communicating information to these young women about their legal rights and the prospects of obtaining a monetary recovery, or from recommending that they obtain counsel. DR 2-104(A) merely prohibited him from using the information as bait with which to obtain an agreement to represent them for a fee. The Rule does not prohibit a lawyer from giving unsolicited legal advice; it proscribes the acceptance of employment resulting from such advice.

* * *

B

The state interests implicated in this case are particularly strong. In addition to its general interest in protecting consumers and regulating commercial transac

---

[11] [13] The immediacy of a particular communication and the imminence of harm are factors that have made certain communications less protected than others.

tions, the State bears a special responsibility for maintaining standards among members of the licensed professions. "The interest of the States in regulating lawyers is especially great since lawyers are essential to the primary governmental function of administering justice, and have historically been 'officers of the courts.'" *Goldfarb v. Virginia State Bar*, 421 U.S. 773, 792 (1975). While lawyers act in part as "self-employed businessmen," they also act "as trusted agents of their clients, and as assistants to the court in search of a just solution to disputes." *Cohen v. Hurley*, 366 U.S. 117, 124 (1961).

As is true with respect to advertising, it appears that the ban on solicitation by lawyers originated as a rule of professional etiquette rather than as a strictly ethical rule. *See* H. DRINKER, LEGAL ETHICS 210-211, and n.3 (1953). "[The] rules are based in part on deeply ingrained feelings of tradition, honor and service. Lawyers have for centuries emphasized that the promotion of justice, rather than the earning of fees, is the goal of the profession." But the fact that the original motivation behind the ban on solicitation today might be considered an insufficient justification for its perpetuation does not detract from the force of the other interests the ban continues to serve. While the Court in *Bates* determined that truthful, restrained advertising of the prices of "routine" legal services would not have an adverse effect on the professionalism of lawyers, this was only because it found "the postulated connection between advertising and the erosion of true professionalism to be severely strained." The *Bates* Court did not question a State's interest in maintaining high standards among licensed professionals. Indeed, to the extent that the ethical standards of lawyers are linked to the service and protection of clients, they do further the goals of "true professionalism."

The substantive evils of solicitation have been stated over the years in sweeping terms: stirring up litigation, assertion of fraudulent claims, debasing the legal profession, and potential harm to the solicited client in the form of overreaching, overcharging, underrepresentation, and misrepresentation. The American Bar Association, as amicus curiae, defends the rule against solicitation primarily on three broad grounds: It is said that the prohibitions embodied in DR 2-103(A) and 2-104(A) serve to reduce the likelihood of overreaching and the exertion of undue influence on lay persons, to protect the privacy of individuals, and to avoid situations where the lawyer's exercise of judgment on behalf of the client will be clouded by his own pecuniary self-interest.

We need not discuss or evaluate each of these interests in detail as appellant has conceded that the State has a legitimate and indeed "compelling" interest in preventing those aspects of solicitation that involve fraud, undue influence, intimidation, overreaching, and other forms of "vexatious conduct." We agree that protection of the public from these aspects of solicitation is a legitimate and important state interest.

III

Appellant's concession that strong state interests justify regulation to prevent the evils he enumerates would end this case but for his insistence that none of those evils was found to be present in his acts of solicitation. He challenges what he characterizes as the "indiscriminate application" of the Rules to him and thus attacks the validity of DR 2-103(A) and DR 2-104(A) not facially, but as applied to his acts of solicitation. And because no allegations or findings were made of the specific wrongs appellant concedes would justify disciplinary action, appellant terms his solicitation "pure," meaning "soliciting and obtaining agreements from Carol McClintock and Wanda Lou Holbert to represent each of them," without more. Appellant therefore argues that we must decide whether a State may discipline him for solicitation per se without offending the First and Fourteenth Amendments.

*   *   *

We agree that the appropriate focus is on appellant's conduct. And, as appellant urges, we must undertake an independent review of the record to determine whether that conduct was constitutionally protected. But appellant errs in assuming that the constitutional validity of the judgment below depends on proof that his conduct constituted actual overreaching or inflicted some specific injury on Wanda Holbert or Carol McClintock. His assumption flows from the premise that nothing less than actual proved harm to the solicited individual would be a sufficiently important state interest to justify disciplining the attorney who solicits employment in person for pecuniary gain.

Appellant's argument misconceives the nature of the State's interest. The Rules prohibiting solicitation are prophylactic measures whose objective is the prevention of harm before it occurs. The Rules were applied in this case to discipline a lawyer for soliciting employment for pecuniary gain under circumstances likely to result in the adverse consequences the State seeks to avert. In such a situation, which is inherently conducive to overreaching and other forms of misconduct, the State has a strong interest in adopting and enforcing rules of conduct designed to protect the public from harmful solicitation by lawyers whom it has licensed.

The State's perception of the potential for harm in circumstances such as those presented in this case is well founded.[12] The detrimental aspects of face-to-face selling even of ordinary consumer products have been recognized and addressed by the Federal Trade Commission, and it hardly need be said that the potential for overreaching is significantly greater when a lawyer, a professional trained in the art of persuasion, personally solicits an unsophisticated, injured, or distressed lay person.[13] Such an individual may place his trust in a lawyer, regardless of the latter's qualifications or the individual's actual need for legal representation, simply in response to persuasion under circumstances conducive to uninformed acquiescence. Although it is argued that personal solicitation is valuable because it may apprise a victim of misfortune of his legal rights, the very plight of that person not

---

[12] [22] Although our concern in this case is with solicitation by the lawyer himself, solicitation by a lawyer's agents or runners would present similar problems.

[13] [24] Most lay persons are unfamiliar with the law, with how legal services normally are procured, and with typical arrangements between lawyer and client. To be sure, the same might be said about the lay person who seeks out a lawyer for the first time. But the critical distinction is that in the latter situation the prospective client has made an initial choice of a lawyer at least for purposes of a consultation; has chosen the time to seek legal advice; has had a prior opportunity to confer with family, friends, or a public or private referral agency; and has chosen whether to consult with the lawyer alone or accompanied.

only makes him more vulnerable to influence but also may make advice all the more intrusive. Thus, under these adverse conditions the overtures of an uninvited lawyer may distress the solicited individual simply because of their obtrusiveness and the invasion of the individual's privacy,[14] even when no other harm materializes.[15] Under such circumstances, it is not unreasonable for the State to presume that in-person solicitation by lawyers more often than not will be injurious to the person solicited.

The efficacy of the State's effort to prevent such harm to prospective clients would be substantially diminished if, having proved a solicitation in circumstances like those of this case, the State were required in addition to prove actual injury. Unlike the advertising in *Bates*, in-person solicitation is not visible or otherwise open to public scrutiny. Often there is no witness other than the lawyer and the lay person whom he has solicited, rendering it difficult or impossible to obtain reliable proof of what actually took place. This would be especially true if the lay person were so distressed at the time of the solicitation that he could not recall specific details at a later date. If appellant's view were sustained, in-person solicitation would be virtually immune to effective oversight and regulation by the State or by the legal profession, in contravention of the State's strong interest in regulating members of the Bar in an effective, objective, and self-enforcing manner. It therefore is not unreasonable, or violative of the Constitution, for a State to respond with what in effect is a prophylactic rule.

On the basis of the undisputed facts of record, we conclude that the Disciplinary Rules constitutionally could be applied to appellant.

The court below did not hold that these or other facts were proof of actual harm to Wanda Holbert or Carol McClintock but rested on the conclusion that appellant had engaged in the general misconduct proscribed by the Disciplinary Rules. Under our view of the State's interest in averting harm by prohibiting solicitation in circumstances where it is likely to occur, the absence of explicit proof or findings of harm or injury is immaterial. The facts in this case present a striking example of the potential for overreaching that is inherent in a lawyer's in-person solicitation of professional employment. They also demonstrate the need for prophylactic regulation in furtherance of the State's interest in protecting the lay public. We hold that the application of DR 2-103(A) and 2-104(A) to appellant does not offend the Constitution.

Accordingly, the judgment of the Supreme Court of Ohio is *Affirmed.*

---

[14] [25] Unlike the reader of an advertisement, who can "effectively avoid further bombardment of [his] sensibilities simply by averting [his] eyes," the target of the solicitation may have difficulty avoiding being importuned and distressed even if the lawyer seeking employment is entirely well meaning.

[15] [26] By allowing a lawyer to accept employment after he has given unsolicited legal advice to a close friend, relative, or former client, DR 2-104(A)(1) recognizes an exception for activity that is not likely to present these problems.

IN RE PRIMUS
436 U.S. 412 (1978)

non-profit

MR. JUSTICE POWELL delivered the opinion of the Court.

We consider on this appeal whether a State may punish a member of its Bar who, seeking to further political and ideological goals through associational activity, including litigation, advises a lay person of her legal rights and discloses in a subsequent letter that free legal assistance is available from a nonprofit organization with which the lawyer and her associates are affiliated. Appellant, a member of the Bar of South Carolina, received a public reprimand for writing such a letter. The appeal is opposed by the State Attorney General, on behalf of the Board of Commissioners on Grievances and Discipline of the Supreme Court of South Carolina. As this appeal presents a substantial question under the First and Fourteenth Amendments, as interpreted in *NAACP v. Button*, 371 U.S. 415 (1963), we noted probable jurisdiction.

Issue

I   *FACTS*

Appellant, Edna Smith Primus, is a lawyer practicing in Columbia, S.C. During the period in question, she was associated with the "Carolina Community Law Firm," and was an officer of and cooperating lawyer with the Columbia branch of the American Civil Liberties Union (ACLU).[16] She received no compensation for her work on behalf of the ACLU, but was paid a retainer as a legal consultant for the South Carolina Council on Human Relations (Council), a nonprofit organization with offices in Columbia.

non-profit.

During the summer of 1973, local and national newspapers reported that pregnant mothers on public assistance in Aiken County, S.C., were being sterilized or threatened with sterilization as a condition of the continued receipt of medical assistance under the Medicaid program. Concerned by this development, Gary Allen, an Aiken businessman and officer of a local organization serving indigents, called the Council requesting that one of its representatives come to Aiken to address some of the women who had been sterilized. At the Council's behest, appellant, who had not known Allen previously, called him and arranged a meeting in his office in July 1973. Among those attending was Mary Etta Williams, who had been sterilized by Dr. Clovis H. Pierce after the birth of her third child. Williams and her grandmother attended the meeting because Allen, an old family friend, had invited them and because Williams wanted "[to] see what it was all about . . . ." At the meeting, appellant advised those present, including Williams and the other women who had been sterilized by Dr. Pierce, of their legal rights and suggested the possibility of a lawsuit.

sterilizing mothers?

---

[16] [2] The ACLU was organized in 1920 by individuals who had worked in the defense of the rights of conscientious objectors during World War I and political dissidents during the postwar period. It views itself as a "national non-partisan organization defending our Bill of Rights for all without distinction or compromise." ACLU, *Presenting the American Civil Liberties Union* 2 (1948). The organization's activities range from litigation and lobbying to educational campaigns in support of its avowed goals.

Early in August 1973 the ACLU informed appellant that it was willing to provide representation for Aiken mothers who had been sterilized. Appellant testified that after being advised by Allen that Williams wished to institute suit against Dr. Pierce, she decided to inform Williams of the ACLU's offer of free legal representation. Shortly after receiving appellant's letter, dated August 30, 1973 — the centerpiece of this litigation — Williams visited Dr. Pierce to discuss the progress of her third child who was ill. At the doctor's office, she encountered his lawyer and at the latter's request signed a release of liability in the doctor's favor. Williams showed appellant's letter to the doctor and his lawyer, and they retained a copy. She then called appellant from the doctor's office and announced her intention not to sue. There was no further communication between appellant and Williams.

On October 9, 1974, the Secretary of the Board of Commissioners on Grievances and Discipline of the Supreme Court of South Carolina (Board) filed a formal complaint with the Board, charging that appellant had engaged in "solicitation in violation of the Canons of Ethics" by sending the August 30, 1973, letter to Williams. Appellant denied any unethical solicitation and asserted, inter alia, that her conduct was protected by the First and Fourteenth Amendments and by Canon 2 of the Code of Professional Responsibility of the American Bar Association (ABA). The complaint was heard by a panel of the Board on March 20, 1975. The State's evidence consisted of the letter, the testimony of Williams,[17] and a copy of the summons and complaint in the action instituted against Dr. Pierce and various state officials.[18] Following denial of appellant's motion to dismiss, she testified in her own behalf and called Allen, a number of ACLU representatives, and several character witnesses.[19]

The panel filed a report recommending that appellant be found guilty of soliciting a client on behalf of the ACLU, in violation of Disciplinary Rules of the Supreme Court of South Carolina, and that a private reprimand be issued. It noted that "[the] evidence is inconclusive as to whether [appellant] solicited Mrs. Williams on her own behalf, but she did solicit Mrs. Williams on behalf of the ACLU, which

---

[17] [7] Williams testified that at the July meeting appellant advised her of her legal remedies, of the possibility of a lawsuit if her sterilization had been coerced, and of appellant's willingness to serve as her lawyer without compensation. Williams recounted that she had told appellant that because her child was in critical condition, she "did not have time for" a lawsuit and "would contact [appellant] some more." She also denied that she had expressed to Allen an interest in suing her doctor. On cross-examination, however, Williams confirmed an earlier statement she had made in an affidavit that appellant "did not attempt to persuade or pressure me to file [the] lawsuit."

[18] [8] This class action was filed on April 15, 1974, by two Negro women alleging that Dr. Pierce, in conspiracy with state officials, had sterilized them, or was threatening to do so, solely on account of their race and number of children, while they received assistance under the Medicaid program. The complaint sought declaratory and injunctive relief, damages, and attorney's fees, and asserted violations of the Constitution and 42 U.S.C. §§ 1981, 1983, 1985(3), and 2000d.

[19] [9] Appellant also offered to produce expert testimony to the effect that some measure of solicitation of prospective litigants is necessary in safeguarding the civil liberties of inarticulate, economically disadvantaged individuals who may not be aware of their legal rights and of the availability of legal counsel; that the purpose of the ACLU is to advance and defend the cause of civil liberties; and that the ACLU relies on decisions such as *NAACP v. Button*, 371 U.S. 415 (1963), in advising its attorneys of the extent of constitutional protection for their litigation activities. These offers of proof were rejected as not germane to the disciplinary proceeding.

would benefit financially in the event of successful prosecution of the suit for money damages." The panel determined that appellant violated DR 2-103(D)(5) "by attempting to solicit a client for a non-profit organization which, as its primary purpose, renders legal services, where respondent's associate is a staff counsel for the non-profit organization." Appellant also was found to have violated DR 2-104(A)(5) because she solicited Williams, after providing unsolicited legal advice, to join in a prospective class action for damages and other relief that was to be brought by the ACLU.

After a hearing on January 9, 1976, the full Board approved the panel report and administered a private reprimand. On March 17, 1977, the Supreme Court of South Carolina entered an order which adopted verbatim the findings and conclusions of the panel report and increased the sanction, sua sponte, to a public reprimand.

On July 9, 1977, appellant filed a jurisdictional statement and this appeal was docketed. . . . We now reverse.

II

This appeal concerns the tension between contending values of considerable moment to the legal profession and to society. Relying upon *NAACP v. Button*, 371 U.S. 415 (1963), and its progeny, appellant maintains that her activity involved constitutionally protected expression and association. In her view, South Carolina has not shown that the discipline meted out to her advances a subordinating state interest in a manner that avoids unnecessary abridgment of First Amendment freedoms. Appellee counters that appellant's letter to Williams falls outside of the protection of *Button*, and that South Carolina acted lawfully in punishing a member of its Bar for solicitation.

The States enjoy broad power to regulate "the practice of professions within their boundaries," and "[the] interest of the States in regulating lawyers is especially great since lawyers are essential to the primary governmental function of administering justice, and have historically been 'officers of the courts.'" *Goldfarb v. Virginia State Bar*, 421 U.S. 773, 792 (1975). For example, we decide today in *Ohralik v. Ohio State Bar Assn., post*, that the States may vindicate legitimate regulatory interests through proscription, in certain circumstances, of in-person solicitation by lawyers who seek to communicate purely commercial offers of legal assistance to lay persons.

Unlike the situation in *Ohralik*, however, appellant's act of solicitation took the form of a letter to a woman with whom appellant had discussed the possibility of seeking redress for an allegedly unconstitutional sterilization. This was not in-person solicitation for pecuniary gain. Appellant was communicating an offer of free assistance by attorneys associated with the ACLU, not an offer predicated on entitlement to a share of any monetary recovery. And her actions were undertaken to express personal political beliefs and to advance the civil-liberties objectives of the ACLU, rather than to derive financial gain. The question presented in this case is whether, in light of the values protected by the First and Fourteenth

Amendments, these differences materially affect the scope of state regulation of the conduct of lawyers.

III

In *NAACP v. Button, supra*, the Supreme Court of Appeals of Virginia had held that the activities of members and staff attorneys of the National Association for the Advancement of Colored People (NAACP) and its affiliate, the Virginia State Conference of NAACP Branches (Conference), constituted "solicitation of legal business" in violation of state law. Although the NAACP representatives and staff attorneys had "a right to peaceably assemble with the members of the branches and other groups to discuss with them and advise them relative to their legal rights in matters concerning racial segregation," the court found no constitutional protection for efforts to "solicit prospective litigants to authorize the filing of suits" by NAACP-compensated attorneys.

This Court reversed: "We hold that the activities of the NAACP, its affiliates and legal staff shown on this record are modes of expression and association protected by the First and Fourteenth Amendments which Virginia may not prohibit, under its power to regulate the legal profession, as improper solicitation of legal business violative of [state law] and the Canons of Professional Ethics." The solicitation of prospective litigants, many of whom were not members of the NAACP or the Conference, for the purpose of furthering the civil-rights objectives of the organization and its members was held to come within the right " 'to engage in association for the advancement of beliefs and ideas.' "

Since the Virginia statute sought to regulate expressive and associational conduct at the core of the First Amendment's protective ambit, the Button Court insisted that "government may regulate in the area only with narrow specificity." The Attorney General of Virginia had argued that the law merely (i) proscribed control of the actual litigation by the NAACP after it was instituted, and (ii) sought to prevent the evils traditionally associated with common-law maintenance, champerty, and barratry. The Court found inadequate the first justification because of an absence of evidence of NAACP interference with the actual conduct of litigation, or neglect or harassment of clients, and because the statute, as construed, was not drawn narrowly to advance the asserted goal. It rejected the analogy to the common-law offenses because of an absence of proof that malicious intent or the prospect of pecuniary gain inspired the NAACP-sponsored litigation. It also found a lack of proof that a serious danger of conflict of interest marked the relationship between the NAACP and its member and nonmember Negro litigants. The Court concluded that "although the [NAACP] has amply shown that its activities fall within the First Amendment's protections, the State has failed to advance any substantial regulatory interest, in the form of substantive evils flowing from [the NAACP's] activities, which can justify the broad prohibitions which it has imposed."[20]

---

[20] [14] The *Button* Court described the solicitation activities of NAACP members and attorneys in the following terms:

Typically, a local NAACP branch will invite a member of the legal staff to explain to a

IV

We turn now to the question whether appellant's conduct implicates interests of free expression and association sufficient to justify the level of protection recognized in Button and subsequent cases. The Supreme Court of South Carolina found appellant to have engaged in unethical conduct because she " '[solicited] a client for a nonprofit organization, which, as its primary purpose, renders legal services, where respondent's associate is a staff counsel for the non-profit organization.' " It rejected appellant's First Amendment defenses by distinguishing Button from the case before it. Whereas the NAACP in that case was primarily a " 'political' " organization that used " 'litigation as an adjunct to the overriding political aims of the organization,' " the ACLU " 'has as one of its primary purposes the rendition of legal services.' " The court also intimated that the ACLU's policy of requesting an award of counsel fees indicated that the organization might " 'benefit financially in the event of successful prosecution of the suit for money damages.' "

V

Appellee contends that the disciplinary action taken in this case is part of a regulatory program aimed at the prevention of undue influence, overreaching, misrepresentation, invasion of privacy, conflict of interest, lay interference, and other evils that are thought to inhere generally in solicitation by lawyers of prospective clients, and to be present on the record before us. We do not dispute the importance of these interests. This Court's decision in Button makes clear, however, that "[broad] prophylactic rules in the area of free expression are suspect," and that "[precision] of regulation must be the touchstone in an area so closely touching our most precious freedoms." Because of the danger of censorship through selective enforcement of broad prohibitions, and "[because] First Amendment freedoms need breathing space to survive, government may regulate in [this] area only with narrow specificity."

A

The Disciplinary Rules in question sweep broadly. Under DR 2-103(D)(5), a lawyer employed by the ACLU or a similar organization may never give unsolicited advice to a lay person that he retain the organization's free services, and it would

---

meeting of parents and children the legal steps necessary to achieve desegregation. The staff member will bring printed forms to the meeting authorizing him, and other NAACP or [NAACP Legal] Defense Fund attorneys of his designation, to represent the signers in legal proceedings to achieve desegregation. On occasion, blank forms have been signed by litigants, upon the understanding that a member or members of the legal staff, with or without assistance from other NAACP lawyers, or from the Defense Fund, would handle the case. It is usual after obtaining authorizations, for the staff lawyer to bring into the case the other staff members in the area where suit is to be brought, and sometimes to bring in lawyers from the national organization or the Defense Fund. In effect, then, the prospective litigant retains not so much a particular attorney as the firm of NAACP and Defense Fund lawyers . . . .

These meetings are sometimes prompted by letters and bulletins from the Conference urging active steps to fight segregation. The Conference has on occasion distributed to the local branches petitions for desegregation to be signed by parents and filed with local school boards, and advised branch officials to obtain, as petitioners, persons willing to 'go all the way' in any possible litigation that may ensue.

seem that one who merely assists or maintains a cooperative relationship with the organization also must suppress the giving of such advice if he or anyone associated with the organization will be involved in the ultimate litigation.

* * *

B

* * *

Where political expression or association is at issue, this Court has not tolerated the degree of imprecision that often characterizes government regulation of the conduct of commercial affairs. The approach we adopt today in Ohralik, that the State may proscribe in-person solicitation for pecuniary gain under circumstances likely to result in adverse consequences, cannot be applied to appellant's activity on behalf of the ACLU. Although a showing of potential danger may suffice in the former context, appellant may not be disciplined unless her activity in fact involved the type of misconduct at which South Carolina's broad prohibition is said to be directed. The record does not support appellee's contention that undue influence, overreaching, misrepresentation, or invasion of privacy actually occurred in this case.

* * *

The State's interests in preventing the "stirring up" of frivolous or vexatious litigation and minimizing commercialization of the legal profession offer no further justification for the discipline administered in this case. The Button Court declined to accept the proffered analogy to the common-law offenses of maintenance, champerty, and barratry, where the record would not support a finding that the litigant was solicited for a malicious purpose or "for private gain, serving no public interest," The same result follows from the facts of this case. And considerations of undue commercialization of the legal profession are of marginal force where, as here, a nonprofit organization offers its services free of charge to individuals who may be in need of legal assistance and may lack the financial means and sophistication necessary to tap alternative sources of such aid.

At bottom, the case against appellant rests on the proposition that a State may regulate in a prophylactic fashion all solicitation activities of lawyers because there may be some potential for overreaching, conflict of interest, or other substantive evils whenever a lawyer gives unsolicited advice and communicates an offer of representation to a layman. Under certain circumstances, that approach is appropriate in the case of speech that simply "[proposes] a commercial transaction," In the context of political expression and association, however, a State must regulate with significantly greater precision.

* * *

We conclude that South Carolina's application of DR 2-103(D)(5)(a) and (c) and 2-104(A)(5) to appellant's solicitation by letter on behalf of the ACLU violates the First and Fourteenth Amendments. The judgment of the Supreme Court of South Carolina is

Reversed.

MR. JUSTICE MARSHALL, concurring in part and concurring in the judgment.

[This opinion applies both to *Ohio v. Ohralik* and *In re Primus.*]

I agree with the majority that the factual circumstances presented by appellant Ohralik's conduct "pose dangers that the State has a right to prevent," and accordingly that he may constitutionally be disciplined by the disciplinary Board and the Ohio Supreme Court. I further agree that appellant Primus' activity in advising a Medicaid patient who had been sterilized that the American Civil Liberties Union (ACLU) would be willing to represent her without fee in a lawsuit against the doctor and the hospital was constitutionally protected and could not form the basis for disciplinary proceedings. I write separately to highlight what I believe these cases do and do not decide, and to express my concern that disciplinary rules not be utilized to obstruct the distribution of legal services to all those in need of them.

I

While both of these cases involve application of rules prohibiting attorneys from soliciting business, they could hardly have arisen in more disparate factual settings. The circumstances in which appellant Ohralik initially approached his two clients provide classic examples of "ambulance chasing," fraught with obvious potential for misrepresentation and overreaching. Ohralik, an experienced lawyer in practice for over 25 years, approached two 18-year-old women shortly after they had been in a traumatic car accident. One was in traction in a hospital room; the other had just been released following nearly two weeks of hospital care. Both were in pain and may have been on medication; neither had more than a high school education. Certainly these facts alone would have cautioned hesitation in pressing one's employment on either of these women; any lawyer of ordinary prudence should have carefully considered whether the person was in an appropriate condition to make a decision about legal counsel.

But appellant not only foisted himself upon these clients; he acted in gross disregard for their privacy by covertly recording, without their consent or knowledge, his conversations with Wanda Lou Holbert and Carol McClintock's family. This conduct, which appellant has never disputed, is itself completely inconsistent with an attorney's fiduciary obligation fairly and fully to disclose to clients his activities affecting their interests. And appellant's unethical conduct was further compounded by his pursuing Wanda Lou Holbert, when her interests were clearly in potential conflict with those of his prior-retained client, Carol McClintock.[21]

---

[21] [1] Appellant's advice to Wanda Lou Holbert that she could get money from the McClintocks' insurance policy created the risk that the financial interests of his two clients would come into conflict.

II

The facts in *Primus*, by contrast, show a "solicitation" of employment in accordance with the highest standards of the legal profession. Appellant in this case was acting, not for her own pecuniary benefit, but to promote what she perceived to be the legal rights of persons not likely to appreciate or to be able to vindicate their own rights. The obligation of all lawyers, whether or not members of an association committed to a particular point of view, to see that legal aid is available "where the litigant is in need of assistance, or where important issues are involved in the case," has long been established. *In re Ades*, 6 F. Supp. 467, 475 (Md. 1934); *see NAACP v. Button*, 371 U.S. 415, 440 n.19 (1963). Indeed, Judge Soper in Ades was able to recite numerous instances in which lawyers, including Alexander Hamilton, Luther Martin, and Clarence Darrow, volunteered their services in aid of indigent persons or important public issues. The American Bar Association Code of Professional Responsibility itself recognizes that the "responsibility for providing legal services for those unable to pay ultimately rests upon the individual lawyer," and further states that "[every] lawyer, regardless of professional prominence or professional workload, should find time to participate in serving the disadvantaged."

*   *   *

III

polar opposites - hard to figure out* for staff b/w them.

Our holdings today deal only with situations at opposite poles of the problem of attorney solicitation. In their aftermath, courts and professional associations may reasonably be expected to look to these opinions for guidance in redrafting the disciplinary rules that must apply across a spectrum of activities ranging from clearly protected speech to clearly proscribable conduct. A large number of situations falling between the poles represented by the instant facts will doubtless occur. In considering the wisdom and constitutionality of rules directed at such intermediate situations, our fellow members of the Bench and Bar must be guided not only by today's decisions, but also by our decision last Term in *Bates v. State Bar of Arizona*, 433 U.S. 350 (1977). . . .

The state bar associations in both of these cases took the position that solicitation itself was an evil that could lawfully be proscribed. While the Court's *Primus* opinion does suggest that the only justification for nonsolicitation rules is their prophylactic value in preventing such evils as actual fraud, overreaching, deception, and misrepresentation, I think it should be made crystal clear that the State's legitimate interests in this area are limited to prohibiting such substantive evils.

A

*   *   *

B

Not only do prohibitions on solicitation interfere with the free flow of information protected by the First Amendment, but by origin and in practice they operate in a discriminatory manner. As we have noted, these constraints developed as rules of "etiquette" and came to rest on the notion that a lawyer's reputation in his community would spread by word of mouth and bring business to the worthy lawyer.[22] The social model on which this conception depends is that of the small, cohesive, and homogeneous community; the anachronistic nature of this model has long been recognized. If ever this conception were more generally true, it is now valid only with respect to those persons who move in the relatively elite social and educational circles in which knowledge about legal problems, legal remedies, and lawyers is widely shared.

The impact of the nonsolicitation rules, moreover, is discriminatory with respect to the suppliers as well as the consumers of legal services. Just as the persons who suffer most from lack of knowledge about lawyers' availability belong to the less privileged classes of society, so the Disciplinary Rules against solicitation fall most heavily on those attorneys engaged in a single-practitioner or small-partnership form of practice — attorneys who typically earn less than their fellow practitioners in larger, corporate-oriented firms. Indeed, some scholars have suggested that the rules against solicitation were developed by the professional bar to keep recently immigrated lawyers, who gravitated toward the smaller, personal injury practice, from effective entry into the profession. *See* J. AUERBACH, UNEQUAL JUSTICE 42-62, 126-129 (1976). In light of this history, I am less inclined than the majority appears to be, to weigh favorably in the balance of the State's interests here the longevity of the ban on attorney solicitation.

C

By discussing the origin and impact of the nonsolicitation rules, I do not mean to belittle those obviously substantial interests that the State has in regulating attorneys to protect the public from fraud, deceit, misrepresentation, overreaching, undue influence, and invasions of privacy. But where honest, unpressured "commercial" solicitation is involved — a situation not presented in either of these cases — I believe it is open to doubt whether the State's interests are sufficiently compelling to warrant the restriction on the free flow of information which results from a sweeping nonsolicitation rule and against which the First Amendment ordinarily protects. While the State's interest in regulating in-person solicitation may be somewhat greater than its interest in regulating printed advertisements, these concededly legitimate interests might well be served by more specific and less restrictive rules than a total ban on pecuniary solicitation. For example, the Justice Department has suggested that the disciplinary rules be reworded "so as to permit

---

[22] [6] The Court's opinion in *Bates* persuasively demonstrated the lack of basis for concluding that advertising by attorneys would demean the profession, increase the incidence of fraudulent or deceptive behavior by attorneys, or otherwise harm the consumers of legal services. It is interesting in this connection to note that for many years even those in favor of the rules against solicitation by attorneys agreed that solicitation was not "malum in se." H. DRINKER, LEGAL ETHICS 211 n.3 (1953). Dr. Johnson, a venerable commentator on mores of all sorts, expressed well the prevailing view of the profession when he stated: "I should not solicit employment as a lawyer — not because I should think it wrong, but because I should disdain it." Quoted in R. POUND, THE LAWYER FROM ANTIQUITY TO MODERN TIMES 12 n.3 (1953). As *Bates* made clear, "disdain" is an inadequate basis on which to restrict the flow of information otherwise protected by the First Amendment.

all solicitation and advertising except the kinds that are false, misleading, undignified, or champertous."

To the extent that in-person solicitation of business may constitutionally be subjected to more substantial state regulation as to time, place, and manner than printed advertising of legal services, it is not because such solicitation has "traditionally" been banned, nor because one form of commercial speech is of less value than another under the First Amendment. Rather, any additional restrictions can be justified only to the degree that dangers which the State has a right to prevent are actually presented by conduct attendant to such speech, thus increasing the relative "strength of the State's countervailing interest in prohibition." As the majority notes, and I wholeheartedly agree, these dangers are amply present in the *Ohralik* case.

Accordingly, while I concur in the judgments of the Court in both of these cases, I join in the Court's opinions only to the extent and with the exceptions noted above.

NOTES, QUESTIONS, AND EXAMPLES

1.   Ohralik committed many violations of the ethics codes in addition to his in-person solicitation.

- he taped conversations with his clients (if they were yet his clients) without their knowledge or consent.

- he gave a "tip" to a prospective client (Wanda Lou) that was adverse to the interests of his current client (Carol McClintock).

- he entered into a contingent fee agreement whose terms were unclear, and certainly not in writing.

- he refused to be discharged by his clients.

- he lied to the disciplinary committee.

2.   Professor Monroe Freedman argues, in a book chapter titled, "The Lawyer's Duty to Chase Ambulances," that lawyers are under an obligation to make legal services available to clients, especially clients who are vulnerable to an opposing party, typically an insurance carrier intent on obtaining a quick release of liability in exchange for a settlement check.

3.   The solicitation rules include an exception for solicitation of those with whom the lawyer has a prior relationship. In an interesting case, the Alabama Supreme Court dismissed disciplinary charges against a lawyer who had solicited the estate settlement business of a bank president. The lawyer sought the assignment of handling estate and trust matters for a friend of the lawyer whose estate and trust matters were in the hands of the bank. *Goldthwaite v. Disciplinary Board*, 408 So. 2d 504 (Ala. 1982).

4.   There are additional restrictions on solicitation of specific prospective clients or those known to be in need of specific services.

- "We don't want any!": Once a prospective client makes known her desire not to be contacted by the lawyer, the lawyer may not contact that prospective client. MR 7.3(b)(1).

- Disclaimer: Written or recorded communications to those known to be in need of specific services must include the words "Advertising Material" on the outside of any envelope used and at the beginning and end of any recorded communication. MR 7.3(c).

5. Historically, "encroachment" (approaching another lawyer's client for the purpose of attracting that client to become the encroaching lawyer's client) was regarded with great disdain. *See* HENRY DRINKER, LEGAL ETHICS 190 (1953). Competition among lawyers to represent litigants in the Supreme Court has produced a conflict requiring the Court's attention. In *Illinois v. Wardlow*, 528 U.S. 119 (2000), and *United States v. Drayton*, 536 U.S. 194 (2002), two criminal procedure cases of note, James Koch of Chicago's Gardner Koch & Weisberg approached the indigent litigants while their cases were pending before the Supreme Court with offers to represent them without fee, eventually asserting that he represented each client. According to the lawyers (both public defenders) Koch sought to replace, Koch made false and misleading statements to the clients in his attempt to move them to dismiss their current lawyers and retain him. According to Koch, because he offers to represent such clients pro bono, *Primus* protects his solicitation. How should the Court treat this issue? *See* Tony Mauro, *Bitter Battle Between Lawyers Reaches High Court*, AM. LAW. MEDIA, Mar. 2, 2002.

E.   IS TARGETED DIRECT MAIL ADVERTISING, SOLICITATION, OR SOMETHING ELSE?

SHAPERO v. KENTUCKY BAR ASSOCIATION
486 U.S. 466 (1988)

JUSTICE BRENNAN announced the judgment of the Court and delivered the opinion of the Court as to Parts I and II and an opinion as to Part III in which JUSTICE MARSHALL, JUSTICE BLACKMUN, and JUSTICE KENNEDY join.

This case presents the issue whether a State may, consistent with the First and Fourteenth Amendments, categorically prohibit lawyers from soliciting legal business for pecuniary gain by sending truthful and nondeceptive letters to potential clients known to face particular legal problems.

I

In 1985, petitioner, a member of Kentucky's integrated Bar Association, applied to the Kentucky Attorneys Advertising Commission for approval of a letter that he proposed to send "to potential clients who have had a foreclosure suit filed against them." The proposed letter read as follows:

> It has come to my attention that your home is being foreclosed on. If this is true, you may be about to lose your home. Federal law may allow you to keep your home by ORDERING your creditor [sic] to STOP and give you more time to pay them.

You may call my office anytime from 8:30 a.m. to 5:00 p.m. for FREE information on how you can keep your home.

Call NOW, don't wait. It may surprise you what I may be able to do for you. Just call and tell me that you got this letter. Remember it is FREE, there is NO charge for calling.

The Commission did not find the letter false or misleading. Nevertheless, it declined to approve petitioner's proposal on the ground that a then-existing Kentucky Supreme Court Rule prohibited the mailing or delivery of written advertisements "precipitated by a specific event or occurrence involving or relating to the addressee or addressees as distinct from the general public." Ky. Sup. Ct. Rule 3.135(5)(b)(I).[23] The Commission registered its view that Rule 3.135(5)(b)(I)'s ban on targeted, direct-mail advertising violated the First Amendment and recommended that the Kentucky Supreme Court amend its Rules. Pursuing the Commission's suggestion, petitioner petitioned the Committee on Legal Ethics (Ethics Committee) of the Kentucky Bar Association for an advisory opinion as to the Rule's validity. Like the Commission, the Ethics Committee, in an opinion formally adopted by the Board of Governors of the Bar Association, did not find the proposed letter false or misleading, but nonetheless upheld Rule 3.135(5)(b) (I) on the ground that it was consistent with Rule 7.3 of the American Bar Association's Model Rules of Professional Conduct (1984).

On review of the Ethics Committee's advisory opinion, the Kentucky Supreme Court felt "compelled by the decision in *Zauderer* to order [Rule 3.135(5)(b)(I)] deleted," and replaced it with the ABA's Rule 7.3, which provides in its entirety:

"A lawyer may not solicit professional employment from a prospective client with whom the lawyer has no family or prior professional relationship, by mail, in person or otherwise, when a significant motive for the lawyer's doing so is the lawyer's pecuniary gain. The term 'solicit' includes contact in person, by telephone or telegraph, by letter or other writing, or by other communication directed to a specific recipient, but does not include letters addressed or advertising circulars distributed generally to persons not known to need legal services of the kind provided by the lawyer in a particular matter, but who are so situated that they might in general find such services useful." 726 S.W.2d at 301 (quoting ABA, Model Rule of Professional Conduct 7.3 (1984)).[24]

The court did not specify either the precise infirmity in Rule 3.135(5)(b)(I) or how Rule 7.3 cured it. Rule 7.3, like its predecessor, prohibits targeted, direct-mail solicitation by lawyers for pecuniary gain, without a particularized finding that the solicitation is false or misleading. We granted certiorari to resolve whether such a

---

[23] [2] Rule 3.135(5)(b)(I) provided in full:

A written advertisement may be sent or delivered to an individual addressee only if that addressee is one of a class of persons, other than a family, to whom it is also sent or delivered at or about the same time, and only if it is not prompted or precipitated by a specific event or occurrence involving or relating to the addressee or addressees as distinct from the general public.

[24] [Model Rule 7.3 was later amended to delete the reference to targeted letters or writings. —Ed.]

blanket prohibition is consistent with the First Amendment, made applicable to the States through the Fourteenth Amendment, and now reverse.

* * *

II

* * *

In *Zauderer*, application of these principles required that we strike an Ohio rule that categorically prohibited solicitation of legal employment for pecuniary gain through advertisements containing information or advice, even if truthful and nondeceptive, regarding a specific legal problem. We distinguished written advertisements containing such information or advice from in-person solicitation by lawyers for profit, which we held in *Ohralik v. Ohio State Bar Assn.*, 436 U.S. 447 (1978), a State may categorically ban. The "unique features of in-person solicitation by lawyers [that] justified a prophylactic rule prohibiting lawyers from engaging in such solicitation for pecuniary gain," we observed, are "not present" in the context of written advertisements.

Our lawyer advertising cases have never distinguished among various modes of written advertising to the general public. Thus, Ohio could no more prevent Zauderer from mass-mailing to a general population his offer to represent women injured by the Dalkon Shield than it could prohibit his publication of the advertisement in local newspapers. Similarly, if petitioner's letter is neither false nor deceptive, Kentucky could not constitutionally prohibit him from sending at large an identical letter opening with the query, "Is your home being foreclosed on?," rather than his observation to the targeted individuals that "It has come to my attention that your home is being foreclosed on." The drafters of Rule 7.3 apparently appreciated as much, for the Rule exempts from the ban "letters addressed or advertising circulars distributed generally to persons . . . who are so situated that they might in general find such services useful."

The court below disapproved petitioner's proposed letter solely because it targeted only persons who were "known to need [the] legal services" offered in his letter, rather than the broader group of persons "so situated that they might in general find such services useful." Generally, unless the advertiser is inept, the latter group would include members of the former. The only reason to disseminate an advertisement of particular legal services among those persons who are "so situated that they might in general find such services useful" is to reach individuals who actually "need legal services of the kind provided [and advertised] by the lawyer." But the First Amendment does not permit a ban on certain speech merely because it is more efficient; the State may not constitutionally ban a particular letter on the theory that to mail it only to those whom it would most interest is somehow inherently objectionable.

The court below did not rely on any such theory. *See also* Brief for Respondent 37 (conceding that "targeted direct mail advertising" — as distinguished from "solicitation" — "is constitutionally protected"). Rather, it concluded that the State's blanket ban on all targeted, direct-mail solicitation was permissible because of the "serious potential for abuse inherent in direct solicitation by lawyers of potential clients known to need specific legal services." By analogy to *Ohralik*, the court observed:

> Such solicitation subjects the prospective client to pressure from a trained lawyer in a direct personal way. It is entirely possible that the potential client may feel overwhelmed by the basic situation which caused the need for the specific legal services and may have seriously impaired capacity for good judgment, sound reason and a natural protective self-interest.

Such a condition is full of the possibility of undue influence, overreaching and intimidation.

Of course, a particular potential client will feel equally "overwhelmed" by his legal troubles and will have the same "impaired capacity for good judgment" regardless of whether a lawyer mails him an untargeted letter or exposes him to a newspaper advertisement — concededly constitutionally protected activities — or instead mails a targeted letter. The relevant inquiry is not whether there exist potential clients whose "condition" makes them susceptible to undue influence, but whether the mode of communication poses a serious danger that lawyers will exploit any such susceptibility.

Thus, respondent's facile suggestion that this case is merely *"Ohralik* in writing" misses the mark. In assessing the potential for overreaching and undue influence, the mode of communication makes all the difference. Our decision in *Ohralik* that a State could categorically ban all in-person solicitation turned on two factors. First was our characterization of face-to-face solicitation as "a practice rife with possibilities for overreaching, invasion of privacy, the exercise of undue influence, and outright fraud." Second, "unique . . . difficulties," would frustrate any attempt at state regulation of in-person solicitation short of an absolute ban because such solicitation is "not visible or otherwise open to public scrutiny." Targeted, direct-mail solicitation is distinguishable from the in-person solicitation in each respect.

Like print advertising, petitioner's letter — and targeted, direct-mail solicitation generally — "poses much less risk of overreaching or undue influence" than does in-person solicitation, Neither mode of written communication involves "the coercive force of the personal presence of a trained advocate" or the "pressure on the potential client for an immediate yes-or-no answer to the offer of representation." Unlike the potential client with a badgering advocate breathing down his neck, the recipient of a letter and the "reader of an advertisement . . . can 'effectively avoid further bombardment of [his] sensibilities simply by averting [his] eyes,' " A letter, like a printed advertisement (but unlike a lawyer), can readily be put in a drawer to be considered later, ignored, or discarded. In short, both types of written solicitation "conve[y] information about legal services [by means] that [are] more conducive to reflection and the exercise of choice on the part of the consumer than is personal solicitation by an attorney." Nor does a targeted letter invade the recipient's privacy any more than does a substantively identical letter mailed at large. The invasion, if any, occurs when the lawyer discovers the recipient's legal affairs, not when he confronts the recipient with the discovery.

Admittedly, a letter that is personalized (not merely targeted) to the recipient presents an increased risk of deception, intentional or inadvertent. It could, in certain circumstances, lead the recipient to overestimate the lawyer's familiarity with the case or could implicitly suggest that the recipient's legal problem is more dire than it really is. Similarly, an inaccurately targeted letter could lead the recipient to believe she has a legal problem that she does not actually have or, worse yet, could offer erroneous legal advice.

But merely because targeted, direct-mail solicitation presents lawyers with opportunities for isolated abuses or mistakes does not justify a total ban on that mode of protected commercial speech. The State can regulate such abuses and minimize mistakes through far less restrictive and more precise means, the most obvious of which is to require the lawyer to file any solicitation letter with a state agency, giving the State ample opportunity to supervise mailings and penalize actual abuses. The "regulatory difficulties" that are "unique" to in person lawyer solicitation — solicitation that is "not visible or otherwise open to public scrutiny" and for which it is "difficult or impossible to obtain reliable proof of what actually took place," — do not apply to written solicitations. The court below offered no basis for its "belie[f] [that] submission of a blank form letter to the Advertising Commission [does not] provid[e] a suitable protection to the public from overreaching, intimidation or misleading private targeted mail solicitation."

III

The validity of Rule 7.3 does not turn on whether petitioner's letter itself exhibited any of the evils at which Rule 7.3 was directed. Since, however, the First Amendment overbreadth doctrine does not apply to professional advertising, see Bates, 433 U.S. at 379-381, we address respondent's contentions that petitioner's letter is particularly overreaching, and therefore unworthy of First Amendment protection. In that regard, respondent identifies two features of the letter before us that, in its view, coalesce to convert the proposed letter into "high pressure solicitation, overbearing solicitation," which is not protected. First, respondent asserts that the letter's liberal use of underscored, uppercase letters (e.g., "Call NOW, don't wait"; "it is FREE, there is NO charge for calling") "fairly shouts at the recipient . . . that he should employ Shapero." Second, respondent objects that the letter contains assertions (e.g., "It may surprise you what I may be able to do for you") that "stat[e] no affirmative or objective fact," but constitute "pure salesman puffery, enticement for the unsophisticated, which commits Shapero to nothing."

The pitch or style of a letter's type and its inclusion of subjective predictions of client satisfaction might catch the recipient's attention more than would a bland statement of purely objective facts in small type. But a truthful and non-deceptive letter, no matter how big its type and how much it speculates can never "shou[t] at the recipient" or "gras[p] him by the lapels," as can a lawyer engaging in face-to-face solicitation. The letter simply presents no comparable risk of overreaching.

To be sure, a letter may be misleading if it unduly emphasizes trivial or "relatively uninformative fact[s]," *In re R.M.J., supra,* at 205 (lawyer's statement, "in large capital letters, that he was a member of the Bar of the Supreme Court of the United States"), or offers overblown assurances of client satisfaction, *cf. In re*

Von Wiegen, 63 N.Y.2d 163, 179, 481 N.Y.S.2d 40, 470 N.E.2d 838, 847 (1984) (solicitation letter to victims of massive disaster informs them that "it is [the lawyer's] opinion that the liability of the defendants is clear"), *cert. denied*, 472 U.S. 1007 (1985); *Bates, supra*, at 383- 384 ("Advertising claims as to the quality of legal services . . . may be so likely to be misleading as to warrant restriction"). Respondent does not argue before us that petitioner's letter was misleading in those respects. Nor does respondent contend that the letter is false or misleading in any other respect. Of course, respondent is free to raise, and the Kentucky courts are free to consider, any such argument on remand.

The judgment of the Supreme Court of Kentucky is reversed, and the case is remanded for further proceedings not inconsistent with this opinion.

It is so ordered.

FLORIDA RULE 4-7.4 Direct Contact with Prospective Clients

(a) Solicitation. A lawyer shall not solicit professional employment from a prospective client with whom the lawyer has no family or prior professional relationship, in person or otherwise, when a significant motive for the lawyer's doing so is the lawyer's pecuniary gain. A lawyer shall not permit employees or agents of the lawyer to solicit in the lawyer's behalf. A lawyer shall not enter into an agreement for, charge, or collect a fee for professional employment obtained in violation of this rule. The term "solicit" includes contact in person, by telephone, telegraph, or facsimile, or by other communication directed to a specific recipient and includes any written form of communication directed to a specific recipient and not meeting the requirements of subdivision (b) of this rule.

(b) Written Communication.

(1) A lawyer shall not send, or knowingly permit to be sent, on the lawyer's behalf or on behalf of the lawyer's firm or partner, an associate, or any other lawyer affiliated with the lawyer or the lawyer's firm, a written communication to a prospective client for the purpose of obtaining professional employment if:

    (A) the written communication concerns an action for personal injury or wrongful death or otherwise relates to an accident or disaster involving the person to whom the communication is addressed or a relative of that person, unless the accident or disaster occurred more than 30 days prior to the mailing of the communication;

    (B) the written communication concerns a specific matter and the lawyer knows or reasonably should know that the person to whom the communication is directed is represented by a lawyer in the matter;

    (C) it has been made known to the lawyer that the person does not want to receive such communications from the lawyer;

    (D) the communication involves coercion, duress, fraud, overreaching, harassment, intimidation, or undue influence;

(E) the communication contains a false, fraudulent, misleading, deceptive, or unfair statement or claim or is improper under rule 4-7.1; or

(F) the lawyer knows or reasonably should know that the physical, emotional, or mental state of the person makes it unlikely that the person would exercise reasonable judgment in employing a lawyer.

(2) Written communications to prospective clients for the purpose of obtaining professional employment are subject to the following requirements:

(A) Each page of such written communications shall be plainly marked "advertisement" in red ink, and the lower left corner of the face of the envelope containing a written communication likewise shall carry a prominent, red "advertisement" mark. If the written communication is in the form of a self-mailing brochure or pamphlet, the "advertisement" mark in red ink shall appear on the address panel of the brochure or pamphlet. Brochures solicited by clients or prospective clients need not contain the "advertisement" mark.

(B) A copy of each such written communication and a sample of the envelopes in which the communications are enclosed shall be filed with the standing committee on advertising either prior to or concurrently with the mailing of the communication to a prospective client, as provided in rule 4-7.5. The lawyer also shall retain a copy of each written communication for 3 years. If identical written communications are sent to 2 or more prospective clients, the lawyer may comply with this requirement by filing 1 of the identical written communications and retaining for 3 years a single copy together with a list of the names and addresses of persons to whom the written communication was sent.

(C) Written communications mailed to prospective clients shall be sent only by regular U.S. mail, not by registered mail or other forms of restricted delivery.

(D) No reference shall be made in the communication to the communication's having received any kind of approval from The Florida Bar.

(E) Every written communication shall be accompanied by a written statement of the lawyer's or law firm's qualifications conforming to the requirements of rule 4-7.3.

(F) If a contract for representation is mailed with the written communication, the top of each page of the contract shall be marked "SAMPLE" in red ink in a type size 1 size larger than the largest type used in the contract and the words "DO NOT SIGN" shall appear on the client signature line.

(G) The first sentence of any written communication concerning a specific matter shall be: "If you have already retained a lawyer for this matter, please disregard this letter."

(H) Written communications shall be on letter-sized paper rather than legal-sized paper and shall not be made to resemble legal pleadings or other legal documents. This provision does not preclude the mailing of brochures and pamphlets.

(I) If a lawyer other than the lawyer whose name or signature appears on the communication will actually handle the case or matter, or if the case or matter will be referred to another lawyer or law firm, any written communication concerning a specific matter shall include a statement so advising the client.

(J) Any written communication prompted by a specific occurrence involving or affecting the intended recipient of the communication or a family member shall disclose how the lawyer obtained the information prompting the communication.

(K) A written communication seeking employment by a specific prospective client in a specific matter shall not reveal on the envelope, or on the outside of a self-mailing brochure or pamphlet, the nature of the client's legal problem.

FLORIDA BAR v. WENT FOR IT, INC.
515 U.S. 618 (1995)

Justice O'Connor delivered the opinion of the Court.

Rules of the Florida Bar prohibit personal injury lawyers from sending targeted direct-mail solicitations to victims and their relatives for 30 days following an accident or disaster. This case asks us to consider whether such Rules violate the First and Fourteenth Amendments of the Constitution. We hold that in the circumstances presented here, they do not.

I

In 1989, the Florida Bar (Bar) completed a 2-year study of the effects of lawyer advertising on public opinion. After conducting hearings, commissioning surveys, and reviewing extensive public commentary, the Bar determined that several changes to its advertising rules were in order. In late 1990, the Florida Supreme Court adopted the Bar's proposed amendments with some modifications. Two of these amendments are at issue in this case. Rule 4- 7.4(b)(1) provides that "[a] lawyer shall not send, or knowingly permit to be sent, . . . a written communication to a prospective client for the purpose of obtaining professional employment if: (A) the written communication concerns an action for personal injury or wrongful death or otherwise relates to an accident or disaster involving the person to whom the communication is addressed or a relative of that person, unless the accident or disaster occurred more than 30 days prior to the mailing of the communication." Rule 4-7.8(a) states that "[a] lawyer shall not accept referrals from a lawyer referral service unless the service: (1) engages in no communication with the public and in no direct contact with prospective clients in a manner that would violate the Rules of Professional Conduct if the communication or contact were made by the lawyer." Together, these rules create a brief 30-day blackout period after an accident during which lawyers may not, directly or indirectly, single out accident victims or their relatives in order to solicit their business. In March 1992, G. Stewart McHenry and his wholly owned lawyer referral service, Went For It, Inc., filed this action for declaratory and injunctive relief in the United States District Court for the Middle District of Florida challenging Rules 4-7.4(b)(1) and 4-7.8 as violative of the First and Fourteenth Amendments to the Constitution. McHenry alleged that he routinely sent targeted solicitations to accident victims or their survivors within 30 days after accidents and that he wished to continue doing so in the future. Went For It, Inc., represented that it wished to contact accident victims or their survivors within 30 days of accidents and to refer potential clients to participating Florida lawyers.

The District Court referred the parties' competing summary judgment motions to a Magistrate Judge, who concluded that the Florida Bar had substantial government interests, predicated on a concern for professionalism, both in protecting the personal privacy and tranquility of recent accident victims and their relatives and in ensuring that these individuals do not fall prey to undue influence or overreaching. Citing the Florida Bar's extensive study, the Magistrate Judge found that the Rules directly serve those interests and sweep no further than reasonably necessary. The Magistrate recommended that the District Court grant the Florida Bar's motion for summary judgment on the ground that the Rules pass constitutional muster.

The District Court rejected the Magistrate Judge's report and recommendations and entered summary judgment for the plaintiffs, relying on *Bates v. State Bar of Ariz.* and subsequent cases. The Eleventh Circuit affirmed on similar grounds. The panel noted, in its conclusion, that it was "disturbed that Bates and its progeny require the decision" that it reached. We granted certiorari, and now reverse.

II

A

*   *   *

Nearly two decades of cases have built upon the foundation laid by Bates. It is now well established that lawyer advertising is commercial speech and, as such, is accorded a measure of First Amendment protection. Such First Amendment protection, of course, is not absolute. We have always been careful to distinguish commercial speech from speech at the First Amendment's core. " 'Commercial speech [enjoys] a limited measure of protection, commensurate with its subordinate position in the scale of First Amendment values,' and is subject to 'modes of regulation that might be impermissible in the realm of noncommercial expression.' " We have observed that " 'to require a parity of constitutional protection for commercial and noncommercial speech alike could invite dilution, simply by a leveling process, of the force of the Amendment's guarantee with respect to the latter kind of speech.' "

Mindful of these concerns, we engage in "intermediate" scrutiny of restrictions on commercial speech, analyzing them under the framework set forth in *Central Hudson Gas & Elec. Corp. v. Public Serv. Comm'n of N.Y.*, 447 U.S. 557 (1980). Under *Central Hudson*, the government may freely regulate commercial speech that concerns unlawful activity or is misleading. Commercial speech that falls into neither of those categories, like the advertising at issue here, may be regulated if the government satisfies a test consisting of three related prongs: First, the government must assert a substantial interest in support of its regulation; second, the government must demonstrate that the restriction on commercial speech directly and materially advances that interest; and third, the regulation must be " 'narrowly drawn.' "

B

"Unlike rational basis review, the *Central Hudson* standard does not permit us to supplant the precise interests put forward by the State with other suppositions," *Edenfield v. Fane*, 507 U.S. 761, 768 (1993). The Florida Bar asserts that it has a substantial interest in protecting the privacy and tranquility of personal injury victims and their loved ones against intrusive, unsolicited contact by lawyers.[25] This interest obviously factors into the Bar's paramount (and repeatedly professed) objective of curbing activities that "negatively affect the administration of justice." Because direct mail solicitations in the wake of accidents are perceived by the public as intrusive, the Bar argues, the reputation of the legal profession in the eyes of Floridians has suffered commensurately. The regulation, then, is an effort to protect the flagging reputations of Florida lawyers by preventing them from engaging in conduct that, the Bar maintains, " 'is universally regarded as deplorable and beneath common decency because of its intrusion upon the special vulnerability and private grief of victims or their families.' "

We have little trouble crediting the Bar's interest as substantial. On various occasions we have accepted the proposition that "States have a compelling interest in the practice of professions within their boundaries, and . . . as part of their power to protect the public health, safety, and other valid interests they have broad power to establish standards for licensing practitioners and regulating the practice of professions."

Under *Central Hudson's* second prong, the State must demonstrate that the challenged regulation "advances the Government's interest 'in a direct and material way.' " That burden, we have explained, " 'is not satisfied by mere speculation or conjecture; rather, a governmental body seeking to sustain a restriction on commercial speech must demonstrate that the harms it recites are real and that its restriction will in fact alleviate them to a material degree.' " In *Edenfield*, the Court invalidated a Florida ban on in-person solicitation by certified public accountants (CPA's). We observed that the State Board of Accountancy had "presented no studies that suggest personal solicitation of prospective business clients by CPA's

---

[25] [1] At prior stages of this litigation, the Bar asserted a different interest, in addition to that urged now, in protecting people against undue influence and overreaching. Because the Bar does not press this interest before us, we do not consider it. Of course, our precedents do not require the Bar to point to more than one interest in support of its 30-day restriction; a single substantial interest is sufficient to satisfy *Central Hudson's* first prong.

creates the dangers of fraud, overreaching, or compromised independence that the Board claims to fear." Moreover, "the record [did] not disclose any anecdotal evidence, either from Florida or another State, that validated the Board's suppositions." In fact, we concluded that the only evidence in the record tended to "contradict, rather than strengthen, the Board's submissions." Finding nothing in the record to substantiate the State's allegations of harm, we invalidated the regulation.

The direct-mail solicitation regulation before us does not suffer from such infirmities. The Florida Bar submitted a 106-page summary of its 2-year study of lawyer advertising and solicitation to the District Court. That summary contains data — both statistical and anecdotal — supporting the Bar's contentions that the Florida public views direct-mail solicitations in the immediate wake of accidents as an intrusion on privacy that reflects poorly upon the profession. As of June 1989, lawyers mailed 700,000 direct solicitations in Florida annually, 40% of which were aimed at accident victims or their survivors. A survey of Florida adults commissioned by the Bar indicated that Floridians "have negative feelings about those attorneys who use direct mail advertising." Fifty-four percent of the general population surveyed said that contacting persons concerning accidents or similar events is a violation of privacy. A random sampling of persons who received direct-mail advertising from lawyers in 1987 revealed that 45% believed that direct-mail solicitation is "designed to take advantage of gullible or unstable people"; 34% found such tactics "annoying or irritating"; 26% found it "an invasion of your privacy"; and 24% reported that it "made you angry." Significantly, 27% of direct-mail recipients reported that their regard for the legal profession and for the judicial process as a whole was "lower" as a result of receiving the direct mail.

The anecdotal record mustered by the Bar is noteworthy for its breadth and detail. With titles like "Scavenger Lawyers" (The Miami Herald, Sept. 29, 1987) and "Solicitors Out of Bounds" (St. Petersburg Times, Oct. 26, 1987), newspaper editorial pages in Florida have burgeoned with criticism of Florida lawyers who send targeted direct mail to victims shortly after accidents. The study summary also includes page upon page of excerpts from complaints of direct-mail recipients. For example, a Florida citizen described how he was " 'appalled and angered by the brazen attempt' " of a law firm to solicit him by letter shortly after he was injured and his fiancée was killed in an auto accident. Another found it " 'despicable and inexcusable' " that a Pensacola lawyer wrote to his mother three days after his father's funeral. Another described how she was " 'astounded' " and then " 'very angry' " when she received a solicitation following a minor accident. Still another described as " 'beyond comprehension' " a letter his nephew's family received the day of the nephew's funeral. One citizen wrote, " 'I consider the unsolicited contact from you after my child's accident to be of the rankest form of ambulance chasing and in incredibly poor taste. . . . I cannot begin to express with my limited vocabulary the utter contempt in which I hold you and your kind.' "

In light of this showing — which respondents at no time refuted, save by the conclusory assertion that the rule lacked "any factual basis" — we conclude that the Bar has satisfied the second prong of the *Central Hudson* test. In dissent, Justice Kennedy complains that we have before us few indications of the sample size or selection procedures employed by Magid Associates (a nationally renowned con sulting firm) and no copies of the actual surveys employed. As stated, we believe the evidence adduced by the Bar is sufficient to meet the standard elaborated in *Edenfield v. Fane*, 507 U.S. 761 (1993). In any event, we do not read our case law to require that empirical data come to us accompanied by a surfeit of background information. Indeed, in other First Amendment contexts, we have permitted litigants to justify speech restrictions by reference to studies and anecdotes pertaining to different locales altogether.

In reaching a contrary conclusion, the Court of Appeals determined that this case was governed squarely by *Shapero v. Kentucky Bar Assn.*, 486 U.S. 466 (1988). Making no mention of the Bar's study, the court concluded that " 'a targeted letter [does not] invade the recipient's privacy any more than does a substantively identical letter mailed at large. The invasion, if any, occurs when the lawyer discovers the recipient's legal affairs, not when he confronts the recipient with the discovery.' " 21 F.3d at 1044, quoting *Shapero*, *supra*, at 476. In many cases, the Court of Appeals explained, "this invasion of privacy will involve no more than reading the newspaper."

While some of *Shapero's* language might be read to support the Court of Appeals' interpretation, *Shapero* differs in several fundamental respects from the case before us. First and foremost, *Shapero's* treatment of privacy was casual. Contrary to the dissent's suggestions, the State in *Shapero* did not seek to justify its regulation as a measure undertaken to prevent lawyers' invasions of privacy interests. Rather, the State focused exclusively on the special dangers of overreaching inhering in targeted solicitations. Second, in contrast to this case, *Shapero* dealt with a broad ban on all direct-mail solicitations, whatever the time frame and whoever the recipient. Finally, the State in *Shapero* assembled no evidence attempting to demonstrate any actual harm caused by targeted direct mail. The Court rejected the State's effort to justify a prophylactic ban on the basis of blanket, untested assertions of undue influence and overreaching. Because the State did not make a privacy-based argument at all, its empirical showing on that issue was similarly infirm.

We find the Court's perfunctory treatment of privacy in *Shapero* to be of little utility in assessing this ban on targeted solicitation of victims in the immediate aftermath of accidents. While it is undoubtedly true that many people find the image of lawyers sifting through accident and police reports in pursuit of prospective clients unpalatable and invasive, this case targets a different kind of intrusion. The Florida Bar has argued, and the record reflects, that a principal purpose of the ban is "protecting the personal privacy and tranquility of [Florida's] citizens from crass commercial intrusion by attorneys upon their personal grief in times of trauma." The intrusion targeted by the Bar's regulation stems not from the fact that a lawyer has learned about an accident or disaster (as the Court of Appeals notes, in many instances a lawyer need only read the newspaper to glean this information), but from the lawyer's confrontation of victims or relatives with such information, while wounds are still open, in order to solicit their business. In this respect, an untargeted letter mailed to society at large is different in kind from a targeted solicitation; the untargeted letter involves no willful or knowing affront to or invasion of the tranquility of bereaved or injured individuals and simply does not cause the same kind of reputational harm to the profession unearthed by the Florida Bar's study.

*   *   *

Here, in contrast, the harm targeted by the Florida Bar cannot be eliminated by a brief journey to the trash can. The purpose of the 30-day targeted direct-mail ban is to forestall the outrage and irritation with the state-licensed legal profession that the practice of direct solicitation only days after accidents has engendered. The Bar is concerned not with citizens' "offense" in the abstract, but with the demonstrable detrimental effects that such "offense" has on the profession it regulates.[26]

Passing to *Central Hudson's* third prong, we examine the relationship between the Florida Bar's interests and the means chosen to serve them. With respect to this prong, the differences between commercial speech and noncommercial speech are manifest. In *Fox*, we made clear that the "least restrictive means" test has no role in the commercial speech context. "What our decisions require," instead, "is a 'fit' between the legislature's ends and the means chosen to accomplish those ends,' a fit that is not necessarily perfect, but reasonable; that represents not necessarily the single best disposition but one whose scope is 'in proportion to the interest served,' that employs not necessarily the least restrictive means but . . . a means narrowly tailored to achieve the desired objective." Of course, we do not equate this test with the less rigorous obstacles of rational basis review.

Respondents levy a great deal of criticism, echoed in the dissent, at the scope of the Bar's restriction on targeted mail. "By prohibiting written communications to all people, whatever their state of mind," respondents charge, the rule "keeps useful information from those accident victims who are ready, willing and able to utilize a lawyer's advice." This criticism may be parsed into two components. First, the rule does not distinguish between victims in terms of the severity of their injuries. According to respondents, the rule is unconstitutionally overinclusive insofar as it bans targeted mailings even to citizens whose injuries or grief are relatively minor. Second, the rule may prevent citizens from learning about their legal options, particularly at a time when other actors — opposing counsel and insurance adjusters-may be clamoring for victims' attentions. Any benefit arising from the Bar's regulation, respondents implicitly contend, is outweighed by these costs.

We are not persuaded by respondents' allegations of constitutional infirmity. We find little deficiency in the ban's failure to distinguish among injured Floridians by the severity of their pain or the intensity of their grief. Indeed, it is hard to imagine the contours of a regulation that might satisfy respondents on this score. Rather than drawing difficult lines on the basis that some injuries are "severe" and some situations appropriate (and others, presumably, inappropriate) for grief, anger, or emotion, the Florida Bar has crafted a ban applicable to all post-accident or disaster solicitations for a brief 30-day period. Unlike respondents, we do not see "numerous

---

[26] [2] Missing this nuance altogether, the dissent asserts apocalyptically that we are "unsettling leading First Amendment precedents." We do no such thing. There is an obvious difference between situations in which the government acts in its own interests, or on behalf of entities it regulates, and situations in which the government is motivated primarily by paternalism. The cases cited by the dissent focus on the latter situation.

and obvious less-burdensome alternatives" to Florida's short temporal ban. The Bar's rule is reasonably well tailored to its stated objective of eliminating targeted mailings whose type and timing are a source of distress to Floridians, distress that has caused many of them to lose respect for the legal profession.

Respondents' second point would have force if the Bar's rule were not limited to a brief period and if there were not many other ways for injured Floridians to learn about the availability of legal representation during that time. Our lawyer advertising cases have afforded lawyers a great deal of leeway to devise innovative ways to attract new business. Florida permits lawyers to advertise on prime-time television and radio as well as in newspapers and other media. They may rent space on billboards. They may send untargeted letters to the general population, or to discrete segments thereof. There are, of course, pages upon pages devoted to lawyers in the Yellow Pages of Florida telephone directories. These listings are organized alphabetically and by area of specialty. These ample alternative channels for receipt of information about the availability of legal representation during the 30-day period following accidents may explain why, despite the ample evidence, testimony, and commentary submitted by those favoring (as well as opposing) unrestricted direct-mail solicitation, respondents have not pointed to — and we have not independently found — a single example of an individual case in which immediate solicitation helped to avoid, or failure to solicit within 30 days brought about, the harms that concern the dissent. In fact, the record contains considerable empirical survey information suggesting that Floridians have little difficulty finding a lawyer when they need one. Finding no basis to question the commonsense conclusion that the many alternative channels for communicating necessary information about attorneys are sufficient, we see no defect in Florida's regulation.

III

Speech by professionals obviously has many dimensions. There are circumstances in which we will accord speech by attorneys on public issues and matters of legal representation the strongest protection our Constitution has to offer. *See, e.g., Gentile v. State Bar of Nevada,* 501 U.S. 1030 (1991); *In re Primus,* 436 U.S. 412 (1978). This case, however, concerns pure commercial advertising, for which we have always reserved a lesser degree of protection under the First Amendment. Particularly because the standards and conduct of state-licensed lawyers have traditionally been subject to extensive regulation by the States, it is all the more appropriate that we limit our scrutiny of state regulations to a level commensurate with the " 'subordinate position' " of commercial speech in the scale of First Amendment values. We believe that the Florida Bar's 30-day restriction on targeted direct-mail solicitation of accident victims and their relatives withstands scrutiny under the three-pronged Central Hudson test that we have devised for this context. The Bar has substantial interest both in protecting injured Floridians from invasive conduct by lawyers and in preventing the erosion of confidence in the profession that such repeated invasions have engendered. The Bar's proffered study, unrebutted by respondents below, provides evidence indicating that the harms it targets are far from illusory. The palliative devised by the Bar to address these harms is narrow both in scope and in duration. The Constitution, in our view, requires nothing more.

The judgment of the Court of Appeals, accordingly, is

Reversed.

JUSTICE KENNEDY, with whom JUSTICE STEVENS, JUSTICE SOUTER, and JUSTICE GINSBURG join, dissenting.

Attorneys who communicate their willingness to assist potential clients are engaged in speech protected by the First and Fourteenth Amendments. That principle has been understood since *Bates v. State Bar of Arizona*, 433 U.S. 350 (1977). The Court today undercuts this guarantee in an important class of cases and unsettles leading First Amendment precedents, at the expense of those victims most in need of legal assistance. With all respect for the Court, in my view its solicitude for the privacy of victims and its concern for our profession are misplaced and self-defeating, even upon the Court's own premises.

I take it to be uncontroverted that when an accident results in death or injury, it is often urgent at once to investigate the occurrence, identify witnesses, and preserve evidence. Vital interests in speech and expression are, therefore, at stake when by law an attorney cannot direct a letter to the victim or the family explaining this simple fact and offering competent legal assistance. Meanwhile, represented and better informed parties, or parties who have been solicited in ways more sophisticated and indirect, may be at work. Indeed, these parties, either themselves or by their attorneys, investigators, and adjusters, are free to contact the unrepresented persons to gather evidence or offer settlement. This scheme makes little sense. As is often true when the law makes little sense, it is not first principles but their interpretation and application that have gone awry.

*   *   *

I

*   *   *

To avoid the controlling effect of *Shapero* in the case before us, the Court seeks to declare that a different privacy interest is implicated. As it sees the matter, the substantial concern is that victims or their families will be offended by receiving a solicitation during their grief and trauma. But we do not allow restrictions on speech to be justified on the ground that the expression might offend the listener. On the contrary, we have said that these "are classically not justifications validating the suppression of expression protected by the First Amendment." And in *Zauderer v. Office of Disciplinary Counsel of Supreme Court of Ohio*, where we struck down a ban on attorney advertising, we held that "the mere possibility that some members of the population might find advertising . . . offensive cannot justify suppressing it. The same must hold true for advertising that some members of the bar might find beneath their dignity."

We have applied this principle to direct-mail cases as well as with respect to general advertising, noting that the right to use the mails is protected by the First

Amendment. In *Bolger*, we held that a statute designed to "shield recipients of mail from materials that they are likely to find offensive" furthered an interest of "little weight," noting that "we have consistently held that the fact that protected speech may be offensive to some does not justify its suppression." It is only where an audience is captive that we will assure its protection from some offensive speech. Outside that context, "we have never held that the Government itself can shut off the flow of mailings to protect those recipients who might potentially be offended." The occupants of a household receiving mailings are not a captive audience, and the asserted interest in preventing their offense should be no more controlling here than in our prior cases. All the recipient of objectional mailings need do is to take "the 'short, though regular, journey from mail box to trash can.'" As we have observed, this is "an acceptable burden, at least so far as the Constitution is concerned." If these cases forbidding restrictions on speech that might be offensive are to be overruled, the Court should say so.

In the face of these difficulties of logic and precedent, the State and the opinion of the Court turn to a second interest: protecting the reputation and dignity of the legal profession. The argument is, it seems fair to say, that all are demeaned by the crass behavior of a few. The argument takes a further step in the amicus brief filed by the Association of Trial Lawyers of America. There it is said that disrespect for the profession from this sort of solicitation (but presumably from no other sort of solicitation) results in lower jury verdicts. In a sense, of course, these arguments are circular. While disrespect will arise from an unethical or improper practice, the majority begs a most critical question by assuming that direct-mail solicitations constitute such a practice. The fact is, however, that direct solicitation may serve vital purposes and promote the administration of justice, and to the extent the bar seeks to protect lawyers' reputations by preventing them from engaging in speech some deem offensive, the State is doing nothing more (as amicus the Association of Trial Lawyers of America is at least candid enough to admit) than manipulating the public's opinion by suppressing speech that informs us how the legal system works. The disrespect argument thus proceeds from the very assumption it tries to prove, which is to say that solicitations within 30 days serve no legitimate purpose. This, of course, is censorship pure and simple; and censorship is antithetical to the first principles of free expression.

* * *

IV

It is most ironic that, for the first time since *Bates v. State Bar of Arizona*, the Court now orders a major retreat from the constitutional guarantees for commercial speech in order to shield its own profession from public criticism. Obscuring the financial aspect of the legal profession from public discussion through direct-mail solicitation, at the expense of the least sophisticated members of society, is not a laudable constitutional goal. There is no authority for the proposition that the Constitution permits the State to promote the public image of the legal profession by suppressing information about the profession's business aspects. If public respect for the profession erodes because solicitation distorts the idea of the law as most lawyers see it, it must be remembered that real progress begins with more rational speech, not less. I agree that if this amounts to mere "sermonizing," *see Shapero*, 486 U.S. at 490 (O'Connor, J., dissenting), the attempt may be futile. The guiding principle, however, is that full and rational discussion furthers sound regulation and necessary reform. The image of the profession cannot be enhanced without improving the substance of its practice. The objective of the profession is to ensure that "the ethical standards of lawyers are linked to the service and protection of clients."

Today's opinion is a serious departure, not only from our prior decisions involving attorney advertising, but also from the principles that govern the transmission of commercial speech. The Court's opinion reflects a new-found and illegitimate confidence that it, along with the Supreme Court of Florida, knows what is best for the Bar and its clients. Self-assurance has always been the hallmark of a censor. That is why under the First Amendment the public, not the State, has the right and the power to decide what ideas and information are deserving of their adherence. "The general rule is that the speaker and the audience, not the government, assess the value of the information presented." By validating Florida's rule, today's majority is complicit in the Bar's censorship. For these reasons, I dissent from the opinion of the Court and from its judgment.

F.   THE SPECIAL CASE OF SPECIALIZATION

Until the 1970s, state bars were quite restrictive in their regulation of lawyers' indications of practice concentration, specialization, or certification in areas of practice. The largely outdated Model Code permitted a lawyer to identify a specialty only if that specialty was in patent, trademark, or admiralty law. It also permitted a lawyer to indicate subject matter areas of practice in which the lawyer engaged only if the lawyer used a prescribed list of words provided by the state bar. DR 2-105. More recently, the restrictions on areas of practice, specialty, and certification in a particular area have been constrained by the First Amendment but continue to be real restrictions, all under the rubric of the false and misleading limitation. MR 7.4.

As long as the words used by the lawyer to designate areas in which the lawyer practices fairly communicate those areas, they will be protected commercial speech and will not subject the lawyer to discipline. Whether the lawyer chooses to designate areas of practice as "torts" or "personal injury," "contracts" or "commercial litigation," "property" or "real estate transfers" will not matter for disciplinary purposes. All are permitted. *In re R.M.J.*, 455 U.S. 191 (1982).

Claiming a certification in a particular area presents additional concerns.

PEEL v. ATTORNEY REGISTRATION AND DISCIPLINARY COMMISSION OF ILLINOIS
496 U.S. 91 (1990)

JUSTICE STEVENS announced the judgment of the Court and delivered an opinion in which JUSTICE BRENNAN, JUSTICE BLACKMUN, and JUSTICE KENNEDY join.

The Illinois Supreme Court publicly censured petitioner because his letterhead states that he is certified as a civil trial specialist by the National Board of Trial Advocacy. We granted certiorari to consider whether the statement on his letterhead is protected by the First Amendment.

I

This case comes to us against a background of growing interest in lawyer certification programs. In the 1973 Sonnett Memorial Lecture, then Chief Justice Warren E. Burger advanced the proposition that specialized training and certification of trial advocates is essential to the American system of justice. That proposition was endorsed by a number of groups of lawyers who were instrumental in establishing the National Board of Trial Advocacy (NBTA) in 1977.

The groups sponsoring NBTA include the National District Attorneys Association, the Association of Trial Lawyers of America, the International Academy of Trial Lawyers, the International Society of Barristers, the National Association of Criminal Defense Lawyers, the National Association of Women Lawyers, and the American Board of Professional Liability Attorneys.

Since then, NBTA has developed a set of standards and procedures for periodic certification of lawyers with experience and competence in trial work. Those standards, which have been approved by a board of judges, scholars, and practitioners, are objective and demanding. They require specified experience as lead counsel in both jury and nonjury trials, participation in approved programs of continuing legal education, a demonstration of writing skills, and the successful completion of a day-long examination. Certification expires in five years unless the lawyer again demonstrates his or her continuing qualification.

* * *

II

Petitioner practices law in Edwardsville, Illinois. He was licensed to practice in Illinois in 1968, in Arizona in 1979, and in Missouri in 1981. He has served as president of the Madison County Bar Association, and has been active in both national and state bar association work. He has tried to verdict over 100 jury trials and over 300 nonjury trials, and has participated in hundreds of other litigated matters that were settled. NBTA issued a petitioner a "Certificate in Civil Trial Advocacy" in 1981, renewed it in 1986, and listed him in its 1985 Directory of "Certified Specialists and Board Members."

Since 1983 petitioner's professional letterhead has contained a statement refer ring to his NBTA certification and to the three States in which he is licensed. It appears as follows:

Gary E. Peel

Certified Civil Trial Specialist

By the National Board of Trial Advocacy

Licensed: Illinois, Missouri, Arizona

In 1987, the Administrator of the Attorney Registration and Disciplinary Commission of Illinois (Commission) filed a complaint alleging that petitioner, by use of this letterhead, was publicly holding himself out as a certified legal specialist in violation of Rule 2-105(a)(3) of the Illinois Code of Professional Responsibility. That Rule provides:

> A lawyer or law firm may specify or designate any area or field of law in which he or its partners concentrates or limits his or its practice. Except as set forth in Rule 2-105(a), no lawyer may hold himself out as "certified" or a "specialist."

The complaint also alleged violations of Rule 2-101(b), which requires that a lawyer's public "communication shall contain all information necessary to make the communication not misleading and shall not contain any false or misleading statement or otherwise operate to deceive," and of Rule 1-102(a)(1), which generally subjects a lawyer to discipline for violation of any Rule of the Code of Professional Responsibility. Disciplinary Rule 2-101(b), 1-102(a)(1) (1988).

After a hearing, the Commission recommended censure for a violation of Rule 2-105(a)(3). It rejected petitioner's First Amendment claim that a reference to a lawyer's certification as a specialist was a form of commercial speech that could not be " 'subjected to blanket suppression.' " Although the Commission's "Findings of Facts" did not contain any statement as to whether petitioner's representation was deceptive, its "Conclusion of Law" ended with the brief statement that petitioner,

> by holding himself out, on his letterhead as "Gary E. Peel, Certified Civil Trial Specialist — By the National Board of Trial Advocacy," is in direct violation of the above cited Rule [2-105(a)(3)].

> We hold it is "misleading" as our Supreme Court has never recognized or approved any certification process.

The Illinois Supreme Court adopted the Commission's recommendation for censure. It held that the First Amendment did not protect petitioner's letterhead because the letterhead was misleading in three ways. First, the State Supreme Court concluded that the juxtaposition of the reference to petitioner as "certified" by NBTA and the reference to him as "licensed" by Illinois, Missouri, and Arizona "could" mislead the general public into a belief that petitioner's authority to practice in the field of trial advocacy was derived solely from NBTA certification. It thus found that the statements on the letterhead impinged on the court's exclusive authority to license its attorneys because they failed to distinguish voluntary certification by an unofficial group from licensure by an official organization.

Second, the court characterized the claim of NBTA certification as "misleading because it tacitly attests to the qualifications of [petitioner] as a civil trial advocate." The court noted confusion in the parties' descriptions of the NBTA's requirements, but did not consider whether NBTA certification constituted reliable, verifiable evidence of petitioner's experience as a civil trial advocate. Rather, the court reasoned that the statement was tantamount to an implied claim of superiority of the quality of petitioner's legal services and therefore warranted restriction under our decision in *In re R.M.J.*, 455 U.S. 191 (1982).

Finally, the court reasoned that use of the term "specialist" was misleading because it incorrectly implied that Illinois had formally authorized certification of specialists in trial advocacy. The court concluded that the conjunction of the reference to being a specialist with the reference to being licensed implied that the former was the product of the latter. Concluding that the letterhead was inherently misleading for these reasons, the court upheld the blanket prohibition of Rule 2-105(a) under the First Amendment.

III

*   *   *

In this case we must consider whether petitioner's statement was misleading and, even if it was not, whether the potentially misleading character of such statements creates a state interest sufficiently substantial to justify a categorical ban on their use.

The facts stated on petitioner's letterhead are true and verifiable. It is undisputed that NBTA has certified petitioner as a civil trial specialist and that three States have licensed him to practice law. There is no contention that any potential client or person was actually misled or deceived by petitioner's stationery. Neither the Commission nor the State Supreme Court made any factual finding of actual deception or misunderstanding, but rather concluded, as a matter of law that petitioner's claims of being "certified" as a "specialist" were necessarily misleading absent an official state certification program. Notably, although petitioner was originally charged with a violation of Disciplinary Rule 2-101(b), which aims at misleading statements by an attorney, his letterhead was not found to violate this rule.

In evaluating petitioner's claim of certification, the Illinois Supreme Court focused not on its facial accuracy, but on its implied claim "as to the quality of [petitioner's] legal services," and concluded that such a qualitative claim " 'might be so likely to mislead as to warrant restriction.' " This analysis confuses the distinction between statements of opinion or quality and statements of objective facts that may support an inference of quality. A lawyer's certification by NBTA is a verifiable fact, as are the predicate requirements for that certification. Measures of trial experience and hours of continuing education, like information about what schools the lawyer attended or his or her bar activities, are facts about a lawyer's training and practice. A claim of certification is not an unverifiable opinion of the ultimate quality of a lawyer's work or a promise of success, but is simply a fact, albeit one with multiple predicates, from which a consumer may or may not draw an inference of the likely quality of an attorney's work in a given area of practice.

We must assume that some consumers will infer from petitioner's statement that his qualifications in the area of civil trial advocacy exceed the general qualifications for admission to a state bar. Thus if the certification had been issued by an organization that had made no inquiry into petitioner's fitness, or by one that issued certificates indiscriminately for a price, the statement, even if true, could be misleading. In this case, there is no evidence that a claim of NBTA certification suggests any greater degree of professional qualification than reasonably may be inferred from an evaluation of its rigorous requirements. Much like a trademark, the strength of a certification is measured by the quality of the organization for which it stands. The Illinois Supreme Court merely notes some confusion in the parties' explanation of one of those requirements. We find NBTA standards objectively clear, and, in any event, do not see why the degree of uncertainty identified by the State Supreme Court would make the letterhead inherently misleading to a consumer. A number of other States have their own certifications plans and expressly authorize references to specialists and certification, but there is no evidence that the consumers in any of these States are misled if they do not inform themselves of the precise standards under which claims of certification are allowed.

*   *   *

The court relied on a similarly cramped definition of "specialist," turning from Webster's — which contains no suggestion of state approval of "specialists" — to the American Bar Association's Comment to Model Rule 7.4, which prohibits a lawyer from stating or implying that he is a "specialist" except for designations of patent, admiralty, or state-designated specialties. The Comment to the Rule concludes that the terms "specialist" and "specialty" "have acquired a secondary meaning implying formal recognition as a specialist and, therefore, use of these terms is misleading" in States that have no formal certification procedures. ABA Model Rule of Professional Conduct 7.4 and Comment (1989). We appreciate the difficulties that evolving standards for attorney certification present to national organizations like the ABA.[27]

However, it seems unlikely that petitioner's statement about his certification as a "specialist" by an identified national organization necessarily would be confused with formal state recognition.

---

[27] [12] Prior to its revision in 1989, the Comment to ABA Model Rule of Professional Conduct 7.4 also prohibited any statement that a lawyer's practice "is limited to" or "concentrated in" an area under the same explanation that these terms had "a secondary meaning implying formal recognition as a specialist." Model Rule 7.4 Comment (1983). When Rule 7.4 was originally proposed in 1983, proponents of unsuccessful amendments to drop all prohibition of terms argued that "the public does not attach the narrow meaning to the word 'specialist' that the legal profession generally does. The public would perceive no distinction between a lawyer's claim that he practices only probate law and a claim that he concentrates his practice in probate law." ABA, The Legislative History of the Model Rules of Professional Conduct 189 (1987). The amendments' opponents argued that allowing lawyers to designate themselves as specialists would undermine the States' ability to set up and control specialization programs. This position essentially conceded that these terms did not yet have "a secondary meaning implying formal recognition," but only that they could develop such a secondary meaning if state programs came into being.

. . . The two state courts that have evaluated lawyers' advertisements of their certifications as civil trial specialists by NBTA have concluded that the statements were not misleading or deceptive on their face, and that, under our recent decisions, they were protected by the First Amendment. Given the complete absence of any evidence of deception in the present case, we must reject the contention that petitioner's letterhead is actually misleading.

We prefer to assume that the average consumer, with or without knowledge of the legal profession, can understand a statement that certification by a national organization is not certification by the State, and can decide what, if any, value to accord this information.

IV

Even if petitioner's letterhead is not actually misleading, the Commission defends Illinois' categorical prohibition against lawyers' claims of being "certified" or a "specialist" on the assertion that these statements are potentially misleading. In the Commission's view, the State's interest in avoiding any possibility of misleading some consumers with such communications is so substantial that it outweighs the cost of providing other consumers with relevant information about lawyers who are certified as specialists.

We may assume that statements of "certification" as a "specialist," even though truthful, may not be understood fully by some readers. However, such statements pose no greater potential of misleading consumers than advertising admission to "Practice before: The United States Supreme Court," *In re R.M.J.*, 455 U.S. 191 (1982), of exploiting the audience of a targeted letter, *Shapero v. Kentucky Bar Assn.*, 486 U.S. 466 (1988), or of confusing a reader with an accurate illustration, *Zauderer v. Office of Disciplinary Counsel*, 471 U.S. 626 (1985). In this case, as in those, we conclude that the particular State rule restricting lawyers' advertising is " 'broader than reasonably necessary to prevent the' perceived evil." *Shapero*, 486 U.S. at 472 (quoting *In re R.M.J.*, 455 U.S. at 203). *Cf. Ohralik v. Ohio State Bar Assn.*, 436 U.S. 447 (1978) (restricting in-person solicitation). The need for a complete prophylactic against any claim of specialty is undermined by the fact that use of titles such as "Registered Patent Attorney" and "Proctor in Admiralty," which are permitted under Rule 2-105(a)'s exceptions, produces the same risk of deception.

* * *

We do not ignore the possibility that some unscrupulous attorneys may hold themselves out as certified specialists when there is no qualified organization to stand behind that certification. A lawyer's truthful statement that "XYZ Board" has "certified" him as a "specialist in admiralty law" would not necessarily be entitled to First Amendment protection if the certification was a sham. States can require an attorney who advertises "XYZ certification" to demonstrate that such certification is available to all lawyers who meet objective and consistently applied standards relevant to practice in a particular area of the law. There has been no showing — indeed no suggestion — that the burden of distinguishing between certifying boards that are bona fide and those that are bogus would be significant, or that bar associations and official disciplinary committees cannot police deceptive practices effectively.

Petitioner's letterhead was neither actually nor inherently misleading. There is no dispute about the bona fides and the relevance of NBTA certification. The Commission's concern about the possibility of deception in hypothetical cases is not sufficient to rebut the constitutional presumption favoring disclosure over concealment. Disclosure of information such as that on petitioner's letterhead both serves the public interest and encourages the development and utilization of meritorious certification programs for attorneys. As the public censure of petitioner for violating Rule 2-105(a)(3) violates the First Amendment, the judgment of the Illinois Supreme Court is reversed and the case is remanded for proceedings not inconsistent with this opinion.

It is so ordered.

JUSTICE MARSHALL, with whom JUSTICE BRENNAN joins, concurring in the judgment.

Petitioner's letterhead is neither actually nor inherently misleading. I therefore concur in the plurality's holding that Illinois may not prohibit petitioner from holding himself out as a civil trial specialist certified by the National Board of Trial Advocacy. I believe, though, that petitioner's letterhead statement is potentially misleading. Accordingly, I would hold that Illinois may enact regulations other than a total ban to ensure that the public is not misled by such representations. Because Illinois' present regulation is unconstitutional as applied to petitioner, however, the judgment of the Illinois Supreme Court must be reversed and the case remanded for further proceedings.

The scope of permissible regulation depends on the nature of the commercial speech in question. States may prohibit actually or inherently misleading commercial speech entirely. They may not, however, ban potentially misleading commercial speech if narrower limitations could be crafted to ensure that the information is presented in a nonmisleading manner.

I agree with the plurality that petitioner's reference to his NBTA certification as a civil trial specialist is not actually misleading. . . .

The statement is nonetheless potentially misleading. The name "National Board of Trial Advocacy" could create the misimpression that the NBTA is an agency of the Federal Government. Although most lawyers undoubtedly know that the Federal Government does not regulate lawyers, most nonlawyers probably do not; thus, the word "National" in the NBTA's name does not dispel the potential implication that the NBTA is a governmental agency. Furthermore, the juxtaposition on petitioner's letterhead of the phrase "Certified Civil Trial Specialist By the National Board of Trial Advocacy" with "Licensed: Illinois, Missouri, Arizona" could lead even lawyers to believe that the NBTA, though not a governmental agency, is somehow sanctioned by the States listed on the letterhead.

*   *   *

The potential for misunderstanding might be less if the NBTA were a commonly recognized organization and the public had a general understanding of its requirements. The record contains no evidence, however, that the NBTA or, more importantly, its certification requirements are widely known.

Because a claim of certification by the NBTA as a civil trial specialist is potentially misleading, States may enact measures other than a total ban to prevent deception or confusion. This Court has suggested that States may, for example, require "some limited supplementation, by way of warning or disclaimer or the like, . . . so as to assure that the consumer is not misled." *Bates, supra*, at 384. *Accord, In re R.M.J.*, 455 U.S. at 203 ("The remedy in the first instance is not necessarily a prohibition but preferably a requirement of disclaimers or explanation"). The Court's decisions in *Shapero* and *Zauderer* provide helpful guidance in this area. In *Shapero*, the Court held that States may not categorically prohibit lawyers from soliciting business for pecuniary gain by sending personalized letters to potential clients known to face particular legal problems. The Court said that States could, however, enact less restrictive measures to prevent deception and abuse, such as requiring that a personalized letter bear a label identifying it as an advertisement or a statement informing the recipient how to report an inaccurate or misleading letter. In *Zauderer*, the Court held that a State could not ban newspaper advertisements containing legal advice or illustrations because the State had failed to show that it could not combat potential abuses by means short of a blanket ban. But the Court held that the State could require attorneys advertising contingent-fee services to disclose that clients would have to pay costs even if their lawsuits were unsuccessful to prevent the possibility that people would erroneously think that they would not owe their attorneys any money if they lost their cases.

Following the logic of those cases, a State could require a lawyer claiming certification by the NBTA as a civil trial specialist to provide additional information in order to prevent that claim from being misleading. The State might, for example, require a disclaimer stating that the NBTA is a private organization not affiliated with or sanctioned by the State or Federal Government. The State also could require information about the NBTA's requirements for certification as a specialist so that any inferences drawn by consumers about the quality of services offered by an NBTA-certified attorney would be based on more complete knowledge of the meaning of NBTA certification. Each State, of course, may decide for itself, within the constraints of the First Amendment, how best to prevent such claims from being misleading.[28]

In any event, this Court's primary task in cases such as this is to determine

---

[28] [2] The precise amount of information necessary to avoid misunderstandings need not be decided here. The poles of the spectrum of disclosure requirements, however, are clear. A State may require an attorney to provide more than just the fact of his certification as a civil trial specialist by the NBTA. But a State may not require an attorney to include in his letterhead an exhaustive, detailed recounting of the NBTA's certification requirements because more limited disclosure would suffice to prevent the possibility that people would be misled. *Cf. Zauderer v. Office of Disciplinary Counsel*, 471 U.S. 626, 663-664 (1985) (Brennan, J., concurring in part, concurring in judgment in part, dissenting in part) ("Compelling the publication of detailed fee information that would fill far more space than the advertisement itself . . . would chill the publication of protected commercial speech and would be entirely out of proportion to the State's legitimate interest in preventing potential deception").

whether a state law or regulation unduly burdens the speaker's exercise of First Amendment rights, not whether respect for those rights would be unduly burdensome for the State. Because Illinois can prevent petitioner's claim from being misleading without banning that claim entirely, the State's total ban is unconstitutional as applied in this case. The burden is on the State to enact a constitutional regulation, not on petitioner to guess in advance what he would have to do to comply with such a regulation.

NOTES, QUESTIONS, AND EXAMPLES

In *Ibanez v. Florida Department of Business and Professional Regulation*, 512 U.S. 136 (1994), the Supreme Court struck down the discipline imposed by the Florida Department of Business and Professional Regulation. Ibanez was a member of the Florida Bar; she was also a Certified Public Accountant (CPA) licensed by the Florida Board of Accountancy, and was authorized by the Certified Financial Planner Board of Standards, a private organization, to use the designation "Certified Financial Planner" (CFP). She referred to these credentials in her advertising and other communication with the public concerning her law practice, placing CPA and CFP next to her name in her yellow pages listing and on her business cards and law offices stationery. Notwithstanding the apparent truthfulness of the communication, the Board reprimanded her for engaging in "false, deceptive, and misleading" advertising. The Court ruled that the use of the CPA and CFP designations was neither false nor misleading in light of the common understanding of the designations.

Chapter X

JUDICIAL CONDUCT

Examination of judicial conduct requires a different lens from the rest of the law governing lawyers: It is about the role of judge rather than the role of lawyer. The two roles are significantly different and as a result, discussion of judicial conduct proceeds from a different set of premises than those from which a discussion of lawyer conduct proceeds. For example, judges are neutrals not partisans, so the lawyer's duty of loyalty to a client is simply not a part of a judicial conduct discussion. Likewise, judges are not confided in by either of the parties, so the lawyer confidentiality discussion drops out of judicial conduct discussions.

Conflicts of interest, in the judicial conduct context, are about impairments of a judge's impartiality rather than about impairments of loyalty to a client. The limits on what judges may say and do come from a source different from the loyalty to client that drives the lawyer role limitations. Judge's limitations come largely from the public trust that is placed in judges in their central role in our justice system.

Even more than lawyers, judges are central to the public's view of the justice system. As such, the avoidance of the appearance of impropriety notion that gets only limited respect in the analysis of lawyer conduct gets much more attention in the judicial conduct area.

A. SOURCES OF JUDICIAL CONDUCT LAW

As is true of the law governing lawyers, the law governing judges comes from a wide range of sources. Like its Model Rules of Professional Conduct and Model Code of Professional Responsibility, the American Bar Association has adopted a Model Code of Judicial Conduct (CJC). Like its lawyer conduct models, the CJC is not directly applicable to anyone. Rather, it becomes so when adopted by a state's legislature or court system as the applicable rules of judicial conduct for the particular jurisdiction. The 1972 Model CJC was adopted by 47 states, the District of Columbia, and the United States Judicial Conference. In 1990, the ABA adopted a relatively modest revision of the Model CJC. States have been switching from the 1972 model to the 1990 model since its adoption by the ABA. The ABA issued a major revision to the CJC in 2007.

A few federal statutes modify the CJC in federal court, particularly as it relates to judicial disqualification procedures and standards:

- 28 U.S.C. § 455 is the federal analogue to the CJC disqualification section.

- 28 U.S.C. § 47 prohibits an appellate judge from sitting on a case that she decided as a trial judge.

- 28 U.S.C. § 144 prohibits a judge from hearing a case in which the judge has actual bias against a party.

- 28 U.S.C. § 372 sets forth the procedure in cases of complaints against federal judges. This statute permits any person to file a complaint with the clerk's office of a federal Court of Appeals alleging that a judge sitting in the appropriate circuit has engaged in conduct that is prejudicial to the administration of justice.

Most judges are also lawyers and to the extent they remain relevant to the judge's role, the professional ethics rules governing lawyers apply to judges as well. Some of the lawyer rules have general applicability, such as those relating to assistance with bar admissions and general licensure rules. These apply to judges who are also lawyers. Some of the lawyer rules are really about judges. Model Rule 1.12, for example, governs lawyer conflicts of interest that arise when a judge leaves the bench and moves into practice.

As with lawyer ethics rules, the constitution, case law, and bar ethics opinions are also important sources of judicial conduct law.

INTERNATIONAL NOTE

The European Union does not have a single, unified code of ethics for judicial conduct. James E. Moliterno with U.S. Agency for Int'l Dev. & Nat'l Ctr. for State Courts, *Lawyer Ethics/Responsibility of Lawyers: Serbian Standards with a Comparative View* 1, 173 (2005). However, several charters have been drafted, discussing the role of judges. In 1997, participants from 13 European Countries met in Strasbourg to assess the status of judges in Europe. European Charter on the Statute for Judges, Council of Europe, July 8–10, 1998, *in* CENTRAL EUROPEAN AND EURASIAN LAW INITIATIVE: LEGISLATIVE ASSISTANCE AND RESEARCH PROGRAM, COMPILATION OF INTERNATIONAL STANDARDS ON JUDICIAL REFORM AND JUDICIAL INDEPENDENCE   51,   *available*   *at* http://www.coe.int/t/e/legal_affairs/legal_cooperation/ legal_professionals/judges/instruments_and_documents/charte%20eng.pdf.   The participating countries took into account the UN Basic Principles and the Council of Europe's recommendations on the independence, efficiency and role of judges in drafting the European Charter. *Id.* at ¶ 1.1. The following year, judges representing 41 European and Asian Countries met in Taiwan and adopted the Universal Charter of the Judge. Universal Charter of the Judge, Cent. Council of the Int'l Ass'n of Judges, art. 15, Nov. 17, 1999, in CEEIL Compilations, at 8–9. The Charter consists of 15 articles covering independence, impartiality, personal autonomy, efficacy, remuneration, appointment, and disciplinary action. In 2002, the Judicial Group on Strengthening Judicial Integrity met in Bangalore to draw up an international code of judicial conduct to combat judicial corruption, promote accountability, and to ensure a competent, independent, and impartial judiciary. The Bangalore Principles of Judicial Conduct 1.1 (Nov. 25–26, 2002), *available at* www.unodoc.org/pdf/crime/corruption/judical_group/Bangalore_principles.pdf. The principles are used around the world as guidelines for developing national codes of judicial conduct and as a reference tool for revising existing national codes. The principles outline and explain six major aspects of ethical judicial conduct:

independence, impartiality, integrity, propriety, equality, and competence and diligence. *Id.*

B.   GENERAL JUDICIAL ATTRIBUTES: INDEPENDENCE, INTEGRITY, AND IMPARTIALITY

Our system of justice requires that judges and the judiciary be independent of outside influences, including those of the legislative and executive branches.[1] A fundamental expectation of judges is that they have integrity.[2] Most of the assumptions underlying our judicial system hinge on the impartiality of judges.

INTERNATIONAL NOTE

The Japanese judicial system is unitary and centralized under the federal government. David M. O'Brien & Yasuo Ohkoshi, *Stifling Judicial Independence from Within: The Japanese Judiciary, in* JUDICIAL INDEPENDENCE IN THE AGE OF DEMOCRACY: CRITICAL PERSPECTIVES FROM AROUND THE WORLD 37, 41 (Peter H. Russell & David M. O'Brien eds., 2001). The Supreme Court, the Chief Justice and General Secretariat control personnel issues involving judges and judicial staff, and oversee the training, nomination reappointment, assignments, and salaries of lower court judges. As a result, Japanese judges and courts are tightly controlled, as opposed to the more decentralized and independent federal courts in the United States. *Id.* at 45. During the course of a judge's career, he will be reassigned on many occasions to different courts. Judges in civil law countries like Japan face pressures from government in the form of incentives to decide cases a certain way. J. Mark Ramseyer & Eric Rasmusen, *Judicial Independence in a Civil Law Regime: The Evidence form Japan*, 13 J.L. ECON. & ORG. 259, 260 (1997). The practice of frequently reassigning judges serves as an incentive to decide cases favorably for the government. Even though the judicial system appears to be based on productivity and efficiency, judges who tend to decide cases against the government tend to receive less favorable assignments.

C.   PERSONAL CONDUCT AND ACTIVITY OUTSIDE THE JUDICIAL ROLE

Judges play *the* central role in our system of justice and they, even more than lawyers, must maintain high standards of personal, out-of-role conduct. Public perception of judges has a significant effect on the public confidence in the justice system. As such, the notion of avoiding even the appearance of impropriety has greater force in judicial conduct law than it does in lawyer conduct law.[3]

    1.   The CJC cautions judges about engaging in conduct that "would create in reasonable minds a perception that the judge's ability to carry out judicial

---

[1]   *In re Advisory Opinion to Governor*, 276 So. 2d 25 (Fla. 1973).

[2]   CJC Canon 1.

[3]   CJC § 2A, Comment.

responsibilities with integrity, impartiality and competence is impaired."[4] This standard is an objective one. Because the standard is so vague, clear rules of conduct are difficult to establish. In *In re Blackman*, 591 A.2d 1339 (N.J. 1991), a judge attended a party hosted by a long-time acquaintance who had recently pleaded guilty and been convicted of racketeering. Approximately 200 guests attended the party. The judge was disciplined for failing to avoid the appearance of impropriety in his out-of-role activities. In *In re Whitaker*, 463 So. 2d 1291 (La. 1985), a judge's association with prostitutes and drug dealers led to the judge's one year suspension without pay.

2.   Judges are expected to comply with the law.[5] Substantial violations of law may result in judicial discipline. No conviction is necessary for discipline on these grounds to occur. A judge who engages in illegal drug abuse, for example, even if the conduct does not result in a conviction may be disciplined.[6] Intentional or bad faith refusal to follow precedent and other mandatory authority can subject a judge to discipline.[7]

3.   Judges are prohibited from lending the prestige of their offices to private interests. Using court stationary for either personal business or to advance private interests, for example, violates this principle.

4.   Because of the judge's potentially excessive influence on a fact finder, there are some limitations on the use of judges as witnesses. The limitations, in fact, however, are minimal. As long as the judge is not presiding over the proceeding, a judge may be called as a fact witness. In other words, the fact that a percipient witness is a judge does not affect his or her availability as a witness. The mere fact that a judge may be an influential witness is insufficient reason to excuse the judge-witness from the obligation to testify when called as a fact witness. By contrast, a judge is prohibited from voluntarily testifying as a character witness.[8] A judge must be subpoenaed in order to obtain her presence and testimony as a character witness. Consistent with the CJC, a judge may testify as a character witness when subpoenaed. Indeed, a judge must obey the subpoena.

5.   A judge is not permitted to be a member of an organization that "practices invidious discrimination on the basis of race, sex, religion or national origin."[9]

6.   Within certain constraints, judges are permitted to teach, speak and write about the law, the legal profession, and the justice system.[10] Judges are required to be cautious in their discussion of pending cases. They must

---

[4] CJC § 2A, Comment 2.

[5] CJC § 2A.

[6] *Starnes v. Judicial Retirement Commission*, 680 S.W.2d 922 (Ky. 1984).

[7] *In re Hague*, 315 N.W.2d 524 (Mich. 1982).

[8] CJC § 2.

[9] CJC § 2C.

[10] CJC § 3B.

refrain from making either public or non-public comments that risk the fairness of the proceedings. Speaking, teaching, and writing activities must be secondary in importance to the judge's judicial responsibilities. A judge must be careful to avoid creation of an appearance that the judge would not enforce the law or decide cases fairly. For example, a judge who wrote editorial letters opposing the death penalty in a state that has the death penalty may give the impression that the judge will not impose the death penalty when the law calls for its imposition in his court.

7. Judges may serve as directors, board members, or trustees of not-for-profit organizations unless the organization would be likely to come before the judge's court or will regularly be involved in litigation in any court.[11] Judges may not, however, engage in direct fund-raising for such organizations.[12]

8. Except for closely-held family businesses, judges may not be director, officer, manager, partner, advisor, or employee of a business.[13]

9. Except for providing fiduciary duties for family members, a judge is prohibited from serving as executor, administrator, trustee, guardian, or other fiduciary.[14]

10. Except for serving interests of herself or her family members, full-time judges are not permitted to practice law.[15]

11. When judges are permitted to earn outside income (teaching, writing, speaking, etc.), that income must be limited to reasonable amounts for the services rendered and must not appear to compromise the judge's integrity and impartiality. For example, a judge who is paid an honorarium for a speaking engagement that is substantially more than the organization pays for others to speak is subject to discipline. Judges may not accept gifts or favors from a person whose interests are or are likely to be before the judge. Gifts that are appropriate to special occasions (wedding or anniversary, for example) are permitted. Judges must file annually as a public document a statement of the nature and amount of compensation received.[16]

INTERNATIONAL NOTE

In Italy, many judges have held political positions. In the 1996 national election, 50 members of the magistracy participated in the electoral race as representatives of various parties, and 27 were elected. Not only are judges allowed to hold positions, but they are permitted to return to their judicial roles after playing prominent political roles. The unique Italian system of promotions creates a

---

[11] CJC § 4C.

[12] CJC § 4C(3)(b).

[13] CJC § 4D(3); *In re Intemann*, 540 N.E.2d 236 (N.Y. 1989).

[14] CJC § 4E; Georgia Ethics Advisory Opinion 80 (1986).

[15] CJC § 4G.

[16] CJC § 4H(2).

structure that facilitates the process for a judge who desires to take a leave of absence to pursue a political position. Promotions to different levels of the judiciary are not based on examination or on the evaluation of written judicial work and extended leaves of absence to perform other activities in the executive or legislative branches do not impair a magistrate's chance for promotion. *See* Giuseppe Di Federico, *Independence and Accountability of the Judiciary in Italy: The Experience of a Former Transitional Country in a Comparative Perspective, in* JUDICIAL INTEGRITY 181, 193 (Andras Sajo ed., 2004), *available at* http://siteresources.worldbank.org/INTECA/Resources/DiFedericopaper.pdf.

D. JUDICIAL DUTIES

The defining characteristic of the judge is the performance of judicial duties, that is, deciding cases. Perhaps the most central attribute of the judge's role in our justice system is impartiality. All of the other rules and assumptions flow from this central notion.[17] Judges are required to be diligent in the discharge of their duties. The old saying is "Justice delayed is justice denied." Thus, judges must process and resolve cases and motions filed in their court without unnecessary delay.[18] Judges must also have and maintain competence in the law and decision-making.[19] In some jurisdictions, this requirement has been interpreted to require judges to attend continuing judicial education classes.

Judges are authorized and required to maintain courtroom decorum.[20] This means that judges have power (the contempt power) to discipline those in their courtrooms for disruptive behavior. For example, lawyers may be removed for failure to follow a judge's rulings. The power must not, however, be abused. Judges may not, for example, remove lawyers from court simply because the judge is unhappy with the lawyer's arguments. Even while maintaining courtroom decorum and disposing of the court's business diligently, a judge must exhibit patience.[21]

In order to remain impartial, a judge must avoid bias and prejudice.[22] In addition to racial, sexist, and ethnic biases, judges must avoid bias in favor of friends and associates and against particular causes or groups of lawyers.[23]

An ex parte communication is a communication, whether written or oral, that involves less than all of the parties or their counsel to a matter, that is about a

---

[17] *Tumey v. Ohio*, 273 U.S. 510 (1927).

[18] CJC § 3A(5); *Starnes v. Judicial Retirement Commission*, 680 S.W.2d 922 (Ky. 1984).

[19] CJC § 3B(2); *McCullough v. Commission on Judicial Performance*, 776 P.2d 259 (Cal. 1989).

[20] CJC § 3B(3).

[21] CJC § 3B(4).

[22] CJC § 3B(5). Judges have been disciplined for a wide variety of slurs against women, *Kennick v. Commission on Judicial Performance*, 787 P.2d 591 (Cal. 1990); Italian-Americans, *In re Carr*, 593 So. 2d 1044 (Fla. 1992); Mexican-Americans, *Gonzalez v. Commission on Judicial Performance*, 657 P.2d 372 (Cal. 1983); African-Americans, *Id.;* Jews, *Id.;* and Arabs, *In the Matter of Ain*, (New York Comm. on Judicial Conduct, Sept. 21, 1992). Claims by judges that they were "joking" have not been treated as a defense. *Gonzalez v. Comm. on Judicial Performance*, 657 P.2d 372 (Cal. 1983).

[23] *McCullough v. Commission on Judicial Performance*, 776 P.2d 259 (Cal. 1989); *Matter of Albano*, 384 A.2d 144 (N.J. 1978).

pending or impending matter, and that is made by or to the judge presiding in the matter.[24] Except in limited circumstances, judges may not engage in ex parte communications. Our adversarial justice system operates on the premise that all parties have an opportunity to be heard on all matters relevant to a case. Ex parte communications undermine the premise by affording some parties opportunities to influence the judge's decision-making in the absence of other parties. Even when a judge engages in ex parte communications for good, but not authorized-by-law reasons, the judge is subject to discipline.[25] In the absence of evidence to the contrary, a private communication between a judge and a lawyer with a matter pending before the judge will be presumed to have been about the pending matter.[26] A case continues to be a pending matter until its final disposition. As such, even after a trial judge has ruled, the judge is not permitted to have ex parte communications with counsel while appeals are pending.

The CJC permits ex parte communications in a few distinct situations. Communications for scheduling or administrative purposes do not violate the ex parte communication rules provided the judge "reasonably believes that no party will gain [an] advantage [from the communication] and the judge promptly notifies all parties and affords them an opportunity to respond."[27] Judges may consult with other judges and with disinterested experts on the law if the judge identifies the person consulted to the parties and affords the parties an opportunity to respond.[28] For example, a judge who is presiding over a case in which a thorny professional responsibility issue arises is permitted to call her former Professional Responsibility professor, outline the issue and ask for Professor's opinion regarding the law of Professional Responsibility. Provided the judge notifies the parties, informs them of Professor's name and of Professor's advice, and gives the parties an opportunity to be heard, then Judge will have obtained excellent legal advice without violating the ex parte communication rules. Central to a judicial clerk's job is the giving of advice to the judge. Judges may consult with clerks about the law in the absence of the parties without restriction. Even judicial clerks, however, may not do independent fact investigation and then communicate the results to the judge.[29] Other law authorizes ex parte communications in various, limited circumstances, such as requests for emergency temporary restraining orders including those in spousal and child abuse cases, applications for wire taps, and when a party has been given notice of a hearing but fails to appear.

Aside from expressing appreciation of jurors' service, judges may neither compliment nor criticize jurors' decisions.[30]

---

[24] Canon 3A(4), 1972 CJC.

[25] *In re Sturgis*, 529 So. 2d 281 (Fla. 1988); *In re Yaccarino*, 502 A.2d 3 (N.J. 1985).

[26] *Kennick v. Commission on Judicial Performance*, 787 P.2d 591 (Cal. 1990).

[27] CJC § 3B(7)(a).

[28] CJC § 3B(7)(b).

[29] CJC § 3B(7)(c); *Price Bros. Co. v. Philadelphia Gear Corp.*, 629 F.2d 444 (6th Cir. 1980) (Clerk went to Plaintiff's factory and observed the operation of machines that were the subject of a fact dispute between the parties. The clerk reported the results to Judge. The clerk's communication to Judge violates the ex parte communication rules.).

[30] CJC § 3B(10).

Judges have duties to report misconduct of other judges and of lawyers under certain circumstances.[31] In a duty that is roughly analogous to the lawyer's misconduct reporting duty under Model Rule 8.3, judges have obligations to report both lawyers' and other judges' misconduct under certain circumstances. Judges have not been particularly diligent about compliance with this mandate.

Springing from the central impartiality principle, judges may be disqualified from presiding over matters when their impartiality might reasonably be questioned. Provisions for waiver of many of the reasons for disqualification exist as well. Largely because of the motivation of the litigants, disqualification is among the most important and most litigated areas of judicial conduct. Both CJC Canon 3E and federal statutes govern this topic. A judge who voluntarily removes herself from hearing a matter is said to have recused herself.[32]

The basic standard for judicial disqualification is an objective one, "A judge shall disqualify himself or herself [when] the judge's impartiality might reasonably be questioned."[33] The central federal statute is similar.[34] A judge must also, however, be subjectively free from bias.

Occasionally, an issue arises that would disqualify every judge that is sitting on a court with jurisdiction to resolve the issue. When this phenomenon occurs, the "rule of necessity" says that judges are not disqualified. For example, when the state legislature passed changes to the state employee retirement program, the changes had a financial effect on every state court judge. A challenge was brought to the changes, and had to be presided over by some judge, all of whom were to be affected by the outcome. Under those circumstances, the judge is not disqualified from hearing the case because every state court judge would be similarly disqualified.[35]

A wide variety of specific categories of reasons may cause a reasonable person to question a judge's impartiality.

Naturally, a judge's bias may be reason to question her impartiality. Bias, however, will only be grounds for disqualification when the bias is against a party as opposed to the legal rules governing the case and when the bias against a party arises from a source outside the present litigation. A judge's bias regarding the governing legal rules is insufficient to warrant disqualification. Only bias for or against a party is disqualifying. For example, where a judge has made public statements that criticize strikes by public employees, and later, when the local teacher's union goes on strike, a case is filed in the judge's court that requests the teachers be ordered back to work, the judge is not disqualified by virtue of his fixed and preexisting views regarding teacher strikes.[36]

---

[31] CJC § 3D; *In re Laurie*, 84-CC#5 (Ill. Courts Commission 1985).

[32] 28 U.S.C. §§ 47, 144, 455.

[33] CJC § 3E(1).

[34] 28 U.S.C. § 455.

[35] *Hughes v. Oregon*, 838 P.2d 1018 (Or. 1992).

[36] *Papa v. New Haven Federation of Teachers*, 444 A.2d 196 (Conn. 1982).

The source of the judge's bias will affect its disqualifying nature. When a judge becomes biased during judicial proceedings based on what happens inside the judicial proceedings, that bias is not disqualifying. Only a bias that has its source outside the judicial proceeding in question is disqualifying. For example, a judge's intense displeasure at a lawyer's tactics during trial will not produce a disqualifying bias.

A judge is disqualified when the judge's spouse or a "person within the third degree of relationship" is a party, a lawyer or a material witness in a matter.[37] A "person within the third degree of relationship" is a great-grandparent, grandparent, parent, uncle, aunt, brother, sister, child, grandchild, great-grandchild, nephew, or niece.[38]

Except in unusual circumstances, a judge is not disqualified when a judge's former law clerk or intern represents a party before the judge. When the former clerk was a clerk during the early stages of the same matter before the court, and later undertook representation of a party in the matter, or when the clerk or intern was simultaneously working for the court and in practice with a firm representing a party in a matter pending before the court, disqualification should result.[39] A judge is not disqualified when an ordinary judicial election campaign contributor of the judge is a party or a lawyer in a matter. The contributions are relevant to the disqualification analysis, but are not per se disqualifying.[40] The judge is disqualified, however, when the judge's campaign coordinator or a campaign committee member is a party or lawyer in a matter.[41]

Only rather close social relationships between judge and party, lawyer, or material witness are disqualifying. Ordinarily, a judge can be expected to put all but the closest social relationships aside when exercising the judicial function. Ordinarily, judges may hear cases in which one of the parties is represented by the judge's former law partners and other associates in practice. When the judge was associated with the lawyer during the pendency of the action, however, the judge is disqualified.[42]

Judges may have prior relationships to the matter before them as well as to the parties and lawyers, some of which are disqualifying. When the judge was formerly a lawyer on the same or a substantially related matter, the judge is disqualified.[43] When a judge has been a material witness in a matter, the judge is disqualified.[44]

---

[37] CJC § 3E(1)(d); *Morelite Construction Corp. v. New York City District Council Carpenters Benefit Funds*, 748 F.2d 79 (2d Cir. 1984).

[38] CJC Terminology 19.

[39] *Fredonia Broadcasting Corp. v. RCA*, 569 F.2d 251 (5th Cir. 1978); *Simonson v. General Motors*, 425 F. Supp. 574 (E.D. Pa. 1976).

[40] *Nathanson v. Korvick*, 577 So. 2d 943 (Fla. 1991).

[41] *MacKenzie v. Super Kids Bargain Store*, 565 So. 2d 1332 (Fla. 1990).

[42] CJC § 3E(1)(b).

[43] *Sharp v. Howard County*, 607 A.2d 545 (Md. App. 1992).

[44] CJC § 3E(1)(b).

When a judge has prior personal knowledge of disputed evidentiary facts regarding the matter, the judge is disqualified.[45]

A judge is disqualified from hearing the matter when she has more than a de minimis (very small) economic interest in the outcome of the matter. In *Aetna Life Insurance Co. v. Lavoie*,[46] Plaintiff filed a case for bad-faith denial of insurance claim. After several appeals the state supreme court affirmed (5-4) the granting of punitive damages even though a partial payment had been made. The state supreme court decision was authored by a judge who had filed as plaintiff two other cases which were similar to the case filed by Plaintiff. The change in the law instituted by the state supreme court affected the decisions in the cases filed by the judge. The judge's interest was direct, personal, substantial, and economic, and the judge had, in essence, acted as a judge in his own case. The Supreme Court reversed the state supreme court because of the judge's bias.

The disqualifying economic interest may be held by the judge personally or as a fiduciary or by a member of the judge's family residing in the judge's household or by the judge's spouse or a person within the third degree of relationship to the judge. The interest must be one that "could be substantially affected by the proceeding." However large the interest might be, minor or highly speculative effects on it are not disqualifying. A de minimis (very small) interest in the subject matter or a party to the proceeding is not disqualifying.[47] Only those interests that are known to the judge are disqualifying, but a judge has a duty to keep informed about the judge's and the judge's spouse and minor children's economic interests. When an otherwise disqualifying interest is divested immediately upon discovery, a judge will be permitted to continue to preside.[48] The judge also has a duty to make reasonable efforts to be informed of the economic interests of family members.

Most sources of disqualification can be waived by the parties and the judge permitted to continue in the matter, provided the appropriate procedures are followed.[49] Under the CJC, parties may not waive the judge's personal bias regarding a party. They may waive any other form of disqualification. Under federal law, the parties may waive disqualification when it follows only from the general standard, that is, when the judge's "impartiality might reasonably be questioned."[50] They may not waive any of the more specific reasons for disqualification, including personal bias regarding a party, personal knowledge of disputed facts, prior service as a lawyer in the matter, financial interest, or family interests. Thus, disqualification is less waivable under federal law than under the CJC.

For the waiver to be effective, the judge must disclose the nature of the disqualifying interest on the record, and the parties must all agree, without the participation of the judge, that the judge should continue in the matter. If the judge

---

[45] CJC § 3E(1)(a).

[46] 475 U.S. 813 (1986).

[47] CJC §§ 3E(1)(c), 3E(1)(d).

[48] CJC §§ 3E(1)(c), 3E(1)(d), 3E(2); *Kidder, Peabody & Co., Inc. v. Maxus Energy Corp.*, 925 F.2d 556 (2d Cir. 1991).

[49] CJC § 3F; 28 U.S.C. § 455.

[50] 28 U.S.C § 455.

is willing to continue under those circumstances, then she may do so after incorporating the parties' agreement into the record.[51]

E.   POLITICAL ACTIVITIES

Judges must maintain a separation from the give and take of politics. As a result, a variety of restrictions on the political activities of judges and judicial candidates exist.[52]

Because states have so many varied systems for selecting judges, including a variety of appointive and elective systems, the CJC drafters suggest that jurisdictions choose from among the CJC provisions as may be appropriate to the particular jurisdiction's systems. As a result the CJC provisions are in some respects internally inconsistent. Some general points may be made nonetheless.

Both judges and candidates are prohibited from the following activities:

- Lead, hold office in, or make speeches for political organizations.

- Publicly endorse or oppose candidates for office.

- Solicit funds for or contribute to political organizations.

A judge is required to resign from judicial office when the judge becomes a candidate for a non-judicial office. Candidates for judicial office must maintain the dignity of the judicial office they seek. The constitutionality of the CJC's command that judicial candidates refrain from making promises or pledges other than to faithfully and impartially discharge the judicial function is in doubt. Although not addressing the "Pledges and Promises" Clause, the Supreme Court in *Republican Party of Minnesota v. White*, 536 U.S. 765 (2002), held that Minnesota's CJC violated the First Amendment by prohibiting judicial candidates from announcing their views on legal or political issues.

F.   JUDICIAL IMMUNITY

When judges engage in the core judicial function of deciding cases, they are absolutely immune from civil damage suits.[53] This immunity is needed to protect judges from fear of retaliation for difficult decisions. If a judge could be sued for judicial decisions, there might be no end to the cases in which judges would be required to fully defend, and the judicial function would be damaged.

A judge's judicial decision-making immunity does not extend beyond the judicial function. For example, judges may be liable for negligence in driving their automobiles, for breach of contract when they fail to make the installment payments on their CD players, and so on. As well, administrative actions by judges also fall outside the protection of absolute judicial immunity. Judges, for example, have no

---

[51] CJC § 3F.

[52] CJC Canon 5.

[53] *Pierson v. Ray*, 386 U.S. 547 (1967).

immunity from suit for discrimination against court employees.[54]

---

[54] *Forrester v. White*, 484 U.S. 219 (1988).

TABLE OF CASES

[References are to pages]

[References are to pages]

[References are to pages]

[References are to pages]

[References are to pages]

[References are to pages]

INDEX

[References are to sections.]

A

ABUSIVE CONDUCT
Generally . . . VI.B

ADMISSION TO PRACTICE
Generally . . . II.A.3
Education . . . II.A.3.b
Good character . . . II.A.3.b
Knowledge . . . II.A.3.b
Misconduct in application process . . . II.A.3.c
Pro hac vice admission . . . II.A.3.d
Territorial restrictions . . . II.A.3.a

ADVERTISING AND SOLICITATION
Generally . . . IX.A
Blanket ban on advertising breaks down . . . IX.B
Direct mail, targeted . . . IX.E
False advertising . . . IX.C
In-person solicitation . . . IX.D
Misleading advertising . . . IX.C
Specialization . . . IX.F
Targeted direct mail . . . IX.E
Taste, matters of . . . IX.C

AMOROUS RELATIONS WITH CLIENTS
Conflicts of interest . . . V.C.2.d

**ATTORNEY-CLIENT EVIDENTIARY PRIVI-
LEGE**
Generally . . . IV.A; IV.A.1
Application . . . IV.A.2
Exceptions . . . IV.A.3

B

BAR ASSOCIATIONS
Alternative national bar associations . . . II.A.1.b
American Bar Association . . . II.A.1.a
State bar associations . . . II.A.1.c

BAR DISCIPLINE
Generally . . . II.B.1
Criminal conduct . . . II.B.1.b
Deceit . . . II.B.1.c
Dishonesty . . . II.B.1.c
Forms of discipline . . . II.B.1.e
Fraud . . . II.B.1.c
Justice, conduct prejudicial to administration of
. . . II.B.1.d
Moral turpitude, acts indicating . . . II.B.1.a
Procedure . . . II.B.1.e

BARRATRY
Conflicts of interest . . . V.C.2.e

BUSINESS
Ancillary businesses . . . VIII.E
Conflicts of interest, business transactions with cli-
ents as . . . V.C.2.a

C

CHAMPERTY
Conflicts of interest . . . V.C.2.e

CIVIL LIABILITY
Third parties, duties to . . . VI.E

CLIENTS
Attorney-client evidentiary privilege (See
ATTORNEY-CLIENT EVIDENTIARY PRIVI-
LEGE)
Complicity in client conduct, liability for
. . . II.B.3
Conflicts of interest (See CONFLICTS OF INTER-
EST)
Lawyer relationship (See LAWYER-CLIENT RE-
LATIONSHIP)

COMMUNICATION
Lawyer-client relationship . . . III.E
Third parties, communication with
        Represented persons . . . VI.C
        Unrepresented persons . . . VI.D

COMPETENCE
Generally . . . III.D

CONFIDENTIALITY
Application of duty of confidentiality . . . IV.C
Attorney-client evidentiary privilege (See
ATTORNEY-CLIENT EVIDENTIARY PRIVI-
LEGE)
Consent exception . . . IV.D.1
Exceptions to duty of confidentiality
        Consent . . . IV.D.1
        Fees . . . IV.D.2
        Future crimes or frauds or harms . . . IV.D.3
        Orders of court . . . IV.D.4
        Other law . . . IV.D.4
        Self-defense . . . IV.D.2
Fees, exception for . . . IV.D.2
Future crimes or frauds or harms . . . IV.D.3
Persons owned duty of confidentiality . . . IV.B
Self-defense exception . . . IV.D.2
Use of confidential information for lawyer's benefit
. . . IV.E

CONFLICTS OF INTEREST
Aggregate settlements . . . V.C.3.d
Amorous relations with clients . . . V.C.2.d
Barratry . . . V.C.2.e
Business transactions with clients . . . V.C.2.a
Champerty . . . V.C.2.e
Concurrent clients . . . V.C.3.a
Current clients
        Former and . . . V.C.3.f
        Prospective and . . . V.C.3.e
Disqualification for
        Generally . . . II.B.5.a
        Imputed disqualification . . . V.D

[References are to sections.]

[References are to sections.]

DUTIES—Cont.

Role-related duties (See ROLE OF LAWYER, subhead: Duties, role-related)

Society, duties to (See LEGAL SYSTEM AND SOCIETY, DUTIES TO)

Supervising and subordinate lawyers, special duties of (See SUPERVISING AND SUBORDINATE LAWYERS)

Termination of representation, duties on . . . III.F.3

Third parties, duties to (See THIRD PARTIES)

Undertake representation, duty to . . . III.A.1

E

EMPLOYEES, LAWYERS AS

Generally . . . VIII.C; VIII.C.4

Partners as employees . . . VIII.C.3

Partnership decision as employment action . . . VIII.C.2

Wrongful discharge . . . VIII.C.1

ETHICS AND MORALITY

Abusive conduct . . . VI.B

Admission to practice

    Good character . . . II.A.3.b

    Misconduct in application process . . . II.A.3.c

Bar discipline (See BAR DISCIPLINE)

Codes of ethics as source of law governing lawyers . . . II.A.2.a

Complicity in client conduct . . . II.B.3

Confidentiality

    Future crimes or frauds or harms as exception to duty of . . . IV.D.3

    Use of confidential information for lawyer's benefit . . . IV.E

Conflicts of interest (See CONFLICTS OF INTEREST)

Contempt of court . . . II.B.4

Discharge, wrongful . . . VIII.C.1

False advertising . . . IX.C

False statements of material law or fact . . . VI.A.1

Fraud

    Generally . . . II.B.1.c

    Future fraud . . . IV.D.3

Frivolous claims and litigation positions . . . VII.C.1

Future crimes or frauds or harms as exception to duty of confidentiality . . . IV.D.3

Good character . . . II.A.3.b

Harassment . . . VI.B

Intemperate remarks . . . VII.C.4

Law governing lawyers, sources of

    Codes of ethics . . . II.A.2.a

    Opinions on ethics . . . II.A.2.c

Litigation positions, frivolous claims and . . . VII.C.1

Loyalty . . . V.A

Malpractice . . . II.B.2

Misconduct

    Application process . . . II.A.3.c

    Report misconduct, duty to . . . II.A.6

ETHICS AND MORALITY—Cont.

Misconduct—Cont.

    Subordinates, responsibility for misconduct of lawyer or nonlawyer . . . VIII.B.3

Misleading advertising . . . IX.C

Obeying court orders . . . VII.C.3

Opinions on ethics as source of law governing lawyers . . . II.A.2.c

Perjury . . . VII.A.3

Philosophy in relation to law governing lawyers, moral . . . I.A

Report misconduct, duty to . . . II.A.6

Subordinates, responsibility for misconduct of lawyer or nonlawyer . . . VIII.B.3

Truth-telling

    Outside of court context (See THIRD PARTIES, subhead: Truth-telling outside of court context)

    Within court context (See LEGAL SYSTEM AND SOCIETY, DUTIES TO, subhead: Truth-telling within court context)

Unauthorized practice . . . II.A.4

Use of confidential information for lawyer's benefit . . . IV.E

Wrongful discharge . . . VIII.C.1

***EX PARTE* PROCEEDINGS**

Judges, *ex parte* contact with . . . VII.E; VII.E.1

Jurors, *ex parte* contact with . . . VII.E; VII.E.2

Truth-telling in . . . VII.A.2

F

FEES

Generally . . . III.B

Confidentiality, fees as exceptions to duty of . . . IV.D.2

Contingent fees . . . III.B.2

Forfeiture of fees . . . III.B.5

Minimum fee schedules . . . III.B.4

Reasonableness standard . . . III.B.1

Splitting of fees . . . III.B.3

FIDUCIARY DUTIES

Generally . . . III.C

FORFEITURE

Fees, of . . . III.B.5

FRAUD

Bar discipline . . . II.B.1.c

Future fraud as exception to duty of confidentiality . . . IV.D.3

H

HARASSMENT

Generally . . . VI.B

I

IMMUNITY

Judicial . . . X.F

[References are to sections.]

[References are to sections.]